CHILD NEUROPSYCHOLOGY

CHILD NEUROPSYCHOLOGY

Assessment and Interventions for Neurodevelopmental Disorders

PHYLLIS ANNE TEETER
University of Wisconsin—Milwaukee

MARGARET SEMRUD-CLIKEMAN
University of Minnesota Medical Center

Allyn and Bacon

Boston   London   Toronto   Sydney   Tokyo   Singapore

Copyright © 1997 by Allyn & Bacon
A Viacom Company
Needham Heights, MA 02194

Internet: www.abacon.com
America Online: keyword: College Online

Library of Congress Cataloging-in-Publication Data

Teeter, Phyllis Anne.
    Child neuropsychology : assessment and interventions for
neurodevelopmental disorders / Phyllis Anne Teeter, Margaret Semrud-
Clikeman.
    p.   cm.
    ISBN 0-205-16331-9
    1. Pediatric neuropsychology.   2. Pediatric neuropsychiatry.
I. Semrud-Clikeman, Margaret. II. Title.
    [DNLM: 1. Mental Disorders–in infancy & childhood. 2. Mental
Disorders–diagnosis. 3. Mental Disorders–therapy.
4. Developmental Disabilities. 5. Brain–physiopathology.
6. Brain–growth & development. WS 350 T258c 1997]
RJ486.5.T44   1997
618.92´89–dc21
DNLM/DLC
for Library of Congress   96-54722
                                                 CIP

Printed in the United States of America

10 9 8 7 6 5 4 3 2 1   01 00 99 98 97

This book is dedicated to my mother, Mae Ellison,
who taught me the love of words and reading,
and to my brother, Stan Chemacki,
who taught me how to walk, talk, and read.
P. A. T.

This is for all the children
from whom I learned so much.
M. S.-C.

CONTENTS

PART II   CLINICAL ASSESSMENT

PART III   CHILDHOOD AND ADOLESCENT DISORDERS

PART IV   AN INTEGRATED INTERVENTION PARADIGM

LIST OF FIGURES

LIST OF TABLES

FOREWORD

*The boundary between behavior and biology is arbitrary and changing. It has
been imposed not by the natural contours of the disciplines, but by lack of knowledge.
As our knowledge expands, the biological and behavioral disciplines will merge
at certain points, and it is at these points of merger that our understanding of
mentation will rest on particularly secure ground. . . . Ultimately, the joining of these
two disciplines represents the emerging conviction that a coherent and biologically
unified description of mentation and behavior is possible.*
(Kandel, 1985, p. 832)

This book represents a unique perspective with regard to the practice of clinical neuropsychology with child and adolescent populations. In these brief remarks, I will attempt to place the practice of clinical child neuropsychology in its historically important context and articulate in a broad sense exactly why this important volume represents a unique turning point in the practice of clinical child neuropsychology.

As Kandel (1985) has noted, knowledge in the biological and behavioral sciences will merge at certain points, and it can no longer be argued that the study of behavior and its many deviations can be separated from our rapidly evolving understanding of the complexities of the biological organism. One needs only to read the newspaper or watch television to appreciate recent research that addresses the genetic or neurobiological basis of some forms of dementia, depression, or other "behavioral" disorders such as Attention Deficit Hyperactivity Disorder (ADHD) or severe reading disability (dyslexia) to appreciate advances in understanding some of the possible genetic, biological, and environmental interactions that must occur in various neurological or psychiatric disorders. It might be proposed that some 90% of our understanding of the interactions between genetic influences, biological ontogeny, and environmental factors has evolved most significantly in the past century and that the public at large expects this research to continue to have an impact on both our understanding of these interactions and our ability to alter the course of potentially negative outcomes. Necessarily, research that addresses these interactions must be multidisciplinary in nature, and this has both blurred professional boundaries and encouraged a deeper understanding of the importance of communication between scientists and applied clinicians.

Within the past century a number of important developments have fostered our current appreciations of the neurobiological underpinnings of neuro-psychiatric and neurodevelopmental disorders. First, despite the influences of philosophical orientations that argued against understanding behavioral, cognitive, or psychiatric disorders from a neurobiological perspective (e.g., behaviorism), clinicians continued to observe and validate observations made in the 1800s regarding the effects of brain damage on behavior. Reports published in the late 1800s noted the neurological—behavioral relationships observed in aphasic patients and in patients with alexia with and without agraphia. Clinicians in this century continued to observe these relationships, and this led to hypotheses about brain dysfunction or damage in children and adolescents with speech and language disorders, specific learning disability such as dyslexia, mental retardation, and behavioral disturbance.

Second, in the postwar recovery period after World War II, economic influences caused resources to be allocated so that millions of individuals, including veterans, were afforded an opportunity to pursue higher education. Not only did this influence the general educational level in the United States, but it was accompanied by legislation passed in the late 1950s that funded scientific research at a much higher level, in large part in response to the Soviet Union launching Sputnik into space and accelerating the "space race." What this accomplished was that we now had a vastly improved appreciation of the importance of scientific investigation and its potential to answer basic questions about our existence and those genetic, biological, and environmental influences that had an impact on our health and behavior.

Finally, advances in medical, social, and behavioral research in the past three decades have strongly encouraged the belief that basic and applied research could provide hope in improving our health and general welfare. As an example, one can well appreciate the impact that the eradication of smallpox, the prevention of polio, the development of new and more effective medicines for the treatment of epilepsy and infections, and the ability to visualize our internal organs through imaging techniques has had on the public. This may help us to understand why the public at large now expects basic research to lead to positive outcomes in treating conditions that are either life-threatening (e.g., AIDS) or have a negative impact on achieving what are now perceived to be normal health, educational, social, or even financial expectations in life (e.g., ADHD, dyslexia)

Previously published volumes in either child or pediatric neuropsychology, including mine, have focused primarily on providing a basic understanding of the neurobiological bases of child and adolescent cognitive or behavioral disorders due to overt disruptions of neurological integrity, as in cases of brain damage, or due to deviations in neurological development. Until the publication of this book, little attention has been directed at integrating this basic understanding with clinical treatment or intervention practices of proven value, although relevance was generally acknowledged or presumed, but not demonstrated.

This is exactly why this book is such an important contribution! While this book advances our basic understanding of brain—behavior relations in child and adolescent clinical populations, it also provides up-to-date information for the clinician on how to treat neuropsychologically based childhood and adolescent disorders. The integrated transactional intervention paradigm so articulately presented in this volume mandates that all clinicians who work with children and adolescents with neurodevelopmental or neuropsychiatrically based disorders have this volume as a ready resource in providing the most current and effective treatments available. Further, and perhaps most important, the authors clearly understand and address the many different medical, behavioral, and educational treatment approaches summarized and advocated in this book.

These authors recognize so well that children and adolescents with neurodevelopmental and neuropsychiatric disorders can be fully understood only in a transactional context that incorporates neurobiological, medical, familial, social, and educational perspectives. In support of their transactional model, they provide richly described clinical case studies of children and adolescents with learning disabilities, ADHD, seizure disorder, and traumatic brain injury. Clearly, this volume advances the potential impact of clinicians who provide neuropsychological services to children and adolescents in helping their clients to lead more productive and meaningful lives. This volume sets a new standard for those who practice clinical child neuropsychology and thus provides parents, teachers, medical professionals, and other health care providers with an increased level of expectation for the quality and impact of services provided.

In this sense, then, this book marks a turning point for the practice of clinical child neuropsychology. No longer will the neuropsychologist be viewed as a professional who only provides a comprehensive neuropsychological evaluation. It raises the expectation that the clinical child neuropsychologist should indeed provide both a comprehensive and treatment-specific evaluation and should have the knowledge and professional expertise to provide the treatment themselves, whether dealing with a child or adolescent with a neurobehavioral or neuropsychiatrically related disorder.

This volume will be a highly regarded resource for all psychologists who provide neuropsychological services to school-aged children and adolescents. It is current, accurately and comprehensively presents our state of knowledge, and is a wonderful resource for the provision of comprehensive neuropsychologically based strategies of clinical intervention. In this sense, this volume itself serves to illustrate that the boundaries between the neurobiological and behavioral sciences is indeed merging and the resulting perspectives can favorably impact on our abil-

ity to understand and effectively treat neuro-developmental and neuropsychiatric disorders in children and adolescents.

George W. Hynd
Center for Clinical and Developmental
    Neuropsychology
The University of Georgia

REFERENCE

Kandel, E. R. (1985). Cellular mechanisms of learning and the biological basis of individuality. In E. R. Kandel & J. H. Schwartz (Eds.), Principles of neural science (2nd ed.), pp. 816—833.

PREFACE

This book presents to psychologists the most current information about the influences of brain function on the cognitive-perceptual, academic-learning, behavioral, and psychosocial adjustment of children and adolescents. An integrated, transactional framework is explored across various neuropsychiatric and neurodevelopmental disorders, acquired injuries and diseases, biogenetic disorders, and other brain-related disorders of childhood. This framework was developed to show that theory, research, and clinical findings across paradigms that are often discussed in dichotomous or mutually exclusive ways (e.g., neuropsychological versus behavioral, neurocognitive versus psychosocial approaches) can be integrated in meaningful ways. It is essential to view childhood and adolescent disorders from an integrated perspective so that we may better understand the dynamic interplay of biological, neurodevelopmental, and environmental factors on children's learning, psychological, emotional, and social development. Such an approach enables clinicians and researchers alike to address these disorders more comprehensively.

This book is written for psychologists and graduate students from various applied disciplines in psychology (child, clinical, counseling, pediatric, neuropsychological, and school). Other medical, mental health, and educational professionals who work with children and adolescents with learning, behavioral, and psychosocial adjustment problems may also find this book of interest because implications for assessment and treatment are emphasized. The orientation of the book is transactional, so that professionals and students with varying theoretical backgrounds can develop a broader perspective on childhood disorders.

A transactional framework is important for a number of reasons. First, biogenetic factors influence and set the stage for early brain development long before the impact of the environment comes into play. The manner in which the developing brain affects the child's ability to profit from and respond to the environment is of interest to psychologists. Furthermore, disturbances in early cell proliferation, migration, and myelination underlie a number of childhood disorders (e.g., learning disabilities, autism, seizure disorders), which in turn ultimately affect cognitive, neuropsychological, academic, and psychosocial development.

Second, in many instances brain function and psychosocial-behavioral manifestations are so closely linked that it is difficult to make distinctions among contributing factors (e.g., biogenetic and neuropsychological) and their psychological outcomes. Third, numerous neurodevelopmental and acquired disorders can be altered with appropriate environmental stimulation and systematic intervention (i.e., educational or remedial strategies). Thus, biogenetic and/or neuropsychological factors can be modified such that negative learning and psychosocial outcomes (e.g., reading disabilities, attentional deficits, and psychological disorders) can be minimized with interventions that address the underlying neuropsychological substrates of the disorders (e.g., phonological awareness deficits, disinhibition of executive control functions). Further, interventions for neurodevelopmental and biogenetic disorders often require medical or pharmacological as well as behavioral, academic, and psychosocial strategies, so an integrated, transactional assessment—intervention paradigm is crucial.

This book includes five major sections. Chapters 1 and 3 provide an introduction to child neuropsychology. This includes a discussion of the various components of the transactional model (i.e., behavioral, cognitive, neuropsychological, and psychosocial paradigms), and professional training issues in Chapter 1. An overview of anatomy and physiology, including neurodevelopmental stages, is explored in Chapter 2.

Chapters 3, 4, and 5 present techniques for neuropsychological assessment. Neurophysiological and neuroimaging techniques are described in Chapter 3, with guidelines for referring children for neurological, neuroradiological, and neuropsychological evaluations presented in Chapter 4. Descriptions of standard neuropsychological batteries and tests are presented in Chapter 5, and a "process approach" to neuropsychological assessment is described.

Chapters 6 through 10 review selected childhood and adolescent disorders within a transactional framework. Neuropsychiatric disorders, including internalized and externalized disorders (Chapters 6 and 7); language and learning disorders (Chapter 8); metabolic, biogenetic, and neuromotor disorders (Chapter 9); and finally acquired disorders and diseases of childhood (Chapter 10) are reviewed. Each chapter presents an overview of the biogenetic and environmental factors that affect the neuropsychological functioning of children with these various disorders. The effects of neuropsychological and/or neurochemical anomalies associated with each disorder are explored, including the effects on the cognitive, perceptual, attentional, and memory functions. Finally, the impact of neuropsychological and environmental factors on the child's academic, behavioral, and psychological development is explored. Implications for

assessment and intervention practices are also considered for each major disorder.

An integrated intervention paradigm is presented in Chapter 11. Specific methods for addressing neurodevelopmental, acquired, and neuropsychiatric disorders are reviewed. Combined techniques are explored, and the need for collaboration among professionals is highlighted. A number of proven educational techniques for addressing language, learning, and psychosocial problems are presented. The potential benefits and side effects of major classes of medications are also discussed. Finally, case studies are offered in Chapter 12 as examples to illustrate the dynamic neuropsychological—environmental transaction, and to show how a comprehensive process-oriented neuropsychological assessment can inform intervention planning.

Our intent in writing this book was to review and to integrate childhood disorders within a transactional, neuropsychological paradigm. We hope that by integrating research and clinical findings across different theoretical orientations, we have shown the interaction among neuropsychological and environmental factors in affecting the child's cognitive, behavioral, and psychosocial functioning. We also showed that neurodevelopmental, biogenetic, and acquired brain-related disorders can be altered with appropriate educational, behavioral, pharmacological, and psychosocial interventions. Thus, although biogenetic factors influence neurodevelopment and brain functioning in children and adolescents, this relationship can be influenced in meaningful ways.

ACKNOWLEDGMENTS

Writing this book was an exhilarating experience in much the same way that finishing a marathon is–in the beginning it seemed like such a good idea, in the middle we forgot what was so great about the half-brained idea in the first place, and in the end we forgot how long it had taken to reach the finish line. But we never forgot why the goal was worth pursuing. Our interest in children and adolescents, particularly those with neurodevelopmental and neuropsychiatric disorders, was the driving force behind this project. A desire to understand and to articulate this understanding to others was paramount. There were so many children and families who brought the theory and research to life, who made the face of neurologically based disorders so real and poignant. We will always remember your courage and dignity. We learned so much from all of you.

My own process of understanding has evolved over the years and has been shaped by a number of people. Many friends and colleagues have influenced my thinking about brain—behavior relationships in children. I must acknowledge my co-author, Margaret Semrud-Clikeman. She has been a true collaborator and friend. Her research has been informative and serves as a solid contribution to our knowledge about the neuropsychological foundations of dyslexia and ADHD. I thank her for the many hours she spent on this project and for her sense of humor on those tedious rewrites and hours spent on Medline.

There are many others who contributed to my professional development, including Bill Gibson, who taught me so much about neuroanatomy, neurophysiology, and neurodevelopment; John Obrzut, who demonstrated the power and elegance of pursuing a line of research to answer those basic questions about how children learn; and Philip Smith, who provided his research and statistical experience to many projects. George Hynd has been both a mentor and a friend. His research has advanced the field of child neuropsychology in too many ways to mention here. His body of work serves as a model of the excellence to which we all aspire.

Finally, my family and friends have been forgiving of my "too busy to come" schedule that kept me away from summer visits to Connecticut and longer Christmas breaks. Your love and support was really a godsend.

P.A.T.

I would like to acknowledge my gratitude to Anne Teeter, my co-author, for introducing me to neuropsychology and encouraging the development of my career. I would also like to acknowledge my debt to George Hynd, Dennis Norman, Pauline Filipek, Ronald Steingard and Joseph Biederman for my research potential and understanding of child neuropsychology. I am most indebted to my husband, John Clikeman, for making the many moves to advance my career, for supporting me through dark days, and for always being my first and foremost cheerleader.

M.S.-C.

We both owe a debt of gratitude to Dr. Sharon Murphy, Professor of Psychiatry at the University of Chicago, for her helpful comments and suggestions during early drafts of the book. We would like to thank Marilyn Budhl, our graphics artist, for her wonderful and detailed drawings of the brain. Our editor, Mylan Jaixen, also deserves thanks for his patience when we were past our deadlines, and for his encouragement to develop this project in the first place. Mylan passed the baton to Carla Daves, who helped us through the final stages of editing. We thank her for her assistance. Finally, our thanks are extended to Judy Ashkenaz for her meticulous editing and helpful comments.

CHAPTER 1

INTRODUCTION TO CHILD CLINICAL NEUROPSYCHOLOGY

THEORETICAL ORIENTATION: AN INTEGRATED PARADIGM

Child neuropsychology is the study of brain function and behavior in children and adolescents. Because brain functioning has a direct impact on the behavioral, cognitive, and psychosocial adjustment of children and adolescents, disorders must be addressed within an integrated model of child clinical neuropsychology. Further, the development of the central nervous system (CNS) and the neurodevelopmental course of childhood disorders are of importance within an integrated framework.

Clinical child neuropsychologists study developmental disorders, such as dyslexia (Obrzut & Hynd, 1991; Hynd & Cohen, 1983; Hynd, Marshall, & Semrud-Clikeman, 1991) and pervasive developmental disorders (Kinney, Woods, & Yurgelun-Todd, 1986; Ritvo et al., 1990); psychiatric disorders including attention deficit hyperactivity (Hynd, Semrud-Clikeman, Lorys, Novey, & Eliopulos, 1990; Hynd, Hern, et al., 1993), obsessive-compulsive (Luxenberg et al., 1988), and conduct disorders (Weintraub & Mesulam, 1983); traumatic brain injury (Brown, Chadwick, Shaffer, Rutter, & Traub, 1981); acquired disorders as a result of exposure to teratogenic substances such as alcohol, cocaine, lead, and radiation (Cook & Leventhal, 1992); and other neurological disorders including seizure (Huttenlocher & Hapke, 1990) and Tourette syndrome (Cohen, Shaywitz, Caparulo, et al., 1978; Comings, 1990). Studies routinely have identified the importance of intact functional cortical and subcortical systems in the overall adjustment of children and adolescents. Further, researchers have recently begun to address specific strategies for treating various brain-related disorders. Initial results suggest reason to be optimistic when interventions consider the child's functional neuropsychological status.

EMERGENCE OF CHILD CLINICAL NEUROPSYCHOLOGY

Child clinical neuropsychology has emerged as an important theoretical, empirical, and methodological perspective for understanding and treating developmental, psychiatric, psychosocial, and learning disorders in children and adolescents. Although a relatively young science, child clinical neuropsychology has been significantly advanced by the use of medical technologies including magnetic resonance imaging (MRI), positron emission tomography (PET), computerized tomography scans (CAT), and regional cerebral blood flow (rCBF) (Hynd & Willis, 1988). The potential for employing functional magnetic resonance imaging techniques (fMRI) for investigating brain activity by monitoring regional changes in blood flow in children with neurodevelopmental disorders also appears promising. In 1988, Lewis Judd, the director of the National Institute of Mental Health, stated that 95% of what we know about the brain—behavior relationship had been discovered in the preceding five years, primarily as a result of the medical technology available in the brain sciences (Yudofsky & Hales, 1992).

The study of the brain—behavior relationship has been revolutionized by these medical technologies. Many psychiatric disorders of childhood once thought to be mental or functional in nature (Yudofsky & Hales, 1992), and behavioral disorders presumed to be related to noncontingent reinforcement systems and other environmental factors (Gresham & Gansle,

1992) have been found to have a neurodevelopmental or neurochemical basis.

For example, children and adolescents with attention deficit hyperactivity disorders (ADHD) may have dysfunction in alternate cortical pathways depending on the primary behavioral manifestations of the disorder, such as overarousal, uninhibited, or cognitive deficits (Hunt, Lau, & Ryu, 1991; Hunt, Mandl, Lau, & Hughes, 1991). Further, the presumed central nervous system dysfunction attributed to reading disabilities in some children (Hynd & Cohen, 1983; Obrzut & Hynd, 1986) has been traced to specific cortical regions in the left hemisphere that mediate phonemic awareness and linguistic-semantic processing (Galaburda & Kemper, 1979; Obrzut & Hynd, 1991; Semrud-Clikeman, Hynd, Novey, & Eliopulos, 1991).

The manner in which disturbances are approached has been revolutionized by neuroscience and medical technologies, such that any serious study of developmental problems must consider neuropsychological theories, methodologies, and empirical findings if the science of childhood and adolescent disorders is to be advanced. Child clinical neuropsychology can be formulated and articulated within an integrative perspective for the study and treatment of child and adolescent disorders. By addressing brain functions and the environmental influences inherent in complex human behaviors, such as thinking, feeling, reasoning, planning, and inhibiting, clinicians can begin to meet more adequately the needs of children with severe learning, psychiatric, developmental, and acquired disorders.

A neurodevelopmental perspective is necessary for a better understanding of childhood disorders for several reasons: (1) the influence of developing brain structures on mental development is sequential and predictable; (2) the effects of brain injury in children have been documented by numerous studies; (3) the nature and persistence of learning problems is dependent on an interaction between dysfunctional and intact neurological systems; and (4) the developing brain is highly vulnerable to numerous genetic and/ or environmental conditions that can result in severe disorders of childhood (Hooper & Boyd, 1986). Moreover, attention to the scope and sequence of development of cortical structures and related behaviors that emerge in the child is important to ascertain the intactness of the child's development and to assess further the impact of the environment (i.e., enrichment, instructional opportunities, and intervention strategies) on this process. This book incorporates theories and research findings from diverse fields, including the neurosciences, neurobiology, behavioral neuropsychology, clinical neuropsychology, cognitive and developmental psychology, social and family systems psychology, and behavioral psychology. Thus, an integrated neurodevelopmental framework serves to inform clinical approaches for the study and treatment of childhood and adolescent disorders.

In this book, child clinical neuropsychology incorporates theories, approaches, and interventions that address the brain—behavior relationship in select neurodevelopmental, acquired, and neuropsychiatric disorders of childhood and adolescence. A transactional perspective is advanced to illustrate the following: (1) how abnormalities or complications in brain development interact with environmental factors in various childhood disorders; (2) how disorders develop over time depending on the nature and severity of neuropsychological impairment; and (3) how neurodevelopmental, neuropsychiatric, and acquired disorders (i.e., traumatic injury) need to be assessed and treated within an integrated clinical protocol addressing neuropsychological, cognitive, psychosocial, and environmental factors. In summary, this book presents child clinical neuropsychology within an integrated framework, incorporating behavioral, psychosocial, cognitive, and environmental factors into a comprehensive model for the assessment and treatment of brain-related disorders in children and adolescents.

PERSPECTIVES FOR THE STUDY OF CHILDHOOD DISORDERS

Theoretical orientations have often been pitted one against another–"medical" versus "behavioral," "within-child" versus "environmental," "neuropsychological" versus "psychoeducational." Further, some have adopted one approach over others in an attempt to describe and treat childhood disorders. Although each orientation provides slightly, or in some cases significantly, different perspectives about childhood disorders, research that compares orientations often oversimplifies the complexity and dynamic interaction inherent in many disorders of childhood (Gaddes & Edgell, 1994). Various theoretical orientations to be considered for clinical child study will be discussed briefly and will be integrated throughout the text whenever possible. An integrated paradigm serves as the foundation of our conceptualization of clinical child neuropsychology.

Teeter and Semrud-Clikeman (1995) assert that diverse perspectives should be integrated for a comprehensive approach to neurodevelopmental disorders and for the advancement of the science of childhood psychopathology. To conduct a comprehensive child study, clinicians need to incorporate various paradigms. Child clinical neuropsychology is then viewed as one essential feature to consider when assessing and treating childhood and adolescent disorders. Differential diagnosis, developmental course, and intervention efficacy should be explored utilizing psychosocial, cognitive, behavioral, and neuropsychological paradigms.

Neuropsychological Paradigm

Neuropsychology is the study of brain—behavior relationships and assumes a causal relationship between the two variables (Obrzut & Hynd, 1990). Neuropsychology offers the following advantages for child study:

1. It is a well-established science with knowledge relevant to childhood disorders (Gaddes & Edgell, 1994).
2. There is a growing body of evidence suggesting that "behavior and neurology are inseparable" (Hynd & Willis, 1988, p. 5).
3. It provides a means for studying the long-term sequelae of head injury in children (Goldstein & Levin, 1990).
4. It provides a means for investigating abnormalities in brain function that increase the risk for psychiatric disorders in children (Tramontana & Hooper, 1989).

5. It provides a means for early prediction and treatment of reading disabilities (Felton & Brown, 1991).

Gaddes and Edgell (1994) state that "All behavior–including cognitive processes, which are essentially psychological–is mediated by the brain and central nervous system and their integrated and supporting physiological systems" (p. 473). Although this statement seems abundantly obvious, the exact nature of brain functioning and behavior is complex, and our knowledge is incomplete, particularly concerning the developing brain. Gaddes and Edgell (1994) argue that this should not deter us from considering child neuropsychology or lead us to ignore what we do know about the developing brain when investigating and treating childhood disorders. Although behavioral psychologists argue that neuropsychology diverts attention from behavioral techniques with documented treatment validity (Gresham & Gansle, 1992; Reschly & Gresham, 1989), clinical child neuropsychologists utilize techniques that consider the interaction of psychosocial, environmental, neurocognitive, biogenetic, and neurochemical aspects of behaviors in an effort to understand more fully the relationship between physiological and psychological systems, and frequently incorporate these same behavioral techniques.

Although neuropsychological approaches provide useful information for understanding and treating childhood disorders, they should not be employed to the exclusion of other theories or methods of assessment (Gaddes & Edgell, 1994). Behavioral, psychosocial, and cognitive variables also should be addressed in a comprehensive child clinical study. Critical aspects of each of these paradigms will be reviewed briefly in the following sections.

Behavioral Paradigm

Behavioral approaches have long been recognized for their utility in assessing and treating childhood and adolescent disorders (Kratochwill & Bergan, 1990; Shapiro, 1989; Shinn, 1989). Analysis of the antecedents and consequences of behaviors is an essential feature of behavioral approaches with attention to the impact of the environment on the understanding and remediation of learning and behavioral difficulties in children (Shapiro, 1989). Assessment and intervention techniques in a behavioral paradigm are closely related and often occur simultaneously. For example, a functional analysis of behavior is ongoing assessment of the efficacy of a treatment plan (Kratochwill & Plunge, 1992). Within this perspective, behaviors are targeted for analysis, and subsequent treatment plans are developed to address areas of concern.

Although some might suggest that behavioral and neuropsychological approaches are mutually exclusive, important information may be lost about a child when these two approaches are not integrated (Teeter & Semrud-Clikeman, 1995). The integration of behavioral assessment and intervention into a clinical neuropsychological paradigm is an important aspect for developing ecologically valid treatment programs of children and adolescents with brain-related disorders (Horton & Puente, 1986). Behavioral factors that interact with neuropsychological functioning include: effects of malnutrition on the developing brain (Cravioto & Arrieta, 1983); effects of parental care and early stimulation on the developing brain; the impact of environmental demands on the child (e.g., school, home, and peer/family interactions) when making predictions about recovery from brain impairment (Rourke, Bakker, Fisk, & Strang, 1983); "psychosocial adversity, family reactions, and pre-accident behavior or temperamental features" on the development of psychiatric disorders following brain injury (Rutter, Chadwick, & Shaffer, 1983, p. 103); and interventions that facilitate recovery after brain injury (Gray & Dean, 1989).

Horton and Puente (1986) argue that there is sufficient evidence that behavioral techniques are effective with brain-injured and learning-disabled children. However, they suggest that more research beyond single case reports is needed to determine whether neuropsychological assessment can be useful for selecting specific behavioral treatments. Rourke (1989) also provides evidence that deficits (social/emotional, cognitive, adaptational, behavioral, and academic) as-

sociated with right-hemisphere dysfunction (i.e., nonverbal learning disabilities syndrome) can be identified with common neuropsychological measures and can be remediated with specific behavioral and cognitive approaches.

Some behavioral psychologists argue that knowledge about the neuropsychological substrates of childhood disorders is not necessary for designing effective treatment plans (Gresham & Gansle, 1992). Others encourage the use of drug treatments and ignore environmental factors contributing to childhood disorders (Schmitt, 1975). Although the accumulated body of research is limited regarding specific types of behavioral therapies or techniques to utilize with various brain injuries (Lovell & Starratt, 1992), there is a growing literature to support the practice of integrating these perspectives with various neurologically based childhood disorders (Semrud-Clikeman & Hynd, & 1991b; Rourke et al., 1983; Teeter & Semrud-Clikeman, 1995). Further, behavioral interventions are frequently incorporated in treatment programs for children with disorders known to have a central nervous system basis, including learning disabilities (Wong, 1991), attention deficit hyperactivity disorders (Pelham, 1993a), and traumatic brain injury (Deaton, 1990).

Psychosocial and cognitive factors are also considered in an integrated clinical neuropsychological model for studying and treating childhood disorders. The importance of these nonneurologic factors will be discussed briefly in the following section.

Psychosocial and Cognitive Paradigms

The fact that various neurodevelopmental, psychiatric, and behavioral disorders have associated psychosocial and cognitive deficits increases the importance of investigating these features in child clinical neuropsychological assessment and of addressing these deficits in treatment programs. The relationship among cognitive functioning, psychosocial characteristics, and neuropsychological deficits for various childhood disorders is multidirectional or transactional in nature. In some instances neuropsychological functioning may help to explain many of the behavioral, cognitive, and psychosocial deficits found in childhood disorders such as ADHD and dyslexia (Semrud-Clikeman & Hynd, 1993; Teeter & Semrud-Clikeman, 1995). In other instances cognitive and/or psychosocial features, such as premorbid intelligence, language and reasoning abilities, and/or social-emotional adjustment, have an impact on the recovery of functions following traumatic brain injury in children and adolescents (Bigler, 1990).

The relationship between brain morphology and activity on cognitive and psychosocial functioning has been investigated in children with neuropsychiatric disorders, including ADHD. Apparently brain-related ADHD symptoms—inattention, overactivity, poor impulse control, and behavioral disinhibition—often result in significant social and peer difficulties (Hynd, Lorys, et al., 1991). Moreover, children with ADHD frequently experience learning disabilities (Semrud-Clikeman, Biederman, et al., 1992), depression (Biederman et al., 1992), and anxiety (Steingard, Biederman, Doyle, & Sprich-Buckminster, 1992). Thus, the impact of abnormal brain functioning can be quite profound and broad-reaching in terms of the child's overall functional picture. Further, stimulants that are known to modify the neurochemical activity of the brain appear to have positive impact on cognitive and social functioning in the majority of children with ADHD.

Deficits in regulation, planning, and organization skills have been found to have a negative impact on the social and emotional adjustment of children and adolescents with ADHD. For example, children with ADHD are characterized as noncompliant and rebellious (Johnston & Pelham, 1986) and are often described as rigid, domineering, irritating, and annoying in social situations (Milich & Landau, 1989). Peer rejection is also common among children with ADHD (Hynd, Lorys, Semrud-Clikeman, et al., 1991), particularly when aggression is present (Milich & Landau, 1989). The extent to which these social outcomes are related to impulsivity, distractibility, and disinhibition, which have been found to have a neurobiological basis, need to be explored within an integrated paradigm. What appears evident is that

ADHD can produce persistent social isolation and that it has been found in adults after major symptoms of hyperactivity are no longer present (Weiss & Hechtman, 1986). Reports of depression (75%), juvenile delinquency (23% to 45%), and alcoholism (27%) in older ADHD individuals further suggest the limiting influences of this biogenetic disorder on psychosocial adjustment even into adolescence and adulthood (Barkley, 1989).

Children and adolescents with ADHD also have associated cognitive disturbances that are severe and chronic in nature. For example, school failure (Barkley, 1990), academic underachievement, and learning disabilities (Epstein, Shaywitz, Shaywitz, & Woolston, 1992; Lambert & Sandoval, 1980; Semrud-Clikeman, Biederman, et al., 1992) are frequently reported in children and adolescents with ADHD; and few adolescents with ADHD complete college (Barkley, 1990). Difficulties in self-regulation and response inhibition may result in academic decline, decreases in verbal intelligence, and related psychosocial problems (Barkley, 1994). Thus, basic neurochemical and neuropsychological abnormalities interact with social, psychological, and behavioral factors to create significant adjustment problems for children with ADHD.

There are several distinct neurophysiological and neuroanatomical findings that may be related to the associated psychosocial and cognitive problems found in children and adolescents with ADHD, including the following: (1) underactivation or hypoarousal of the reticular activating system (RAS), a subcortical region that activates the cortex (Klove, 1989); (2) subtle anatomical differences in the right caudate nucleus (near the lateral ventricles) (Filipek, Semrud-Clikeman, et al., in press), and the frontal lobes (Hynd, Hern, Voeller, & Marshall, 1991; Semrud-Clikeman, Filipek, et al., 1994); or (3) smaller genu and/or splenium in the corpus callosum (Hynd, Semrud-Clikeman, et al., 1991; Semrud-Clikeman, Filipek, et al., 1994). Right-hemisphere structures also appear to be involved in the regulation of attention (Riccio, Hynd, Cohen, & Gonzalez, 1993; Semrud-Clikeman, Filipek, et al., 1994; Voeller, 1995).

Lou, Henriksen, and Bruhn (1984) found that children with ADHD displayed hypoperfusion of the mesial frontal regions, particularly in the white matter. The frontal cortex has been shown to modulate motor output, to organize and execute goal-directed behavior, and to inhibit responding (Kolb & Whishaw, 1985). Frontal lobe arousal apparently occurs when methylphenidate is administered. Once activated, the frontal lobes exert a regulatory influence over subcortical and cortical regions of the brain that ultimately monitors motor activity and distractibility (Heilman, Voeller, & Nadeau, 1991). Further, the frontal lobes have been found to be underactivated in ADHD parents who also have ADHD children (Zametkin et al., 1990). Barkley (1994) has argued that ADHD is not an attentional disorder but, rather, a disorder of dysregulation. Thus, specific symptoms of ADHD (i.e., response disinhibition and poor self-regulation), are likely a result of impairment in executive functions mediated by the frontal cortex (Barkley, 1994).

While various neuropsychological functional systems are involved, children with learning disabilities (LD) also exhibit psychosocial and cognitive deficits that may be related to underlying neural mechanisms. Nussbaum, Bigler, and Koch (1986) suggest that LD children with low verbal skills and intact visual-spatial abilities tend to have high rates of depression. Nussbaum et al. (1986) postulate that the unique pattern of neuropsychological deficits observed in this subgroup of LD children may further exacerbate personality and behavioral adjustment. Further, children with nonverbal learning disabilities (NLD), presumed to result from right-hemisphere dysfunction, tend to have high rates of suicide (Bigler, 1989a; Rourke, Young, & Leenaars, 1989; Semrud-Clikeman & Hynd, 1991b). Rourke (1989) suggests that poor social interaction skills, inappropriate verbal interchanges, and poor social adjustment are a result of underlying neuropsychological assets and deficits found in children with NLD.

Investigating data across divergent paradigms makes it possible to build an integrated model for understanding, assessing, and treating children and adolescents with various disorders. Child clinical neuropsychology can serve as a vehicle for an integrated assessment to determine the nature of distur-bances and to develop treatment programs for childhood disorders such as ADHD, dyslexia, and other learning disabilities. Psychiatric disorders such as anxiety and depression also may need to be investigated from a neuropsychological perspective. Once neuropsychological status is assessed, the interaction of environmental-behavioral, psychosocial, and cognitive factors can then be more fully explored.

Transactional Paradigm

To date, a transactional neuropsychological paradigm has not been studied systematically across different types of childhood psychopathology. Emerging literature suggests that this is a promising endeavor for studying learning disabilities, ADHD, traumatic head injury, and other neurodevelopmental disorders. This text discusses the neuropsychological correlates of psychiatric, neurodevelopmental, and acquired (e.g., traumatic brain injury) disorders of childhood; the neurodevelopmental course of these disorders; and the impact of moderator variables such as cognitive, social, and behavioral aspects on the overall adjustment of children and adolescents with various disorders. The extent to which neuropsychological weaknesses limit cognitive and psychosocial adjustment or change across different age ranges will be explored within a transactional model.

In isolation, neuropsychological approaches have limitations in terms of definitive answers about the relationship between brain dysfunction and the cognitive, psychosocial, and behavioral characteristics of childhood disorders because this is a relatively young science. Within a transactional model, however, it is possible to investigate how intact versus impaired functional neuropsychological systems interact with and limit cognitive-intellectual and psychosocial adjustment in children and adolescents. This text presents a transactional model of child clinical neuropsychology.

In a transactional model, basic biogenetic and environmental factors, including prenatal and postnatal toxins or insults, influence the development and maturation of the central nervous system. This relationship is depicted in Figure 1.1. Subcortical and corti-

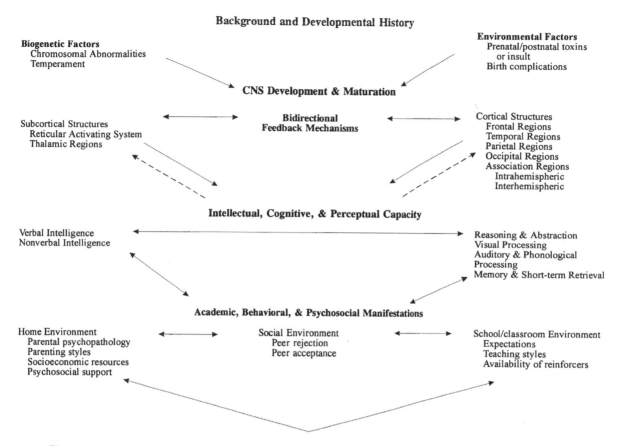

Figure 1.1. Transactional Neuropsychological Model for Understanding Childhood and Adolescent Disorders

cal regions have a bidirectional influence on various neural functional systems affecting the intellectual and perceptual capacity of the child. These functional systems ultimately interact with and influence the expression of various behavioral, psychological, and cognitive manifestations of childhood disorders. Social, family, and school environments also interact in mutually influential ways to exacerbate childhood disorders or to facilitate compensatory or coping skills in the individual child.

Sameroff and colleagues (1975, 1989) have hypothesized that behavioral and biological functioning needs to be incorporated into a model for developmental regulation. In other words, biological vulnerabilities influence and are influenced by coping skills and stresses experienced in the child's life. Sameroff and Emde (1989) further state that psychopathology should be understood not only in terms of the child's ability to cope or not cope with situations but also in relation to the "continuity of ordered or disordered experience across time interacting with an individual's unique biobehavioral characteristics" (pp. 20—21). Sameroff's developmental approach attempts to identify the variables that impact the child's organization of his or her experience into a method of adaptation. Such adaptation may or may not be efficient or "healthy" but can be viewed as the child's attempt to achieve self-stabilization (Sameroff & Emde, 1989). In such a paradigm, the individual reacts to both internal and external environments as he or she attempts to make his or her way in the world.

In our transactional model, Sameroff's theory of a biobehavioral interaction plays a major role. The transactional model presented in this text assumes a dynamic interaction among the biogenetic, neuropsychological, environmental, cognitive, and psychosocial systems. Further, biogenetic forces shape the child's experiences and are most predominant during embryogenesis and early infancy (Sameroff & Emde, 1989). As the child becomes more independent, he or she begins to experience influences from the social as well as the cultural environment. In turn, the child's basic temperament also interacts with the social environment and causes changes in that environment. For example, an infant or toddler who is "easy" to manage will fare reasonably well with a caregiver (parent) regardless of the parent's temperamental characteristics (i.e., calm or disruptive). In contrast, a more "difficult," fussy, demanding infant or toddler will not mesh well with a caregiver who is also fussy and demanding (Scarr & McCartney, 1983). This same "difficult" infant would be more likely to prosper under the care of a parent with an even temperament. The "difficult"—"difficult" dyad will interact in mutually unsatisfactory ways. This parent—child interaction may be characterized as distant and nonreinforcing, which is more likely to result in attachment or bonding problems. In this manner, the child's constitutional temperament forms a template on which psychopathology develops or is forestalled. By contrast, a "difficult" child—"easy" parent match may be advantageous in that the parent can help reduce the adverse affects of the child's inborn biological tendencies. So, although parental caretaking may not change the biological tendencies of the child, it may buffer biological vulnerabilities (Teeter, in preparation).

While our transactional model acknowledges the role of the developing nervous system, it also recognizes that severe childhood disturbances are not necessarily inevitable. Appropriate psychosocial, cognitive, and/or educational interventions, in conjunction with changes in the ecological systems of the child (i.e., home, school, and social environment) can reduce the negative effects of many neuropsychological

or biogenetically based disorders. For some childhood disorders, psychopharmacological therapy can also be beneficial. The important point to emphasize is that brain—behavior relationships are dynamic and fluid, and this dynamic transaction should be investigated in the clinical assessment and treatment of childhood disorders. Thus, an integrated model will be used throughout this book as a method to inform neuropsychological assessment and intervention.

NEUROPSYCHOLOGICAL PERSPECTIVES ON ASSESSMENT AND INTERVENTION

Child clinical neuropsychological assessment originally focused on identifying the presence or absence of brain damage in individuals, comparing cognitive differences among children and adults following injury, and determining the specific type and nature of cognitive deficits associated with brain damage (Boll & Barth, 1981). During this phase, the search for a single item or test to localize and lateralize brain damage was of primary importance (Lezak, 1994). A functional organizational approach to child clinical neuropsychology is recommended by others, with the emphasis placed on assessment of the sequence and rate of skill development and on the measurement of how disabilities interfere with and disrupt normal development (Fletcher & Taylor, 1984). Further, psychological tests are frequently being used in conjunction with more direct measures of brain function, such as MRI and CT scans, in cases involving traumatic brain injury or tumor processes (Hynd, 1988).

Trends in neuropsychological assessment with children and adolescents focus on the following variables:

1. Neuropsychology distinguishes behaviors that are considered to be within a normal developmental framework from those considered to be alterations of the central nervous system given the child's social-environmental context (Hynd, 1988).
2. Neuropsychology seeks to identify and explain the various learning deficits or disorders that are as-

sociated with impaired brain function (Obrzut & Hynd, 1991).

3. Neuropsychology is concerned with evaluating the neurodevelopmental course of specific subtypes of learning disabilities to improve early identification and intervention (Rourke, 1989).

4. Neuropsychologists monitor the recovery of function following brain injury and neurosurgery, and measure the effects of possible deterioration of function associated with degenerative brain diseases (Chadwick & Rutter, 1983).

5. Neuropsychologists focus on understanding the cognitive, behavioral, intellectual, attentional, motoric, memory, and personality deficits associated with traumatic brain injury (Bigler, 1990).

6. Neuropsychology investigates the psychiatric disorders of children with severe neurological disorders (Tramontana & Hooper, 1989).

7. Neuropsychology assists in the design of remediation programs, particularly when used within an integrated clinical framework (Sohlberg & Mateer, 1989).

Therefore, this book advances the perspective that clinical neuropsychological assessment should be comprehensive enough to answer referral questions while integrating the behavioral, cognitive-intellectual, psychosocial, and environmental variables within a developmental framework. In a multidisciplinary setting these areas are frequently evaluated by various professionals. In other settings, the child clinical neuropsychologist is responsible for evaluating all of these variables. In both cases, a comprehensive evaluation addresses the main referral question while also screening for additional explanations for the child's areas of concern. Regardless of who actually conducts the evaluation of psychosocial, educational, and family systems problems, the child clinical neuropsychologist will consider these results when formulating diagnostic and intervention plans.

Neurodevelopmental Framework for Child Neuropsychology

Fletcher and Taylor (1984) provide a theoretical foundation for child clinical neuropsychology and describe

several fallacies that now exist in the field. Fletcher and Taylor (1984) point out the danger in: (1) assuming that signs of adult brain-related disorders are similar for children; (2) assuming that tests designed for adults measure the same skills in children; (3) assuming that specific behavioral deficits are direct reflections of brain disease or damage; and (4) assuming that behavioral deficits represent brain impairment or deviancy on some clear continuum.

In an effort to avoid these fallacies, Fletcher and Taylor (1984) describe a procedure for conceptualizing developmental neuropsychology. The basic postulates of this model, termed the functional organization approach, emphasize the significance of dividing the behavioral characteristics of developmental disorders into those that form the basis of the disability and identifying those deficits that are correlated with the disability. One should also consider how moderator variables, including environmental and social factors, influence the basic competencies and disabilities of the child where the central nervous system is viewed as one of several influences. Questions in child clinical neuropsychology begin to focus on the sequence in which skills are developed, the rate at which skills are developed, and the ways these skills change at each developmental stage. Further, Fletcher and Taylor (1984) suggest a need to focus on how disabilities interfere with or disrupt normal development, rather than on identifying which brain areas are deficient.

Early attempts at utilizing a developmental model for investigating childhood learning disorders have shown promise. For example, Satz and Sparrow (1970) found a relationship between the types of tests used and the discriminatory power of the tests based on the developmental age of the child with reading disabilities. Younger and older children show different patterns of disabilities in such a way that those skills developing earlier are deficient for younger children, whereas skills developing at a later age tend to be impaired in older children. For example, younger children tended to show deficits in visual-perceptual, visual-motor, and directional-spatial skills, whereas language based and reasoning deficits appeared more prominent in older children. Consequently, a lag in early skills may be overcome, and lags in skills that are more complex and develop at later ages may become obvious in older children. Others have shown that specific patterns of cognitive and neuropsychological abilities and deficits vary with age in learning-disabled groups (Fletcher, Taylor, Morris, & Satz, 1982; Morris, Blashfield, & Satz, 1986). Still others have shown that reading difficulties are associated with early language-related deficits (i.e., phonemic awareness deficits) that are highly responsive to early interventions (Cunningham, 1989, 1990). These findings have implications both for assessment and for treatment.

Rationale for an Integrated Neuropsychological Model

An integrated neuropsychological paradigm is recommended for making accurate clinical diagnoses, for determining the course and prognosis, and for designing treatment interventions for childhood and adolescent disorders. Adherence to a single theoretical perspective or the adoption of one paradigm to the exclusion of others leads to missed opportunities for more fully understanding the nature of complex human behaviors in children (Teeter & Semrud-Clikeman, 1995). Comprehensive clinical practice, accurate diagnosis, and effective intervention rely on an integrated perspective. Further, educational programming, psychosocial interventions, and psychopharmacological regimes must be multifaceted to be most effective for many childhood disorders.

There are several reasons that an integrated approach is necessary when assessing and treating child and adolescent disorders. First, research demonstrates that neurodevelopmental deficits identified in young children are associated with later learning disabilities and adjustment problems (Berninger, 1990). In some cases a fairly predictable course of development can be anticipated when specific neurocognitive deficits are present, including nonverbal learning disorders (Rourke, 1989), verbal-language-related reading disabilities (Pirrozolo, 1981), phonemic awareness deficits (Stanovich, 1986), and impaired temporal processing deficits of auditory information (Stark & Tallal, 1988). Neuropsychological and neurocognitive assessment procedures have been used for identifying children with early learning problems. Recent evidence suggests that remediation can be successful for reading-disabled children with phonemic awareness deficits (Cunningham, 1990; Korkman & Peltomaa, 1993); however, Torgesen (1991b) suggests that children with phonological core deficits are more resistant to intervention than other children with reading problems. Tallal et al. (1996) also report that children with linguistic or cognitive impairments show remarkable progress in language comprehension when the rate of acoustic stimuli is modified using computer programs. Rourke (1989) also found that children who display arithmetic disabilities have distinct neuropsychological strengths and weaknesses that are responsive to treatment. Understanding the nature of the neuropsychological features underlying specific childhood disorders allows the developmental course of the disorder to be described and treatment planning to be enhanced. Emerging literature suggests that for some learning disorders, the adverse affects of neurodevelopmental abnormalities can be altered with effective and highly specific early intervention.

Second, the nature and severity of traumatic brain injury are related to cognitive, psychosocial, and adjustment problems in children (Berg, 1986). Approximately 1 million children a year sustain brain injuries, with about 20% requiring hospitalization (Eiben et al., 1984). Careful evaluation and monitoring of these children is imperative, and recent federal legislation recognizes traumatic brain injury as a special education need. Nearly 50% of children with severe brain injury have been found to develop new psychiatric disturbances postinjury, and related behavioral problems persist long after cognitive deficits improve (Brown, Chadwick, Schaffner, Rutter, & Traub, 1981). Further, social disinhibition is frequently observed in children with closed head injuries. Even mild head injuries can result in various cognitive difficulties, including grade retention, underachievement, and in some cases increased need for special education or resource support (Bigler, 1990). Knowing the neuropsychological systems involved, the level and degree of injury, the pervasive nature of the injury, and the developmental course of the injury is imperative to successful rehabilitation and reintegration into the school, social, and familial milieu for the child or adolescent with head injuries.

Third, converging data suggest that many psychiatric disorders have a biochemical basis, and some require psychopharmacological therapy in conjunction with more traditional behavioral and psychosocial interventions. Many childhood disorders are chronic in nature and severely limit the long-term adjustment of children. There is a growing need to utilize an integrated model so that presenting problems and the core features of disorders can be understood in relationship to biological indices (Ewing-Cobbs & Fletcher, 1990). Further, the extent to which non-neurological/environmental moderator variables influence this interaction is also of interest. Ewing-Cobbs and Fletcher (1990) suggest starting at the level of behavior and proceeding to the biological level of analysis to understand this complex interaction. In this manner, behavior, biology, and environment interact with resulting cognitive, social, and emotional functioning.

PROFESSIONAL TRAINING

Professional Training Standards

The International Neuropsychological Society (INS), Division 40 (Clinical Neuropsychology) of the American Psychological Association (APA), and the National Academy of Neuropsychology (NAN) are major professional organizations comprising researchers and clinicians in neuropsychology and child neuropsychology. Professional training standards have been of particular interest to these organizations in an effort to assure the expertise of those individuals practicing clinical child neuropsychology. Table 1.1 summarizes guidelines established and endorsed by INS.

Clinicians interested in becoming experts in child neuropsychology should consider the recommended curricula and internship standards. INS recommends Ph.D. training, with core course work in general psychology, general clinical psychology, basic neurosciences, and clinical neuropsychology. Internship guidelines specify 1800 hours, with 50% time devoted

Table 1.1. Guidelines for Doctoral Training in Neuropsychology

Education
May be accomplished through a Ph.D. program in Clinical Neuropsychology offered by a psychology department or medical facility or through completion of a Ph.D. program in a related specialty (e.g., clinical psychology) that offers sufficient specialization in clinical neuropsychology.

Required Core
  A. Generic psychology core:
      1. Statistics and methodology
      2. Learning, cognition, and perception
      3. Social psychology and personality
      4. Physiological psychology
      5. Life span development
      6. History

  B. Generic clinical core:
      1. Psychopathology
      2. Psychometric theory
      3. Interview and assessment techniques
         a. Interviewing
         b. Intellectual assessment
         c. Personality assessment
      4. Intervention Techniques
         a. Counseling and psychotherapy
         b. Behavior therapy/modification
         c. Consultation
      5. Professional ethics

  C. Neurosciences: Basic human and animal neuropsychology:
      1. Basic neuroscience
      2. Advanced physiological and psychopharmacology
      3. Neuropsychology of perceptual, cognitive, and executive processes
      4. Research design and research practicum in neuropsychology

  D. Specific clinical neuropsychology training:
      1. Clinical neuropsychology and neuropathology
      2. Specialized neuropsychological assessment techniques
      3. Specialized neuropsychological intervention techniques
      4. Assessment practicum with children and/or adults
      5. Clinical neuropsychology internship of 1800 hours, preferably in a university setting

Internship
The internship must devote at least 50% of a one-year full-time training experience to neuropsychology. In addition, at least 20% of the training must be devoted to general clinical training to ensure competent background in clinical psychology. Supervisors should be board-certified clinical neuropsychologists.

Source: INS-APA Division 40 Guidelines for Doctoral Training Program," *Clinical Neuropsychologist, 1,* 15—16.

to clinical neuropsychology, including specialization in neuropsychological assessment and intervention techniques, and clinical neurology and neuropathology (Hynd & Willis, 1988).

Other Professional Training Issues

The guidelines described here are provided for clinicians who may function as child clinical neuropsychologists. Other professionals working with children and adolescents should consider different levels of training. Psychologists in private practice or in schools as well as educational professionals, including diagnosticians and regular, exceptional, and remedial education teachers, may want to adhere to guidelines suggested by Gaddes and Edgell (1994):

> The in-depth study of the neurologically impaired learning disabled student should include a synthesis of educational, psychological, social, and neurological data. Such an approach is ambitious and requires educational diagnosticians to learn some basic neurology and neuroanatomy and a useful body of neuropsychology, in addition to their expertise in professional education and psychology. (p. 1)

Others have made similar recommendations suggesting that educational professionals need to become knowledgeable about neuropsychology and neurodevelopment (see Gaddes, 1980; Haak, 1989; Hynd & Obrzut, 1981, 1986; Hynd, Quackenbush, & Obrzut, 1980).

Although professionals in the schools typically do not conduct neuropsychological evaluations (Haak, 1989) and are cautioned against making "diagnostic statements about a child's brain" (Gaddes & Edgell, 1994, p. 17), there are a number of important roles that educational professionals can assume with proper knowledge about the brain—behavior relationship. First, working in teams with medical professionals, education professionals can be helpful in designing educational interventions and psychosocial conditions that improve the opportunity for the successful integration of children with severe brain injury, trauma, or disease (e.g., leukemia or brain tumors). Without adequate knowledge, serious problems can arise when

the child returns to school after brain surgery or trauma. This is illustrated in the story of a child who underwent surgery to remove a large portion of the left hemisphere and received intracranial irradiation as part of his medical treatment for a brain tumor. When the child returned to school after his surgery, the educational staff were unaware of his subsequent neurological status. They were unsure of how his neurological status was related to his present level of academic and intellectual performance, and they did not know what to expect in terms of the course of recovery of function for skills that were impaired.

Further, the school staff had little confidence in their ability to design effective educational experiences for the child and had little information about what to expect from him in terms of psychosocial functioning. By working with the child neurologist, the neuropsychologist, and the clinical psychologist, the school staff were able to develop reasonable expectations and to provide a more appropriate education for this child. When the tumor reappeared and later proved fatal, school professionals, again in conjunction with the medical team, were better able to provide the needed psychological support to the child and his family. School staff also were able to help peers and other school personnel deal with the untimely loss of a classmate. By working in this way as part of a collaborative team, education professionals knowledgeable about brain function and recovery can work effectively to promote the adjustment of children following treatment for brain tumors and other diseases or injuries affecting the CNS.

In an another case, school staff were not prepared to integrate a child back into the school system following severe brain injury. Medical records indicated that the child had suffered severe language and memory losses following a prolonged (one-week) coma. When the child returned to school, he was immediately referred for a multidisciplinary (M-team) evaluation. When the school psychologist observed the child, his language processes were significantly better than described in the medical records, although he was struggling with his academic work. Further, in discussions with the mother it became apparent that the family was dealing with a great deal of stress because the child's injury was sustained during a beating from the mother's boyfriend. At the time, the mother was cooperating in a police investigation of the incident and was unable to participate fully in the school's attempt to evaluate her child. In this instance the school staff were unsure about how to proceed in this complex case and needed help in determining the best course of action for designing an educational intervention plan for the child.

Second, educational professionals are often the front line individuals who first observe behavioral, psychological, and cognitive problems exhibited by children with brain-related disorders. In this position, knowledge about when to refer for further neuro-psychological, neurodiagnostic, or medical evaluations is crucial for the proper diagnosis and treatment of some disorders (e.g. seizures, brain tumors, or neurodegenerative diseases).

Third, early childhood specialists often play a pivotal role in identifying subtle neurodevelopmental disorders that respond positively to early intervention or in providing educational interventions for previously diagnosed children. A better understanding of various neurodevelopmental anomalies, normal and abnormal brain development, and effective treatments will no doubt aid in rigorous early and effective intervention programs. Early interventions are particularly important for the optimal development of some children, particularly low-birth-weight babies, infants with intrauterine exposure to prenatal drugs and alcohol, infants with congenital acquired immune deficiency syndrome (AIDS) infection, and toddlers and preschool children with significant cognitive, speech/language, and/or motor delays.

Fourth, a number of children and adolescents receive medication for various disorders (e.g., Tourette syndrome, seizures, ADHD, depression, and schizophrenia). Education professionals are in a unique position to provide detailed, systematic feedback to physicians and parents concerning the side effects and efficacy of such medications. Knowledge of common medications and their impact on cognitive, social, and behavioral functioning will greatly facilitate this process. A knowledgeable professional is better informed about the benefits and risks of psychopharmacotherapy and understands the need for combined psychosocial and behavioral treatments for medicated children.

Finally, by understanding the neuropsychological basis of other childhood disorders, educational professionals can help design and implement effective interventions. For example, children with phonological core deficits are at risk for developing serious reading deficits (Felton & Brown, 1991; Stanovich, Cunningham, & Cramer, 1984). Children with phonological core deficits are unable to access and utilize speech—sound relationships necessary for early reading. These linguistic deficits are highly resistant to educational and remedial interventions (Wong, 1991). However, specific training in phonological awareness and metacognitive strategies in preschool and kindergarten has proved to be an effective educational intervention for increasing decoding and reading development (Byrne & Fielding-Barnsley, 1993; Cunningham, 1989). Without systematic and specific training, children with phonological deficits continue to lag seriously behind in reading despite adequate math achievement (Torgesen, 1991b).

The task of understanding the multiple factors affecting the cognitive, academic, psychosocial, and behavioral development of children is challenging. Increased knowledge will require an expanded curriculum and will no doubt be difficult to manage in rigorous undergraduate and graduate programs in education and psychology that are already packed with numerous course, practica, and internship requirements. At the very least, all education professionals should be required to take a course in the biological basis of behavior, a requirement that APA enforces for all professional psychology training programs. The potential benefits that children may reap from coming into contact with educational professionals who are knowledgeable about neuropsychology, neurodevelopment, and effective interventions for brain-related disorders can hardly be ignored or underestimated.

OVERVIEW OF BOOK CHAPTERS

Since the purpose of this book is to provide practical guidance to beginning child clinical neuropsychologists, the remainder of the text addresses practical issues related to the assessment, diagnosis, and treatment of childhood and adolescent disorders. Chapter

2 presents an overview of the functional neu-roanatomy of neurons, subcortical regions, and cortical structures and discusses the functions of these various structures. This chapter describes the stages of brain development and discusses factors affecting this process. Chapter 3 reviews neuroimaging and neurophysiological procedures for assessing brain functions in children. Chapter 4 presents guidelines for making referrals for neurological and neuropsychological examinations and for integrating these results with psychological assessments. Chapter 5 reviews available procedures for neuro-psychological assessment, including the Halstead-Reitan batteries, the Luria-Nebraska battery, the Boston Hypothesis approach, and other related techniques. A framework for investigating neuropsycho-logical functioning within an integrated assessment paradigm, incorporating measures of psychological, behavioral, and cognitive-intellectual functioning is also presented.

Chapter 6 reviews severe disorders of childhood, including Tourette syndrome, pervasive developmental disorders, Asperger syndrome, and externalized neuropsychiatric disorders including ADHD and conduct and oppositional disorders. In Chapter 7, the neuropsychological correlates of various internalized psychiatric disorders of childhood and adolescent are presented within an integrated neuro-

psychological perspective. Chapter 8 presents a discussion of neurodevelopmental disorders, including language and articulation impairments, reading disabilities resulting from phonological core deficits, written language disorders, and nonverbal reading disabilities. Select metabolic, biogenetic, seizure, and neuromotor disorders are presented in Chapter 9. Acquired neurological disorders and diseases of childhood are reviewed in Chapter 10. Traumatic brain injury, exposure to teratogenic agents (e.g., alcohol and cocaine), childhood cancer, and infectious diseases including meningitis and encephalitis are discussed. The core characteristics of each disorder, the neuropsychological correlates and the developmental course, and the effects of neuropathology and the impact of moderator variables such as the environment will be explored. Implications for assessment and intervention are briefly discussed.

Chapter 11 presents interventions and treatment approaches for various childhood and adolescent disorders within an integrated neurodevelopmental paradigm. Metacognitive, academic, behavioral, psychosocial, and classroom management techniques will be integrated for a comprehensive, multidimensional intervention plan to address neuropsychologically based disorders. Finally in Chapter 12, case studies will be presented that represent typical neuro-developmental disturbances.

CHAPTER 2

FUNCTIONAL NEUROANATOMY

The manner in which structures in the developing brain are related to changes in psychological and cognitive development is of interest to child neuropsychologists. There are several ways that this relationship can be explored, including: (1) correlating structural changes in the developing brain with behavioral changes, (2) investigating behavioral changes and making inferences about structural maturation of the brain, and (3) studying brain dysfunction and its relationship to behavioral disorders (Kolb & Fantie, 1989). Although these approaches can yield useful information about the developing brain, they are not without shortcomings. For example, because of the plasticity of the developing brain following damage, injury in a specific brain region may produce behavioral losses that vary greatly depending on the age of the child. Environmental factors, such as enrichment opportunities and social-cultural experiences, also influence the developing brain and the manner in which behaviors are expressed (Kolb & Fantie, 1989). Thus, the study of the brain—behavior relationship is particularly complex in children, and these factors must enter the equation when drawing conclusions about this relationship.

Some have criticized neuropsychological approaches because of the level of inferences made when relating behavior to brain structure and function, and because of the correlational nature of the research (Fletcher & Taylor, 1984). Medical technologies and new research protocols that avoid some of these shortcomings are now available. It is now possible to explore the brain during craniotomies under local anesthesia (Ojemann, Cawthon, & Lettich, 1990), to investigate dendritic morphology with electron microscopic techniques (Scheibel, 1990), and to measure sequential brain processing during cognitive tasks using visual evoked potentials (Halgren, 1990). Further, our basic understanding of the brain and its rela-

tionship to complex human behaviors has been greatly facilitated by technological advances in modern neuroimaging techniques, including computed tomography (CT), magnetic resonance imaging (MRI), regional blood flow (rCBF), and positron-emission tomography (PET) (Yudofsky & Hales, 1992). Neuroimaging techniques allow researchers to gather direct evidence linking cognitive, behavioral, and psychosocial disorders to anatomical, physiological, and biochemical processes in the brain (Daniel, Zigin, & Weinberger, 1992). Research findings from these various approaches and methodologies for understanding the developing brain will be used throughout this chapter in an effort to explore the biological basis of childhood disorders. These findings will be further discussed in Chapter 3.

To appreciate fully the brain—behavior relationship in children, an overview of the structure and function of the brain is necessary. This chapter reviews the structures and functions of the neuron and the subcortical and cortical regions from a neurodevelopmental perspective. This review serves as a foundation for exploring the complex interaction between anatomical development of the brain and the emergence of childhood behaviors and disorders.

STRUCTURE AND FUNCTION OF THE NEURON

The neuron, the basic cellular structure of the nervous system, transmits nerve impulses throughout a complex network of interconnecting brain cells (Rayport, 1992). The brain contains approximately 180 billion cells, 50 billion of which transmit and receive sensory-motor signals in the central nervous system (CNS) via 15,000 direct physical connections (Kolb & Whishaw, 1990). Investigation of the structure and function of neurons and their synaptic connections provides insight into basic psychopharmacology at the molecular level (Cooper, Bloom, & Roth, 1986) and may provide a method for describing how various neuropsychiatric disorders emerge and progress (Rayport, 1992).

The CNS comprises two major cell types, neurons and neuroglia (Shepard, 1994). While neurons conduct nerve impulses, the neuroglia ("nerve glue") provide structural support and insulate synapses (the connections between neurons). Glial cells make up about 50% of the total volume of the CNS (Shepard, 1994). Glial cells serve various functions, including transmission of signals across neurons, structural support for neurons, repair of injured neurons, and production of CNS fluid (Kandel, 1991a). Neuroglia infiltrate or invade surrounding tissue in both the gray and white matter, and in rare instances these cells replicate uncontrollably during tumor activity (Cohen & Duffner, 1994). Though still relatively infrequent, pediatric brain tumors are the second most common neoplasms in children under 15 years of age, and as many as 1000 to 1500 cases per year are estimated to occur (Hynd & Willis, 1988).

Gray matter is located in the core of the CNS, the corpus striata at the base of the right and left hemispheres, the cortex that covers each hemisphere, and the cerebellum (Kelly, 1993). The cell bodies, the neuroglia, and the blood vessels that enervate the CNS are gray-brown in color and constitute the gray matter (Kolb & Whishaw, 1990). White matter covers the gray matter and the long axons that extend from the neuron. Axons are generally covered by a myelin sheath, which contains considerable amounts of neuroglia and appears white upon inspection. White matter has fewer capillaries than are found in gray matter (Reitan & Wolfson, 1985b).

As the basic functional unit of the CNS, the neuron transmits impulses in aggregated communities or nuclei that have special behavioral functions. Neurons can be modified through experience, and they are said to learn, to remember, and to forget as a result of experiences (Hinton, 1993). Pathological changes in neurons can occur as a result of early abnormal experiences. Although these alterations are thought to have a profound effect on the mature organism, the exact nature of these changes is still under investigation (Rayport, 1992). Genetic aberrations also play a role in the way in which neurons develop and function (Malaspina, Quitkin, & Kaufman, 1992). Damage to or destruction of neurons is also of concern because neurons typically do not regenerate (Swaiman, 1994b). Neurodevelopmental disorders and issues related to recovery of function following brain trauma will be discussed in detail in later chapters (see Chapter 10).

Anatomy of the Neuron

The neuron contains four well-defined cellular parts, including the cell body, dendrites, axons, and axon terminals. The cell body, or soma, is the trophic or life center of the neuron (Shepard, 1994; see Figure 2.1. Cell bodies vary in size and shape and contain the RNA and DNA of the neuron. RNA, the cite of protein synthesis, transmits instructions from DNA directing the metabolic functions of the neuron. Biochemical processes of the neuron, which take place in the cytoplasm of the cell body, include the energy-producing functions, the self-reproducing functions, and the oxidating reactions, whereby energy is made available for the metabolic activities of the cell (Shepard, 1994). Destruction or damage to the cell body can result in the death of the neuron.

Dendrites branch off the cell body and receive impulses from other neurons (Rayport, 1992). Dendrites are afferent in nature, whereby nerve impulses are conducted toward the cell body. Dendritic spines are the major point of the synapse, the area of transmission from one cell to another. It has been found that individuals with cognitive retardation have fewer spines or points of contact across neurons (Kandel & Schwartz, 1993; Purpura, 1975).

The axon is a long projection or axis from the cell body. Most neurons have only one axon, usually efferent in nature, that conducts nerve impulses away from the cell body (Rayport, 1992). Axons are typically longer than dendrites and can be as much as a yard in length. For example, giant pyramidal cells in the motor cortex send axons to the caudal tip of the spinal cord. The axon hillock is a slender process close

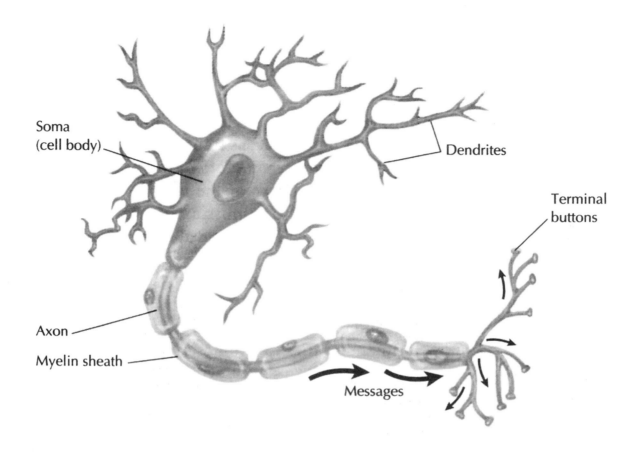

Figure 2.1. Anatomy of the Neuron
Source: From Neil R. Carlson, *Physiology of Behavior,* 5th edition, p. 21. Copyright © 1994 by Allyn and Bacon. Reprinted by permission.

to the cell body where action potentials arise. The axon hillock is highly excitable and is activated through electrochemical processes, thereby "turning on" the neuron (Kolb & Whishaw, 1985).

Axons are covered by a myelin sheath made up of neurilemma (or Schwann), which surround the axon (Shepard, 1994). The myelin sheath gives the axon a white appearance and constitutes most of the white matter in cortical and subcortical areas. Most axons are myelinated at birth, although this process continues into early childhood (Hynd & Willis, 1988) and may not be completed until after puberty (Yakovlev

& Lecours, 1967). Changes in postnatal brain weight are generally related to increases in dendritic connections and to increases in the number of glial cells that form the myelin sheath along the axon (Shepard, 1994). Axons allow the nerve cells to transmit impulses rapidly, particularly along the Nodes of Ranvier. During cell activation, nerve impulses skip from node to node, where the myelin sheath is very thin or nonexistent (Thompson, 1975). Myelinated axons permit more rapid transmission of signals, and anesthetics seem to be more effective at the Nodes of Ranvier.

The terminal branches of the axon end at the synaptic telodendria (Kolb & Whishaw, 1990). The presynaptic and postsynaptic sites are both referred to as the synapse. Synapses are specialized for the release of chemicals known as neurotransmitters. Neurotransmitters are released from synaptic knobs at the end foot of the neuron in the presynapse, and they activate neurons at the postsynapse (Shepard, 1994). Neurotransmitters are released from the presynapse (neuron A), travel across the synaptic cleft, and influence the activity of the adjoining neuron (neuron B) (see Figure 2.2 for a depiction of these activities). There is a collection of vesicles at the synaptic knob at the end of each synapse, where neurotransmitters are stored. Most neurons have thousands of synapses, and each dendritic spine serves as a synapse that is excitatory in nature, which causes neurons to fire (Thompson, 1975).

Synapses are quite large for motor neurons and are smaller in the cerebellum and other cortical regions. Synapses usually occur between the axon of one cell and the dendrite of another (axon—dendritic connections) (Kolb & Whishaw, 1990). Although they can connect onto the soma or cell body of another neuron (axosomatic connection), synapses rarely occur from axon to axon (axo-axonal connections).

Types of Neurons

There are two basic types of neurons–efferent and afferent. Efferent neurons originate in the motor cortex of the CNS, descend through vertical pathways into subcortical regions, and culminate in the muscles in the body (Carpenter & Sutin, 1983). These large descending tracts form columns from the motor cortex connecting higher cortical regions, through the

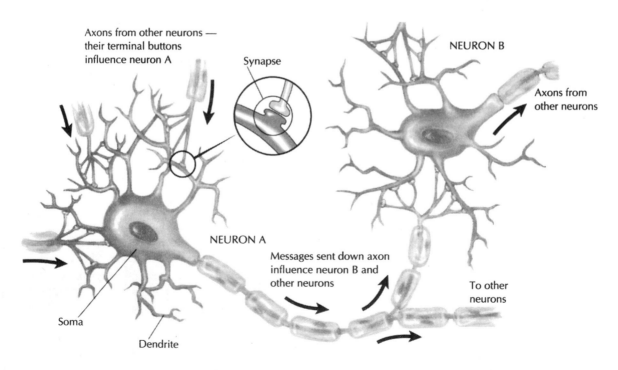

Figure 2.2. Anatomy Showing Connections between Neuron A and B with Synaptic Cleft
Source: From Neil R. Carlson, *Physiology of Behavior,* 5th edition, p. 23. Copyright © 1994 by Allyn and Bacon. Reprinted with permission.

brain stem and spinal cord, to the body for the activation of single muscles or muscle groups. Various motor pathways begin to develop prenatally (Carmichael, 1970), while postnatal development is marked by changes in primitive reflexes (the Babinski reflex) and automatic reflexes (head and neck righting) (Shepard, 1994).

Afferent neurons, sensory receptors found throughout the body, transmit sensory information into specific cerebral areas. For example, afferent neurons consist of rods and cones in the visual system that project into the occipital cortex; hair cells in the auditory system that project into the temporal cortex; and, pain, touch, temperature, and pressure sensors in the skin that project into the parietal cortex (Gardner, 1975). Somesthetic senses are the first to become functional in the fetus, as early as 7 to 8 weeks gestation, while auditory and visual neural maturation occurs later in embryonic development (Shepard, 1994).

Types of Neuroglia

The three major types of neuroglia–astrocytes, oligodendroglia, and microglia–have distinct functions and serve multiple purposes in the CNS (Kolb & Whishaw, 1985).

Astrocytes have three primary functions: (1) forming the blood—brain barrier; (2) supporting the cellular structure of the brain; and (3) directing the migration of neurons during early development (Rayport, 1992). Astrocytes are the largest in size and the most abundant type of neuroglia (Reitan & Wolfson, 1985b). These star-shaped glial cells attach to capillary blood vessels and cover approximately 80% of each capillary. Astrocytes, found primarily in the pia matter (fine membrane on the surface of the brain), cover large blood vessels. When injury occurs to the spinal cord or to the brain, through either disease or trauma, astrocytes go into hypertrophy (Rosman, 1994). These cells multiply quickly, forming a glial scar that fills in gaps in the cellular structure caused by injury. Astrocytes may also serve a phagocytic function by removing destroyed tissue and cleaning up the site of injury. Astrocytoma, a type of primary

neoplasm that frequently reoccurs after surgery, is the second most common brain tumor in adults (Cohen & Duffner, 1994); though rare, astrocytomas do occur in children as well. Astrocytomas in childhood most frequently occur in the cerebellum and the brain stem. These tumors are found equally in males and females. Although astrocytomas can occur at any age, the most frequent incidence is between 5 and 9 years of age (Cohen & Duffner, 1994).

Oligodendroglia cells form and maintain the myelin sheath and, when injured, swell in size. Tumors rarely occur in oligodendroglia cells, but when they do they are slow growing and are found primarily in the cortex and white matter (Cohen & Duffner, 1994). While about 40% to 60% of these tumors can be detected by skull X-rays after they calcify (Reitan & Wolfson, 1985b), radionuclid brain scans, angiography, and computed tomography scans have been helpful in the diagnostic phase of tumor processes (Vonofakos, Marcu, & Hacker, 1979).

Finally, microglia cells are predominantly found in the gray matter (Shepard, 1994). Following disease or injury, microglia proliferate, move to the site of injury, and perform a phagocytic function by cleaning up damaged tissue. Tumors rarely occur in microglia cells.

The neuroglia cells serve a number of important functions in the CNS: (1) providing structural support to neurons; (2) aiding in the regeneration of injured nerve fibers; (3) occupying injured sites by producing scar tissue; and (4) transporting gas, water, and metabolites from blood, and removing wastes from nerve cells (Kolb & Whishaw, 1990). The prenatal and postnatal developmental course of the neuron will be explored next.

NEURONAL DEVELOPMENT

Prenatal Course

The fastest rate of brain growth occurs prenatally, when it is estimated that every minute 250,000 brain cells are formed through mitosis (Papalia & Olds, 1992). The increase in the number of cell bodies occurs most rapidly between 25 and 40 weeks gestation

(Caesar, 1993). The human brain develops in orderly stages, beginning in the neural tube at 25 days gestation and, though not fully mature, assumes adult features at birth (Rayport, 1992). The spinal cord, the brain stem, and a large portion of the forebrain are developed at 40 weeks gestation, while the cerebellum has maximum growth by the time of birth and during the first year (Jacobson, 1991).

Six neuronal layers make up the cytoarchitectonic structure of the cerebral cortex (Polyakov, 1961). Kolb and Fantie (1989) describe the sequential migration process of the cortical layers across six prenatal periods. In the 5-month-old fetus, Layer I is developing; Layers V and VI are immature; and Layers II, III, and IV are unrecognizable. At 7 months fetal age, all six layers are present; and by 7.5 months fetal age, Layer I and portions of Layer III are highly developed. During postnatal development, the cortical layers become fully developed. Layers I and portions of Layers III, V, and VI are highly developed in the newborn; by 8 months of age, Layer II is the only cortical layer that still is not highly developed. A select portion of neurons actually begin a process of degeneration in the postnatal period, particularly neurons in Layer IV of the motor cortex (Kolb & Fantie, 1989).

These cortical layers develop in an inside-out fashion, where neurons move into specific regions and are passed by later migrating layers (Kolb & Fantie, 1989). For example, neurons in Layer IV, which reside farther away from external cortical surfaces, migrate the earliest. These layers migrate into various regions, forming the structural organization of the cortex (Sidman & Rakic, 1973). See Luria (1973) and Sidman and Rakic (1973) for more details.

While neurons proliferate and migrate to different cytoarchitectonic regions during various prenatal stages, numerous factors can interrupt this process. Environmental toxins (e.g., alcohol and drugs) pose a particular threat to the migration process; and depending on the time and stage of fetal development, different brain regions can be impaired causing significant cognitive and behavioral deficits later in life.

Proliferation and Cell Migration

The manner in which cells migrate is largely defined at birth, and the time and place of migration appear regulated by physical as well as chemical processes (Rayport, 1992). The developmental process is marked by an intricate neuron—glial interaction, where neurons are guided along radial glial fibers to their proper location. The migration process occurs rapidly, and several cortical layers appear visible during the fifth month of fetal development (Kolb & Fantie, 1989). The cortex begins to thicken and shows signs of developing sulci during this period. Dooling, Chi, and Gilles (1983) indicate that sulci develop early, with the longitudinal fissure apparent at 10 weeks, the lateral sulcus at 14 weeks, the parieto-occipital sulcus at 14 weeks, and the central sulcus at 20 weeks gestational age.

Within six months of inception, neurons are genetically programmed to proliferate so that the proper number of cells is available (National Institute of Neurological and Communicative Disorders, 1979). During the neonatal and postnatal periods neurons also differentiate and migrate into genetically predetermined regions of the brain (Shepard, 1994). Aberrant neuronal development can lead to cell migration to wrong locations or may cause neurons to make inappropriate synaptic connections (Rayport, 1992). For example, Weinberger (1987) suggests that schizophrenia may result from abnormal neuronal connections where mesocortical regions (dopaminergic systems) fail to connect to frontal cortical regions.

Cell death occurs during these early developmental stages because more neurons are generated than are necessary; thus, strategic or "selective cell death" appears critical in the developing fetal brain (Rakic & Riley, 1983). Kandel (1985) suggests that approximately 25% to 33% of neurons in the developing brain die during the process of neuronal proliferation and migration; Brodal (1992) indicates that as many as 50% of motor neurons in the spinal cord are eliminated. Brodal (1992) hypothesizes that neurons probably compete for a limited amount of the "trophic substance" that keeps the cells alive, so that only a portion of fetal neurons can survive. Neurodevelopmental disorders caused by abnormal cell proliferation, migration, or cell death can have significant impacts on children's cognitive, behavioral, and psychosocial potential (Falconer et al., 1990). The impact of these neurodevelopmental anomalies is reviewed in later chapters of the text.

Axon and Synaptic Formations

Once they reach their destination, neurons continue to develop and differentiate. Axons appear to follow or to "grow along" other pioneer axons with high concentrations of chemicals that seem to set the course or direction of growth (Brodal, 1992). Brodal (1992) suggests that axons may recognize their developmental path as a result of "chemoaffinity" between the axon terminals and target neurons. Further, chemical markers may be present only in specific phases of development and then may disappear to ensure selective contact with target neurons. The peripheral nervous system is known to have specific proteins– nerve growth factor (NGF)–that stimulate the outward movement of axons, so that axons grow into these regions and away from areas without NGF. Brodal (1992) suggests that other proteins–brainderived neurotrophic factor (BDNF)–may play a similar function in the brain.

Axons grow at a rapid rate, while cells are still migrating, and cross to form commissural pathways (Kolb & Fantie, 1989). The anterior commissure appears first, at about 3 months' gestation, while the corpus callosum develops at a slower rate (Carpenter & Sutin, 1983). The hippocampal commissure appears after 3 months' gestation, followed by the appearance of another set of fibers that eventually develop into the corpus callosum (Gilles, 1983). The corpus callosum continues to develop postnatally and is fairly well formed at 5 years of age (Witelson, 1989).

Dendritic and spine growth (visible at about 7 months' gestation) occurs at a slower rate than axon development and usually starts after cells have reached their final destination. Dendritic development continues postnatally and is affected by environmental stimulation after birth.

Synaptic development is less well understood, although synapses have been observed during the fifth month of fetal development (Kolb & Fantie, 1989). The relationship between synaptic density and cognitive abilities may be an inverse one, because synaptic density appears to decrease with age. Whereas synaptic density was once thought to be indicative of increased functional abilities, the reduction of synapses may be related to efficiency and refinement of function in some qualitative sense (Kolb & Fantie, 1989). Early synaptic redundancy and selective elimination of synapses in later development have been verified in PET studies (Caesar, 1993). The high levels of glucose metabolism recorded during the first year of life begin to decrease during the second year through adolescence.

A process similar to selective cell death occurs to eliminate axon collaterals (Brodal, 1992). According to Brodal, this process is best understood in the study of the motor neurons that enervate skeleton muscles. Whereas early stages of development are marked by the emergence of numerous neurons connecting to one muscle, multiple synapses are eliminated in later stages of development. Once motor neurons begin to send signals to the muscle, it appears that the process of synaptic elimination occurs. Brodal (1992) indicates that it is this process of synaptic elimination, once normal activity begins, that allows for precise neural connections. Apparently, according to Brodal (1992), "meaningful" information rather than simple activity is a key factor in this process.

The migration of cells may be disrupted by disorders in genetic programming or as a result of external disruption due to viral infections and disturbances to vascular circulation (Caesar, 1993). Recent advances in brain imaging techniques have begun to shed light on differences between genetic and acquired disorders that disrupt cell migration (Nadich, 1992).

Finally, synaptic networks become more elaborate in the postnatal period, where dendritic arborization increases in complexity (Brodal, 1992). In the third trimester the brain enters a major prenatal growth spurt, which continues postnatally until 2 years of age (Gardner, 1975). Antenatal insults during the third trimester may result in cerebral palsy syndromes (Lyon & Gadisseux, 1991).

Postnatal Course

An individual's full quota of neurons is reached by 6 months' gestational age, but postnatal development is marked by increased cortical complexity (Shatz, 1993). In general, myelination increases brain weight from approximately 400 grams at birth to 850 grams at 11 months, to 1100 grams at 36 months, to 1350 to 1410 grams at age 15, and continues to increase through age 60 (Kolb & Whishaw, 1985, 1990). Myelination allows for rapid conduction velocity of nerve impulses, increasing from 2 meters to 50 meters per second (Caesar, 1993).

Four postnatal growth spurts have been found that correspond to Piaget's stages of cognitive development: from 2 to 4 years, from 6 to 8 years, from 10 to 12 years, and from 14 to 16+ years (Kolb & Fantie, 1989). Although Epstein (1978, 1979) found that these growth spurts were correlated with changes in mental test performance, conclusions based on these data must be used cautiously (Marsh, 1985). Although cognitive development follows time lines similar to anatomical and physiological growth patterns, the manner in which environmental factors affect brain development through these growth spurts is unknown (Berk, 1989). However, myelination does appear to account for age differences in latency times for acoustic, visual, and sensory evoked potentials during development (Caesar, 1993).

"It is not myelination as such which is important but whether centers of the brain which are intensely interacting are provided with fast signal-conducting pathways" (Caesar, 1993, p. 106). Further, increased myelination does not affect all brain areas at the same time. Myelination occurs first in the primary sensory and motor cortices (prior to birth); the secondary areas myelinate within 4 months postnatally, while the myelination process begins postnatally in the frontal and parietal association regions and continues until about 15 years of age (Kolb & Fantie, 1989). Myelination appears correlated to the development of and changes in visual, motor, social, and cognitive behaviors. Malnutrition, disease, injury, and inadequate stimulation can affect the myelination process, which in turn may affect the learning capacity of the individual. Schwaab (1991) also suggests that the ef-

fects of medication and other toxic substances on the developing brain during embryonic, fetal, or postnatal development may have such devastating and long-term impact because these events occur before neurotransmitters are detected or are fully operational as receptor sites in the young brain. External medications may interfere with this process, affecting neurological and psychosocial development.

Although genetic factors certainly map the nature and course of neuronal development, environmental factors have a significant influence on the developing nervous system. Brodal (1992) suggests that "use-dependent stimulation" is crucial during early stages of postnatal development. That is, the developing brain requires proper and adequate stimulation for optimal development. This aspect of neurodevelopment will be explored in later sections of this chapter.

This brief overview of the structure, function, and development of neurons serves as a foundation for understanding the basic structure of the CNS and will be explored in more detail in a discussion of brain tumors and head trauma (Chapter 10) and in the discussion of psychopharmacology (Chapter 11). In the following sections, the basic divisions of the nervous system will be explored. The structure, function, and development of subcortical and cortical regions are discussed.

STRUCTURE AND FUNCTION OF THE HUMAN BRAIN

The nervous system is divided into two basic systems– the peripheral (PNS) and the central nervous system (CNS). The PNS consists of the spinal, cranial, and peripheral nerves that connect the CNS to the rest of the body (Shepard, 1992). Table 2.1 lists the cranial nerves and their functions.

The CNS is completely encased in bone, is surrounded by protective coverings, and consists of two major structures: (1) the spinal cord in the vertebral column, and (2) the brain within the skull. Aspects of the CNS will be further elaborated.

The spinal cord serves two major functions: connecting the brain and the body via large sensory-mo-

Table 2.1. Cranial Nerves

NUMBER	NAME	FUNCTIONS
I	Olfactory	Smell
II	Optic	Vision
III	Oculomotor	Eye movement
IV	Trochlear	Eye movement
V	Trigeminal	Masticatory movement
VI	Abducens	Eye movement
VII	Facial	Facial movement
VIII	Auditory	Hearing
IX	Glossopharyngeal	Tongue and pharynx
X	Vagus	Heart, blood vessels, viscera, larynx, and pharynx movement
XI	Spinal accessory	Movement, strength of neck and shoulder muscles
XII	Hypoglossal	Tongue muscles

tor tracts and integrating motor activity at subcortical levels (Kolb & Whishaw, 1985). The spinal cord comprises gray matter and white matter. Gray matter is the central, interior region of the spinal cord and is shaped like a butterfly. It appears gray on inspection and is made up of cell bodies. Neurons leave the spinal cord in segments called dermatomes and enter into muscles and organs. Motor commands from higher cortical centers are conducted at these sites (Shepard, 1994).

Sensory receptors connect with motor neurons in the gray matter of the spinal cord, via interneurons. Interneurons remain in the spinal cord and mediate motor activity with sensory stimuli (Brodal, 1992). Interneurons also provide for cooperation among different spinal segments, which control distant muscle groups. For example, interneurons connect cervical and lumbar regions of the spinal cord to coordinate forelimbs and hindlimbs for walking (Brodal, 1992).

White matter surrounds the gray matter and consists of the myelin sheath (Brodal, 1992). The spinal cord conducts signals to and from higher cortical regions, including the brain stem, the cerebellum, and the cortex. The posterior root of the spinal cord is afferent in nature, where sensory fibers enter into the gray matter, synapse with other neurons, and ascend into higher cortical areas in pathways. Conversely,

the anterior root is efferent in nature and is made up of motor fibers that receive motor signals from higher cortical areas and communicate to muscle groups for movement.

Nerve fibers enter and leave the spinal cord at regular intervals (dermatomes) and provide sensory and motor innervation to specific body segments (Martin, 1993). There are a total of 30 segments innervating the spinal cord–8 cervical, 12 thoracic, 5 lumbar, and 5 sacral (Brodal, 1992). Damage to the spinal cord at specific sites produces localized sensory and motor dysfunction in the body.

Unlike the brain, the spinal cord has little diversification or specialization, but it does carry out sensory, motor, and integrative functions. Four such functions are carried out in the spinal cord: (1) reflex activity, whereby a stimulus is followed by a coordinated motor response; (2) reciprocal activity, whereby one activity starts or stops another (i.e., excitatory or inhibitory); (3) monitoring activity, whereby incoming messages are controlled, coded, and transmitted; and (4) transmission activity, whereby messages are transmitted to and from the brain through the white matter (Gardner, 1975).

In summary, the spinal cord is one major division of the CNS, and the brain is the other major division (see Table 2.2). There are three major anatomical structures of the brain, including the brain stem (myelencephalon, metencephalon, mesencephalon, and diencephalon), the cerebellum (hindbrain), and the forebrain (telencephalon). These major anatomical structures will be reviewed briefly.

STRUCTURE AND FUNCTION OF THE BRAIN STEM

The brain stem comprises five areas, including the fourth ventricle, the medulla oblongata, the pons (bridge), the midbrain (mesencephalon), and the diencephalon (Kolb & Whishaw, 1990). See Figure 2.3 for a sagittal view of these regions. Figure 2.4 shows a magnetic resonance image of these same structures. The major regions of the brain stem are discussed in detail in the following sections.

Table 2.2. Major Divisions of the Nervous System

BRAIN DIVISIONS	BRAIN STRUCTURES	FUNCTIONAL DIVISIONS
Telencephalon (endbrain)	Neocortex Basal ganglia Limbic system	Forebrain
	Olfactory bulb Lateral ventricles	
Diencephalon (between-brain)	Thalamus Epithalamus Hypothalamus Pineal gland Third ventricle	
Mesencephalon (midbrain)	Tectum Tegmentum Cerebral aqueduct	Brain stem
Metencephalon (across-brain)	Cerebellum Pons Fourth ventricle	
Myelencephalon (spinal brain)	Medulla oblongata Fourth Ventricle	Spinal cord

Source: Adapted with permission from *Fundamentals of Human Neuropsychology,* 3rd edition, by B. Kolb and I. Q. Whishaw (1990). San Francisco: W. H. Freeman.

Ventricles

The ventricles, large cavities filled with cerebrospinal fluid, reside in various regions of the brain. The fourth ventricle, also referred to as the aqueduct of Sylvius, resides in the brain stem at the level of the pons and the medulla (Brodal, 1992). The third ventricle is located in the diencephalon; and, the lateral ventricles are found in the forebrain region (see Figure 2.5). Enlargement of these ventricles can be useful for diagnosing tumor or disease processes, including, hydrocephalus, encephalitis, and meningitis (Trauner, 1994).

Medulla Oblongata

The medulla is a continuation of the spinal cord and contains nerve tracts similar to those found in the spinal cord (Brodal, 1992). Groups of sensory and motor nuclei are arranged in ascending (i.e., afferent—sensory tracts) or descending (i.e., efferent—motor

tracts) cell columns. Projections of the major cranial nerves occur at the level of the medulla (Carpenter & Sutin, 1983), including the hypoglossal (tongue), the glossopharyngeal (pharynx and larynx), and the accessory (neck muscles) nerves (Brodal, 1992).

Neural decussation takes place at the medulla, where sensory and motor tracts cross over into the opposite side of the brain (Brodal, 1992). The somatosensory (touch, pressure, pain, and temperature) and the motor systems are organized in contralateral fashion, such that sensory information and movement on the right side of the body are primarily controlled by the left hemisphere (Shepard, 1994). Conversely, the left side of the body is controlled by the right hemisphere. The auditory and visual systems are also crossed. These functional systems will be discussed in more detail in this chapter.

The reticular activating system (RAS) comprises a major portion of the medulla, extends into the midbrain region (Kelly, 1993), and has numerous connections and functions (Brodal, 1992). For example, some RAS functions control blood pressure, blood volume in organs, and heart rate, whereas others regulate sleep and wakefulness (Brodal, 1992). The RAS receives input from most sensory systems and connects to all levels of the CNS (Reitan & Wolfson, 1985b). Because the RAS is directly or indirectly connected to much of the CNS, it can modulate CNS activity. Selective stimuli activate the RAS, which then alerts the cortex to incoming stimuli.

The RAS, considered the arousal system, plays an important role in maintaining consciousness and attentional states for the entire brain. The RAS has been hypothesized as one of the critical mechanisms involved in ADHD (Sagvolden & Archer, 1989). Researchers espousing a bottom-up model hypothesize that the RAS may be filtering too much sensory information and thereby not allowing stimulation to reach higher cortical regions as is necessary for adequate direction and maintenance of attention (Klove, 1989). When enough information reaches the RAS, it signals the cortex and produces cortical arousal and wakefulness (Gardner, 1975; Kelly, 1993). Thus, in children with ADHD this subcortical filter may not allow sufficient stimuli to reach higher cortical re-

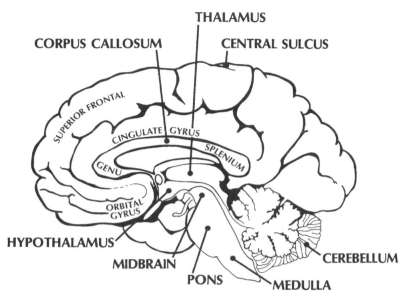

Figure 2.3. Sagittal Section of the Brain Showing Brain Stem, Midbrain, and Forebrain Structure

Source: Adapted from M. Semrud-Clikeman and P. A. Teeter, "Personality, Intelligence, and Neuropsychology," in D. Saklofske (Ed.), *International Handbook of Personality and Intelligence in Clinical Psychology and Neuropsychology,* copyright © 1995 by Plenum Press, New York.

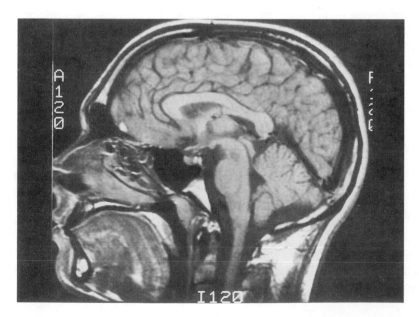

Figure 2.4. MRI Sagittal Section of CNS Analogous to Brain Areas Depicted in Figure 2.3

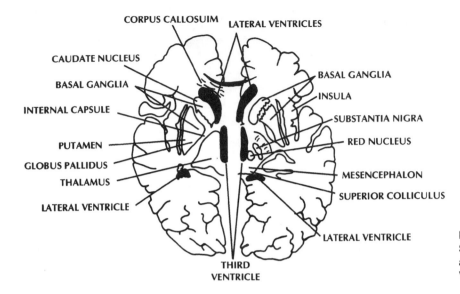

CORPUS CALLOSUIM LATERAL VENTRICLES

CAUDATE NUCLEUS

BASAL GANGLIA

INTERNAL CAPSULE

PUTAMEN

GLOBUS PALLIDUS

THALAMUS

LATERAL VENTRICLE

BASAL GANGLIA

INSULA

SUBSTANTIA NIGRA

RED NUCLEUS

MESENCEPHALON

SUPERIOR COLLICULUS

LATERAL VENTRICLE

THIRD
VENTRICLE

Figure 2.5. Coronal Section
Showing Structures of the Right
and Left Hemisphere with
Ventricular Systems

gions. This theory and others will be explored in later chapters.

Secretion of serotonin takes place at the pons, probably in the raphe system. The raphe nuclei are cells located across the medulla, pons, and midbrain regions, with afferent connections to the hypothalamus and limbic system (Reitan & Wolfson, 1985b). This region also contains the locus ceruleus (LC), which produces 70% of norepinephrine in the brain, which serves as a modulator for other neurotransmitters (Comings, 1990). The norepinephrine-rich cells in the locus ceruleus connect with the serotonin-rich cells in the raphe nuclei, and each type has a reciprocal affect on the other. Norepinephrine plays a role in vigilance, arousal, filtration of stimuli, and habituation.

Finally, the continuation of the RAS at the pontine level, appears to mediate sleep. Serotonin inhibits arousal of the RAS, which then allows the thalamus to bring the cortex to a slow-wave sleep state (Gardner, 1975; Kelly, 1993). Anesthetics appear to depress the RAS, which ultimately depresses the cortex. Fibers in the RAS also project to the limbic system and serve behavioral and emotional mechanisms

for the control of pain. Morphine and opiate-like drugs may produce analgesic actions most likely in the raphe system (Shepard, 1994).

Pons

The pons, between the medulla and midbrain and above the cerebellum, serves as a bridge across the right and the left hemispheres. Major sensory and motor pathways move through the pons, a continuation from the spinal cord and brainstem regions, and enter into higher cortical areas. The pons, in coordination with the cerebellum, receives information concerning movements from the motor cortex and helps modulate movements (Brodal, 1992). Information from the visual cortex is also received at the pontine level, which serves to guide visually determined movements. Finally, information from the hypothalamus and the limbic system converge in the pons and may influence the impact of emotional and motivational factors on motor activity (Brodal, 1992).

A number of cranial nerves converge in the pontine region. Cranial nerves innervating the face and head receive sensory information and transmit signals in the pons for swallowing and chewing (trigeminal nerve), moving facial muscles (nervus facilis), and affecting the hearing and equilibrium in the inner ear (Brodal, 1992). Cranial nerves innervating the eye muscles (abducens) also pass through the pons.

Midbrain

The most anterior region of the brain stem is the midbrain or mesencephalon. The midbrain serves a major relay function for sensory-motor fibers. The two major divisions in the midbrain are the tegmentum, which falls below the ventricle and is separated by the substantia nigra (Reitan & Wolfson, 1985b), and the tectum, which comprises the superior colliculi (upper region involved in vision) and the inferior colliculi (lower region involved in the integration of auditory and kinesthetic impulses). The RAS also continues into the midbrain region.

Several cranial nerves are located in the midbrain region. The oculomotor nerve moves the eye (lateral and downward gaze), and regulates the size of the pupil and the shape of the lens (Brodal, 1992). The trigeminal nerve also resides in the midbrain area and serves as the major sensory nerve of the face.

Diencephalon

The diencephalon, the superior region of the brain stem, contains major relay and integrative centers for all the sensory systems except smell (Kolb & Whishaw, 1985). The diencephalon is not clearly demarcated but includes the thalamus, the hypothalamus, the pituitary, the internal capsule, the third ventricle, and the optic nerve (Brodal, 1992). The thalamus receives input from several sensory sources, including: (1) the visual system (projecting into the lateral geniculate body of the thalamus); (2) the auditory system (projecting into the medial geniculate body); and (3) sensory receptors in the skin for pain, pressure, touch and temperature (i.e., nucleus ventralis posteromedalis of lateral/posterior thalamus). The nucleus ventralis anterolateralis thalamic region receives input from the cerebellum and other motor regions (i.e., globus pallidus and corpus striatum). These

pathways ultimately radiate into the neocortex at specific sites in the frontal, temporal, and occipital cortices (Kolb & Whishaw, 1985).

The hypothalamus, anterior and inferior to the thalamus, plays a role in controlling the autonomic nervous system, including eating, sexual functions and dysfunctions, drinking, sleeping, temperature, rage, and violence (Brodal, 1992). With connections to the limbic system, the hypothalamus influences motivational mechanisms of behavior. The pituitary, following directions from the hypothalamus, secretes hormones that regulate bodily functions (Brodal, 1992).

The internal capsule, situated lateral to the thalamus, contains fibers connecting the cortex to lower brain regions including the brain stem and the spinal cord (Brodal, 1992). Major fibers comprise the internal capsule and connect the frontal cortical regions to the thalamus and to the pons (Kelly, 1993a). The genu forms the apex of the internal capsule and has been implicated in some childhood disorders.

Finally, the optic nerve converges in the diencephalon and forms the optic chiasma (Brodal, 1992). Fibers from the optic nerve cross at the chiasma and project to the lateral geniculate body (occipital cortex) via the optic tract (Brodal, 1992).

Cerebellum

The cerebellum or hindbrain, behind the brain stem, connects to the midbrain, pons, and medulla. The cerebellum receives sensory information about where the limbs are in space and signals where muscles should be positioned. The cerebellum receives information from the semicircular canals (in the inner ear) concerning orientation in space. The cerebellum is involved in the unconscious adjustment of muscles in the body for coordinated, smooth, and complex motor activity. Injury of the cerebellum can result in dystaxia (movement disorders), dysarthria (slurred speech), nystagmus (blurred vision and dizziness), and hypotonia (loss of muscle tone) (Swaiman, 1994a). Though still relatively uncommon, subtentorial tumors involving the cerebellum and the fourth ventricle are the most frequent type of brain tumor affecting young children (Cohen & Duffner, 1994).

ROLE AND FUNCTION OF THE MENINGES

Both the spinal cord and the brain are surrounded by a protective layer of tissue called the meninges. The meninges comprises three layers: the dura mater, the arachnoid, and the pia mater.

The dura mater is the tough outer layer of the spinal cord and the brain, and has the consistency of a thin rubber glove. The dura mater attaches to the bones covering the cranium and receives blood vessels that innervate the brain (Carpenter & Sutin, 1983). Injury to the head may form an epidural hematoma, causing blood to accumulate in the region between the skull and the dura mater. The dura mater is supplied with blood by tiny vessels on its outermost layer near the skull. The subdural space, a fluid-filled layer, separates the dura mater from the arachnoid. Accumulation of blood in the subdural area following injury can put enormous pressure on the brain (Bengali, 1992).

The arachnoid, a spiderlike web, is a delicate network of tissue under the dura mater (Kandel & Schwartz, 1994). Blood accumulation between the dura mater and the arachnoid following injury is referred to as a *subdural hematoma*. Finally, the pia mater is the fragile, innermost layer of the meninges and contains small blood vessels. The pia mater surrounds the arteries and veins that supply blood to the brain; it serves as a barrier keeping out harmful substances that might invade the brain. Bilateral infections that attack the meninges, referred to as *meningitis,* can have serious consequences for the developing brain (Weil, 1985). The first year of life is the time of greatest risk for meningitis (Bharucha, Bharucha, & Bhabha, 1995). The earlier the infection, the higher the mortality rate. Some of the long-term consequences of meningitis are mental retardation, hydrocephalus, seizures, deafness, and hyperactivity (Bharucha et al., 1995; Weil, 1985).

Cerebrospinal fluid (CSF), a clear, colorless fluid, fills the ventricles and the subarachnoid space (Wilkinson, 1986). CSF contains concentrations of sodium, chloride, and magnesium, as well as levels of neurotransmitters and other agents. An assay of the composition of these chemicals can be important for diagnosing disease processes. CSF reproduces at such a rate that total replacement occurs several times a day. The choroid plexus, located in the fourth ventricle, produce the CSF, while the lateral ventricles contain the highest amounts of CSF (Brodal, 1992). Infectious and metabolic disorders, such as meningitis, encephalitis, and tumors, as well as traumatic injury, can cause discernible changes in the CSF (Bharucha et al., 1995; Heffner, 1995).

Cerebrospinal fluid has three major functions. Specifically, it (1) serves protective function against injury to the brain and spinal cord (Reitan & Wolfson, 1985b); (2) diffuses materials into and away from the brain (Kolb & Whishaw, 1990); and (3) maintains a "special environment" for brain tissue (Wilkinson, 1986). The role of the neurotransmitters found in CSF remains unknown (Brodal, 1992). Interference in the circulation and drainage of CSF can result in hydrocephalus, which causes cranial pressure (Brodal, 1992). Hydrocephalus can have a devastating affect on the developing brain and may cause cognitive delays, particularly for nonverbal information; emotional, psychiatric, or behavioral disturbances; and slow motor development (Walsh, 1994). Surgical shunting drains CSF outside the skull (Brodal, 1992). Recent advances in microsurgery in utero have produced successful results by reducing some of the more severe long-term negative effects of brain dysfunction or damage that can occur when hydrocephalus is untreated. Residual effects of hydrocephaly, ranging from mild to severe, depend on individual variables including the age of the child at the time of shunting and the presence of other neurological or medical complications that often accompany this disorder (Wald, 1995).

DEVELOPMENT OF THE CENTRAL NERVOUS SYSTEM

The earliest stages of brain development are marked by rapid changes in the embryo. Within seven days of inception, two layers of tissue, the ectoderm and the endoderm, are present; and, within nine days, a third layer, the mesoderm, develops and moves between the first two layers in a process referred to as *gastrulation* (Shepard, 1994). The ectoderm forms the neural groove, which in turn forms the neural tube. The process of neurulation is initiated in the first two weeks, where in embryonic tissue differentiates, forming the neural tube, and is completed by the fourth gestational week (Brodal, 1992). During this process, embryonic tissues thicken, deepen, and close, forming the basic structures of the nervous system. Neurons and glial cells are formed on the outside wall of the neural tube, and the inside wall is covered with glial cells forming a canal that becomes filled with CSF (Brodal, 1992).

Throughout this course, neural tissues differentiate and migrate forming columns of spinal and cranial nerves that keep the organism alive (Volpe, 1995). The cranial portion of the neural tube eventually develops into the brain, while the caudal portion becomes the spinal cord (Brodal, 1992). Motor and sensory columns develop from separate structures of the neural tube, and by the end of four weeks the neural tube closes (Sarnat, 1995).

Once the process of neurulation ends (fourth week), three brain vesicles appear, forming the hindbrain, the midbrain, and the forebrain. These vesicles further differentiate into (1) diencephalon, which eventually forms the thalamus, hypothalamus, and epithalamus, and (2) the telencephalon, which forms the cerebral hemispheres. The lumina or cavities of the brain vesicles develop into the ventricular system, which can be compromised in various developmental or disease processes, such as hydrocephalus.

The vesicles continue to develop into the major brain regions that are discussed next. Hynd and Willis (1988) caution that the interdependence of prenatal and postnatal development should be considered when viewing structures and functions in child neuropsychology.

STRUCTURE AND FUNCTION OF THE FOREBRAIN

The forebrain (telencephalon) comprises the lateral ventricles, the olfactory bulb, the limbic system, the basal ganglia, and the neocortex (Kolb & Whishaw, 1990). Some textbooks also place the thalamus in the forebrain region, while others refer to this as a diencephalic structure (Brodal, 1992). See earlier discussions of the diencephalon for a review of the thalamus.

Lateral Ventricles

Each hemisphere has a cavity in its center, surrounded by large areas of white matter, that extends from the third ventricle via the interventricular foramen (Brodal, 1992). The lateral ventricles are expansive, with an anterior horn in the frontal lobe, a posterior horn in the occipital lobe, and an inferior horn in the temporal lobe (Wilkinson, 1986). The lateral ventricles are filled with CSF, and when these regions are misshapen, enlarged, or grossly asymmetrical, this may have diagnostic significance for the pediatric neurologist.

Olfactory Bulb

The olfactory system is the only sensory system that converges in the telencephalon (Castellucci, 1985). The olfactory bulb receives sensory information concerning smell directly from the olfactory nerve (Brodal, 1992) and converges with the olfactory tract; at this juncture, axons cross to the bulb in the opposite hemisphere via the anterior commissure (Wilkinson, 1986). The olfactory tract projects to the primary olfactory cortex to a small region called the uncus (Wilkinson, 1986), close to the end of the temporal lobe (Brodal, 1992). Although olfactory assessment is often ignored, the sense of smell is frequently associated with various neuropsychiatric disturbances found in adults, particularly schizophrenia, Parkinson's disease, multiple sclerosis, subfrontal tumors, and some brain injuries (Ovsiew, 1992).

Limbic System

The limbic system is a complex deep structure in the forebrain comprising the hippocampus, septum, and cingulate gyrus (Kolb & Whishaw, 1990). The limbic system has widespread connections with the neocortex and with the autonomic and endocrinological systems, and is considered a primitive brain structure involved with the olfactory senses. It resides between two brain regions (diencephalon and telencephalon) and serves as an intermediary to cognitive and emotional functions (Wilkinson, 1986).

In humans the limbic system has less to do with the olfactory system than with emotional and memory functions that are essential for the survival of the species (Barr & Kierman, 1983). It also has preservation functions for the individual (Wilkinson, 1986). Wilkinson (1986) describes a number of important functions of the limbic system, including: (1) analyzing and responding to fearsome, threatening situations; (2) monitoring sexual responses, including reproducing and nurturing offspring; (3) remembering recent and past events; and (4) sensing and responding to feeling states, including pleasure. Autonomic responses (e.g., heart rate, breathing, blood pressure, and digestive functions) can be influenced by limbic structures, especially the cingulate gyrus (Brodal, 1992). Aggressive reactions and social indifference have been associated with the cingulate gyrus, while feelings of anxiety, déjà vu experiences, and fear have been associated with functions of the amygdala (Brodal, 1992). With its connections with other limbic and cortical structures, the hippocampus has broad functions involving learning and memory.

Seizure activity in limbic structures, particularly the hippocampus (Kolb & Whishaw, 1985), sometimes includes temporal lobe structures as well (Lockman, 1994b). Seizures at this site may result in a temporary loss of consciousness and a loss of memory.

Basal Ganglia

The term *basal ganglia* refers to all or some of the masses of gray matter within the cerebral hemispheres, including the corpus striatum (caudate nucleus, putamen, and globus pallidus) and occasionally the amygdala (Shepard, 1994). The corpus striatum connects to the neocortex and to the thalamus, and has ascending and descending pathways to the midbrain structures (red nucleus and substantia nigra) and to the spinal cord (Reitan & Wolfson, 1985b). Serotonin-rich connections from the raphe

nuclei also reach the striatum, the prefrontal regions, and the limbic system (Comings, 1990). These serotonin pathways serve to inhibit motor actions and emotional responses.

The basal ganglia are intimately involved with motor functions and, when damaged, can produce postural changes, increases or decreases in muscle tone, and movement changes (e.g., twitches, tremors or jerks). Sydenham's chorea, a childhood disease resulting from poststreptoccal rheumatic fever involving the corpus striatum, is characterized by irregular and purposeless movements (Ashwal & Schneider, 1994). This disease usually appears insidiously, gradually worsening with symptoms of hyperkinetic movement disorder, emotional lability, and hypotonia. Rheumatic heart disease is often found in conjunction with Sydenham's chorea and is the cause of mortality in this disorder. The chorea generally dissipates 6 months after onset, but the emotional lability remains (Ashwal & Schneider, 1994).

Neocortex

The neocortex, often referred to simply as the cortex, comprises the highest functional division of the forebrain and makes up about 80% of the human brain (Kolb & Whishaw, 1990). The cortex is wrinkled and convoluted in appearance, with various elevated ridges and convolutions. Ridges are referred to as *gyri,* the deepest indentations are called *fissures,* and the shallower indentations are called *sulci.* The configuration of fissures and large sulci can be identified on visual inspection of the cortex (see Figure 2.6).

The lateral or Sylvian fissure separates the frontal lobe from the temporal lobe, and the central sulcus (fissure of Rolando) separates the frontal from the parietal lobe. The central sulcus is a prominent landmark separating the motor cortex (anterior to the central sulcus) from the sensory cortex (posterior to the central sulcus). The surface areas of posterior temporal and parietal locations are not clearly defined from the occipital regions (Brodal, 1992). Finally, the calcarine sulcus extends from the occipital pole below to the splenium of the corpus callosum (Carpenter & Sutin, 1983).

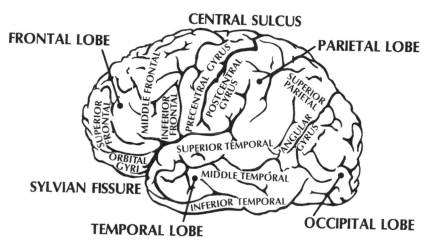

Figure 2.6. Surface of the Left Hemisphere Showing Sulci, Fissures, and Major Subdivisions of the Cortex

Source: Adapted from M. Semrud-Clikeman and P. A. Teeter, "Personality, Intelligence and Neuropsychology," in D. Saklofske (Ed.), *International handbook of Personality and Intelligence in Clinical Psychology and Neuropsychology,* copyright © 1995 by Plenum Press, New York.

CEREBRAL HEMISPHERES

The cerebrum comprises the right and left hemispheres, which appear to have anatomical (asymmetry) as well as functional (lateralization) differences (Brodal, 1992). *Asymmetry* typically refers to the structural or morphological differences between the two hemispheres (Rosen, Galaburda, & Sherman, 1990). Although neuroanatomical differences may underlie behavioral variations documented for each hemisphere, it is not known whether chemical as well as structural differences between the hemispheres also account for functional asymmetries (Witelson, 1987a, 1990).

Cerebral lateralization refers to the degree to which each hemisphere is specialized for processing specific tasks. The right and left hemispheres appear to differ in terms of their efficiency in processing certain stimuli, such that both hemispheres are "not equally good at all tasks" (Brodal, 1992, p. 421). Goldberg and Costa (1981) indicate that significant cytoarchitectural differences exist between the two

hemispheres that may be related to neurobehavioral differences. The left hemisphere has a greater ratio of gray matter to white matter, particularly in the frontal, parietal, and temporal regions, compared to the right hemisphere. Conversely, the right hemisphere has greater white-to-gray matter ratios than the left hemisphere. Major anatomical and functional differences observed in the two hemispheres are described as follows:

1. The left hemisphere has more neuronal representations in modality-specific regions in the three sensory cortices.
2. The right hemisphere has greater association zones, where sensory modalities converge.
3. The left hemisphere is structurally conducive to single modality processing, distinct motor activity, and intraregional integration.
4. The right hemisphere is structurally conducive to multiple modality processing and intraregional integration.

5. The right hemisphere has a greater capacity for handling informational complexity because of its intraregional connections, whereas the left hemisphere seems best suited for processing unimodal stimuli (Goldberg & Costa, 1981; Rourke, 1989; Semrud-Clikeman & Hynd, 1991b). The right hemisphere appears better able to process novel information, whereas the left hemisphere seems able to work more efficiently with information with preexisting codes, such as those found in language activities.

These differences will be further explored in a later discussion regarding nonverbal learning disabilities.

Although the correlations between structure and function are not perfect, cerebral asymmetry has been of great interest to child neuropsychologists (Kinsbourne, 1989). Further, particular anatomical asymmetries between the two hemispheres are present at birth (Kolb & Fantie, 1989). Witelson and Pralle (1973) observed that measurable differences in the left planum temporale (near the auditory cortex) are evident by 39 weeks gestation, which have led some to suggest that the functional lateralization of language in the left hemisphere is determined prenatally (Witelson, 1983, 1987b). In adults, approximately 70% of right-handed individuals show larger planum temporale in the left hemisphere, which has been shown to be the "posterior substrate of language function" (Kolb & Fantie, 1989, p. 30). The typical asymmetry of the left hemisphere has not been observed in those with developmental dyslexias and thus may be related to the difficulty in encoding letters and words (Galaburda, Sherman, Aboitiz, & Geschwind, 1985; Hynd, Semrud-Clikeman, Lorys, Novey, & Eliopulos, 1990; Hoien, Lundberg, & Odegaard, 1990).

Early accounts of cerebral lateralization often listed specific functions for each hemisphere in a dichotomous, all-or-none fashion, implying that all aspects of a given task were carried out by one hemisphere. This all-or-none approach is probably overly simplistic because both hemispheres generally play a role in most complex tasks. One hemisphere, however, is usually considered dominant or most important for a specific task, while the other hemisphere

is recessive or nondominant (Brodal, 1992). Table 2.3 summarizes the developmental milestones for anatomical and functional asymmetries.

Witelson (1990) suggests that it is unclear whether functional differences between the two hemispheres are "relative" or "absolute," in such a way that each hemisphere is able to process tasks but does so less efficiently. Others have proposed that the two hemispheres operate in a domain-specific fashion (Fodor, 1983), whereby each hemisphere acts in an autonomous manner with restricted access to information processed by the other hemisphere.

Zaidel, Clark, and Suyenobu (1990, p. 347) provide some evidence that the hemispheres work in a parallel fashion with a "hierarchical sequence of control." Zaidel et al. (1990) suggest the following: (1) the two hemispheres can operate independently of one another, which reinforces the concept of hemispheric specialization, in some domain-specific functions; (2) hemispheric specialization is "hard-wired" and is apparently innately directed; (3) developmental patterns of the two hemispheres may differ; and (4) while the two hemispheres may share processing resources, they can remain autonomous at any stage of processing. Hemisphere independence appears related to various models of hemispheric functioning, including specialized processing during domain-specific tasks; interactive processing wherein each hemisphere adds to a particular stage of processing; and monitoring processing whereby one hemisphere monitors the processes of the other. Zaidel et al. (1990) hypothesize that these functions can occur in parallel which provides for flexibility and adaptability in processing control. Functional neuroimaging techniques will help answer these questions and will no doubt add to our understanding of the relative contribution of the two hemispheres, as well as specific structures, during certain activities.

Although anatomical differences appear early in development, there is insufficient evidence to conclude that morphological variations between the two hemispheres predict functional capabilities in any perfect sense (Kinsbourne, 1989). This appears most obvious when observing recovery of functions after brain injury. For example, damage to the left hemi-

Table 2.3. Developmental Milestones for Functional Asymmetry and Cerebral Lateralization

FUNCTIONS	AGE	HEMISPHERE	REFERENCE
Motor			
Thumb sucking, right hand preference	15-week fetus	Left	Hepper, Shahidullah, & White (1991)
Head turning[a]	Birth		
Reaching	4 months	Left	Young et al. (1983)
Passive holding		Right	
Moving pegs	3 years	Left	Annett (1985)
Finger tapping	3—5 years	Left	Ingram (1975)
Strength		Left	
Gestures		Left	
Auditory			
Syllables	21 hours	Left	Molfese & Molfese (1979)
Speech	>24 hours	Left	Hammer (1977)
White noise	>24 hours	Right	
Speech sounds	1 wk—10 months	Left	Molfese, Freeman, & Palermo (1975)
Speech (CV)	22—140 days	Left	Entus (1977)
Music sounds	22—140 days	Right	
Conversational speech	6 months	Left	Gardiner & Walter (1977)
Name of child	5—12 months	Left	Barnet, Vicenti, & Campos (1974)
Visual			
Light flashes	2 weeks	Right	Hahn (1987)
Photograph of Mom	4 months	Right	de Schonen, Gil de Diaz, & Mathivet (1986)
Patterns			
Global form	4—10 months	Right	Deruelle & de Schonen (1991)
Tactile			
Dichaptic	4—5 years	Right	Klein & Rosenfield (1980)
Emotions			
Approach expression to sugar H$_2$O	2 days	Left	Fox & Davidson (1986)
Facial expressivity	Infants	Right	Best & Queens (1989)
Happy facial expressions	10 months	Left	Davidson & Fox (1982)
Crying with separation from Mom	10 months	Right	Davidson & Fox (1989)
Discriminate Emotional faces	5—14 years	Right	Saxby & Bryden (1985)
Emotional tones	5—14 years	Right	Saxby & Bryden (1984)
Emotional reaction to negative expression	9 years	Left	Davidson (1984)
	12 years	Right	

[a] Head turning correlated to same side as thumb sucking at birth.

sphere can result in a shift of language functions to the right hemisphere, particularly if both the posterior and anterior speech zones are damaged (Kolb & Fantie, 1989). While language functions can be assumed by the right hemisphere, complex visuospatial functions appear to be in jeopardy (Kolb & Fantie, 1989); further, complex syntactic processing appears vulnerable (Scheibel, 1990). So, although the left hemisphere might be better organized anatomically to deal with the language process, as suggested by the Goldberg-Costa (1981) model, the right hemisphere is able to do so under specific conditions. However, there is a price to be paid when one hemisphere assumes the function of the other, usually involving the loss or compromise of higher level functions. These more complex functions also may be more dependent on the anatomical differences generally found between the two hemispheres that exist early in the developing brain. This difference is most likely a result of the differential ratio of gray to white matter between the two hemispheres described by Goldberg and Costa (1981). Recovery and loss of functions will be covered in more detail in subsequent chapters.

Interhemispheric Connections

Large bundles of myelinated fibers connect various intra- and interhemispheric regions. The two hemispheres are connected via several transverse commissures or pathways, including the corpus callosum and the anterior commissure.

The corpus callosum, comprising the rostrum, the genu, the body, and the splenium, contains approximately 300 million nerve fibers for rapid interhemispheric communication (Carpenter & Sutin, 1983). The genu connects rostral portions of the right and left frontal lobes, while the body has interconnections between the frontal and parietal regions across the two hemispheres. The splenium connects temporal and occipital regions and is reportedly larger in females (Witelson, 1989). The splenium has been implicated in various childhood disorders, including ADHD (Hynd, Semrud-Clikeman, et al., 1991; Semrud-Clikeman, Filipek, et al., 1994). The anterior commissure is smaller than the corpus callosum and connects the temporal lobes of the right and left hemispheres (Kolb & Whishaw, 1990).

Intrahemispheric Connections

Association fibers connect cortical regions within each hemisphere (Kandel & Schwartz, 1985). Association pathways allow for rapid communication within hemispheric regions for the perception and integration of stimuli and for the organization of complex output (e.g., emotional responses to stimuli).

Short association fibers connect one gyrus to another, and longer fibers connect one lobe to another. For example, the arcuate fasciculus connects the frontal and temporal lobes (Broca's area to Wernicke's area); the longitudinal fasciculus connects the temporal and the occipital lobes with the frontal lobe;

the occipitofrontal fasciculus connects the frontal, temporal, and occipital lobes (Reitan & Wolfson, 1985b); and the angular gyrus connects the parietal and the occipital lobes (Williams, 1993). Dysfunction of these pathways can result in a variety of behavioral, cognitive, and personality manifestations (Tranel, 1992), including reading, spelling, and computational disorders in children (O'Donnell, 1991).

STRUCTURE AND FUNCTION OF THE CORTEX

The cortex comprises the right and left hemispheres, each with four major lobes: (1) frontal, motor cortex; (2) parietal, somatosensory cortex; (3) occipital, visual cortex; and (4) temporal, auditory cortex. (See Figure 2.7 for a view of the cortical regions.) The structures and functions of the cortex will be reviewed briefly.

Frontal Lobes

The frontal lobes are the most anterior cortical structures and comprise the primary motor cortex, the premotor cortex, Broca's area, the medial cortex, and the prefrontal cortex (Kolb & Whishaw, 1990). Whereas the frontal lobes have major motor functions, especially the primary and premotor areas, the prefrontal cortex mediates reasoning and planning and monitors other cortical and subcortical functions.

Lesions or damage to the primary motor cortex can result in paralysis to the contralateral side of the body, whereas lesions to the premotor cortex can produce more complex coordination problems because this region directs the execution of the primary motor area (Kolb & Whishaw, 1990). Lesions or damage to the prefrontal cortex, with its intricate connections to other brain regions, including thalamic, hypothalamic, and limbic areas, often result in affective dissociations, impaired executive functions and judgment, and intellectual deficits (Tranel, 1992).

Primary Motor Cortex

The motor system comprises the primary motor, the premotor, and to a lesser degree, the prefrontal, with

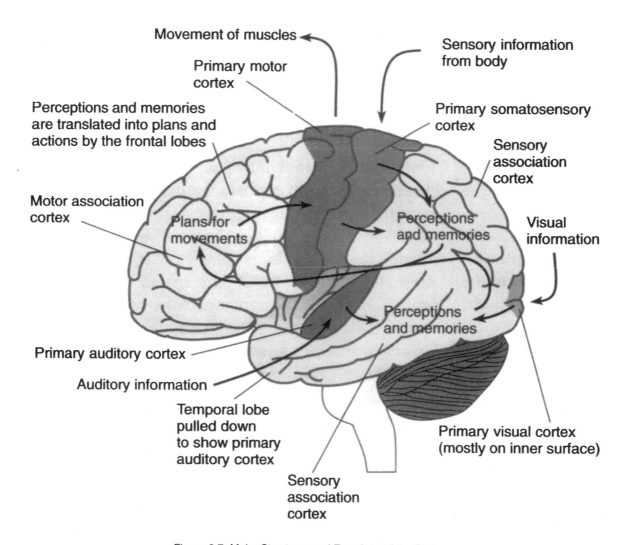

Figure 2.7. Major Structures and Functions of the Cortex

Source: From Neil R. Carlson, *Physiology of Behavior,* 5th edition, p. 91. Copyright © 1994 by Allyn and Bacon. Reprinted with permission.

each region assuming differentiated motor functions. The primary motor cortex is involved with the execution and maintenance of simple motor functions; the premotor cortex directs the primary motor cortex; and the prefrontal cortex influences motor planning and adds flexibility to motor behavior as a result of input from internal and external factors (Kolb & Whishaw, 1990).

The primary motor cortex resides immediately anterior to the central sulcus and contains giant pyramidal cells (Betz), which control fine motor and highly skilled voluntary movements (Ghez, 1993). The primary motor cortex receives afferent (incoming sensory) signals from the parietal lobe, the cerebellum, and the thalamus for the integration of sensory-motor signals, while efferent (outgoing motor) signals are transmitted to the reticular activating system, the red nucleus (midbrain structure), the pons, and the spinal cord for the production of movement (Ghez, 1993).

The primary cortex controls movements to the opposite side of the body and is arranged in a homuncular fashion. Specific muscle groups of the body are represented in an inverted pattern stretching across the primary motor area (Ghez, 1993). Stimulation to specific areas of the primary motor cortex produces contractions of highly localized muscle areas. For example, Broca's area resides near the primary motor area in the left hemisphere, controls facial musculature, and mediates speech production (Kolb & Whishaw, 1990).

Premotor Cortex

The premotor cortex, anterior to the primary motor cortex, plays a role in controlling limb and body movements. More complex, coordinated movements appear to be regulated at this level, especially fluid sequential movements. The premotor cortex directs the primary cortex in the execution and maintenance of simple movements (Reitan & Wolfson, 1985b). The limbic system also influences the motor cortex, directly and indirectly, primarily in terms of attentional and motivational aspects of motor functions (Brodal, 1992).

Prefrontal Cortex

The prefrontal cortex, the most anterior region of the frontal lobe, receives incoming signals from the thalamus, which then project to the hypothalamus. Further, connections to the limbic system allow the prefrontal cortex to mediate, regulate, and control affective, emotional behavior (Kolb & Whishaw, 1990). Prefrontal connections to the temporal, parietal, and occipital association regions allow for a comparison of past and present sensory experiences (Reitan & Wolfson, 1985b). These intricate connections of the prefrontal cortex with cortical and subcortical regions allow for highly integrative, complex functions. Judgments and insights arise out of prefrontal activity, whereas motor planning, consequential thinking, and

ongoing monitoring of behavior also appear to be regulated by prefrontal regions. Though not considered part of the motor area, the limbic system also seems to play a role in complex, intentional, or volitional motor behaviors.

The development of executive control functions is discussed in more detail in later sections of this chapter. Also see Chapter 6 for a discussion of neuropsychiatric disorders (e.g., ADHD and Tourette syndrome) associated with frontal lobe and executive control damage or dysfunction.

Parietal Lobes

The parietal lobe is separated from the frontal regions by the central sulcus and from the temporal lobe by the lateral fissure (Teeter, 1986). The parietal lobes play a central role in the perception of tactile sensory information, including the recognition of pain, pressure, touch, proprioception, and kinesthetic sense. The parietal lobe comprises of three areas: the primary sensory projection area, the secondary somatosensory area, and the tertiary or association area (Carpenter & Sutin, 1983).

Primary Sensory Cortex

The primary sensory projection area is immediately posterior to the central sulcus, adjacent to the primary motor cortex. Some have argued that there is a great deal of functional overlap between the sensory and motor cortical areas (Woolsey, 1958). Penefield and Jasper (1954) found that somatic-sensory perceptions were elicited in approximately 25% of the points that were electrically stimulated in regions anterior to the central sulcus. Regions anterior to the central sulcus are generally referred to as the primary motor cortex. Further, sensory sensations were reported when stimulation was applied both in front of and behind the central sulcus. Woolsey (1958) subsequently referred to the regions posterior to the sulcus as the sensory-motor area, while regions anterior to the sulcus were labeled the motor-sensory area. What seems most evident from this research is that the sensory-motor regions are highly interrelated, which probably results in increased functional efficiency.

The primary sensory projection area has three major functions, including the recognition of the source, quality, and severity of pain; the discrimination of light pressure and vibration; the recognition of fine touch (proprioception); and awareness of the position and movement of body parts (kinesthetic sense) (Kolb & Whishaw, 1985, 1990). Numerous fibers converge in the primary sensory projection area, including afferents coming from the thalamus, skin, muscles, joints, and tendons from the opposite side of the body. Lesions to the primary parietal regions can produce sensory deficits to the contralateral (opposite) side of the body, and other more complex deficits can occur when the temporoparietal and/or inferior parietal regions are involved (Tranel, 1992).

Like the primary frontal cortex, the primary sensory projection area is arranged in a homuncular fashion, with the proportion of cortical representation related to the need for sensitivity in a particular body region (Kandel, 1993a). For example, the region representing the face, lips, and tongue is quite large because speech production requires multiple sensory input from these various muscles to provide sensory feedback to orchestrate a complex series of movements needed for speaking. The proximity of the primary parietal region to the primary motor regions allows for the rapid cross-communication between sensory-motor systems that is necessary for the execution of motor behavior.

Secondary and Association Cortices

Input from the primary sensory projection regions is synthesized into more complex sensory forms by secondary parietal regions (Kolb & Whishaw, 1990). The tertiary or association region, the most posterior area of the parietal lobe, receives input from the primary sensory projection area and sends efferents into the thalamus. The association region is involved with the integration and utilization of complex sensory information (Brodal, 1992). Pandya and Yeterian (1990) indicate that the association regions synthesize infor-

mation, whereas the primary areas are involved with finer distinctions and analysis of information.

The association region overlaps with other cortical structures, including temporal and occipital areas for the integration of sensory information from different modalities (Brodal, 1992). Although damage to the association region does not produce visual, auditory, or sensory deficits, damage to the association area can result in disorders of the integration of complex sensory information. Cross-modal matching of visual with auditory and sensory stimuli takes place in the association region, which is considered to be the highest level of sensory analysis. Some argue that this region regulates much of what is measured by intelligence tests, including cognitive and mental functions such as thinking, reasoning, and perception (Kolb & Whishaw, 1990).

Occipital Lobes

The most posterior region of the cortex comprises the occipital lobe (primary visual cortex), which is further divided into dorsal (superior) and ventral (inferior) areas (Tranel, 1992). The inferior and superior regions are divided by the lateral-occipital sulcus, while the calcarine fissure extends from the occipital pole into the splenium of the corpus callosum (Reitan & Wolfson, 1992).

The visual cortex receives projections from the retina in each eye via the lateral geniculate nucleus in the thalamus (see Figure 2.8). The rods and cones in the retina respond to photic stimulation, and photochemical processes result in nerve impulses in the optic nerve (Carlson, 1994). The optic nerve forms the optic chiasm once inside the cranium; where nerve fibers partially cross, project to the lateral geniculate in the thalamus, and converge in the visual cortex. Damage anywhere along this pathway can produce a variety of visual defects.

The occipital lobe comprises primary, secondary, and tertiary or association regions (Kolb & Whishaw, 1990). The primary occipital cortex receives afferents from the thalamus, which pass through the temporal cortex (Kelly, 1993). Damage to this tract, even if it occurs in the temporal lobe, can produce visual

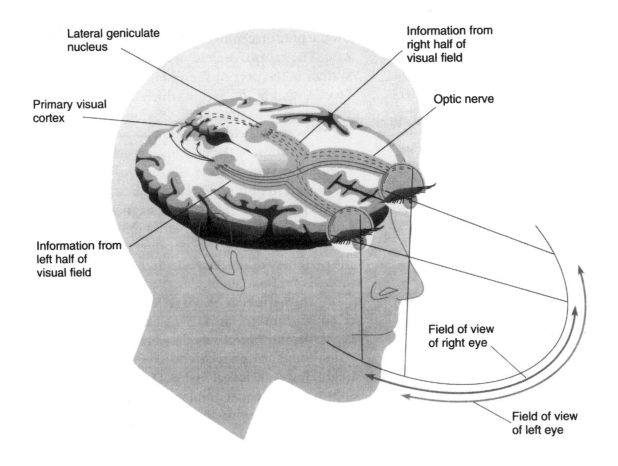

Figure 2.8. Visual Fields and Cortical Visual Pathways

Source: From Neil R. Carlson, *Physiology of Behavior,* 5th edition, p. 149. Copyright © 1994 by Allyn and Bacon. Reprinted by permission.

field defects. The association region is involved with complex visual perception, relating past visual stimuli to present stimuli for the recognition and appreciation of what is being seen (Kolb & Whishaw, 1985). Damage to the association region, particularly in the right hemisphere, can produce a variety of visual deficits, including recognition of objects, faces, and drawings.

Temporal Lobes

The temporal lobe, has three major divisions: (1) the posterior region of the superior temporal gyrus, which

is referred to as Wernicke's area in the left hemisphere; (2) the inferior temporal region, including the occipitotemporal association region; and (3) the mesial temporal aspect, including the hippocampal and amygdala regions (Tranel, 1992). The temporal lobe has complex interconnections, with afferent fibers coming from the parietal lobe; efferent fibers projecting into the parietal and frontal lobes; and the corpus callosum and the anterior commissure connecting the right and left temporal lobes (Kolb & Whishaw, 1990). Three major pathways connect the temporal lobe with other cortical regions for complex integrated functions. The arcuate fasciculus connects the frontal and temporal lobes; the superior longitudinal fasciculus connects the temporal to the occipital and frontal cortices (i.e., the sensory and motor regions of Wernicke's and Broca's areas); and the occipitofrontal fasciculus connects the frontal-temporal-occipital regions (Hynd & Cohen, 1983).

The anatomical complexity, including large association regions, suggest that the temporal lobes have diverse functions, including: the perception of auditory sensations, the analysis of affective tone in auditory stimuli, and long-term memory storage. Although the temporal lobe has primary auditory perception and association functions related to speech and language processing, it also plays a significant role in memory functions and in facial (prosopagnosia) and object recognition (Shepard, 1994).

The primary temporal cortex is involved with the perception of speech sounds, particularly in the left hemisphere, and nonverbal tonal sequences, particularly in the right hemisphere, while the secondary and association regions are more complex and varied in function. The secondary and association regions add the affective quality to stimuli that is essential for learning to take place. When positive, negative, or neutral affective qualities are attached to stimuli, information takes on motivational or emotional importance to the learner. Without this association, all stimuli would be judged as equal and we would respond to all stimuli with the same affect or emotion (Kolb & Whishaw, 1990).

The mesial temporal region, including the adjoining hippocampus and amygdala, appears to be linked to memory processes and plays a role in learning or acquiring new information (Tranel, 1992). Lesions in this area result in impaired retention of new memories, as this region appears to be related to the process by which new memories are stored or are retrieved from storage (Kupfermann, 1991).

Asymmetry of functions is evident in the temporal lobes. Memory functions appear to be lateralized. The recall of verbal information, including stories and word lists presented either orally or visually, is stored in the left hemisphere, whereas nonverbal recall for geometric drawings, faces, and tunes is stored in the right hemisphere (Kolb & Whishaw, 1990).

THE DEVELOPMENT OF HIGHER CORTICAL REGIONS

The relationship between cognitive-behavioral development and neuroanatomical development is relatively uncharted in young children, with two exceptions—motor and language functions (Kolb & Fantie, 1989). Changes in myelin formation in specific brain regions are correlated with increased complexity of functions and increased cognitive abilities in children from birth to 5 years of age. See Table 2.4 for an overview of this interaction.

Kolb and Fantie (1989) caution that it is unclear which of these correlations is meaningful. Although there is an obvious interaction among developing brain structures, many of which are developing simultaneously, and behavioral changes, this relationship is highly variable (Majovski, 1989). Brains are distinct in their individual cellular and neural growth patterns, but this process is affected by acculturation (Majovski, 1989) and chemical-environmental factors (Cook & Leventhal, 1992). Despite individual variations in this process, developmental trends in structural and behavioral interactions can be interpreted with these limitations in mind.

The following sections address maturational processes in specific cortical regions. In some instances, there is not sufficient research to determine when structures are fully developed and how structural changes relate to cognitive development; however, there is sufficient evidence to suggest that meaningful patterns are emerging. The following review summarizes the current available research in this area.

Frontal Lobe Maturation

Conel (1939—1959) mapped postnatal frontal lobe development, showing rapid changes in density from birth until 15 months. Synaptic density increases until 2 years of age, when it is about 50% above that of adults, and decreases until about 16 years of age (Huttenlocher, 1979). Kolb and Fantie (1989) suggest that a decrease in the number of synapses in the frontal lobes may represent a "qualitative refinement" in the functional capacity of the neurons. That is, cognitive complexity cannot be defined in simple

Table 2.4. Myelination and Cognitive Development

AGE	VISUAL/MOTOR FUNCTIONS	SOCIAL/INTELLECTUAL FUNCTIONS	MYELINATION
Birth	Sucking reflex, rooting, swallowing, Moro reflex, grasping, and blinking to light		Motor root +++; sensory root ++; medial lemniscus ++; superior cerebellar peduncle ++; optic tract ++; optic radiation —/+
6 weeks	Neck turning and extension when prone; regards mom's face; follows objects.	Smiles when played with.	Optic tract ++; optic radiation +; middle cerebellar peduncle; pyramidal tract +
3 months	Infantile grasp; volitional sucking; holds head up; turns to objects in visual field; may respond to sound.	Watches own hands.	Sensory root +++; optic trace & radiation +++; pyramidal tract ++; cingulum +; frontopontine tract +; middle cerebellar peduncle +; corpus callosum +/—; reticular formation +/—
6 months	Grasps with both hands; puts weight on forearms; rolls; supports weight on legs brief periods.	Laughs and shows pleasure. Makes primitive sounds. Smiles at self in mirror.	Medial lemniscus +++; superior cerebellar peduncle ++; middle cerebellar peduncle +; pyramidal tract ++; corpus callosum +; reticular formation +; association areas +/—; acoustic radiation +
9 months	Sits and pulls self to sitting position; thumb—forefinger grasp; crawl.	Waves bye-bye; plays pat-a-cake; uses *Dada, Baba*; imitates.	Cingulum +++; fornix ++; others as described
12 months	Releases objects. Cruises and walks with one hand held; plantar reflex flexor in 50 %.	Uses 2—4 words with meaning; understands nouns; may kiss on request.	Medial lemniscus +++ pyramidal tract +++; fornix +++; corpus callosum +; intracortical neuropil +/—; association areas +/—; acoustic radiation ++
24 months	Walks up and down stairs; (two feet-step); bends and picks up object; turns knob; partially dresses; plantar reflex flexor 100%.	Uses 2—3 word sentences; uses *I, me,* and *you*; plays simple games; names 4—5 body parts; obeys simple commands.	Acoustic radiation +++ corpus callosum ++; association areas +; nonspecific thalamic radiation ++
36 months	Goes up stairs (one foot) pedals tricycle; dresses self fully except shoelaces, belts, and buttons; visual acuity 20/20/OU.	Asks numerous questions; says nursery rhymes; copies circles; plays with others.	Middle cerebellar peduncle +++
5 years	Skips; ties shoelaces; copies triangles; gives age.	Repeats 4 digits; names 4 colors.	Nonspecific thalamic radiation +++; reticular formation ++; corpus callosum +++; intracortical neuropil & association areas ++
Adult			Intracortical neuropil & association areas ++ to +++

Source: Adapted with permission "Development of the Child's Brain and Behavior" by B. Kolb and B. Fantie (1989), in C. R. Reynolds and E. R. Janzen, eds., *Handbook of Clinical Child Neuropsychology*, pp. 17—40. New York: Plenum Press.
Note: +/— minimal amounts; + mild amounts; ++ moderate amounts; +++ heavy.

quantitative terms, such as the number of synapses. These structural changes appear to correspond to the development of behaviors mediated by the frontal lobes, namely speech, executive, and emotional functions.

Using EEG data to map brain activity, Thatcher (1991, 1994) suggests that there are "growth spurts" of cortical connections from the parietal, occipital, and temporal lobes to the frontal lobes. These growth spurts occur at three intervals: (1) from age 1.5 to 5 years; (2) from 5 to 10 years; and (3) from 10 to 14 years. After age 14 the frontal lobes develop at the same rate and continue until age 45. These corticocortical connections differ between hemispheres. The left hemisphere shows a developmental sequence of gradients involving anterior-posterior and lateral-mesial regions, with *lengthening* of connections between posterior sensory regions, and frontal areas, while the right hemisphere involves a *contraction* of long-distance frontal connections to posterior sensory areas. Thatcher (1994) suggests that the expansion of the left hemisphere is due to functional differentiation of new subsystems, whereas the contraction of the right hemisphere is the functional integration of previously existing subsystems. Thus, experience and stimulation play a direct role in the process of redefining and differentiating neuroanatomy.

Expressive Speech Functions

Scheibel (1990) examined dendritic structures in the frontal lobe to determine the relationship between functional speech abilities and cortical development. In a series of postmortem studies, electron microscopic techniques were applied to brain tissue taken from 17 subjects between the ages of 3 months and 6 years. Structural changes in dendritic growth patterns appear related to differences in language functions across the ages and are summarized as follows:

1, Initially, dendritic growth is greater in the right opercular region (motor speech area) than on the left at 3 months.
2. Dendritic systems on the left increase in higher order speech zones at 6 months and eventually surpass the right hemisphere.

3. The hemispheres develop in an uneven pattern for the next 5 years.
4. The dendritic system in the left hemisphere appears more complex by the age of 6, and Broca's area resembles the development of adults at this age (Scheibel, 1990).

Further, these structural changes appear related to differences in functional speech mechanisms present at each stage.

Speech during the first 6 to 12 months of age is characterized by affective communication patterns, which probably account for dendritic growth in the right frontal regions (Scheibel, 1990). Syntactic and propositional aspects of language, developed in later stages, appear related to the development of left frontal regions. Development of dendritic processes in the language regions in the left hemisphere catches up to and eventually exceeds development in the right hemisphere corresponding to increases in the use and complexity of language skills. Further, Scheibel (1990, p. 263) hypothesizes that "structural maturation develops concomitantly with, and may in fact depend on, functional activity."

Scheibel (1990) found that proximal and distal segments of the dendritic branches also differed depending on the hemisphere. Proximal segments (near the cell body) develop early, with distal segments (far) appearing later in development. Proximal segments are longer in the right hemisphere, with distal segments more pronounced in the left hemisphere. The proximal/distal ratio appears complementary, where proximal segments are longer in the absence of distal segments. The importance of distance from the cell body in determining the role of the dendritic processes is unknown. However, Scheibel (1990) does suggest that distinct dendritic processes in the two hemisphere are probably related to functional differences between the two regions.

Executive Functions

Studies have also focused on the neurobehavioral correlates of frontal lobe development, specifically the emergence of "executive" functions (e.g., planning, flexibility, inhibition, and self-monitoring) that have been attributed to this area. Whereas prefrontal regions have been hypothesized to be involved primarily in executive functions (Dennis, 1991; Welsh, Pennington, & Grossier, 1991), striatal regions also have been investigated (Denckla, 1996; Voeller, 1991). Because there are rich connections between the frontal lobes and striatal regions (Hynd et al., 1993), it is reasonable to believe that these two areas are intimately involved in executive functions.

Pribram (1992) suggests that executive functions are subdivided between these anatomical regions: dorsal frontal, lateral frontal, and orbital frontal. The dorsal frontal region is thought to be responsible for determining how important a situation is; the lateral frontal is involved in determining if the selected action is worth the effort needed to obtain the result; and the orbital frontal is responsible for determining the social and situational appropriateness of actions. Thatcher (1991) suggests that the interaction of these three functionally relevant areas provides the behavior known as executive function.

In keeping with our transactional model, Denckla (1994) suggests that executive functions have two influences, one neuroanatomical and the other "psychodevelopmental," and that these influences not only interact but also modify each other. Moreover, there appear to be age-related variables that demarcate the possession of different functions believed to be executed in nature (Welsh et al., 1991). For example, Denckla (1994) cites the example that construct validity of executive function is demonstrated by convergent (a child X age can do this when he or she can do that) and divergent (a child of X age can do this but not that) validity.

Some suggest that the frontal lobes of children develop rather markedly between the ages of 4 and 7 years, with steady but less dramatic increases from 12 years of age to adulthood (Luria, 1973). Others suggest that development begins in adolescence and continues up to about 24 years of age (Golden, 1981). Still others suggest that the frontal lobes develop in cycles rather than with variable development between the hemispheres (Thatcher, 1994). Experimental studies have shown that children do exhibit behaviors thought to be mediated by the frontal lobes much earlier than adolescence or adulthood.

Similar to Denckla's (1994) convergent/divergent validity approach to executive functions, Becker, Isaac, and Hynd (1987) found age variation in skill attainment. Skills thought to be mediated by the frontal lobes were found to be mastered by 10 and 12 year olds; these included the capability of inhibiting motor responses, remembering the temporal order of visual designs, using strategies for memory tasks, attending to relevant details and ignoring distractors, and employing verbal mediators to enhance performance. Six-year-olds had more difficulty inhibiting motor responses and remembering the temporal order of visual designs. There appeared to be a developmental shift for 8-year-olds, who were able to inhibit motor responses. While subjects at all age levels were able to verbalize directions, younger children, especially those under the age of 8, were not always able to inhibit perseverative responses.

Passler, Isaac, and Hynd (1985) also found that children progress through developmental stages showing mastery of some frontally mediated tasks at 6 and at 8 years, while other tasks were not mastered even at the age of 12. Six-year-olds gave flexible, correct responses for a verbal conflict task but were unable to respond accurately to a nonverbal conflict task. Although 8-year-olds mastered both tasks and also were able to complete a perseveration task, they were unable to complete a series of drawings consistently or to respond correctly respond to verbal and nonverbal proactive inhibition task. Finally, even the 12-year-olds did not obtain full mastery of the verbal and nonverbal retroactive inhibition tasks. These findings suggest that the greatest period of development for executive functions occurs between the ages of 6 and 8, with continued growth beyond the 12-year-old level for more complex tasks.

Kolb and Fantie (1989) also measured age-related increases in tests of frontal lobe functioning. On the Wisconsin Card Sorting Test, children reached adult levels of performance by 10 years of age but did not reach adult levels of performance on a word fluency test even by the age of 17. Emerging research suggests some correlation between structural and cognitive development, but much more information is needed to understand this dynamic process fully.

Emotional Functions

Models of the neuropsychological basis of emotions indicate that the frontal lobes play a central role in the processing of emotional responses (Heller, 1990). The two hemispheres appear differentially involved in adults, with damage to the left hemisphere resulting in depression and catastrophic reactions; whereas damage to the right hemisphere results in inappropriate emotional reactions, including indifference or euphoria (Heller, 1990). Developmental patterns have been documented showing that the left hemisphere may be more reactive to emotional stimuli in younger children (9 years of age) than the adolescents (14 years of age) and adults (Davidson, 1984). Heller (1990) suggests that as the right hemisphere matures, it has a modulating effect on the more reactive left hemisphere. Moreover, as the corpus callosum matures, the right hemisphere can inhibit or control the left hemisphere more effectively.

Heller (1990) postulates that depression in children and adults may be a function of underactivation of the frontal regions, or the right hemisphere may be overactivated. Apparently, it is the ratio of activation between the two hemispheres that is important rather than the level of activation of either one. Heller (1990) further speculates that neurodevelopmental patterns may help to explain why depression seems to increase around puberty, which corresponds to the time when later-developing corpus callosal structures are becoming mature. Kolb and Taylor (1990) also describe the role of the temporal lobes in the perception of emotions (e.g., facial or tonal), and suggest that differences between the anterior/posterior regions may be just as important as the right/left hemisphere differences in the control of emotions.

Parietal Lobe Maturation

Although it is assumed that the sensory systems are functional prior to birth, very little is known about tactile-sensory development. Whereas evidence suggests that somesthetic senses are the first to develop embryonically, the course of development in infancy and early childhood is less well articulated (Martin, 1993). Proton magnetic resonance spectroscopy tech-

nology has been used to measure brain metabolism in order to determine regional differences in brain development from childhood into early adulthood (Hashimoto et al., 1995). There was a significant correlation between age and metabolic activity in the right parietal regions, suggesting rapid brain maturation in this region from one month up to the age of 2 or 3 years. The frontal regions showed less metabolic activation during the same time frame, suggesting slower development of these regions. The frontal lobes, dense with gray matter, are slower to myelinate and to form synaptic and dendritic connections than are the more posterior brain regions.

The course of development for tactile perception has been most thoroughly researched for hemispheric asymmetries. Tactile form perception increases with age (from 8 to 12 years); children usually show a slight superiority in scores using their preferred hand (dominant hand); and scores on the nonpreferred hand were much more variable than on the preferred (Benton, Hamsher, Varney, & Spreen, 1983a). For the 12- to 14-year-old group, children show a more even range of scores and reach adultlike performance on these measures. Tactile finger localization develops more slowly, and most preschool children are unable to name or point to the finger that has been touched (Benton et al., 1983a). For most 6-year-old children, this is a difficult task, but by the age of 9 few errors are present. When errors do appear, they occur more frequently on adjacent fingers (37.5%). 4 times higher than for adults.

Children apparently respond differentially to tactile localization tests on the right and left hands, depending on the type of response mode required (Bakker, 1972). Verbal responses seem to increase accuracy when identifying touch to the right hand, whereas nonverbal responses enhance accuracy with the left hand. Witelson and Pallie (1973) found that children do recognize nonsense forms better with the left hand, but recognition of letter shapes does not appear to have a right or left hand advantage.

Occipital Lobe Maturation

The visual system is slow to develop in humans (Hynd & Willis, 1988). Myelination of the optic tract is moderately developed at 6 weeks of age but is heavily developed by 3 months of age (Kolb & Fantie, 1989). The myelination of the optic radiation is somewhat slower, with minimal development at 3 months of age and mild development at 6 weeks of age. However, heavy myelination occurs in the optic radiation at about the same time as the optic tract.

Developmental trends in visual asymmetries have also been investigated in children. Kolb and Fantie (1989) found that the right hemisphere may be specialized for facial recognition in children as young as 4 years of age, and shows a steady increase in accuracy up to 5 years of age, with slower acceleration after this age. Kolb and Fantie hypothesize that the structural hardwire of the brain is sufficiently mature by age 5 and that further growth in accuracy is dependent on experience. While the 6-year-old is adept at facial recognition, matching expressions to situations is not well developed until about 14 years of age. This finding implies that the later task may also require frontal lobe maturation as well as posterior cortical development (Kolb & Fantie, 1989).

Temporal Lobe Maturation

Developmental patterns have also been investigated for hemispheric asymmetry in the temporal lobes. Asymmetries of the temporal lobe appear to have some relationship between cortical maturation and the development of the corpus callosum (Rosen, Galaburda, & Sherman, 1990). There is sufficient evidence that the left planum temporale is larger than the right and that these differences are present at birth (Wada, Clark, & Hamm, 1975; Witelson & Pallie, 1973). This developmental course is likely related to functional differences between the two hemispheres in their ability to process information. Infants appear to discriminate speech sounds at a young age, as early as 1 to 4 monthsof age (Eimas, 1985). Further, researchers have found functional lateralization of the left hemisphere for speech sounds in infants (Molfese & Molfese, 1986) and for music and nonspeech sounds in the right hemisphere in infants (Entus, 1977). See Table 2.3 for a summary of developmental ages when asymmetry between the two hemispheres appears.

Rosen et al. (1990) investigated the ontogeny of lateralization and have generated some hypotheses about the mechanisms of asymmetry. In these studies, symmetry in the brain was found to be related to the size of the planum temporale in the right hemisphere. In brains with normal patterns of asymmetrical organization, there was a corresponding decrease in the size of the right hemisphere. This correspondence was not observed in brains that were symmetrical, as there was an abundance of neurons in the temporal regions of the right hemisphere (Duane, 1991). Further, the corpus callosum in symmetrical brains was found to be larger than in those with the normal patterns of asymmetry (Rosen et al., 1990). Rosen et al. (1990) hypothesize that this variation in volume is likely a result of "pruning" of the axons in the corpus callosum that takes place in early developmental stages. Asymmetry may be related to withdrawal of neurons in the corpus callosum, while ipsilateral connections are maintained (Rosen et al., 1990).

Numerous factors impinge upon normal brain development, affecting the manner in which neural systems function and the way in which traits and behaviors are expressed. Genetic as well as environmental factors influence neurodevelopment. These factors will be reviewed briefly in the following sections.

GENETIC FACTORS AFFECTING BRAIN DEVELOPMENT

Brain development appears to follow relatively fixed sequences of growth and changes in the biological processes that are genetically specified. Defects in the genetic program, intrauterine trauma (e.g., toxins), or other factors can result in serious malformations in brain size and structural organization. See Table 2.5 for a summary of these neurodevelopmental abnormalities. Cell migration, axonal/dendritic formation and growth, synaptic development, and myelination appear compromised.

These neurodevelopmental anomalies produce a variety of functional/behavioral deficits, ranging from life-threatening to severely symptomatic to asymptomatic. While a number of these anomalies are related to defects in embryogenesis (dysplasias, agen-

Table 2.5. Neurodevelopmental Abnormalities Associated with Neurogenesis or Abnormal Neural Migration

ABNORMALITIES	SYMPTOMS	POSSIBLE CAUSES
Size Micrencephaly	Brain is smaller than normal. Involves cognitive deficits, epilepsy.	Genetic, malnutrition, inflammatory diseases (e.g., rubella), radiation, maternal exposure to poisons
Megalencephaly	Brain is larger than normal. Intelligence ranges from subnormal to gifted, behavioral deficits.	Genetic
Abnormal Tissue Growth Holoprosencephaly	Hemispheres fail to develop. Single hemisphere or ventricle is present. Medical problems (e.g., apnea, cardiac) exists. Mental and motor retardation are present.	Neurotoxicity, genetic (trisomy 13—15)
Agenesis of corpus callosum	Corpus callosum fails to develop (partial or complete). Linguistic and intellectual deficits are present. Found with other neurological disorders (i.e., hydrocephaly, spina bifida)	Genetic
Cerebellar agnesis Cerebellum fails to develop		Genetic
Cortical Malformations Lissencephaly	Sulci and gyri fail to develop. Found with agenesis of corpus callosum. Severe mental retardation, epilepsy. Early death.	Etiology unknown
Micropolygyria or polymicrogyria	Numerous small, and poorly formed gyri. Severe retardation to LD.	Intrauterine infections
Abnormalities with Hydrocephaly Dandy-Walker malformation	Cerebellar malformations, with fourth ventricle enlargement. Other abnormalities (e.g., agenesis of corpus callosum).	Genetic
Abnormalities in Neural Tube and Fusion Anencephaly	Hemispheres, diencephalon, and midbrain fail to develop.	Genetic
Hydranencephaly	Hemispheres fail to develop, CDF-filled cystic sac. Looks like hydrocephaly early. Appears normal at birth.	Umbilical cord strangulation. Vascular blockage, ischemia
Porencephaly	Large cystic lesion (bilateral). Mental retardation, epilepsy. Agenesis of temporal lobe. Early death.	Neonatal hemorrhaging following trauma, ischemia
Spina bifida	Neural tube fails to close. Skeletal, gastrointestinal, cardiovascular, and pulmonary abnormalities, bulging dura mater.	Maternal fever, virus, hormonal imbalance, folic acid deficiency

Source: Adapted from G. W. Hynd and W. G. Willis, *Pediatric Neuropsychology,* Table 4.1, pp. 73—77. Copyright © 1988 by Grune & Stratton, Orlando, Florida. Adapted by permission of The Psychological Corporation, Orlando, Florida 32887.

esis of the corpus callosum, malformations of the cortex, etc.), both genetic and environmental factors appear to be causative factors (Garg et al., 1994).

The extent to which other childhood and adolescent disorders, particularly dyslexia and schizophrenia, are genetically transmitted has been investigated. Developmental dyslexia has been the focus of studies demonstrating autosomal dominant (generation-to-generation) inheritance (Smith, Kimberling, Pennington, & Lubs, 1983). Lubs et al. (1991) suggest that autosomal recessive inheritance (normal parents with affected siblings) are also reported, but autosomal dominant inheritance seems most frequent. Volger, Defries, and Decker (1984) found that less than half of persons with dyslexia have parents with a history of reading problems. According to Lubs et al. (1991), the genetic linkage will likely increase when cases of dyslexia resulting from injury or environmental damage are excluded from studies. Lubs et al. (1991) conclude that "developmental dyslexia is a heterogeneous group of disorders, some of which are inherited" (p. 74).

Malaspina, Quitkin, and Kaufman (1992) indicate that a number of other neuropsychiatric disorders of childhood and adolescents have a genetic component. Individuals with an affected relative seem to be at a higher risk of also developing some disorders, including a 45% morbid risk for dyslexia; a 50% morbid risk for Gerstmann-Straussler syndrome (degenerative disease with motor signs and dementia), acute porphyria (motor neuropathy with psychiatric features), and myotonic dystrophy (motoric, intellectual, and psychiatric deterioration); a 25% to 50% risk for leukodystrophy (hyper- or hypotonicity with psychotic symptoms); a 25% risk for Lesch-Nyhan syndrome (spastic and movement disorders with retardation); a 24% risk for Wilson disease (liver disorder with neuropsychological symptoms); a 12.8% risk for schizophrenia; an 8% risk for bipolar disorders; a 4% risk for epilepsy; and, a 3.6% risk for Tourette syndrome (major behavioral disorder with motor and vocal tics). See Malaspina et al. (1992) for an in-depth discussion of the epidemiology and genetic transmission of these and other neuropsychiatric disorders.

The specific abnormal gene(s) involved in these disorders are unknown; further, the role of environmental factors in the expression of these illnesses cannot be overlooked (Malaspina et al., 1992). Even when single autosomal genes are known, the exact nature or presentation of various disorders is unknown. Variable expression of neuropsychiatric disorders depends on a variety of factors, including age at onset of the illness. Further, Malaspina et al. (1992) hypothesize that one genotype may result in multiple phenotypes or vice versa. The latter situation, where one phenotype arises from several genotypes, seems most likely for disorders with heterogeneous etiologies. For example, Malaspina et al. (1992) suggest that psychosis may be the inherited trait found in both schizophrenia and bipolar disorders. The critical point at this juncture is that the systematic linking of hereditary factors with environmental factors will likely be useful in advancing our understanding of childhood disorders. This linkage may ultimately provide some insight for preventing and treating some neuropsychiatric abnormalities (Malaspina et al., 1992).

Selected environmental factors known to affect brain development are briefly examined in the following sections.

THE INTERACTION OF BIOLOGICAL AND ENVIRONMENTAL FACTORS ON BRAIN DEVELOPMENT

It has long been recognized that biogenetic (e.g., chromosomal abnormalities), environmental factors, (e.g., pre- and postnatal toxins and insults), and birth complications all affect the developing brain. Traumatic brain injury at an early age and a lack of environmental stimulation are also known to have long-term affects on optimal brain development. Prenatal and postnatal factors known to have an impact on the developing brain will be briefly reviewed.

Prenatal Risk Factors

With the advent of X-ray technology in the 1920s and 1930s, it became apparent that the developing fetus was susceptible to various environmental agents known as *teratogens* (Berk, 1989). Moore (1983) identified critical periods during the embryonic (second to eighth week of development) and the fetal stage (ninth week to birth) in which the exposure to teratogens produced different outcomes. The central nervous system was particularly vulnerable from the fifth week of embryonic development up to birth. Berk (1989) discussed several detrimental environmental influences, including alcohol, narcotics, pollutants, maternal disease, and malnutrition, as prenatal risk factors affecting neurodevelopment.

Maternal Stress, Nutrition, and Health Factors

Maternal stress. In addition to numerous prenatal factors that place the developing child at risk for neurological complications, maternal stress, malnutrition, poor health, and age also play a role in the ultimate expression of these risk factors (Berk, 1989). Extreme maternal stress is known to increase levels of stress in the fetus and has been associated with low-birth-weight babies and irritable, restless, colicky infants. Reinis and Goldman (1980) suggest that maternal stress creates vasoconstriction reducing circulation that ultimately produces fetal asphyxia, which is known to cause brain damage in the developing fetus.

Maternal nutrition. Nutritional deficiencies during the last 3 months of fetal life and during the first 3 months of infancy also can have severe effects on the developing brain, particularly seen as a decrease in the number of brain cells and brain weight (Berk, 1989). Although proper maternal nutrition can reverse infant mortality rates (Papalia & Olds, 1992), the affects of pre- and postnatal malnutrition on the child's intellectual and behavioral development are difficult to measure (Berk, 1989).

Maternal health. Maternal health during pregnancy is generally monitored to ensure normal fetal development. Duane (1991) suggests that maternal hypotension may have an adverse affect on the fetal brain. A reduction of blood pressure in the pregnant woman can result in circulation failures in the developing brain (Humphreys, Kaufman, & Galaburda, 1990). Fibromyeline plaques or lesions form in cortical areas called "watershed regions." These ischemic-induced alterations, caused by a temporary loss of blood (perfusion), have been found in the brains of individuals with dyslexia (Duane, 1991). Ischemia may also be induced by maternal or fetal autoimmune mechanisms.

The extent to which these morphological variations are related to or contribute to reading disability will be explored in later chapters. The important point here is that maternal health directly affects the developing fetal brain. Glial cells and specific molecules that direct the migration of cells may be involved in such a way as to alter the cortical architecture of the child's brain (Duane, 1991).

Another maternal health factor that has known effects on the developing brain is rubella (German measles), which often results in deafness in babies if the mother contracts this disease in the first trimester of pregnancy (Papalia & Olds, 1992). Berk (1989) notes that eye and heart involvement are other likely outcomes if rubella occurs in the first 8 weeks of pregnancy, whereas deafness is more likely to occur if the illness occurs between 5 and 15 weeks. Maternal herpes simplex 2 is also known to produce mental retardation and learning difficulties because this virus attacks the developing central nervous system of the fetus (Samuels & Samuels, 1986).

Concerns have been recently raised about the effects of acquired immune deficiency syndrome (AIDS) on the developing fetus. Berk (1989) reports that embryonic and fetal malformations are likely results of prenatal AIDS infection. Microcephaly often appears, together with other facial deformities, and babies who are infected with the AIDS virus often die within 5 to 8 months of symptom onset (Minkoff, Deepak, Menez, & Firkig, 1987). Central nervous system involvement has been estimated to be as high as 78% to 93% of children with human immunodeficiency virus (HIV), with signs of motor, visual-perceptual, language, and reasoning delays (Belman, Lantos, et al., 1986; Belman, Ultmann, et al, 1986; Ultmann et al., 1985, 1987).

Diamond et al. (1987) investigated the cognitive

status of children with congenital HIV infection. In this longitudinal study, children (aged 4-2 to 8-7 years) were found to have prominent visual-spatial organization problems, with generalized cognitive impairment and motor involvement (e.g., spastic diparesis, hypotonia, clumsiness, and coordination difficulties). CAT scans also revealed mild atrophy (Diamond et al., 1987), with progressive encephalopathy and basal ganglia calcification.

Mothers who are likely to contact AIDS often come from high-risk populations, including intravenous drug abusers, so other health factors may play a role in the manifestation of symptoms (Berk, 1989). The extent to which other psychosocial factors play a role in the long-term outcome for children with congenital HIV infection needs further study.

Maternal age during pregnancy also can play a role in the outcome of the developing fetal brain. Major medical complications in older women and poverty or a lack of "psychological readiness" in younger women have been found to be risk factors for the developing fetus (Berk, 1989). When health, poverty, and psychological factors are controlled, infants born to teenagers and mothers over 35 do not appear to be at higher risk for complications (Berk, 1989).

Maternal Alcohol and Drug Addiction

Alcohol. Heavy maternal alcohol consumption has serious consequences for the developing fetal brain, whereas the effects of drug addiction are less clear (Berk, 1989). Fetal alcohol syndrome (FAS) occurs frequently in infants born to alcohol-dependent mothers, and estimates suggest that 40,000 children are born with alcohol-related birth defects every year (Papalia & Olds, 1992). Characteristic symptoms in children with FAS include pre- and postnatal growth delays, facial abnormalities (e.g., widely spaced eyes, shortened eyelids, small nose), mental retardation; and behavioral problems (e.g., hyperactivity and irritability) (Berk, 1989). Central nervous system symptoms early in life include brain-wave abnormalities, impaired sucking responses, and sleep problems, with attentional, behavioral, motor, and learning

problems developing and continuing into later childhood (Papalia & Olds, 1992).

The developing fetal brain is highly susceptible to alcohol damage, and pregnant mothers are advised to eliminate alcohol consumption entirely (Surgeon General's Advisory on Alcohol and Pregnancy, 1981). Even moderate alcohol consumption (i.e., one to two drinks a day) in mothers who are breast feeding can produce mild delays in motor development, including crawling and walking delays (Little, Anderson, Ervin, Worthington Roberts, & Clarren, 1989). Although not all children are equally affected, maternal alcohol consumption during pregnancy and lactation is definitely a risk factor, with deleterious affects on the developing brain.

Marijuana. Infant and fetal central nervous system signs have been shown to result from heavy maternal consumption of drugs during pregnancy, including marijuana, cocaine, and heroin. Physical signs (i.e., low weight and premature infants), neurological complications, and central nervous system involvement (e.g., tremors and startles) have been found in infants born to mothers with high marijuana usage (Lester & Dreher, 1989; Fried, Watkinson, & Willan, 1984).

Cocaine. Cocaine use appears to affect blood flow into the placenta and may affect neurotransmitters in the fetal brain (Papalia & Olds, 1992). Infants born to mothers who use cocaine are at risk for various complications, including spontaneous abortions, prematurity and low birth weight, small head size, and behavioral symptoms (lethargy, unresponsiveness, irritability, and a lack of alertness) according to numerous studies reported in Papalia and Olds (1992) (see Chasnoff, Griffith, MacGregor, Dirkes, & Burns, 1989; Chavez, Mulinare, & Cordero, 1989; Hadeed & Siegel, 1989; Zuckerman et al., 1989, for a more in-depth treatment of this topic).

Howard (1989) described the social interaction and play characteristics of children with intrauterine cocaine exposure. Drug-exposed toddlers were more disorganized, showed signs of abnormal play patterns, and had trouble interacting with peers and adults. Allen, Palomares, DeForest, Sprinkle, and Reynolds

(1991) also suggest that cognitive and behavioral problems in cocaine-exposed children may not be obvious until later childhood, when damage to frontal lobes and basal ganglia is evident.

The long-term effects of cocaine use on the developing brain are difficult to differentiate from the effects of other environmental conditions that might accompany maternal drug use. However, mother—child and child—peer relationships are at risk because infants with symptoms described previously often have trouble with bonding and attachment (Papalia & Olds, 1992). Allen et al. (1991) also suggest that confounding factors, such as maternal drug addiction, may seriously interfere with the mother's ability to care for her infant properly.

Heroin. Heroin addiction during pregnancy produces risk factors including high mortality rates, prematurity, malformations, and respiratory complications (Berk, 1989). Infants display withdrawal symptoms at birth (tremors, vomiting, fevers, etc), and even though these decrease within months, mothers often have difficulty coping with the behavioral problems (i.e, irritability) that persist in heroin exposed infants (Stechler & Halton, 1982).

Postnatal Risk Factors

Many of the prenatal risk factors mentioned previously (infant nutritional deficiencies, maternal stress, etc.) continue to have an effect on the developing brain in the postnatal period.

Nutritional Deficiencies

Although it is often difficult to isolate the effects of nutritional deficiencies from other socioeconomic complications, severe vitamin deficiencies have a direct influence on the developing brain (Reinis & Goldman, 1980). Vitamin B_1 depletion can produce neurologic symptoms including ataxia, loss of equilibrium, and impairment of righting reflexes. Neurons and the myelin sheath can be destroyed, moving from peripheral to central brain regions. Thus, numb-

ness and other sensorimotor symptoms appear as early signs (e.g., tingling, muscle tenderness, with mental confusion and learning and memory problems appearing in later stages (Reinis & Goldman, 1980). Vitamin B_{12} and folic acid deficiencies also have been implicated in structural changes in myelination. Further, low levels of folic acid caused by nutritional deficiencies in breast milk may delay the normal course of EEG development in infants.

Other postnatal factors have been known to have long-standing effects on the developing brain, including birth complications, traumatic brain injury, exposure to environmental toxins, and lack of environmental stimulation. The way in which these factors affect the developing brain will be reviewed briefly.

Birth Complications

Birth complications during labor and delivery often produce neurological insults that have been associated with numerous childhood disorders, including psychiatric disorders (Yudofsky & Hales, 1992). Of particular concern are complications resulting in significant or prolonged loss of oxygen to the fetus. During the normal delivery process, contractions constrict the placenta and umbilical cord reducing the amount of oxygen to the fetus (Berk, 1989). In extreme situations, infants produce elevated levels of stress hormones to counterbalance oxygen deprivation and to ensure an adequate blood supply during delivery. Neurological insults are known to follow extreme oxygen deprivation, so electronic fetal monitoring provides needed information about the fetal heartbeat and oxygen level (Papalia & Olds, 1992).

Nasrallah (1992) lists a number of birth complications found in adults with psychotic symptoms that are consistent with schizophrenia, including long labor, breech presentation, abruptio placenta, neck-knot of umbilical cord, Apgar scores under 6, vacuum extraction, meconium aspirated, large placenta infarcts, birth weight under 2500 or above 4000 grams, and hemolytic disease. Although these obstetric complications (when in excess) have been found in adult schizophrenics, Nasrallah (1992) cautions that the exact neuropathology of this disorder is unknown. However, research employing a neurodevelopmental model is recommended.

Environmental Toxins

Exposure to lead, even in low levels, can produce a variety of cognitive and behavioral problems in children (Cook & Leventhal, 1992). Children with acute lead encephalopathy present severe symptoms, including seizures, lethargy, ataxia, nerve palsy, intracranial pressure, and death in some cases (25%) (Cook & Leventhal, 1992). In about 20% to 40% of cases, children develop epilepsy, severe motor symptoms (hemiplegia and spasticity), and blindness. Inattention and hyperactivity are also known sequelae of lead exposure, although this relationship is not as strong in cases with lower level exposure (Fergusson et al., 1988).

Environmental Stimulation

Postnatal stimulation is a critical factor affecting brain development and the child's capacity for learning. Although the infant appears genetically programmed for many abilities (e.g., sitting, walking, talking), the role of the environment can affect maturation rates in some areas (e.g., vision) (Papalia & Olds, 1992). Babies who are well nourished, receive maternal attention and care, and are allowed physical freedom to practice and explore generally will show normal motor development. In extremely deficient environments (e.g., orphanages), motor delays have been documented.

Although infants are born with the ability to learn, learning occurs through experience (Papilia & Olds, 1992). Language development, intellectual capacity, and social adaptations are influenced by the environment. The way mothers interact with, talk to, and respond to their infants affects the child's ability to de-

velop into competent children. However, there appears to be an interplay among these genetic-environmental influences. Children evoke differential responses from individuals in their environment depending on their genotypes (Berk, 1989). These responses can reinforce original predispositions and result in more positive interactions with adult caretakers. Infants are highly responsive to attentive, warm, stimulating environments that encourage self-initiated efforts. Inadequate early environments can have a negative impact on a child's early development, but children can recover if they are placed in more responsive environments before the age of 2 years (Berk, 1989).

Neurodevelopmental investigations are beginning to explore how changes in brain structures are related to cognitive development, but this undertaking is far from complete (Kolb & Fantie, 1989). Further, this area of investigation should be viewed as exploratory and as an emerging field of study that no doubt will evolve with more research and better techniques of inquiry. The extent to which morphological differences are related to various behavioral deficits found in children with learning and reading deficits will be explored in more detail in subsequent chapters. The interaction of environmental factors with neuro-development and cognitive-behavioral development is also critical.

Summary

This chapter reviewed the structural and functional organization of the brain within a transactional framework. This review serves as a foundation for understanding how various brain regions mediate specific behaviors in children. Neurological and clinical neuropsychological assessment mthods for children and adolescents will be explored next.

CHAPTER 3

ELECTROPHYSIOLOGICAL AND NEUROIMAGING TECHNIQUES IN NEUROPSYCHOLOGY

Technological advances have come about in all areas of medicine, and the techniques utilized for diagnosis of neuropsychological problems are no exception. These advances have moved neuropsychology from a practice emphasizing assessment to determine focal and diffuse lesions to one of developing interventions to compensate for brain damage or neurodevelopmental differences. Historically, neuropsychology has concentrated on the ability to diagnose cerebral lesions on the basis of behavioral data. This emphasis was necessary because technology was unable to provide the evidence for such diagnoses. With the advent of magnetic resonance imaging (MRI), lesions, brain tumors, and brain conditions that previously could be seen only with surgery or at autopsy can now be observed in the *living* patient.

Because the neuropsychologist will consult on cases that utilize neuroradiological and electrophysiological techniques, it is important to understand what these basic techniques involve and what they can tell the clinician. This chapter will provide information about common neuroradiological and electrophysiological techniques.

ELECTROPHYSIOLOGICAL TECHNIQUES

Procedures utilizing an electrophysiological technique provide an assessment of electrical activity associated with incoming sensory information. Electrodes are attached to the scalp and electrical brain activity is recorded through the use of a computer and an amplifier for the signals. Electrical brain activity is very weak and requires a differential amplifier to record

these signals through a recorder attached to a personal computer. Each electrode is placed on the scalp according to various conventions, the most common of which is the 10—20 universal system (Jasper, 1958). Figure 3.1 provides an overview for electrode placement.

Each electrode provides a signal from a particular region, and each signal is referred to a common reference electrode. The function of the reference electrode is to provide a reference to be used to subtract the signals from the individual electrodes. Because each electrode provides some natural interference to the signal, the reference electrode serves as a baseline for this interference, and the interference is thus subtracted from each electrode. In this way, each electrode provides information about the unique degree of electrical activity from that selected region of the scalp. Because muscle contractions, muscle movement, and eye movement can interfere with the signal, the patient is observed carefully and brain waves that show such movement are removed.

These techniques include electroencephalography and event and evoked potentials. Each of these techniques will be discussed in this chapter as well as research using such techniques for the study of neurodevelopmental disorders such as learning disabilities and attention deficit disorders.

Electroencephalography

Electroencephalographs (EEGs) are recorded in patients who are considered at risk for seizure disorders and abnormal brain activity resulting from brain tumors. They also have been found helpful for use with

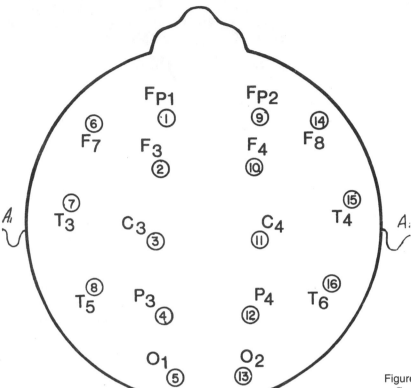

Figure 3.1. Electrode Placement
  Courtesy of Beverly Wical, M.D., pediatric
neurologist, University of Minnesota.

children who have experienced febrile convulsions, cerebral malformations, brain trauma, vascular events, and coma (Blume, 1982; Lombroso, 1985).

Different electrode selections can help in the localization or quantification of EEG results. For example, if seizures are thought to be temporally located, more electrodes will be placed in this region. Different montages can allow for the evaluation of seizure activity as well as activation patterns for seizures.

EEGs are not foolproof for identifying some types of seizure disorders (Bolter, 1986). At times an EEG may come out normal when in fact there is seizure activity or, conversely, may appear abnormal when no seizure activity exists (Dodrill & Willkus, 1978). For example, a study of normal children found that 68% had normal EEGs, with 42% having abnormal EEGs, whereas 33% of normal adolescents were found to have abnormal EEGs (Harris, 1983).

For some cases, activation procedures can be used to document neurodevelopmental abnormalities more carefully. These activation procedures include induction of sleep, sleep deprivation, hyperventilation, stimulation with flashing lights, and the use of pharmacological agents. These techniques may bring on seizure activity, which can then be recorded through the EEG procedure.

Reading an EEG is a complex and difficult task, particularly with children. Significant variability is found among EEG recordings from different children, with the greatest amount of variability found in neonates (Hynd & Willis, 1988). Cerebral maturation also can have an impact on EEG recordings. Therefore, it is recommended that children's mental age rather than their chronological age be used for reading the EEG (Lombroso, 1985). Conditions such as illness and metabolic disturbances can also have an impact on the EEG and alter it in such a way that it appears abnormal (Harden, Glaser, & Pampiglione, 1968; Pampiglione, 1964).

Evoked Potentials

An *evoked potential* is recorded using electrodes connected to a microcomputer and amplifier. Evoked potentials are recorded in the same manner as EEGs and utilize similar electrode placements. Because an evoked potential is considered to be a direct response to external sensory stimulation, it is considered to be relatively free from the influence of higher cortical processes. This type of potential is felt to be an inexpensive and noninvasive method for assessing the integrity of sensory pathways.

Evoked potentials pose one difficulty that is less problematic with EEGs, the difficulty of screening out artifacts. Another problem is that evoked potentials have extremely low amplitude ($0.1-20 \mu V$), and with such a low voltage, artifacts can have significant impact on the results (Molfese & Molfese, 1994). The actual brain waves occurring during the artifact can be rejected when compared to typical brain waves associated with the type of evoked potentials. There are distinctive patterns associated with auditory and visual evoked potentials. These will be discussed in more detail.

Auditory evoked potentials. Auditory evoked potentials (AEPs) are measures of brain activity from the brain stem to the cortex. The brain stem contains the auditory pathways leading to the cortex. AEPs are one way to assess the integrity of these auditory pathways in infants and young children. The common paradigm is to present auditory stimulation in the form of tones and to evaluate the child's responses to this stimulation. The responses have three phases: early ($0-10$ μsec), middle ($10-50$ μsec), and late (>50 μsec). Each of these phases will be discussed in turn.

Early phase. The early phase is also called the brainstem auditory evoked response (BAER). It consists of 5 to 7 waves that are thought to coincide with various brain stem nuclei along the auditory pathway (Hynd & Willis, 1988). Figure 3.2 represents a commonly found BAER, in which the first five waves are found in the first 5 to 6 milliseconds. Waves 6 and 7 are not found in all people. Eighty-four percent of people have wave 6, and 43% show wave 7 (Chiappa, 1985).

Wave 5 is considered the most diagnostically important for latency measurement (Chiappa, 1985). This wave appears to be related to the nuclei at the level of the pons or midbrain. It is relevant not only for diagnosing hearing problems but also for the diagnosis of hydrocephalus, coma, and the effects of toxins, among others (Menkes, 1985a). Wave 5 is also important for mapping the neurodevelopment of neonates. As the preterm child develops, the latency for auditory stimulation is found to decrease and approach that of full-term babies at 38 weeks (Monod & Garma, 1971).

Research has found that the BAER is useful in mapping the progression of a disorder of the central nervous system. Disorders such as asphyxia, autism, mental retardation, and hyperglycemia have been found to have differences in the amplitude and latency of various components (Hynd & Willis, 1988).

Visual evoked potentials. A visual evoked potential (VER) is a technique to evaluate the integrity of the visual system. Generally, two techniques are used. One involves uses a flashing light; the other presents a reversible black and white checkerboard pattern. The pattern-shift paradigm is felt to provide a more significant reading for visual deficits. This paradigm results in three peaks, which occur at the following latencies: 70, 100, and 135 milliseconds.

The VER has been shown to assist in evaluating the integrity of the visual system in cases of neurofibromatosis (Jabbari, Maitland, Morris, Morales, & Gunderson, 1985). In this study, children with neurofibromatosis (NF) were frequently found to experience tumors on the optic nerves which are difficult to detect in the early stages of growth. These

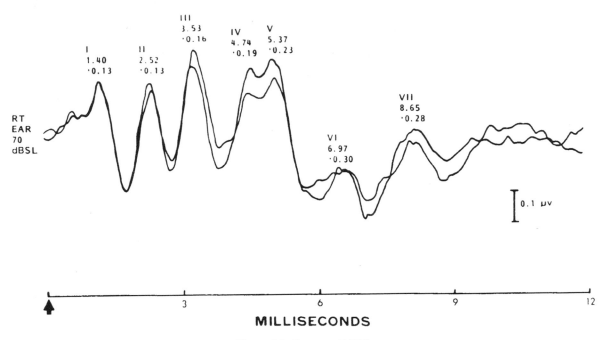

Figure 3.2. Common BAER

Source: From G. W. Hynd and G. Willis, 1988, *Pediatric Neuropsychology,* p. 179. Copyright © 1977 by Allyn and Bacon. Reprinted by permission.

early signs were later confirmed through the use of computed tomography (CT) scans.

Similar to the BAER, the VER has been found to be useful in determining the integrity of the visual system in preterm infants (Weiss, Barnet, & Reutter, 1984). In studies with preterm infants, the latency and amplitude of the waves appears normal with ensuing development (Moskowitz & Sokol, 1980).

Thus, the VER has been found to be useful with children for an inexpensive screening device for optic tumors as well as for monitoring the development of the visual system in preterm infants.

Event-Related Potentials

In contrast to evoked potentials, *event-related potentials* (ERPs) provide an assessment of later compo-

nents of the electrical wave forms that are thought to be associated with cognition. Another difference is that an ERP requires the client to participate in the data-gathering process, whereas the client is passive with evoked potentials. ERPs are collected in the same manner as evoked potentials and EEGs, with electrodes, amplifiers, and a computer. The difference lies in stimulus presentation and in the use of later wave components.

ERPs consist of complex wave forms comprising several components. Measurements of these components can be for amplitude (size of the wave) and latency (time from stimulus onset). Some components are *exogenous* (automatic responses to stimuli); others are *endogenous* (elicited by psychological characteristics of stimuli). The endogenous ERPs are thought to reflect cognitive processes.

Dyslexia. Research utilizing event-related potentials has found differences in brain electrical activity in children with developmental dyslexia. Generally, these differences have been found in the amplitude of the brain wave for both auditory and visual stimuli (Fried, Tanguay, Boder, Doubleday, & Greensite, 1981; Livingstone, Rosen, Drislane, & Galaburda, 1991; Shucard, Cummins, & McGee, 1984; Zambelli, Stamm, Maitinsky, & Loiselle, 1977), with children with dyslexia showing smaller amplitude to words, auditory stimuli, and shape/sound-matching tasks. In addition, those with dyslexia have been found to be less efficient in their processing to auditory material and to function similarly to much younger children (Hynd et al., 1988). Livingstone and colleagues (1991) found differences in responses of those with dyslexia to visual evoked potentials. These findings may be related to neuroanatomical differences that subserve these functions found during autopsy studies of dyslexic brains.

Research utilizing event-related potentials with people with dyslexia has been problematic in regard to subject selection. Heterogeneous groups of dyslexics have been utilized, and some studies utilized dyslexics who would not qualify for such a diagnosis in current educational practice. There has been little to no attention paid to *subtypes* in reading deficits and possible differences in their event-related potentials. It is not known whether dyslexic children who experience difficulty with sight word reading but not with phonics development (surface dyslexia) vary on electrophysiological measures from children with phonological coding disabilities (phonological dyslexia). Moreover, programs for wave form analysis have now been developed that allow not only for comparison across subjects but also for intrasubject comparisons. This development allows for comparisons of reading performance with different types of reading material. For example, material that requires phonetic processing can be compared with material that primarily requires visual processing.

In addition to identification of subtypes being problematic, the sample source for studying dyslexia is also problematic. For example, when children identified as learning disabled by objective standardized tests were compared with previously school-identified children for learning disabilities, an over-representation of boys in the school-identified sample was found, whereas the objective standardized test method found approximately equal numbers of girls and boys (Shaywitz, Shaywitz, Fletcher, & Escobar, 1990). Similarly, when groups were selected on the basis of objective test results, males have been found to show a more severe type of reading disability than girls (Berninger & Fuller, 1992).

Attention deficit disorders. ERPs have also been found to be helpful with children with attention deficit disorders (ADD). Difficulties in *sustained attention* may cause children with attentional disorders to respond more slowly and variably, and make more mistakes when presented with stimuli. Difficulties with *selective attention* may cause children not to respond to relevant stimuli (Douglas, 1983). Therefore, it has been important to evaluate both the amplitude and the latency of responses to stimulation. To evaluate this hypothesis, event-related potentials (ERP) have been used to measure sustained and selective attention.

P3b. One component of *sustained attention* that has been most frequently studied in children with attentional disorders has been the P3b component. The P3b is a late positive wave with a latency of 300 to 800 msec with maximal expression in the parietal region of the cerebral cortex. Amplitude of P3b can be increased through directing attention to novel features presented with low probability. Several studies have found smaller amplitude on P3b for children with ADD for both frequent and rare stimuli (Holcomb, Ackerman, & Dykman, 1985; Klorman et al., 1988; Loiselle, Stamm, Maitinsky, & Whipple, 1980). However, studies have also found smaller amplitude in diagnostic groups ranging from autism to mental retardation, which suggests that a reduced P3b may reflect cognitive disturbance rather than a unique characteristic of attention deficit disorder (Klorman, 1991).

Administration of stimulant drugs has been found to improve accuracy and speed of judgment and to increase P3b amplitude in children diagnosed as having attention deficit disorder (Klorman, Brumaghim, Borgstedt, & Salzman, 1996). This finding has been replicated with children with pervasive attention deficit disorder and children with attention deficit disorder with oppositional/aggressive features, and across age groups (Coons, Klorman, & Borgstedt, 1987; Klorman et al., 1988).

Holcomb et al. (1985) compared attention deficit disorder with hyperactivity (ADD/H), attention deficit disorder without hyperactivity (ADD/noH), and reading-disabled groups and found that only children with ADD/noH had significantly smaller amplitude of their P3b wave to stimuli they were asked to attend to (called target stimuli) than did controls. In a later study (Harter & Anllo-Vento, 1988), children with ADD/H were found to display larger difference in brain wave amplitudes between targets versus nontargets than did nondisabled children, whereas children with learning disabilities showed the opposite tendency.

In contrast to the amplitude component, the latency of the P3b has not been as fully studied comparing subtypes of children with attention deficit disorder to other groups. Holcomb et al. (1985) found that children with reading deficits and children with ADD/H and ADD/noH showed longer latencies than did nondisabled children. Although this procedure would not be diagnostically specific for attention deficit disorder, it does indicate differences in P3b components for ADD/noH children compared to controls and suggests that there may be differences between the subtypes in brain electrical activity.

MMN. Children with attentional problems may have deficits in brain processes that are automatic and not under voluntary control (Hynd, Semrud-Clikeman, et al., 1991). *Mismatch negativity* (MMN) has been carefully studied in normal children and adults and is believed to reflect the basic mechanism of automatic attention switching to stimulus changes without conscious attention (Näätänen, 1990). MMN is the difference in the N200 (N2) amplitude comparing rare targets and nontargets. Because the MMN component is thought to be automatic, if children with

ADHD showed lower amplitude or slower responses to incoming stimuli, it may well be that the deficits in ADHD children often found on behavioral measures of automatized skills are due to hard-wired neurological deviations.

Processing negativity. Selective attention differences using event-related potentials have also been detected in children with attention deficit disorders compared to control children. Children with attention deficit disorders have been found to have smaller waves for target detection than did control children for the processing negativity (N2) component (peak latency at 265 msec) independent of the electrode site (Loiselle et al., 1980; Satterfield, Schell, & Backs, 1988; Zambelli et al., 1977). These findings have been interpreted to reflect poorer selective attention in children with attention deficit disorder, particularly when subjects are required to ignore sets of stimuli. When only a single dimension of a target is presented and selective attention is not so overloaded, these differences no longer occur (Callaway, Holliday, & Naylor, 1983; Harter & Anllo-Vento, 1988). Therefore, it would be important to gather data on stimuli that require the subject to attend to one task at a time and conditions that require the subject to split her or his attention across tasks.

Conclusions

In summary, brain wave differences have been found in selective and sustained attention tasks in children with attention deficit disorders, particularly when complex tasks are utilized. There is emerging evidence that the subtypes may differ in brain electrical activity, with children with ADD/noH showing the largest difference from normal controls. If children with ADHD have different patterns of selective attention that can be measured through ERPs, it may well be possible to demonstrate changes in these differences following treatment.

For example, children with ADD/H were found to have a larger than normal response to rare stimuli, which may be interpreted to mean that they overreact to novel stimuli. This finding is similar to the behavioral observation that ADD/H children tend to be *very* attentive to rare and/or novel situations, tasks, and experiences. The findings of the processing negativity study indicates that it is almost impossible for these children to inhibit their responses. Therefore, not only do children with ADD/H show better attention to novel stimuli, but they also find it extremely difficult to ignore or inhibit responses to these rare occurrences. Thus, differences in how the brains of children with ADHD (ADD/H and ADD/noH) respond to the environment may provide information for the development of interventions as well as furthering our understanding of the underpinnings of these disorders.

NEUROIMAGING TECHNIQUES

While ERPs allow for a dynamic assessment of brain activity, computed tomography (CT) and magnetic resonance imaging (MRI) techniques allow for comparison of possible structural differences in children with developmental disorders compared to normal controls. Both of these techniques will be briefly discussed in the following sections.

Computed Tomography

Computed tomography (CT) allows for the visualization of the brain anatomy to determine the presence of focal lesions, structural deviations, and tumors. A CT scan uses a narrow X-ray beam that rotates 360 degrees around the area to be scanned. Each CT slice is acquired independently, and that slice can be repeated if a movement artifact occurs (Filipek, Kennedy, & Caviness, 1992). Scanning time is 15 to 20 minutes per slice. The resulting data are transformed by Fourier analysis into gray scale to create the image. Table 3.3 illustrates a CT scan image.

One advantage of a CT scan is the short acquisition time. Another is the ability to repeat single slices if movement or other artifacts occur. Limitations of CT scans are the relatively poor resolution of gray and white matter structures. Moreover, CT slices are obtained in the axial plane, which limits visualization of the temporal lobes and posterior fossa (Filipek

& Blickman, 1992). You may recall from Chapter 2 that the pediatric population is susceptible to tumors of the posterior fossa, which cannot be easily visualized by CT scanning. Although within acceptable ranges, radiation is used in CT scans in order to produce the images (Filipek & Blickman, 1992).

Magnetic Resonance Imaging

Recent advances in magnetic resonance imaging (MRI) procedures allow for noninvasive investigation of neuroanatomical structures in a *living* brain. MRIs allow for visualization of brain tissue at about the level of postmortem studies, with clarity superior to that of CT scans. Table 3.4 presents a representative MRI scan.

The MRI consists of a large magnet with magnetic field strengths up to 2.0 Tesla (Filipek et al., 1992). The patient lies on a movable table, which goes inside a doughnut-hole opening. A coil covers the area, to be scanned with an opening over the face in the use of the head coil.

To understand how MRI works, it is important to review briefly the physics behind MRI. In a magnetic field, hydrogen photons align in the same direction as the field. A radio-frequency pulse will deflect these photons into an angle predetermined by the clinician. Once the pulse ceases, the photons return to their original alignment through a series of ever-relaxing and slowing circles (Filipek & Blickman, 1992). Altering the rate, duration, and intensity of the radio frequency pulses allows for the differing visualization of the brain. An MRI is actually several complementary sequences, each an average of 7 to 10 minutes in length.

In clinical use, routine MRI scans utilize T_1 and T_2- weighted sequences. T_1-weighted scans provide visualization generated photons involved in the pulse, whereas T_2-weighted scans involve the interaction of the neighboring photons (Cohen, 1986). T_1-weighted scans provide excellent anatomical detail with myelin and structural abnormalities easily visible. In contrast, T_2-weighted scans are sensitive to water content in the tissues and are used to determine the extent of the lesions.

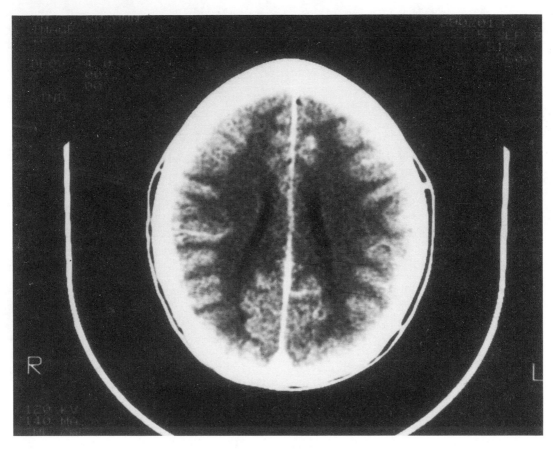

Figure 3.3. Normal CT Scan
Courtesy of William Dobyns, M.D., pediatric neurologist, University of Minnesota.

Becayse MRIs are noninvasive and do not use radiation, they are fairly risk-free. MRIs are expensive and are generally used only when there is suspicion of brain abnormality. They are more sensitive than CTs for locating lesions, and, when a contrast agent such as gadolinium DTPA is used, the tumor can be differentiated from surrounding swelling (Filipek et al., 1992). In the past, neuropsychological assessment was used to try to localize brain tumors, lesions, and the like. The MRI has supplanted neuropsychological assessment for this process in cases where tumors or lesions are suspected. Neuropsychological assessment is used for intervention planning and for determining *how* the person solves the difficulty. Neuropsycho-

logical assessment continues to be sensitive to subtle damage or damage at the microcellular level that the MRI is unable to pinpoint.

Functional MRI

Functional MRI (fMRI) is a relatively new technique, which at present is used mostly for research. It allows for the mapping of cerebral blood flow or volume as well as changes in cerebral blood volume, flow, and oxygenation (Fox & Raichle, 1986). fMRI allows for the study of brain activation through the use of echoplanar imaging (EPI). This technique may or may not use contrast agents that are injected into

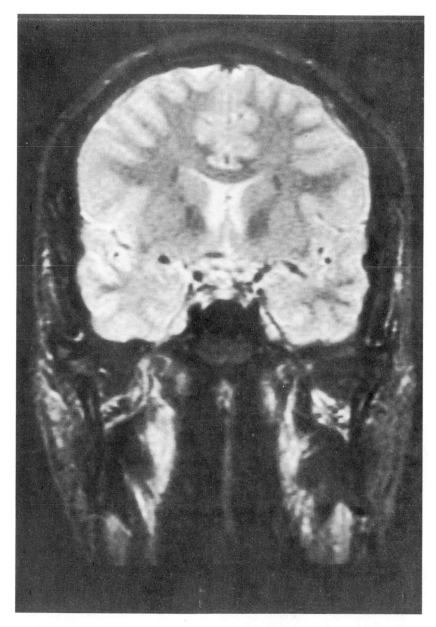

Figure 3.4. Normal Coronal MRI
Scan
    Courtesy of William Dobyns, M.D.,
pediatric neurologist, University of
Minnesota.

the vascular system and exposed to EPI and thus are able to be visualized in a magnetic field. T_2-weighted images are obtained which allow for visualization of the blood flow. Two maps are obtained: one at a resting state and one after activation.

This technique does not use radioactive agents for the contrast agent and is currently believed to be risk-free. It is so new that only very limited applications are available outside of research use. The sensory, motor, and language centers have been mapped with fMRI, and future use of the technique to map these areas prior to neurosurgery looks promising (Jack et al., 1994; Morris et al., 1994).

Research with fMRI. Binder (personal communication, September 1994) and associates at the Medical College of Wisconsin are in the forefront of exploring functional studies in adolescents with dyslexia. fMRI technology is one of the most advanced techniques available for measuring brain functions by detecting changes in blood flow during activation. This noninvasive technique allows researchers to explore the relationship between increases in metabolic activity in various local brain regions during cognitive or perceptual tasks; thereby, mapping or identifying cortical regions involved in various functions. Binder et al. (1994) found that several regions were activated during a single-phoneme monitoring task, including Heschl's gyrus and the transverse temporal sulcus (regional proximity to the primary auditory cortex); the lateral surface of the anterior/superior temporal gyrus; the planum polare (anterior to Heschl's gyrus) and, the planum temporale (superior temporal gyrus). Roa et al. (1992) found bilateral activation in the superior temporal gyrus during passive processing of lengthy phoneme clusters. The rate of stimulus presentation produced an interesting finding, as Binder et al. (1994) reported that as rate increased there was an analogous increase in bilateral temporal activation.

These fMRI findings suggest that more static or indirect measures of brain function may not be capturing the richness and complexity of brain function, in that both hemispheres were activated during a task thought to be mediated primarily by left temporal regions. These results expand and may challenge fairly well established patterns (using PET scans) of unilateral left temporal-parietal activation for phonological processing in adult populations of normal readers. Medical College of Wisconsin researchers are also using fMRI scans to investigate younger subjects identified as dyslexic with phonological awareness deficits in order to test empirically whether bilateral temporal-parietal activation also occurs in this population.

Research with MRI

MRI technology now allows us to obtain pictures of the brain from living children and also to assess the impact of treatment on the brain's development (Filipek et al., 1989). Because it may be possible to detect neuroanatomical differences before the behavioral problems emerge in response to school requirements, investigation of brain measures may allow us to begin studying children at a much younger age and thus to provide interventions earlier.

Dyslexia

Research by Hynd, Semrud-Clikeman et al. (1990) and Semrud-Clikeman, Hynd, Novey, and Eliopulos (1991) utilizing MRI scans found differences specific to dyslexia in the neuroanatomical regions involved with language processing. These findings were replicated in several subsequent studies (Duara et al., 1991; Jernigan, Hesselink, Sowell, & Tallal, 1991; Larsen, Hoien, Lundberg, & Odegaard, 1990). Additional findings in these studies indicated no differences in cerebral hemispheric area or posterior areas in dyslexic subjects.

The fact that these findings so strongly implicate areas thought to be important in language processing is very important. No differences were found in brain size, so reported regional differences more strongly implicate the likelihood of a neurodevelopmental process active during gestation of these regions. Abnormal development is thought to occur somewhere between the twenty-fourth and twenty-eighth week of gestation.

ADHD

For a regional difference to be predictive, it needs to be unique to a specific disorder. The consistent finding of smaller splenial (the posterior portion of the corpus callosum) measurements in ADHD may be unique to ADHD (Hynd, Semrud-Clikeman, Lorys, et al., 1991; Semrud-Clikeman, Filipek, Biederman, et al., 1994). Recent studies have documented no differences in the splenial callosal regions between normal controls and those with developmental dyslexia (Hynd et al., 1995; Larsen, Hoien, & Odegaard, 1992) or autistic patients (Gaffney, Kuperman, Tsai, & Hassanein, 1987).

Using a carefully diagnosed sample of ADHD with overactivity symptoms and no codiagnoses compared to a matched nondisabled control subjects, Semrud-Clikeman, Filipek, Biederman, et al. (1994) were able to demonstrate differences through MRI analysis in the posterior regions of the corpus callosum, with particularly smaller splenial regions for the ADHD group. No differences were found in the anterior regions of the corpus callosum, in callosal length, or callosal total area. When response to medication was evaluated, a trend also was found that may suggest structural differences for the ADD/H sample based on medication response. Subjects who did not respond to methylphenidate but did respond to desipramine or imipramine showed a trend toward a smaller corpus callosum splenial measure compared to subjects who were positive methylphenidate responders or control subjects. These results indicate that medication response may be partially mediated by fewer connections between posterior regions of the brain. Given the small number of subjects, the area of medication response and its relationship to brain structure needs further study.

Additional studies of brain structure differences between ADHD and normal children using MRI scans have found no difference in brain area (Hynd et al., 1990; Filipek, Semrud-Clikeman, et al., in press). Although a significant difference in total brain volume was not found by Filipek, Semrud-Clikeman, et al. (in press), a 5% smaller volume in children with ADHD, which was not related to age, height, weight, or IQ, was found by these researchers as well as by Castellanos et al. (1994).

One of the more intriguing findings of the Filipek, Semrud-Clikeman, et al. (in press) study was that of bilaterally smaller white matter in the region of the posterior to the corpus callosum. This region may be related to the findings of smaller splenial measures of the corpus callosum in two previous studies of children and adolescents with ADHD (Hynd et al., 1991; Semrud-Clikeman et al., 1994). It is possible

that fewer transmission fibers in the retrocallosal region of the brain may result in less activation in the frontal parts of the brain. The findings of Zametkin et al. (1990) indicate less metabolic activity in the parietal and occipital regions. These regions correspond roughly to the regions that were found to have less matter volumetrically in the Filipek, Semrud-Clikeman, et al. (in press).

Caudate findings. Hynd et al. (1995) found two-dimensional areas of the left caudate to be smaller in the ADHD sample than in a normal control group. These researchers found asymmetry differences using MRI in the caudate region of ADD/H children compared to normal controls. In this study, children with ADD/H showed reversed asymmetry (L > R) of the caudate nucleus. The caudate has rich connections to the frontal lobes. Such reversed asymmetry may have a negative impact on these children's ability to inhibit motor behavior. These results relate directly to the clinical finding that hyperactivity is a common symptom in caudate infarcts (Caplan et al. 1990). Hynd et al. (1995) suggested that such a difference may be related to lower levels of neurotransmitter being relayed to the frontal lobes and resulting in compromised levels of complex attentional skills. In contrast, Castellanos et al. (1994) found the right caudate to be smaller and symmetrical with the left caudate in their ADHD sample, while the control sample evidenced $R > L$ caudate volumes. Castellanos et al. (1994) also found that the volume of the caudate decreased significantly with age for the normal controls, with no difference in the ADHD group.

Filipek, Semrud-Clikeman, et al. (in press) found smaller volumetric measurements in the left anterior caudate of the ADHD sample compared to normals. This finding is consistent with the results of Hynd et al. (1995). Symmetrical caudate volume was found for the ADHD group as a result of a smaller than expected left caudate. The control group possessed left greater than right caudate volume. Moreover, there was significant medication effect related to smaller left caudate volume with the ADHD sample who responded favorably to methylphenidate showing the smallest left caudate volume, followed by the ADHD sample who did not respond to methylphenidate, and with the normal control group showing the largest left caudate volume.

Although there are conflicting findings as to the direction of the caudate asymmetry, the studies to date have found that there are structural differences in the caudate regions of ADHD children compared to normal children. The caudate is intimately involved in the dopaminergic system–a system in which methylphenidate is believed to correct suspected imbalances. Moreover, lesions to the caudate in adults and animals has resulted in behaviors that are very similar to those seen in hyperactive children (Posner & Raichle, 1994). Further study is needed in determining the role of the caudate in ADHD as well as the contributions of structural differences in this disorder.

These studies are preliminary and must be interpreted with caution because of small numbers and differing methodologies. However, their results suggest that neurodevelopmental anomalies may characterize the brains of children with ADHD and that deviations in structure may be associated and related to prenatal deviations in cellular migration and maturation (Geschwind & Galaburda, 1985; Hynd & Semrud-Clikeman, 1989).

The use of three-dimensional MRI as well as subgrouping ADHD may provide further information about the neurodevelopmental underpinnings of this disorder. Investigators have hypothesized that the brain areas implicated in ADD/H are in the anterior regions involved in motor activity modulation, whereas ADD/noH is hypothesized to be related to central-posterior regions affecting attention (Pennington, 1991; Posner & Petersen, 1990; Schaughency & Hynd, 1989). These hypotheses have not been tested empirically, and MRI results may well show anatomical differences among the subtypes.

As there appear to be differences in behavior between the subtypes, it is likely that the subtypes differ neurologically. Moreover, the finding that the subtypes of attention deficit disorder respond differentially to medication further indicates that differing brain mechanisms may be implicated in the subtypes (Urion, 1988). Therefore, since the MRI studies to date have utilized subjects with ADD/H, it would

appear that the next step would be to look at subjects with differing expressions of ADHD to determine if there are neuroanatomical differences exist between the subtypes.

NEURORADIOLOGICAL TECHNIQUES

Although techniques involving neuroradiology are not used by neuropsychologists and are of necessity research-based, it is important for neuropsychologists to be familiar with the burgeoning evidence these techniques provide. These techniques generally involve the use of radioactive isotopes and require very expensive equipment. These techniques are also seldom used with children given that radioactivity is administered. However, results from studies using these measures can provide information on the brain processes at the metabolic level.

PET and SPECT Scans

Positron emission tomography (PET) imaging can provide a direct measure of cerebral glucose metabolism. Zametkin, Nordahl, Gross, et al. (1990) studied ADD/H adults through the use of PET with 5 to 6 mm resolution. A radioactive tracer injected into the subjects is partially metabolized by the neurons and emits radiation imaged through the PET scanner.

These 25 ADD/H adults had onset of ADD/H in childhood and also were parents of ADD/H children. Subjects with conduct disorder or use of stimulant medication in childhood were eliminated from the sample.

Cerebral glucose metabolism (CGM) was measured in 60 regions and the ADD/H group was found to have a CGM approximately 8% lower than the controls, with 50% of the regions showing significantly lower metabolism than the controls ($p < .05$). The regions with significant hypometabolism were in the cingulate, right caudate, right hippocampal, and right thalamic regions. In addition, reduced metabolism was found in the left parietal, temporal, and rolandic structures for the ADHD subjects.

Statistical difficulties are present in this study in

that 60 *t*-tests were used for analysis, introducing the possibility of inflated significant results due to experiment-wise error. Zametkin has written additional information about his study, and when his results were studied using the Bonferonni method of correction, the areas that continued to be significant were in the superior prefrontal and premotor regions (Zametkin & Cohen, 1991).

In contrast to PET scans, single photon emission tomography (SPECT) is a direct measure of regional cerebral blood flow (rCBF) with neuronal glucose metabolism inferred from the rCBF. Thus SPECT is a vascular measure, whereas PET is a neuronal measure. Results from PET and SPECT studies may not be directly comparable because of this difference in acquisition.

Lou, Henriksen, and Bruhn (1984) utilized SPECT in 13 children with dysphasia and ADHD. Only two of these children had pure ADHD. The remaining 11 had variations of dysphasia, mental retardation, and visual-spatial delays, although two did not have a diagnosis of ADHD. All children were attending a school for children with learning disorders. The contrast group was selected from the siblings of these children. Given that Lou et al. (1984) did not provide information about the functioning of these children and of the finding of substantial learning and attentional problems in siblings of ADHD children (Barkley, 1990; Biederman, Faraone, Keenan, Knee, & Tsuang, 1990; Goodman & Stevenson, 1989), it may well be that the contrast group was not a true control group.

Despite these methodological problems, the findings from this study are intriguing. All children with ADHD (*n* = 11) were found to have less blood perfusion in the white matter of the middle frontal regions, including the region of the genu of the corpus callosum. Hypoperfusion was also found in the caudate region. It must be pointed out that the caudate region was inferred from the scan, as the caudate nucleus is smaller than the 17 mm resolution of the scanner. Therefore, the hypoperfusion may also have involved the lateral wall of the anterior horn of the lateral ventricle as well as the caudate, in addition to other areas of the basal ganglia. When methylphenidate was ad-

ministered to the ADHD group, increased flow was found in the central region of the brain most likely encompassing the basal ganglia region.

Theoretically these findings make sense. Frontal regions have feedback loops into the caudate. However, the primary output for the caudate is the thalamus, and it is not clear why the thalamus was not found to be hypoperfused also. The thalamic region was found to have lower perfusion in only 3 of the children; 2 with mental retardation and 1 *without* ADHD.

Lou, Henriksen, Bruhn, Borner, and Nielson (1989) expanded their study to include 19 additional subjects, 6 of whom were identified as "pure ADHD." The remaining 13 had ADHD as their primary diagnosis, along with other neurological deficits. Of these 13, 3 had mild mental retardation, 9 had dysphasia, and 6 had visuospatial problems. The control group was the same as in the initial study. In this follow-up study, the mesial frontal region was not found to show significant hypoperfusion as was found in the 1984 study. Instead, the ADHD group found hypoperfusion in the right striatal area encompassing the anterior corpus callosum, internal capsule, and part of the thalamus in addition to the caudate. Hyperperfusion was found in the occipital region for the ADHD groups and in the left anterior parietal and temporal regions. Methylphenidate normalized perfusion in the left striatal area but not the right, as well as in the association regions in the posterior region of the brain.

In a 1991 letter to the *New England Journal of Medicine,* Lou stated that statistical analysis was not performed on the SPECT scans in the initial 1984 study. Scans were analyzed through "visual analysis," and when the prefrontal region measures were statistically analyzed with corrections for multiple analyses performed, the regional difference was not statistically different.

Therefore, Lou et al.'s (1989) statistically significant finding of hypoperfusion in the striatal region and hyperperfusion in the posterior regions may implicate these regions in ADHD. With statistical correction Zametkin and Cohen (1991) reported that the superior prefrontal and premotor areas continued to show significant differences. Further study with con-

trolled statistical procedures as well as subjects without co-morbid diagnoses would clarify knowledge in
this area, and it is hoped that these researchers will
pursue this end.

Conclusions

In summary, MRI imaging of the brains of ADHD
children and adults has found differences in the frontal regions of the brain as well as in the corpus callosum. The recent finding of differences in the caudate
nucleus is particularly interesting and important, as a
structural anomaly in the caudate region in other disorders has been found to be important for the ability
to inhibit behavior (Pennington, 1991). Studies have
not addressed issues of comorbidity of disorders nor
of adult-child similarities in these structures when
both present with ADHD. Most important, the rela-

tionship between structural differences and behavioral
measures needs to be investigated. The question of
behavioral measures predicting structural differences
in ADHD remains largely unexplored.

The areas found to differ on MRI may also show
differences in metabolism/blood flow as measured by
the SPECT and PET studies of Lou and Zametkin.
Methodological problems in these metabolism/blood
flow studies make their results equivocal and further
investigation appears to be warranted. The development of these techniques is promising not only for
clinical reasons but also for furthering our knowledge
of brain function and links to behavior. fMRI, spectroscopy, and PET scans allow for the evaluation of
structure and function. It is likely that the next decade will add exponentially to our understanding of
various disorders and we hope, lead to the development of appropriate interventions.

CHAPTER 4

INTEGRATING NEUROLOGICAL, NEURORADIOLOGICAL, AND PSYCHOLOGICAL EXAMINATIONS IN NEUROPSYCHOLOGICAL ASSESSMENT

This chapter provides guidelines to help psychologists make decisions about when to refer a child or adolescent neuropsychological assessment, for neurological examination, or other neurodiagnostic testing (e.g., CT scan or MRI). Children and adolescents often need neurological, neuroradiological, and/or neuropsychological assessments. Although not every child seen for cognitive, academic, psychiatric, or behavioral problems requires further assessment apart from traditional psychoeducational evaluations, some disorders do need further attention by specialists to investigate the child's neurological or neuropsychological status.

Clinical and school psychologists need to be apprised of conditions that typically require further attention. The nature of neurologic, neuroradiologic, and neuropsychological assessment will be discussed, along with guidelines for making referrals. Further, aspects of psychological, psychosocial, and academic functioning are discussed, as these areas may be seriously compromised by brain-related disorders of childhood. Integration of these various evaluation findings are discussed.

THE NEUROLOGICAL EXAMINATION

Neurological examinations are conducted by neurologists generally specializing in childhood and adoles-

cent neurology. Because it is sometimes difficult to differentiate normal developmental variations from abnormal neurodevelopment in the first few years of life, it is important to access child neurologists when there is a question about chronic and serious neurodevelomental delays. The neurologist is generally interested in identifying disease, injury, developmental, or genetic processes that interfere with CNS functioning.

The neurological examination usually consists of the following: (1) an in-depth review of medical and developmental history; (2) an assessment of mental status; (3) an assessment of the functional capacity of the CNS, including the cranial nerves; (4) an evaluation of motor systems; (5) an assessment of sensory functions; and (6) an assessment of autonomic functions (Swaiman, 1994b). Each area is systematically evaluated through a series of activities designed to measure muscle tone, cranial nerves, and primitive and autonomic reflexes. Interpreting information from the neurological examination is complicated by the child's age and intellectual and functional capacity.

A look inside the examination room with a neurologist and patient would show the physician initially conducting an in-depth developmental interview. In most cases the child is present during this procedure and the physician notes the child's participation, attention, and language. Moreover, the child's facial movements are noted with attention to head nodding, eye blinking, staring, tics, and movement disorders. In addition, the physician observes the child's behavior as far as his or her impulsivity, dependence on the parent, and activity level. Additional observations of parent—child interaction are obtained. Swaiman (1994b) suggests that the physician ask him or herself the following questions: "Does the child respond positively to the parent's interaction? Does the child attempt to manipulate the parent? Is the response transient or persistent? Is the parent's attitude one of caring or hostility?"

After age 4, a motor screening examination is conducted. The neurologist has the child stand in front of him or her and demonstrates the required motor acts. The child is asked to hop on one foot and then the other, to walk forward and backward, to walk on tiptoes, and to walk on heels with toes pointed up. Additionally, the child is asked to rise from a squatting position, and to stand with feet together, eyes closed and arms and hands outstretched from the body and parallel with the floor. These maneuvers are designed to check for balance, extraneous unnecessary movement, and the Romberg sign. The Romberg sign is the inability of the child to stand still when his or her eyes are closed (Swaiman, 1994b). The child then is asked to touch his or her nose with the finger, both with eyes closed and with eyes open. On the basis of this initial screening, the neurologist will follow up on any abnormalities in motor coordination.

The next portion of the examination involves testing reflexes. Both deep tendon reflexes (also known as muscle stretch reflexes) and reflexes appropriate at various ages are assessed. For the deep tendon reflexes, the neurologist elicits the reflex with a rubber reflex hammer while the child is seated quietly. Hyperreflexes (contraction of muscles that generally are not involved in the reflex) are a sign of corticospinal dysfunction. Hyporeflexes are most often associated with motor unit abnormalities of the spinal cord (Swaiman, 1994a) or of the cerebellum. Cerebellar functions are assessed by asking the child to first touch his or her nose and then the examiner's finger at various positions. The child is also asked to run his or her heel down the shin of the opposite leg. Inability to complete these tasks smoothly may indicate cerebellum dysfunction.

Cranial nerves are evaluated next. Congenital anomalies as well as traumatic injury can produce observable neurological signs. See Table 4.1 for a review of some common anomalies that might be identified when conducting an examination of the cranial nerves.

The sensory system is next assessed during the neurological examination. The ability to sense vibrations, position of limb, and joint sense is evaluated. For evaluation of the child's ability to localize tactile information, the neurologist touches various places both unilaterally and bilaterally with the child's eyes closed. The inability to localize touch is associated with parietal lobe dysfunction (Swaiman, 1994b). The child is also asked to recognize various objects which are placed in his or her hand (stereognosis) with eyes closed. Parietal lobe dysfunction is measured by this means, but attention to task can interfere with performance.

Muscle strength is also assessed. The child is asked to push against the examiner's hand with his or her hand or foot as hard as possible. He or she also may be requested to push his/her head against the neurologist's hand as hard as possible. The child may also be asked to walk on his or her hands while the examiner holds the child's feet. Once the child's feet are placed on the floor, the child is asked to stand up. Inability to stand without use of aid is another measure of muscle strength.

To evaluate gait, the child is asked to walk back and forth and to run. Running exacerbates problems with gait and can show additional signs of spasticity or jerking movements (Swaiman, 1994a).

This section was a brief overview of a typical neurological examination. The interested student may wish to observe a neurological examination in order to obtain a first-hand experience. You may wish to ask a parent if you can accompany him or her to such an examination.

WHEN TO REFER FOR NEUROLOGICAL EVALUATION

A neurological examination should be considered under the following conditions:

Table 4.1. Common Anomalies Revealed during Examination of the Cranial Nerves

NUMBER	NAME AND FUNCTION	ANOMALIES	CONTRIBUTING FACTORS
I	Olfactory (smell)	Asnomia–loss of smell	Severe head trauma Frontal lobe gliomas Olfactory groove meningiomas Temporal lobe epilepsy
II	Optic (vision)	Uncoordinated movement Asymmetric nystagmus Exophthalmos Papilloedema Macula discoloration Retinal bleeding	Congenital blindness Gliomas or craniopharyngiomas Congenital disorders Increased cranial pressure Tay-Sachs, metachromatic dystrophy, Batten's disease Intracranial pressure, bleeding, or leukemia
III	Oculomotor (eye movement	Pupil dilation Eyes downward	
IV	Trochlear	Depression of eye movement	
VI	Abducens	Eye turns medially Restricted lateral eye movement	
V	Trigeminal (masticatory movement)	Hyperactive jaw Hypoactive jaw	Cerebral trauma Pseudobulbar palsy Bulbar palsy
VII	Facial (facial movement)	Symmetry, upper and lower face Odd auditory perceptions Impaired taste and salivation	Lesions Lesions Bell's palsy
VIII	Auditory (hearing)	Vestibular dysfunction Vertigo, nystagmus, ataxic gait Audition Tinnitus (ear ringing)	 Medication Neuromas or skull factures Otosclerosis or toxins (streptomycin or aspirin)
IX	Glossopharyngeal (tongue and pharynx)	Taste buds	
X	Vagus (heart, blood vessels, viscera, larynx, and pharynx)	Swallowing Language expression	
XI	Spinal accessory (movement, strength of neck and shoulder muscles)	Paralysis of head/neck muscles Atrophy	Lesions
XII	Hypoglossal (tongue muscles)	Atrophy of tongue Protrusion of tongue Eating problems Dysarthria	Lesions

Note: See Hynd and Willis (1988) for more details on cranial nerve damage.

1. Sudden, unexplained, and prolonged nausea accompanied by high fever, headache, and lethargy that might suggest meningitis or encephalitis
2. Rapid blinking eye movements, visual aura (auditory and sensory auras are not uncommon), blank stares, or head or muscle jerks/spasms that might suggest seizure activity
3. Visual or olfactory hallucinations
4. Sudden motor clumsiness or cerebellar ataxia
5. Prolonged viral infections producing symptoms listed under item 1
6. Head trauma producing nausea, blurred vision, loss of consciousness, or dilated pupils
7. Cranial nerve involvement producing unilateral or bilateral motor weaknesses (e.g., droopy mouth, eyes, or facial muscles, or tongue protrusion)
8. Sudden, unexplained diminution of cognitive, language, speech, memory, or motor functions following normal development

A number of tumor processes, CNS leukemia, CNS infections (meningitis, encephalitis, and intracranial abscesses), neuromuscular diseases, and genetic disorders (e.g., neurofibromatosis, Sturge-Weber syndrome, and tuberous sclerosis) produce some of these symptoms (Hynd & Willis, 1988). These conditions typically require ongoing neurological examination and follow-up.

Neurologic examination is usually part of the diagnostic and treatment protocol that follows when children display the symptoms described here. In some instances, neurologists will recommend further neuroradiological follow-up to ascertain the nature and range of CNS involvement. In other instances (head injury or suspected brain tumor or lesion), CAT scans and MRI studies may be warranted immediately. CT scans, MRI scans, and regional cerebral blood flow (rCBF) procedures were described in detail in Chapter 3.

NEURORADIOLOGICAL EVALUATION

Despite their research potential, CT scans and MRI procedures are not necessarily part of the typical diagnostic process for identifying developmental disorders unless there are other accompanying neurologic signs (e.g., seizures, dysphasia). CT/MRI techniques are relatively expensive and for the most part are reserved for diagnosing and treating medical or neurological conditions affecting the CNS.

When to Refer for Neuroradiological Evaluation

A physician generally refers a child or adolescent for neuroradiological techniques under the following conditions:

1. Head trauma
2. CNS tumor processes
3. CNS disease processes involving white matter degeneration
4. Neurodevelopmental anomalies affecting the size or formation of brain structures, such as hydrocephaly or agenesis of the corpus callosum
5. Cerebrovascular diseases (e.g., sickle cell anemia)
6. Dyslexia or other neurodevelopmental disorders when there is a history of seizures, neurological signs, and/or significant language or speech delays.

Positive signs on the neurological examination (see previous section) also may warrant further neuroradiologic evaluation.

Children with neurodevelopmental disorders that affect brain size, tissue growth, cortical formations, and neural tube and fusion abnormalities usually require initial diagnostic and ongoing neuroradiological follow-up. See Table 2.5 for a list of select neurodevelopmental disorders. Finally, repeated neuroradiologic evaluations are routinely conducted on children with brain trauma to measure changes in neurologic status (Bigler, 1990).

Neuropsychological evaluations utilize measures and methods for determining the neurobehavioral status of children with various disorders. Guidelines for referral for neuropsychological evaluation will be explored next.

NEUROPSYCHOLOGICAL ASSESSMENT

Neuropsychological assessment procedures are described in detail in Chapter 5. Neuropsychological tests are generally administered to investigate the brain—behavior relationship in children and adolescents and to determine whether cognitive, academic, and psychiatric disorders are related to abnormal brain function.

When to Refer for Neuropsychological Evaluation

Neuropsychological evaluations are generally recommended under the following conditions:

1. Conditions affecting the CNS that were previously described under neurological and neuroradiological referrals (e.g., head trauma, CNS diseases)
2. Chronic and severe learning disabilities that do not respond to traditional special education or remedial programming, particularly when there is evidence of a pattern of right or left hemisyndrome (lateralizing sensory-motor neurological signs)
3. Severe emotional or behavioral disturbances accompanied by significant learning, intellectual or developmental delays (e.g., motor, speech/language, perceptual) that are particularly resistant to traditional psychopharmacological, psychological, or behavioral interventions
4. Acute onset of memory, cognitive, academic, motor, speech/language, behavioral, and personality deficits that cannot be explained by other psychoeducational evaluations.

Neuropsychological evaluations can be useful for diagnosing various neurodevelopmental disorders (e.g., LD), brain injuries, and CNS diseases, and for measuring treatment efficacy and recovery of function (Coutts et al., 1987). See later chapters for methods of developing interventions for specific childhood disorders.

INTEGRATION OF NEUROLOGICAL, NEURORADIOLOGICAL, AND NEUROPSYCHOLOGICAL DATA

Medical and university labs and clinics are exploring integrated research protocols including neuroradiological and neuropsychological data in an effort to understand more fully the nature of childhood disorders. Clinicians and researchers that are prominent in this effort include Bigler (1991) and associates (Bigler, Yeo, & Turkheimer, 1989); Denckla, LeMay, and Chapman (1985); Duffy, Denckla, McAnulty, & Holmes (1988); Hynd, Semrud-Clikeman, et al. (1990); Witelson and Kigar (1988); and Zaidel, Clarke, and Suyenobu (1990). In these efforts, researchers are revealing evidence linking neurocognitive and neuropsychological deficits to functional brain regions or systems. In essence, these investigators are providing information establishing the bidirectional nature of the neuroanatomical/morphological— neuropsychological/functional link. (This relationship is depicted in Figure 1.1.) While the link between anatomy and function has generally been downward, these efforts start at the functional/neuropsychological level and build upward, establishing a function-to-structure linkage that may lead to a better understanding of childhood disorders.

Researchers postulate neurobiological models of childhood disorders, such as dyslexia, and, in an effort to test these models empirically, information from divergent sources is analyzed. Typically theories about how the brain functions are tested by administering neuropsychological tests to carefully defined groups of children (e.g., dyslexic children with language-related deficiencies) and then by studying morphological variations in brain structures using neuroimaging techniques and, more recently, fMRI procedures. The degree to which specific neurolinquistic deficiencies are related to morphological abnormalities or functional differences in brain activation can thus be investigated. In doing so, researchers are beginning to answer questions such as these: Do children with language-related reading disorders have atypical symmetry in regions presumably mediating language processes? And, are the measured linguistic difficulties a function of these unique patterns of brain asymmetry? Hynd et al. (1991) discussed these morphological-functional relations for dyslexics in detail. The reader is also referred to Teeter and Semrud-Clikeman (1995) for a better understanding of these brain—behavior interactions in children with ADHD.

The next logical and critical step in developing a neurobiological model of childhood disorders is to investigate the extent to which children with cognitive-processing and/or linguistic deficits respond to differential intervention programs. Efforts at identifying cognitive correlates of reading deficits have been conducted by Shankweiler and Liberman (1989), Stanovich (1988, 1993), Sternberg (1985), and Wagner and Torgeson (1987). Further, attempts at designing specific remediation programs for increasing reading achievement for children with specific cognitive deficiencies are underway. Tallal et al. (1996) found that children with language deficits improved dramatically after four weeks of computer-based instruction teaching listening and speech discrimination skills. Cunningham (1990) also reports positive gains in children who received phonemic awareness training and strategy instruction to increase reading achievement. Rourke (1989) is also exploring an integrative neurobiological model in a group of children with nonverbal learning disabilities with presumed right-hemisphere weaknesses. These will be explored in more detail in Chapter 8.

In summary, efforts linking neuroradiological and neuropsychological findings are underway establishing the bidirectional nature of the relationship between brain structure and brain function. Integrated research paradigms are important in this effort, and will advance our basic understanding of childhood disorders. In the clinical setting, children referred for neuropsychological evaluation do not necessarily receive neurological or neuroradiological testing unless there is accompanying brain damage or suspected CNS disease.

Cognitive, academic, behavioral and psychosocial functioning are also of interest to the neuropsychologist because these factors may affect test performance on neuropsychological measures. Thus

it is important to explore alternative hypotheses (e.g., attentional deficits, motivational variations, depression, anxiety, and/or oppositional defiance) before making inferences about brain pathology on the basis of neuropsychological test results.

Tests of psychological functioning that are commonly incorporated into neuropsychological evaluations are reviewed next. Psychological factors that have a negative impact on the neuropsychological evaluation are also explored.

PSYCHOLOGICAL ASSESSMENT OF CHILDREN WITH NEURODEVELOPMENTAL, NEUROPSYCHIATRIC, AND OTHER CNS DISORDERS

Achenbach (1990) suggests that at least six micro-paradigms be incorporated in the study of childhood disorders: biomedical, behavioral, psychodynamic, sociological, family systems, and cognitive. By drawing from each of these diverse approaches, questions about childhood disorders can be framed into an integrated "macroparadigm." Achenbach describes a model of multiaxial assessment with specific suggestions for measuring child behavior:

Axis I: Parent reports, Child Behavior Checklist (Achenbach, 1991)
Axis II: Teacher reports, Child Behavior Checklist–Teacher's Report Form
Axis III: Cognitive assessment, WISC-III or WAIS-R
Axis IV: Physical assessment, height, weight, and neurological/medical exam
Axis V: Direct assessment, Semistructured Clinical Interview (Achenbach & McConaughy, 1989) and Youth Self Report (Achenbach & Edelbrock, 1987).

Neuropsychological evaluations could be appropriately incorporated into Axis IV of this model.

Various components and techniques recommended for use in a comprehensive psychological evaluation are discussed briefly. Information gathered from this evaluation inform the neuropsychologist and others about the child's overall cognitive-intellectual, psychosocial, and academic functioning. This information is helpful in describing the extent to which brain-related dysfunction affects these important functional areas of the child.

Although the neuropsychologist working in a multidisciplinary setting may not necessarily administer these tests, psychological evaluation results can be further analyzed from a neuropsychological perspective. Interpretation of psychological findings within a neuropsychological framework will be explored after a selective review of available instruments/methods.

Background and Developmental History

Developmental and background history is important for a number of reasons. First, developmental history can be important for identifying risk factors during pregnancy and delivery that have been associated with neurodevelopmental disorders of childhood of a specific (e.g., learning disabilities) or global (e.g., cognitive disabilities) nature. Second, previous head trauma and/or other health factors (e.g., recurring ear infections, high fevers, or febrile seizures) can be uncovered in a review of developmental history. Third, a careful history is important for determining the presence of similar or related disorders in other family members or hereditary linkages that might be helpful for understanding the etiology of a particular disorder. Fourth, a history of when the child attained motor and language milestones (walking, talking, etc.) is essential for determining the nature and extent of the developmental correlates of the child's problem.

Fifth, background history is essential for determining the presence of coexisting disorders (e.g. conduct disorders, depression, anxiety) that affect long-term outcomes for children with various neurodevelopmental disorders. These conditions often must be addressed separately in treatment plans. Finally, background information also sheds light on the child's educational, psychosocial, and academic opportunities, which may assist in the proper diagnosis of a disorder (i.e., reading deficits). The extent to which environmental, genetic, and experiential factors affect the manner in which some CNS disorders progress or influence treatment approaches can be explored with a complete review of the child's history. This information is crucial for accurate differential diagnoses, particularly when the clinician is trying to determine whether the problem is neurodevelopmental in nature or the result of a lack of opportunity to learn or the absence of appropriate modeling, stimulation, or reinforcement.

There are several methods for obtaining reliable background information, including the structured parent and child interviews from the Child Behavior Checklist (Achenbach, 1991) and the Behavior Assessment for Children (Reynolds & Kamphaus, 1992). Most neuropsychological clinics use structured interviews (i.e., K-SADS; Puig-Antich & Chambers, 1978) for gathering information, and many utilize questionnaires designed specifically to investigate a particular disorder, such as ADHD (see Barkley, 1990; DuPaul & Stoner, 1994).

Medical and school records also provide crucial information for identifying the child's biogenetic, health, and environmental history of the child. A careful review of these materials often reveals risk factors and predisposing conditions that may interact with the child's specific problem, and this information may be useful in designing effective interventions.

Intellectual, Cognitive, and Perceptual Functioning

Selected instruments for measuring cognitive-intellectual functioning are reviewed including the following: (1) the Woodcock-Johnson Cognitive Battery-Revised (WJ-R); (2) the Weschler Intelligence Scale for Children–III (WISC-III); (3) the Differential Ability Scale (DAS); and (4) the Kaufman Assessment Battery for Children (K-ABC).

Woodcock-Johnson Tests of Cognitive Ability—Revised

The Woodcock-Johnson Tests of Cognitive Ability (WJ) was developed by Woodcock and Johnson (1977) and was later revised (WJR) by Woodcock and Johnson (1989). The WJR is based on the intellectual model of crystallized and fluid intelligence (Cattell & Horn, 1978) and has been found useful for measuring cognitive ability, scholastic aptitude, and achievement (Woodcock, 1990). There are seven scales on the WJR: Long-term Retrieval (Glr), Short-Term Memory (Gsm), Processing Speed (Gs), Auditory Processing (Ga), Visual Processing (Gv), Comprehension Knowledge (Gc), and Fluid Reasoning (Gf).

Woodcock (1990) analyzed the factor structure of the WJR and found that it was unique in its measure of Gf and Ga. Further, the Gc factor was related to the WISC-III Verbal Comprehension factor, and Gv was related to the Perceptual Organization Factor. In this study comparing the WJ-R and the WISC-III, there was little empirical support for the Freedom from Distractibility (FD) factor of the WISC-III.

Although it is sometimes difficult to abandon the verbal-perceptual organization model of intelligence underlying the Weschler scales, the WJR offers a conceptual alternative to this framework that might be extremely useful for some childhood disorders, particularly learning disabilities. The WJR has strong psychometric properties and offers a method of gathering benchmark measures of visual and auditory processing, memory and retrieval, and reasoning abilities in children and adolescents.

Wechsler Intelligence Scale for Children—III

The Wechsler scales have enjoyed a long history of use for measuring intelligence in children and adolescents (Sattler, 1988), and the Wechsler Intelligence Scale for Children–III (WISC-III) is the latest revision for children (Wechsler, 1991). The WISC-III provides scores on the following: Verbal Intelligence Quotient (VIQ), Performance IQ (PIQ), Full Scale IQ (FSIQ), Verbal Comprehension Index (VCI), Perceptual Organization Index (POI), Freedom from Distractibility Index (FDI), and Processing Speed Index (PDI).

Though not originally developed as a measure of brain functioning, the Wechsler scales are almost always used as part of a neuropsychological evaluation (Wechsler, 1991). In studies with LD and ADHD males, the WISC-III shows moderate correlations (.36 to —.64) with various Halstead-Reitan scales: Performance IQ with TPT Total Time (—.64), TPT Mem (.45), TPT Loc (.42), Trails A (—.57), and Trails B (—.42); Freedom from Distractibility Index with TPT Total Time (—.41), Trails A (—.59), and Trails B (—.40); and Processing Speed Index with Trails A (—.51). Verbal intelligence measures typically show lower correlations with neuropsychological measures.

The WISC-III or the WJR: Which is best? Generally, primarily because of time constraints, neuropsychologists do not incorporate both the WISC-III and the WJR in an evaluation of children. However, deciding which cognitive-intelligence instrument to use may be a difficult choice. In making this determination, consider using the WISC-III (1) when the impact of injury or CNS disease on the child's intelligence is of concern, (2) when long-term intellectual competencies are in question, and (3) when identifying functional sequelae of focal injury is of interest (i.e., verbal comprehension deficits related to injury of temporo-parietal regions or perceptual-organization weaknesses following injury to parieto-occipital regions). The WJR may be more useful (1) when perceptual processing and memory functions are of primary interest (i.e., phonological core deficits); (2) when deficits of concept formation and abstract reasoning are of concern (i.e., injury to frontal regions); (3) when there are signs of visual agnosia, aphasia, or significant academic deficits in language-related or math skills (i.e., dyslexia); or (4) when the WISC-III or other cognitive measures do not seem to reflect adequately the child's ability, as evidenced by adaptive behavior levels.

There also seems to be historical precedence for selecting the WISC-III, although important data can be gleaned from the WJR that are quite distinct from those obtained with other intelligence measures. The WJR was developed with multiple intelligences as the theoretical framework, which may prove to be very useful for articulating more clearly the complexities of specific cognitive abilities as they relate to specific brain function. Further research exploring the relative contributions of the WISC-III and the WJR to neuropsychological evaluation is needed to clarify these issues.

Differential Ability Scale (DAS)

The Differential Ability Scale (DAS) comprises a cognitive and an achievement scale and was developed for children and adolescents between the ages of 2 1/2 and 17 years (Elliott, 1990). The Cognitive Battery has a total of 17 subtests for the Preschool and the School-Age Level. The Preschool Level measures the following cognitive abilities General Cognitive Ability (GCA), which comprises Block Building, Vocabulary Comprehension, Picture Similarities, and Naming Vocabulary for children aged 2-6 to 3-5. The CGA is divided into Verbal Ability (Verbal Comprehension and Naming Vocabulary), Nonverbal Ability (Picture Similarities, Pattern Construction, and Copying), and Early Number Concepts for children 3-6 to 5-11. For children between the ages of 6-0 and 17-11, the GCA consists of erbal Ability (Word Definitions and Similarities), Nonverbal Reasoning Ability (Matrices, Sequential, and Quantitative Reasoning), and Spatial Ability (Recall of Designs and Pattern Construction).

The normative sample for the DAS includes children who are learning-disabled; speech- and language-impaired, cognitively retarded, gifted and talented, severely emotionally disturbed, and mildly impaired on visual, auditory, or motoric functions. The DAS was designed to measure profiles of cognitive abilities as well as differences between cognitive and achievement abilities. The achievement battery includes three tests: Basic Number Skills, Spelling, and Word Reading. Both batteries were normed on the same group so that discrepancy scores would be objective and meaningful (Elliott, 1990).

In their review of the DAS, McIntosh and Gridley (1992) indicate that this measure has several advantages in that it has strong psychometric properties (i.e., validity and reliability) and the standardization is sound. The separation between cognitive abilities apart from processing skills is also viewed as a strength, particularly for LD populations. The conorming of the cognitive and achievement batteries is also judged positively. Initial studies with the scale indicate its utility for describing subgroups of LD students (McIntosh & Gridley, 1992). The extent to which the DAS becomes a useful tool for clinical neuropsychologists is undetermined at this time, but the DAS appears to have minimized some of the weaknesses inherent in less psychometrically sound batteries.

Kaufman Assessment Battery for Children (K-ABC)

The Kaufman Assessment Battery for Children (K-ABC; Kaufman & Kaufman, 1983) was developed on the basis of neuropsychological theory (i.e., Sperry and Luria) as a measure of simultaneous and sequential processing (Kamphaus, Kaufman, & Harrison, 1990). The K-ABC was designed to measure how a child processes information, where simultaneous processing is thought to be holistic in nature and consistent with right-hemisphere processing, whereas sequential processing is linear and analytic, reflecting left-hemisphere processing. The battery has four global scales: Sequential, Simultaneous, Mental Processing Composite, and Achievement.

The K-ABC is nonverbal and was intended for use with minority, bilingual, speech- or language-impaired, and/or learning-disabled children. The K-ABC has received mixed reviews, although strengths were noted in the psychometric properties of the instrument, the theoretical orientation of the battery, the empirical nature of the scales, and the novelty of many of the subtests. Weaknesses include the limited "floor" of the test, which affects its use with very young or cognitively limited children, and its insufficient "ceiling," which affects measurement of gifted children (Kamphaus et al., 1990).

The K-ABC has been relatively well researched

and has been shown to be positively correlated (.47 to .65) with the Luria Nebraska Neurological Battery–Children's Revised for LD students (Leark, Snyder, Grove, & Golden, 1982). It was found to have higher correlations with independent measures of hemispheric function for a brain-injured group than the Wechsler scales (Morris & Bigler, 1985). The correlation between brain function and processing fell within the predictable direction following the theoretical underpinnings of the test, where right hemisphere and simultaneous processing and left hemisphere and sequential processing were related. Shapiro and Dotan (1985) also reported significant relationships between hemispheric functioning and the simultaneous and sequential scales in the predicted direction. Despite these results, the K-ABC should not be used to localize brain dysfunction in children (Kamphaus et al., 1990). Further research is needed to determine the usefulness of the K-ABC for designing intervention plans.

Academic Functioning

Most psychological evaluations include a measure of academic achievement in a comprehensive evaluation of children. Generally the Wide Range Achievement Test (WRAT) or the WRAT-Revised are used as screening measures. To obtain more comprehensive measures of achievement, the Woodcock-Johnson Tests of Achievement–Revised (WJA-R) or the Wechsler Individual Achievement Tests (WIAT) are recommended.

Woodcock-Johnson Tests of Achievement—Revised

The WJR Tests of Achievement include Reading, Mathematics, Written Language, and Knowledge. Three discrepancy scores can be generated comparing intracognitive discrepancies (e.g., Auditory versus Visual Processing), intra-achievement discrepancies (e.g., Reading versus Mathematics), and cognitive-achievement discrepancies when the WJ-R cog-

nitive and achievement batteries are both employed.

There are several advantages to incorporating these tests into a neuropsychological battery. First, the WJR Tests of Achievement have strong technical properties, Second, these measures are conormed with the same population as the WJR Tests of Cognitive Ability. This reduces the weaknesses inherent in comparing a child's intellectual and achievement abilities on tests with different standardization groups and norms. Third, there has been considerable research with the WJR scales on LD children. Finally, the discrepancy scores provide a method for making normative comparisons and for determining individual strengths and weaknesses across various measures.

Wechsler Individual Achievement Test (WIAT)

The Wechsler Individual Achievement Test (WIAT) was developed and conormed with the WISC-III. Conorming intelligence and achievement tests on the same population decreases statistical and measurement error present when comparing tests that were separately normed. The WIAT provides measures of reading, math, and written language.

Although the Wide Range Achievement Test (WRAT) or the revised version (WRAT-R) is often used for screening purposes, these measures are not sufficient for making a diagnosis of learning disabilities in children. The WJ-R or the WIAT should be included to assess fully the academic performance of children.

Psychosocial Functioning

Assessment of a child's psychosocial adjustment is best accomplished using behavioral rating scales, clinical interviews, and observational techniques. These techniques are useful for determining comorbid psychiatric problems and for ruling out other disorders that may result in reasoning, problem solving, and social interaction difficulties that affect overall adjustment and impact on treatment plans.

Clinicians may want to start out with instruments that measure broad-band personality disorders, then utilize tests designed for specific problems such as ADHD, depression, and/or anxiety. Several instruments will be described briefly.

Child Behavior Checklist (CBL)

The Child Behavior Checklist (CBL) is a well-developed, psychometrically sound instrument measuring two broad-band personality syndromes–externalizing and internalizing disorders (Achenbach, 1991). The CBL can be used for children and adolescents across a wide age range (6 to 18 years) and includes rating scales for parents and teachers and a self-report form for older children (Achenbach & Edelbrock, 1987). Structured Interview and Observation forms have also been developed for the CBL.

Externalizing disorders measured by the CBL include aggressive, hyperactive, schizoid, delinquent, and sex problems. Internalizing disorders comprise depressive, anxious, and social withdrawal problems (Witt, Heffer, & Pfiffer, 1990). Teacher ratings are highly correlated with observations of the child, and parent ratings are associated with other well-established measures of behavior problems (Witt et al., 1990). The CBL offers a comprehensive method for obtaining data from a variety of sources in an effort to identify comorbid personality disorders in children and adolescents. See Witt et al. (1990) and Mash and Terdal (1988) for a more in-depth discussion of these techniques.

Behavior Assessment System for Children

The Behavior Assessment System for Children (BASC; Reynolds & Kamphaus, 1992) was developed as a "multimethod, multidimensional approach to evaluating the behavior and self-perceptions of children aged 4 to 18 years" Reynolds & Kamphaus, 1992, p. 1). The BASC includes five methods for assessment of the child's behavior:

1. A self-report for children aged 8 to 18 years, which allows the child to answer "true" or "false" to questions about feelings and perceptions of the self and of others
2. A teacher behavioral rating scale
3. A parent behavioral rating scale
4. A structured developmental history than can be used as an interview or questionnaire format
5. A system for systematically observing and recording the child's behavior

The BASC allows for the measurement of both adaptive and clinical dimensions of the child's behavior. The wording on the BASC allows for ratings of observable behavior, thus decreasing subjectivity on the part of the rater. The system allows for measurement of the child's behavioral and emotional functioning from a variety of sources to provide a more comprehensive picture of the total child.

The BASC is not intended to provide a diagnosis, placement decision, or treatment plan. It is, rather, designed to provide information about the child's behavior from many sources and to contribute to designing and determining the most appropriate intervention. The BASC can provide useful data to be used as a follow-up for further interviews and evaluation.

Personality Inventory for Children (PIC)

The Personality Inventory for Children (PIC), a parent rating scale, measures a variety of disorders in young children and adolescents (Lachar, 1990). The PIC includes the following scales: three profile scales (Lie, Frequency, and Defensiveness); an Adjustment Scale; three cognitive scales (Achievement, Intellectual Screening, and Development); and nine clinical scales (Somatic, Depressive, Family Relations, Delinquency, Withdrawal, Anxiety, Psychosis, Hyperactivity, and Social Skills). The PIC utilizes a branching rules system for determining profile types, and provides seven classification options (Lachar, 1990).

Scores on the PIC have been shown to correlate

with placement in regular education or special education classrooms for children with emotional, learning, and cognitive impairments. Lachar, Kline, and Boersma (1986) systematically investigated the utility of the PIC for decision making about educational placements. Lachar et al. (1986) found that children across divergent categories (ED and LD) do not possess independent profiles, as they share some common behavioral and personality characteristics.

The CBL, BASC, and PIC measure broad-band behavioral and psychosocial problems. When elevated scores are present in specific areas, the clinician may want to use tests designed to measure narrow-band disorders, such as the Children's Depression Inventory (Kovacs & Beck, 1977) and the Reynolds Adolescent Depression Scale (W. M. Reynolds, 1989) for depression, and the Revised Children's Manifest Anxiety Scale (C. R. Reynolds & Richmond, 1978); and/or the Conners Rating Scales (Conners, 1969) for hyperactivity. See Reynolds and Kamphaus (1990) for an in-depth discussion of other personality and behavioral assessment measures.

Social interaction problems have been found in a variety of disorders, including ADHD and LD. The extent to which a child is isolated, ignored, or rejected may have an impact on how well the child adjusts in school and at home. A measure of social skills adjustment will be discussed briefly.

Social Skills Questionnaire

Gresham and Elliot (1990) developed the Social Skills Questionnaire (SSQ) in an effort to measure social skills problems in children and adolescents systematically. The SSQ contains rating scales for parents, teachers, and the child and provides a method for determining the child's social interaction skills, problem behaviors in school, and overall adjustment. This is a relatively new instrument and may prove to be a valuable addition to a comprehensive evaluation of child and adolescent disorders.

Psychological factors can have a negative impact on a child's performance on neuropsychological measures. It is important to determine if this is the case. The astute, experienced clinician investigates the na-

ture of the child's psychosocial status and assesses how this affects on the neuropsychological evaluation. A number of these factors are explored in the following discussion.

IMPACT OF PSYCHOLOGICAL FUNCTIONING ON NEUROPSYCHOLOGICAL RESULTS

A number of psychological conditions or factors have an impact on neuropsychological evaluations that should be considered when evaluating children and adolescents. These factors may interact differentiately depending on whether the child's condition is a result of acquired anomalies (e.g., traumatic brain injury) or developmental anomalies (e.g., learning or neuropsychiatric disorders).

First, children sustaining traumatic brain injury may display symptoms of "psychic edema" that interfere with performance on neuropsychological tests. Inattention, distractibility, and motivational problems may be present soon after injury. Although these features frequently subside within weeks of injury, once the child has stabilized, initial or baseline neuropsychological evaluation may be contaminated by these short-term problems. Furthermore, these psychological aspects may mask other deficits that may ultimately be long-lasting (e.g., impaired reasoning and planning). For example, tests of executive functioning (e.g., Wisconsin Card Sort or Category Test) may be sensitive to these psychological problems. If a child is inattentive and distractible, then careful and thoughtful analysis is lacking. Impulsive responses may be inaccurate. Some children with TBI do continue to display ADD-like symptoms long after recovery, but the clinician is advised to consider the initial impact on test results if inattention and distractibility are observed, particularly when the child's history does not suggest that the problems were present preinjury.

Second, language and/or reading delays may make some neuropsychological items difficult. If a child does not understand the verbal directions of a test and responds inaccurately, this may indicate a language comprehension problem rather than a deficit in the underlying neuropsychological function of interest. For example, instructions on the Trails B (Halstead-Reitan) test may prove too complicated for a child with a receptive language delay. In this instance, it is imperative to determine whether low scores result from true reasoning/planning deficits or from problems in comprehension. Testing the limits or simplifying instructions may be helpful in this determination. Further, cognitive delays also may produce poor performance on measures of global (e.g., reasoning, abstract formation, memory) versus specific brain functioning (e.g., motor speed).

Third, children with conduct-related or oppositional defiant disorders may show signs of passive aggressiveness and poor motivation. Refusal or poor effort should not be confused with neuropsychological deficits. It is also not uncommon for children with these psychiatric problems to have poor frustration tolerance. They may give up quickly and may be easily frustrated when they begin to struggle on items that are difficult (e.g., reasoning tasks). Efforts to improve frustration tolerance may include using reinforcers (e.g., a soda, a candy bar) or shorter testing intervals.

Fourth, children with ADHD also may make care-less, impulsive errors. Testing on and off medication often gives the clinician a better picture of the child's underlying neuropsychological problems beyond the impulsivity and distractibility that may be paramount in ADHD. Breaking testing periods into shorter periods may also improve performance.

Finally, depression and/or anxiety may interfere with a child's ability to put forth sustained effort. Children may appear apathetic, withdrawn, or overly nervous. It is important to build rapport with the child and to create a supportive, reinforcing testing climate. Again, testing the child both on and off medication may be indicated, especially for children who take antidepressants. The neuropsychological report should reflect any special testing administration changes or modifications, and should describe the conditions under which the behaviors were elicited. It may be helpful to conduct a follow-up evaluation (3 to 6 months later) if the clinician believes that psychological factors have rendered the interpretation of neuropsychological findings suspect or contaminated.

The next chapter discusses the neuropsychological evaluation process in depth. It includes an overview of the most frequently utilized batteries as well as suggestions for a transactional approach to assessment.

CHAPTER 5

NEUROPSYCHOLOGICAL ASSESSMENT APPROACHES AND DIAGNOSTIC PROCEDURES

The purpose of this chapter is twofold. First, we will briefly review three generally accepted approaches to neuropsychological assessment. Second, we will present our transactional assessment approach. This discussion will include methods of evaluation for selected functional areas of the central nervous system. The conceptual framework underlying each battery and research with each approach will also be presented.

APPROACHES TO CHILD CLINICAL NEUROPSYCHOLOGICAL ASSESSMENT

Halstead-Reitan-Indiana Assessment Procedures

The Halstead-Reitan neuropsychological procedures are considered the most popular commercial batteries available in this country (Howieson & Lezak, 1992). Halstead originally developed a series of tests to measure frontal lobe dysfunction in adults, and Reitan later added new tests and recommended the battery for various types of brain damage (Howieson & Lezak, 1992). Between 1951 and 1953, Reitan modified the adult battery and developed new items for children (Teeter, 1986). Although Reitan procedures have been criticized as being atheoretical (Luria & Majovski, 1977), Hynd and Willis (1988) argue that Reitan's contributions have been influential for a number of reasons. First, Reitan offered evidence that intelligence was not simply a frontal lobe function and that the frontal lobes were more involved

in the organization and execution of behaviors than in intelligence per se. Second, Reitan further developed and validated clinical neuropsychological assessment procedures and provided a rich body of empirical and clinical work in child and adult neuropsychology. Although the debate over the theoretical contributions of Halstead and Reitan's approaches remains lively, Reitan and Wolfson (1985a) argue that his methods have a conceptual framework that is useful for advancing the science of neuropsychology. Further, the Halstead-Reitan batteries contain measures necessary for understanding the brain—behavior relationship in children and adolescents.

Conceptual Model for the Halstead-Reitan Methods

Reitan and Wolfson (1985a) indicate that attempts to develop a set of assessment measures resulted in a conceptual model of brain function that is incorporated in the Halstead-Reitan Battery. The battery consists of six categories representing the behavioral correlates of brain function: (1) input measures; (2) tests of concentration, attention, and memory functions; (3) tests of verbal language abilities; (4) tests of visual-spatial, sequential, and manipulatory functions; (5) tests of abstraction, reasoning, concept formation, and logical analysis; and (6) output measures (Reitan & Wolfson, 1985a, p. 4).

Reitan and Wolfson (1985a) further argue that a neuropsychological battery must have three components: (1) items that measure the full range of psychological functions of the brain; (2) strategies that allow for interpretation of individual brain functions;

and (3) valid procedures demonstrated through empirical and clinical evaluation and applications. The neuropsychological batteries for children and adolescents were developed with these components in mind (Hynd & Willis, 1988).

Halstead-Reitan Neuropsychological Batteries for Children

Reitan designed two batteries for children, the Halstead-Reitan Neuropsychological Battery for Older Children (9—14 years) and the Reitan-Indiana Test Battery (5—8 years) (Teeter, 1986); see Table 5.1.

Adolescents 15 years and older are evaluated using the Halstead-Reitan Battery for Adults. See Reitan and Wolfson (1985a) for an in-depth description of the adult battery. The interested reader is referred to Nussbaum and Bigler (1989), Reitan

(1986a, 1987), and Teeter (1986) for descriptions of the various measures and scoring criteria. Table 5.2 lists the various subtests and the abilities associated with each of these measures.

Interpretation of the Reitan Neuropsychological Batteries

Over the years Reitan has developed and expanded his approach for analyzing the Halstead Neuropsychological Test Battery for Children (9—14 years) and the Reitan-Indiana Test Battery (5—8 years). Reitan typically focuses on a Multiple Inferential Approach, including an investigation of Level of Performance, Pathognomonic Signs, Patterns of Performance, and Right—Left Comparisons. Reitan (1986a, 1987) also developed the Neuropsychological Deficit Scale (NDS), a scoring and interpretation model for these batteries, which incorporates multiple fac-

Table 5.1. Subtests of the Halstead-Reitan Neuropsychological Test Batteries

FUNCTIONAL SKILLS	HALSTEAD-REITAN BATTERY (9–14 YEARS)	REITAN-INDIANA BATTERY (5–9 YEARS)
Motor Functions	Finger Tapping Grip Strength Tactual Performance Test (total time)	Finger Tapping Grip Strength Tactual Performance (total time) Marching Test
Visual-Spatial[a]	Trails Part A	Matching Figures Matching V's Matching Pictures Star Drawing Concentric Squares Target
Sensory-Perceptual	Tactile Perception Tactile Form Recognition Tactile Localization Fingertip Writing	Tactile Perception Tactile Form Recognition Tactile Localization Fingertip Writing
Alertness and Concentration[b]	Speech Sound Perception	Progressive Figures
Immediate Memory	TPT-Memory TPT-Localization	TPT-Memory TPT-Localization
Reasoning	Category Test Trails Part B	Category Test Color Form

[a] Reitan includes Picture Arrangement, Block Design, and Object Assembly from Wechsler scales.
[b] Reitan includes Coding from Wechsler scales.

Table 5.2. Abilities Assessed by the HRNB and HINB in Children and Adolescents

FUNCTION	SUBTEST	REQUIREMENTS	R/L DIFFERENTIATION	ABILITIES	LOCALIZATION
Motor	Finger Tapping	HINB and NRNB: Children tap mounted key 5—10 second trials with dominant and nondominant hand	Dominant hand expected 10% faster	Motor speed and coordination	Frontal lobe
Motor	Grip Strength	HINB and HRNB: Squeeze on dynamometer, alternate hands, 3 trials dominant/nondominant	Dominant hand expected to be stronger	Sensitive to R/L weaknesses in motor cortex	Frontal lobe
Motor	Tactual Performance Test (TPT)	HINB & HRNB: (a) Place 6 blocks onto board while blindfolded with dominant/nondominant	Expect 1/3 improvement over trials	Motor and sensory functions, kinesthetic functions	Frontal lobe
Memory		(b) Draw location of blocks from memory	No	Spatial memory	Global
Visual	Trails A[a]	HRNB: Child connects circles sequentially as quickly as possible	No	Motor speed Visual-perception and symbol recognition	
Sensory	Tactile Perception Test	HRNB and HINB: Back of hand and face are touched either separately or together with eyes closed	Errors on RH-implicates left hemisphere and LH errors implicate right hemisphere	Sensory stimulation	Contralateral parietal lobe
	Auditory Perception Test	Examiner stands behind child and lightly rubs fingers together. Child indicates where sound is (unilateral or bilateral presentations).	Yes	Auditory stimulation	Temporal lobe
	Visual Perception	Examiner produces a finger movement at eye level, above and below eye level.	Yes	Visual fields Peripheral, unilateral, and bilateral	Visual pathway Visual fields
	Tactile Form Recognition TRF	Child extends hand through opening in board, and a cross, square, or triangle is placed in hand.	Yes	Tactile form recognition (stereognosis)	Parietal lobe
	TRF	Child points to same shape on front of board.			

Table 5.2. *(Continued)*

FUNCTION	SUBTEST	REQUIREMENTS	R/L DIFFERENTIATION	ABILITIES	LOCALIZATION
Sensory *(Continued)*	Fingertip Writing (FTW)	HRNB: Numbers are traced on palm while child watches. Then, 3, 4, 5, and 6 are traced on fingertips with eyes closed. HINH: X's and O's are traced.	Yes	Tactile perception, attention can be a factor in performance.	Peripheral nervous system Parietal lobe
	Finger Localization Test	Examiner lightly touches each of child's fingers with eyes closed. Child indicates which finger was touched.	Yes. Errors on RH implicates left hemisphere and RH errors implicates right hemisphere.	Tactile perception discrimination and attention to tactile stimulation.	Unilateral errors implicatecontra-lateral parietal lobe–can also occur with bilateral errors.
Alertness and Concentration	Speech[a] Sounds Perception Test	60 nonsense words presented on tape recorder. Child underlines correct sound from 4 alternatives.	No	Attention Auditory discrimination cross-modal matching.	Global Anterior left-hemisphere deficits (Teeter, 1986)
	Rhythm[a]	Thirty pairs of rhythms are presented on tape recorder. Child writes S or D if pair is same or different.	No	Attention, auditory perception, and concentration.	Global
Abstract Reasoning Logical Analysis	Category Test	80 items HINB, 168 items HRNB: Visual stimulus is projected on screen, and child selects one of four stimuli that corresponds to the original. If correct, bell rings. Incorrect: A buzzer sounds.	No	Abstract concept formation, mental efficiency and flexibility, learning skills.	Global Sensitive to right frontal lobe dysfunction in older children (Rourke et al., 1983)
	Trails B[a]	Series of circles alternating between letters (A—G) and numbers (1—8). Child connects circles alternating numbers-letters-numbers, etc.	No	Simultaneous processing, flexibility in planning.	Global
Language	Aphasia Screening Test	HRNB items: Naming, drawing, reading, math, and spelling.	Yes	Receptive language and expressive language, dyspraxia, word naming,	Language items relate to left hemisphere. Constructional items related to right hemisphere.

(Continued)

Table 5.2. *(Continued)*

FUNCTION	SUBTEST	REQUIREMENTS	R/L DIFFERENTIATION	ABILITIES	LOCALIZATION
Language *(Continued)*				reading, calculation, articulation, right/left discrimination.	

The following items are in HINB for younger children only:

FUNCTION	SUBTEST	REQUIREMENTS	R/L DIFFERENTIATION	ABILITIES	LOCALIZATION
Visual-Spatial	Matching Pictures	Matching pictures that are identical, then in same category.	No	Perception Generalization Reasoning	Global
	Matching V's and Figures, Concentric Square, and Star	Matching group of figures, or group of V's of differing widths; copying complex concentric square and star	No	Visual-perception and motor abilities.	Association areas
	Target Test	Consists of large cardboard poster with nine printed dots. Examiner taps out a series of dots and after 3-second delay child reproduces series on protocol.	No	Visual and spatial memory abilities.	Association areas
Motor	Marching Test	Child follows a sequence of circles connected by lines up a page touching each circle as quickly as possible, using right, left, and both hands.	Yes	Gross motor function and coordination	Global
Alertness and Concentration	Progressive Figures	8 large shapes with small shapes inside. Child moves from the small shape inside to a large figure with same shape.	No	Visual perception, motor speed, concentration, and cognitive flexibility	Global
Reason	Color Form Test	Geometric shapes of different colors on board. Child touches one figure then another, moving from shape-color-shape-color, etc.	No	Simultaneous processing and flexibility in planning	Global

Note: Reitan Indiana Neuropsychological Battery (HINB); Halstead-Reitan Neuropsychological Battery (HRNB).
[a]In HRNB for older children only.

tors. The Functional Organization Approach, proposed by Fletcher and Taylor (1984), is less inferential and places neuropsychological measures within a developmental and contextual framework. Each of these approaches will be briefly described and critiqued.

Multiple Levels of Inference

Reitan (1969) and Selz and Reitan (1979b) developed an interpretive system using four levels of inference: Level of Performance, Pathognomonic-Sign, Differential/Pattern of Scores, and Right—Left Differences.

Level of Performance

Interpretive guidelines for the Reitan batteries have discussed the importance of determining the Level of Performance by comparing the child's scores to those of a normative group (Nussbaum & Bigler, 1986; Teeter, 1986). Normative data are available from Spreen and Gaddes (1969), Knights and Norwood (1980), and Reitan (1969, 1986a, 1987). Standard score comparisons are typically employed in this method, where two standard deviations below the mean is often used as the benchmark for consideration as significantly below normal and 1.5 standard deviations below the mean suggests mild impairment.

While a normative approach has been described as essential for children in the 5- to 15-year range (Rourke, 1981), there are reasons for using caution with a Level of Performance analysis in isolation. First, normal or abnormal levels of performance do not unequivocally confirm or disconfirm abnormal/normal brain function (Rourke, 1981). Recovery of function may effect a child's level of performance such that a brain-injured child may reach normal performance. Other children may be falsely identified as neuropsychologically impaired as a result of other factors, including motivation, psychopathology or significant language deprivation (Teeter, 1986). To be most reliable and valid, the Level of Performance approach should be used in conjunction with other interpretive factors.

Pathognomonic Sign Approach

One of the most common methods of analyzing neuropsychological data has been the deficit or pathognomonic sign approach (Rourke, 1981). This approach was developed from research findings showing that certain items on neuropsychological batteries, particularly those items from the Aphasia Screening Test, occurred almost exclusively in brain-damaged individuals and not in normal individuals (Wheeler & Reitan, 1962).

The pathognomonic approach has been moderated by other findings demonstrating that false negatives can be common when this approach is used in isolation (Boll, 1974). Analyzing these signs is also particularly complicated in children because of wide developmental variations in acquiring some skills in normal children (Teeter, 1986). To be considered pathognomonic, it must be proved that the child at one time had acquired the skill prior to injury or insult. Although this is usually easier to establish in older children and adults, the pathognomonic sign approach is rarely advocated in isolation.

Pattern of Performance Approach

The differential score or Pattern of Performance approach involves developing an overall gestalt of the various performance patterns of the individual. In this method, the examiner builds a profile of individual strengths and weaknesses on test scores and begins to make inferences about the neuropsychological status of specific and global brain function based on these patterns. For example, a pattern of clear right-handed weaknesses on sensory and motor measures (e.g., elevated time for the right hand TPT score and low tapping speed with the right hand), in conjunction with poor performance on the Speech Sounds Perception test and borderline Verbal Intelligence (IQ) scores (compared to normal Performance IQ), might suggest a pattern of left-hemisphere weaknesses. Reitan (1971) also reports that children and adults show similar patterns of performance on some tests: low scores on Part B of Trails compared to good scores on Part A has been found in individuals with left-hemisphere weaknesses, and poor performance on the Speech

Sounds Perception Test is often found in individuals with left-hemisphere impairment. See Teeter (1986) for a review.

Rourke, Bakker, Fisk, and Strang (1983) indicate that this method of interpretation is problematic for young, severely involved children. However, the Pattern of Performance approach has been broadly adopted by some neuropsychologists in their quest to identify meaningful subtypes of learning disabilities (Nussbaum & Bigler, 1986; Pirozzolo, 1981; Rourke, 1989).

Right–Left Differences

Reitan (1986a, 1987) suggests that Right—Left Differences can be a useful adjunct to understanding a child's neuropsychological performance. Table 5.3 reports right—left sensory and motor signs based on the Halstead-Reitan batteries for children. Reitan (1987) states that right-left indices can be a useful method for comparing the status of the two cerebral hemispheres, because even young children (5—8 years) have developed consistent hand preferences for simple motor tasks. Reitan (1987) further argues that right—left differences rely on "basic neuroanatomical structure and organization rather than higher-level neuropsychological functions that have been developed through educational and environmental influences and experiences" (p. 6).

The extent to which right—left differences differentiate between brain-damaged and normal children is also of interest. Reitan (1987) found that this method of analysis had less overlap between normals and brain-damaged children when compared to the Level of Performance or the Aphasia Screening Test. Reitan also argues that it is important to identify children who lag behind in the basic biological organization of the brain (e.g., sensory and motor functions), which can be related to learning problems that may require remediation. Sensory and motor pathways are "essentially equivalent among younger children, older children and adults" (Reitan, 1987, p. 40). While the right—left approach can differentiate brain-damaged from normal children, it is not recommended in isolation or as a substitute for a comprehensive neuropsychological evaluation.

Neuropsychological Deficit Scale Approach

The Neurological Deficit Scale (NDS) incorporates a method for determining the child's Level of Performance, Right—Left Differences, Dysphasia and Related Deficits, and cutoff scores for differentiating brain-damaged from normal youngsters for each battery. The NDS also provides a total score for measuring the overall adequacy of neuropsychological functioning in children. Raw scores are weighted as Perfectly Normal (score = 0), Normal (score = 1), Mildly Impaired (score = 2), or Significantly Impaired (score = 3) on the basis of normative comparisons.

When using the NDS approach, the examiner takes the following steps: (1) converts raw scores on each test to corresponding weights, 0, 1, 2, or 3, based on

Table 5.3. Right–Left Sensory and Motor Signs on the Halstead-Reitan Neuropsychological Test Battery

MOTOR AND SENSORY ITEMS	LEFT-HEMISPHERE SIGNS[a]	RIGHT-HEMISPHERE SIGNS
Finger-tapping	Lower right hand tapping	Lower left hand tapping
Tactual performance test	Lower right hand scores	Lower left hand scores
Grip strength	Lower right hand scores	Lower left hand scores
Finger localization	Higher errors–right hand	Higher errors–left hand
Fingertip writing	Higher errors–right hand	Higher errors–left hand
Tactile perception	Higher errors–right hand	Higher errors–left hand

Note: Right-dominant individuals.
[a]Divide nondominant hand by dominant hand and subtract from 1. Use Neuropsychological Deficit Scale to determine significant differences between right and left hands.

normative tables provided by Reitan (1986a, 1987); (2) calculates right—left difference scores by dividing the score of the nondominant hand by that of the dominant hand, subtracting from 1.00, and converting to weighted scores; (3) makes clinical judgments following Reitan's (1984) guidelines for scoring the Aphasia Screening Test and assigns NDS scores; (4) sums weighted scores across each factor, Level of Performance, Right—Left Differences, and Aphasia Test; and, finally, (5) sums the weighted scores on 45 variables for older children and 52 variables for younger children to obtain a Total NDS Score. Reitan provides cutoff scores for brain-damaged versus normal children on the Total NDS score and for each of the factor scores.

Separate tables are available for analyzing the neuropsychological test results of older children (Reitan, 1986a) and younger children (Reitan, 1987). Although the NDS approach seems to be an extension of an earlier standardized scoring procedure ("Rules for Neurological Diagnosis"; Selz & Reitan, 1979a), the normative group used to develop the weighted scores reported in the tables is not clearly described in recent test manuals available for the child batteries.

Research Findings with HRNB and HINB

Selected research studies utilizing the HRNB and HINB are reported in Table 5.4. These studies sought to determine the ability of these batteries either to distinguish between children with brain damage and those with learning disabilities or to elucidate the profiles achieved by differing disorders (e.g., conduct disorder, psychiatric disorders). The Category test has been found to be the best discriminator for learning-disabled children. For example, the results of studies attempting to distinguish learning-disabled children from brain-damaged and normal children found normal motor development with consistent weaknesses on the Category test (Coutts et al., 1987; Strang & Rourke, 1983; Shurtleff et al., 1988). Moreover, a relationship between reading and/or math difficulty and the Category test has been found consistently

(Strang & Rourke, 1983; Shurtleff et al., 1988; Strom, Gray, Dean, & Fischer, 1987).

Intelligence scores have been found to show moderate correlations with the HRNB (Shurtleff et al., 1988). In a review of studies that attempted to differentiate learning-disabled from brain-damaged children using the HRNB, Hynd (1992b) suggested that differential performance on intelligence tests may account for much of the ability of the HRNB to discriminate between the two groups. On the other hand, Strom et al. (1987) found that the HRNB provided unique data that were not redundant with data from the WISC-R. Because the issue of the overlap between the WISC-R and the HRNB has not been resolved, it is important that the clinician recognize the overlap between the two measures and take intelligence into consideration in the interpretation of results.

In addition to the caution as to the influence of intelligence on performance on this battery, children with psychiatric disorders also have been found to perform poorly on the HRNB (Berman & Siegel, 1976; Tramontana, Sherrets, & Golden, 1980; Tramontana & Sherrets, 1985; Tramontana, Hooper, & Nardillo, 1988). The HRNB's ability to distinguish children with psychiatric disorders from brain-damaged children is not clear from existing research. This finding is consistent with the adult Reitan Battery, which also is not diagnostically specific for brain damage versus psychiatric disorder (Hynd & Semrud-Clikeman, 1992).

A further area of concern is the length and expense of the battery for general use with clients. The average amount of time for administration of the battery ranges from 6 to 12 hours. Reitan (1986b) has suggested that although reducing the length of the battery or developing a screening protocol would have value, the information necessary to answer referral questions makes the development of a screening protocol problematic. Although Reitan has demonstrated a remarkable hit rate for his ability to determine brain damage (Reitan & Boll, 1973; Selz & Reitan, 1979a, 1979b), there has not been sufficient documentation of the battery's ability to localize dysfunction or predict recovery from brain injury (Hynd, 1992b).

Table 5.4. Selected Research with the Halstead-Reitan Neuropsychological Batteries

REFERENCE	POPULATION	AGE	MAJOR FINDINGS
Batchelor & Dean (1993)	Learning	9—14 years	1. Two distinct clusters across ages. Group 1 = diffuse deficits. Group 2 = spatial memory deficits. 2. Diffuse deficits may not change with age. 3. Specific deficits deem to change with age.
Berman & Siegal (1976)	CD, normal		1. CD > normals on every HRNB task. 2. CD lowest on verbal mediation, concept formation, and perceptual.
Boyd, Tramontana, & Hopper (1986)	Psychiatric	9—16 years	1. DE = WISC-R + Aphasia test. 79% rate for prediction. LNNB-C status 2. DE valid as screening device.
Coutts et al. (1987)	LD, non-LD	11—12 years	1. LD > non-LD on Category test. 2. Minimal practice effect after 3 weeks for LD. 3. Category test may be useful for measuring treatment efficacy.
Gamble, Mishra, & Obrzut (1988)	Referred-learning	6—8 years	1. Category test loaded on Psychomotor Speed Factor. 2. TPT loaded on Memory Factor. 3. Use Reitan-Indiana with caution with young LD children.
Newby & Matthews (1986)	Clinic-referred	6—14 years	1. Specific neuropsychological function not predicted by PIC.
Nussbaum et al. (1988)	Referred-learning	7—12 years	1. Anterior deficits related to Social Withdrawal, Aggression, Hyperactivity, and Externalized scales on CBCL. 2. Posterior deficits high on ANX.
Reitan & Boll (1973)	Normal, MBD, BD	5—8 years	1. BD > MBD > normals. 2. 84% overall accuracy rate classification. 3. 96% BD, 89% MBD, 64% normals.
Selz & Reitan (1979a)	Normal, LD, BD	9—14 years	1. LD normal on motor tasks. 2. LD similar to BD on cognitive and attentional tasks. 3. 80% accuracy, error-impaired groups as less impaired.
Selz & Reitan (1979b)	Normal, LD, BD	9—14 years	1. Classification rules. 2. BD > LD > normals performance. 3. 73% accuracy rate for classification.
Shurtleff, Fay, Abbott, & Berninger (1988)	Learning	10—12 years	1. Low to moderate correlations of HRNB and WISC-R. 2. Speech Sounds related to Reading decoding and spelling. 3. Category related to math.
Strang & Rourke (1983)	LD	9—14 years	1. Low math/normal reading/spelling group scores low on Category, bilateral tactile-motor, and visual-perceptual-organization. 2. Low math related to low reasoning and sensory-motor.
Strom et al. (1987)	LD	11 years	1. 28% variance in reading accounted for by HRNB. 2. 15% variance in math accounted for by HRNB. 3. Unique contributions of HRNB not measured by WISC-R.

Table 5.4   *(Continued)*

REFERENCE	POPULATION	AGE	MAJOR FINDINGS
Teeter (1985)	Normal	5—8 years	1. RINB accurate for discriminating high, average, and low readers. 2. RINB more predictive than McCarthy Scales for spelling, reading, and math. 3. Predictive variable stable over two years.
Tramontana et al. (1980)	Psychiatric	9—15 years	1. 60% mild impairment on HRNB using Selz and Reitan rules. 2. 25% moderate impairment. 3. Impairment > chronic psychiatric.
Tramontana & Hooper (1987)	CD, depression		1. No distinct neuropsychological features for INT and EXT disorders.
Tramontana & Sherrets (1985)	Psychiatric		1. 50% abnormal HRNB or LNNB-C. 2. Impairment > young boys with chronic psychiatric history.
Tramontana, Hooper, & Nardillo (1988)	Psychiatric	8—16 years	1. Impairment > with more severe behavior problems. 2. Mostly in young children with INT disorders. 3. EXT disorders no distinct neuropsychological features.

Notes: BD = brain damaged; MBD = minimal brain dysfunction; LD = learning-disabled; CD = conduct-disordered; RINB = Reitan Indiana Neuropsychological Battery; HRNB = Halstead-Reitan Neuropsychological Battery; LNNB-CR = Luria Nebraska Neuropsychological Battery for Children–Revised; INT = Internalized Scale on the Child Behavior Checklist; EXT = Externalized Scale on the Child Behavior Checklist.

Finally, the HRNB requires intensive training for administration and interpretation of results, which also can be problematic for its use in general clinical or school environments. It may be more appropriate for general clinicians to use other measures to screen for possible neuropsychological involvement and to refer clients to a trained neuropsychologist for a full evaluation if areas of concern are identified. Some of the available screening instruments are discussed in the second half of this chapter.

LURIA-NEBRASKA ASSESSMENT PROCEDURES FOR CHILDREN

Few would question the importance of the contributions made by the Russian neuropsychologist A. R. Luria, although some have been skeptical about the manner in which his clinical procedures have been standardized into a battery for assessing brain func-

tions (Lezak, 1983). Luria originally described assessment procedures that varied from patient to patient depending on the specific brain area of concern (Teeter, 1986). Attempts to standardize these procedures have been met with enthusiasm by some neuropsychologists and criticism by others.

The conceptual model underlying the standardized approach will be reviewed briefly, and subtests of the Luria-Nebraska Neuropsychological Battery for Children–Revised (LNNB-CR) will be described. The research and clinical validity of the battery will also be discussed. Computer scoring options and computer-generated reports are also available for the battery (Golden, 1987).

Conceptual Model for the Luria-Nebraska

Luria (1980) described brain activity in terms of functional systems or units that incorporated elements of localization and equipotential theories. Localization theorists argued that specific brain regions were responsible for discrete brain functions–visual functions in the occipital lobe, auditory functions in the temporal lobe, and so on (Kolb & Whishaw, 1985). Equipotential theorists pointed out that complex human behaviors are controlled by functional CNS regions in such a way that when one portion is damaged, another adjacent or analogous region can assume its function (Kolb & Whishaw, 1985).

Luria's theory was different from other hypotheses at the time because he made four major assumptions:

1. Luria assumed that only specific parts, not all parts, of the brain are involved in forming a behavior.
2. No equipotentiality of brain tissue is hypothesized. Rather, brain tissue is conceptualized as being specialized for function, both psychologically and physiologically.
3. Behavior is conceived as a function of systems of brain areas working in concert rather than unitary and specific areas producing set behaviors. Therefore, a given behavior will be impaired when any part of the functional system responsible for the behavior is impaired.
4. Luria proposed that alternative functional systems exist–that is, that a given behavior can be produced by more than one functional system. Therefore, the clinician will at times see no deficits when such deifcits are expected given the locus of damage and at other times see deficits when no known damage is present. If the nature of the task is changed, then the locus of information processing will be changed and another input or output modality utilized. Thus, damage to areas controlling lower skills can be compensated for by areas controlling higher skills.

Research supports aspects of each of these theories in various degrees because functions appear localized to some extent; however, a particular behavior may be impaired because of damage to a number of different brain areas. Kolb and Whishaw (1990) suggest that the important question is: "How is performance affected following damage to a particular site?"

Luria's functional systems approach conceptualizes brain function as follows. Luria (1980) discussed three functional units as: (1) the arousal unit; (2) the sensory receptive and integrative unit; and (3) the planning, organizational unit (see Table 5.5). The nature of each functional unit is briefly described.

Functional Unit I

In Luria's theory (1980) the arousal system is the first unit and comprises the retricular activating system (RAS), the midbrain, the medulla, the thalamus, and the hypothalamus. Visual, auditory, and tactile stimulation comes through this unit to higher cortical regions. The structures work together in concert in Unit I to regulate energy level and to maintain cortical tone. This unit raises or lowers cortical arousal depending on internal needs. When cortical tone is too low, the brain loses its ability to discriminate between stimuli. Another function of this unit is to filter out irrelevant stimuli. The RAS prevents the cortex from being flooded by unimportant stimuli that could interfere with cortical functioning. If the RAS filters out too much stimulation, sensory deprivation and hallucinations may be present as the cortex attempts to generate its own activity to keep itself aroused.

Severe injury to Unit I can result in marked deterioration of wakefulness, with loss of consciousness and possible death. Less severe injury can result in disorganization of memory, distractibility, attentional problems and insomnia. If Units II and III are functional, then in later development or in adulthood these units can take over the functions of Unit I and can monitor hyperactive and/or impulsive behavior. Methylphenidate has also been found to activate Unit I and thereby decrease behaviors of impulsivity and poor attention.

Functional Unit II

Unit II is considered the sensory system and consists of the parietal, temporal, and occipital lobes; its major function is sensory reception and integration.

Table 5.5. Major Systems and Behavioral Correlates of Luria's Functional Units

FUNCTIONAL SYSTEMS	BRAIN UNITS	BEHAVIORAL CORRELATES
Unit 1: Arousal System	Reticular activating system pons and medulla through thalamus to cortex	Modulate cortical arousal Filters incoming stimuli Attention and concentration
Unit 2: Sensory System	Primary temporal lobes Secondary temporal lobes	Auditory perception Analysis and synthesis acoustic sounds and sequential analysis Phoneme, pitch, tone, and rhythm
	Primary parietal lobes Secondary parietal lobes	Tactile perception Two-point discrimination Movement detection Recognition of complex tactile stimuli (e.g., shapes)
	Primary occipital lobes Secondary occipital lobes	Visual perception Visual discrimination (letters, shapes, etc.) Cross-modal integration
	Tertiary parietal occipital/ temporal region	Simultaneous processing "Intelligence" (e.g., reading, writing, math, language, syntax, grammar, stereognosis, spatial rotation, angle discrimination)
Unit 3: Output/Planning	Primary frontal lobes Secondary frontal lobes	Simple motor output Sequencing motor activity Speech production
	Tertiary frontal lobes	Decision making and evaluation Impulse control Delay of gratification Focused attention

Therefore, the areas of Unit II correspond to their sensory modality (temporal for auditory, parietal for sensory tactile, and occipital for vision).

Unit II has been hypothesized to be guided by three functional laws: (1) hierarchical structures of cortical zones do not remain the same during ontogenesis; (2) hierarchical zones decrease in their specificty of function with development; and, (3) progressive lateralization of function within hierarchical zones increases with development (Luria, 1980). This hierarchy is further divided into three zones: primary, secondary, and tertiary. The primary zones are responsible for sorting and recording sensory information. The secondary zones organize the sensory information and code it for later retrieval. The tertiary zones combine data from various sources in order to lay the basis for organized behavior.

Primary zones. The primary zones generally consist of sense receptors with point-to-point relationships to the peripheral sense organs. These zones are predetermined by genetics and are the most hard-wired of the areas. The primary auditory zone is in the temporal lobe and involves auditory perception. The primary tactile zone is in the sensory strip of the parietal lobe and involves tactile perception. Finally, the primary visual zone is in the occipital lobe and involves visual perception.

Secondary zones. The secondary zones are generally involved in input of data and integration of information. These zones process information sequentially and have a link, with more than one stimulus being received by the brain at a time. For the auditory secondary zone, the locus is in the secondary regions of the temporal lobe and involves the analysis and synthesis of sounds and the sequential analysis of phonemes, pitch, tone, and rhythm. The secondary tactile zone is in the parietal lobes next to the sensory strip and is involved in two-point discrimination, movement detection, and recognition of complex tactile stimuli (i.e., identifying shapes by touch). The secondary visual zone surrounds the primary visual center of the occipital lobe and is involved in visual discrimination of letters, shapes, and figures.

There is specialization in the secondary zones, with the left hemisphere predominantly responsible for analyzing verbal material and language while the right hemisphere is important for the analysis of nonverbal material such as music, environmental sounds, and prosody of language. Both hemispheres play a role in reading, with the right hemisphere important for recognizing unfamiliar shapes. Once words and letters have been learned, recognition of these shapes becomes a process of the left hemisphere. Both hemispheres are involved in comprehension, with the left hemisphere more involved with semantic and syntactic analysis and the right hemisphere with processing the emotional quality and tone of the passage. Lateralization of function is also found for writing, with the right hemisphere activated primarily when the task is a novel visual-motor task and the left hemisphere activated primarily once a task is learned.

Intelligence tests are hypothesized to measure Unit II functions. Given that Unit II is the center for the analysis, coding, and storage of information, damage to this region results in difficulty in learning basic reading, writing, and mathematics skills.

Tertiary zones. Tertiary zones allow for cross-modal integration of information from all sensory areas. Information is processed simultaneously and involves integration of various modalities. For example, the reading process is an integration of auditory and visual material; language is an integration of grammatical skills, analysis of auditory information, and comprehension of auditory material; and mathematics involves the integration of visual material with knowledge of number and quantity. These zones are the primary region that intelligence tests are thought to

measure directly. Damage to this association area can result in lowered IQ, poor reading, writing, and mathematics ability, and understanding of language.

Functional Unit III

Unit III is considered to be responsible for output and planning. It is located in the frontal lobes which are further demarcated into three hierarchical zones. The primary zone, in the motor strip of the frontal lobe, is concerned with simple motor output. The secondary zone, in the primary premotor regions, is involved in sequencing motor activity and speech production. The tertiary zone is located in the orbitofrontal region of the frontal lobe, also referred to as the prefrontal region. This zone is the last region to myelinate and develop, with development continuing until the third decade of life.

The tertiary zone of Unit III is primarily involved with planning, organization, and evaluation of behavior, functions similar to the executive functions described in Chapter 2. Damage to this area has been linked to problems in delaying gratification, controlling impulses, learning from past mistakes in behavior, and focusing attention. In many cases damage to this zone can be difficult to distinguish from psychiatric and behavior problems. When dysfunction occurs in Unit I, later development of Unit III can compensate or modulate levels of arousal. Moreover, Unit III can activate other parts of the brain and has rich connections to all regions of the brain (Shepard, 1994).

The LNNB-CR procedures are based on a neurodevelopmental model of assessment, which is discussed in the following section.

Developmental Considerations

The LNNB-CR is based on the theory that certain skills are acquired at different rates depending on the neurodevelopmental stage of the child (Golden, 1981). Further, specific problem-solving strategies, behaviors, and skills are dependent on biochemical as well as physiological maturation, including myelination and the growth of cells, dendritic networks, and interconnecting neuronal pathways. Although physiological development is related to psychological maturation, this relationship can be altered by adverse environmental events. These factors will be explored in later chapters investigating childhood disorders and brain injury. Table 5.6 outlines the five major developmental stages described by Golden (1981).

Injury during any one of these stages is thought to produce various deficits depending upon the site and severity of injury. Golden (1981) suggests that damage to the developing brain during Stage 1 is likely to produce deficits in arousal and that, when severe damage ensues, death or mental retardation may result. Damage after 12 months of age is less likely to produce attentional deficits, although physiological hyperactivity is associated with damage prior to 12 months. Paralysis, deafness, blindness, or tactile deficits may result from unilateral injury to the primary sensory areas during Stage 2 development. In some instances, sensory or motor functions may be transferred to the opposite hemisphere if damage occurs during this stage. Although damage after this developmental stage is likely to produce more serious deficits, there are still compensatory factors that play a role in recovery of function. Golden cautions, however, that bilateral damage is more serious, producing deafness, blindness, and/or paralysis, where compensation is less likely.

During Stage 3 development, the two hemispheres begin to show differentiation of function in terms of verbal and nonverbal abilities (Golden, 1981). Unilateral damage is likely to result in loss of language functions if injury is sustained in the left hemisphere once verbal skills are present, at about the age of 2 years. Damage prior to age 2 may result in transfer of language to the right hemisphere, whereas damage after age 2 begins to mimic recovery of functions similar to what is seen in adults (Golden, 1981). However, Golden (1981) suggests that plasticity (i.e., transfer of function) is less likely when injuries are diffuse in nature, or in cases of mild injury. Thus, small injuries early in development can have more deleterious effects than larger injuries later in life. Recovery of function will be explored in more detail in later chapters.

Table 5.6. Developmental Sequences of Luria's Functional Units

DEVELOPMENTAL STAGE	AGE RANGES	FUNCTIONAL SYSTEMS	DEFICITS/DAMAGE
Stage 1	Birth—12 months	Arousal Unit 1	Disorders of arousal Physiological hyperactivity Death in some severe cases Severe retardation
Stage 2	Birth—12 months	Primary zones Sensory Unit 2	Sensory-motor deficits in contra- lateral hemisphere

Stage 3	Birth—5 years	Secondary zones
		Sensory Unit 2
			Hemispheric differentiation
			  (language–left hemisphere)
			Damage prior to 2 years–some
			  transfer of function
			Small injury–no transfer
			Diffuse injury–no transfer
			Single modality deficits

Stage 4	5—8 years	Tertiary zones Sensory Unit 2	Learning deficits Mental retardation Learning disabilities
Stage 5	Adolescence– 24 years	Tertiary zones Unit 3	Frontal lobe symptoms

Golden (1981) suggests that learning during the first five years of life is primarily unimodal in nature, with little cross-modal, integrative processing. Early reading during this stage is characterized by rote strategies involving memorization of individual letters, words, or letter sounds. The visual symbol is meaningful only in its relationship to spoken language. Cross-modal learning is possible during Stage 4 when tertiary, association regions of the sensory cortices are developing. Injury to these association regions can result in significant learning impairments, such as mental or cognitive retardation or learning disabilities. The type of deficit depends on the location and severity of the injury, and even small insults can affect the integration of one or more sensory modalities (Golden, 1981).

Golden (1981) suggests that injuries to tertiary regions are not always evident until Stage 4 development. Injury in one stage may not produce observable deficits until a later stage because the brain regions subserving specific psychological and behavioral functions are not mature. For example, a child sustaining injury to tertiary regions at the age of 2 may appear normal at age 3 but may show serious learning deficits at age 10 (Golden, 1981). Golden further indicates that prediction of future deficits is complicated by these neurodevelopmental factors, and that neuropsychologists must consider these issues when injury is sustained early in life.

Finally, according to Golden (1981), Stage 5 involves the development of the prefrontal regions of the brain, which begins during adolescence. The LNNB-CR thus does not attempt to measure prefrontal activities. According to this neurodevelopmental theory, deficits resulting from injury to frontal regions may not begin to emerge until 12 to 15 years of age or later. Others have argued that frontal lobe development may occur at earlier stages than suggested by Golden (1981). For example, Becker et al. (1987) and Passler et al. (1985) describe a progression of frontal lobe development beginning at age 6. In these studies it was found that some tasks thought to be mediated by the frontal lobes begin at 6 years of age (e.g., flexibility during verbal conflict tasks), continue to emerge at age 8 (e.g., inhibition of motor responses),

and still are incomplete at age 12 (e.g., verbal proactive inhibition). Neurodevelopmental stages are of primary importance in child neuropsychology, and further research is needed to map more clearly these stages of brain development.

Although the question of frontal lobe development will be of continued interest to researchers and clinicians in the next decade, the relationship between brain development and psychological and behavioral function has a strong empirical base as previously described in Chapter 2. In the design of the LNNB-CR, Golden and associates have utilized the stages of development discussed earlier.

LURIA-NEBRASKA NEUROPSYCHOLOGICAL BATTERY—CHILDREN'S REVISION

Although Anne-Lise Christiansen first provided a description of Luria's neuropsychological methods and compiled these into a battery format, it was Golden and associates who formalized and standardized these procedures for adults and children. The Luria-Nebraska Neuropsychological Battery–Children's Revision (LNNB-CR) went through four revisions (Plaisted, Gustavson, Wilkening, & Golden, 1983) and was developed for children between 8 and 12 years of age. An advanced scoring procedure is available for computers (Golden, 1987).

The battery consists of 11 clinical scales: motor, rhythm, tactile, visual, receptive speech, expressive language, writing, reading, arithmetic, memory, and intelligence (Golden, 1981, 1989; Plaisted et al., 1983). A brief description of each scale follows.

C1: Motor

The Motor Scale consists of 34 items to measure motor coordination, motor speed, and constructional apraxia. At times the child must repeat a motor pattern demonstrated by the examiner, or draw geometric designs (Teeter, 1986). Golden (1989) suggests that elevations on this scale typically result from secondary frontal lobe lesions, although poor scores may occur with some parietal and temporal lobe or anterior frontal lobe problems. T-scores above 80 are most frequently associated with the motor system.

C2: Rhythm

Eight items of this scale measure the child's ability to perceive, discriminate, and reproduce rhythmic patterns. Auditory perception and motor reproductions of rhythmic patterns, tones, or melodies are required (Teeter, 1986). Lesions in either the right or the left hemisphere may interfere with performance on this scale (Golden, 1989). Golden further suggests that in combination with high scores on the Arithmetic (C9) and Memory (C10) scales, high scores on C2 right anterior regions are likely to be involved. Left anterior lesions also may result in this profile especially with verbal skill deficits. Golden adds that the Visual Scale (C4) may help to differentiate anterior or posterior cortical problems, with C4 implicating posterior regions.

C3: Tactile

Right and left sided tactile perceptual abilities are measured using 16 items. The child identifies and localizes tactile stimuli under unilateral and bilateral conditions. Elevated scores on this scale may be caused by lesions in the secondary parietal region or the parietal-occipital regions when visual and tactual functions are both impaired (Golden, 1989).

C4: Visual

Visual perception and visual-spatial discrimination are measured on a variety of tasks. For example, the child is asked to identify pictures, memorize and draw figures, or determine similarities and differences between visual stimuli (Teeter, 1986). C4 elevations often accompany impairment in posterior-occipital regions of the right hemisphere or in anterior (parietal) regions when complex visual tasks are the only visual deficits observed (Golden, 1989). Although the left hemisphere may be implicated, this is uncommon.

C5: Receptive Speech

Speech-language abilities are measured on this scale. The child discriminates phonemes, reads words, comprehends the meaning of words and sentences, and follows verbal commands (Teeter, 1986). Left hemisphere impairment often results in elevated scores on the Receptive Language Scale (Golden, 1989).

C6: Expressive Language

Expressive language and grammar skills are measured on this scale. The child is asked to repeat simple and complex phrases, describe pictures, and make speeches on a given topic after seeing a picture or hearing a short story. Left-hemisphere function are primarily the target of this scale, although right-hemisphere weaknesses are implied when impairment is observed on some items when sequencing or spontaneous speech is the focus (Golden, 1989).

C7: Writing

This scale measures writing, spelling, and copying skills. The child must write sounds, letters, and words from dictation; copy letters and words; and write names (Golden, 1989). The angular gyrus of the left hemisphere (temporal-parietal-occipital regions) is thought to be the underlying mediating structure for these tasks (Golden, 1989).

C8: Reading

Simple to complex reading activities make up this scale. The posterior region of the left hemisphere is most frequently involved with these activities, although Golden (1989) suggests that other regions (temporal lobe or occipital-parietal or right hemisphere) may also produce difficulties on these items, particularly when specific error patterns are present.

C9: Arithmetic

The Arithmetic scale comprise computation problems (addition, subtraction, and multiplication), number recognition, and number reasoning (Teeter, 1986).

Posterior, left-hemisphere regions are most likely involved with these tasks when reading skills have been acquired (Golden, 1989). Right-hemisphere regions may be implicated if reading has not been acquired.

C10: Memory

The Memory Scale consists of both verbal and nonverbal items, under immediate recall, interference, and cued/noncued conditions (Teeter, 1986). This scale is most susceptible to verbal deficits, although moderate elevations may accompany right-hemisphere lesions (Golden, 1989).

C11: Intelligence

This scale comprises a variety of measures similar to items on the Wechsler intelligence scale, including similarities, vocabulary, comprehension, picture arrangement and completion, and arithmetic (Teeter, 1986). Both hemispheres may be implicated with elevated scores on C11, although the left parietal region is most likely involved (Golden, 1989). Again, laterality may be determined on the basis of the pattern of scores from other scales. For example, right-hemisphere involvement is likely with elevated C11, in combination with C2, C4, C9, and C10, while the left hemisphere may be implicated with associated elevations in C6, C8, and C7 (Golden, 1989).

Interpretation of the Luria-Nebraska Battery

Scoring procedures and clinical interpretation of the scales include both qualitative and quantitative approaches. These are described next, with a summary of select research findings with the battery.

Scoring Procedures

The scoring procedures for these scales are fairly uniform and are based on three criteria: (0) for a normal performance; (1) for a performance falling 1 to 2 standard deviations below the mean; and, (2) for performance more than 2 standard deviations below the

mean (Gustavson et al., 1981; Golden, 1987). Developmental norms are available for each item and are incorporated into the test protocol. A computer scoring and computer-generated test report service is also available (Golden, 1987). The battery is fairly well self-contained, and the test protocol is easy to use. T-scores are calculated for each scale.

Clinical Interpretation

There are several levels of interpretation of the LNNB-CR incorporating qualitative, as well as quantitative analysis of the child's performance. Golden (1989) discusses four levels of qualitative interpretation.

1. It is important to determine whether the child has sustained brain injury, and, if so, the neuropsychologist should refer for further evaluation. Golden suggests that this level of interpretation is most frequently employed when there may have been some insult or injury, when screening for unexplained or unusual behaviors, or when a neurological evaluation does not yield significant findings post injury.

2. It is important to describe what the child is and is not capable of doing (Golden, 1989). Inferences are not drawn at this point.

3. It is important to determine the underlying causes of the behaviors observed in the evaluation. Theoretical models of how the brain relates to behavior are applied, and extensive knowledge is required for this level of interpretation.

4. It is important to integrate the neuropsychological findings and to draw conclusions about the brain functioning of the child under study. Golden (1989) outlines numerous factors that might affect this level of interpretation (e.g., sites of injury, when the injury occurred, emotional sequelae, preinjury status, subcortical involvement) and cautions that this level of interpretation is complex. Further, at this level identifying or localizing the site of injury is not of primary importance; rather, the ability to make hypotheses about the child's deficits and possible recovery process is of interest. Identifying the anatomical site of the lesion is in most cases only an

intermediary step, and is useful insofar as it helps in understanding the nature of the deficits, the course of the injury, and what might be expected given this particular injury. Golden does, however, acknowledge that site of injury may be of utmost importance in legal cases, when it is important to determine whether a set of behaviors or deficits is related to a particular injury.

From a quantitative perspective, the LNNB-CR provides a method for determining a Critical Level of performance to determine abnormal functioning that is likely a result of brain injury (Golden, 1989). The Critical Level approach uses an age-adjusted formula (i.e., Critical level = 82.01 — (0.14 × age in months) and represents the highest score that is still within a normal range on the LNNB-CR. The number of scales (C1 to C11) above this level are then calculated, and scales above this score is considered abnormal. Three or more scales above the Critical Level are generally judged to be an indication of brain damage; while no scales or one scale above the critical level probably indicates an absence of damage, and two scales above may be considered borderline (Golden, 1987, 1989).

Golden (1987, 1989) provides useful guidelines to be considered when interpreting scale patterns, and cautions that an experienced neuropsychologist should make diagnoses of brain damage. Factors of interest to be considered when interpreting the child's performance include the following:

1. Receptive and expressive language skills may affect a large number of items.
2. Children with severe peripheral or brain stem damage may appear more impaired; acute damage may produce significant elevations in scores compared to 3 to 6 months postinjury.
3. The size and location of the injury is important, and the LNNB-CR tends to be more sensitive to left-hemisphere deficits.
4. The cause of the damage may affect the child's performance, such as focal or diffuse disorders (e.g., epilepsy).
5. The premorbid status of the child, such that a child

with higher abilities prior to injury will have higher skills postinjury than will a child with generally lower preinjury cognitive abilities (Golden, 1989).

Research and Clinical Validation of the LNNB-CR

Research with the LNNB-CR has been extensive, and the battery has been continually modified based on these research findings. Table 5.7 summarizes selected research studies with the LNNB-CR.

Three factors have been found to be present on the LNNB-CR: Language-General Intelligence; General Academic; and Sensory-Motor (Snow & Hynd, 1985a, 1985b). The scales are heterogeneous and have been found to be highly correlated with each other with a fair amount of redundancy of items (Karras et al., 1987). Such redundancy makes interpretation difficult and compromises the ability to determine whether specific brain damage exists is compromised. Moreover, Snow and Hynd (1985a, 1985b) found the effects of general ability on performance on the LNNB-CR to be significant and advise caution as to the interpretation of such overlap.

As Table 5.7 shows, the LNNB-CR has shown ability to discriminate learning-disabled from non-learning-disabled children with a significant amount of accuracy on some subscales (Geary, Jennings, Schultz, & Alpers, 1984; Lewis, Hutchens, & Garland, 1993; Teeter, Uphoff, Obrzut, & Malsch, 1986). These discriminatory scales appear to be language-based and academically oriented subtests, which Hynd (1992) suggests can be better assessed by instruments designed for that specific purpose.

The battery has not been shown to be as effective in the discrimination of ADHD children. Moreover, the ability of the battery to discriminate brain-damaged from normal controls is not as strong as its ability to select LD from non-LD populations (Hynd, 1992b; Karras et al., 1987). It has been suggested that other clinical groups, such as those with genetic disorders and neurologically based disorders, be assessed by the LNNB-CR to determine if the scales can identify these children (Tuma & Pratt, 1982). Little evidence has been provided that correlates known lesions

Table 5.7. Selected Research Findings with the LNNB-CR

REFERENCE	POPULATION	AGE	MAJOR FINDINGS
Geary, Jennings, Schultz, & Alper (1984)	LD, non-LD	9—15 years	1. 87% classification accuracy 2. Motor with WISC-R, $r = .30$ Writing with WISC-R, $r = .70$ 3. LD > non-LD on 10 of 11 LNNB scales
Lewis, Hutchens, & Garland (1993)	LD, non-LD	13—18 years	1. LD > non-LD on 12 of 14 scales 2. 95% classification accuracy criteria 3+ scales elevated 3. 81% classification accuracy criteria localization scales
Myers, Sweet, Deysach, & Myers (1989)	RD, normals	8—12 years	1. RD > Normals overall 2. RD > Reading, Writing, and Expressive Speech 3. RD > Normals Rhythm, Motor and Tactile scales 4. 81% classification accuracy 12.5% false negatives 6% false positives
Nolan, Hammeke, & Barkley (1983)	Reading LD, Math LD Control		1. READ LD > Expressive Speech Writing and Reading scales. 2. LNNB did not discriminate MATH group from control or READ LD.
Schaughency et al. (1989)	ADHD	8—12 years	1. ADD/H did not differ from ADD/WO on LNNB-CR. 2. No neuropsychological deficits for ADD/H or ADD/WO.
Snow, Hynd, & Hartlage (1984)	Mld LD,		1. Severe LD > Mild LD on Receptive Language, Writing Reading, and Arithmetic scales. 2. Three-factor structure language–general IQ, academic-achievement, and sensory-motor. 3. Critical cutoff criteria 2+ scales may result in too many false positives. 4. Critical cutoff level not appropriate for LD.
Teeter, Uphoff, Obrzut, & Malsch (1986)	LD, Non-LD		1. LD > Non-LD all LNNB except Visual scale. 2. T > 70 Receptive Language Expressive Language, 3. 95% classification accuracy criteria 2+ elevated scales.

Note: LD = learning-disabled; RD = reading disabled; ADHD = attention deficit hyperactivity disorder; ADD/H = attention deficit with hyperactivity; ADD/WO = attention deficit without hyperactivity.

with performance on these scales and determination of brain damage from them is speculative at best. Further, Teeter et al. (1986) found that suggested cutoff scores for identifying brain damage are too liberal, in that a large number of children with LD without known brain injury would be considered brain-damaged.

One of the major criticisms of the LNNB-CR may stem from the theoretical base provided by Golden. There is little or no empirical data to support the five stages of development (Hynd, 1992b; McKay et al., 1985). Hynd (1992b) makes the point that Golden's assumption that the prefrontal region of the brain does not mature until adolescence is not supported by Luria's (1980) theory nor by the research literature (Becker et al., 1987; Passler et al., 1985). This assumption resulted in too few items to assess executive function and thus removed a whole domain from being assessed. Moreover, Hynd (1992b) takes exception to the use of above-average-achieving children in the standardization of the LNNB-CR in order to determine items and instructions as to which items required modifications.

In summary, the LNNB-CR should be used with caution. In many instances it may be more useful to use different measures to assess reading, math, language, and writing skills and to employ those scales that are not redundant with other materials (e.g., rhythm, motor, and tactile). Because the battery requires 1.5 to 2.5 hours to administer, Hynd (1992b) suggests the use of items by Karras and colleagues (1987) that do not appear to be redundant with other items and/or measures (see Table 5.8).

The complexity of child neuropsychological evaluation seems evident from the foregoing discussions, and various batteries approach this task quite differently. While the Halstead-Reitan and the Luria batteries are prominent instruments with theoretical as well as empirical support, a number of other approaches and instruments are currently in use in different medical centers across the country. Various neuropsychological protocols adopted by major medical centers, including the Boston and Austin Neurological Clinics, are discussed next. Other measures not previously described are also briefly reviewed.

Table 5.8. Factors from the LNNB-CR Determined by Karras and Colleagues (1987)

FACTOR DESCRIPTIONS	ITEM NUMBERS
Academic Skills	91–92, 105–106, 110–112, 115–121, 123, 126
Spatial Integration	11–12, 65, 79, 127, 149
Spatially Based Movements	4–7, 13–14
Motor Speed	1–3, 15–17
Drawing Quality	21, 23, 25, 27, 29, 31
Drawing Time	22, 24, 26, 28, 30, 32
Rhythm Perception and Reproduction	39–42
Somatosensory	43–48, 51–52
Receptive Language	67–69, 71, 75
Abstract Verbal Reasoning	142, 144–145, 147

NEUROPSYCHOLOGICAL PROTOCOL: AUSTIN NEUROLOGICAL CLINIC

Nussbaum et al. (1988) describe a neuropsychological protocol that reflects neurobehavioral functioning along an anterior/posterior (A/P) axis or gradient. This framework is formulated on the anatomical divisions of the cortex along the frontotemporal and parieto-occipital axis. Frontal (A) regions have been associated with motor, attentional, sequential processing, reasoning, and abstract thinking abilities, while parietotemporal (P) regions have been associated with tactile, visual perceptual, word recognition, and spelling functions (Nussbaum et al., 1988).

On the basis of theoretical and research findings with children and adults, Nussbaum et al. (1988) have included test items from the Halstead-Reitan battery (i.e., finger tapping, tactual performance test, sensory perceptual exams), the Benton Visual Retention Test (BVRT), the Kaufman Assessment Battery for Children (K-ABC) (i.e., Number Recall, Word Order, Gestalt Closure, and Spatial Memory), the Wechsler Scales for Children–Revised (WISC-R) (i.e., Similarities, Digit Span), and the Wide Range Achievement test (WRAT). See Table 5.9 for a detailed description of Anterior and Posterior measures.

While Nussbaum et al. (1988) recognize that this conceptualization is somewhat artificial, they provide this model for heuristic purposes and discuss the importance of developing models to investigate functional asymmetries in children with various learning and personality disorders. Initial findings with the A/P model suggest that children with weaknesses on anterior measures are likely to exhibit psychological and behavioral problems. These findings may be important for clinicians when developing behavioral management interventions.

BOSTON PROCESS APPROACH

The Boston Hypothesis Testing Approach utilizes an initial cadre of tests to sample specific behaviors, including memory, language, visual-motor skills, and attention. From these measures, addi-

Table 5.9. Austin Neurological Clinic: A Paradigm of Anterior/Posterior Measures

NEUROPSYCHOLOGICAL MEASURES	ANTERIOR FUNCTION ASSESSED
Finger oscillation, dominant and non-dominant hands	Fine motor coordination
Similarities–WISC-R	Verbal abstract reasoning, cognitive flexibility
Digit span–WISC-R	Sequential processing, attention, cognitive flexibility
Number recall–K-ABC	Sequential processing, attention
Word order–K-ABC	Sequential processing, attention
Tactual Performance Test (TPT)–both hands[a]	Motor coordination
	Posterior Function Assessed
Sensory Perceptual Exam	
Tactile	Tactile perception
Visual	Visual perception
Finger Recognition	Tactile gnosis
	Sensory integration
Fingertip Number Writing	Tactile graphesthesia, Sensory integration
TPT–both hands[a]	Tactile perception, Spatial abilities, Sensory integration
TPT memory	Memory for tactile information
TPT localization	Spatial memory
Testalt Closure–K-ABC	Simultaneous visual processing, Figure-ground discrimination
Spatial Memory–K-ABC	Visuospatial memory
Wide Range Achievement Test	
Reading	Reading recognition skills
Spelling	Spelling skills

aThe TPT for Both Hands is included in the Anterior composite score when the TPT–Both Hands is impaired, and when the Sensory Perceptual Exam (SPE) and the Benton Visual Retention Test (BVRT) are in the normal range. The TPT for Both hands is included in the Posterior composite score when the TPT–Both Hands is impaired, and when the SPE and the BVRT are impaired.

Source: Adapted from *Archives of Clinical Neuropsychology,* Vol. 3, N. L. Nussbaum, E. D. Bigler, W. R. Koch, J. W. Ingram, L. Rosa, & P. Massman, "Personality/Behavioral Characteristics in Children: Differential Effects of Putative Anterior versus Posterior Cerebral Asymmetry," pp. 127—135, copyright © 1988, with kind permission from Elsevier Science Ltd., The Boulevard, Langford Lane, Kidlington 0X5 1GB, UK.

tional tests may be added to further evaluate areas of possible deficit.

The Boston Process Approach is not a published approach and can vary depending on the clinician. It is also called the Boston Hypothesis Testing Approach. The approach suggests that basic areas of functioning are screened and from this screening hypotheses are developed and additional measures are added (Lezak, 1983). The Boston Process Approach has its foundation in the belief that both the qualita-tive nature of behaviors and the quantitative scores are important in order to understand the client's deficits and to develop the treatment programs (Milberg, Hebben, & Kaplan, 1986).

The Boston Process Approach emphasizes the utilization of information about the client's age, handedness, and previously developed skills, which is gathered through the interview process. Such information not only informs the conduct of the evaluative process but also puts into focus how these skills are affected or spared from brain damage. In addition, these skills are assessed to determine which strategies the client may employ to compensate for his or her impairments. Emphasis is also placed on "testing the limits"–that is, asking the client to answer questions above the ceiling level. Because patients with brain damage have been found to be able to do difficult tasks past their ceiling level (Milberg & Blumstein, 1981), it is important to determine these limits through testing, whether the reason for failure lies in the client's inability, retrieval problems, or less efficient strategies due to brain damage. This modification is important not just for verbal tasks but also for timed performance tasks. On these timed tasks it is important to determine whether the problem is one of power (mastery) or speed.

A process approach allows flexibility in assessment with an eye to how this assessment informs the treatment plan. Kaplan (1988) suggests that the process approach is helpful to provide insights into brain—behavior relationships. Both standardized and experimental measures are utilized. Therefore, the goal of the process approach is to evaluate the current behavioral functioning in light of intuited brain—behavior relationships.

The initial tests suggested for the Boston Approach with children are listed in Table 5.10. Instruments

Table 5.10. Neuropsychological Test Procedures: Modified Boston Battery

History
Neuropsychological Screening Examination
Wechsler Intelligence Scale for Children–3rd Edition
Symbol Digit Modalities Test (optional if Digit Symbol not used)
Wisconsin Card Sorting Test
WRAML
Rey Auditory Verbal Learning Test
Neuropsychological Screening Test
Boston Naming Test
Rey-Osterreith Complex Figure
Finger Tapping Test
Hooper Visual Organization Test
Wide Range Achievement Test–Revised (optional)

Note: September 1986.

utilized in the Boston Process Approach are described in the following section; they include tests of reasoning, verbal language and memory, and perception.

Tests of Reasoning

Stroop Color Word Test

The Stroop, modified as described in Comalli, Wapner, and Werner (1962), consists of 100 words (random color names) printed in three different colors. In separate trials, the child will be asked to read the color word (maybe printed in different color) then to call out the color (maybe a different color word). The time taken to read the color words is usually recorded. Young ADHD children had trouble inhibiting habitual responding on this task (Boucugnani & Jones, 1989).

Wisconsin Card Sorting Test

The Wisconsin Card Sorting Test (WCST) was developed by R. Heaton (1981) as a measure of frontal lobe dysfunction. The child must match 128 cards to 4 key cards on the dimensions of color, form, or number. The criteria for correct responses change unexpectedly, and the child must alter the response pattern. Several scores can be derived from the test, including the total number of errors and the number of perserverative errors. Heaton, Chelune, Talley, Kay, and Curtiss (1993) provide a revised and expanded manual for the WCST, with extensive norms for children and adolescents.

The WCST measures reasoning, concept formation, and flexibility, and has been shown to be sensitive to frontal lobe activity in children (Chelune, Ferguson, Koon, & Dickey, 1986).

WRAML

The Wide Range Assessment of Memory and Learning (WRAML; Sheslow & Adams, 1990) contains a Screening Index for memory and new learning ability. This screening index includes the ability to scan pictures and then recall items that have been changed. In addition, the child is shown four pictures of increasing complexity and, after a 10-second delay, is asked to reproduce the figure. The screening index also includes a measure of verbal learning. This subtest, requires the child to learn a list of simple words within four trials. This test yields a learning curve over trials. The child then goes on to an additional test with delayed recall of this list following the intervening task. Finally, the child is read two stories and is asked to recite the stories back to the examiner. The child is asked to recall these stories after an intervening task. An optional story recognition format presents the details from a story in a multiple-choice manner. Children who are unable to recall story details spontaneously may be able to elicit this information from memory when prompts are provided.

Rey-Osterreith Complex Figure Test

The Rey-Osterreith Complex Figure Test was standardized by Osterreith in 1944. This task requires the child to copy a complex figure, which is presented in Figure 5.1. The child is asked to draw the figure using six different colors: red, orange, yellow, blue, green, and purple. Every 45 seconds, the child is asked to switch colors. If the child completes the figure before using all colors, the examiner notes the final color utilized and the time needed. After 20 minutes, the child is asked to draw the figure from memory. The figure can be scored using the various methods developed by Waber and Holmes (1986) and as presented in Lezak (1983). The method includes analyzing how many of the original elements are present, as well as the process the client used to draw the figure. See Kolb and Whishaw (1990) for a suggested scoring method.

Additional measures thatcan be utilized depending upon the referral questions under study are listed next. For a more detailed list and explanation of tests, see Lezak (1994) and Spreen and Strauss (1991).

Tests of Verbal Language and Memory

Boston Naming Test

The Boston Naming Test (BNT), developed by Kaplan, Goodglass, and Weintraub (1978), requires the child to name increasingly difficult black and white pictures. If the child misperceives or fails to recognize a picture, he or she is given a cue as to a category (i.e., if a banana is called a "cane," the examiner might say, "No, it's something to eat"). Phonemic cues are also provided by giving the child the beginning sound of the target word. This cue is to be given after an incorrect responses or no response. Norms for children are being developed for this test but remain incomplete at this time.

The BNT has been found to be successful in differentiating children with reading problems from those without (Wolf & Goodglass, 1986; Klicpera, 1983). Results from children with language disorders found their performance to be similar to that of learning-disabled children (Rubin & Liberman, 1983). McBurnette et al. (1991) also found that conduct disordered males show significantly discrepant scores on this measure, suggesting that these children have verbal expressive disabilities. A total error score can be derived for this instrument.

Controlled Oral Word Association Test

The Controlled Oral Association Test (COWA), developed by Benton et al. (1983), requires the child to say as many words as he/she can think in one minute which begin with the letter F, then the letter A, then S. These letters were selected by how frequently they appear in the English language. This test has been found to be sensitive to brain dysfunction in adults, particularly in the left frontal region followed by the right frontal area (Lezak, 1994).

California Verbal Learning Test

The California Verbal Learning Test–Children's Version (CVLT-C) was developed to assess memory-

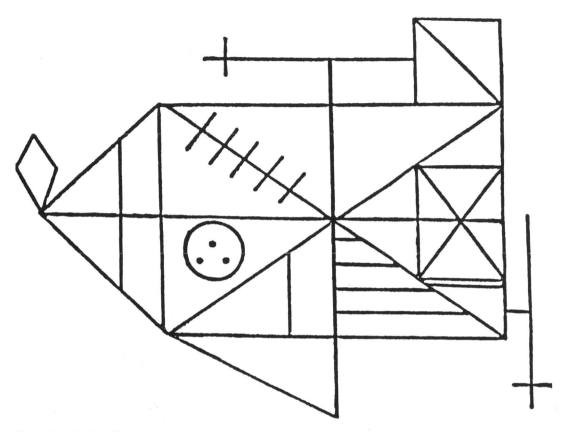

Figure 5.1. The Rey-Osterreith Complex Figure

related strategies and processes for verbal material for children 5 to 16 years of age (Delis, Kramer, Kaplan, & Ober, 1994). The test was developed to be used as an adjunct to intellectual and neuropsychological evaluations for children with learning, attentional, intellectual, psychiatric, and other neurological disorders. The test measures memory and verbal learning skills using a hypothetical shopping list in an effort to use everyday, meaningful stimuli. Learning strategies, learning rate, interference (proactive and retroactive conditions), memory enhancement using cuing, and short and longer delay retention are variables of interest in the CVLT-C.

The CVLT-C comprises the following subtests: List A, Immediate Free-Recall; List B, Immediate Free-Recall; List A, Short-Delay Free-Recall; List A, Short-Delay Cued-Recall; List A, Long-Delay Free-Recall; List A, Long-Delay Cued-Recall; and List A, Long-Delay Recognition. The Test Manual presents normative data; a description of the standardization group; administration, scoring, and interpretation guidelines; and reliability and validity studies with the CVLT-C. Nine hundred twenty children were selected from a representative sample across gender, racial, and age categories using U.S. Bureau of Census data.

Initial research suggests that the CVLT-C has adequate reliability and validity (Delis et al., 1994). The CVLT-C may have some utility for investigating memory and verbal learning abilities of children with various disorders, including Down syndrome and fetal alcohol syndrome (FAS) (Mattson, Riley, Delis, Stern, & Jones, 1993), ADHD (Loge, Staton, & Beatty, 1990), developmental verbal learning disability without ADHD (Shear, Tallal, & Delis, 1992), and dyslexia (Knee, Mittenburg, Burns, DeSantes, & Keenan, 1990). Developmental differences appear on the use of semantic clustering (Levin et al., 1991) and on beginning (primacy) and ending (recency) portions of the lists. Learning curves (average number of words learned across five trials) also were found to differ across ages, with older children displaying steeper curves than younger children (Delis et al., 1994). Finally factor analysis yielded six major factors that appear consistent with the theoretical principles of the CVLT-C. The factor structure is also similar to the solution found on the Adult CVLT.

At present, the CVLT-C appears psychometrically sound and appears to measure skills not readily measurable with other neuropsychological tests.

Neurosensory Center Comprehensive Examination for Aphasia

The Spreen-Benton Aphasia Tests or the Neurosensory Center Comprehensive Examination for Aphasia (NCCEA) comprises 20 subtests measuring language functions and 4 subtests measuring visual and tactile skills (Spreen & Benton, 1969). Spreen and Benton (1977) describe the revised NCCEA tests in detail and list the following tests for the language domain: Visual Naming, Description of Use, Tactile Naming (right hand), Tactile Naming (left hand), Sentence Repetition, Repetition of Digits, Reversal of Digits, Word Fluency, Sentence Construction, Identification by Name, Identification by Sentence (Token Test), Oral Reading (Names), Oral Reading (Sentences), Reading Names for Meaning, Reading Sentences for Meaning, Visual-Graphic Naming, Writing Names, Writing to Dictation, Writing from Copy, and Articulation.

The NCCEA items cover a range of language functions and were selected to be sensitive to aphasic symptoms but not to mild intellectual impairment. Gaddes and Crockett (1973) provide detailed normative data for 6- to 13-year-old males and females who are free from medical, neurological, and achievement impairments. The sample was selected from western Canada, and these data may not generalize to children in the United States.

Tests of Perception

Hooper Visual Organization Test

The Hooper Visual Organization Test comprises 20 cut-up pictures and the subject is asked to write or name the object. The test has been shown to be related to frontal lobe functioning in children (Kirk & Kelly, 1986). A total accuracy score can be derived.

Benton Visual Perceptual Tests

The Benton Visual Retention Test, the Benton Facial Recognition Test, the Benton Judgment of Line Orientation Test, and the Benton Visual Form Recognition Test are described in detail by Benton, Hamsher, Varney, and Spreen (1983a,1983b, 1983c). Hynd (1992b) reports that these measures are well validated and that developmental norms are available for children between the ages of 6 and 14 years. Hynd (1992b) further suggests that the Facial recognition and the Line Orientation tests may be most the useful clinically.

Judgment of Line Orientation

The Judgment of Line Test requires the child to estimate the relationship between line segments by matching a sample to an array of 11 lines in a semicircular array of 180°. The test includes 30 items, with 5 practice items to teach the test. There are two forms, H and V, which present identical items in different order. This test has been found to be sensitive to posterior right hemispheric deficits (Benton et al., 1983c).

Test of Facial Recognition

This test requires the child to match faces with three different conditions: identical view orientation, matching front view with three-quarter views, and front view with lighting differences. The first 6 items require a match of only one pose with six selections. The final 16 items require the child to match three selections to the sample. This test is sensitive to language comprehension difficulties as well as to visual-spatial processing problems. Bilateral posterior deficits have been found to be most significantly identified by this task (Benton et al., 1983b).

Cancellation Tasks

The Cancellation Task requires the child to select a target visually and repetitively, as quickly as possible. One task may be used is the D2 task. This task requires the child to cross out all the D's with two marks above them. There are 15 lines of D's, and the child is asked to cross out the D's in each line for 20 seconds and then to switch to the next line. Lower scores may indicate problems in visual scanning, inhibition problems, and inattention. It has been found that clients with difficulties in sequencing and inattention do poorly on this task compared to those individuals without these problems (Spreen & Strauss, 1991; Sohlberg & Mateer, 1989). The Symbol Search task from the WISC-III and the Visual Matching and Cross-Out Tasks from the Woodcock-Johnson are additional tasks that require quick visual scanning and attention to task and which may be utilized if this area is of concern.

There are several more measures which may be utilized to more fully evaluate various aspects of functioning. The astute clinician will seek out these measures in order to determine their appropriateness for various children or adolescents.

Summary and Conclusions

In summary, the Boston Process Approach begins with a sampling of behaviors and then fine-tunes the evaluation depending on the initial findings. The strength of the Boston Process Approach is also its weakness–namely, the ability to determine the client's areas of strengths and deficits through qualitative data. Qualitative information has been found

to improve greatly the prediction of brain damage found on radiological evidence to upwards of 90% (Milberg et al., 1986). Heaton, Grant, Anthony, and Lehman (1981) also found that qualitative data gathered by clinicians using the Reitan battery also showed significant improvement over quantitative scales.

The weakness of the Boston Process Approach lies within the examiner. To avail him- or herself of this approach, the clinician not only must have a wide array of measures in his or her knowledge base, but also must have sufficient experience in which to apply behavioral observations to brain—behavior relationships. It is also imperative that the clinician have a good database of a "normal" child's performance at various ages.

Although there is a beginning database for the use of the Boston Process Approach with adults (Lezak, 1994; Milberg et al., 1986), data on its efficacy with children are limited. The astute clinician will recognize that best practice will always dictate careful observation of how the child solves the tasks presented to him or her. Although the Boston Approach may be intuitively appealing, further research is needed to determine the benefit of this approach with children.

A TRANSACTIONAL APPROACH TO NEUROPSYCHOLOGICAL ASSESSMENT

Neuropsychological assessment from a transactional model encompasses evaluation of a child's functioning in many areas of his or her life. Given the basic premise of our model that the child's biobehavioral status acts and is acted on by the environment, it is important that this assessment evaluate home, school, and community functioning as well as neuropsychological performance. The assessment is generally based on the referral question but also must address additional issues that may be raised during the evaluation process.

This approach is consonant with the functional organization approach of Fletcher and Taylor (1984) for interpreting neuropsychological data. This approach avoids many of the shortcomings inherent in other methods of interpretation. The functional approach emphasizes the major behavioral characteristics of each disorder, analyzes how behavioral and cognitive variables correlate with one another, analyzes how these behaviors affect development and change over time, and investigates the neurological substrates of behavioral and cognitive characteristics of a disorder (Teeter & Semrud-Clikeman, 1995). Further emphasis is placed on determining how non-neurological factors (e.g., family and education) interact with and moderate biological factors (i.e., neurochemical imbalances or structural damage).

In concordance with the functional organizational approach, the transactional neuropsychological approach includes the following: (1) a description of the neuropsychological correlates of the disorder; (2) identification of behavioral characteristics of various childhood disorders; (3) takes into consideration moderator variables such as family, school, and community interactions; and (4) determines how the existing neuropsychological constraints interact with the child's coping ability and developmental changes that occur at various ages.

The transactional model further provides a systematic study of the interaction of the child's behavior with his or her neurobiology not only as a means of assessment but also for measuring treament efficacy. This approach is ecologically valid and recognizes the interplay of the child's acts and predispositions to his or her environment and the resulting neuropsychological findings. Thus medical interventions such as psychopharmacology will be measured in juxtaposition with psychosocial interventions and vice versa.

In keeping with these assumptions, a neuropsychological assessment based on the transactional approach includes several domains for examination. The initial approach would be a comprehensive developmental interview with the parents. Such an interview would detail information from the child's birth, temperament, developmental milestones, and social, medical, family, and school history. Medical history needs to include information about the existence of seizure disorder, head injury, illnesses, and any medications the child's currently taking. Not only is it important to gather this information, it is also crucial to gather as much information from parents about their perceptions of the child's strenghts and weaknesses, as well as questions they may have about their child's neuropsychological functioning.

The evaluation also needs to contain reports from the child's teacher, which should include the completion of behavior rating scales by at least two teachers who know the child well. We find it instructional to use the main teacher plus a teacher of a subject that is less structured than formal academics, such as art or gym. These less structured classes can provide a window onto the child's ability to handle situations that may be less predictable. Art, music, and gym classes also frequently provide additional information about the child's social skills. If a special education teacher is providing any services to the child, it is very important that this teacher also complete a behavior rating scale.

The next part of the evaluation involves direct observation of the child. If the child is to be observed in his or her classroom, this should be done *before* the assessment begins. Although it is always good practice to observe the child in the classroom setting, clinicians in private practice or in clinics generally are unable to do so. If this is the case, then a phone interview (with the parents' permission, of course) with the teacher is strongly suggested to ascertain areas of concern in that setting, consistency of behavior across settings (particularly important with regard to assessment of behavioral problems such as ADHD, conduct disorders, and social skills deficits), and interventions that have been attempted and that have failed or succeeded. Observation of the child also takes place during the assessment process. How the child separates from his or her parents, how he or she relates to the examiner and copes with a novel situation; and his or her language skills, affect, and problem-solving strategies during the session are all important areas of observation.

Finally, the transactional assessment process includes information about the presenting problem and selection of measures for that concern as well as any additional areas that emerge during the assessment. Incorporation of these data and evolution of an evaluation strategy are integral parts of the transactional approach to neuropsychological assessment. The domains to be assessed will vary depending on the referral question and on the child's age and developmental level. Screening of areas not believed to be involved is desirable but not always possible. For example, a child who is suspected of having ADHD but who is performing adequately academically does not need a full achievement battery–if there are recent standardized test scores or group achievement tests exhibit, then further evaluation is not required. The examiner can then concentrate on measures of distractibility, attention, impulse control, and activity level. In contrast, a child referred for an assessment of a possible learning disability may not need a full assessment of attention or emotional functioning particularly when there is no evidence that these are problem areas. The assessment should be tailored to the child and not the child to an assessment protocol. Therefore, we recommend this approach over a battery approach.

Table 5.11 contains the various domains that are often evaluated in a neuropsychological assessment, along with some suggested measures. It is hoped that these suggestions will assist the clinician in using these measures either to determine the existence of a problem that requires a full neuropsychological evaluation or to gain needed information for the development of an intervention program.

Several of these measures were described earlier in Chapter 4. The interested reader is also referred to the test manuals of standardized tests for more details (e.g., Woodcock-Johnson Psychoeducational Battery–Revised: Cognitive; Clinical Evaluation of Language Fundamentals; Token Test; Differential Ability Test). Many of these measures take little time to administer and can be used as screening devices to rule out or rule in a diagnosis or area of concern.

Many of the measures listed in Table 5.11 are routinely used by the generally trained clinical or school psychologist. The interpretation of these measures from a functional neuropsychological perspective is what differs between the evaluations. In the transactional approach it is important to be able to assess the varying domains and to determine how the results affect the child's ability to relate to his or her environment and to adapt to the resulting environmental reaction. The transactional model interprets the results of these measures and develops an appropriate intervention program. Further discussion of the process underlying this type of assessment is contained in descriptions in the case studies presented in Part III.

Table 5.11. Domains for Neuropsychological Assessment and Suggested Measures

GROSS MOTOR	FINE MOTOR	VISUAL-PERCEPTUAL
Marching (HINB) Motor Scale (MSCA) Motor Scale (LNNB-CR) Grip Strength Test	Grooved Pegboard Purdue Pegboard Finger Tapping Tactual Performance Test Bender-Gestalt Test Trails A Rhythm (LNNB-CR)	Matching Figures, V's, Concentric Squares, and Stars (HINB) K-ABC subtests Rey-Osterreith Complex Figure Judgment of Line Test Facial Recognition Bender-Gestalt Test Beery Visual-Motor Integration Test Hooper Visual Organization Test

SENSORY-MOTOR	VERBAL FLUENCY	EXPRESSIVE LANGUAGE
Tactile, Visual, Auditory (HRNB, HINB) Tactile Form Recognition Fingertip Writing (HRNB, HINB)	Controlled Oral Word Association–FAS Verbal Fluency (MSCA)	Clinical Evaluation of Language Fundamentals (CELF-R) Vocabulary Subtest (SB:FE & WISC-III) Boston Naming Test Aphasia Screening Test (HRNB)

RECEPTIVE LANGUAGE	MEMORY	ABSTRACTION/REASONING
CELF-R Token Test Peabody Picture Vocabulary–Revised Picture Vocabulary (WJ-R)	Benton Visual-Retention Tactual Performance Test Wide Range Assessment of Memory and Learning (WRAML) Children's Auditory Verbal Learning Test (CAVLT) Rey Auditory Verbal Learning Test Sentence Memory (SB:FE)	Category Test (HRNB, HINB) Wisconsin Card Sort (WCST) Concept Formation Test (WJ-R) Trails B (HRNB) Color Form Test (HINB) Ravens Progressive Matrices

LEARNING	EXECUTIVE FUNCTIONS	ATTENTION
CAVLT WRAML Rey-Auditory Verbal Learning Test Auditory-Verbal Learning (WJ-R)	Wisconsin Card Sort Category Test Matching Familiar Figures (HINB) Verbal Fluency Tasks	Continuous Performance Test Cancellation Tests (WJ-R; D2) Stroop Test Seashore Rhythm Test (HRNB) Speech-Sounds Perception Test (HRNB) Progressive Figures Test (HINB) Serial 7's

Note: Halstead-Indiana Neuropsychological Battery (HINB); Halstead-Reitan Neuropsychological Battery for Children (HRNB); Kaufman Assessment Battery for Children (K-ABC); Luria Nebraska Neuropsychological Battery–Children Revised (LNNBB-CR); McCarthy Scales of Children's Ability (MSCA); Stanford-Binet Intelligence Scale, Fourth Edition (SB:FE); Woodcock-Johnson Cognitive Battery–Revised (WJ-R); Wechsler Intelligence Scales for Children–Third (WISC-III).

CHAPTER 6

SEVERE NEUROPSYCHIATRIC AND EXTERNALIZED DISORDERS OF ADOLESCENCE AND CHILDHOOD

Externalizing disorders have been defined as those disorders in which overt behavior is present (American Psychiatric Association [APA], 1994). Externalized disorders are characterized by numerous dysfunctional behaviors, which pose difficulties in management in the social and psychological aspects of the child's life. The externalized disorders to be reviewed include attention deficit hyperactivity disorder and conduct disorder. Severe neuropsychiatric disorders, including Tourette syndrome, Asperger's disorder, and autism (pervasive developmental disorders of childhood), are discussed here because of the similarities in the brain areas that are implicated and in the neurotransmitter systems that are thought to be involved. Comings (1990) suggests that many of the symptoms of ADHD and frontal lobe dysfunction are also shared with autism and Tourette syndrome.

Biochemical and neuropsychological models of these disorders will be discussed in more detail in the following sections, including the effects on these neuropsychiatric disorders on the psychosocial and academic functioning of children.

BIOCHEMICAL AND NEUROPSYCHOLOGICAL MODELS OF PSYCHIATRIC DISORDERS OF CHILDHOOD

Investigation into the causes of neuropsychiatric disorders of childhood has led researchers to appreciate the role of neurochemicals, specifically neurotransmitters, and their effect on behavior. Three major neurotransmitters have received attention: (1) serotonin (SE), (2) dopamine (DA), and (3) norepinephrine (NE). Neurotransmitters are not evenly distributed throughout the brain but appear concentrated in specific brain regions (Comings, 1990) (see Table 6.1). High levels of DA appear in the caudate, putamen (striatum), and frontal lobes. In general, NE is more widespread in the brain. The hypothalamus has high concentrations of SE and NE, while the limbic and frontal lobes also have high levels of SE. These various brain regions play different roles in the control and regulation of motor activity, emotional responsivity, and emotions. Neurotransmitters are part of the electrochemical mechanisms by which neurons communicate to initiate, regulate, and inhibit simple and complex activities.

An over- or underabundance of neurotransmitters appear related to some psychiatric problems in children and adults (Comings, 1990). See Table 6.2 for a summary of the behavioral effects of neurochemical levels and psychiatric disorders. Although evidence suggests that neurotransmitter models are viable explanations for psychiatric disorders, there are billions of neurons in the brain and the complexity of the interactions are almost unfathomable (Comings, 1990). The chemical balance of neurotransmitters is interactive; that is, increases or decreases in one neurochemical affect the levels of other chemicals in various brain regions. For example, decreased SE levels that may be present individuals with Tourette syndrome (TS) interact with levels of NE (in the locus ceruleus) which subsequently affect DA metabolism (Comings, 1990). Furthermore, medications that move one transmitter to normal levels may influence other transmitters in negative directions.

Table 6.1. Neurotransmitter Circuits, Brain Regions, and Functional Activity

NEUROTRANSMITTERS	BRAIN CIRCUITS	FUNCTIONAL ACTIVITY
Dopamine (DA)	• Nigrostriatal pathway 　Substantia nigra → caudate 　　→ striatum	Stimulates movement ↓ DA ↑ muscle rigidity & tremors (e.g., Parkinson's) ↓ DA ↑ jerky movements, tics (e.g., Tourette)
	• Mesocortical-limbic pathway 　Brain stem → prefrontal 　Brain stem → limbic system	Modulates emotions ↑ DA ↑ hallucinations and paranoia (e.g., schizophrenia) ↓ DA disinhibition of subcortex ↓ DA ↑ hyperactivity 　　↑ inattention 　　↑ temper 　　↑ aggression
	• Tuberoinfundibular pathway 　Hypothalamus ® pituitary	
Norepinephrine (NE)	• Locus ceruleus (LC) → spinal cord • LC → cerebellum • LC → thalamus • LC → frontal → limbic	Regulaes DA and NE in prefrontal Alternative hypothesis for Tourette syndrome and ADD
Serotonin	• Caudal raphe nuclei → cerebellum • Rostral raphe nuclei → thalamus • Rostral raphe nuclei → prefrontal 　　→ limbic	Inhibits large brain regions • Frontal (ADHD) • Striatum (tics) • Hippocampus (memory and learning) • Septum and limbic (emotional lability)
	• Feedback loop 　Raphe nuclei inhibits 　Habenual → feedback → inhibits 　　raphe nuclei	May increase/decrease symptoms Decreased serotonin • Alcoholism • ADHD • Aggression • Borderline personality • Bulimia • Depression • Impulsivity & inattention • Self-mutilation (Lesch-Nyhan) • PMS • Tourette syndrome • Violent behavior • Violent suicide

Table 6.2. Neurotransmitter Levels, Psychiatric Disorders, and Behavioral Effects

PSYCHIATRIC DISORDERS	NEUROTRANSMITTERS	BEHAVIORAL EFFECTS
Tourette syndrome	↓ DA frontal regions ↑ DA nucleus accumbens and striatum ↓ DA substantia nigra ↓ SE	Frontal lobe syndrome Motor and vocal tics ADHD symptoms Learning and conduct problems Mimics frontal lobe syndrome Aggression and self-injury Hypersuxuality
ADHD	↓ DA frontal regions ↓ SE	Disinhibition of subcortex Hyperactivity and irritability Aggression
Schizophrenia	↑ NE ↑ SE ↓ SE	Hyperarousal Particularly in brain atrophy Two types of schizophrenia
Depression	↓ NE ↑ NE ↓ SE	Depression Mania Severe depression
Anxiety	↑ NE	Anxiety and fear
Obsessive-compulsive disorder (OCD)	Hypersensitive SE receptors	OCD symptoms Linkage of depression, anxiety, and aggression in OCD

Note: DA = dopamine; SE = serotonin; NE = norepinephrine.

Dopamine Activity and Psychiatric Disorders

DA pathways are found in three brain regions: (1) the substantia nigra to the caudate and striatum or putamen; (2) the brain stem to the prefrontal and limbic regions; and (3) the hypothalamus and pituitary (Comings, 1990; Heimer, 1983). Disturbances in DA activity can result in various disorders, which are briefly reviewed next.

DA Hypothesis of Tourette Syndrome

In this model, there is a deficiency of DA in the prefrontal lobes with a corresponding sensitivity of DA receptors in the striatal and nucleus accumbens regions, resulting in disinhibition of subcortical regions (Comings, 1990). The changes in striatal regions produce motor and vocal tics, while subcortical disinhibition produces characteristics of frontal lobe syndrome.

Genetic links (e.g., Gts gene) may account for this dynamic neurochemical and behavioral interaction. Injury to brain stem regions also can cause TS-like symptoms, especially when mesolimbic and mesocortical DA pathways are involved. Damage to the caudate nucleus also results in full TS symptoms. Other evidence shows that acute encephalitis may result in TS symptoms.

Haldol stimulates the synthesis and turnover of DA at the presynapse and decreases DA release at the postsynapse. This balance in effect reduces the presence of Tourette symptoms. Medications that stimulate DA receptors (e.g., Ritalin and Cylert) increase TS symptoms and tics.

DA Hypothesis of Schizophrenia

The same theories underlying TS symptoms appear to explain the presence of schizophrenia.

DA Hypothesis of ADHD

When there is too little DA in the prefrontal regions, subcortical regions are disinhibited which increases hyperactivity and irritability (Comings, 1990), Stimulants facilitate prefrontal DA, which in turn inhibits subcortical regions, returning activity and behaviors back to "normal" levels. Ritalin also may affect the action of norepinephrine.

Comings (1990) suggests that frontal lobe syndrome, resulting from an imbalance of DA in the prefrontal lobes, accounts for many of the symptoms associated with ADHD and Tourette syndrome. Further, it may explain the comorbidity of schizophrenia, ADHD, and Tourette symptoms in some children and adolescents.

While DA appears to play a role in psychiatric disorders, SE and NE levels also have been implicated. Further, the delicate interaction among neurotransmitters with behavioral and psychiatric disturbances may help explain comorbidity of disorders (Tourette syndrome with ADHD, ADHD with depression, etc.).

Norepinephrine Activity and Psychiatric Disorders

Norepinephrine (NE) activity also seems related to psychiatric disturbances. NE functions as a modulator of other neurotransmitters and is structurally very similar to DA (Comings, 1990). [The adrenal glands, connected by pathways to the locus ceruleus, produce the majority of NE, and NE nerves pass into almost every other region of the brain (e.g., cerebellar and cerebral cortices, limbic system, brain stem, and spinal cord) (Heimer, 1983).] The interaction of NE and DA has been the focus of recent studies, and stress has been found to affect this interaction.

Clonidine is the most effective medication for TS, and its action stimulates receptor sites that ultimately inhibit the release of NE (Comings, 1990). Clonidine also may increase SE in the and DA in the prefrontal region.

Serotonin Activity and Psychiatric Disorders

Serotonin (SE) plays a central role in impulse control disorders because of its inhibitory affects on the striatal and limbic system regions (Comings, 1990; Panksepp, 1982; Soubrie, 1986). SE is derived from tryptophan, which must come from the diet (aided by vitamin B_6) because the body does not produce it (Comings, 1990). SE is concentrated in the raphe systems in the midbrain and nerve fibers project to the prefrontal, limbic, thalamic/hypothalamic, striatal, and cerebellar regions. Defects in these SE pathways can result in ADHD (frontal signs), motor tics (striatal signs), learning and memory problems (hippocampal signs), and emotional disturbances (limbic signs), which are all symptoms associated with Tourette syndrome (Comings, 1990). When functioning properly, SE excites or inhibits these various brain regions for dynamic impulse control.

The frontal lobes have the highest concentration of SE receptor sites, and SE deficiencies may result in numerous behavioral disorders (see Table 6.1 for a summary of these various behavioral disorders). A number of antidepressant medications, including chlorimipramine, flenfluramine, fluoxetine (Prozac), and trazedone, alter SE levels in the brain, and haldol inhibits SE. Antidepressants affect SE as well as DA and NE (Comings, 1990). Violent suicide attempts are also high in individuals with low levels of SE (vanPraag, 1982). Extremely violent criminals (convicted of murder or attempted murder) have been found to have low levels of SE, and all these individuals also had histories of ADHD and/or conduct disorders and violent suicide attempts (Linnoila et al., 1983).

Comings (1990) also describes a cycle of SE depletion and alcoholism, where alcohol ingestion produces a short-lived "high" as SE levels increase. SE levels ultimately decrease, leading to more alcohol consumption. The behavioral picture that results from imbalances of SE is complex, although a susceptibility to increased aggression, impulsivity, and depression seems likely (Comings, 1990).

Medication Effects on Neurotransmitters

Neurotransmitters are released at the synaptic cleft (see Chapter 2 for an explanation of the neuroanatomy of the neuron), and if they remained at the synapse the neuron would continue to fire (Comings, 1990). To keep neurons from constant firing, neurotransmitters are either broken down or reabsorbed into the presynapse (neuron originating the signal). Monoamine oxidase (MAO) is one of the enzymes that breaks down neurotransmitters. Thus, medications that inhibit this breakdown process (MAO inhibitors) allow for the neuron to continue firing. MAO inhibitors are used to treat depression and serve to increase the amount of neurotransmitters at the synapse. Other antidepressants, such as the tricyclics, inhibit the reuptake process thereby enhancing the activity of dopamine, norepinephrine, and serotonin.

Transmitters can stimulate or inhibit neural activity and are classified as either agonists, because they stimulate receptor activity, or antagonists, because they inhibit receptors (e.g., Haloperidol inhibits dopamine). Further, neurotransmitters can serve to stimulate or inhibit cell activity (e.g., serotonin inhibits cellular activity). See Table 6.3 for a summary of medication effects on neurotransmitter systems.

Although the neurochemical model of psychiatric disorders is far from complete, many researchers suggest that the biochemistry of neurotransmitter systems holds the key to better understanding and treating many severe disorders of childhood. Further, research that investigates the effects of combined psychopharmacology and psychosocial interventions may shed further light on how biochemical and environmental factors interact. It may also indicate how psychosocial or behavioral therapies augment medication and vice versa. Future clinical and research

Table 6.3. Medication Effects on Neurotransmitters

MEDICATIONS	NEUROTRANSMITTER EFFECTS	BEHAVIORAL EFFECTS
Stimulants	↑ DA in frontal regions	Frontal lobe inhibits subcortex Decreases ADHD symptoms Increases Tourette symptoms
Haldol	Stimulates synthesis and turnover of DA ↑ SE	Decreases aggression Decreases Tourette symptoms Decreases self-injury
Cylert	↑ SE	Decreases ADHD symptoms
Clonidine	↓ NE ↑ SE ↑ DA frontal regions Inhibits production of NE	Decreases anxiety and panic attacks Decreases ADHD Decreases Tourette symptoms
Tricyclics	↓ Locus ceruleus activity ↑ NE	Decreases depression
Imipramine	Inhibits reuptake of NE	Decreases depression
Clomipramine	↑ SE	Decreases obsessive-compulsive symptoms Decreases panic attacks
Prozac	↑ SE Increases synthesis or decreases reuptake of SE	Decreases depression

Note: DA = dopamine; SE = serotonin; NE = norepinephrine.

trials should investigate this interaction. Pelham et al. (1993) have initiated such research for combined treatments for ADHD. Efforts of this nature may prove useful for other disorders, such as conduct disorders and depression.

The following sections provide a review of select severe neuropsychiatric disturbances, including Tourette syndrome, Asperger's syndrome, and autism.

TOURETTE SYNDROME

Tourette syndrome (TS) is classified as a tic disorder that is marked by multiple motor and vocal tics (APA, 1994). TS is associated with significant social impairment and often interferes with normal school adjustment. For diagnostic purposes, symptoms of TS must be present before 18 years of age and must not result from medication effects (e.g., stimulants) or other medical conditions (e.g., encephalitis).

Tics may include the following: facial regions (e.g., eye-blinking, eye rolling, squinting, licking lips, sticking tongue out, smacking lips, etc.); head and neck movements (touching shoulder to chin, throwing head back); shoulders (e.g., shrugging); arms (failing, extension, or flexion); hands (e.g., biting nails, finger signs or copropraxia, picking at skin); diaphragm (e.g., inhaling or exhaling); legs and feet (e.g., kicking, stooping, stamping, tapping, toe curling); or others (e.g., banging, chewing on clothes, flapping arms, smelling fingers, body jerking, picking lint) (Comings, 1990). Complex tics involve several muscle groups, are frequently stereotypic in nature (e.g., grooming, kicking, stamping, smelling, facial grimaces), and may occur in sequences like compulsive behaviors. Comings (1990) list the most common tics as eye-blinking (69%), shoulder shrugging (47%), mouth opening (40%), arm extending (25%), facial grimacing (23%), and licking lips (21%).

Vocal tics present unique problems for individuals with TS and are involuntary in nature. These may include (in order of frequency) throat clearing (56%), grunting (48%), yelling/screaming (29%), sniffing (28%), barking (22%), and snorting (20%) (Comings, 1990). Compulsive swearing or coprolalia is one of the more disturbing features of TS, with *fu* and *sh*

words being quite common. The compulsive, repetitive nature of the swearing has a negative impact on the individual's ability to interact with others. Although swearing may be high in severe TS (60%), in milder cases swearing appears to occur less frequently (from 8% to 33%) (Comings, 1990).

An interesting aspect of the disorder is the child's ability to control the tics for periods of time during the day. This often leads to misunderstanding and misdiagnosis, as the child may display the symptoms while at home but not in school. Stress appears to increase the rate of tics, and the presence of early TS symptoms appears related to more severe cases of the disorder.

Biogenetic Correlates of TS

Although TS appears to be an inherited disorder in a majority of children, approximately 35% of cases may not be inherited (Comings, Comings, Cloninger, & Devor, 1984). Single-gene rather than multiple-gene transmission is most likely, and in some cases obsessive-compulsive disorders are seen in some family members. Pauls and Leckman (1986) found that approximately 1 in 83 people are carriers of the gene that transmits TS.

TS appears to be transmitted through the Gts gene and visual-field defects are associated with defects in Gts (Comings, 1990). Comings (1990) further indicates that TS is a semidominant, semirecessive trait carried on the Gts gene, and that a "percentage of individuals in the general population with ADHD, learning disabilities, obsessive-compulsive behaviors, conduct disorder, phobias, depression, addictive behaviors including alcoholism and compulsive eating, and other related disorders may have these same problems because they are carrying a Gts gene" (p. 519).

Frequency of TS

TS may occur more often than previously suspected. While early studies reported rates at about 1 in 1000 in boys to 1 in 10,000 in girls (Burd, Kerbeshian, Wikenheiser, & Fisher, 1986), others report that school-aged males observed over a two-year period demonstrated higher rates, about 1 in 100 (Comings, 1990). The fact that TS may occur with other disorders also may mask an accurate diagnosis when symptoms are mild.

Associated Features of TS

TS has been found to coexist with numerous other childhood disorders, including autism, Asperger's syndrome, ADHD, borderline personality disorder, schizophrenia, and manic-depressive and depressive disorders (Comings, 1990). The linkages among these various disorders may depend on activity levels and the intricate balance among the neurotransmitters (DA, SE, and NE), as well as on the site of primary neurological involvement (frontal, striatal, or limbic regions). Other associated features of TS include learning problems, reading and speech deficits, motivational problems, sleep disorders, attentional deficits, and motor coordination problems (Comings, 1990).

Implications for Assessment

Comings (1990) suggests that TS is often misdiagnosed for the following reasons: (1) misunderstanding that the child *must* swear; (2) mislabeling TS as "habits"; (3) failing to ask about tics; (4) discomfort in making the diagnosis; (5) ignoring parental reports of symptoms, particularly if the tics did not appear during evaluation; (6) inadequately exploring family history; (7) reaching inaccurate conclusions about the symptom picture; (8) failing to consider longitudinal history so that when tics subside, other disorders (e.g., alcoholism) appear primary; (9) failing to identify tics when individual is on medication; and (10) lacking knowledge about TS. Further, TS can range from mild symptoms to severe tics with the associated behavioral deficits described here. Careful consideration should be given especially when behaviors are mild in nature.

The diagnosis of TS depends on a comprehensive evaluation, including careful history taking and behavioral descriptions. An assessment of psychosocial interactions and cognitive-academic functioning should be included. Neuropsychological evaluation may be helpful for identifying frontal lobe deficits, speech, language, memory, and learning problems associated with TS. Visual-field defects were found in a number of TS subjects (Enoch et al., 1988a, 1988b), so neuropsychological evaluation may uncover these related problems. Medical consultation may be helpful for identifying genetic linkages and for ruling out other neurological disorders (e.g., Lesch-Nyhan and myoclonus) that may present like TS symptoms.

Implications for Interventions

Interventions may include medication in conjunction with other psychosocial and behavioral therapies depending upon the diagnostic picture. The selection of intervention strategies also depends on the number and severity of other comorbid disorders (e.g., ADHD, depression). Individual case analysis with careful monitoring is then the key to successful programming for children with TS.

Pharmacological Interventions

Comings (1990) indicates that medication should be considered only when the child's behaviors significantly interfere with adjustment, and when the behavioral pattern cannot be controlled through other behavioral and psychosocial interventions. Increased structure at home or in school may be warranted, and educational interventions such as tutoring may alleviate learning and academic difficulties.

Common medications that control TS symptoms are haloperidol and clonidine. The child's overall quality of life should be considered when assessing the need for medication. Dosage levels should be "the smallest dose that provides just enough change in the chemical balance so the child, or adult, can function as near to normal as possible" (Comings, 1990, p. 538). Tics may be the easiest to control for, while other associated behaviors may require additional medications. For example, stimulants may be useful for ADHD symptoms. In some instances, haloperidol and clonidine are administered together, and clonopin may be added for children who do not respond to single medications (Comings, 1990). It is always best to start with low doses and to increase dosage levels when needed. This basic approach may reduce the negative side effects associated with medications.

Psychosocial and Behavioral Interventions

It should be clear that nonpharmacological interventions will do nothing to reduce tics but may be helpful for reducing associated behavioral problems (Comings, 1990). It should also be emphasized that many children do not get better when the only treatment is medication, so combined interventions are recommended.

Medication may be the first line of treatment when TS significantly interferes with the child's functioning, and may increase the likelihood of success of nonpharmacological treatments (Comings, 1990). Comings (1990) suggests that parents can and should discipline for antisocial behavioral problems (e.g., lying, stealing, refusal to complete chores, disrespect, talking back, oppositional/confrontational, temper tantrums) but not for tics, attentional problems, obsessive-compulsive behaviors,or learning problems. Thus, parenting techniques may be the focus of intervention plans.

Some techniques that Comings (1990) has found useful in his treatment of 1400 TS patients include short-term natural consequences, rewards, behavioral contracts, skill building for appropriate behaviors, and family/sibling therapy. Avoid prolonged restrictions, spankings, arguing back and being drawn into the angry outburst, abdicating the parenting role, and inconsistent parenting. A careful plan for handling rage attacks is needed. Some parents find that holding the child until the rage subsides works well, while others find that removing themselves from the the angry outburst works, too. For example, if the child loses control and begins to yell obscenities, the parent disengages by repeating that the decision stands and that the conversation is over. Other techniques for controlling physical or verbal outbursts can be gleaned

from Patterson's work with oppositional and conduct-disordered youth. The clinician should work closely with the parent to have a plan of action and to seek out alternatives if the plan fails. These types of interventions are time-consuming and can be taxing for the family, so family therapy may be necessary to address the stress involved in raising a child with TS.

It is important to address family dynamics and stress factors. A patient who was treated by one of the authors was placed in an out-of-state residential treatment facility because his parents could no longer tolerate his behavioral problems and he was an embarrassment to the family. When discussing his feelings about this rejection, the teenager became more agitated, and his tics and involuntary swearing increased. It was important to improve the family cohesion and to initiate efforts to reinstate the youngster back into the family.

School-based interventions should focus on the child's strengths and should attempt to bypass weaknesses if possible (Comings, 1990). Strength approaches may include untimed tests, small work units, simple instructions, child-paced work, reduced work load, reduced rote activities, oral exams, the use of tape recorders and computers, and individual tutoring. Children with TS may require special-education services, and an individualized educational plan (IEP) may be needed.

Autism and Asperger's syndrome are reviewed next.

AUTISM/PERVASIVE DEVELOPMENTAL DISORDERS

Although autism and pervasive developmental disorders (PDD) are relatively rare, Cook and Leventhal (1992) indicate that autism is one of the most severe forms of childhood neuropsychiatric disorders. Incidence estimates range from 4 to 5 cases per 100,000 (Rutter, 1978b) to 10 to 11 per 10,000 (Bryson, Clark, & Smith, 1988; Tanoue, Oda, Asano, & Kawashima, 1988). The ratio of females to males is approximately 3 or 4 to 1 (Rutter & Lockyear, 1967), with females having somewhat lower Full Scale IQs than males

(Lord & Schopler, 1985). Autistic disorders are characterized as impaired social reciprocity, communication disorders, and cognitive deficits (Cook & Leventhal, 1992).

Comparisons between autistic and cognitively retarded children have found a differing cognitive profile. Autistic children show high scores on measures of visual-spatial ability and rote memory, with very poorly developed verbal comprehension, whereas cognitively retarded children generally show uniformly delayed performance (Dawson & Castelloe, 1995). Moreover, autistic children have a poorer prognosis for employment compared to cognitively retarded children. Therefore, although both populations show severe impairment, they are believed to be different syndromes (Dawson & Castelloe, 1995).

One of the cardinal symptoms of autism is significant impairment in social reciprocity, which is evident soon after birth (Rutter, 1978b, 1985). Autistic infants generally do not show normal patterns of social responsiveness when being held, and do not engage in social smiling. Impaired mother—child reciprocity (Mundy & Sigman, 1989), regression or arrested social interactions (Dahl, Cohen, & Provence, 1986), and ritualistic or stereotypic behaviors (Rutter, 1985) appear as basic characteristics of this disorder. Language and communication disorders are also major features of autism, with signs of delayed speech; echolalia; idiosyncratic speech; vocabulary and comprehension disorders; grammatical immaturity; and rate, tone, and pitch abnormalities (APA, 1994). Rutter (1985) indicates that some features (i.e., stereotypic behaviors and gaze avoidance) may be most evident between 3 and 5 years of age, while communication and social interaction patterns persist throughout the life span. Preschool children with autism show severely impaired language and social skills as well as a paucity of imaginative play. In addition, these children also show deficits in understanding of object permanence and spatial relations (Dawson & Adams, 1984). In contrast, autistic adolescents show severely impaired abilities in language and concept development, with average to superior visual spatial skills (Dawson & Levy, 1989; Firth, 1993).

Associated Features

Children with autism have high rates of cognitive retardation (70%), epilepsy (25%), attentional deficits, and aggressive and impulsive disorders (Cook & Leventhal, 1992). Comings (1990) also indicates that autism and TS overlap and share common behavioral problems (e.g., eye-blinking, echolalia, hyperactivity, mood lability, perseverations, poor speech control, and stereotypic movements). Other associated features of autism include self-injury; hypersensitivity to touch, sounds, or odors; eating disorders (e.g., pica); sleep disturbances; and mood or affect disorders (i.e., lack of emotional response or inappropriate emotional response) (APA, 1994). Minshew and Goldstein (1993) also found that high-functioning autistic individuals (aged 12 to 40 years) have difficulty organizing information and may use rigid, inflexible strategies for encoding visual material.

Prenatal and Postnatal Factors

An increase in the incidence of prenatal and perinatal complications in autistic individuals compared to normal children has been found (Funderbuck, Carpenter, Tanguay, Freeman, & Westlake, 1983). Some of the more frequent complications are meconium in the amniotic fluid, bleeding during pregnancy, and use of doctor-prescribed hormones (Deykin & MacMahon, 1980; Gillberg & Gillberg, 1983).

Genetics

The heritability of autism is supported by two important findings: the rate of autism in siblings of autistic individuals is approximately 50 times that of the general population (Smalley, Asarnow, & Spence, 1988; Rutter et al., 1990); and there is a high concordance rate of autism in monozygotic twins compared to dyzygotic twins (Ritvo, Freeman, Mason-Brothers, Mo, & Ritvo, 1985). Genetic subtypes in autism may also exist, and the disorder has been linked to other genetic disorders such as fragile X syndrome and untreated phenylketonuria (Folstein & Rutter, 1987).

Neurological Features

Theories suggesting impaired parent—child relationships as causative factors in the development of autism have been replaced by neurodevelopmental theories (Minshew & Goldstein, 1993). Hypotheses concerning the neurological mechanisms of autism include reports of EEG abnormalities (APA, 1994), hippocampal abnormalities (Minshew & Goldstein, 1993), ventricular enlargement (Bigler, 1989a; Hauser, DeLong, & Rosman, 1975), cortical atrophy (Bigler, 1989a), right—left asymmetry abnormalities (Prior & Bradshaw, 1979), reticular activating system dysfunctions (Rimland, 1964), limbic system involvement (Boucher & Warrington, 1976), and cerebellum abnormalities (Courchesne, 1989). Further, Chiron et al. (1993) found that autistic children between the ages of 4.5 and 17 years had a range of abnormalities using rCBF and SPECT imaging, including slight subcortical atrophy, ventricular enlargement, and hypofunction of the left hemisphere. Individuals with autism had similar activation patterns as a control group in posterior brain regions, with significant differences apparent in sensorimotor, temporal, and Broca's regions. These findings correspond roughly to differences revealed on neuropsychological measures (e.g., impaired motor and language functions with intact visual-spatial abilities).

Neurodevelopmental anomalies have been postulated given that abnormal cell density and reduced dendritic growth have been observed (Raymond, Bauman, & Kemper, 1989). Hynd and Willis (1988) also indicate that autistic children have high rates of associated neurological disorders, including PKU, seizures, and tuberous sclerosis.

Although the exact etiology of autism is still unknown, results from electrophysiological and dichotic listening techniques suggest that autistic children may not show the expected pattern of hemispheric specialization. Research has documented that normally the two hemispheres are functionally and structurally asymmetric at birth (Best, Hoffman, & Glanville, 1982; Molfese & Molfese, 1979). Autistic children do not show such hemispheric specialization. The dichotic listening technique requires the child to listen to a simultaneous presentation of differing auditory stimuli to each ear while wearing headphones. When asked to report what they hear, most individuals report only one of the stimuli–linguistic stimuli are reported from the right ear (left hemisphere). Studies have repeatedly found that autistic individuals report stimuli to the left ear (right hemisphere) or no ear preference (Blackstock, 1978; Prior & Bradshaw, 1979; Hoffman & Prior, 1982). Further, (Chiron et al. 1995) contend that children with more severe structural abnormalities are most resistant to interventions because of the cognitive disorders associated with autism.

Data from electrophysiological studies are consistent with the results of dichotic listening techniques; that is, autistic children tended to either have dominant right-hemisphere response to linguistic stimuli (Dawson, Finley, Phillips, & Galpert, 1986) or no dominant language hemisphere (Ogawa et al., 1982; Tanguay, 1976). When EEG recordings are made during completion of cognitive tasks, a reversed pattern of brain activity during language tasks and use of the right hand (normally left-hemispheric-mediated tasks) has been found (Dawson et al., 1982; Dawson, 1983). These researchers concluded that autistic individuals exhibit abnormal brain activity and development (Dawson & Levy, 1989).

Consistent with the above-average findings are the results from the P300 component of the event-related potential (ERP). As you will recall from Chapter 3, the P300 component has been associated with the detection of novel and unpredictable stimuli. In autistic individuals this component has been found to have an extended latency; that is, it occurs later than expected (Courchesne, Lincoln, Kilman, & Galambos, 1985; Dawson, Finley, Phillips, Galpert, & Levy, 1990), and the amplitude (degree of response) is smaller (Dawson et al., 1990). Additional work in this area has led researchers to hypothesize that the foregoing results may be due to the possibility that autistic children react to novel stimuli as aversive and/or as overstimulating (Dawson & Levy, 1989). Moreover, there is emerging evidence that autistic individuals are chronically overaroused (Kootz, Marinelli, & Cohen, 1982). Furthermore, lower functioning autistic individuals showed the highest level of overarousal compared to higher functioning autistic individuals. Such overarousal has been found to be negatively associated with good information-processing abilities.

These findings have led some researchers to hypothesize that autism involves dysfunction of the cortical-limbic-reticular system (Heilman & Van Den Abell, 1980). Courchesne's study (1987) found that the first exposure of a novel stimulus on a P300 resulted in a large amplitude. Following additional exposure, the amplitude decreased. Dawson and Levy (1989) interpreted these findings as reflecting overarousal from novel stimuli experienced as aversive, with failure to attend to subsequent stimuli. Therefore, there does not appear to be a mechanism in place that can assist in filtering out perceived aversive stimuli and reducing cortical arousal. Dawson and Levy (1989) further speculate that social processing, which is fraught with novelty, would be perceived by autistic individuals as extremely aversive and therefore would be avoided. Furthermore, the more control the autistic individual has over the novelty of the stimuli, the more likely he or she is to interact with it.

Neuropsychological Factors

On measures of executive control and frontal lobe function, children with autism have performed below expected levels (Bishop, 1993). Perseverative errors were noted high on the Wisconsin Card Sorting Task, and performance on the Tower of Hanoi was inefficient (Ozonoff, Pennington, & Rogers, 1990). The Tower of Hanoi was the single best predictor for discriminating normal from autistic children, although performance was impaired for children with Asperger's syndrome as well (Ozonoff, Pennington, & Rogers, 1991). Bishop (1993) suggests that frontal lobe and limbic systems are implicated in autism, although our understanding of the neurobiological nature of the disorder is still incomplete.

Neurochemical Factors

Mean levels of serotonin in autistic individuals have been found to be higher than normal (Anderson &

Hoshino, 1987), with approximately 40% having SE levels in the top 5% of the population. High levels of SE also have been found in cognitively retarded individuals.

Dopamine may also play a role in the expression of autistic behaviors. Autistic children have been found to have an elevated level of the DA marker, which has been linked to symptom severity (Garreau et al., 1980). Elevated levels of DA excretion also have been found in psychotic children.

Implications for Assessment

The DSM-IV (APA, 1994) provides separate diagnostic criteria for autistic disorders that are to be differentiated from Rett's disorder (more frequent in females), Childhood Disintegrative Disorders (two years of normal development), Asperger's disorder (language development is normal), and Pervasive Developmental Disorder (including atypical autism). Cook and Leventhal (1992) indicate that assessment may include the following: Autism Diagnostic Interview (Le Couteur, Rutter, Cord, et al., 1989); Childhood Autism Rating Scale (Mesibov, Schoper, Schaeffer, et al., 1989); and Autism Diagnostic Observation Schedule (Lord, Rutter, Goode, et al., 1989).

Intellectual assessment will be helpful in identifying the nature of verbal and visual-spatial strengths and weaknesses. Verbal fluency, language comprehension, and word knowledge should also be assessed. Measures of frontal lobe function (e.g., WCST and Tower of Hanoi) may yield important information.

Implications for Intervention

Psychopharmacological Treatment

Interventions for children with autism often are similar to programs for children with cognitive retardation, although Cook and Leventhal (1992) recommend employing intervention techniques to reduce stereotypic behaviors and to improve communication skills. Medication to reduce anxiety and compulsive behaviors includes anticonvulsants, stimulants, neuroleptics, fluoxetine and clomipramine, fenfluramine, and most recently opiate antagonists. Stimulants, lithium, and megavitamin therapy have not been found to be helpful (Aman, 1982; Campbell et al., 1972; Gualteri, Evans, & Patterson, 1987). Neuroleptics have been found to be most useful for reducing severe aggressive and self-injurious behaviors (Cohen et al., 1980; Dalldorf & Schopler, 1981).

Unfortunately the side effects of these medications can be severe (Dawson & Castelloe, 1995). Fenfluramine, a serotonin reducer, has been found to have good effects early on autistic symptoms, but this response diminishes with time and an increase in dosage has been found to be only moderately helpful (Holm & Varley, 1989). The newest type of psychopharmacological intervention is the use of opiate receptor antagonists such as naloxone or naltreione. Opiate receptor antagonists do not allow the postsynaptic receptors to absorb the brain endorphins. Beginning evidence shows that low doses of this agent have reduced many maladaptive behaviors while high doses improve the child's ability to relate to others (Campbell et al., 1988).

Behavioral Treatments

Behavioral interventions have been most successful with autistic children, although the long-term prognosis for children with this disorder is guarded. In the current view, some behaviors seen in autistic children–self-stimulation, self-injury, and aggression–are seen as attempts by the child to communicate with the outside world (Donnellan, Mirenda, Mesaros, & Fassbender, 1984). Behavioral techniques are used to teach the child alternative communication methods. These techniques also have been used to improve language skills, imitative abilities, and play skills (Lovaas, 1987; Koegel, Firestone, Kremme, & Dunlap, 1974).

Psychoeducational strategies have also utilized behaviorally based paradigms. Programs that have been successful stress early intervention, predictability and structure, and parent involvement (Schopler, Mesibov, Shigley, & Bashford, 1984; Simeonsson, Olley, & Rosenthal, 1987; Strain, Jamieson, & Hoyson, 1985). For example, an innovative program

by Strain and colleagues (Strain et al., 1985) utilizes typically developing children to facilitate social interactions with autistic children. Preliminary results from this program following a two-year involvement showed increases in motor, academic, and play skills, as well as an increase in social interactions.

Language and Communication Interventions

These interventions emphasize the need to teach preverbal skills as a necessary foundation for spoken language. Some of the preverbal skills necessary for intensive training are communicative intent (Prizant & Wetherby, 1987) and turn-taking (Dawson & Galpert, 1986). In addition, the teaching of these skills have been found to be facilitated by treatment occurring in naturalistic settings (Carr, 1985; Koegel & Johnson, 1989).

Motivational aspects have been found to be very important and when combined with traditional language training approaches, have been successful in improving generalization of language ability (Koegel & Johnson, 1989). Autistic children's language skills are found to improve with age, as well as their social interactions with adults (Baltaxe & Simmons, 1983) but not with peers (Attwood, Firth, & Hermelin, 1988).

Conclusion

The etiology, effective psychopharmacological treatments, and productive educational interventions for autism are currently being developed and researched. Much is unknown about this disorder, but gains are being made in our understanding. It is likely that a transactional approach, utilizing neurological/neuropsychological knowledge of this disorder in conjunction with work with the child's two major environments, namely home and school, will be most effective. Evidence of an exquisite sensitivity to environmental stimulation has led to a new understanding of the autistic child's behavior and language skills.

Effective pharmacological treatment continues to elude practitioners, and additional work is needed in that regard. Researchers are beginning to develop programs across the life span for individuals with autism, and promising vocationally based programs have been started for adolescents and adults (see VanBourgondiem & Mesibov, 1989).

ASPERGER'S SYNDROME

Asperger's disorder is characterized by significant and chronic impairment of social interaction and/or repetitive patterns of behavior (APA, 1994). Asperger's differs from autism in that language impairment is not present, and speech and cognitive developmental may be age-appropriate. Self-help skills are adequate, although school, occupational, and social attainment is often compromised.

Prevalence rates vary depending on the study, but estimates have suggested that Asperger is a rare disorder occurring in approximately 0.26% of the population (Gillberg & Gillberg, 1989). Using a comprehensive two-stage evaluation process, Ehlers and Gillberg (1993) found higher rates in children between the ages of 7 and 16 years (0.71% of the population), and of the children who were identified, 0.97% were males and 0.44% were females. See the following discussion for more details about a possible assessment battery for diagnosing Asperger syndrome.

Characteristics of Asperger's Syndrome

Children with Asperger's syndrome often are described as having flat affect and dull, monotonous speech patterns (Asperger, 1944). Social interactions are impaired, with little reciprocity. Generally, children with Asperger syndrome show a lack of interest in others and appear to lack empathy. Individuals may appear apathetic and withdrawn, and nonverbal interactions (e.g., eye contact, facial expressions and gestures) are impaired. Stereotypic behaviors, where body movements (e.g., hand flapping, twisting), and preoccupation with objects or idiosyncratic interests are present.

Asperger syndrome often appears before the age of 4 years (Comings, 1990), and the developmental course suggests a chronic, lifelong disturbance. Many of the behaviors displayed by children with Asperger are similar to TS symptoms, and TS may develop with age (Comings, 1990). Associated features include resistance to change, good rote memory, and obsessive-compulsive rituals.

Implications for Assessment

At present, there is no general agreeement on diagnostic characteristics (Ehlers & Gillberg, 1993; Szatmari, 1991). Gillberg and Gillberg (1989) suggest using a two-tiered assessment approach. Stage 1 includes screening for social impairment, narrowness of interests, presence of repetitive routines, speech and language problems, nonverbal communication difficulties, and motor difficulties. Stage 2 involves a more comprehensive assessment employing reports from the child's parents and teachers.

Clinicians should rule out Autism, Pervasive Developmental Disorder, Schizophrenia, Obsessive Compulsive Disorder, and other dissociative or schizoid disorders (APA, 1994). Behavioral and psychosocial evaluations may be the primary focus, with a qualitative analysis of the child's social interactions and interests. High-functioning children with Asperger's syndrome may be difficult to differentiate from children with TS (Comings, 1990). Ehlers and Gillberg (1993) also suggest including neuropsycholgical (e.g., the Token Test and a neurolinguistic test), intelligence, language, and neuropsychiatric measures (e.g., parent/teacher interviews and rating scales).

Implications for Interventions

Interventions for children with Asperger syndrome often focus on reducing bizarre and stereotypic behaviors. Medication may be warranted, particularly if obsessive-compulsive, attentional, or Tourette-like symptoms are present. Individuals with Asperger syndrome can be intellectually capable and, depending on their degree of social isolation, may lead semi-independent lives. Even in these individuals, however, social withdrawal and isolation often remain.

ATTENTION DEFICIT HYPERACTIVITY DISORDER

Attention Deficit Hyperactivity Disorder (ADHD) has been conceptualized as a disorder involving disturbances in attention span, self-regulation, activity level, and impulse control. ADHD includes symptoms of poor attention to task, impulsive behavior, motoric overactivity, and an inability to consider consequences of behaviors. As a heterogeneous disorder, ADHD is thought to affect between 3% and 5% of the school population (Barkley, 1989). The disorder has been found to persist into adulthood and has been linked to psychopathology in later life (Gittelman, Mannuzza, Shenker, & Bonagura, 1985; Weiss & Hechtman, 1986, 1993).

The literature on attention deficit disorder in childhood is replete with contradictions. Confusion is present in the diagnosis, behavioral characteristics, and etiology for this disorder. Over the past 45 years, attention deficit disorder has been variously termed minimal brain damage; hyperkinetic syndrome; hyperkinetic reaction in childhood; attention deficit disorder with and without hyperactivity; attention deficit hyperactivity disorder (Barkley, 1990); and, finally, attention deficit hyperactivity disorder predominantly inattentive, predominantly overactive, and combined (APA, 1994).

Inhibition difficulties are particularly important for the understanding of ADHD. An inability to delay a response long enough to evaluate various alternative behaviors makes it difficult to learn new behaviors or to develop compensatory skills. Children with ADHD often have difficulty delaying their responses to environmental stimuli. They have also been found not to respond readily to environmental feedback concerning their behavior (Douglas, 1983). This inability to utilize feedback may be grounded in difficulty in inhibiting their responses long enough to profit from this feedback.

Neuropsychological Correlates

Given the heterogeneity of attention deficit disorder, it is not surprising that there have been 11 different neuroanatomically based theories about the underlying causes (Zametkin & Rapaport, 1986). These various formulations include hypotheses ranging from dysfunctional diencephalic (thalamus, hypothalamus) structures (Laufer & Denhoff, 1957), decreased reticular activating system excitation (Wender, 1974), and deficient forebrain inhibition (Dykman, Ackerman, Clements, & Peterson, 1971). Depending on how the ADHD pie was sliced, different behavioral characteristics, neurological underpinnings, and treatment choices could be made. In this way ADHD became like the proverbial elephant being described by the blind man. Whatever characteristic was salient (whether attention or activity level) became a definition for this disorder. These difficulties are now being resolved as research continues to develop our understanding of this complex disorder. Further discussion of the neuroanatomical correlates of ADHD can be found in Chapter 4.

The experimental literature strongly suggests that ADHD encompasses clinically meaningful and distinct subtypes. A large number of factor-analytic studies using a variety of scales with diverse samples to describe ADHD symptoms consistently indicate two largely independent dimensions: (1) symptoms describing motor hyperactivity and (2) symptoms describing inattention (Frick & Lahey, 1991; Lahey et al., 1988). These dimensions may also be thought of in terms of inhibitory systems. Motor hyperactivity can be conceptualized as difficulty with motor inhibition, which is thought to be a task mediated by the frontal and prefrontal regions of the brain. Inattention may be viewed as interference sensitivity. Interference sensitivity involves difficulty in filtering out extraneous stimulation, which is the mechanism involved in sustained and divided attention.

Interference sensitivity likely corresponds to the classification of Attention Deficit Disorder without Hyperactivity (ADD), and motor inhibition relates to the diagnosis of Attention Deficit Disorder with Hyperactivity (ADD/H). The subtypes probably also differ in facets other than the presence or absence of motoric activity. In fact, there are likely differences in attention processing for the subtype. Inconsistent differences have been found between ADD/H and

ADD/noH on neuropsychological measures. ADD/H have been found to have longer reaction time than ADD/noH or control children (Hynd et al., 1988; Sargeant & Scholten, 1985a, 1985b) and more difficulty in completing finger sequential tasks and frontal lobe tasks than ADD/noH, whereas ADD/noH children were found to have deficiencies in perceptual-motor tasks (Barkley, 1996); and ADD/noH were found to have a cognitively sluggish style versus impulsive and sloppy responding by ADD/H (Hart, Lahey, Loeber, & Hanson, 1990; Healy et al., 1987).

Attention is complex and multifaceted. It is made up of multiple processes/components that interact with motor, cognitive, and social development (Sohlberg & Mateer, 1989). Thus, disruption of any component may compromise the efficiency of the total system. Moreover, disruption of a component will have a negative impact on aspects lower in the hierarchical chain (i.e., ability to shift set may be disturbed and may consequently affect responses to temporally presented information or vigilance).

Mental control of attention may involve two distinct but interconnected pathways (Benson, 1991). *Basic mental control* refers to the level of general awareness that activates either increases or decreases in arousal (via midbrain reticular activating systems) and the ability to maintain attention in a fully alert state (via the posterior, inferior medial areas of frontal lobes). *Higher mental control* refers to the ability of the executive function to monitor and regulate widely distributed networks of complex operations, such as motor activity, motivation, and abstract thinking (via the prefrontal lobes).

Because attentional processes are widely distributed throughout many brain structures, the ability to select, sustain, and control attention may involve the ability to access and direct resources on both sides of the brain (Colby, 1991). When a stimulus is highlighted for potential action, a competition among responses may occur that requires the mutual inhibitory interaction of structures on opposite sides of the brain that are responsible for directing attention. This interhemispheric regulation may be compromised in children with ADHD (Hynd, Semrud-Clikeman, Lorys, Novey, Eliopulos, & Lyytinen, 1991).

Stress on the attentional system occurs when there is conflict between signals. Activating any of the components of attention involves the conscious processing of input with some mental operations while preventing access of other signals to those same levels of processing (Posner, 1988). Even simple cognitive tasks involve the orchestration of a network of brain areas. It is likely that a breakdown in the processing of temporal information would have an impact on classroom tasks, which often require bit-by-bit information processing as well as reconstruction of information into a whole. In line with these findings, children with ADHD have been found to experience difficulty in selective and sustained attention while not experiencing problems in orienting or reactive attention (Douglas & Peters, 1979; Porges, Walter, Korb, & Sprague, 1975; Sykes, Douglas, & Morgenstern, 1973; Sykes, Douglas, Weiss, & Minde, 1971).

Barkley (1994) presents a transactional approach to understanding the underlying mechanisms in ADHD. He suggests that measures of attention need to assess the interrelationship between the environment the child is in and his or her behavior. Further, there is a functional relationship between the behavior and the environment; that is, each influences the other. Thus, in his view, attentional problems are deficits in facilitating, sustaining, or disengaging these behaviors in relation to the environment. Moreover, attention involves rules and instructions that are associated with the task either explicitly or implicitly. Given that ADHD children have been consistently found to be contingency-governed, the rules inherent in tasks are not effective in interventions with them.

Differences in subtypes of ADHD have been suggested by Barkley (1994) and Denckla (1994). Children with ADD: Combined Type show poor sustained attention, with improved response to novel stimulation. Those with ADHD: Inattentive Type show problems in focused attention, and this appears to be more of a cognitively driven (as opposed to behavioral) disorder.

Behavioral Inhibition

Behavioral disinhibition or the inability to control and direct attention to the demands of a task is central to ADHD (Loge, Staton, & Beatty, 1990). In fact, attention problems may be secondary to a disorder of behavioral regulation and inhibition, and poor regulation with inhibition of behavior, rather than inattention, may be the hallmark of ADHD (Barkley, 1990). The term *distractibility* is often used to describe a deficit in *focused attention* pr an inability to focus attention (Mirsky, 1987; Posner & Boies, 1971). Brain structures in Luria's first functional unit, the reticular formation, control basic alertness and attention, with higher functions of disinhibition controlled by the network of connections to the upper brain or cortex. Focused attention is thought to be one of the first aspects of attention to develop.

Research on distractibility has found ADHD children to be no more distractible than normal children (Barkley, 1990). Instead, the problem appears to be one of declining persistence or effort in responding to tasks that have little intrinsic appeal or minimal immediate consequences for completion. When alternative activities are available that promise immediate reinforcement or gratification, children with ADHD may appear distracted because their attention shifts off task in order to engage in the more rewarding competing activity. Thus, the problem may be one of disinhibition rather than distraction. The child with ADHD is capable of orienting to specific stimuli but unable to resist or disinhibit responses to competing stimuli that appear more interesting and reinforcing.

Disinhibition of response to extraneous stimulation is also implicated in the second component of attention to develop: *sustained attention,* or the ability to maintain a behavioral response for a continuous or repetitive activity. *Vigilance* is the term often used to describe this type of attention. This component of attention is most easily measured using a continuous performance test and K-ABC hand movements. Difficulties with maintaining attention while resisting other impulses indicate that there may be a basic problem at the arousal level within Luria's first functional level and may explain why the use of stimulants helps attention, because stimulants may raise the level of basic arousal to within a normal range.

Sustained attention for more complex tasks is probably controlled in later development by the fron-

tal lobes, which regulate behavior. Because the frontal lobes are the last areas of the brain to develop fully, it may be that hyperactive symptoms are due in part to a significant maturational lag in the development of the inhibitory mechanisms of motor responses controlled by the frontal lobes (Becker, Isaac, & Hynd, 1987; Passler, Isaac, & Hynd, 1985). Suggestion that these regions are at least partially compromised has been found in the perfusion studies of Lou et al. (1984, 1989) and the metabolism studies of Zametkin et al. (1990), where hypometabolism has been found in striatal areas believed to control motor activity.

Selective attention is a complex behavior that requires the maintenance of a response involving activation or inhibition of another response. These filtering mechanisms, which are necessary to block out or attend to input, probably involve maintaining arousal of the first functional unit as well as the information-processing capacity of the primary and secondary zones of the second functional unit. This component of attention is most easily measured using cancellation tasks, the Stroop, and the Trails tests.

Dysfunction in selective attention would certainly compromise academic achievement, especially when the information presented is complex and of some length, requiring both sustained attention and information processing simultaneously. This area is also thought to be implicated in sensory localization. When the symptoms of cognitive sluggishness, confusion, hypoactivity, and anxiety are displayed, finger agnosia on the left side was found with ADD/noH and may relate to difficulties in selective attention (Goodyear & Hynd, 1992; Lorys, Hynd, & Lahey, 1990).

There is support for the hypothesis that children with ADD/H may have difficulties in sustained attention while selective attention is related to ADD/noH. Trommer, Hoeppner, Lorber, and Armstrong (1988) found significant differences between the ADD subtypes in impulse control. ADD/noH children were as impulsive as ADD/H children on a choice task in the initial portion of the task. However, ADD/noH children displayed significant improvement as training continued, while ADD/H showed no lessening of impulsivity. Similarly, ADD/noH have exhibited slower rates of processing speed and more difficulties in selective attention than children with ADD/H (Barkley, Fischer, Edelbrock, & Smallish, 1990; Sargeant & Scholten, 1985b).

The most complex forms of attention are *alternating attention* and *divided attention*. Both of these involve the ability to time-share mental operations when there is competition for attention. Alternating attention includes measures such as the WSCT and the Category test. There is no current measure for divided attention. These functions are highly dependent on the executive functioning of Luria's third unit to organize and orchestrate the associated complex responses. Dysfunction at the executive level would be seen in diminished complex problem-solving strategies, organizational skills, and less efficient memory strategies characteristic of ADHD children (Barkley, 1990). The impact of executive control dysfunction has profound effects on the child's overall adjustment and may be more devastating than effects of overactivity or inattention. This line of research may provide a better understanding of ADHD and warrants further inquiry.

Transactional Model of ADHD

Our conceptual model of ADHD is transactional in nature, where neuropsychological dysfunction arises from genetic factors and/or temperamental variations. While prenatal or postnatal insult may result in ADHD characteristics, environmental factors are not considered causal. See Table 6.4 for an overview of the interactional nature of ADHD.

Neuropsychological tests that measure complex problem solving, response inhibition, and sustained effort believed to be primarily frontal lobe functions are more likely than other tests to reveal differences between children with ADHD and normal children (Chelune et al., 1986). Given the complexity of the third unit, it may well be that the neuroanatomic analysis will not provide insight into ADHD. The use of SPECT and PET may eventually provide answers about the mechanisms involved, and it is likely that differences will be at the neuronal and metabolic substrates rather than at the gross anatomical level.

In addition to interhemispheric disinhibition, frontal lobe inhibitory mechanisms are also believed to play a role in ADHD (Chelune et al., 1986). The prefrontal regions of the frontal lobes have a rich network of reciprocal pathways with the reticular formation and diencephalic structures that regulate arousal and the ability to suppress responses to stimuli that are not task-relevant. The failure of children with ADHD to inhibit inappropriate responses and sustain goal-directed behavior may be due to their inability to suppress and control higher level inhibitory cortical reflexes. This theory would support age-related changes in some of the symptoms of ADHD children as they grow up. During adolescence, many of the hyperactive symptoms diminish in intensity, and the teenager seems to have calmed down (Mendelson, Johnson, & Stewart, 1971; Minde et al., 1971; Weiss, Kruger, Danielson, & Elman, 1975). However, this does not completely explain the fact that although the primary symptom of hyperactivity may diminish, many of the secondary symptoms persist and cause increasingly greater difficulty for the adolescent (Fischer, Barkley, Edelbrock, & Smallish, 1990).

Genetic Factors

A family history of ADHD has been found to be four times more common for children with ADHD than for a sample of normal controls (Cantwell, 1975). Biederman et al. (1990) found that the first degree relatives of children with ADHD not only have an increased incidence of ADHD but also are more likely to have members diagnosed with antisocial or mood disorders. Lahey et al. (1988) found a higher rate of parental psychopathology in the fathers of children with ADHD. Frick et al. (1992) found that 80% of their sample of children with ADHD had at least one first-degree biological relative who had ADHD as a child. Although it is likely that a form of genetic transmission for this disorder is present, this hypothesis is speculative at this time. It is presently unclear whether the familial association is genetic, psychosocial, or both in nature. Further study is needed to separate out genetic factors from environmental and familial difficulties.

Table 6.4. A Summary of Specific Deficits Associated with Attention Deficit Hyperactivity Disorder (ADHD)

Biogenetic Factors
— 59%—84% MZ
— 33%—29% DZ
— Independent genetic code differs from reading
— Familial ADD transmitted single gene
— Single gene has not been isolated; probably domapamine receptor gene

Environmental Factors/Prenatal/Postnatal
— Multifactorial, polygenetic, cultural, and environmental transmission seem unlikely
— Poverty, overcrowding, chaotic family style, pollution, food additives account for very little variance
— Common environmental factors: 0—30% variance

Temperament
— Genetic linkage
 • Activity level
 • Distractibility
 • Psychomotor activity
 • Attentional problems, school competence, and behavioral problems

Birth Complications
— No known correlates

CNS Factors
— Underactivated frontal lobe
— Bilaterally smaller anterior cortex
— Reversed asymmetry of anterior cortex (right < left)
— Reversed asymmetry of caudate nucleus (left < right)
— Reduced metabolic activity in right caudate region
— Smaller left caudate nucleus
— Right-hemisphere deficits (disinhibition of left hemisphere)
— Left-hemisphere underactivation
— Genu (corpus callosum) smaller
— Rostrum and rostral bodies smaller

Intellectual
— Range of IQ
— Low coding

Perceptual

Memory
— Low verbal
— Less efficient

Attentional
— Sustained
— Selective
— Alternatiting/divided

Reasoning
— Response inhibition
— Sustained effort
— Complex problem solving
— Executive functions
— Organizational skills

Academic/Behavioral
— Motivational problems
— Underachievers
— Comorbid LD
— Work completion

Psychosocial
— Rejected
— Ignored
— Comorbid INT/EXT
— Comorbid aggression

Family
— Disorder exacerbates
— Parental psychopathology
— Related to CD/ADHD

Note: DZ = dyzgotic; MZ = monzygotic; INT = internalized disorders; EXT = externalized disorders; LD = learning disabilities; CD = conduct disorders; ADHD = attention deficit hyperactivity disorder.

Family Factors

Given that a higher incidence of parental psychopathology is present in families of children with ADHD, it may well be that a chaotic and/or conflictual family environment exacerbates or increases the signs of this disorder. Some researchers have found that psychiatric difficulties in the parents of these children are related more to the child's conduct problems than to the ADHD (Frick et al., 1990; Stewart, deBlois, & Cummings, 1980).

Just as ADHD children have negative interactions with their peers, they also experience similar difficulties in the home environment. Dysfunctional interaction patterns have been found in families with ADHD children, with these parents frequently engaging in highly directive, controlling, and negative interactions with their child. Fewer incidences of reward and responsivity to the child's needs has also been found (Befera & Barkley, 1985; Mash & Johnston, 1982). Moreover, these interactions have been found to improve when the child begins medication and parent—child relationships improve (Barkley, Karlsson, Strzeleck, & Murphy, 1984). Therefore, while the symptoms of ADHD appear to be improved or worsened depending on environmental factors as well as by adding psychopharmocotherapy (Horn & Ialongo, 1988), the disorder is most likely neurologically based (Frick & Lahey, 1991).

Intellectual, Perceptual, Attention, and Memory Functioning

Qualitative differences in cognitive processing deficits and in types of attentional difficulties were also suggested in the Barkley, DuPaul, and McMurray study (1991). Children with ADD/noH had fewer problems with off-task behavior during a vigilance task, performed worse on the Coding subtest of the WISC-R, and had greater problems on a measure of consistent retrieval of verbal information from memory than children with ADD/H.

Other studies have not found differences between these subtypes on measures of achievement, cognitive skills, or verbal learning skills (Carlson, Lahey, & Neeper, 1986; Conte, Kinsbourne, Swanson, Zirk, & Samuels, 1986). However, many of these studies have not controlled for conduct disorder/oppositional disorder or learning disabilities, nor have they separately evaluated children who respond differentially to treatment–namely, children who are treatment resistant versus those who respond to treatment.

The emerging behavioral/cognitive profile indicates that children with ADD/noH may have more of a problem with the information-processing component of attention, speed of cognitive processing, and mental preoccupation. They are exquisitely sensitive to environmental interference. In contrast, children with ADD/H may possess more of a deficit in sustained attention and the disinhibition component of attention. They are unable to inhibit their motoric behavior, which in turn negatively correlates with maintaining attention to task.

Children with ADD/H evidenced problems with behavioral organization and disinhibition, whereas those with ADD/noH demonstrated a slow cognitive tempo and inwardly directed attention problems. Thus, a different cognitive and attentional pattern is suggested for children with ADD/H and those with ADD/noH.

Studies using teacher ratings of DSM-III symptoms for clinic-referred and nonreferred samples isolate two factors in both samples in diagnosing ADHD (Hart et al., 1994; Lahey et al., 1988). These studies identified inattention and hyperactivity as the factors, with impulse control items being split between the two factors. Disorganization and need for adult supervision were related to the attention factor while items dealing with an impulsive tempo were associated with the hyperactivity factor.

Academic and School Adjustment

ADD/noH children more often show difficulty with social isolation and nonverbal reasoning than do ADD/H children who, in turn, tend to be more frequently socially rejected and have a higher incidence of oppositional defiant disorder/conduct disorder than ADD/noH (Cantwell & Baker, 1988; Hynd et al., 1989; Lahey et al., 1987). When children with ADD/H have significant conduct problems, they also appear to be at higher risk for learning problems and poorer information-processing ability (Semrud-Clikeman, Hynd, Lorys, & Lahey, 1993).

Barkley et al. (1991) reported several differences that distinguished children with ADD/H from children with ADD/noH. Children with ADD/H were rated by their parents and teachers as more aggressive and antisocial than children with ADD/noH. Children with ADD/H had been suspended from school more frequently and were more likely to have been placed in special education programs for children with behavior disorders. They were described as more noisy, disruptive, messy, irresponsible, and immature. Families of children with ADD/H exhibited more substance abuse and aggression compared with families of children with ADD/noH.

In contrast, children with ADD/noH displayed a different behavioral profile (Barkley et al., 1991). They showed less aggression, impulsivity, and overactivity, both at home and at school, and less situational pervasiveness of their behavioral problems as rated by parents and teachers; they were more likely to be ignored rather than rejected as were the ADD/H children. Moreover, children with ADD/noH were rated as more confused, daydreamy or lost in thought, apathetic, and lethargic. Families of children with ADD/noH were more likely to have anxiety disorders and learning problems compared to families of children with ADD/H.

Implications for Assessment

Objective assessment of attention and behavioral disinhibition may have inherent difficulties with ecological validity; that is, many tasks may not be demanding enough to tax the attentional system. Often the tasks utilized are initially interesting, last only a few minutes, and are administered under direct adult supervision. To measure the component of sustained attention accurately, for example, the tasks must be of sufficient length and repetition to ensure potential boredom. In addition, adult supervision must not be seen as a discriminating stimulus to remain on task. These findings suggest that neuropsychological tasks should not be used alone to diagnose ADHD; however, such tasks may be useful in describing the cognitive and neuropsychological functioning of a subgroup of ADHD (Schaughency & Rothlind, 1991).

Denckla (1994) suggests that assessment of attention and executive functions need tasks that provide a delay between stimulus and response, require an internally represented view of the task, require response inhibition and efficiency of response, and require active and flexible strategies for solutions. All of these aspects need not be present, but the majority should be for a complete assessment of attentional-executive functions.

The role of frontal dysfunction in ADHD continues to be widely discussed (Benson, 1991). Beyond the neuroanatomical findings of possible frontal involvement in ADHD, recent research has suggested that children diagnosed with ADHD display neurological deficits with greater consistency on tests evaluating neuropsychological functions mediated by the frontal and prefrontal cortex (Hynd, Voeller, Hern, & Marshall, 1991). The frontal lobes are important in the regulation of motor output and in the organization and management of behavior, such as developing plans, allocating resources, and inhibiting behaviors that interfere with goal achievement. An individual suffering frontal disturbance may have totally normal basal-posterior functions, including normal or even high intelligence, but be unable to use these abilities effectively.

Chelune et al. (1986) found that subjects with attention deficits were impaired in the Wisconsin Card Sorting Task (WCST). The WCST, which requires sustained attention, cognitive flexibility, and regulation of goal-directed activity through the use of environmental feedback, is believed to reflect frontal lobe functioning (Heaton, 1981). Chelune et al. (1986) suggest that the WCST may be assessing disinhibition and not hyperactivity or attentional deficits. Other studies (Fischer et al., 1990; Loge et al., 1990) failed to find any differences in performances on sorting and verbal fluency tasks. Reports from other measures, such as the Stroop Test, also have been inconsistent in finding differences between subjects with ADHD and normal controls. These inconsistent results may be a function of the use of varying ADHD subtypes, failure to control for co-occurrence of comorbid disorder, or severity of ADHD. Each of these factors may influence the subject's performance on the WCST.

A study utilizing attentional components training found significant improvement in posttraining information processing in an ADHD sample. This improvement generalized from test materials to classroom materials and was maintained at a 90-day post-test (Williams, 1989). In this unpublished dissertation, however, these subjects were also learning-disabled. Therefore, it is not clear whether the effects of the attentional training were due to the learning problems or to the attentional difficulties.

On a continuous-performance test developed by Gordon (1987), hyperactive subjects showed significantly poorer sustained attention and impulse control on the vigilance task but not on the distractibility task (Fischer et al., 1990). These results suggest that tasks presumed to reflect attention that are relatively short in length and administered under direct adult supervision may not be measuring the problems that children with attentional difficulties experience when tasks are tedious and not directly supervised.

More complicated tasks pose greater demands for planning, organization, and executive regulation of behavior. Children with ADHD display fewer attentional or behavior problems in novel or unfamiliar settings or when tasks are unusually different, colorful, or highly stimulating (Barkley, 1990). Symptoms of ADHD are noticeable when the demands of the environment or the task exceed the child's capacity to sustain attention, regulate activity, and/or restrain impulses. Examples of this poor regulation and inhibition of behavior include responding quickly to situations without understanding what is required, failing to consider consequences, having difficulty waiting one's turn, and seeking immediate gratification or rewards that require less work to achieve rather than working toward a long-term goal and a larger reward. Thus, poor inhibition and regulation of behavior may appear as an attention deficit but is explained more clearly as a dysfunction of behavioral inhibition. This complex interplay of attention, behavioral inhibition, motivation, overactivity, and brain maturation needs to be addressed in treatment of ADHD children.

In addition to attentional difficulties in ADHD, recent studies have supported a hypothesis of a generalized self-regulatory deficit that affects information processing, inhibition of responses, arousal/alertness, planning, executive functions, metacognition, and self-monitoring abilities that span the various sensory modalities (Douglas, Barr, O'Neill, & Britton, 1988). An inability to inhibit excess behavior and stimulation has a negative impact on the child's ability to learn in the classroom not only in terms of negative classroom behavior but also in terms of impacting on attentional resources. Because attention is not directed, the child takes in irrelevant as well as relevant detail. Thus, an interaction between inattention and disinhibition would have a negative impact on information processing and thus on school achievement.

These deficits may also be dependent on the situation the child faces. For children with ADHD, attentional problems become more evident in situations where attention is required to be sustained on a repeated task (Milich, Loney, & Landau, 1982) or in structured situations (Porrino et al., 1983). Moreover, on tasks that are novel or when behavioral consequences are immediate, children with ADHD show great ability to contain attentional problems (Douglas, 1983). Some suggest that the primary difference in ADHD children may not be in attention but in the way the child's behavior is regulated by consequences (Barkley, 1989; Frick & Lahey, 1991). Other investigators suggest that children whose hyperactivity is "pervasive" across situations have a poorer prognosis, more comorbid diagnoses, and more differences in neurodevelopment than children with "situational" hyperactivity (Rutter, 1983a). There may also be differences in how children with ADD/H and ADD/noH respond to consequences and to their environment. All of these areas deserve further empirical investigation.

Children with ADHD frequently have been found to experience concomitant learning difficulties (Lambert & Sandoval, 1980; Semrud-Clikeman, Biederman, et al., 1992). A review of the literature by Semrud-Clikeman, Biederman, et al. (1992) found that 30% of children with ADHD also have learning disabilities while another 25% to 35% have learning delays. The extent of learning difficulties found in over 50% of the ADHD population may relate not only to attentional problems but also to the self-regulatory deficit proposed by Douglas et al. (1988). If children with ADHD cannot learn to plan, organize, and evaluate their learning (i.e., metacognitive skills), it is likely that they will experience significantly more problems performing academically as they develop, since most of their educational experiences after grade 3 will require independent work skills. Moreover, if, as Sohlberg and Mateer (1989) propose, attentional resources are hierarchical, then difficulties with selective or sustained attention may predispose a child to self-regulatory deficits. Thus, regulation of self and others and attention are not dichotomous characteristics of ADHD. It is reasonable to speculate that regulation and attention may be inextricably interrelated and mutually reciprocal.

Thus, a child who is motorically active may not necessarily show significant attentional problems or learning deficits once the overactivity is controlled. These children respond readily to medication and may be the children who are later found to "outgrow" their hyperactivity. Conversely, a child who has attentional and self-regulatory deficits may respond partially to medication but often will continue to have learning difficulties and require additional support (Barkley, 1990). It is these children who may need continuing support throughout life (Weiss & Hechtman, 1986, 1993).

Tasks that have been found to be sensitive to frontal lobe functioning (i.e., executive function deficits) include perseveration score on the WCST, Tower of Hanoi and London, Go/No-Go tasks, motor sequencing, and continuous-performance tests. These tasks require either flexible problem solving (WCST, Tower of Hanoi or London) or response inhibition (continuous performance test, Go/No-go).

Developmental Contributions

Barkley et al. (1991) found that several of the attentional measures demonstrated significant changes within both hyperactive and control subjects as a function of the age groupings (12—14 years versus 15—20 years). Older adolescents made fewer errors of omission on the distractibility task and exhibited less off-task behavior than did younger adolescents, suggesting that sustained attention continues to improve across these age levels of development. Older adolescents improved in the inhibition and regulation of activity (reflected in significantly less fidgeting, vo-

calizing, playing with objects, and out-of-seat behaviors during independent performance of math problems) and were significantly better at abstract problem-solving skills as assessed by the WCST. To the extent that these measures reflect neuropsychological functions mediated by the frontal lobes, these results suggest that the maturation of frontal lobe functions continues well into late adolescence and are consistent with patterns of neuroanatomical maturation of these brain regions.

Age. Differences in age at diagnosis differ between ADD/H and ADD/noH children. ADD/H children are generally identified approximately 6 months younger than ADD/noH children (Lahey, Schaughency, Hynd, Carlson, & Nieves, 1987). This finding suggests that ADD/H children may be identified younger than ADD/noH because their behaviors are more noticeable and more disturbing for parents and teachers.

Gender. Gender also plays a part in identification in that most of the ADHD population is male. However, studies that have not utilized clinic-referred children, have found more females with ADHD than did studies with referred subjects (Berry, Shaywitz, & Shaywitz, 1985; Lahey, Schaughency, Frame, & Strauss, 1985). There may well be an under-identification of girls with ADHD, and currently it is unknown if girls are more likely to show ADD/H or ADD/noH than males. This area of interest requires further evaluation.

Therefore, an assessment of a child for possible ADHD needs to be multifaceted and take into consideration developmental, familial, and environmental variables. It is important not only to assess whether an attentional difficulty exists, but also to determine the extent to which it impairs the child's functioning. Such impairment needs to be present in two or more of the child's environments and should be significant enough to cause difficulties (APA, 1994).

Implications for Treatment

Reviews of the literature suggest that the most efficacious understanding of ADHD would combine educational, medical, and environmental components (Conners & Wells, 1986). Although teachers and parents struggle daily with the behaviors associated with ADHD, its treatment has historically been medically based. Double-blind medication trials have found improvement for 70% to 90% of ADHD children (Barkley, 1977; Conners & Werry, 1979; Pelham, 1993a). Moreover, medication shows differential results with ADD/H and ADD/noH children. Both groups respond to stimulant drugs, but dosage differs between the groups (Barkley et al., 1991; Dykman, Ackerman, & McGray, 1980) and there are fewer nonresponders among the ADD/H group (Barkley et al., 1991).

In conjunction with stimulant medications, the major targets of cognitive-behavioral intervention have been the child's poor attention span, lack of self-control, and noncompliance with authority figure directives (DuPaul, Stoner, Tilly, & Putnam, 1991). In any treatment paradigm, it is important to take into consideration the child's age and developmental level. In infancy and toddlerhood emphasis is recommended to be placed on building positive parent—child relationships (Teeter, 1991). Teeter (1991) suggests that a warm and responsive style coupled with flexibility would be the best parenting response to an infant and toddler with ADHD. As the child matures the parents need to develop effective parenting skills that utilize consistent limit setting and tying consequences to both appropriate and inappropriate behaviors. In addition work with children in developing appropriate social skills, self-control, and organization/problem-solving techniques needs to be started in elementary school and continued throughout the school experience (Abramowitz & O'Leary, 1991). In adolescence, additional instruction in social judgment, problem solving, and management of typical teen-age concerns, including substance abuse, sex, and peer pressure (Robin & Foster, 1989).

CONDUCT DISORDER

Aggressive behaviors that do not take into consideration the feelings of others and that can be dangerous and hurtful are becoming more visible in today's society. Individuals who display such behaviors often have a history of antisocial behavior stretching back into early childhood. Conduct disorder is defined as chronic and severe antisocial behaviors that include some combination of physical and verbal aggression, stealing, lying, and lack of feeling for other people (Short & Shapiro, 1993). These behaviors are frequent and severe and have an impact the child's academic and social functioning.

The diagnosis of conduct disorder appears to be stable across environments and informants (Patterson, 1986). It has been hypothesized that there are three major subtypes of conduct disorder: solitary aggressive, group, and undifferentiated (APA, 1994). The solitary aggressive type possesses aggressive behavior, poor self-control, and interpersonal difficulty (Quay, 1986b). The group type of conduct disorder includes children who engage in delinquent behaviors in a group context and has a more positive prognosis. Finally, the undifferentiated subtype includes a combination of the other two types.

Children with serious conduct disorder appear to evidence symptoms at a very early age, with the disorder developing into delinquency and antisocial behavior in adolescence and adulthood (Wolf, Braukmann, & Ramp, 1987). Wolf et al. (1987) suggest that severe conduct disorder runs in families and is treatment-resistant. Although the prognosis for conduct disorder is poor (Dumas, 1989; Loeber, 1990), only 50% of children with severe conduct disorder have been found to develop adult antisocial personality disorder (Kazdin, 1987; Robins, 1966). A family history of conduct disorder/antisocial personality disorder appears to be the most predictive variable for the course of conduct disorder (Tramontana & Hooper, 1989).

Incidence

The incidence of conduct disorder in the general population ranges from 3% to 7% (Costello, 1989). Conduct disorder has been found to be the most common reason for referral to mental health services (Wells & Forehand, 1985). Moreover, children with conduct disorder are heavily represented in school classrooms for children with behavioral disturbances (Epstein, Kaufman, & Cullinan, 1986; McGinnis & Forness, 1988; Pullis, 1991).

Gender

Conduct disorder may vary as a function of sex (Gilbert, 1957). Males are three times more likely to be diagnosed with conduct disorder than females (Graham, 1979). Sex differences are also present in the age of onset of conduct disorder, with males showing conduct problems at a much earlier age than girls (Robins, 1966). For example, the mean onset of symptoms for males was in the 8- to 10-year-old level, while for girls it was 14 to 16 years of age. The pattern of characteristics was also different, with boys showing aggression as a reason for referral while for girls it was sexual acting out.

Developmental Course

There is a high concordance between conduct problems in early childhood and these same difficulties in adolescence (Loeber, 1990; Rutter, 1983a). It has been suggested that there may be at least two differing expressions of conduct disorder (Patterson, DeBaryshe, & Ramsey, 1990). The first is that of the child who begins with oppositional behaviors in preschool and the elementary years and develops into aggressive behavior and lying and stealing in middle childhood, with significant behavioral difficulties in adolescence. The second pathway is that of the child who first evidences conduct problems in adolescence after a fairly normal childhood. The prognosis is poorer for the early starter than the later starter; further, oppositional defiant disorder in early childhood is considered a significant risk factor (White, Moffitt, Earls, & Robins, 1990).

Genetic Factors

It is likely that conduct disorder is the result of the interaction of several genetic correlates and environmental variables. Moreover, children with a genetic predisposition to conduct disorder have been hypoth-

esized to seek out situations that trigger aggressive behavior (Plomin, Chipuers, & Loehlin, 1990). Biederman and colleagues (Biederman, Munir, & Knee, 1987, Biederman et al., 1990) have found a relationship between parental antisocial personality disorder and childhood conduct disorder.

Twin studies have found a higher incidence and concordance of criminality and antisocial behavior among monozygotic than dizygotic twins (Christiansen, 1974; Cloninger, Christiansen, Reich, & Gottesman, 1978). Adoption studies of monozygotic and dizygotic twins have found that antisocial behavior occurs more frequently than would be expected by chance alone in those twins with a family history of conduct problems (Cadoret, 1978; Crowe, 1974). Moreover, these studies found that in cases where antisocial behavior is present in both adoptive and biological parents, the impact of the biological parents' influence is more pronounced (Mednick & Hutchings, 1978).

Kazdin (1991) suggests that the concordance of conduct disorder in twins from families with a history of antisocial personality disorder may point to the fact that while genetics plays some role in the development of this disorder, environment also contributes a significant amount of influence. For example, siblings of conduct-disordered children also are more frequently conduct-disordered than would be expected solely on the basis of genetic factors (Cloninger, Reich, & Guze, 1975). Particular contributions to conduct disorder are family characteristics such as marital discord, psychiatric dysfunction, discontinuous mothering, and substance abuse (Hutchings & Mednick, 1975). These studies suggest that there is an interplay of genetics and environment for the development of this disorder. These studies are just beginning to attempt to document the complex relationship between environmental and genetic influences on this disorder.

Family Factors

The most well documented related variable to conduct disorder is parent and family attributes and behaviors. Families of children with conduct disorder evidence considerable stress (McGee, Silva, & Williams, 1984; Patterson, 1982), with frequent substance abuse and criminal activity (West, 1982) and a higher incidence of familial psychopathology (Frick, Lahey, Christ, Loeber, & Green, 1991).

Particularly problematic in families with a history of conduct disorder are patterns of inconsistent and highly punitive child control procedures (Dumas, 1989; Loeber & Dishion, 1983). Similarly, these families very infrequently reinforce positive behaviors or evidence prosocial relationships (Dumas & Wahler, 1985). Therefore, the parent—child interactions are fraught with negative interactions and very few positive exchanges and are highly predictive of childhood conduct disorder (Pettit, Bates, & Dodge, 1993).

In addition to negative parent—child interactions, the families of children with conduct disorder are more likely to engage in substance abuse than are those of other children (Frick et al., 1992; Lahey, Piacentini, et al., 1987). These parents also have a higher incidence of antisocial personality disorder (Cadoret, Troughton, & O'Gorman, 1987). In studies designed to untangle the relationship between substance abuse, parental antisocial personality disorder, and childhood conduct disorder, parental substance abuse was not associated with criminality in children, while parental antisocial personality disorder was highly associated (Frick et al., 1992; McCord, 1991). Children with conduct disorder have been found to be more likely than control children to have parents with antisocial disorders (Faraone, Biederman, Keenan, & Tsuang, 1991; Frick et al., 1992; Lahey, Piacentini, et al., 1987). Finally, a study of adopted children found that these children's conduct problems were highly correlated with antisocial personality disorder in their biological parentage and not correlated with their adoptive family (Jarey & Stewart, 1985). Therefore, a specific relationship between parental antisocial personality disorder and conduct disorder has been documented and appears specific to this disorder.

Neuropsychological Correlates

Children with conduct disorder have not been found to differ from normal controls in perinatal develop-

ment except that they tend to be small for their gestational age (McGee et al., 1984). There are few studies of young conduct-disordered children. Most of the studies are related to older children. Given the high frequency of accidental head injury in this population (Pincus & Tucker, 1978), the neuropsychological profile of these children is confounded by these injuries.

Cognitive factors have been found to be related to conduct problems (Dodge, 1993). Children with conduct disorder have been found to have a negative response bias and to interpret even ambiguous stimuli as negative and hostile toward them (Dodge, Price, Bachorowski, & Newman, 1990). Difficulties with problem-solving skills, a rigid response style, and stereotyped responses to conflictual situations have frequently been found in children with conduct disorder (Short & Shapiro, 1993; Spivack, Platt, & Shure, 1976).

In a study designed to isolate neuropsychological correlates of frontal lobe dysfunction in two groups of adjudicated adolescents, Linz, Hooper, Hynd, Isaac, and Gibson (1990) did not find a profile of neuropsychological dysfunction to be diagnostic of conduct disorder. Some studies have found that verbal mediation does not appear to be as well developed in children with conduct disorder as in other children (Hare & Jutal, 1988; Raine, O'Brien, Smiley, Seerbo, & Chan, 1990). Similarly, Moffitt (1993) found deficits in verbal and auditory-verbal memory skills in conduct-disordered children compared to normal controls. In this study the children with conduct disorder scored more poorly on the Rey Auditory Verbal Learning Test; Verbal Fluency; and the WISC subtests of Information, Similarities, Arithmetic, and Vocabulary. Tramontana and Hooper (1989) suggest that this difficulty in language may translate into impulsive acting out when the child faces a provoking situation because verbal reasoning and judgment skills are deficient. Support for this hypothesis comes from studies that have found 15-point verbal < performance scores on the WISC-R to be highly predictive of recidivism in adjudicated delinquents (Haynes & Bensch, 1981).

Moffitt (1988, 1993) and colleagues (Moffitt &

Henry, 1989) have found executive function deficits in a sample of children with conduct disorder. When conduct disorder co-occurred with ADHD, the scores were poorer than for either disorder alone. White et al. (1991) found that children with conduct disorder showed higher measures of impulsivity than other groups even with IQ and social class controlled. Pennington and Bennetto (1993) suggest that children with conduct disorder with concomitant verbal and executive function deficits are at higher risk for significant aggressive and antisocial behaviors.

Children with conduct disorder also have been studied as to their response to reward and punishment. These children have been found to show a greater tendency to respond to the cues of a reward (Gorenstein & Newman, 1980; Newman, Patterson, & Kosson, 1987) and are unable to delay responding for a reward (Shapiro, Quay, Hogan, & Schwartz, 1988). A study investigating sensitivity to reward found that conduct-disordered children are exquisitely sensitive to reward and unable to inhibit responding in mixed-incentive situations (Shapiro et al., 1988). Daugherty and Quay (1991) also found a perseverative response set for reward in conduct-disordered children. Children in this study continued maladaptive response patterns even though such responses resulted in loss of rewards.

School and Academic Correlates

Children with conduct disorder have been frequently found to be poor readers (Bale, 1981) and to experience poor academic performance (Frick et al., 1991; Tremblay et al., 1992), in addition to their commonly expected disruptive behavior and poor school attendance (Finn, 1988; Herbert, 1987; Rincker, 1990). Children with conduct disorder also have been found to have poorer verbal skills, difficulty with information processing (Semrud-Clikeman et al., 1992), and deficient reasoning abilities.

In addition to difficulties in learning, children with conduct disorder experience peer rejection (Ladd, Hart, & Price, 1990; Patterson et al., 1990). Perhaps in reaction to such rejection, children with similarly disruptive and aggressive behavior tend to group to-

gether and form gangs that become involved in delinquent behaviors in adolescence (Cairns, Cairns, Neckerman, Gest, & Gariepy, 1988; Dishion & Loeber, 1985).

Implications for Assessment

Because conduct disorder is rarely diagnosed before age 6, most young preschoolers with behavioral difficulties are frequently diagnosed as having oppositional defiant disorder (Webster-Stratton, 1993). A diagnosis of conduct disorder requires that the behavioral difficulties must have lasted for at least six months and that at least three of the following symptoms are present (APA, 1994):

- Cruelty to people and/or animals
- Stealing or breaking and entering
- Lying and cheating in school activities
- Aggression
- Setting fires
- School truancy
- Running away from home at least twice

Diagnosis of conduct disorder is behavioral in nature, and a clinical structured interview is the preferred method of analysis (Webster-Stratton, 1993). The key elements for diagnosing a severe conduct disorder are as follows: (1) early onset of conduct problems; (2) presence of the problem behaviors in many settings; (3) greater frequency, intensity, and severity of conduct difficulties; (4) presence of several types of misbehavior; (5) covert behavioral difficulties such as stealing and lying; and (6) family characteristics (Kazdin, 1987).

Implications for Intervention

Given the finding that the earlier the child develops oppositional and conduct problems, the more severe the problem, it is surprising that there so few early screening and intervention programs. Webster-Stratton (1993) suggests that early intervention programs would be appropriate to allow parents and teachers to modify target behaviors before peer rejection has taken place and negative school reputations are in place.

Intervention programs have focused mainly on parent training programs. An exemplary training program was developed by the Oregon Social Learning Center (Patterson, Reid, Jones, & Conger, 1975). The parents are taught parenting skills by utilizing a task analysis approach that breaks down the task and builds each succeeding skill on skills already mastered. As part of this approach, the parent is directly taught how to reward appropriate behavior and modify inappropriate behavior, as well as discipline procedures, how to supervise children, and problem-solving and child negotiation skills. Patterson and Chamberlain (1988) reported that almost one-third of the time in training is devoted to dealing with parental adjustment issues.

Another program developed by McMahon and Forehand (1984), based on a model introduced by Hanf and Kling (1973), was specifically developed for working with younger conduct-disordered children. This program stresses teaching the parent to play with his or her child and, in so doing, to teach prosocial behaviors. The goal is to teach the parent to reward appropriate behavior and forestall the punitive parenting process frequently seen in these families.

Finally, a program developed by Webster-Stratton (1984) combines the McMahon and Forehand approach with the Patterson strategies. In addition, a program to deal with the parents' personal issues of the parent has been developed that encompasses skills such as anger management, developing coping skills for negative feelings, promoting effective communication skills, and improving problem-solving skills (Webster-Stratton, 1993). This program utilizes videotaped vignettes of models appropriately demonstrating the necessary skills as well as less appropriate methods of discipline.

All of these programs have evidenced good reviews from parents and short-term evaluation (Cross Calvert & McMahon, 1987; Webster-Stratton, 1989; Webster-Stratton, Hollinsworth, & Kolpacoff, 1989). Improvement has been documented in parental change through home observation (Patterson, 1982; Webster-Stratton, 1985) and generalization of appropriate be-

haviors to other settings (Patterson & Fleischman, 1979; Webster-Stratton, 1984) and to untreated behaviors (Arnold, Levine, & Patterson, 1975; Forehand & Long, 1986; Webster-Stratton, 1990).

Unfortunately, these improvements do not generalize to the school setting (Breiner & Forehand, 1981). Direct child training combined with the parent programs has been found to be the most effective and ecologically valid method of intervention. These programs include social skills training (Gresham & Nagle, 1980), academic and social skills training (Coie & Krehbiel, 1984), and training in behavioral self-control skills (Bierman, Miller, & Stabb, 1987). Additional programs target helping children to develop cognitive awareness of their feelings and their ability to see situations from more than one perspective (Camp & Bash, 1985; Kendall & Braswell, 1985).

Lochman, Lampon, Gemmer, and Harris (1987) developed a school-based anger control program for CD youth between the ages of 9 and 12 years. Eighteen sessions are designed to teach interpersonal problem solving, awareness of anger signals, self-talk, and self-control strategies. Role playing, modeling, behavioral contracting, goal setting, reinforcement, and monitoring are built into this program.

Teacher training programs are also an important ingredient in working with conduct-disordered children. Interventions with conduct-disordered children generally have not involved their teachers. Such an oversight might help to explain the difficulties with generalization outside the clinic and home settings.

Kellam and Rebok (1992) have conducted one of the few studies utilizing a school-based intervention. In this study, children in first grade are trained in cooperative behavior. Significant improvements have been found in academic performance, social relationships and disruptive behaviors.

Thus, it appears that, given the myriad of difficulties of conduct-disordered children, the most appropriate intervention plan must include parent, home, and school. Moreover, these interventions must be appropriate to the age of the child; be initiated at an early age; teach prosocial behaviors; provide consequences for inappropriate behaviors; and develop academic, verbal, and reasoning skills. In this manner, the frequent finding of adult antisocial personality disorder resulting from childhood conduct disorder can be forestalled and reversed.

Conclusion

Futher research is necessary to shed light on the neurological and neuropsychological underpinings of severe psychiatric and externalized disorders of children. Although there appear to be strong neurochemical models that help to explain the high rates of comorbidity of these disorders, it is still unclear why neurotransmitter imbalances result in different behavioral patterns (e.g., TS versus ADHD or TS versus conduct disorders). The picture is further complicated by the repeated finding that frontal lobe dysfunction is prominent in so many neuropsychiatric disorders (e.g., TS, ADHD, autism). It may be that further research using rCBF imaging techniques will be helpful in this investigation, particularly if this technology can more clearly demonstrate differences in activation in the various frontal-limbic regions that correspond to specific neurochemical pathways (e.g., NE, DA, and SE brain circuits).

In externalizing disorders, the environment, genetics, and behavior interact with the child, and he or she in turns acts on the environment. The genetic and neurochemical evidence discussed in relation to the disorders in this chapter sets the stage and needs to be considered as a constraint the child works against, works with, or works around. Family interactions are another level that overlay the child's genetic background and development. Assessment of all of these areas is crucial to a full understanding not only of the child but also of brain-behavior functioning.

Research on the neuropsychological and neurochemical underpinnings of these disorders is in its infancy, and the contribution of neuropsychological measures to treatment planning is just beginning. The extent to which executive control deficits can be reliably measured and ultimately altered through psychosocial or behavioral interventions may presage future models of neuropsychiatric disorders of childhood.

The child neuropsychologist and the clinical or school psychologist have a wealth of information among them, none of which is solely within the purview of one specialty. Neuropsychological assessment should add to an educational assessment or a child clinical assessment and can provide knowledge about the child's functional level. Differential diagnosis of ADHD versus depression or anxiety of conduct disorder versus information-processing deficits and of obsessive-compulsive disorder versus ADHD are just some of the possibilities.

This chapter was designed to give the reader an overview of the genetic and neuropsychological correlates of the more commonly seen neuropsychiatric disorders. A further goal of this chapter was to discuss these disorders so that astute school and clinical psychologists, in addition to the neuropsychologist, recognize the interplay of brain function and behavior and glean suggestions for assessment that are within his or her expertise. The two roles are complementary and not distinct. One of the purposes of this book is to provide the child clinician with basic understanding of these disorders, as well as methods for screening these possibilities when confronted with the dilemma of differential diagnosis.

CHAPTER 7

NEUROPSYCHOLOGICAL CORRELATES OF CHILDHOOD AND ADOLESCENT PSYCHIATRIC DISORDERS: INTERNALIZED DISORDERS

Neuropsychiatric disorders in children are believed to "occur because the normal processes of brain maturation do not occur in a sufficiently organized manner" (Cook & Leventhal, 1992, p. 640). These disorders arise as a result of pathoanatomic differences present either pre- or postnatally. Axons myelinate, synaptic connections are formed, and the arrangement of these synapses into networks continues into adolescence and young adulthood and corresponds to the develop of complex human behavior. Abnormalities in the regulation of axonal-synaptic processes have been hypothesized to underlie such childhood disorders as obsessive compulsive-disorder, attention deficit hyperactivity disorder, and Tourette syndrome (Cook & Leventhal, 1992). Moreover, interference in the developmental process of one brain region most likely affects the development of other areas as well (Reitan & Wolfson, 1985a; Tranel, 1992). For example, preschool children with developmental delays in language frequently experience developmental delays in cognition and motor skills (Semrud-Clikeman & Hynd, 1991a).

Neuropsychological difficulties have been found in groups of children with undifferentiated psychiatric diagnoses. Tramontana and Sherrets (1985) compared CAT scans and neuropsychological test data for children with psychiatric diagnoses without a history of brain damage. The results of this study found that 50% of the sample had neurologic abnormalities with signs of lower density in the right hemisphere and anterior regions on the CT scans. These children also had neuropsychological deficits consistent with right-hemispheric-mediated disorders. Thus, children with psychiatric difficulties appear also to experience neuropsychological difficulties.

Environmental variables may well interact with neuroanatomical differences to produce various types of comorbid disorders. In a review of 100 studies, Werry, Reeves, and Gail (1987) concluded that children with attention deficit hyperactivity disorder (ADHD) with comorbid anxiety disorder showed less disturbed and deprived backgrounds than did children with conduct disorder and comorbid anxiety disorder. It was also concluded that the ADHD-plus-anxiety children exhibited more internalizing than externalizing problems, were less impulsive, and had fewer neurodevelopmental disorders than those with conduct disorder plus anxiety.

Neuropsychiatric disorders have generally had the emphasis placed on the psychiatric portion of the label and not on the *neuro* segment. Although much of the data available for these disorders comes from the psychiatry and clinical psychology literature, neuropsychologists are frequently faced with distinguishing between attentional problems due to ADHD and those due to depression; the overlap of anxiety and depression with some types of learning disabilities (Rourke, Young, & Leenaars, 1989) and ADHD (Biederman, 1990), and distinguishing psychiatric disorders from organic disorders. While many of the same measures may be utilized by the child clinical psychologist and the child neuropsychologist to identify psychiatric disorders, the interpretation of the data may differ. The child neuropsychologist gives additional emphasis to possible organic involvement and a thorough understanding of the brain—behavior function. Utilizing a transactional approach to assessment enables both types of clinicians to recognize the interplay between the environment and the individual. Thus, a child who is biologically predisposed to an affective disorder will interact with the environment–and the environment in turn will react and then act on the individual–in a manner different from that of a typically developing child. These transactional differences likely shape the child's perceptions of the environment, and in turn, how he or she reacts to the world.

As you will read in this chapter and the next, it is important to recognize that there is a great deal of overlap between clinical psychology, school psychology, and neuropsychology. Very few measures are within the sole domain of any one specialty. It is, rather, the interpretation and the planning that may differ between the specialties.

Although there is evidence that some disorders have specific neuropsychological profiles (i.e., Tourette; Sutherland, Kolb, Schoel, Whishaw, & Davis, 1982), and others do not (i.e., schizophrenia; Heaton, Badde, & Johnson, 1978), Kolb and Whishaw (1990) suggest that use of neuropsychological knowledge in assessment of the traditional psychiatric patient can add valuable information about cognitive abilities and aid in establishment of appropriate treatment protocols. With this view in mind, the following sections briefly review the neuropsychological underpinnings of selected neuropsychiatric disorders.

This chapter will explore childhood internalizing disorders within a transactional model. Genetic, prenatal, and postnatal history will be discussed in light of how these factors interact with neuropsychological, cognitive, perceptual, and memory functioning. Moreover, the impact of these factors will be interpreted in the framework of the influence of these factors on the child's functioning (family, school, and social interactions).

INTERNALIZING DISORDERS

Internalizing disorders have been defined as those disorders that are covert in nature and are experienced internally by the client. Such disorders include the diagnoses of anxiety, depression, obsessive-compulsive disorder, pervasive developmental disorder, and somatic disorders. These disorders have recently become of interest to researchers and clinicians alike, perhaps because of the emergence of cognitive-behavioral perspectives (Meichenbaum, Bream, & Cohen, 1985, Reynolds, 1990a). For example, knowledge of the nature and correlates of depression, anxiety, obsessive-compulsive disorder and somatic disorders has appeared in the past 10 to 15 years (Reynolds, 1990b).

In contrast to externalizing disorders (discussed in Chapter 6), which are characterized as behavioral in nature, internalizing disorders are viewed as emotionally driven. As with all taxonomies, the distinction between externalizing and internalizing disorders becomes blurred in real practice with children and adolescents qualifying for both diagnoses. For example, a sizable minority of children with attention deficit hyperactivity disorder (ADHD, an externalizing disorder) have also been found to present with depression (Biederman, Baldessarini, Wright, Knee, & Harmatz, 1989) or anxiety (Biederman, Munir, Keenan, & Tsuang, 1991). Moreover, some children with depression can be found to experience significant behavioral difficulties (Semrud-Clikeman & Hynd, 1991a). Further, internalizing disorders also may comorbid with one another (Strauss, Last, Hersen, & Kazdin, 1988). To complicate matters further, there is considerable disagreement as to the methods for diagnosis and treatment (Cantwell, 1988; Quay, 1986a). Given the very nature of internalizing disorders, the severity and observability of symptoms may not be easily recognized by the child's caretakers and/or teachers. Therefore, these disorders are challenging for the main players in the child's life as well as for clinicians. Neuropsychological correlates of these disorders are just beginning to be assessed, and research in this area is sketchy at best.

The following sections are not meant to be exhaustive of all internalizing disorders. The disorders that are included in this review are depression and anxiety.

Childhood Depression

Childhood depression as defined by DSM-IV requires that child must have experienced the following symptoms for 6 months or longer nearly every day: sad or dysphoric mood (in children, mood can be irritable), loss of interest in previously enjoyable events, significant weight gain or loss, sleeping problems (e.g., too little or too much sleep), lack of energy; excessive guilt or feelings of worthlessness, difficulty with concentration, and thoughts of death or suicide (APA, 1994, p. 327). In the school setting, children with depression may appear withdrawn, resist social contact, at times refuse to attend school and show academic difficulties (Shaw, 1988).

Depression in childhood may last for years and extend into adulthood (Kovacs, 1985; Kovacs et al., 1984), lead to suicidality (Reynolds, 1990a), and be more widespread than has previously been recognized (Silver, 1988). Silver (1988) reported that a diagnosis of depression was present in 17.9% of all children under age 18 admitted to psychiatric hospitals. Overall prevalence has been estimated to be between 6% and 12% in adolescents (Kashani, Rosenberg, & Reid, 1989), with a lower incidence present in childhood (Anderson, Williams, McGee, & Silva, 1987; Reynolds, 1990a). There are no gender differences in childhood depression until the middle to late teenage years (Semrud-Clikeman & Hynd, 1991a).

Depression has been found to occur concurrently with anxiety disorders (Munir, Biederman, & Knee, 1987; Strauss et al., 1988), conduct disorders (Alessi & Magen, 1988), and attention deficit hyperactivity disorder (Steingard, Biederman, Doyle, & Sprich-Buckminster et al., 1992; Biederman et al., 1989). It has been hypothesized that a child with a dual diagnosis will evidence a more severe disorder, with a poorer prognosis (Kovacs, 1989).

It is also important to recognize that major depression can be subdivided into bipolar and unipolar forms. The bipolar form of depression requires that one or more episodes of mania occur, in addition to bouts of depression. Twenty to thirty percent of children and adolescents with depression have been found to have a bipolar disorder when followed over time (Waterman & Ryan, 1993). Bipolar depression is rare in children, with greater frequency of occurrence found in adolescents (Goodwin & Jamison, 1990). Unipolar depression has been found to be more heterogeneous in genetic origin as well as more susceptible to familial and environmental contribution (Waterman & Ryan, 1993).

Issues of comorbidity need to be considered, as depression may underlie disorders that are classified as externalizing in nature.

Comorbidity

Depression in childhood has been found to co-occur with anxiety, ADHD, and conduct disorder. Kovacs et al. (1984) found in their sample of depressed and dysthymic children that 33% of the depressed children and 36% of the dysthymic children also had anxiety disorders. Tisher (1983) found that 42% of children with school refusal had low self-esteem and depressive symptoms. He concluded that the high proportion of school refusers with a comorbid major depression may raise the hypothesis that children with school phobia represent a subgroup of those with major depression.

Biederman et al. (1991) found that depression co-occurs with attention deficit hyperactivity disorder at approximately an incidence level of 30% to 40%. For these children, prescription of an antidepressant resolved the depressive symptoms as well as the inattention and hyperactivity.

Puig-Antich (1982) found that approximately one-third of his sample of preadolescents with major depressive disorder also met the criteria for conduct disorder. A strong majority of these children responded favorably to antidepressants for the depressive symptoms, with the conduct problems also being resolved following medication. Kovacs et al. (1984) found that conduct disorder predated the major depressive symptoms in 7% of a depressed sample as well as in 11% of the sample of children with dysthymic disorder. Therefore, it may well be that major depression puts the child at risk for the development of anxiety disorders and externalizing behaviors. It is crucial that the child be evaluated for these disorders as well as for the presenting problem of depression. It is also possible that there is a tendency to develop an affective disorder and that the environmental and familial aspects of the particular child mediate how the disorder is expressed. Although work in the area of comorbidity is currently progressing, there are few studies that have evaluated these disorders outside of a clinical sample.

Genetic Factors

Bipolar and unipolar depressive disorders have been found to differ not only in terms of symptomatology but also in terms of genetic contributions (Gershon, 1990). Bipolar depression has been found to be most likely a genetically based disorder, whereas unipolar depression is related to both genetic and environmental contributions. Torgesen (1986) studied 151 same-sex twins for incidence of bipolar and unipolar depression. He found that 10 had bipolar depression, 92 had major depression, 35 had dysthymia, and 14 had adjustment disorder with depressed mood. He further found a 75% concordance rate for bipolar depression in monozygotic twins and close to 0% concordance in dizygotic twins. Furthermore, he found a 27% concordance rate for major depression in monozygotic twins and a 12% rate for dizygotic twins, with a 40% concordance rate for psychotic depression in monozygotic twins compared to 15% in dizygotic twins. Torgesen (1986) concluded that unipolar and bipolar depression are two different disorders, with bipolar and severe (i.e., psychotic) depression more likely to be genetically transmitted.

Prenatal and Postnatal Factors

A study by Geraldine Dawson and colleagues (1992) of depressed teenage mothers with 11- to 17-month-old infants found similar slowing of the left frontal EEG brain waves in both mothers and infants. No such slowing was found in a matched group of teenage mothers and their babies. There was no differ-

ence between the two groups in terms of demographics, health, or other maternal health areas. There were three conditions: (1) mother playing with the infant, (2) mother walking to the door, and (3) mother out of the room. The groups differed in the EEG patterns for all conditions. There was less frontally based arousal during all of the conditions in the depressed infants. These electrophysiological findings were significant for the conditions even when the behavioral manifestations of the babies did not appear to be observably different.

Neuropsychological Correlates

Childhood depression has been found to be associated with a high frequency of neurological soft signs compared to normal children (MacAuslan, 1975), and has also been found to be a frequent sequela to head injury in children (Rutter, 1983b). Several studies have found evidence of right-hemispheric involvement in children with depression, with antidepressants improving performance on tasks sensitive to frontal and right-hemisphere functioning (Staton, Wilson, & Brumback, 1981; Tramontana & Hooper, 1989).

Electrophysiology has been found to be helpful in evaluating the neuropsychological correlates of depression. Right-hemisphere cognitive dysfunction and EEG hyperarousal in unipolar depression were found, whereas bipolar depression was found to be associated with right-hemispheric abnormalities in depression and lef- hemispheric abnormalities during the manic episodes of this disorder (Sackheim, Decina, & Malitz, 1982). Other studies have produced conflicting results, with some finding EEG patterns differing in depressed children (Mendlewicz, Brown, Minichiello, Millican, & Rapoport, 1984; Rochford, Weinapple, & Goldstein, 1981), while others have not found evidence of specific hemispheric abnormalities on EEG (Knott, Waters, Lapierre, & Gray, 1985). Therefore, it appears that additional studies investigating the neuropsychological correlates of childhood depression are needed in order to determine more firmly which brain abnormalities exist in depression. Moreover, research that evaluates different types of depression and their relationship to child psychopathology needs to be completed in order to provide us with more information about the underpinnings of this disorder.

Intellectual, Perceptual, Attention, and Memory Functioning

PET scans and blood flow studies (Kolb & Whishaw, 1990) have indicated a bilateral reduction of cerebral activity. This diffuse reduction of activity may be neuropsychologically reflected in poorer cognitive processing on many tasks. It is believed that the severity of the deficit would be related to the difficulty of the task rather than to any specific type of task. Therefore, overall intellectual functioning would be depressed, as would attention span and memory. Difficulties would not necessarily be related to these tasks but would relate to the ability of the subject to garner cortical arousal to solve the problems. Children with depression often are found to experience difficulty with new learning, completion of work assignments, and concentration. These difficulties may be related to lower cortical arousal than to any regional or task-related deficit.

Another strategy for studying the neuropsychological correlates has been to evaluate the performance of depressed children on neuropsychological measures. Kaslow, Rehm, and Siegel (1984) found that higher scores on the Children's Depression Inventory (CDI) were negatively correlated with scores on Block Design, Coding and Digit Span on the WISC-R. Similarly, Blumberg and Izard (1985) found that their sample of girls performed more poorly on the Block Design, particularly when elevated scores on the CDI are found.

Children with bipolar depression also have been found to experience difficulty on performance-based tasks rather than on verbal measures (Dencina et al., 1983). Tramontana and Hooper (1989) suggest that children with depression may show these types of patterns because of their depressed concentration and motor speed rather than as a result of right-hemispheric dysfunction per se.

Family and Home Factors

Children with depression frequently have been found to have parents with affective disorders (Reid & Morrison, 1983). Beardslee, Keller, and Kierman (1985) found the presence of depression in 24% of the children from 37 families in which at least one parent was found to be diagnosed with major depression. Moreover, severity of depression in the parent was strongly positively correlated with greater impairment in children. Beardslee et al. (1985) also found that maternal depression was strongly related to greater impairment in the child. No such relationship was established for paternal depression. Beardslee et al. (1985) concluded that this finding may suggest an X-linked transmission of depression and/or environmental factors involved in the etiology of depression.

Similarly, in a sample of mothers with affective disorder, Hammen (1990) found that children of affectively ill mothers had higher lifetime rates of psychopathology as well as higher lifetime rates of affective disorders compared to children from parents who were medically ill or without psychiatric disorders. Hammen (1990) found that when both parents possessed affective disorders, the child had an 80% risk for development of psychopathology; when one parent was affected, the risk dropped to approximately 67%. Weissman (1987) found that a child who had an affective disorder and was younger than 20 at onset was 1.6 times more likely to have a family history of depression compared to a normal control population. For this sample, the peak onset of depression was at 12 years of age. Moreover, alcoholism was found 2.3 times more often in these children than in the normal control sample.

Implications for Assessment

Depression has been found to affect performance on neuropsychological and psychological assessment (Flor-Henry, 1986). Slower response time and depressed completion times on speeded tasks are an area the examining neuropsychologist needs to pay particular attention. For example, a child or adolescent who is severely depressed may have decreased attention to detail or lowered reaction speed which can reduce scores on the performance subtests of the WISC-III as well as on timed tasks such as Trails A and B, the Tactual Performance Test, Stroop, and others.

In addition to attention problems, depressed clients have been found to experience problems with new learning (Caine, 1986). When the same information is presented in a very structured format, learning improves dramatically (Weingarten, Gold, Ballenger et al., 1981). Therefore, it is not a learning problem per se but, rather, a presentation problem. For something to be learned, it must first be attended to, and if attention is deficient poorer performance follows (Cohen, Weingarten, Smallberg, & Murphy, 1982). Retrieval deficits are also frequently seen in depressed clients (Firth, Stevens, Johnstone, et al., 1983). Problems in both remote and newly acquired information are found. These difficulties ameliorate after recovery from depression (Caine, 1986).

Therefore, clients with depression may present in much the same manner as those with organic problems. The astute clinician will recognize such overlap and sekk to differentiate, if at all possible, between the two types of disorders. Clues for differentiation may be found in specific areas of the child's social functioning/relationships (e.g., isolation, rejection, withdrawal, etc.) and emotional adjustment/wellbeing (e.g., overwhelming feelings of sadness, prolonged/chronic feelings of sadness/depression, etc.). In cases where such a distinction is not possible, retesting should be pursued after a trial of medication and/or therapy is attempted.

Diagnosis of depression involves gathering information about the client and matching this information to the DSM-IV criteria for a diagnosis of depression. Table 7.1 presents these criteria. It is recommended that the diagnosis be made on the basis of a multi-informant, multimethod procedure. Although multimethod procedures provide the best information, it is important to recognize that poor concordance has been found between raters (Semrud-Clikeman & Hynd, 1991a). Particularly important is the finding that the child/adolescent is a reliable source of information about his or her subjective feelings of

Table 7.1. Diagnostic Criteria for a Diagnosis of Major Depression Using the DSM-IV

Major Depressive Episode
1. At least five of the following signs which have been present for two consecutive weeks with an accompanying depressed mood or loss of interest or pleasure:
   a. Depressed or irritable mood for most of the day and nearly every day (can be by self-report or observation)
   b. Pronounced diminishment of interest and pleasure in previously enjoyed activities
   c. Significant weight loss or gain; a decrease or increase in appetite
   d. Difficulty sleeping or too much sleeping nearly every day
   e. Agitation or lethargy
   f. Lack of energy or overwhelming feelings of fatigue
   g. Feelings of excessive or inappropriate guilt and worthlessness
   h. Difficulty with concentration and ability to make everyday decisions
   i. Thoughts of death or suicidal ideation

Under DSM-IV criteria (APA, 1994) these symptoms must also cause significant distress or impairment in an important part of the client's life. These symptoms also must not be due to physiological effects of a substance, be due to a general medical condition, or be associated with delusions or hallucinations. In addition, if the symptoms are due to the loss of a loved one, the symptoms must be present for more than two months and involved functional impairment.

Source: Reprinted with permission from the *Diagnostic and Statistical Manual of Mental Disorders,* Fourth Edition. Copyright 1994 American Psychiatric Association..

depression (Kazdin, 1987). Therefore an assessment for suspected depression needs to include information directly from the child or adolescent as well as information from teachers and parents.

Clinical interviews. Clinical interviews have been found to be one of the most sensitive methods of assessment (Puig-Antich & Gittelman, 1982; Reynolds, 1990b). Interviews allow information to be gathered from multiple sources, answers more fully queries about the severity, duration, and frequency of depressive symptoms and provides a comparison of the child or adolescent's feelings with his or her developmental and mental age. For the interested reader, a review of the various clinical interviews is presented in Semrud-Clikeman and Hynd (1991a).

Rating scales. The Children's Depression Inventory (CDI; Kovacs, 1979) is the most frequently utilized rating scale and has had the greatest amount of research. The CDI consists of 27 items with three alternatives to each question measuring severity of symptoms (the higher the number, the more severe). A cutoff of 13 is recommended for a diagnosis of depression (Kovacs, 1979). However, a cutoff this low has been found to overidentify children (Semrud-Clikeman & Hynd, 1991a). The CDI may be best used as a screening measure, after which further diagnosis may rest on clinical interviews and other rating scale measures.

Other rating scales include the Reynolds Child Depression Scale (W. M. Reynolds, 1989), the Children's Depression Rating Scale (Poznanski et al., 1984), and the Hamilton Depression Rating Scale (Hamilton, 1967). Although these scales may also be used (or if the CDI has been used most recently), the results may be redundant with the CDI, and all of these measures take a longer time to administer.

If depression is suspected, use of both the structured interview and the CDI can most efficiently and reliably answer the diagnostic questions posed to the examiner. In cases where difficulty remains in diagnosis due to an unwillingness by the child or adolescent to discuss his or her feelings, projective techniques such as the Rorschach, Roberts Apperception Test, or Thematic Apperception Test should be considered. These measures are beyond the confines of this book, and the interested reader is referred to Martin (1988) or Exner (1993). If an omnibus rating scale is indicated, then the Self-Report Scale of the Behavioral Assessment Scale for Children (Reynolds & Kamphaus, 1992) is recommended. See Chapter 5 for a brief review.

Implications for Intervention

Treatment of depression must be conducted by professionals with training and sensitivity to the subjectively felt distress of the child or adolescent. Disturbances in concentration, feelings of guilt and worry, self-destructive thoughts, and social withdrawal are extremely painful and have repercussions for present and future adjustment. Relapses following treatment or poor progress in the initial stages of treatment may exacerbate the disorder and prolong the subjective feelings of hopelessness, helplessness, and sadness (Reynolds, 1990a). Treatment of depression often combines pharmocotherapy and psychotherapy. Each of these treatment strategies will be discussed further.

Pharmocotherapy. The etiology of depressive disorders has been explored through examining neurotransmitter systems affected by antidepressant medications. Antidepressant medications affect the systems in which the primary neurotransmitters are norepinephrine and/or serotonin. These medications affect the ability of systems to increase or decrease the release of these neurotransmitters or to affect the ability of the postsynaptic receptors to absorb these neurotransmitters (Kandel, Schwartz, & Jessel, 1993). Although it is not clear what the pathophysiology of unipolar or bipolar depression is, both of these systems appear to be involved in mood disorders (Comings, 1990; Waterman & Ryan, 1993).

For bipolar depression in children and adolescents, lithium carbonate is the most commonly used pharmacological agent. When lithium carbonate is utilized, kidney and thyroid functions need to be monitored every six months. The primary pharmacotherapy for unipolar depression is the use of tricyclic antidepressants. These medications block the reuptake of norepinephrine and/or serotonin, which in turn increases the effect of these neurotransmitters on the synapse (Waterman & Ryan, 1993). Several studies have found improvement in children and adolescents when these compounds are used (Preskorn, Weller, & Weller, 1982; Preskorn, Weller, & Hughes, 1987; Puig-Antich et al., 1987). Other studies have not conclusively found improvement from the use of antidepressants (Geller, Cooper, & McCombs, 1989; Kramer & Feiguine, 1981).

In a review of psychopharmacology in childhood and adolescent depression, Waterman and Ryan (1993) suggest that studies demonstrating the efficacy of medications for depression do not now exist. Despite this finding, these clinicians suggest that given the long-term course of depression, the possible morbidity, and the psychic pain experienced, medication is warranted if the child shows a severe form of depression, psychosocial treatment has not been successful, and hospitalization is considered. Frequent communication between home, school, and physician is recommended, particularly with regard to assignment completion and rate of social interaction.

Therefore, it is important that the child's progress be closely monitored; that consultation between school, home, and physician be maintained; and finally, that psychosocial interventions be continued.

Psychosocial interventions. Treatment case studies of depressed children have indicated that a multimodal (psychotherapy plus pharmocology) treatment for depression is effective (Frame, Matson, Sonis, Fialkov, & Kazdin, 1982; Petti, Bornstein, Dalamater, & Conners, 1980). Control group treatment of depression have been found to have mixed results. One of the few treatment studies conducted in a school setting found children who received social skills training or cognitive restructuring therapy improved (Butler, Miezitis, Friedman, & Cole, 1980). However, a control group of depressed children also improved during this same time. Another study utilized cognitive-behavioral treatments including problem-solving therapy, training in self-monitoring, and self-control training (Stark, Reynolds, & Kaslow, 1987). This study found an 88% improvement rate for the self-control group, in contrast to a 67% improvement rate for the control group. Similar findings were presented in a study by Kahn, Kehle, Jenson, and Clark (1990). Thus, it appears that psychosocial training that involves cognitive restructuring, training in self-monitoring, and problem solving can be successful when used by a trained clinician.

In summary, the efficacy of psychopharmocological intervention for childhood depression is not clear at this time. The beginning emergence of studies that utilize psychosocial intervention indicates improvement when cognitive-behavioral treatment is used. As controlled studies of psychopharmocology and therapeutic techniques appear, the field may well discover the most efficacious methods of treatment. Unipolar depression may be related to environmental factors as much as to biological factors. Treatment of familial difficulties along with psychopharmocology and child treatment may bethe best avenue for success.

Anxiety Disorders

There are three major subdivisions of anxiety disorders as defined by DSM-IV (APA, 1994): Separation Anxiety Disorder, Overanxious Disorder, and Avoidant Disorder. The common theme in these disorders is intense subjective distress which in turn is related to maladaptive behaviors developed as a means for coping with the child or adolescent's feelings. The manifestations of the disorder vary in relation to the object of fear or anxiety. For separation anxiety disorder the emphasis is on separation from a caregiver; for overanxious disorder the crux of the anxiety is related to worry and fear concerning a myriad of different situations and events; finally, for avoidant disorder social interactions are excessively feared. Francis, Last, and Strauss (1992) found that in clinic-referred children anxiety accounts for 84% of diagnoses with 16% having a diagnosis of avoidant disorder. Table 7.2 presents the criteria associated with each of these types of anxiety disorders. Overanxiousness is found to be comorbid with depression and with avoidant disorder; rarely is avoidant disorder a reason for referral.

Additional types of anxiety disorders found in childhood include obsessive-compulsive disorder and posttraumatic stress disorder. Obsessive-compulsive disorder is diagnosed when recurrent and distressing thoughts or drive lead to a repetitive or irrational behavior, which in turn causes anxiety when resisted (Baer & Jenike, 1990). This disorder more typically is found in adolescence (Strauss, 1990) but can also be found in childhood (Hollingsworth, Tanguay, Grossman, & Pabst, 1980; Rapoport et al., 1981). In the early stages of this disorder, the child or adolescent may experience relatively little impairment and the symptoms are generally manageable (Adams, Waas, March, & Smith, 1995). The symptoms in-

Table 7.2. Anxiety Disorders as Defined by the DSM-IV

Separation Anxiety Disorder
Anxiety that is developmentally excessive and inappropriate involving separation from home or caretakers, and with three of the following signs present:

1. Extreme distress when separated from home or caretakers
2. Fear of losing or harm happening to the caretakers
3. Fear of permanent separation from caretakers
4. Inability to go to school or anywhere without the caretakers
5. Fear of being home without the caretaker
6. Inability to sleep without the caretaker close by
7. Nightmares having separation themes
8. Physical symptoms such as frequent headaches and stomach aches happening when separation from the caretakers is imminent

These symptoms must occur for at least four weeks, and onset is before 18 years of age.

Overanxious Disorder of Childhood
Recurrent anxiety and worry occurring for at least six months nearly every day with an inability to control these thoughts. This anxiety is associated with at least one of the following:

1. Overactivity and restlessness
2. Feelings of fatigue, problems sleeping
3. Problems with concentration
4. Irritability
5. Tight muscles

Obsessive-Compulsive Disorder

Obsessions   Recurrent and persistent thoughts and image occur, causing anxiety.

These are not excessive worries about current experiences.

Attempts are made to ignore or suppress such obsessions.

The person recognizes that these obsessions are a product of his or her own imagination.

Compulsions   The person is driven to perform repetitive behaviors.

The behaviors are performed to decrease or prevent distress and/or some event.

The person recognizes that the obsessions/compulsion are excessive or unrealistic. The obsessions and compulsions cause great distress and interfere with the person's life.

Posttraumatic Stress Disorder
The person has been involved either directly or indirectly with a situation that involved extreme stress to the self or others, and the person's response involved an intense emotion. The event is reexperienced in one of the following manners:

1. Recurrent recollections of the events–for children, there may be repetitive play involving these themes
2. Recurrent dreams or dreams that are frightening but not well formed
3. Reenactment of the event; flashbacks
4. Overreaction, both physically and emotionally, to cues that represent the traumatic event

Avoidance of any stimuli associated with the traumatic event and numbing, including at least three of the following:

1. Avoidance of thoughts, feelings, or talk about the event
2. Avoidance of places, activities, or people associated with or resembling the event
3. Amnesia for the event or important parts of the event
4. Diminished interest in previously enjoyed activities
5. Detachment and separation from others
6. Constricted affective behavior
7. Sense of not expecting to live long or to fulfill commonly experienced life events

Persistent behaviors including at least two of the following:

1. Problems with insomnia or hypersomnia
2. Irritability and volatility
3. Problems with concentration
4. High awareness of environment; on guard for environmental threats
5. Jumpy and nervous

Source: Reprinted with permission from the *Diagnostic and Statistical Manual of Mental Disorders,* Fourth Edition. Copyright 1994 American Psychiatric Association.

crease in severity over time and eventually the child or adolescent becomes dysfunctional (Leonard & Swedo, 1996).

Posttraumatic stress disorder is characterized by anxiety symptoms following a emotionally distressing event that is unusual in normal human experience. A summary of the criteria for a diagnosis of posttraumatic stress disorder is also contained in Table 7.2.

Incidence

The incidence of anxiety disorders is approximately 7% to 8% in children (Graziano, DeGiovanni, & Garcia, 1979). In a study utilizing a sample from a general population, Anderson et al. (1987) found that separation anxiety was the most common type of anxiety disorder (3.5%); overanxious disorder and simple phobia were in an intermediate range (2.9% and 2.4%, respectively); and avoidant disorder (0.9%) was the rarest type of anxiety disorder. Girls have been found to report more separation anxiety and avoidant disorder than boys (Francis et al., 1992; Last, Hersen, Kazdin, Finkelstein, & Strauss, 1987), while overanxious disorder was found to be comparable between the sexes (Strauss et al., 1988).

Comorbidity

Children with anxiety disorders have been found to be at higher risk for the development of concurrent depression (Brady & Kendall, 1992; Finch, Lipovsky, & Casat, 1989; King, Ollendick, & Gullone, 1991). In a school-based study of children in grades 4 through 7, Laurent, Hadler, and Stark (1995) found 5.5% of the sample of 746 children exhibited an anxiety disorder, while 25% of the children with anxiety disorder also had a diagnosis of childhood depression. Children and adolescents with school refusal have been found to possess a major depressive disorder as well (Bernstein & Garfinkel, 1986; Kolvin, Berney, & Bhate, 1984). In a sample of inpatient children, Alessi and Magen (1988) found that 25% of those children who were diagnosed with a major depressive disorder and 88% of those diagnosed with dysthymia were found to have a concurrent anxiety disorder.

External behavioral difficulties also have been found to co-occur with anxiety disorders. Last et al. (1987) found that attention difficulties and oppositional behavior are highly associated with anxiety disorders. Further, these researchers found that between 15% and 27% of children with diagnosed anxiety disorder also met criteria for a diagnosis of attention deficit hyperactivity disorder or oppositional defiant disorder.

Genetic Factors

Proneness to develop an anxiety disorder may be inherited. Studies utilizing twins have found a high concordance rate for anxiety disorder in identical twins (Torgesen, 1986). There is a tendency for children who are behaviorally inhibited at an early age to have parents who are under treatment for panic disorder and agoraphobia (Rosenbaum, 1988). On follow-up these children were found to be at increased risk for anxiety disorders in late adolescence and early adulthood (Biederman, 1990; Rosenbaum, 1988). It appears that biological dispositions may interact with environmental stressors and result in the increase of anxiety disorder in children born to parents who have been diagnosed as affectively dis-

ordered. A review of twin studies by Rapoport (1986) found a concordance of 80% for obsessive-compulsive disorder in monozygotic and dizygotic twins. This high rate of concordance is suggestive of genetic transmission and needs to be studied further. This area of study is just beginning, and further information is needed to determine the relationship of genetics and environment to the risk factor of later development of an anxiety disorder.

Neuropsychological Correlates

Elevated blood pressure and heart rate responses have been found to be related to anxiety arousal (Beidel, 1988; Matthews, Manuck, & Saab, 1986). Evidence for the existence of increased arousal in the limbic system of inhibited children has been found through the use of electrophysiology (Kagan, Arcus, Snidman, & Feng-Wang-Yu, 1994). It has been hypothesized that such arousal may contribute to the development of anxiety disorders. It also may be that biological dispositions interact with environmental stressors, subsequently resulting in the higher-than-expected incidence of anxiety disorder in children of parents with anxiety and/or depressive disorder (Biederman et al., 1990). Evidence gained through PET and CT scans has found increased metabolic rates for glucose, particularly bilaterally in the left orbital gyrus and caudate nucleus, in OCD clients (Baxter et al., 1987; Luxenberg et al., 1988)

Academic and School Adjustment

Anxiety disorders have not been found to be related to low intelligence. In contrast, children with anxiety disorders tend to have at least average ability (Rachman & Hodgson, 1991). Anxious children have been found to experience significant psychosocial difficulty, including impaired peer relations, depression, low self-concept, poor attention span, and deficits in academic performance (Strauss, Frame, & Forehand, 1987). Children with anxiety disorder have been found to be as disliked by their peers as those children with conduct disorder (Strauss et al., 1988). Anxious children also have been found to be socially neglected, isolated, withdrawn, and lonely (Strauss, 1990). Anxious children have also been found to be more likely to experience test anxiety and difficulty in presenting before their classmates. Children with obsessive-compulsive disorder have been found to be absent from school frequently because of peer ridicule (Clarizio, 1991) and social isolation (Allsop & Verduyn, 1990), and are at higher risk for suicide (Flament et al., 1988, 1990) and substance abuse (Friedman, Utada, Glickman, & Morrissey, 1987).

It is important to note that anxious children rarely pose significant overt behavioral difficulties in school and often are not referred for assessment by their teacher. Teachers have frequently described these children as well behaved and eager to please (Strauss, 1990). However, such anxiety has been found to impair the child's social and academic functioning, and teachers need to be familiarized with these difficulties through inservice and direct training.

Family and Home Factors

There appears to be a relationship between socioeconomic status and anxiety in children (Strauss, 1990). Separation anxiety disorder has been found to be more prevalent in families of lower socioeconomic status (SES) (Last et al., 1987), while overanxious children are found in greater concentration in middle to higher SES families. Moreover, avoidant disorder also has been found to be more prevalent in middle to higher SES families than in lower SES families (Francis et al., 1992). In addition, there is an increased incidence of psychopathology in close relatives of obsessive-compulsive-disordered (OCD) children and adolescents (Templer, 1972). Families of children with OCD have been found to be highly verbal, were socially isolated and withdrawn, emphasized cleanliness and etiquette, and had a tendency to be extremely frugal with money (Adams et al., 1995). Clark and Bolton (1985) found that OCD adolescents believed their parents held very high expectations for them, and these expectations were higher than those perceived by adolescents with anxiety disorders. These authors reported that the parents of OCD and anxious adolescents did not differ in their expectations for their children.

Implications for Assessment

As with depression, it is important to utilize a multimethod approach to the diagnosis of anxiety disorders. Semistructured interviews, rating scales, self-report scales, and observations are important pieces of an assessment. As discussed in the section on childhood depression, semi-structured interviews are helpful in diagnosing anxiety disorders. Last et al. (1987) has found good concordance across informants using a semistructured clinical interview to diagnose anxiety disorders. Children have been found to report more anxiety symptoms than parents, possibly indicating that because of the internal nature of these signs, children are more aware of these types of difficulties than their caregivers (Edelbrock, Costello, Dulcan, Kalas, & Conover, 1986).

Rating scales. Self-report rating scales frequently are used to assess general anxiety levels. These scales are not developed to determine various types of anxiety disorders. One of the most popular rating scales used is the Revised Children's Manifest Anxiety Scale (Reynolds & Richmond, 1978), which provides a global score. It is confounded by symptoms of depression in the scale and may be best utilized as a general measure of psychic distress.

Behavioral rating scales such as the Achenbach and BASC are useful for screening for anxiety disorders with children showing elevated scores on more intensive measures, including a structured clinical interview and observations. Such a multistage method of evaluation can serve to decrease false positives and increase the specificity of diagnosis in order to facilitate selection of the most appropriate treatment.

Implications for Treatment

A number of strategies exist for treatment of anxiety disorders. These methods include behavioral techniques, cognitive-behavioral therapy, psychodynamic therapy, and psychopharmacology. Psychopharmacology will be discussed in Chapter 11 in this book. Behavioral approaches view anxiety as a combination of three variables: motor, subjective, and physiological (Izard, Kagan, & Zajonc, 1984) and devise techniques for reducing all of these components. Specific techniques include systematic desensitization, flooding, modeling, and reinforcement (Strauss, 1990). Systematic desensitization involves the gradual exposure of fear-evoking situations paired with a non-anxiety-arousing situation. This technique has been most successful with phobias (Strauss, 1990). Flooding involves placing the child in the feared situation for an extended period of time to evoke an intense reaction which gradually diminishes. Although this technique has been found to be most effective with school phobia (Kennedy, 1965), it is not recommended for other types of disorder because of the aversive nature of the treatment and the availability of less stressful methods. The use of positive reinforcement, shaping, and extinction has been found to be most helpful with phobias. One of the most important components of this technique is to reduce parental attention when the child becomes fearful, thus removing a very powerful reinforcement for the anxious behavior. Modeling is another behavioral technique in which the child watches a model become involved in the feared situation. This technique has been found to be helpful in reducing common childhood fears (Strauss, 1990).

Cognitive-behavioral interventions are used to modify cognitions that underlie the anxiety and emotional distress. Included in this type of intervention are methods of cognitive restructuring, self-instruction, and self-monitoring. These techniques have been found to be successful in treatment of anxiety disorders in childhood and are continuing to be developed (Ross, 1981).

CHAPTER 8

LANGUAGE-RELATED AND LEARNING DISORDERS

Neurodevelopmental disorders of childhood, including language-related and learning disabilities, constitute a large percentage of the disorders of children seen by child clinical neuropsychologists. Language impairments and learning disabilities resulting from phonological core deficits are featured, as are math difficulties resulting from nonverbal, reasoning, and perceptual deficits.

Each of these neurodevelopmental disorders will be explored within a transactional model, where the genetic and prenatal/postnatal history affecting neuropsychological, cognitive, perceptual, and memory functions will be reviewed. The manner in which family, school, and social factors interact with and ultimately influence the manifestation of these disorders will also be discussed. Research and clinical literature will be incorporated, and implications for assessment and intervention will be addressed.

NEURODEVELOPMENTAL DISORDERS OF CHILDHOOD

Language Impairment

Language impairment and speech disorders are considered to be communication disorders, and are often discussed with reading impairment (Stark & Tallal, 1988). Further, Montgomery, Windsor, and Stark (1991) indicate that impairment of spoken language and the underlying neuropsychological mechanisms may be the common thread between production and comprehension language difficulties, reading problems, mathematics problems, and social difficulties in children with learning disabilities. Stark and Tallal (1988) hypothesize that language disorders are a result of impaired temporal processing of auditory in-

formation, they summarize 15 years of research efforts exploring this possibility.

The extent to which temporal processing deficits underlie language disorders in children is reviewed, with an emphasis on the relationship among difficulties with processing auditory signals presented at a rapid rate, phonological awareness in language processes, and reading impairment (Montgomery et al., 1991).

Specific Language Impairment

Children with specific language impairment (LI) or developmental dysphasia have been to found to have a number of difficulties, including significant deficits in expressive and/or receptive language, with normal abilities in nonverbal areas (Montgomery et al., 1991); deficits in speech perception and poor vocabulary skills, including naming, memory, syntax (grammar), and semantics (word meaning) (Mann, 1991); and impaired temporal sequence of nonverbal auditory stimuli and poor discrimination of sounds, particularly when auditory signals are presented rapidly (Tallal & Percy, 1973). Speech articulation, syntactic, and semantic deficits may also be present.

Neuropsychological Correlates of LI

It is difficult to determine a causal link between brain functions and language impairment in children (Montgomery et al., 1991). However, several tentative hypotheses have been proffered. One is that atypical patterns of symmetry of the planum temporale are associated with verbal comprehension problems, phonological processing deficits, and expressive language difficulties (Morgan & Hynd, in press, Semrud-

Clikeman et al., 1991). The other assumes that perisylvian temporal cortical activation is present for processing auditory speech stimuli (Galaburda et al., 1985).

Both the right- and left-hemisphere temporal regions appear activated, and each hemisphere may have a different role to play in the analysis of sounds (Binder et al., 1994). Preliminary studies using fMRI technology in adults with normal language abilities suggest that the superior temporal lobes are involved in the decoding of acoustic signals of speech, whereas the left frontal lobes are involved in semantic operations (Binder et al., 1994). Binder et al. (1994) suggest that language processing is probably hierachical in nature, involving primary sensory levels and intermodal association regions for higher cognitive activities. As processing demands move from simple (unimodal) to complex (multimodal), more brain regions are likely to be involved. Further research into these mechanisms is underway and will undoubtedly shed more light onto the neurological basis of language, and further clarify the role of selective attention, memory, cognitive associations, and semantic functions on language processes.

Other research indicates that children with LI are less efficient on neuropsychological tasks involving rate of motor performance (rapid alternating finger movements); dihaptic stimulation (simultaneous perception of bilateral tactile stimulation); and left—right discrimination (Stark & Tallal, 1988). LI children also had less control over involuntary movements than did control children; and although signs of involuntary movements are observed in both groups, LI children have movements of longer duration. Stark and Tallal (1988) were careful to screen for children with severe LI and to exclude other children with disabilities so that these findings would not be confounded with disorders also known to have mild neurocognitive deficits (e.g., articulation or reading disorders).

Cognitive-Processing Features of LI

Children with language impairments evidence problems with rate-processing deficits; that is, children with LI have auditory-processing deficits or difficulty in processing auditory signals that have short segments or are presented rapidly in a series (Montgomery et al., 1991). Some suggest that this is the basic deficit that underlies many of the neuropsychological and cognitive features associated with LI (Stark & Tallal, 1988). Rate-processing weaknesses were found in rapid speech production; finger identification (two fingers); association of consonants and vowels (*ba* versus *da*); processing of cross-modal, nonverbal stimuli; and simultaneous tactile stimulation (face and hand). Auditory masking may explain some of the auditory deficits found in LI children, where the rapid presentation of signals runs on top of or masks other, later occurring signals. Masking also may account for other problems observed in both the tactile and motor areas, where a sequence of stimuli or movements interferes with discrete single stimuli.

Tallal (1988) concludes that there may be common though interacting neural substrates for both speech and nonverbal processing that "incorporate rapidly changing temporal cues" that appear to be deficient in children with LI (p. 163). In fact, normal infants were able to discriminate subtle temporal signals (i.e., speech and nonverbal stimuli), that were problematic for LI children 5 to 9 years of age. Their research suggests that children with LI are characterized by deficits in the ability to perceive and to produce information in rapid time sequences. This deficit is not specific to language but includes other processes (e.g., motor, tactile, memory). Stark and Tallal (1988) hypothesize that "a basic neural timing mechanism" interferes with the simultaneous processing and production of information. While other higher level linguistic deficits may also be present, the timing mechanism deficit seems to have a significant negative impact on various processing skills. Ways to alter the functioning of this "neural timing mechanism" are explored in the discussion on intervention implications.

Although rate-processing deficits appear in both LI and LD children, Montgomery et al. (1991) indicate that language impairment is not a direct result of these difficulties, and, "It may be that auditory perceptual and linguistic disabilities co-occur in LI children and are related to a third variable, that is, a more general information-processing deficit" (p. 581).

Academic Correlates of LI

Children with LI frequently develop later reading problems, and as many as 40% of kindergarteners with impaired language also show math difficulties and reading problems in elementary school (Aram & Nation, 1980). Tallal (1988) suggests that the underlying mechanism involved in language impairment is shared with other learning disabilities. Others estimate that children with speech and language deficits show reading problems at six times the rate of control children (Ingram, Mason, & Blackburn, 1970).

Social-Psychological Correlates of LI

The psychosocial functioning of children with language problems often is not investigated separately from that of children with learning disabilities. In general, discussions of social difficulties in children with learning diabilities have focused on the communicative competency of children in social situations, level of moral development, perspective taking, and empathy for others, understanding of nonverbal cues, and problem-solving abilities (Bryan, 1991). Further, in a review of childhood psychopathology and learning disabilities, Nieves (1991) summarized findings of various research showing that low verbal intelligence is correlated with high rates of conduct disorders and juvenile delingency, regardless of socioeconomic and race variables.

The extent to which social-emotional difficulties are related to language-impaired children without learning disorders in general needs further exploration. It does seem evident that communication and verbal intelligence are important variables in determining social adjustment, in conjunction with other cognitive and behavioral factors. Further, Spreen (1989) suggests that constitutional as well as environmental factors contribute to emotional and learning problems in children. Again, this supports the theoretical orientation of a transactional model of childhood disorders, in which biological factors and environmental conditions are interdependent.

Articulation Impairment

In the past, children with articulation impairments (AI) were considered to have primary motor system problems, and therapies were devised to address motor-learning patterns (Stark & Tallal, 1988). Recent conceptualizations suggest that linguistic abilities, particularly phonological processing skills, play an important role in AI. From this perspective, speech sound production is viewed in light of global language functions, including syntax, semantics, and pragmatics (Tallal & Percy, 1973). Although attempts have been made to determine whether children with articulation disorders also have general language deficits, it is unclear whether AI should be considered a linguistic (phonological disorder) or a neurogenic (developmental motor apraxia) disorder.

Neuropsychological Correlates of AI

On a number of measures of nonverbal sensory-motor skills, children with AI performed in a manner similar to normals (Stark & Tallal, 1988). AI children did have more difficulty on items where flashes of different hues were projected in a rapid sequence. Difficulty on tasks of cross-modal, serial memory were also evident.

Differences were pronounced on tests of verbal sensory-motor skills, when language-impaired and articulation-impaired children were contrasted. Children with LI had more trouble on speech perception capabilities, whereas children with AI performed better than control children on these measures (Stark & Tallal, 1988). Speech production errors were made by children with AI, although their errors were less serious than those of the LI group (AI children had fewer omisions, transpositions, and syllable additions than LI children).

In a multivariate analysis differentiating AI from normal children, the following variables were predictive of group membership: weight, temporal ordering of visual graphemes (*e* and *k*), and identification of syllables /bae/ compared to /dae/ (Stark & Tallal, 1988). In a smaller group of children with AI, weight, family history of speech disorders, history of motor delays, difficulty identifying syllables (/bae/—

/dae/), and problems discriminating light flashes were significant in differentiating AI children from normal controls. In this study, AI and LI children were all heavier and taller than the control group. There are no clear-cut answers as to why weight is associated with LI and AI, but speculations suggest that heavy children may be more socially awkward, particularly if they are also clumsy; that low self-esteem may be manifested in less spontaneous speech, especially if accompanied by poor expressive language skills; or that uneven or rapid growth periods may place challenges on speech musculature (Stark & Tallal, 1988). Other unknown genetic linkages may account for this relationship.

While children with AI also had difficulty controlling involuntary movements of arms and had trouble with rapid fine-motor coordination tasks, they were able to produce CV syllables in rapid succession when speaking (Stark & Tallal, 1988). Compared to LI groups, children with articulation disorders did not show difficulty on measures of verbal auditory processing or speech discrimination. Further, children with AI who also had mild expressive language problems had similarities to both normal and LI children, and in general very few children with articulation disorders looked like the more serious language-impaired groups.

Implications for Assessment

There is a paucity of decent measures for language impairments in both young and older children (Montgomery et al., 1991). It is especially difficult to find one adequate test that measures phonemic awareness, syntax, and semantic skills; and analyzing subtests from more than one instrument presents psychometric measurement problems (e.g., comparison of grade or age levels from different tests with dissimilar reliability and validity standards). Language pragmatics also are often overlooked, so it is difficult to determine the effects of LI on communication in general.

The following list has been found helpful in the assessment of language-related deficits in children:

1. Token Test (Teaching Resources Corporation, Boston, Massachusetts, 1978): Comprehension of auditory commands with increasing length and grammatical complexity
2. Curtiss and Yamada Comprehensive Language Evaluation–Receptive (CYCLE-R) (unpublished): Grammar, morphology and syntax
3. Goldman-Fristoe-Woodcock Diagnostic Auditory Discrimination Test (American Guidance Service, Circle Pines, Minnesota, 1974): Speech-sound discrimination
4. Goldman-Fristoe Test of Articulation (American Guidance Service, Circle Pines, Minnesota, 1986): Speech articulation

Implications for Interventions

Interventions for language disorders may be (1) preventive, by reducing the probability of reading disorders; (2) remedial, by addressing the language or communication deficits; or (3) compensatory in nature (Stark, 1988). Early identification and intervention are crucial and are best initiated at the preschool age, when the associated features of severe communication disorders are best prevented. However, most intervention research has focused on children with cognitive delays or hearing impairments, a fact that complicates the picture when evaluating the efficacy of such research when these disorders are not also present. Stark (1988) suggests that the heterogeneity of children with language impairments further complicates the intervention process and that speech, reading, and articulation disorders vary from child to child.

Recently, Tallal et al. (1996) found that children with language-learning impairments (LLI) showed significant improvement following a four-week training program to improve language processing. The intervention consisted of two-stage computer-generated lessons. In stage 1 of the training, speech was temporally modified by lengthening the speech signal by 50%; during stage 2, fast (3 to 30 Hz) transitional features of speech were enhanced by as much as 20 db. The speech tracks were presented on CD-ROMs. The speech sounds had a staccato quality, with consonants (usually fast elements of speech sounds) exaggerated compared to vowels (typically slower speech sounds).

After training LLI children, who had originally showed speech—language delays from one to three years below their chronological age, made remarkable gains. Speech discrimination and language comprehension improved significantly with approximately two years' growth in a four-week period. Further these gains generalized to natural speech conditions.

Intervention outcome may be best for children with expressive language problems who do not have accompanying receptive language disorders (Tallal, 1988). It appears that auditory-processing deficits may result in both expressive and receptive language deficits, while speech motor deficits may result in expressive problems. Further, if auditory-processing abilities are intact, these abilities may facilitate the development of expressive language and speech motor problems; while the opposite does not appear to be the case. That is, intact speech motor abilities have little impact on improving language problems resulting from auditory processing deficits.

The best treatment approach is not always evident. Should intervention address the deficit or should it be compensatory in nature? Stark (1988) provides some general guidelines for determining whether strengths or weaknesses should be the focus. First, if remediation is the focus, weaknesses should be considered. For example, children with articulation disorders and intact auditory processing skills may profit from speech therapy where the placement of articulators in the speech musculature and successive phonetic segments are emphasized. Conversely, if the disorder is phonological in nature, then the focus should be on developing the phonological rules of language, with an emphasis on semantic contrasts and auditory sensitivity.

Second, intact mechanisms should be coupled with impaired functions. It is important to fully assess the child's functional skills across all domains of language (e.g., speech motor, speech perception, visual, and linguistic) in order to provide an integrated intervention plan (Stark, 1988). Therapeutic interventions then should begin at the level where the language breakdown or weakness occurs. For example, Stark (1988) suggests that intervention should not jump too quickly into the strength area, such as vocabulary, if receptive phonological abilities are weak. Intervention in this case would begin with helping the child distinguish CV, then CVC syllables, words, or words in sentences. This approach allows for a progressive development of skills that might not be possible if intervention focused on vocabulary development at the start. In situations where the deficit is profound, intervention may need to focus on compensation using special technologies (e.g., touch-talker or other computer systems).

Motivational, attentional, and impusive problems may also interfere with intervention programs for both young and older children and efforts should be taken to minimize these effects (Montgomery et al., 1991). Children with severe language-related deficits are apt to demonstrate behavioral problems, including resistance and opposition when challenged, particularly at the end of long therapy sessions. Reinforcers, praise, and other management techniques may be helpful in these instances. The length of therapy sessions should also be monitored; shorter sessions can be lengthened as the child becomes more successful and less resistant or fatigued. In summary, Stark (1988) indicates: "Failure to adhere to the principle of beginning at the child's own lowest level of functioning may be positively harmful and may inhibit language development" (p. 178). See Chapter 11 for issues related to addressing neurocognitive strengths and weaknesses when designing remedial interventions.

Learning disabilities, particularly reading disabilities, often accompany language disorders and may arise from the same neuropsychological weaknesses—phonological awareness deficits, especially in early reading. Learning disabilities are reviewed next.

LEARNING DISABILITIES

Children with learning disabilities (LD) constitute the largest and fastest growing population of special-needs children in schools (Lerner, 1993; Torgesen, 1991b). Currently the field is replete with controversies affecting how we think about, diagnose, and design educational interventions for children identified as LD. These issues may even threaten the existence of the field (Torgesen, 1991b). Torgesen (1991b) suggests that the major controversies focus on: (1) defining LD, (2) establishing LD's diagnostic integrity separate from other achievement or adjustment problems in school, (3) determining whether LD has a different developmental course than other school-related difficulties, and (4) determining whether children with LD require unique educational interventions. Research efforts addressing these controversies have questioned the assumption that LD is a biologically based disorder and have investigated the heterogeneity of the disorder (Torgesen, 1991b). Selected research findings addressing these controversies may shed light on a number of these issues.

First, learning problems can arise from divergent sources including genetic, neuropsychological, cognitive-perceptual, social-psychological, and environmental (i.e., home and school or classroom) factors. The extent to which we can identify reliably which factors or combination of factors affects a child's learning may be helpful in distinguishing children with LD from other slow learners or "garden-variety" poor readers. For example, we might expect to see differences across variables depending on whether the learning difficulties result from neurobiological, cognitive-perceptual, intellectual, or instructional opportunities and experiences. Research on this issue has yielded mixed results.

LD and nonidentified slow learners do not differ in terms of demographics or psychoeducational test scores, including both cognitive and affective measures (Ysseldyke, Algozzine, Shinn, & McGue, 1982). Further, slow learners and LD groups show similar skills on cognitive tasks related to reading (Seigel, 1989), including phonological awareness, and on measures of reading achievement. However, LD and garden-variety poor readers do differ on cognitive tasks not directly related to reading, such as nonverbal reasoning skills and verbal-conceptual abilities which in turn may ultimately affect intervention efficacy (Torgesen, 1991b). Stanovich (1993) suggests that garden-variety poor readers have global deficits across a variety of cognitive measures, whereas dyslexic subjects have core deficits in the phonological

area and thus have more domain-specific deficits. Further, Stanovich (1993) states that problems in phonological awareness are shared by the two groups and that these deficits serve as causal factors for reading problems. However, members of the dyslexic group, unlike garden-variety or other slow learners, have key performance deficits specific to the phonological domain.

Second, "developmental lag" theories may be more appropriate for children with mild reading problems than for children with severe reading deficits or dyslexia (Stanovich, Nathan, & Vala-Rossa, 1986). Stanovich et al. (1986) illustrated this point in a study in which groups were matched on reading levels. In this research design, third-grade readers were compared to a less skilled fifth-grade group. The less skilled older children appeared similar to younger children on measures of vocabulary development, pseudo—word decoding, phonological processing, verbal fluency, and picture naming tasks. These findings lend preliminary support to the developmental lag theory for children with mild reading problems.

The developmental lag theory is not as robust for severe reading disabled and dyslexic groups. When matched on reading skills with younger children, studies of children with specific reading disabilities show mixed results. Some studies indicate that LD children have lower scores on measures of phonology but are higher than younger reading-matched subjects on vocabulary knowledge and strategic skills (Olson, Kliegl, Davidson, & Foltz, 1985); others have not found this pattern (Treiman & Hirsch-Pasek, 1985). In a meta-analysis of numerous studies, Rack, Snowling, and Olson (1992) conclude that older dyslexic children do have phonological deficits compared to younger children when matched on reading ability. See Stanovich (1993) for an in-depth discussion of this meta-analysis.

In a critical review of studies, Stanovich et al. (1986) concluded that, "The presently available evidence would appear to suggest the hypothesis that the 'garden-variety' poor reader is characterized by a developmental lag; whereas the much rarer, dyslexic child displays a specific phonological deficit, in conjunction with compensatory use of other skills and knowledge sources" (p. 280). Stanovich et al. (1986) also suggest that the majority of children with reading problems possess mild but pervasive, rather than specific cognitive deficits. Further, although mildly reading-impaired children should not be overlooked in our schools, they may be expected to progress in reading when given instructional resources and will eventually develop reading abilities similar to their other cognitive skills (Stanovich et al., 1986). The same may not be the case for the more severe and specific reading problems found in LD and dyslexic children.

Third, LD and garden-variety poor readers may have a different developmental course and outcome. This assumption seems to be supported by research findings. In one study, garden-variety poor readers achieved at higher reading rates than children with higher IQs who had severe reading disabilities (Rutter & Yule, 1975). Conversely, the reading disabled group obtained higher achievement in the math domain. Torgesen (1991b) also reports that LD children with specific phonological coding deficits made markedly less progress in reading than another group of LD children with similar IQs. Children with severe phonological deficits showed a 1.3 grade level increase in reading over a 10 year period (9 to 19 years), while other LD children in the same class increased reading skills by 6.3 grade levels. This differential learning pattern was not observed in nonreading areas, as the two groups made similar progress in math over the same period. Further, some studies have shown that once decoding skills have been attained, comprehension skills may be slightly better for children with specific reading disabilities than for children with generalized cognitive deficits (Stanovich, 1989).

Finally, evidence that children with severe reading disabilities respond differently to specific intervention techniques than garden-variety poor readers has not been clearly established (Torgesen, 1991b). Reading programs emphasizing phonemic awareness training have been successful for preschool children (Byrne & Fielding-Barnsley, 1993; Cunningham, 1990; Lundberg, Frost, & Peterson, 1988), at-risk readers (Iverson & Tunmer, 1993), and children with severe reading deficits (Wise & Olson, 1991; Wise et al., 1989). Although these studies indicate that specific instruction in phonemic awareness instruction improves reading, that is not necessarily to suggest that different models of instruction are needed across

groups. Phonological awareness appears essential to early reading achievement, and a variety of children respond favorably to techniques employing these principles. The data lend support to Stanovich's (1993) contention that phonological deficits underlie reading deficits for both groups, although garden-variety poor readers may have more generalized cognitive deficits beyond the phonological weaknesses.

Other studies suggest that students respond differently to instruction based on cognitive factors. For example, Torgesen, Dahlem, and Greenstein (1987) suggest that adolescents with specific reading deficits may respond better to comprehension enhancement techniques than adolescents whose IQ scores are consistent with their reading levels (i.e., both reading and intelligence low). Wong and Jones (1982) also found that self-questioning techniques increased comprehension for reading-disabled students, while this method lowered the performance of non-LD adolescents. However, Swanson (1989) found that strategy instruction benefited gifted, average, and slow learners but was not effective for reading-disabled groups. Research in strategy instruction is inconclusive; thus, Torgesen (1991b) and Stanovich (1989) argue that more research is needed to help resolve this issue.

The extent to which researchers and clinicians are more explicit when classifying children with specific reading problems and/or dyslexia, and particularly when differentiating these from garden-variety poor readers, may make definitional and intervention issues less controversial. Further, when reading disabled groups are more clearly defined, empirical and theoretical inconsistencies seem to be less pronounced. Despite these findings, definitional issues remain controversial.

Defining Learning Disabilities

Controversies over definitions of learning disabilities have been long-standing (Lerner, 1993). Stanovich (1993) and others (Shepherd, 1988; Torgesen, 1988) advocate that we stop using the term *learning disabilities,* particularly in scientific realms, and adopt terms such as *reading disability* or *arithmetic disability* to describe the specific domain or deficit area where the problem exists. Berninger and

Abbott (1994) call for a redefinition of LD, departing from the concept of discrepancy between aptitude and achievement; they advocate defining LD instead as a failure to respond to validated intervention and treatment programs. Further, Berninger and Abbott (1994) indicate a need to develop validated treatment approaches, so that variability in instructional patterns can be reliably excluded as a causative factor contributing to learning disabilities.

At present, the definition of LD revised in 1988 by the National Joint Committee on Learning Disabilities (NJCLD) represents the broadest consensus in the field to date (Torgesen, 1991b). The definition states:

> Learning disabilities is a general term that refers to a heterogeneous group of disorders manifested as significant difficulties in the acquisition and use of listening, speaking, writing, reasoning, or mathematical abilities. These disorders are intrinsic to the individual, presumed to be due to central nervous system dysfunction, and may occur across the lifespan
>
> Problems in self-regulatory behaviors, social perception, and social interaction may exist with learning disabilities but do not by themselves constitute a learning disability.
>
> Although learning disabilities may occur concomitantly with other handicapping conditions (for example, sensory impairment, mental retardation, serious emotional disturbance) or with extrinsic influences (such as cultural differences, insufficient or inappropriate instruction), they are not the result of those conditions or influences (NJCLD Memorandum, 1988, cited in Torgesen, 1991b).

Although there appears to be acceptance of the NJCLD definition, Torgesen (1991b) suggests that the definition is so broad and inclusive that it creates difficulties, particularly when comparing research. Research findings across laboratories and clinics are fairly consistent when more homogeneous groups are considered (Hynd & Cohen, 1983), specifically children with reading disabilities as a result of phonological core deficits and math disabilities as a result of nonverbal learning disabilities (Morrison & Siegel, 1991). The cognitive, neuropsychological, and academic correlates of specific reading and arithmetic disorders will be explored separately.

Reading Disabilities: Phonological Core Deficits

Phonological awareness deficits have been found to be a primary cause of reading deficits (Liberman & Shankweiler, 1985; Mann, 1986; Stanovich, 1986; Wagner & Torgesen, 1987). Fletcher, Shaywitz, and Shaywitz (1993) indicate that "It is presently difficult to imagine a study of reading disability without reference to the role of phonological awareness skills in decoding" (p. 109). Torgesen (1994) indicates that children with phonological reading disabilities (PRD) experience trouble in early reading and also have associated difficulties in speech perception, speech production, and naming tasks. Wagner and Torgesen (1987) report that phonological skills predict later reading achievement better than any other measure for preschool children. Further, Montgomery et al. (1991) suggest that rapid auditory-processing deficits may be at the root of reading deficits and may result in inefficient decoding skills.

Phonological awareness is the ability to use the phonemic segments of speech (Tunmer & Rohl, 1991), including the awareness and use of the sound structure of language (Mattingly, 1972). Mann (1991) identifies other language-processing deficits that appear related to phoneme awareness deficits, including difficulties with speech perception when listening, naming and vocabulary ability, and short-term memory involving phonetic representations in linguistic tasks. Reading requires learning the relationship between graphemes (written letters) and phonemes (sound segments) (Iverson & Tunmer, 1993). Thus, children with phonological deficits have difficulty applying the "alphabetic principle" when reading unfamiliar words (Torgesen, 1993). Another group of children may struggle in the reading process as a result of deficits in their ability to process the visual or orthographic features of printed words (Stanovich, 1992; Stanovich & West, 1989). Orthographic or visually based disorders will be reviewed briefly following the description of phonologically based reading disorders (PRD).

Children with PRD exhibit a variety of disorders that may be related or associated with their linguistically based learning disorder. The nature and extent of the interaction between neurocognitive deficits, intellectual and academic progress, and psychosocial adjustment needs further research. However, available research addressing these factors will be reviewed.

Transactional Model of PRD

In order to clarify some of these issues, conceptualizing PRD within a transactional model maybe helpful. Table 8.1 summarizes selected research findings.

Table 8.1. A Summary of Specific Deficits Assocviated with Reading Disabilities: Phonological Core Deficits (PRD)

Biogenetic Factors
– 40% variance in word recognition is genetic
– h2g = .62 phonology/reading deficits
– h2g = .22 orthographic/reading deficits

Environmental Factors: Prenatal and Postnatal
– Orthographic deficits related to exposure to print and learning opportunities
– Development of speech and vocabulary related to language acquisition and reading
– Growth spurt in phonemic awareness at 6 years related to reading efforts
– Despite strong heritability of phonological awareness, deficits can be modified

Temperament
– No known correlates

Birth Complications
– No known correlates

CNS Factors
– Gray matter dysfunction
– Left temporal anomalies
– Larger plana in right hemisphere
– Symmetrical R/L[a] temporal lobes
– Symmetrical or reversed parieto-occipital regions
– Abnormal asymmetry (R > L) in prefrontal regions
– Abnormal asymmetry in parietal regions

Neuropsychological Factors
– Rapid naming
– Abnormal hemispheric lateralization
– Attention activation of RH interferes with LH verbal processing
– Attentional control mechanisms between hemispheres
– Phonemic hearing, segmenting, and blending

Intellectual
– Verbal weaknesses
– Vocabulary knowledge
– Verbal associations
– Word similarities
– Verbal fluency
– Receptive language
– Expressive language
– Verbal IQ
– Comprehension

Perceptual
– Phonemic
– Speech

Memory
– Digit span
– Speech sounds
– Word series
– Letter strings
– Phonetic strategies

Attentional
– Strong comorbidity of reading problems and ADHD
– Attention to phonemes

Academic/Behavioral
– Motivational problems
– Chronic reading problems
– Disengaged in learning
– Spends less time reading
– Reading and spelling

Psychosocial
– Research is sparse
– RD in general show internalized disorders (e.g., depression)

Family
– Research is sparse on PRD
– Prenatal and postnatal risk factors related to general learning and behavioral problems
– "Disorganized" and/or poverty, environment more important with age

Note: PRD refers to phonological reading disabilities, while RD refers to reading disabilities in general. L and LH refer to left hemisphere, R and RH to right hemisphere.

Guidelines for classifying and treating LD may be more clearly articulated and systematically investigated within this transactional framework. Although not every child is expected to demonstrate all of the associated features presented, Table 8.1 suggests an interaction among the neuropsychological, cognitive, academic, and psychosocial problems that may accompany reading disabilities resulting from phonological core deficits.

Genetic Factors

The search for the genetic basis of reading disabilities has been helpful in determining the relationship between environmental and genetic factors. The Colorado Reading Project (Decker & Vanderberg, 1985; DeFries, 1985), one of the largest studies of its type, found a strong relationship between reading disabilities in identical or monozygotic twins (MZ) and in same-sex fraternal or dizygotic twins (DZ). The concordance rate was 71% for MZ twins and 49% for DZ twins, confirming a strong genetic basis of reading disabilities in children. DeFries and Fulker (1985, 1988) proposed a regression model to measure the proportion of variance accounted for by both genetic and environmental factors, and reported that genetic factors were more important than environmental factors for explaining differences in reading between MZ and DZ twins.

Olson, Wise, Conners, Rack, and Fulker (1989) also investigated the role of heredity in examining reading skills. Specifically, Olson et al. (1989) reported a greater similarity in reading abilities in MZ than in DZ twins, even though both twin groups had similar environments. Further, genetic factors accounted for approximately 40% of the variance in word recognition deficits. Phonological coding problems were linked more strongly to reading deficits than were orthographic deficits. With more precise measures (described by DeFries & Fulker, 1985), Olson et al. (1989) found even higher covariance factors with phonological deficits and reading problems (h^2g = .62) than with orthographic factors (h^2g = .22). Scarborough (1990) also found that 2-year-olds with a family history of reading problems and difficulties in syntactic fluency had an extremely high risk for also developing reading problems.

Wise and Olson (1991) suggest that orthographic skills may be due largely to environmental factors such as opportunity and exposure to printed material, whereas, phonological skills are more dependent on genetic influences. Further, when disabled readers who had good phonological skills were excluded from group comparisons, the heritability indices dropped significantly (Olson, Rack, Conners, DeFries, & Fulker, 1990). Olson, Fosburg, Wise, and Rack (1994) report that although the group deficient in phonological decoding was influenced largely by genetic factors, computer-based remediation techniques in reading have been quite successful for this group (Olson, 1994).

In summary, genetic studies suggest that phonological decoding problems are largely genetic and that these deficits have a negative impact on a child's ability to develop word recognition skills and to sound out new words. However, with specific interventions genetically based deficits can improve.

Prenatal/Postnatal Factors

To date, prenatal factors affecting a child's capacity to develop phonological awareness deficits are virtually unknown; however, there are several environmental factors that have been found to be related to general language deficits and reading disabilities. Although a biogenetic foundation for language is virtually indisputable, postnatal factors associated with language development typically emphasize the influence of environmental stimulation. Infants 1 to 4 months of age are quite adept at discriminating speech sounds, and can make discriminations between *ba* and *ga, ma* and *na* (Eimas & Tartter, 1979), and preschool children seem to utilize phonetic representations when processing language in short-term memory (Eimas, 1975). Mann (1991) suggests that children at this age may be aware of and able to discriminate phonemes, even though they may not be aware that phoneme units exist. For reading to develop, the child must become aware of phonemes when approaching written language (Mann, 1991). Mann (1991) indicates that experience plays a role in the child's development of speech perception and vocabulary, both of which are related to language acquisition and reading; however, the role of the environment on these factors have not been adequately investigated for poor readers.

Mann (1991) illustrates how the environment influences phonemic awareness. A predictable growth spurt in phonemic awareness occurs in children at about the age of six years, which appears related to efforts in teaching children to read (Liberman, Shankweiler, Fisher, & Carter, 1974; Liberman, Shankweiler, Blackman, Caurp, & Werfelman, 1980). However, Mann (1991) does suggest that while experience plays a prominent role in the development of phonemic awareness, children with phonological deficits appear to have some biogenetic factor that limits their ability to profit from exposure. Like Olson (1994), Mann (1991) stresses the importance of phonetically based remedial techniques, and cites numerous studies facilitating phonemic awareness in children using such techniques.

Neuroanatomical Variations and Neuropsychological Correlates

CNS variations. Children with a language-based reading disability, particularly with PRD, have been found to show behavioral as well as neuropsychological delays (Torgesen, 1991b). When discussing the etiology of problems associated with reading, Torgesen (1991b) indicates that developmental anomalies in the left temporal region of the brain are causative factors in phonological processing deficits. Further, Torgesen (1993) suggests that children with phonological reading disabilities have gray matter rather than white matter dysfunction, which has been associated with nonverbal learning disabilities).

Although a number of CNS irregularities are found in subjects with dyslexia, these studies should be viewed as preliminary (Hynd, Semrud-Clikeman, & Lyytinen, 1991; Morgan & Hynd, in press). First, the planum temporale in the left hemisphere is consistently larger in a majority of adults (Galaburda, Corsiglia, Rosen, & Sherman, 1987; Geschwind & Livitsky, 1968; Steinmetz et al., 1989) and in fetuses, newborns, and infants (Chi, Dowling, & Gilles, 1977; Witelson & Pralle, 1973). The left planum temporale is thought to be the primary site for linguistic processes and reading (Morgan & Hynd, in press) because of its proximity to the auditory association region and Wernicke's area (Geschwind & Levitsky, 1968). The expected leftward asymmetry is rare in dyslexics, whereas symmetry in the temporal regions is more frequent (Hynd et al., 1990; Larsen et al., 1990; Leonard et al., 1993). A number of studies report that the symmetrical patterns appear to be the result of larger plana in the right hemisphere (Galaburda, 1989; Larsen et al., 1990). Although others found smaller left plana (Hynd et al. 1990), different measurement techniques may be responsible for these divergent findings (Galaburda, 1993; Morgan & Hynd, in press).

Second, dyslexics show symmetrical or reversed asymmetry (R > L) in parieto-occipital regions, which is found less frequently in normal groups (Haslam, Dalby, Johns, & Rademaker, 1981; Hier, LeMay, Rosenberger, & Perlo, 1978; LeMay, 1976; Rumsey et al., 1986). Third, Jernigan, Hesselink, Sowell, and Tallal (1991) found rightward asymmetry in prefrontal regions (R > L), as well as aberrant asymmetry in parietal regions. While Jernigan et al. (1991) did not find abnormal asymmetry in the plana region, this may be a result of the method of measurement utilized in this study. Jernigan et al. (1991) included the plana, a larger cortical region, so that actual differences in the planum temporale may have been inadvertently masked by methodological differences in measurement.

Semrud-Clikeman et al. (1991) specifically addressed the relationship between atypical symmetry of the plana and linguistic deficits. Semrud-Clikeman et al. (1991) found that atypical symmetry was related to reduced verbal comprehension abilities and to expressive language deficits. Other corroborating evidence supports these findings; in particular, Larsen et al. (1990) also found that dyslexic subjects with phonological deficits all had symmetrical plana.

Although dyslexics and normals differ in their pattern of symmetry/asymmetry in the left planum temporale, the exact nature of this relationship is not fully understood (Morgan & Hynd, in press). The relationship between symmetry/asymmetry of the planum temporal and dyslexia is still unclear because this feature alone does not necessarily result in dyslexia (Steinmetz & Galaburda, 1991). Further research may help to clarify whether patterns of symmetry/asymmetry are related to dyslexia or if this pattern varies in a predictable manner with linguistic skills in other nondyslexic populations (Morgan & Hynd, in press).

Wise and Olson (1991) suggest that even though phonological deficits have a neurobiological basis and appear highly heritable, these deficits can be modified. However, Wise and Olson (1991) do acknowledge that "extraordinary efforts" may be required to improve these phonological deficits. Effective instructional techniques will be explored in a later section.

Neuropsychological correlates. Although further research investigating the relationship between morphological variations in the plana and neuropsychological/linguistic deficits is needed, there are some initial results clarifying this relationship. Semrud-Clikeman et al. (1991) found that atypical patterns of symmetry in the planum temporale were related to word attack skills, passage comprehension skills, and rapid naming abilities. Thus, the left planum was postulated as a central language processing center. Atypical symmetry of the planum has also been associated with phonological processing deficits (Larsen et al., 1990; Semrud-Clikeman et al., 1991). Rourke (1994) also reports that children with phonological deficits show deficits on neuropsychological measures, including phonemic hearing, segmenting, and blending; verbal reception, repetition, and memory storage; and verbal output.

Researchers have also explored other neuropsychological postulates and have focused on deficient or abnormal patterns of hemispheric lateralization related to attentional activation processes as plausible explanations for the academic deficiencies exhibited by LD children. In a series of dichotic listening studies, Obrzut (1988, 1991), Obrzut, Conrad, and Boliek (1989), Obrzut, Conrad, Bryden, and Boliek (1988), and Boliek, Obrzut, and Shaw (1988) investigated the role of attention and its effect on asymmetry during language tasks. In general, these studies found that LD children have deficits in auditory processing in the left hemisphere (Obrzut, 1991). Apparently, right-hemisphere "attentional activation interferes with left-hemisphere verbal processing," and "learning disabled children experience a greater imbalance in ac-

tivation between hemispheres suggestive of an attentional-control dysfunction" (Obrzut, 1991, p. 195). Obrzut (1991) further suggests that the "source of the reading-disabled child's difficulties may be primarily in the inability of either the left or the right hemisphere to assume a dominant role in the processing of only verbal material" (p. 191). These studies raise questions about whether learning disabled children have attentional imbalances between the two hemispheres or whether there are problems in interconnected attentional systems (Obrzut, 1991).

Further research is necessary to determine the relationship between morphology and attention control mechanisms during language tasks in children with LD. The extent to which these neuropsychological aspects are further related to the cognitive, academic, and perceptional deficits associated with LD also needs further exploration. These will be reviewed briefly in the following sections.

Intellectual, Perceptual, Memory, and Attentional Functions

Intellectual functions. Children with phonological core deficits evidence weaknesses on a variety of verbal measures, including vocabulary knowledge (Mann, 1991); auditory memory and verbal associations (Rourke, 1994); receptive vocabulary, word similarities, and verbal fluency (Fletcher & Satz, 1985); and receptive and expressive language (Newby & Lyon, 1991). However, Stanovich (1993) argues that performance on intelligence measures, particularly verbal abilities, may be directly related to the child's reading disabilities. Specifically, reading problems interfere with vocabulary development, comprehension abilities, and Verbal IQ (Stanovich, 1986).

Stanovich (1986, 1993) refers to the Matthew effect to describe the reading—IQ relationship, where reading has "reciprocal causation effects" on other cognitive skills. Further, impaired listening comprehension and verbal intelligence may in fact be a "result of poor reading" (Stanovich, 1993, p. 293). Children with reading deficits read less, acquire less general and specific knowledge, and in essence may fall further and further behind in achievement and verbal skills (Wong, 1991). Stanovich (1993) cautions against the use of intelligence measures in the diagnosis of reading disabilities (see implications for assessment below).

Perceptual functions. Difficulty in phonemic processing underlie reading deficits in many children (Liberman & Liberman, 1990; Mann, 1991). The child's ability to perceive spoken words appears related to reading difficulties and is less than accurate, particularly under adverse or noisy conditions (Mann, 1991). Deficient speech perception seems evident, but children with phoneme awareness deficits may also have poor memory for speech sounds as well.

Memory functions. Research does provide evidence that children with reading disabilities do poorly on a variety of memory functions, including deficits on digit span, recall of letter strings, nonsense words, and word order (Mann, 1991). Mann and Liberman (1984) investigated the developmental course of recall and found that the ability to remember a series of words preceded reading disabilities rather than being a consequence of reading problems. Poor readers are unable to use the phonological structure of language for holding letter strings in short-term memory (Mann & Liberman, 1984; Shankweiler, Liberman, Mark, Fowler, & Fischer, 1979).

There is little evidence to suggest that poor readers avoid phonetic strategies during memory tasks. Mann (1991) further suggests that poor readers rely on word meaning in an effort to remember words, and do not appear to use visual rather than phonetic memory strategies. Error pattern analysis suggests that poor readers make "phonetically principled errors" in a manner similar to good readers, but that their error scores are quite high (Mann, 1991, p. 145).

Attentional functions. The extent to which children with learning disabilities also have attentional deficits is of interest. Rourke (1994) indicates that children with phonological deficits often fail to attend to auditory-verbal material. Further, the overlap between ADHD and learning disabilities is quite high, ranging from 26% to 80% depending on the study (Teeter, 1991). In their review, Fletcher et al. (1994) indicate that the comorbidity between these two disorders is strong and that there is a strong heritability for both. However, genetic studies appear to show that the two disorders are independent (Gilger, Penningon, & DeFries, 1992). Fletcher et al. (1994) indicate the necessity of differentiating attentional problems that are a result of cognitive deficits from those that are primarily a function of noncompliance, failure to follow rules, and difficulty sustaining attention, as is typically found in children with ADHD.

Academic and School Adjustment

Early reading failure has been shown to create motivational problems in children (Torgesen, 1977). Children with chronic reading problems often hate school, and develop secondary self-esteem problems (Wong, 1991). These motivational problems generalize to other academic areas, where children become more disenfranchised from the learning process (Butkowsky & Willows, 1980). Wong (1991) further reports that remedial classes often drill in phonics or word recognition but may deemphasize passage comprehension, so that the child spends less time reading. Eventually the child develops more generalized cognitive deficits involving numerous subject areas.

Social-Psychological Adjustment

Research addressing the socioemotional functioning of children with phonological core deficits is sparse. Other research shows that LD children who demonstrate distinctively lower verbal abilities with intact visual/spatial skills were rated by their parents as having more internalizing disorders, particularly depression (Nussbaum, Bigler, & Koch, 1986). These authors conclude that the "unique pattern of neuropsychological deficits exhibited in this LD subgroup may be serving to accentuate their personality and behavioral characteristics" (Nussbaum et al., 1986, p. 66). The extent to which this applies specifically to children with phonological core deficits is yet to be established.

Rourke (1994) suggests that children with basic phonological processing disorders may develop psychosocial disturbances if parents and teachers have unrealistic expectations or if social reinforcers are available for acting out. Further, Rourke (1994) suggests that when psychopathology does occur, it may be expressed in acting-out behaviors or in anxious/depressed symptoms. Others have found that children with conduct disorders (CD) also have lower verbal intelligence (Teeter & Smith, 1993). The extent to which CD and language-based difficulties are associated with poor achievement and learning problems needs further study (Nieves, 1991).

Spreen (1989) suggests that brain dysfunction is the underlying common feature of learning disabilities, psychopathology, and other disorders of children and adolescents, although these disorders may coexist. While Spreen (1989) did not find evidence of LD subtypes and specific forms of psychopathology, he did find that LD children with neurological signs were more likely to experience emotional disturbance. See Nieves (1991) for an in-depth discussion of this topic. The LD/psychosocial line of inquiry needs to be explored more fully before definitive answers are available, particularly for children with phonological core deficits.

Family and home factors. There are few studies addressing family home factors and reading disabilities, specifically for children who display phonological awareness deficits. The research that has been conducted generally shows genetic linkage to be stronger than environmental variables (DeFries & Gillis, 1991).

Studies investigating family and home influences on learning disabilities in general have found that prenatal and postnatal conditions are highly related to risk factors, including the development of general behavioral or learning problems during the first 20 months of life (Werner & Smith, 1982). Further, risk conditions were found in families that were characterized as "disorganized" and/or in poverty, and these environmental factors became more significant as the children became older. Children who continued to demonstrate moderate to severe problems tended to come from families with low economic status and with a high degree of disruption and psychopathology in the family. Badian (1988) also found that socioeconomic status, home conditions, and educational attainment of family members may act as compensatory variables for children initially

identified as at risk for reading problems but who later show normal achievement progress. See Keogh and Sears (1991) for a more in-depth review of these studies.

It is premature to generalize conclusions reported in studies investigating children with general learning problems to students with phonological core deficits. However, stable and consistent home situations, strong emotional family bonds, and child characteristics (e.g., easy temperament) appear to be important factors associated with the "resilient" child who appears less susceptible to the adverse effects of risk factors (Keogh & Sears, 1991).

Implications for Assessment

At least average intellectual functioning or potential has been one of the hallmarks of learning disabilities, and historically definitions include the criteria of an aptitude—achievement discrepancy (Lerner, 1993). Despite this history, aptitude-achievement discrepancies have been criticized for statistical and methodological weaknesses (C. R. Reynolds, 1990) and on developmental grounds as well (Stanovich, 1993). C. R. Reynolds (1990) recommends using a multiple regression approach rather than an intelligence—achievement discrepancy method for determining eligibility. Stanovich (1993) is critical of the use of intelligence for defining reading disabilities on the basis of questionable construct validity. These criticisms are briefly discussed.

First, Stanovich (1986) found that the relationship between intelligence and reading changes with age. There is a developmental trend such that intelligence and reading skills are more highly correlated for older children. Second, Stanovich, Cunningham, and Feeman (1984) report that, although intelligence is clearly related to reading ability, intelligence measures do not have an advantage over other variables (e.g., verbal comprehension, phonological awareness, decoding speed) for predicting reading problems in children. Finally, Stanovich (1993) challenges the practice of using intelligence measures when defining reading disorders, because reading problems may in effect be a causal factor in reduced intelligence, particularly verbal IQ. Stanovich (1993) advocates employing other cognitive measures (e.g., listening comprehension) for assessing reading disabilities.

A number of neuropsychologists employ Stanovich's theoretical orientation when evaluating children with PRD. In research and clinical trials, Felton and Brown (1991) have found that the following measures are useful for predicting reading abilities in young children.

Language, Verbal Memory, and Learning

1. Phonological awareness: Final Consonant Different and Strip Initial Consonant Tasks; Lindamood Auditory Conceptualization Test and Mann and Liberman's syllable counting test
2. Phonological recoding in lexical access: Rapid automatized naming tasks and Boston Naming Test
3. Verbal memory and learning: Rey Auditory Verbal Learning Test

Visual-Spatial and Visual Memory

1. Perceptual organization: Rey's Complex Figure Test
2. Visual-spatial: Judgment of Line Test.

Achievement

1. Woodcock Psychoeducational Battery– Reading Cluster.
2. Wechsler Individual Achievement Test–Reading.

Felton and Brown (1991) found that the measures of phonological awareness and lexical access were the strongest predictors of reading skills, whereas visual-memory, verbal learning, perceptual organization, and visual-spatial skills were less powerful. Early reading was dependent on phonological awareness skills rather than intelligence. However, Felton and Brown (1991) suggest that intelligence may be related to overall prognosis in that children with specific cognitive deficits may compensate for weaknesses, whereas children with more generalized cognitive deficits may not have the same intellectual resources to overcome academic weaknesses.

Felton and Pepper (1995) reviewed other tests of phonological processing that might prove useful in the assessment of reading readiness skills in kindergarden and early elementary school. These include the following:

1. Tests of Phonological Awareness (Torgesen & Bryant, 1994): Standardized measure of individual sound awareness for children in grades K—2
2. Test of Word Finding (German, 1989): Standardized measure of speed and accuracy of word retrieval
3. Comprehensive Test of Phonological Skills (Torgesen, in development, available in 1997; cited in Felton & Pepper, 1995): Standardized measure of phonological awareness, word identification, and rapid naming for grades K—2
4. Kaufman Brief Survey of Early Academic and Language Skills (Kaufman & Kaufman, 1991): Standardized measure of reading readiness, expressive and receptive language, prereading, and premath readiness skills, articulation, and word naming for 3- to 6-11-year-old children.

These measures are used to identify children who are at risk for reading problems. Thus, finding deficits in phonological awareness and/or word naming skills would be helpful in that early intervention programs could be implemented prior to the development of serious reading disorders.

Implications for Intervention

Evidence indicates that phonologically impaired children show normal progress in math but continue to show severe delays in reading despite remedial attempts in school (Torgesen, 1991b). When remedial techniques specifically address phonological core deficits, the outcome is more positive for at-risk students and children with PRD (Byrne & Fielding-Barnsley, 1993; Cunningham, 1990; Iverson & Tunmer, 1993; Molter, 1993; Vellutino & Scanlon, 1987). Studies also have shown increased reading abilities when phonological awareness is combined with metacognitive techniques (Cunningham, 1990); and, when phoneme awareness is contextualized within the reading curriculum (Cunningham, 1989).

The Reading Recovery Program (Clay, 1993) has proved effective in increasing reading achievement of children (Stahl & Kuhn, 1995). The program incorporates aspects of whole language while also emphasizing decoding instruction. Decoding is taught in the context of reading and writing, where the teacher selects strategies depending on the child's unique reading problems. Iverson and Tunmer (1993) found that a modified version of the Reading Recovery teaching word families (*ight* in *sight, light, fight,* etc.) was extremely effective.

Early identification and remediation also seem imperative to avoid some of the secondary motivation and psychosocial deficits that may accompany chronic academic failure (Felton & Pepper, 1995; Wise & Olson, 1991). Specific training in phonemic awareness for young children in kindergarten and early elementary grades has proved successful and seems preferable to control conditions where children are not exposed to these skills (Ball & Blackman, 1991; Felton, 1993). Further, Scarborough (1990) found that children as young as 2 years of age are at extreme risk for severe reading problems when they have a family history of dyslexia and they also possess even mild syntactic fluency problems in language development. See Wise and Olson (1991) and Stahl and Kuhn (1995) for a more in-depth review of remedial programs for reading disabilities, including whole language, learning styles, Comprehension Strategy, and computer-assisted instruction. Also see Foorman (1995) for clarification of the whole language versus decoding debate, and a review of related research.

These data suggest that intervention techniques must specifically address the phonological core deficit that seems to be the basis of many reading deficits. Although phonemic awareness is essential for early reading success, several researchers have found that orthographic and visual-spatial deficits are present in some children with severe reading disabilities. These correlates will be briefly reviewed next.

Visual/Orthographic Deficits in Reading

Although PRD seems well established, there also appears to be a smaller group of children who have major difficulties accessing the orthographic or visual features of written words (Stanovich, 1992). Chase and Tallal (1991) describe the sequential order of reading proposed by Firth (1985), including the logographic,

alphabetic, and orthographic. During the logographic stage, reading occurs through a visual or graphic analysis of letters and words (lexical system). Visual memory plays an important role during this stage, and the child begins to develop a sight-word vocabulary. The alphabetic stage is characterized by the phonological decoding (phonological system) of words using grapheme—phoneme (letter-to-sound) conversions. To develop into a fluent reader, the child must then proceed to the orthographic stage, where larger morpheme units (i.e., syllables) are used. Decoding is quicker during this last stage, and this model assumes that later stages are dependent on skills acquired at earlier stages. This sequential model has been challenged, and recent research suggests that reading is most likely an interactive process whereby children "decode from sound to print as well as print to sound" (Chase & Tallal, 1991, p. 208).

Olson et al. (1994) describe numerous measures of orthographic coding skills and methods for assessing the lexical processes of reading. A number of research tasks have been employed to measure orthographic coding skills, including pseudohomophone choice (e.g., *rain—rane*), letter verification, homonym verification, recognition of orthographic patterns, rhyme judgments with orthographically dissimilar words (e.g., *great—state*), and brief exposure of words (Olson et al., 1994).

Lexical impairments have been found in a small proportion of children with dyslexia, although impairment in the phonological system seems to be a more consistent finding across studies. Written language disorders are briefly reviewed next.

WRITTEN LANGUAGE DISORDERS

Written language impairments are often overlooked in discussions of learning disabilities. However, written language disorders (WLD) can have profound effects on the academic attainment of older children and adolescents. In fact, young learning-disabled children differ from normal children on writing conventions, while older LD children show significant deficits from controls on composition skills (Poplin, Gary, Larsen, Nauikowski, & Mehring, 1980). Further, LD children have difficulty writing narrative text (Nodine, Barenbaum, & Newcomer, 1985), generating expository prose (Thomas, Englert, & Gregg, 1987), and finding ideas to write about (MacArthur & Graham, 1987).

Neuropsychological Correlates of Written Language Disorders

The extent to which written language disorders result from right- or left-hemisphere lesions or dysfunction is still not resolved. Satz (1991) argues that language-related disorders, including reading and written language disorders, may be a function of bilateral hemispheric substrates. The two hemispheres appear to play complementary roles in these processes, with the right hemisphere (anterior, central, and posterior regions) involved in the visual-spatial, emotional, and affective components of language skills, while the left hemisphere (temporal-parietal and anterior regions) is involved in linguistic, speech, and reading processes.

The neuropsychological substrates of WLD have not been researched as thoroughly as reading and speech-language disorders. However, Aram and Ekelman (1988) did investigate the academic sequalae of 32 children who had sustained prenatal or childhood cerebral vascular lesions, insults, or arteriovenous malformations. The majority of the lesioned group had neurological early onset, before the age of 8. In general, the lesioned group was remarkably similar to a control group, except for math aptitude and written language. Written language deficits were associated with the right-lesioned group. Despite relatively high achievement scores, the lesioned group did show high rates of grade retention, special class placement, and/or remedial help.

Cognitive Correlates of Written Language Disorders

Levine (1993) suggests that WLD is a function of multiple developmental processes that impede automatization and sophistication in written language.

Various developmental dysfunctions and their impact on writing include the following. Selective attention problems may result in planning problems, erratic and inconsistent writing, poor self-monitoring, careless errors, and low persistence. Simulataneous production difficulties may affect spatial planning, visualization of words, organization, and spelling. Sequential production deficits may relate to delayed learning of motor movements of letter forms, deficient narrative sequencing, and organization deficits. Memory problems affect word retrieval; spelling; memory for rules of grammar, punctuation and capitalization; and dysfluent writing. Language problems may result in impoverished vocabulary, decreased written expression, dysphonetic (phoneme—grapheme irregularities) spelling patterns, and poor narration. Finally fine motor problems can result in decreased amounts of writing, slow productivity, effortful writing, illegible writing, and awkward pencil/pen grip.

Levine (1993) provides detailed discussion on developmental variations that result in numerous academic and learning problems in children. The extent to which these variations specifically relate to brain dysfunction in children needs further investigation, but this particular model provides a strong theoretical model for understanding how language, attentional, memory, motor, and higher order cognitive processes affect learning processes.

Assessment of Written Language Disorders

Written language disorders can be measured usung writing samples taken from the child's academic work or structured tests. Portfolio or authentic assessment procedures typically include an analysis of writing samples generated by the child. Goetz, Hall, and Fetsco (1990) provide strong arguments, based on cognitive theories, for using alternatives to standardized assessment tools. Task analysis, error pattern analysis, application of the academic skill, dynamic asessment (e.g., learning efficiency), and process assessment using the child's curriculum for determining the learning processes used by the child are sev-

Table 8.2. A Summary of Specific Deficits Associated with Nonverbal Learning Disabilities (NLD)

Biogenetic Factors
– No known correlates

Environmental Factors/Prenatal/Postnatal
– NLD appear at or soon after birth
– Neurodevelopmental disorder or may be caused by traumatic injury
– Few details on environmental impact

Temperament
– No known correlates

Birth Complications
– No known correlates

CNS Factors
– White matter dysfunction
– Intermodal integration (callosal fibers)
– Right-hemisphere involvement

Neuropsychological Factors
– Bilateral tactile deficits (pronounced on left side)
– Visual-spatial-organizational deficits
– Complex psychomotor deficits
– Oral-motor apraxia
– Concept formation and problem-solving deficits

Intellectual	*Perceptual*	*Memory*	*Attentional*
– Concept formation	– Visual discrimination	– Tactile	– Tactile
– Strategy generation	– Visual detail	– Nonverbal	– Visual attention
– Hypothesis testing	– Visual relation	– Complex information	– Attends to simple, repetitive verbal material
– Cause–effect relations			
– Little speech prosody			
– Formal operational thought			

Academic/Behavioral	*Psychosocial*	*Family*
– Graphomotor	– Adapting	– Research is sparse
– Reading comprehension	– Overreliance on rote behaviors	
– Mechanical arithmetic	– Externalized disorders (conduct, acting out)	
– Mathematical reasoning	– Social perception and judgment	
– Science	– Social interaction skills	
	– Social withdrawal or isolation	
	– May develop internalized disorders (e.g., depression, anxiety)	

eral of the alternative methods suggested by Goetz et al. (1990). Also see Shinn (1989) for a discussion of reliability and validity issues related to behaviorally based curriculum assessment procedures. Levine (1993) also describes a unique neurodevelopmental assessment process that may prove helpful to clinicians.

The following standardized instruments have good psychometric properties: (1) Woodcock Psychoeducational Battery—Written Language and (2) Test of Written Language (TOWL).

Interventions for Written Language Disorders

A number of cognitively based intervention procedures have been developed for remediating written language disorders. See Chapter 11 for a discussion of these techniques.

Rourke and his colleagues, who have been exploring the nature of learning disability subtypes over the past 20 years, have investigated a group of children who show relatively normal reading and spelling skills, with deficient math abilities. The nonverbal learning disability (NLD) syndrome will be discussed in the following sections.

NONVERBAL LEARNING DISABILITIES

In a series of studies (Rourke, 1985, 1989, 1991; Rourke & Finlayson, 1978; Rourke & Strang, 1978, 1983), Rourke and colleagues provide empirical support for a syndrome, nonverbal learning disability (NLD), based on the presence of an intact left hemisphere with dysfunctional right-hemisphere systems. The interplay between basic neuropsychological deficits and assets result in complex social-emotional and academic difficulties. See Table 8.2 for an summary of research investigating the neuropsychological, cognitive, academic, and psychosocial features of the NLD syndrome.

The NLD model is a culmination of 20 years of research investigating the neurocognitive basis of learning and social-emotional functioning in children (Rourke, 1989), and is an extension of the Goldberg and Costa model (1981). Rourke (1989) summarizes two major functional-anatomical differences between the hemispheres:

1. The left hemisphere has greater cortical representation in specific sensory modalities (in temporal, occipital, and parietal areas) and in the motor cortex, whereas the right hemisphere has more association cortex (temporoparietal and prefrontal areas) than the left.
2. The left hemisphere has more intraregional connections, while the right has more interregional connections.

These basic differences led Goldberg and Costa (1981) to conclude that the right hemisphere has a greater capacity for dealing with "informational complexity."

Rourke (1989) further incorporates neurodevelopmental theory and discusses the role of the right hemisphere cognitive and emotional adjustment in children. Rourke proposes that the right hemisphere is more important than the left for activating the entire cortex, processing novel information, developing new descriptive systems, and processing complex information. The left hemisphere is more adept than the right at applying already learned descriptive systems that use discrete units of information (like language), and for storing compact codes (Rourke, 1989).

Genetic Factors

To date there are no studies addressing the genetic basis for the NLD syndrome. The extent to which genetic factors play a role in this neuropsychologically based learning disorder certainly warrants investigation.

Prenatal/Postnatal Factors

The NLD syndrome is described as a neurodevelopmental disorder–that is, one that is present at or soon after birth (Rourke, 1989). While Rourke (1989) does assume that the neuropsychological patterns of assets and deficits are developmental in nature, appearing at birth, he does acknowledge that traumatic injury or trauma may result in a similar pattern. Few other details are available describing prenatal and postnatal factors associated with the NLD syndrome.

CNS Variations

The right hemisphere is thought to be primarily implicated in the NLD syndrome (Rourke, 1989). Specifically, Rourke (1989) indicates that "destruction or dysfunction of white matter that is required for intermodal integration" is most likely involved in the NLD syndrome (p. 114). Further, reduction of callosal fibers may be a key to explaining intermodal integration problems, such that right-hemisphere systems cannot be accessed adequately.

Neuropsychological Correlates

Rourke (1989) lists the neuropsychological assets of the NLD child as auditory perception, simple motor skills, rote memory, verbal and auditory memory, attention to verbal and auditory information, and verbal reception, storage, and associations. Normal scores were found on Verbal Scale of the WISC-R (Information, Similarities, Vocabulary, and Digit Span) and the Peabody Picture Vocabulary Test.

Neuropsychological deficits associated with the right-hemisphere NLD syndrome include tactile and visual imperception, impaired complex psychomotor skills, inattention to tactile and visual information, poor memory for tactile and visual information, and some verbal skill deficits (i.e., prosody, semantics, content). Scores are also below average on subtests of the Performance Scale of the WISC-R (Block Design, Picture Arrangement, and Object Assembly): the Tactual Performance Test, left hand; the Pegboard Test, both right and left hands; and the Category test (Rourke, 1989).

Intellectual, Perceptual, Memory and Attentional Functions

Intellectual functions. Children with the NLD syndrome typically demonstrate at least average verbal intelligence, have well-developed vocabulary knowledge, and generally have strong language skills (Rourke, 1989, 1994).

Perceptual functions. Perceptual functions vary depending on the verbal nature of the task. For example, NLD children have excellent phonological decoding skills, especially early in their development (Rourke, 1994). Conversely, NLD children have marked deficits in visual-spatial organization, impaired visual recognition, and failure to appreciate visual details (Rourke, 1989). These visual deficits appear to increase with age and become more problematic in later childhood and adolescence.

Memory functions. Memory skills in children with NLD tend to be extremely well developed for verbal material, with significantly impaired memory for nonverbal material (Rourke, 1989). Children with NLD are more adept with rote memory, especially with information that lends itself to verbal mediation.

Attentional functions. Attentional skills are impaired for tactile and visual information, and these deficits become more pronounced with age (Rourke, 1989). Attention to complex, novel information is particularly difficult, and children with NLD are more attentive to simple, repetitive tasks than to tasks that are verbal or auditory in nature. This attentional bias makes new learning particularly difficult, and this pattern continues to become more prominent with age.

Children with NLD often appear overactive initially, but this apparent hyperactivity does not persist. Rourke (1994) suggests that NLD children eventually look normal on this dimension and may even become hypoactive. The hypoactivity, however, may be a function of psychosocial factors rather than neuropsychological deficits.

Academic and School Factors

The interaction between right-hemisphere weaknesses and left hemisphere assets is manifested in good graphomotor skills (usually later in life), word-decoding skills, spelling skills, and "verbatim memory" (Rourke, 1989). Because NLD children rely heavily on intact left-hemisphere functions, they often develop excellent reading decoding and spelling skills (Rourke, 1994). NLD children tend to perform well on academic tasks that rely on rote verbal memory.

Academic deficits include poor academic achievement in mathematical reasoning and computation and low scores on measures of reading comprehension and science (Rourke, 1989). These academic areas are particularly compromised by difficulties with abstract reasoning and deduction. NLD children fail to develop complex concept formation and problem-solving abilities needed for advanced subject matter such as physics (Rourke, 1989). However, Rourke (1994) suggests that when rote memory strategies are used to teach science and math, NLD children can learn these materials. Although NLD children start out with slow development of early graphomotor skills, these improve with age.

Academically, NLD children appear to be compromised by their extreme difficulties with understanding cause-and-effect relationships, and problems generating age-appropriate problem-solving skills. These deficits are particularly evident during novel tasks, and subsequent learning is negatively affected.

Social-Psychological Functioning

In a series of studies, Rourke (1985, 1989, 1994) found that a complex set of symptoms develop in the social-emotional functioning of NLD children as a result of and as an interaction with the neuropsychological assets and deficits present. Behavioral symptoms associated with the NLD syndrome include the following: (1) poor social judgment as a result of reasoning and problem-solving deficits; (2) difficulties identifying and understanding facial expressions and nonverbal communication as a result of poor visual-spatial-organizational skills; (3) poor social interaction skills as a result of inappropriate verbal interchange (e.g., dull, repetitive speech); (4) reduced physical "intimate" encounters as a result of poor tactile-perceptual and motor skills in conjunction with poor judgment of nonverbal information; and (5) poor overall social adaptation as a result of an interaction of all of the other symptoms (Rourke, 1989).

Children with the NLD syndrome often develop social withdrawal and depression in adolescence due to the interactions of these neuropsychological assets and deficits. According to Rourke (1989), children move "from apparent hyperactivity through normoactive behavior and then on to a hypoactive response style. This occurs largely, if not exclusively, as a result of the rebuffs and outright physical punishments that NLD children experience as a result of their failure to anticipate the consequences of their actions," and "there is good reason to infer that the negative consequences of their behavior will eventuate in the reduction of activity level," resulting in "an even further reduction in exploratory behavior" (Rourke, 1989, p. 99). Rourke (1989) has not identified specific socioemotional or adaptational assets associated with the left hemisphere in NLD children who show right-hemisphere weaknesses. Further, Rourke (1994) cautions that there are no unitary psychological, social, or adaptational patterns character-

istic of all LD children; and, that most LD children are well adjusted.

Implications for Assessment

Comprehensive neuropsychological assessment is necessary to identify the NLD syndrome in children. Rourke (1994) recommends a developmental model of assessment, where evaluations are repeated over time and form the basis for remedial programs. A standardized, comprehensive assessment is recommended, including the following: tactile, visual, and auditory-perceptual components of the Reitan batteries; motor tasks, Trails B; and the Tactile Performance tests from the Reitan; portions of the Klove-Mathews Motor Steadiness test; the Underlining Test; and the WISC Coding subtest (Rourke, 1989, 1994).

Implications for Intervention

According to Rourke, when systems of the right hemisphere are dysfunctional and systems of the left hemisphere are relatively intact, there is a tendency for the child to engage in perseverative or stereotypic responding because of the overreliance on information that has already been learned. This often results in difficulties in developing problem-solving strategies and generating alternative solutions. Children begin to develop compensatory skills that are primarily verbal in nature, and they begin to avoid novel situations. Because of tactile deficits and slow maturation of early psychomotor skills, NLD children have a tendency to avoid active exploration of the environment.

Rourke (1989) recommends intervention programs that incorporate the following. First, in early development intensive physiotherapy including sensory-motor integration may be necessary to "stimulate the functioning of remaining white matter to the maximum" (Rourke, 1989, p. 130). Second, if interventions do not occur early, then compensatory strategies using verbal skills may be effective. Third, intervention should be implemented across all domains (i.e., academic and psychosocial) and should include the child as well as the parent. Fourth, specific methods for increasing social awareness, teaching problem-solving strategies, encouraging generalization of strategies, and improving verbal skills should be part of the intervention plan. Methods for strengthening areas of weakness in visual-spatial areas, interpreting competing stimuli, teaching nonverbal behaviors, providing structure for exploration, using concrete aids, teaching self-evaluation, and developing life skills are described in detail by Rourke (1989).

Summary and Comments about NLD Syndrome

Rourke and his colleagues demonstrate a need to understand the dynamic interaction between psychological and emotional problems in light of neuropsychological assets/deficits in children with learning disabilities. Although further research is necessary to verify these relationships and to determine how learning disabilities change over the ages, an integrated neurodevelopmental model provides the framework for such study.

Although Rourke has developed a model based on a series of related studies spanning two decades, subtypology research has been criticized. Reynolds (1989) asserts that models relying on profile analysis must take into account the reliability (i.e., stability) of profiles. The extent to which profiles change over time and how these changes might affect the original clinical decision need further study. The ratio of subjects to variables is also crucial because random or chance variation "takes maximum advantage of correlated error variance" (Reynolds, 1989, p. 160). Others have pointed out weaknesses in using correlational methods to imply similarity among subjects (Fleiss & Zubin, 1969). Correlational methods also are inappropriate for studies when the linearity of variables is questionable. Satz and Morris (1981) also point to weaknesses in applying Q-techniques for the statistical analysis of subtype data.

Despite criticisms of subtype research, Rourke's NLD model provides a foundation for further research and contributes to our preliminary understanding of how neuropsychological, cognitive, and social-emotional functioning interacts with and influences the development of children. This model describes a complex interaction among deficient and intact neuropsychological systems, early experiences, and learning that is associated with social-emotional functioning. Rourke does provide a viable model for a "right-hemisphere syndrome" that can be tested empirically with children experiencing academic disabilities (primarily in math) and psychosocial adjustment difficulties using standard neuropsychological and psychological tests.

SUMMARY

The purpose of this chapter was to describe the neuropsychology of language disorders and learning disabilities in children. In all these disorders, the child's genetic inheritance and neurological makeup interact with the environment. A child with language and learning disorders is born with neurological constraints that make up the beginning points of the child's interaction with the world. In these disorders, early interventions that combine phonological awareness training and direct instruction of the child in the context of reading have been most successful. The neurobiological constraints are the backdrop for what develops, and, although they are limiting in some manner, they are also malleable through environmental interventions.

A transactional approach allows for a simultaneous understanding of the biology, neuropsychology, and family systems of children with neurodevelopmental disorders. Such an understanding is imperative in order to work effectively with children with neurobiological vulnerabilities. As one parent of a learning-disabled child reminded the second author: "You professionals give us [the mother and father] lots of suggestions–do you not recognize that we also have learning disabilities? How do you expect us to follow through when we have the same problem?" The wisdom of this father's statement cannot be lost on us as we work with families of children with neurodevelopmental disorders. Families frequently share, to some degree at least, the problems of their child. Even when they do not, the stress, concern, frustration, and disappointment families routinely feel is often ignored when developing treatment plans for children and adolescents with disorders. These contextual variables also need to be assessed and planned for in effective interventions.

CHAPTER 9

METABOLIC, BIOGENETIC, SEIZURE, AND NEUROMOTOR DISORDERS OF CHILDHOOD

Various metabolic, biogenetic/chromosomal, seizure, and neuromotor disorders (e.g., cerebral palsy) are the focus of this chapter. These neurological disorders frequently result in accompanying neuropsychological, social/emotional, and behavioral difficulties that place stress on the child, family, and school. As with other neurological and neurodevelopmental disorders, the child neuropsychologist needs to be particularly sensitive to these stressors when assessing and planning intervention programs. Recognition of these variables is just beginning to be studied, but clinical practice indicates that children with these various disorders require support in all environments–home, school, and social. A transactional approach to the deficits experienced by children with these disorders would be most ecologically valid while also providing information for the most appropriate interventions.

A number of select metabolic, biogenetic, seizure, and neuromotor disorders will be discussed in this chapter, with attention not only to the neuropsychological assessment of deficits but also to the contributions of the family and school for remediating these difficulties. Research on intervention outcome and is sparse is sorely needed. For each of these disorders, a review of the literature indicates that more knowledge is needed, not only concerning the neuropsychology of the disorder but also in planning for these children throughout the life span. The demarcation of biogenetic, neurocutaneous, and metabolic disorders is one of convenience and does not imply that a biogenetic basis may underlie some of these various conditions. The demarcations are used only for ease of discussion.

METABOLIC DISORDERS

Metabolic disorders have been linked to various neurological disorders including cognitive retardation, with over 100 single-gene disorders identified in children and adolescents (Menkes, 1990). Phenylketonia (PKU) and Lesch-Nyhan syndrome (LNS) are only two metabolic disorders that will be discussed here. These disorders could easily be listed under chromosomal abnormalities, as each has a genetic basis (Cook & Leventhal, 1992). See Hynd and Willis (1988) for a more in-depth treatment of other disorders affecting metabolic processes that ultimately result in neuropsychiatric disorders in childhood and adolescents.

PKU

Phenylketonia (PKU) is a rare (affecting 1:16,000 to 1:18,000) autosomal recessive disorder that affects males and females equally (Cook & Leventhal, 1992; Hynd & Willis, 1988). Characteristics of the disorder and assessment and intervention implications are briefly discussed.

Characteristics and Associated Features of PKU

PKU is a chronic disorder that affects the metabolism of phenylalanine to tyrosine (Fehrenbach & Peterson, 1989). Tyrosine is a precursor to dopamine (DA), and when phenylalanine is too low, the production of DA may be altered and may result in changes in bones, anemia, antibodies, and cognitive development. Phenylalanine is a protein and, when it is not metabolized, it begins to be stored in the body. When phenylalanine levels are too high they can produce serious negative consequences, including cognitive retardation (Hynd & Willis, 1988; Michaels, Lopus, & Matalon, 1988).

PKU can produce neuropsychiatric disorders in children, including behavioral disruption and antisocial problems (Fehrenbach & Peterson, 1989). Lifetime ADHD was also associated with PKU even after successful dietary control (Realmuto et al., 1986). In rare instances, PKU can result in death (Hanley, Linsoa, Davidson, & Moes, 1970) or in seizure activity, abnormal EEGs, spasticity, and reflex and tremor disorders (Hynd & Willis, 1988). The development of neural tissues appears to be affected, with cellular abnormalities and incomplete myelination resulting.

Implications for Assessment

Early medical screening for PKU is widespread and can be extremely effective in reducing the progressive, deleterious developmental and medical difficulties associated with the disorder (Hynd & Willis, 1988). Neuropsychological assessment may also be important in efforts to identify the presence of cognitive, reasoning, and visuospatial deficits that have been reported in some children with PKU. Psychoeducational evaluation appears effective for determining academic (e.g., learning disabilities, deficits in mathematics), and behavioral adjustment difficulties (e.g., disruptiveness, antisocial behavior, low self-esteem).

Effective interventions focus on dietary control and compliance with these restrictions. Family issues appear to affect dietary compliance, so strategies that address these related factors are discussed.

Implications for Interventions

The negative effects of PKU can be controlled through dietary changes whereby foods containing high levels of phenylalanine (e.g., meats, milk, and milk products) are reduced or eliminated (Fehrenbach & Peterson, 1989). Thus, PKU is clearly a genetic disorder that can be influenced by environmental fac-

tors (intake of foods), which directly affect the manifestation and control of the disorder. It is important to initiate dietary treatment early in life (within the first 3 months) to reduce the possibility of cognitive retardation.

Although early treatment appears to reduce significant cognitive impairment, children with PKU may still have minor cognitive deficits. There is some evidence to suggest that the child's cognitive outcome is dependent on a number of factors, including maternal IQ level, the age at which treatment is initiated, and dietary compliance (Williamson, Koch, Aze, & Chang, 1981).

Family factors related to dietary compliance. Fehrenbach and Peterson (1989) investigated the affects of other family factors, including organization, cohesion, stress, and conflict, on the child's compliance with dietary restrictions. The families of 30 children were followed, and the level of parental problem solving was related to disease control. Specifically, Fehrenbach and Peterson (1989) found that verbal problem-solving abilities were related to children's compliance. Further, parents with highly compliant children were able to provide a number of solutions and parenting options available in problem situations. Family cohesion, level of conflict, and support were not related to compliance.

Although family SES, age, and education of parents were unrelated to problem-solving measures, these variables were related to stress levels and family functioning (Fehrenbach & Peterson, 1989). Induced stress conditions affected both groups of families (high- and low-compliant groups) and thus was not considered predictive of compliance. While stress did reduce the number of alternative strategies that were generated by both groups, the high-compliant parent group demonstrated higher quality solutions and reported stressful situations as less stressful. These findings are important because they point out the need to consider family members in the treatment plans for children with PKU.

Preventive measures. Recent research suggests that maternal hyperphenylalanemia should be monitored during pregnancy (Menkes, 1990). Dietary control (i.e., phenylalanine-restrictions) during pregnancy does have preventive effects, thereby reducing fetal complications including microcephaly.

Ongoing treatment monitoring appears prudent and may increase children's compliance with dietary restrictions and other intervention strategies. Medical, psychological, and educational interventions should be coordinated, with the child and the family as the focus of treatment.

Lesch-Nyhan Syndrome

Lesch-Nyhan syndrome (LNS) is a progressive metabolic disorder that results in cognitive retardation and is often accompanied by choreoathetoid movements (Matthews, Solan, & Barabas, 1995). LNS is a sex-linked disorder that is usually inherited, although it can occur through a spontaneous genetic mutation (Davidson et al., 1991). Females rarely have LNS but can be carriers of the disorder.

LNS is associated with an abnormality or near absence of an enzyme (hypoxanthine-guanine phosphoribosynltransferase, HGPRT) that appears prominent on the X chromosome (Cook & Leventhal, 1992). This abnormality has an effect on the individual's ability to metabolize purines, which in turn has in profound neurological and behavioral consequences (Matthews et al., 1995). Dopamine activity appears altered in various brain regions (putamen, caudate, and nucleus accumbens), with other neurochemical imbalances that may explain the movement and psychiatric problems associated with the disorder (Jankovic et al., 1988).

Characteristics and Associated Features of LNS

At birth, there are no abnormal characteristics, but motor delays and choreoathetoid movements appear within the first year and progressively worsen for infants with LNS (Cook & Leventhal, 1992). Children with LNS often develop normally until about 8 to 24 months of age, when choreoathetosis appears and earlier motor milestones are lost (Matthews et al.,

1995). Hypotonia may be present in infants, but hypertonia and hyperreflexia develop.

Self-mutilation is characteristic of children between the ages of 3 and 5 years, when injuries to facial areas (i.e., eyes, nose, lips) and appendages (fingers and legs) result from chewing and biting oneself (Hynd & Willis, 1988). Almost all children with LNS show self-injurious behaviors by age 8 to 10 years, with spasticity, choreoathetosis, opisthotonos, and facial hypotonia also evident (Matthews et al., 1995). Malnutrition may result from severe self-injury to the mouth or from vomiting (Nyhan, 1976).

Communication is also hampered because of poor articulation from the palsy in speech musculature (Matthews et al., 1995). Although cognitive retardation has been reported, individuals with LNS may be brighter than measured abilities suggest (Nyhan, 1976). Many of the studies to date have relied on single subjects, so it is difficult to ascertain the exact nature of the deficits that have been reported. One study with a comparatively large sample (N = 42) reported that cognitive impairment was not present in 41 subjects, although the study relied on parental reports of the children's mental abilities (Anderson, Ernst, & Davis, 1992). Using the Stanford Binet Intelligence Scale, fourth edition (SB-IV), Matthews et al. (1995) investigated intellectual levels for seven subjects. Subjects showed ability levels ranging from moderate cognitive retardation to low average ability. As a group, the sample performed equally well on verbal and nonverbal tasks, although individually they did show a strong preference for either the visual or the verbal modality. Further, attention and higher level intellectual abilities appeared most compromised in this group. Memory, word definitions, and comprehension of complex speech were impaired. Memory deficits affected mental computation, recall of digits backward, visual reasoning, and verbal reasoning. It is also important to note that the youngest children performed the best, suggesting that there may be a ceiling for cognitive development for individuals with LNS.

Seizure disorders are common in LNS patients (maybe as high as 50%). Other neuropsychiatric problems may include aggression. Finally, the long-term outcome is poor, as LNS usually results in premature death (the patient may reach young adulthood) from renal failure.

Implications for Assessment

Neuropsychologists play a role in the treatment of children with LNS by providing baseline data to substantiate initial cognitive and psychiatric features of the disorder. To date there is no prescribed assessment protocol for this group, but comprehensive, multifactorial assessment is needed to evaluate the full range and extent of deficits across motor, cognitive, academic, and psychosocial areas. Significant physical involvement may restrict the type of intellectual and neuropsychological measures that can be used reliably with this population. Therefore the clinician needs to incorporate functional, ecologically based assessment procedures to ascertain skill levels.

Efforts should be made to assess functional skills through interview and observation of the individual in a natural setting (e.g., in a classroom or home environment). Careful evaluation of family stress and coping patterns will also be helpful to aid in the planning of interventions.

Implications for Interventions

LNS can be detected during the fetal stage, and research into various medical interventions is underway. To date, behavioral interventions have been effective for reducing self-mutilation; although in some cases self-restraints may be required.

Psychopharmacotherapy may be helpful in treating individuals with LNS, but haloperidol, L-dopa, pimozide, diazepam, and clomipramine have been limited in there effectiveness (Watts et al., 1982). Serotonin reuptake inhibitors (e.g., fluoxetine) may prove useful for reducing the compulsively self-injurious behaviors (Cook, Rowlett, Jaselskis, & Leventhal, 1990), and other medications have been suggested for use (i.e., 5-hydroxytryptophan, fluphenazine, and naltreone) (Cook & Leventhal, 1992). Controlled research into psychopharmacological trials is needed before these avenues can be fairly assessed.

Psychoeducational interventions have not been described, although children with LNS may benefit from programs that emphasize functional life skills. Repetition and visual cues may be helpful. The extent to which computer-assisted approaches would be helpful with this group has not been researched, but computer usemay be warranted in individuals with significant motor involvement.

CHROMOSOMAL SYNDROMES

Selected biogenetic disorders of childhood, including Down, Fragile X, and Klinefelter syndromes, are reviewed next. See Dill, Hayden, and McGillivray (1992) for a more extensive review of chromosomal abnormalities.

Down Syndrome

Down syndrome, the most common chromosomal disorder, occurs when there is a triplication of a chromosome (it may result from trisomy 21 or a fragment of 21q22) during meiosis (Cook & Leventhal, 1992) (Papalia & Olds, 1992). Although Down syndrome can be inherited, the majority of cases are noninherited, with as many as 90% of cases resulting from an accident in the chromosomal distribution in the development of the ovum, sperm, or zygote (Smith & Wilson, 1973).

Risk factors increase dramatically depending on the age of the mother, from 1 in 1420 births in mothers in their twenties to 1 in 30 for mothers over 45 years of age (Dill & McGillivray, 1992). Although the mother is typically implicated in the appearance of Down, the syndrome also increases (20% to 30% greater chance of occurrence) when fathers are between 50 and 55 (Erickson & Bjerkedal, 1981). Less frequently, occurrences of Down syndrome are associated with translocation of chromosomes other than 21 (Emery, 1984).

Characteristics and Associated Features of Down Syndrome

Down syndrome is a disorder associated with mild to severe cognitive retardation (Papilia & Olds, 1992).

Physical anomalies include small head; flat nose; folds at the corners of the eyes; protruding tongue; and heart, eye, and ear defects. Although infants with Down syndrome may show slower development, they follow the same sequence of development as normal children (Cicchetti & Beeghly, 1990).

Children with Down syndrome are also prone to spinal cord injuries due to lax ligaments between the first and second cervical vertebrate (Heller, Alberto, Forney, & Schwartzman, 1996). Dislocation of this area may weaken the child's arms and legs or, in rare instances, may result in paralysis; thus, some activities that put strain on the neck (e.g., diving and tumbling) should be avoided (Shapiro, 1992). Children with Down syndrome also have higher than normal rates of hip dislocation and dysplasia (Shaw & Beals, 1992).

Alzheimer's disease may be linked to the same chromosome associated with Down syndrome. Alzheimer's is a progressive loss of memory and brain function associated with tangling/plaguing of nerve tissue (LeFrancois, 1995). Older individuals with Down syndrome have shown physiological abnormalities similar to those seen in Alzheimer's patients, and apparently the underlying pathology in both disorders occurs from a defective gene on chromosome 21 (Goldgarber, Lerman, McBride, Saffiotti, & Gajdusek, 1987).

Implications for Assessment

Amniocentesis and chorionic villus sampling (CVS) can detect Down syndrome (LeFrancois, 1995). In amniocentesis, amniotic fluid is drawn and fetal cells are examined for the presence of chromosomal abnormalities. CVS also involves testing of fetal cells, but these are drawn from samples of chorion (precedes placenta) (Liu, 1991). CVS can be performed early (within 7 weeks after conception) and tests can be conducted on the same day. Amniocentesis requires two- to three-week laboratory time to grow cultures, so that results are not available until well into the second trimester of the pregnancy (LeFrancois, 1995). However, CVS may carry higher risks for complications, resulting in a loss of the fetus in 3% to 4% of cases (Gilmore & Aitken, 1989).

Screening of women presents numerous ethical as well as medical dilemmas. Even though amniocentesis is commonly used on mothers over 35, 95% of pregnant women are under 35 years of age, so initial screening may miss 80% of Down syndrome prenatally (Kloza, 1990). Other measures of detecting high-risk mothers may help. For example, significant low levels of alpha-fetoprotein (AFP) have been found in blood samples of pregnant women, and AFP levels are routinely measured to identify neural tube defects.

Once chromosomal abnormalities have been detected, the treatment options are not always preferred or optimal. Genetic counseling may help parents by providing information about the presence of the disorder so that they can decide for or against a therapeutic abortion (LeFrancois, 1995). Counseling may differ depending on whether the family sees an obstetrician, a clinical geneticist, or a genetic nurse. In a study conducted in England, Marteau, Drake, and Bobrow (1994) found that obstetricians are more directive than genetic nurses, while clinical geneticists fell somewhere between the two other groups. Obstetricians tended to recommend termination of pregnancy more frequently, whereas termination recommendations from the other two professional groups were more related to the specific conditions. For example, 94% of nurses, 57% of geneticists, and 32% of obstetricians recommended termination when Down syndrome was present.

Important ethical and psychological factors influence process counseling. Psychological support for parents-to-be is essential to address the complex emotional reactions that accompany genetic counseling.

Implications for Interventions

The finding that children with Down syndrome can be taught skills that will allow independent living as adults has led educators to increase their expectations for their overall development (Hayden & Harding, 1976). In supportive, enriched environments, young children with Down syndrome can approach normal functioning, particularly when programs are initiated in infancy (Cicchetti & Beeghly, 1990).

Children with Down syndrome may experience

multiple disabilities that influence their physical, communication, cognitive, and psychosocial performance (Heller et al., 1996). The manner in which one designs an intervention program depends on the unique combination of disabilities and the severity of symptoms the child displays. Cognitive retardation affects learning in general and may result in longer learning curves, necessitating repetition and increased drill and practice for academic and/or self-help, daily living skills. Antecedent or response cues may be effective for children with cognitive disabilities (Heller et al., 1996), and increased rates of reinforcement may be required.

Basic instruction in daily self-care skills may be needed using reinforcement and modeling techniques. Social interactions skills also may be enhanced through direct instruction in specific skills and reinforcement of appropriate behaviors in naturally occurring situations.

Heller et al. (1996) suggest that children with congenital heart disorders need to be monitored carefully in the classroom depending on the nature and severity of the heart defects. Physical restrictions may be necessary for those with severe forms of heart defects, while milder forms may not necessitate such restrictions. Adaptive physical education, shortened days or special rest times, and homebound education may be needed in some cases. Further, Heller et al. (1996) suggest that children with congenital heart problems should be taught about heart defects, should be taught to identify their own symptoms, should become aware of their own limitations, and should be encouraged to be their own advocates when decisions about the level of their activities are discussed.

Although Carr (1994) found that individuals with Down syndrome are living longer lives and are in better health than in past years, the long-term outcome is still unsettling. The gradual decline of intellectual abilities into adulthood poses problems and many individuals with Down syndrome lead restricted lives with few interactions with the general population. Many of the individuals who were followed in this study received early intervention, so it is not clear whether children born with Down syndrome today will have a better outcome. It appears that a longer,

more intensive intervention is needed for children with Down syndrome to be more fully integrated into society.

Fragile X Syndrome

Fragile X occurs when the X chromosome is compressed or broken (LeFrancois, 1995). Although Fragile X occurs in females, it is more common in males and may explain why cognitive retardation is more frequent in males than in females (Zigler & Hodapp, 1991). Females with Fragile X syndrome appear to have higher rates of normal intelligence (70%) than do males (20%) affected by the disorder (Dill & McGillivray, 1992).

As a sex-linked genetic disorder, where the X chromosome is abnormal, the defective recessive gene appears to have more of a profound effect on males, who have only one X chromosome, whereas females may inherit one good X chromosome to counterbalance the other defective gene (LeFrancois, 1995). The defective gene is inherited from the mother, who does not manifest the disorder because it is recessive. Fragile X syndrome also increases in frequency for mothers over the age of 40 (Hsu, 1986).

Characteristics and Associated Features of Fragile X

Fragile X syndrome is associated with mild to severe retardation (Papilia & Olds, 1992) and is considered to be the most common cause of inherited cognitive retardation (Wolf-Schein, 1992). Although Down syndrome may account for more cases of cognitive retardation, it is not considered to be inherited from parent to child but occurs from abnormal chromosomal divisions (LeFrancois, 1995). Unlike Down syndrome, cognitive retardation in Fragile X may not be obvious until later stages of development, where marked intellectual deterioration may occur between the ages of 10 and 15 years of age (Silverstein & Johnston, 1990).

Dykens et al. (1989) suggest that the drop in IQ, which may be as dramatic as from a high of 54 points (between 5 and 10) to 38 points (at older ages) may be due to a "plateau" effect rather than a loss of previously acquired intellectual skills. Nevertheless, impairments in visual and sequential processing skills appear prominent (Cook & Leventhal, 1992). Hypersensitivity to auditory stimuli, self-injury, and interest in unusual sensory stimuli (smell) may also be present.

Fragile X is also considered to be one of the primary causes of autism (Papalia & Olds, 1992), with as many as 12% of autistic children display Fragile X (Wolf-Schein, 1992). Males appear to have more severe symptoms, including language delays, slow motor development, speech impairments, and hyperactivity. Rapid speech, echolalia, and impaired communication skills have been reported (Cook & Leventhal, 1992). Social interactions also appear compromised.

Implications for Assessment

Cytogenetic screening can detect Fragile X syndrome in almost all affected males, although false negative rates may be as high as 50% in heterozygotic female carriers (Cook & Leventhal, 1992). However, there are more sensitive molecular genetic probes for diagnosing Fragile X syndrome in males, carrier females, or unaffected males.

Diagnosis may be aided in less severely affected individuals by physical characteristics, including long face; prominent ears, jaw, and forehead; hypermobility and hypertonia; mitral valve prolapse; and macro-orchidism in postpubescent males (Cook & Leventhal, 1992).

Implications for Interventions

The extent to which social interaction, intellectual, and communication abilities are involved may determine the long-term outcome. Recent investigations show that 10 of 17 individuals with Fragile X syndrome also have autistic or pervasive developmental disorders (Reiss & Freund, 1990). Preliminary treatment efficacy suggests that hyperactivity and attentional problems improve with stimulants (Hagerman, Murphy, & Wittenberger, 1988). Therapeutic inter-

ventions are not well investigated to date, and Cook and Leventhal (1992) suggest that "molecular understanding of pathogenesis may contribute directly to the development of therapeutic strategies" (p. 657).

Klinefelter Syndrome

Klinefelter syndrome (KS) is a chromosomal variation whereby an extra X chromosome is present on chromosome 47 (47, XXY) (Sandberg & Barrick, 1995). KS is considered the most common of the chromosomal abnormalities, and estimates suggest that it occurs in approximately 1 in every 1000 male births (Grumbach & Conte, 1985) or 1 in 700 (Hynd & Willis, 1988). Autosomal abnormalities like KS, including Down syndrome (trisomy 21), Edward syndrome (trisomy 18), Patua syndrome (trisomy 13), Cri du Chat syndrome (deletion on Chromosome 5), and Turner syndrome (XO), affect CNS development and are characterized by physical variations (Hynd & Willis, 1988). KS is considered an endocrine disorder resulting from hyposecretion of sex hormones (Sandberg & Barrick, 1995).

Characteristics and Associated Features of KS

Characteristics of KS include: infertility, male breast development, underdeveloped masculine build, and social-cognitive-academic difficulties (Grumbach & Conte, 1985). Physical characteristics (e.g., long legs, tall stature, small testes and penis for body) may be distinguishing features for diagnosing KS (Ratcliffe, Butler, & Jones, 1990).

Psychosocial and psychoeducational correlates of KS. Males with KS often have associated behavioral difficulties (i.e., anxiety, immaturity, passivity, and low activity levels), and may present with various problems in peer relations as well as academic, and behavioral problems (e.g., impulsivity, aggressiveness, withdrawal) (Sandberg & Barrick, 1995). Because KS children appear shy and withdrawn, teachers may describe these boys as lazy or daydreamy. Although most KS males are not psychiatrically disturbed, they may have difficulties with psychosocial adjustment because of passivity and withdrawal (Robinson, Bender, & Linden, 1990). Further, schizophrenia appears higher among KS children (Friedman & McGillivray, 1992).

Language and speech delays may be present in about 50% of individuals with KS (Walzer, 1985), with typically average IQ (Pennington, Bender, Puck, Salbenblatt, & Robinson, 1982). Fine and gross motor delays have been found in some individuals, where dexterity, speed, coordination, and strength may be affected (Mandoki & Sumner, 1991). Considerable evidence of academic weaknesses, including difficulty in reading (Netley, 1987; Ratcliff et al., 1990), spelling (Netley, 1987), and reading comprehension (Graham, Bashir, Stark, Silbert, & Walzer, 1988), has been reported.

Implications for Assessment

Sandberg and Barrick (1995) indicate that most males with KS are not identified in adolescence or in adulthood, so present research may be skewed toward those individuals with more medical and/or psychological difficulties. Chromosomal analysis is necessary to identify KS, and is not routinely conducted. Careful history taking, in light of psychosocial, behavioral, and academic problems, may suggest the need for a medical consultation and genetic screening. Thorough psychological and educational assessment may shed light on other language and academic delays. To date, very little has been written about the neuropsychological correlates of KS; however, neuropsychological assessment may be helpful in determining the nature and extent of motor and language difficulties. Research into this avenue would be useful.

Implications for Interventions

Medical intervention may include testosterone replacement at about the age of 12, when levels are lower than expected; in cases where gynecomastia (breast development) is present, surgery may be warranted (Sandberg & Barrick, 1995). Testosterone replacement may or may not result in a favorable outcome, although for some individuals it has been successful (Nielsen, 1991).

Individual and family therapy may be needed to address the psychosocial needs of the individual with KS. Sandberg and Barrick (1995) suggest implementing opportunities for structured social interactions. Finally, educational interventions may address language- and speech-related difficulties with vocabulary development and comprehension training.

Three of the more common neurocutaneous disorders are discussed separately.

NEUROCUTANEOUS SYNDROMES/DISORDERS

Neurofibromatosis, tuberous sclerosis, and Sturge-Weber syndrome are among the more common neurocutaneous syndromes. Tuberous sclerosis and neurofibromatosis both involve the failure of cells to differentiate and/or proliferate during early neurodevelopmental stages (Cook & Leventhal, 1992). Morphological changes in the brain occur following these early developmental abnormalities, and these morphological differences result primarily from a failure of control of cell differentiation and proliferation. Hynd and Willis (1988) suggest that these abnormalities may occur during the eighth and twenty-fourth week of gestation, when migration of embryonic cells is at its height.

Most of these neurocutaneous disorders are genetically transmitted through autosomal dominant means. Thus, neurocutaneous disorders could just as easily be discussed under biogenetic diseases.

Neurofibromatosis

Neurofibromatosis (NF) is a rare disorder and has been referred to as Von Recklinghausen's disease in honor of the physician who first identified the disorder (Hynd & Willis, 1988). The manner in which NF is expressed varies dramatically; parents may show few abnormalities, while one child may show severe symptoms and a sibling may show no signs (Hynd & Willis, 1988). It has been shown that when the child's father is affected by NF, the child's symptoms are less severe than when the mother is affected (Miller & Hall, 1978). Furthermore, children with affected mothers have higher morbidity, and show symptoms at an earlier age (38% show signs in infancy and 76% by age 3 years). For a more detailed discussion of neurofibromatosis, see Riccardi (1992).

There are two major forms of NF–NF1 and NF2–involving either chromosome 17 (NF1) or chromosome 22 (NF2) (Phelps, in press). NF1 is an dominant, autosomal (nonsex) inherited disorder which occurs in approximately 1 in 3000 births, while NF2 occurs in approximately 1 in 50,000 births. In a cross-cultural study, Garty, Laor, and Danon (1994) found that NF1 may occur at two to five times the prevalence rate. Incidence rates appeared higher for individuals with North African and Asian families as opposed to European and North American. Garty et al. (1994) suggest these higher incidence rates in specific populations may be explained in part by the older age of the parents in these groups. Further research along these lines may prove helpful in addressing this variable. NF1 and NF2 have different features, although NF2 occurs rarely in pediatric populations.

Characteristics and Associated Features of NF

Features of NF1. NF1 is characterized by the following: spots of skin pigmentation that appear like birthmarks (café au lait maculas); benign tumors on or under the skin (neurofibromas); tumors in the iris that are also benign (Lisch nodules); focal lesions in various brain regions (e.g., basal ganglia, subcortical white matter, brain stem, and cerebellum); and freckles in unexposed body areas (e.g., armpit or groin area) (Phelps, in press). NF1 also is associated with learning problems, anxiety related to physical appearance, malignant tumors in the CNS, cluster tumors (plexiform neurofibromas), optic tumors, and seizure disorders (Phelps, in press).

North, Joy, Yuille, Cocks, and Hutchins (1995) found that children with NF1 displayed high rates of learning disabilities; poor adaptive social functioning, and high rates of behavioral problems. A bimo-

dal distribution in intelligence scores was found, suggesting that the group may have subtypes–those with and those without cognitive deficits. Individuals with lower IQs do show abnormal MRI scans (increased T_2 signal intensity) in a number of studies (Hofman et al., 1994; North et al., 1995). These lesions are thought to arise from glial proliferation and aberrant myelination. Speech-language, attentional, organizational, and social difficulties were present, although hyperactivity and oppositional and conduct disorders were not apparent.

The physical features of NF1 vary from mild, with café au lait spots, to extensive pigmentation and neurofibromas all over the body (Phelps, in press). Neurofibromas and brain lesions may not appear until later childhood and adolescence, and with the onset of puberty they have a tendency to increase. While the cafe au lait spots may be present immediately, they too increase with age, along with increased Lisch nodules (Listernick & Charrow, 1990). Symptoms may become so severe in a large number of adolescents that by the age of 15 as many as 50% of individuals with NF1 may have health-related problems (Riccardi, 1992).

Cognitive and psychosocial correlates of NF1. Academic problems including learning disabilities occurs in about 50% of children with NF1 (Riccardi, 1992). Visual spatial disorders, with accompanying reading problems are common (Eliason, 1986; Hofman et al., 1994; Riccardi, 1992). Compared to noninvolved siblings, NF1 patients have lower cognitive skills (Hofman et al., 1994). Global and verbal intelligence appear somewhat compromised, although these skills are within the average range (Phelps, in press).

Psychosocial adjustment appears problematic in that NF1 children are often teased because of their appearance, which worsens with age. Children with NF1 often do poorly in school and have trouble establishing friendships. NF is a disfiguring disorder that produces stress and anxiety in individuals with this disorder (Benjamin et al., 1993). Attempts to hide the condition often lead to isolation, and high levels of anxiety are not uncommon in adolescents (Benjamin et al., 1993).

Features of NF2. NF2 involves the eighth cranial nerve, which results in hearing loss, imbalances, pain, headaches, and ringing in the ears (Phelps, in press). These are late-appearing tumors (in the twenties or thirties), although it is possible to diagnose NF2 in children, particularly when there are multiple skin (absent café au lait or Lisch nodules) or CNS tumors.

Implications for Assessment

The presence of café au lait spots is often used as a clinical marker for the presence of NF1. However, the number of spots needed to make a diagnosis is controversial, ranging from 5 to 6 distinct spots at least 1.5 cm in diameter (Hynd & Willis, 1988). Diagnosis of NF2 is often made following MRI scans, genetic analysis, and review of family history of the disorder, particularly when the physical appearances described above are present (Mautner, Tatagiba, Guthoff, Samii, & Pulst, 1993).

Neuropsychologists may be called on to assess the child to establish a base rate of cognitive and academic deficits and to ascertain any subsequent deterioration that may occur. Thus, the use of a broad-based assessment protocol is advised, including measures of intellectual, language, motor, academic, and psychosocial ability (North et al., 1995).

Implications for Interventions

Although specific treatment plans have not been investigated, techniques for addressing learning, behavioral, and academic difficulties may prove helpful. Access to special education services may be appropriate under the category of "Other Health Impaired" (Phelps, in press). It is apparent that children with NF require academic as well as psychological support. Furthermore, surgical removal of tumors may be necessary (Hynd & Willis, 1988). Long-term follow-up is needed because children with NF may show deficits at a later age as demands increase (Montgomery, 1992).

Parents may also benefit from counseling and realistic planning for the child's future. Family education and support is also recommended, as families

often are not well informed about the disorder (Benjamin et al., 1993). Further research is needed to establish more clearly how these factors affect interventions with this population of children and adolescents.

Tuberous Sclerosis

Tuberous sclerosis (TS) is a neurocutaneous disorder affecting about 1 in 150,000 infants (Dawson, 1954). CNS symptoms are present, with a majority of individuals also showing other physical symptoms involving the heart, lungs, bones, and kidneys. Distinct facial lesions–adenoma sebaceum–that appear like acne are present in approximately 53% of 5-year-olds and 100% of 35-year-olds with the disorder (Bundey & Evans, 1969). Other white spots–amelanotic naevus–may be present on the face, trunk, or limbs in half of patients with TS (Chalhub, 1976). A rough discolored patch also may be observed in the lumbar region in a smaller number of individuals (20& to 50%).

CNS lesions result from an abnormal proliferation of brain cells and glia during embryonic development (Chalhub, 1976). Tubers occur in the convulsions of brain tissue and ultimately interfere with the lamination of the cortex. Tumorlike protrusions also may enter the ventricular regions from an outgrowth of astrocytes. These calcium-enriched tubers are visible on CT scans. White matter heterotopias also may be one of the CNS lesions found in patients with TS. When tumors are present near the lateral ventricular region, hydrocephalus may appear.

Characteristics and Associated Features of TS

Children with TS often show signs including: cognitive retardation, epilepsy, and hemiplegia (Hynd & Willis, 1988). Seizure activity is common in individuals with TS, and maybe as high as 85% to 95% of those affected. Infantile spasms are common and may worsen with age (Friedman & Pampiglione, 1971; Pampiglione & Pugh, 1975). However, there appears to be little connection between physical signs (lesions), seizure activity, and intracranial lesions.

Psychological and behavioral characteristics have been noted in children with TS, including hyperactivity, aggression, destructive tantrums, and other behavioral control problems (Hunt, 1983). Autism also has associated with TS (Cook & Leventhal, 1992), as has schizophrenia (Herkert, Wald, & Romero, 1972).

Implications for Assessment

Children may require medical evaluations including ultrasound to identify tumors in visceral regions and EEGs for seizure activity or spasms. Surgical removal of CNS tumors (near the ventricular region) may be necessary but does not always produce good results and may have a high morbidity rate (Hynd & Willis, 1988). Neuropsychological assessment, including academic and psychological evaluation to identify associated features such as hyperactivity, aggression, autism, and other behavioral/psychiatric disorders, is recommended.

Implications for Interventions

As with other neurocutaneous disorders, little is known about a specific course of action to take for interventions, other than medical treatment and seizure control. Although psychoeducational interventions for school-related difficulties seem reasonable, efficacy and outcome research has not been conducted. Thus, careful follow-up and monitoring of specific interventions need to be conducted on an individual basis to determine which strategies and approaches are most effective for addressing educational and psychological problems. Medical follow-up seems essential.

Sturge-Weber Syndrome

Sturge-Weber syndrome (SWS) is characterized by a number of significant neurodevelopmental anomalies, including seizure disorders, cognitive retardation, behavioral difficulties, and infantile hemiplegia. These anomalies appear to result from various neuropathologies involving (1) intracranial calcification in the occipital and parietal regions, and sometimes in the temporal region, and (2) abnormal production of endothelial cells, which leads to leptomeningeal angioma and, in some cases, to subarachnoid or subdural hemorrhage (Chalhub, 1976). Calcification usually is not observable during infancy but is observable through CT and skull X-rays at a later age. Vascular lesions and abnormal blood flow have also been found using carotid angiography. Facial naevus (port wine staining) is characteristic of SWS.

Characteristics and Associated Features of SWS

SWS is associated with seizure activity usually occurring early in the child's life, within the first two years, and progressively worsening with age (Chalhub, 1976). The extent to which seizures can be controlled often predicts later outcome of the disorder. Cognitive and behavioral problems are common. Some patients also have glaucoma.

Implications for Assessment and Intervention

Medical follow-up is required to identify the nature of neuropathology and to treat seizure activity. In rare cases, hemispherectomy has been completed to control seizures. While the outcome of neurosurgery has been variable, seizure control was effective, although severe cognitive retardation was an outcome when the left hemisphere was removed early in life (Falconer & Rushworth, 1960). Severe behavioral disturbances were also reduced following surgery.

Neurosurgical intervention is used with caution because of the serious complications associated with hemidecortication, including hemorrhaging into the open cavity, hydrocephalus, and brainstem shifts (Cabieses, Jeri, & Landa, 1957; Falconer & Wilson, 1969; McKissock, 1953). Furthermore, improved medications for seizure control have reduced the need for such invasive techniques (Hynd & Willis, 1988).

Seizure disorders are reviewed next, with attention paid to the transactional nature of the associated features and the need for a transactional, multifaceted intervention plan including medical, academic, and psychosocial approaches.

SEIZURE DISORDERS

Seizure disorders can occur in children with developmental disorders and may be caused by metabolic disorders, hypoxia, or other congenital problems (Black & Hynd, 1995; Heller et al., 1996). *Epilepsy* refers to chronic disturbances in brain functions affecting perceptions, movements, consciousness, and other behaviors, while *seizures* refer to individual episodes (Bennett & Krein, 1989). Neppe (1985) describes seizures as paroxysmal firing of neurons, which may cause perceptual, motor disturbances or loss of consciousness. Although epilepsy occurs in only 1% to 2% of the population (Hynd & Willis, 1988), it is considered to be the most prevalent of neurological disorders of childhood (Black & Hynd, 1995; Bolter, 1986). Seizures, or single episodes, caused by high fevers (above 102°F) are the common cause of convulsions. Febrile seizures are most common in children between 3 months and 5 years of age (Hynd & Willis, 1988). Most children (70%) experience only one seizure episode; when a second seizure does occur, it is usually within a year of the first episode (Hynd & Willis, 1988).

There are several classification systems based on changes in EEG activity during (ictal) and between (interictal) seizures (Neppe & Tucker, 1992). Most recent systems ignore neuroanatomical sites of seizure activity, age, gender, and pathological explanations of epileptic seizures, and emphasize major descriptions, including partial (i.e., simple, complex, generalized tonic-clonic), generalized (i.e., absence, myoclonic, clonic, tonic, etc.), or unclassified generalized seizures (Neppe & Tucker, 1992). Older classification systems for seizure disorders (grand mal, petit mal, psychomotor), have been replaced (Hartlage & Hartlage, 1989). Seizures that appear for unknown reasons (idiopathic) typically are differentiated from those occurring from known reasons such as brain trauma or tumor activity (Hynd & Willis, 1988).

Stages of Seizure Activity

The seizure itself may be divided into stages: the prodome, aura, automatism, and postical changes (Besag, 1995). According to Besag (1995), the *prodome* is the time before a seizure or cluster of seizures occurs. The child may show irritability, lethargy, or apathy during this period, with these symptoms ending when the seizure begins. The *aura* occurs just prior to the seizure and has been described as a seizure itself. The aura is a simple partial seizure type that can lead into a complex partial seizure. The aura, which occurs while the child is fully conscious, has been described as more distressing to the child than the actual tonic-clonic seizure (Besag, 1995). The aura is actually a seizure with a focal charge, lasts a few seconds, and can occur many times a day. Besag (1995) reports that auras can result in mood (mainly anxiety) and behavioral change. Thus, the aura may herald not only the beginning of a seizure but also significant behavioral change in the child.

Automatisms have been defined as a "clouding of consciousness, which occurs during or immediately after a seizure and during which the individual retains control of posture and muscle tone but performs simple or complex movements and actions without being aware of what is happening" (Fenton, 1972, p. 59). Automatisms may include lip smacking, hand flapping, eye blinking, twirling, and other similar behaviors.

Postictal changes are behaviors that occur after the seizure and vary depending on the parts of the brain involved, the duration of the seizure, and whether the seizures come in clusters. Behaviors during the postical stage can range from drowsiness to significant behavioral and cognitive changes such as paranoid ideation. Usual symptoms include irritability and confusion. Besag (1995) strongly recommends that parents and teachers realize that these postical changes *are* related to the seizure and require understanding and empathy for the child.

Partial Seizures

Partial seizures are associated with diagnosable structural lesions. These seizures do not involve a loss of consciousness but can evolve into generalized clonic-tonic seizures (Dreifuss, 1994).

Simple partial seizures. This type of seizure results from a specific focus in the gray matter of the brain, which causes an abnormal electrical discharge. The most commonly seen seizure of this type involves the jerking of one part of the body without loss of consciousness. The foci for this type of simple partial seizure is the motor strip area. Other types of simple partial seizures include sensory (simple hallucinations), autonomic (sweating, pallor, hair standing on end on limbs), and psychic (affective problems, speaking, distortion of time sense) seizures with no impairment of consciousness (Hartlage & Telzrow, 1984).

Complex partial seizures. Complex partial seizures generally involve a loss or impairment of consciousness. This alteration of consciousness occurs before the attack or shortly after its beginning. These seizures involve behavioral automatisms such as lip smacking, hair twirling, and hand patting. Problems in orientation in time and space also occur. The focus of this type of seizure is in the temporal lobe as well as the frontal lobes. Some believe the complex partial seizures arising from the frontal lobes are associated with automatisms, while those with a temporal focus relate to a cessation of activity (Delgado-Escueta, Bascal, & Treiman, 1982).

Generalized Seizures

There are three main types of generalized seizures. Of the three, febrile seizures are not considered a seizure disorder. This type of seizure is associated with a fever experienced by a previously neurologically intact child. Although these seizures may reoccur, medication is not used because of the benign nature of the seizure (Hartlage & Telzrow, 1984; Lockman, 1994b). The other two types of generalized seizures are absence and tonic-clonic.

Absence seizures. This type of seizure was previously labeled petit mal. Seizures of this kind involve an abrupt loss of consciousness. The child's eyes may flicker, roll back, or blink rapidly. When the seizure ceases, the child resumes his or her activity as if nothing untoward has occurred (Lockman, 1994a). These seizures may occur very frequently; some children have been known to have over 100 in a day (Hartlage & Telzrow, 1984). Age of onset is 4 to 8 years. School performance is often seen to fall off, and the child may be described as dreamy or unmotivated.

The diagnosis of absence seizures is confirmed by EEG. The EEG will show spikes that are synchronized bilaterally and frontally (normal brain activity is *not* synchronized), with alternating spike and slow wave patterns (Lockman, 1994a). To induce a seizure during an EEG, hyperventilation is used whereby the child is asked to take 60 deep breaths for 3 or 4 minutes (Lockman, 1994a).

Although the etiology of absence seizures is suspected to be genetic in origin (Degen, Degen, & Roth, 1990; Metrakos & Metrakos, 1970), the genetic mechanism has not yet been identified. The risk of siblings also showing absence seizures is approximately three times greater than for the general population (Ottman et al., 1989).

The treatment of absence seizures is generally with one medication. Zarontin is the medication with the fewest side effects (Dooley et al., 1990), followed by valproate (Sato, White, & Penry, 1982) and clonazepam (Hartlage & Telzrow, 1984). Absence seizures have been known to worsen with the use of carbamazepine (Horn, Ater, & Hurst, 1986; Snead, 1985).

The prognosis for absence seizures is favorable, with approximately half of affected children becoming seizure-free. The other 50% may develop tonic-clonic seizures or may continue to experience absence seizures (Lockman, 1994a). Sato et al. (1983) found that 90% of children of normal intelligence and neurological function with no history of tonic-clonic seizures were seizure-free in adolescence. Conversely, those children with automatisms and motor responses during the absence seizures had a poorer prognosis (Loiseau et al., 1983). Lockman (1994a) concluded that typical absence seizures are not necessarily benign and that medical management of these seizures does not necessarily influence the eventual outcome.

Tonic-Clonic Seizures

This type of seizure was formerly called grand mal seizure. Epidemiological studies have shown this type of seizure to be the most commonly found in children (Ellenberg, Hirtz, & Nelson, 1984; Juul-Jensen & Foldspang, 1983).

Tonic-clonic seizures begin with a loss of consciousness and a fall accompanied by a cry. The limbs extend, the back arches, and breathing may cease for short periods of time. This phase can last from several seconds to minutes. The limb extension is then followed by jerking of the head, arms, and legs. This is the clonic phase, which can last for minutes or may stop with intervention (Dreifuss, 1994). Most commonly, the jerking decreases and the child regains consciousness. Headaches and confusion usually ensue. Generally the child falls into a deep sleep lasting from 30 minutes to several hours.

Tonic-clonic seizures can occur after focal discharges and then are labeled as secondary generalization (Dreifuss, 1994). Tonic-clonic seizures have been found to be related to metabolic imbalances, liver failure, and head injury.

On rare occasions, tonic-clonic seizures may persist for extremely long periods of time or may be repeated so close together that no recovery occurs between attacks. This type of seizure is called *status epilepticus* (Lockman, 1994b). Underlying conditions such as subarachnoid hemorrhage, metabolic disturbances, and fevers (e.g., bacterial meningitis) can trigger status epilepticus in children (Phillips & Shanahan, 1989). Treatment for status epilepticus includes medication using very high dosages and in some case inducing a coma (Young, Segalowitz, Misek, Alp, & Boulet, 1983).

Associated Features

While seizures can occur in children with normal cognitive abilities (Hartlage & Hartlage, 1989), seizure disorders occur more frequently in individuals with depressed intelligence (Cook & Leventhal, 1992; Farwell, Dodrill, & Batzel, 1985). Low IQ (less than 80) with intractable epilepsy usually has a poor outcome for remission (Huttenlocher & Hapke, 1990).

Further, increased seizure activity is correlated with more severe cognitive deficits (Farwell et al., 1985). It is also important to note that children with early seizure onset are likely to have lower IQ (Aldenkamp, Gutter, & Beun, 1992).

Curatolo, Arpino, Stazi, and Medda (1995) investigated risk factors associated with the comorbidity of partial seizures, cerebral palsy (CP), and cognitive retardation in a group of children from Italy. Cerebral malformations (e.g., agenesis of the corpus callosum, NF, cortical dysplasia, lissencephaly) were found in half of the group of children. Children with an early onset of seizures were likely also to have CP and cognitive retardation. Children with a family history of epilepsy may have a "genetic predisposition to neurological disorders in general which range from epilepsy to CP" to cognitive retardation (Curatolo et al., 1995, p. 779). Cardiopulmonary resuscitation was also found to be a risk factor only in the group of children who did not have cerebral malformations. These authors suggest that resuscitation may be the first neurological abnormality that appears in this group, rather than a cause of the cerebral palsy.

Academic problems also may occur in children with seizure disorders (Pazzaglia & Frank-Pazzaglia, 1976), and LD may occur in approximately 15% to 30% of children with epilepsy (Matthews, Barabas, & Ferrai, 1983). Epidemiologic studies of children with epilepsy have found that approximately 50% have school difficulty ranging from mild to severe difficulties (Ross et al., 1980; Pazzaglia & Frank-Pazzaglia, 1976; Sillanpaa, 1992). In a study of Finnish children with epilepsy compared to nonepileptic controls, Sillanpaa (1992) found that the most frequent associated problems were mental (cognitive) retardation (31.4%), speech disorders (27.5%), and specific learning disorders (23.1%).

Children with seizure disorders have shown impaired performance on tests of reading, written language, and spelling (Gourley, 1990; Stedman et al., 1982; Seidenberg et al., 1986), as well as on teacher reports of attention, concentration, and information processing (Bennett-Levy & Stores, 1984). Reading comprehension appears to be more compromised than word recognition skills. However, social and cultural factors may also influence academic outcome and IQ for children with epilepsy-related disorders, as family factors (e.g., family setting and parental attitudes) were significantly correlated with underachievement (Mitchell, Chavez, Lee, & Guzman, 1991). Finally, psychomotor and visual-motor coordination problems also have been found to be poorer in children with seizure disorders than in typically developing children (Cull, 1988).

Psychosocial correlates. Although children with epilepsy differ from normal peers on a number of social-emotional variables, they do not appear to have higher rates of psychopathology than do children with other chronic medical or neurological conditions (Hartlage & Hartlage, 1989). Psychosocial features often include external locus of control, poor self esteem (Matthews, Barabas, & Ferrai, 1982), and increased dependency (Hartlage & Hartlage, 1989). Neppe (1985) indicates that individuals with epilepsy do experience psychosocial stress due to the effects of having a chronic illness, anxieties over social interactions, and restrictions in everyday life activities (e.g., driving).

Seizure disorders in childhood are related to other psychiatric conditions. The majority of children (85%) with temporal lobe epilepsy have cognitive retardation (25%) and disruptive behavior disorders including hyperactivity and "catastrophic rage" (Cook & Leventhal, 1992). Psychopathology, including psychoses, has been described in individuals with epilepsy (Neppe & Tucker, 1992), and psychiatric disorders (i,e., cognitive retardation, hyperkinesis, and rage disorders) have been reported in 85% of children with temporal lobe epilepsy (Lindsay, Ounstead, & Richards, 1979). Cook and Leventhal (1992) suggest that the loss of control children may experience as a result of epilepsy may be a special challenge during development, and children may react either passively or aggressively. However, these reactions may be related to how seizure activity affects cognition and impulse control.

Implications for Assessment

Children with seizure disorders require medical diagnosis and follow-up by a child neurologist. On-going assessment of neuropsychological, cognitive, and psychosocial functioning is useful for measuring the long-term effects of chronic seizure disorders. Because many children with epilepsy are not easily categorized, each child would benefit from a team that includes a physician, psychologist, teacher, and counselor (Black & Hynd, 1995).

Moderator Variables

There are a number of moderator variables which need to be recognized when evaluating the performance of a child with a seizure disorder. These variables are etiology of the seizure disorder, age of onset, seizure type, seizure frequency, medication, and family environment. Each of these moderator variables will be discussed in the following sections.

Etiology. The main classes of etiology for seizure disorders are *idiopathic,* where the cause is unknown, and *symptomatic*, where the cause is associated with organic and/or identified neurologic problems (Cull, 1988). Children with symptomatic epilepsy generally have lower IQ scores, with many showing mental (cognitive) retardation (Bourgeois, Prensky, Palkes, Talent, & Busch, 1983; Sillanpaa, 1992), whereas those with idiopathic epilepsy show normal distribution of intellectual ability. Symptomatic epilepsy is also associated with poorer academic and intellectual outcome (Dam, 1990).

Recently, neural developmental abnormalities have been implicated in the development of seizure-related disorders. Specifically, abnormal cell migration has been associated with both mental retardation and epilepsy (Falconer et al., 1990). As cells migrate and move into their final destinations during embryonic development, genetic and/or environmental factors may disrupt this process and ultimately result in epilepsy.

Age of onset. The majority of studies evaluating the significance of age of onset in relation to cognitive development have found a direct relationship between the two, with children with early onset generally showing poorer cognitive attainment (Seidenberg, 1988). Ellenberg and Nelson (1984) reported that children with normal neurological development prior to first seizure have a better prognosis for intellectual development at age 7 than did those who had earlier seizures *and* poorer neurological attainment.

O'Leary, Seidenberg, Berent, and Boll (1981) compared the performance of children with tonic-clonic seizures on the Halstead-Reitan Test Battery for Children. Those children with seizure onset before the age of 5 years were more impaired on measures of motor speed, attention and concentration, memory, and complex problem solving than those with a later onset. These researchers then evaluated the relationship between age of onset and partial seizure type. O'Leary et al. (1981) found that children with partial seizures and early onset performed more poorly than those with later onset, regardless of whether their seizures were partial or generalized.

Similarly, Hermann, Whitman, and Dell (1988) found that children with early onset performed more poorly on 8 of 11 scales of the LNNB-C. Evaluating age of onset with seizure type found that children with complex-partial seizures *and* early onset performed more poorly on Memory, Expressive Speech, and Reading, whereas generalized seizures *and* early onset were associated with poorer performance on Receptive Speech, Writing, Mathematics, and Intelligence Scales.

Duration of seizure has been found to co-occur with age of onset as a crucial variable and is frequently difficult to evaluate apart from age of onset. Generally, the earlier the onset, the longer the duration (Black & Hynd, 1995). Early onset and long duration appear to be associated with a poorer prognosis for learning. The number of seizures over the life span is a contributing factor to poor outcome as well (Aldenkamp, Gutter, & Beun, 1992).

Seidenberg (1988) makes the point that further study is needed in this area to determine whether the neuropsychological impairment is broad-based and general or whether there are specific areas of functioning that are more vulnerable during specific periods of development. This may be a likely case given what we know about neurodevelopment and increased cognitive, language, memory, and reasoning abilities in children. Thus, age of onset and seizure duration

are important variables to consider when evaluating children with seizure disorders, particularly when planning for etheir ducational and vocational needs.

Seizure type. The relationship between seizure type and intellectual and educational attainment is currently unclear. Some investigators have found memory deficits to be associated with partial-complex seizures with a temporal lobe focus (Fedio & Mirsky, 1969), whereas others have found that children with mixed seizures perform more poorly on measures of ability and achievement (Seidenberg et al., 1986). However, O'Leary et al. (1981) found few differences between seizure types, and those significant differences that did appear occurred more frequently in children with generalized seizures. Seidenberg (1988) concluded from his review of this literature that further study is needed using subtypes of seizure disorders. Most research has not identified subtypes of the seizure disorders when evaluating neuropsychological functioning.

Seizure frequency. The relationship between seizure frequency and cognitive development is presently unclear. Methodological considerations may account for this difficulty, as many studies have not subtyped the seizure group, thus possibly obscuring important findings (Dodrill, 1981).

Studies that have looked at seizure subtypes have generally found an inverse relationship between seizure duration and cognitive performance (longer duration = poorer test performance). Seidenberg (1988) found that with increasing frequency of seizure activity, performance on the full, verbal, and performance intelligence scales (FSIQ, VIQ, and PIQ) of the Wechsler, and the Trailmaking and Tactual Performance of the Reitan Battery significantly declined. When seizure type was also factored into the analysis, significant correlations for seizure duration, seizure frequency, and seizure type were found only for tonic-clonic subtype. This finding has been replicated by Dean (1983). Both of these studies used measures of lifetime frequency rather than setting a time frame of the previous month or year.

Seizure control is also related to seizure frequency.

Hermann et al. (1988) found that poor seizure control was related to poorer neuropsychological performance *only* for generalized epilepsies. Such a finding was not present for those children with partial seizures.

Seidenberg (1988) suggests that not only is subtyping of seizures important, but that researchers need to pay attention to seizure frequency, age of onset and duration, seizure type, and seizure control when evaluating neuropsychological functioning. He also suggests that seizure severity may be an overlooked variable in all investigations. Thus, etiology, age of onset of a seizure disorder, duration and frequency, type of seizure disorder, and possibly severity of the seizure all appear to contribute to the neuropsychological impairments that children may experience.

In addition to these intraindividual variables, two major extra individual variables interact with the seizure disorder–namely, medication effects and family environmental influences. Each of these will be developed in the following sections.

Medication. Antiepileptic drugs such as phenobarbital and clonazepam have been associated with cognitive difficulties (Besag, 1995). Others, including ethosuximide, sodium valporate, and carbamazepine generally have been found to be beneficial (Cull, 1988). Carbamazepine has been found to impair memory (Forsythe, Butler, Berg, & McGuire, 1991).

Some researchers have found that decreases in dosage are associated with better performance, while increases show no such effects (Cull, 1988). Moreover, children with more than one antiepileptic medication show more cognitive impairment. Whether polydrug treatment is related to a more severe seizure disorder and therefore to more cognitive impairment is unclear at the current time.

Family influences. Family and environmental influences on children with seizure disorders are just beginning to be explored. Given our transactional model, it would appear very important to gather information concerning important influences such as the family and school environments.

Preliminary data indicate that negative reactions of peers and teachers to the child's behaviors can have a significant deleterious effect on the child's school attainment (Dreifuss, 1994). As discussed earlier, behavioral changes during aura and postictal stages are frequently seen. When peers and teachers interpret these behaviors as willful and deviant, significant adjustment problems can arise. Research evaluating interventions such as educating the child's peers about seizure disorders and any resulting changes in attitudes has not been conducted. Such investigations are sorely needed. These influences on the child with a seizure disorder are probably more easily solved than variables such as age of onset, frequency of seizures, and severity of seizures.

Socioeconomic status (SES) has been found to be significantly related to intelligence. Singhi, Bansai, Singhi, and Pershad (1992) in a study with Indian children, found that SES was the second most powerful indicator of cognitive impairment, second only to status epilepticus. This finding is similar to that of American white and African-American children (Dodson, 1993).

Family variables such as stress, divorce, parental control and dependency, financial difficulty, and fewer family social supports have been shown to have a negative impact on cognitive development in children with seizure disorders (Austin, 1988; Hermann et al., 1988; Mulder & Suurmeijer, 1977; Hoare & Kerley, 1991). Austin, Risinger, and Beckett (1992) sought to evaluate the relative importance of demographics, seizure, and family variables on the behaviors of children with seizure disorders. In this study, no differences were found between boys and girls, children with mono- versus polydrug therapy, oneparent versus two-parent homes, or seizure type in behavioral problems. Significant findings were present for age, seizure frequency, family stress, and extended family social support. When stepwise multiple regression techniques were employed, intrafamily strain and marital strain emerged as the most significant predictors of behavioral problems. This finding is similar to findings linking family discord to psychopathology in nonepileptic children (Breslau, 1985; Austin, 1988).

Hoare and Russell (1995) describe an assessment

measure for identifying quality-of-life issues for children with chronic epilepsy and their families. This scale measures the impact of the illness on the child, the parents, and the family, and the cumulative impact. Further research is needed to determine the efficacy of this scale for intervention planning, but initial reports suggest that parents do have significant concerns, and these appear related to age of onset and seizure frequency.

Austin et al. (1992) suggest that the relationship between seizure variables (age of onset, duration, medication effects, frequency) and family variables (marital stress, lack of extended family support) may be bidirectional. Moreover, it has been hypothesized that family variables may have more influence on the child than seizure variables (Drotar & Bush, 1985). Models such as those of McCubbin and Patterson (1983) and Wallander, Varni, Babani, Banis, and Wilcox (1989) suggest that adaptive skills of families may inoculate the child against stress (i.e., of a seizure disorder). For example, Patterson (1983) hypothesizes that irritable behavior by a child may provoke a like response in the parent and thus provoke an escalating behavior in the child. Given the finding that antiepileptic drugs increase a child's irritability, it is likely that in families with underdeveloped adaptive skills, for example in family interactions, such negative cycles of escalation may frequently occur (Austin et al., 1992). This hypothesis is supported by the finding of Hoare (1984) of a higher prevalence of psychic disturbance in mothers and siblings of children with chronic epilepsy compared to those with newly diagnosed seizure disorders.

Summary

Seizure variables interact with family variables to influence the child's intellectual and educational attainment as well as his or her emotional adjustment. Investigators are just beginning to evaluate these transactional relationships and their contributions to appropriate interventions. It is not clear, at present, whether interventions that target environmental (school and family) influences can improve the child's eventual cognitive attainment. However, these variables are very important to keep in mind in treatment planning for these children, as they have been found to be potent predictors. The following section discusses intervention strategies for children with seizure disorders.

Implications for Intervention

Interventions addressing pharmacological, environmental, and educational strategies are reviewed briefly. In many cases, a dynamic plan may include one or more of the following strategies.

Pharmacological and Surgical Interventions

Anticonvulsant medications are commonly prescribed for children with nonfebrile seizure disorders (Cook & Leventhal, 1992). However, anticonvulsant medications (e.g., phenobarbital) produce side effects (e.g., sedation) that may interfere with academic performance (Cook & Leventhal, 1992) and may increase hyperactivity (Vining et al., 1987) or depression (Brent et al., 1987) in children.

In rare cases of intractable seizures, surgical removal of involved brain tissue may be an option. Several studies document resiliency in the developing brain, where intact brain regions compensate for damaged regions. For example, Meyer, Marsh, Laws, and Sharbrough (1986) found that children who had undergone surgical removal of the dominant temporal lobes, including the hippocampus and amygdala, showed no significant decline in verbal, performance, or full-scale IQ scores. Smith, Walker, and Myers (1988) also found that a 6-year-old made remarkable postoperative recovery following surgical removal of the right hemisphere. The child had perinatal epileptogenic seizures that worsened and spread from the right to the left hemisphere. Postsurgical test scores showed average verbal intelligence (96), low-average performance abilities (87), and average full-scale (90) potential. The extent to which cognitive abilities improve or develop following surgical interventions depends on a number of factors, including the age of the child and the location of the lesion, once intact brain regions are freed from the abnormal influences of the lesioned regions.

Environmental Interventions

Given the findings of Austin et al. (1992) discussed previously, it would appear imperative not only to assess variables such as family strain, behavioral concerns, and discipline, but also to plan interventions taking these factors into consideration. Assistance, as needed, in parenting, stress management, and epilepsy education are likely avenues for intervention.

It is important in the course of epilepsy education to discuss the potential for parents to overcompensate for their child's illness and the possible guilt that may accompany a diagnosis. It has been found that parents who expect to provide lifetime care for their child do not facilitate the development of independent behaviors (Safilios-Rothschild, 1970). Moreover, it has also been found that parents may lower expectations for their child's academic performance (Ferrari, 1989). Therefore, it would appear to be crucial to discuss these possibilities with parents and to help them set realistic goals for their child and encourage coping skills for the epileptic child. When a transactional approach is not taken, the child's program will be incomplete and most likely will be at least partially unsuccessful.

Educational Interventions

It is very important that the school not only be aware of the diagnosis of epilepsy but educational staff should develop and institute a plan for working effectively with the child who has a seizure disorder. The child neuropsychologist can be helpful in the initial planning and implementation phase of the educational program. At the very least, medication monitoring is important. Sachs and Barrett (1995) list behavioral side effects of medication, such as drowsiness, lethargy, overactivity, confusion, and motor signs (e.g., clumsiness), and suggest that teachers should be on the look-out for these signs. Moreover, information on what action should be taken in the event of a seizure in school is very important for teachers and staff. Generally, little action is needed except when the child needs to be protected from injury. It is not appropriate to place items in the child's mouth, to restrain the child, or to perform cardiopulmonary resuscitation (Hartlage & Telzrow, 1984).

Communication between the school and the physician is important for monitoring the child's seizure frequency and medication response (Gadow, 1985). The neuropsychologist may serve a much needed service in interpreting medical information for school personnel and parents. Linking of these services is not only desirable for understanding the child's needs but also crucial for developing a comprehensive intervention program for the child. Formulating the program can assist in planning for psychosocial stressors that may occur at home or in school, monitoring medication compliance and effectiveness, and enhancing the child's school performance in either special or regular education (Sachs & Barrett, 1995). Helping peers to understand the child's needs and his or her occasional unusual behaviors (during seizure activity) may smooth the way for children with seizure disorders to develop healthy peer relationships.

In summary, a transactional approach is an important vehicle for understanding and planning for the needs of children with seizures disorders. Similarly, children with head injuries would benefit from this type of integrated approach. See Chapter 10 for a discussion of interventions for children sustaining traumatic brain injury. Cerebral palsy is reviewed next.

CEREBRAL PALSY

Cerebral palsy is not a unitary disorder but, rather, consists of many subtypes, which share the common symptoms of movement disorder, early onset, and no progression of the disorder (Nelson et al., 1994). Cerebral palsy can be subtyped by the area of the body involved, level of difficulty experienced, and concomitant disorders.

Etiology of Cerebral Palsy

Cerebral palsy (CP) has been estimated to occur in 1.2 to 2.5 children per 1,000, with at least 5,000 new cases diagnosed yearly in the United States (Grether, Cummins, & Nelson, 1992). A minority of identified cases can be traced to documented brain injury from infection or trauma after 4 months of life (Nelson et al., 1994).

Low-Birth-Weight Factors

Low-birth-weight babies are at high risk for the development of CP. As a result of increased rates of survival, CP in low-birth-weight babies is increasing (Hagberg, Hagberg, & Zetterstrom, 1989; Pharoah et al., 1990; Stanley, 1994). Survival rates for CP appear to depend on the severity of the disorder and the level of intelligence. Children with severe motor involvement and extremely low IQ have a shorter life expectancy (Eyman et al., 1990).

Premature infants who are significantly smaller than expectations appear to be at high risk for CP (Nelson et al., 1994). Frequent medical difficulties found in these infants may contribute to the development of CP. These complications include intraventricular hemorrhage, white matter necrosis, and variation in cerebral blood flow (Leviton & Paneth, 1990). Evidence for the involvement of these complications in CP has been found by ultrasonography in infants and neuroimaging for older children and adults (Krageloh-Mann et al., 1992).

Twins who are low birth weight appear to be at special risk for CP as well (Nelson et al., 1994). If one of the twins dies at or before birth, the remaining twin appears to be at high risk for CP (Szymonowicz, Preston, & Yu, 1986). In fact, the incidence of twins in the general population is 2%, with a 10% incidence rate of CP within this sample (Grether et al., 1992).

Newborn Illnesses

Babies born with damaged brains from the delivery are at risk for CP. These infants frequently show low tone, breathing problems, low APGAR scores, delayed reflexes, and seizures (Nelson & Leviton, 1991). When all of these symptoms are present, the child is at high risk for CP, with the risk decreasing as the number of presenting symptoms decreases (Ellenberg & Nelson, 1984; Seidman et al., 1991).

Subtypes of CP appear related to different causes. Most children and adults with CP did not experience oxygen deprivation during birth. Interuterine infection have been associated with CP, as has strokes at birth. Asphyxia has been most closely related to quadriplegia (Nelson & Leviton, 1991). In most cases, however, it is not possible to determine the cause of CP.

Brain Malformations

Children with CP appear to have structural brain disorders which appear to be related to abnormal neuronal migration (Volpe, 1992). In these cases cells have migrated to the wrong place and thus brain layers are disordered, cells are out of place, and/or there are too many or not enough cells in certain critical brain regions. Volpe (1992) estimates that approximately 33% of CP in full-term infants involves some disordered cells and layers due to cortical malformation deficits.

Subtypes of Cerebral Palsy

Six subtypes of CP are currently identified, although some controversy exists in the field as to their delineation. The subtypes presented in this book have been adopted by many pediatric neurologists (Nelson et al., 1994). They are spastic hemiplegia, spastic quadriplegia, spastic diplegia, extrapyramidal, atonic, ataxic, and mixed. These subtypes are based on the motor systems, the body regions, and the amount of impairment involved.

Spastic Hemiplegia

Children with this subtype show difficulties on one side of their body, with more arm than leg involvement. The right side of the body (left hemisphere) appears to be at the highest risk for involvement and is found in two-thirds of patients (Byers, 1941; Crothers & Paine, 1959). The child's walk is characterized by toe-walking and swinging the affected leg in a semicircular movement when taking steps. Moreover, the affected arm does not follow the reciprocal movement usually seen in walking. The foot faces in toward the middle of the body, with hypotonia present throughout the limbs. The affected side often appears smaller and during development becomes noticeably smaller than the unaffected side. This condition frequently causes lower spinal and walking difficulties as the child develops (Nelson et al., 1994).

Children with this type of CP may show cognitive retardation (28%) and seizure disorders (33%) (Aicardi, 1990; Perlstein & Hood, 1955). In addition, brain studies using MRI and CT scans have frequently found atrophy of the affected hemisphere with areas of cortical thinning, loss of white matter, and expansion of the same-side lateral ventricle (Uvebrandt, 1988; Wiklund, Uvebrandt, & Floodmark, 1991).

Spastic Quadriplegia

In contrast to spastic hemiplegia, spastic quadriplegia is characterized by increased muscle tone, with the legs the most involved (Nelson et al., 1994). Some difficulty with articulation and swallowing may be present when the corticospinal tract is involved. Almost half of children with this subtype are cognitively retarded or learning disabled (Crothers & Paine, 1959; Robinson, 1973), and a large percentage have tonic-clonic seizure disorders (Ingram, 1964). These children also frequently have visual impairments (Preakey, Wilson, & Wilson, 1974).

Children with this type of CP often have morphological abnormalities, generally in the white matter, including death of white matter, edema, and cysts (Chutorian et al., 1979). In addition to missing white matter in specific areas, the cortex underlying the white matter is also affected with accompanying thickening of the meninges and gliosis in the white matter (Nelson et al., 1994). Nelson et al. (1994) further report that these lesions can vary from one full hemisphere to one lobe, to a specified portion of a lobe. Some structural deviations are also found in the brainstem (Wilson, Mirra, & Schwartz, 1982).

Spastic Diplegia

Spastic diplegia generally involves both legs, with some arm involvement. This type of CP is commonly found in premature infants, with approximately 80% of infants with motor abnormalities showing this type of CP (Hagberg et al., 1989). These children may later develop ataxia and frequently toe-walk (Nelson et al., 1994). The clinical picture of children with spastic diplegia includes hypertonia with rigidity. Many children show generalized tonic-clonic seizures (27%; Ingram, 1955), strabismus (43%; Ingram, 1955), and cognitive retardation (30%, with increasingly higher rates as more extremely low birth-weight babies survive; Hagberg et al., 1989).

The brains of these children often evidence porencephalic cysts and microgyria (many small gyri) with abnormalities in tracts which serve the legs as they transverse the internal capsule (Christensen & Melchior, 1967). Atrophy, abnormal cortical formation, and periventricular lesions have been found to correlate strongly with severe impairment (Hagberg et al., 1989; Yokochi, Hosoe, Shimabukuro, & Kodama, 1990).

Extrapyramidal Cerebral Palsy

This type of CP involves problems with posture, involuntary movements, hypertonia, and rigidity (Nelson, Swaiman, & Russman, 1994). Extrapyramidal CP can be further divided into choreoathetotic and dystonic CP.

Choreoathetotic cerebral palsy. This type of CP is characterized by involuntary movements that are very large and one marked by slow, irregular, twisting movements seen mostly in the upper extremities. This type of CP has been most clearly associated with birth asphyxia and oxygen deprivation (Nelson et al., 1994). Use of ventilation and brain lesions due to asphyxia are frequently seen directly after birth. Changes in the caudate nucleus are generally found, with cysts present where arteries and veins have swelled and neighboring cells are negatively affected (Volpe, 1987). Demyelinization is often present, with deviations in critical columns and neuronal loss in corticospinal tracts. An MRI study by Yokochi, Aiba, Kodama, and Fujimoto (1991) reported that a majority of children have basal ganglia, thalamic, and white matter lesions.

In this subtype of CP, muscle tone will fluctuate between hypertonic, normal, and hypertonic (Thomas, 1985). Choreiform movements are present in the face and limbs, and are asymmetric, involuntary, and uncoordinated (Nelson et al., 1994).

Children with choreoathetotic CP frequently have speech production problems, with unexpected changes in rate and volume. The upper motor neuron unit appears to be affected, and this is frequently accompanied by seizures and cognitive retardation (Nelson et al., 1994).

Dystonic cerebral palsy. This form of CP is believed to be uncommon, with the trunk muscles being mostly affected. The trunk may be twisted and contorted, which involves the head movement (Nelson et al., 1994).

Atonic Cerebral Palsy

Children with atonic CP have hypertonic and muscle weakness in the limbs. This type of CP is less common than the other subtypes and is associated with delayed developmental motor milestones. Its cause is unknown, and it is not known which brain region is affected in this subtype of CP (Nelson et al., 1994).

Ataxic Cerebral Palsy

Ataxic CP is associated with dysfunction of the cerebellum leading to difficulty with skilled movements (Hagberg, Hagberg, & Olozo, 1975). Hypotonia, poor fine motor skills, and clumsiness are seen and identified late in the first year of life. Walking develops very late (3 or 4 years of age), and frequent falling is observed in children with ataxic CP (Nelson et al., 1994).

Findings of brain pathology in ataxic CP are inconsistent. Some researchers have found abnormality in the cerebellar vermis (Bordarier & Aicardi,

1990), while others have found differences in the cerebral hemispheres (Miller & Cala, 1989).

Neuropsychological Aspects of Cerebral Palsy

There appears to be a progression in deficits as high-risk children mature (Majnemer, Rosenblatt, & Riley, 1994). In a study by Majnemer et al. (1994), 23 healthy and 51 high-risk neonates were tested at birth, 1 year, and 3 years. Findings included 13 (7%) delayed at age 1 year, increasing to 39% at age 3. Those subjects who were high-risk *and* normal at the neonatal stage had the most favorable outcome. Additional studies have found a decline in abilities in life (ages 18—25 years) that is attributed to ongoing psychological stress rather than to medical reasons (Pimm, 1992).

The finding that many children with CP have concomitant learning disabilities, cognitive retardation, and attention deficit disorders has implications for educational planning (Blondis, Roizen, Snow, & Accardo, 1993). This result, coupled with the finding by Majnemer et al. (1994), indicates not only that the needs of these children are multiple but that they become more evident as the child matures.

In addition localization of brain damage also has an impact on the type of learning difficulties experienced by children with CP. Children with motor difficulties appear to be at higher risk for deficits in arithmetic and visual-spatial skills than those who do not have such difficulties (Roussouris, Hubley, & Dear, 1993). In a further study of motor effects on visuospatial abilities, Howard and Henderson (1989) found that compared to athetoid CP and normal children, children with spastic CP showed more difficulty in visual-spatial judgment. These researchers also found that experience and training can improve skills dramatically.

Right-sided hemiplegia (left-hemisphere involvement) has been found to result in language impairment in girls but not in boys (Carlsson et al., 1994). Similarly, in a study by Feldman, Janosky, Scher, and Wareham (1994) preschool boys with CP did not show language impairment. In children with right and left hemiplegia, both boys and girls showed significant impairment on nonverbal tasks. It was not clear why boys showed less language impairment. The extent to which these findings are related to other research showing gender differences between normal males and females for language lateralization is unknown. For example, Witelson (1990) indicates that women have more focused representation of language and speech functions in the anterior left frontal regions than do men. Further research may add to our understanding of these gender differences in language deficits in children with CP.

Working memory, a skill associated with attention, has not been found to be an area of impairment for children with CP (White, Craft, Hale, & Park, 1994). White et al. (1994) taught children with spastic CP to utilize memory strategies such as covert and overt rehearsal in order to improve articulation skills. Impairment was found in phonemic discrimination in children with CP and speech impairment. Bishop, Brown, and Robson (1990) also reported that children with impaired speech and CP show difficulty discriminating same—different nonwords. There were no difficulties found in receptive language skills or in their ability to discriminate altered sounds in real words. Therefore, it appears that CP children with speech impairment do *not* show concomitant language problems but do show phonological-processing difficulty. Speech production ability has been found to correlate significantly with sound-blending skills (Smith, 1989). Reading difficulties have not been found in this population to the same degree as arithmetic-based learning disabilities and visual-perceptual deficits (Rowan & Monaghan, 1989). This is somewhat surprising given the relationship between phonemic awareness deficits and reading disabilities in learning-disabled samples. Reading deficits also have been shown in children who have both phonological and visuospatial deficits; so the absence of high rates of reading problems in CP groups is interesting.

Attentional skills in children with CP have been found to be deficient (Blondis et al., 1993). White, Craft, Park, and Figiel (1994) found that children with bilateral anterior lesions showed significant problems in focussing of attention, while those with bilateral posterior lesions showed slower reaction times. These researchers interpreted their findings to indicate problems in visual attention when anterior lesions, particularly in the left hemisphere, occur. Using a dichotic listening paradigm, Hugdahl and Carlsson (1994) found significant auditory attentional difficulties in children with both left and right hemiplegia.

The most striking finding in the neuropsychology of CP children is the heterogeneity of problems experienced by this varied population. Early identification of CP, development of appropriate intervention program, and the use of a multidisciplinary team approach have been found to relate strongly to later success in school and life (Rowan & Monaghan, 1989). Kohn (1990) found a strong link between psychoeducational, family, and vocational support and positive outcome. She strongly recommends that pediatricians acquaint themselves with community resources and utilize early referrals to appropriate early childhood programs for young children with CP.

Psychosocial Correlates of Cerebral Palsy

Although parents of children with motor disabilities have been found to report more sadness, these symptoms have not been found to be strongly related to the child's rate of development or to parent—child interactions (Smith, Innocenti, Boyce, & Smith, 1993). Further studies of mothers with CP children have found that professionals who interact with these families disregard information provided by mothers (Case-Smith & Nastro, 1993). These difficulties are compounded by the frequent change in professionals who work with families. Perrin, Ayoub, and Willett (1993) found that mothers' feelings of control over their child's program were a potent predictor of the child's adjustment. This finding is important to consider when designing intervention programs for children with CP, and provides further evidence of the need for an integrated, transactional model.

Family interactions have been linked to the psychological adjustment of children regardless of age and socioeconomic status (Perrin et al., 1993). Dallas,

Stevenson, and McGurk (1993a) found that CP children often are more passive and less assertive than their siblings and generally were treated as if they were younger than their chronological age. Maternal intervention between CP children and siblings was found to be more common than with nondisabled siblings. Similarly, Dallas et al. (1993b) found that the tendency toward sibling and maternal control of interactions resulted in lower self-efficacy and poorer development of social skills in children with CP.

The findings of Dallas et al. (1993a, 1993b) were supported by results of a study by King et al. (1993), who found lower self-efficacy and self-control on self-report measures in a group of male and female children with CP. Level of social self-efficacy was found to be a good predictor of the adolescent's later independence and persistence. A follow-up study of adults with motor disabilities found that they were more frequently unemployed, left the parental home at a later age than normal peers, and completed less schooling (Kokkonen et al., 1991). Recommendations were for earlier vocational training and support and additional family assistance for individuals with CP. Moreover, for adults who received such support in adolescence, self-esteem and self-efficacy measures have not found them to differ from typical adults (Magill-Evans &

Restall, 1991). A cognitive-behavioral approach to social skills and assertiveness training appears to meet the needs of adolescents with CP.

CONCLUSIONS

Children with CP are more different from one another than the same on neuropsychological measures. What they seem to have in common is the need for early intervention that is tailored to their specific needs and provides vocational and family support. A transactional approach is particularly relevant for this population given the findings that when psychoeducational objectives, vocational training, and parental support are interwoven, the child's later outcome is most optimal. For these children, the neuropsychologist needs to move beyond the diagnostic role into the role of advocate and counselor (Sachs & Redd, 1993). The Americans with Disabilities Act of 1990 empowers disabled adults, children, and adolescents to gain the vocational and educational training needed for life success. The extent to which we can foster this kind of ecologically valid intervention may mean the difference between developing individuals who are self-reliant, self-sufficient, and independent or semi-independent.

CHAPTER 10

ACQUIRED NEUROLOGICAL DISORDERS AND DISEASES OF CHILDHOOD

Though relatively rare compared to neuro-developmental disorders, acquired neurological disorders and diseases represent some of the more common disorders seen by child clinical neuropsychologists. This chapter reviews traumatic brain injury in children; exposure to teratogenic agents, including alcohol and cocaine; childhood cancer; and infectious diseases of the CNS, including meningitis and encephalitis. Research into these various disorders and diseases suggests the need for a transactional approach to assessing and treating children with these neurological conditions.

TRAUMATIC BRAIN INJURY

Traumatic brain injury (TBI) is a relatively common occurrence in childhood (Berg, 1986). Although trauma can occur at any developmental stage, children are at particular risk of accidents (Hynd & Willis, 1988; Spreen, Tupper, Risser, Tuokko, & Edgell, 1984). Goldstein and Levin (1990) suggest that head trauma to children and adolescents results in high rates of mortality and morbidity, and most estimates suggest that as many as one million children a year sustain closed head injuries. Approximately 500,000 children incur head injuries in bicycle accidents, and about 400 children die each year as a result of these injuries (Department of Health and Human Services, 1989).

Cook and Leventhal (1992) suggest that car accidents involving adolescents and older children, home injuries in preschool children, and falls for children between 6 and 12 years of age account for the major-

ity of head injuries sustained by children. Silver, Hales, and Yudofsky (1992) report that child abuse is the most common reason for head injury in infants, and indicate that the figure is quite high–64% (Department of Health and Human Services, 1989). Despite these figures, Ewing-Cobbs and Fletcher (1990) report that very few systematic studies have been conducted to assess the neuropsychological recovery process in children or to address the educational needs of children sustaining TBI.

Kraus (1987) found that children from birth to age 24 years have higher injury rates than older individuals, and males have twice as many injuries as females (Kraus et al., 1984). Injury rates decrease for females during the first 15 years, while incidence rates increase for males between 5 and 15 years. Children and adolescents may be at risk for TBI as a result of sports activities, including football (Gerberich et al., 1983) and soccer (Tysvaer, Storli, & Bachen, 1989).

Recent evidence suggests that soccer players who engage in repeated "heading," a technique whereby the child hits the soccer ball with his or her head, scored lower on the Trails A and B and the Shipley Estimated IQ (Witol & Webbe, 1994). Others have not found major differences between adolescent and young adult tennis players and soccer players on common neuropsychological measures; however, within-group differences were observed in soccer players who played the most games (Abreau, Templer, Schuyler, & Hutchison, 1990). There was a negative correlation —.41) between the number of soccer games played and scores on a measure of attention and information-processing (Paced Auditory Serial Addition Task). Thus, Abreau et al. (1990) concluded that soccer players do not "warrant a clean bill of neuro-psychological health," and that "soccer provides minor damage or dysfunctioning" (p. 179). Professional soccer players also show signs of mild to moderate neuropsychological impairment (81%), with central cerebral atrophy in one-third of the group (Tysvaer, 1992).

Neurobehavioral Sequelae of Head Injury

The neurobehavioral sequelae of head injury may include declines in nonverbal intelligence; visual-motor impairment; attentional and memory deficits; decreases in oral fluency, comprehension, and verbal association; achievement declines in reading; and an increase in psychiatric disorders (Ewing-Cobbs, Fletcher, & Levin, 1986). Obviously, deficits will vary across children depending on their age at injury and on the nature, type, and severity of injury sustained.

The extent to which TBI alters brain development and functional capacity of the CNS depends on a variety of factors, including the age of injury, the etiology and severity of the injury sustained, the neurological complications, and the treatment protocol (Fletcher, Levin, & Landry, 1984). These factors are reviewed in detail in following sections.

Age of Onset of Brain Injury

Early research investigating the effects of brain injury in childhood revealed that children showed spontaneous or eventual recovery of language functions (i.e., aphasic symptoms) within 6 months of injury (Alajouanine & L'Hermittee, 1965). These findings suggested that children had remarkable resiliency and potential for recovery due to the rapid changes in neurodevelopment that facilitated recovery of function. More recently, these notions have been challenged by findings showing that early injury may have more deleterious effects than later injury (Teeter, 1986). Apparently, transient and permanent effects of injury may have a significant impact on the recovery process, and these factors are particularly sensitive to the age of the child.

Early observations suggested that brain injury in children had less severe and more short-term side effects than in adults (Kolb & Whishaw, 1990). This observation has been challenged by more recent findings, and some conclude that "it first became evident that earlier may not always be better, and then it became apparent that earlier may actually be worse" (Kolb & Whishaw, 1990, p. 695). O'Leary and Boll (1984) further contend that the developing brain is more vulnerable to damage during rapid growth periods, and that factors usually involved in early damage (e.g., toxins, anoxia, nutritional deficiencies) often produce general, diffuse rather than discrete, focal damage. Closed-head injuries may not follow this general rule (O'Leary & Boll, 1984) and may have a better prognosis than injuries caused by other factors (Chelune & Edwards, 1981). However, Isaacson (1975) argues that even with focal injuries, permanent structural changes in the brain occur following early injury.

Kolb and Whishaw (1990) indicate that there are three critical age divisions influencing the loss of function and outcome of the injury: less than 1 year of age; between 1 and 5 years of age; and more than 5 years of age. Damage occurring prior to age 1 most often results in significant impairment compared to later injury, whereas injury between 1 to 5 years often results in reorganization of functions and recovery of language ability (Kolb & Whishaw, 1990). Injury after age 5 likely results in more significant loss of function. Not only are damaged regions impaired, but O'Leary and Boll (1984) argue that the normal process of brain development is impaired as well.

Transient and Permanent Reactions Following Injury

Isaacson (1976) identified ten major transient reactions following brain injury:

1. Cells at the site of injury are destroyed.
2. Cellular activity in nearby cells is disrupted.
3. Phagocytic and astrocytic reactions occur at the border of the injury.
4. Blood vessels are changed at the site of injury.

5. Edema or swelling occurs.
6. Swelling disrupts the functioning of normal, undamaged cells.
7. Cerebrospinal fluid is altered.
8. Undamaged cells are no longer monitored or inhibited by the damaged cells.
9. Newly developed axon collaterals move into regions once occupied by the damaged cells.
10. Cellular makeup and brain size are affected.

Neurobehavioral deficits that result from these transient factors may improve quickly once these transient reactions are stabilized (Teeter, 1986). However, these transient factors may result in more serious permanent changes in brain structure and function that result in dramatic and long-term losses.

Permanent changes in the brain that may occur following early injury include the proliferation of axon collaterals and the development of major abnormal motor tracts. Although newly formed axon collaterals allow for recovery to occur, Isaacson (1976) suggests that abnormal patterns may be formed when these collaterals assume regulation over damaged regions. New synaptic contacts may facilitate recovery, but they also may produce abnormal brain activity as major tracts move into regions normally regulated by areas that have sustained damage (Teeter, 1986). Isaacson (1976) points out that the developing brain is highly susceptible to the influences of these new neuronal contacts compared to the brain of an adult. Further, the reduction of brain size that may accompany early injury is a serious problem. Thus, Isaacson (1976) suggests that "from a structural point of view early damage must be considered to be more disastrous than damage occurring later" (p. 42). Brain damage in adolescents does not result in changes in the size of the brain but begins to follow a course similar to that found in mature adults. Damage for both adolescents and adults thus often results in more discrete and localized deficits than damage to young children.

Isaacson (1975) further suggests that the normal developmental process is altered as a result of structural changes in the brain following injury. Isaacson and Spear (1984) contend that the behavioral and

cognitive consequences of early brain injury are related to the changes in function of the remaining brain systems. Specifically, damage to brain tissue early in life may change growth patterns, "neurogenesis," neuronal proliferation and migration, and neural connections in remaining neural systems (Isaacson & Spear, 1984). Secondary features of brain injury, including alterations in developing structures, neurochemicals, and hormones, affect how behaviors may be compromised as well as the developmental course and adaptation at any given age. Further, Isaacson and Spear (1984) suggest that unanticipated consequences of early damage can result but that effective interventions may alleviate or alter these consequences.

Taylor (1984) indicates that normal cognitive development is extremely complex and that numerous other variables (e.g., learning environment) preclude meaningful generalizations about the effects of early brain injury. Taylor argues that increased emphasis should be placed on determining the conditions that facilitate or impede cognitive and behavioral sparing. Fletcher et al. (1984) propose that neuroimaging technologies be employed with indices of environmental factors and age-appropriate developmental measures to study the effects of early injury on children.

Another critical point to consider when investigating brain injury in young children is that damage to later-developing brain regions (e.g., frontal lobes) may not be obvious until years after injury has occurred (Rourke et al., 1983). Children may actually "grow into a deficit" when developing brain structures that normally control and regulate a particular behavior become more important for the execution of the activity. Kolb and Fantie (1989) concur and indicate that this makes it very difficult to assess the impact of early injuries to frontal and posterior brains regions, as these areas do not assume adult-like functioning until about 10 to 12 years of age. Further, Rourke et al. (1983) found that in some cases initial deficits are replaced by other deficits. In young chikldren attentional problems are more pronounced than cognitive deficits, whereas the opposite pattern is found in older children with brain damage. Rourke et al. (1983) suggest that attentional deficits may actually mask other cognitive problems; once this "psychic edema" subsides, more discrete cognitive deficits may be observed.

Nature, Type, and Severity of Injury

The nature, type, and severity of brain injury affects the outcome and long-term sequelae associated with such injury in children. Further, Kalsbeek, McLaurin, Harris, and Miller (1980) report that injury type (e.g., falling versus being hit on the head) will produce very different cognitive, behavioral, and neuropsychological impairment, which should be carefully assessed and monitored.

The mechanisms of closed-head injury involve several factors, including compression of neural tissues, which are pushed together; tension as tissues are torn apart; shearing as tissues slide over other tissue; and skull deformations that change the volume of cerebrospinal fluid (Berg, 1986). Brain injury may occur in three basic ways. First, acceleration occurs when a moving object (e.g., baseball bat) makes sudden contact with the skull. This type of injury may result in bruising or contusions in the brain stem, under the corpus callosum, in the cerebellum, or in the occipital lobes. Contré coup is common in these conditions and results in more severe damage in regions opposite the point of contact. Berg (1986) indicates that pressure waves spread out from the injury site and cause tissue tearing. The frontal lobes are particularly sensitive to this kind of injury because of the bony protrusions in the anterior skull. Second, deceleration occurs when the head is moving faster than a stationary object (e.g., the dashboard of an automobile), causing abrupt deceleration of the skull. Contusions occur at the site of injury, and contre coup may also result as the brain is thrust back against the skull. Occipital impact may cause frontal and temporal involvement. Midbrain injury also may involve temporal lobe injury to the opposite lobe, while impact to the frontal regions is less likely to result in occipital damage because the surface of the posterior skull is smooth (Berg, 1986). Third, rotations of the neck or head may occur when there is both acceleration and deceleration, and this results in shearing. Although the skull is less rigid in children than in adults, shearing may still cause significant distortions and damage.

Unilateral Damage

The effects of lateralized damage has been investigated extensively, and it has been found that functional loss following injury may be recovered by the intact hemisphere when injury occurs early (Rourke et al., 1983). Although Woods and Teuber (1978) found that the right hemisphere can assume language functions following damage to the left hemisphere, it does so at the expense of reduced right-hemisphere (i.e., visual-spatial) functions. Rasmussen and Milner (1977) also suggest that transfer of language occurs primarily when the speech regions of the left hemisphere are involved. In instances where the Broca's area remains intact, the left hemisphere may reorganize rather than transfer language functions to the right hemisphere.

Evidence from hemidecortications in early childhood provide insight into recovery of function as well. Kolb and Whishaw (1990) indicate that although the two hemispheres are functionally specialized at birth, both are relatively flexible in their capacity to pick up functions of the hemisphere that has been surgically removed. The price of transfer, however, seems to be a loss of functions of higher level abilities and generalized lower intelligence. For example, simple language functions appear intact following left hemispherectomy, but complex language skills (e.g., complex syntax) are compromised. Conversely, right hemispherectomy results in normal language functions and in decreased complex visual-spatial skills (e.g., visual organization, perception of mazes). Thus, while both hemispheres can assume functions of the opposite hemisphere if it has been removed early, neither can mediate all of these functions.

While these findings support the notion of brain plasticity, Boll and Barth (1981) cite studies indicating that surgical removal of one hemisphere following injury may actually produce fewer problems than occur when surgical removal is not feasible. It may be that the damaged hemisphere exerts abnormal influence as the intact hemisphere attempts to assume the functions of the damaged hemisphere, an influence that is not possible when the damaged hemisphere is removed.

Transactional Features of TBI

The neuropsychological, academic, and psychosocial sequelae of TBI depends on numerous factors (e.g., age, severity and site of injury). Further, environmental and premorbid status, including IQ level and presence of psychiatric or behavioral problems, is an important factor affecting outcome.

Table 10.1 presents a summary of select research findings for children sustaining TBI. This summary suggests that a variety of domains are affected by traumatic injury. Individual children will vary in terms of the specific features and dysfunctions manifested following injury. The various domains are reviewed next.

Genetic Factors

Although traumatic brain injury is not a result of genetic factors, there is some evidence that certain children may be at higher risk for sustaining brain injury. In a discussion of risk factors associated with TBI, Goldstein and Levin (1990) indicate that children who sustain injuries may not be a random group. Preexisting conditions often include hyperactivity and antisocial behavioral problems (Craft, Shaw, & Cartlidge, 1972); developmental learning problems, particularly in young males (Klonoff & Paris, 1974); reading difficulties, impulsivity, and overactivity (Brown, Chadwick, Shaffer, Rutter, & Traub, 1981). Goldstein and Levin (1990) suggest that preexisting behavioral patterns may increase risk-taking behaviors, leading to traumatic injuries.

Prenatal/Postnatal Factors

There are no known prenatal factors that predispose a child to TBI, although brain damage can occur during the birth process. Postnatal factors generally are most important, including both child and family characteristics associated with increased rates of TBI in children. See the discussion on genetic factors. The level of violence and child-related homicides appears to be on this rise, and one can only wonder how many children and adolescents sustain TBI as a result of gunshot wounds and physical attacks.

Parental behaviors, particularly avoidable situations such as drinking and driving or not restraining children while driving (Cook & Leventhal, 1992), may also place children at risk for TBI. However, family socioeconomic status and parental employment history do not appear related to increased rates of TBI (Klauber, Barrett-Connor, Hofstetter, & Micik, 1986). Child abuse victims do sustain high levels of brain injury, especially for young children (Department of Health and Human Services, 1989).

Neuropsychological Correlates

Neuropsychological correlates usually relate to the major areas that have been damaged. Patterns in children begin to mimic those of adults in late childhood or early adolescence. See the following discussions for detailed deficits associates with various injury sites.

Intellectual, Perceptual, Memory, and Attentional Functions

Intellectual functions. Persistent intellectual deficits have been found in children sustaining brain injury with coma status for more than 24 hours (Levin & Eisenberg, 1979). Chadwick, Rutter, Brown, Shaffer, and Traub (1981) found that Performance IQ was lower than Verbal IQ in children suffering posttraumatic amnesia. Winogron, Knights, and Bowden (1984) found similar Performance IQ deficits in children with low Glasgow Coma scores (7 or less). Ewing-Cobbs and Fletcher (1990) suggest that intelligence seems most compromised for severe injuries.

While personality factors following injury in children are somewhat similar to patterns found in adults, Berg (1986) reports that cognitive deficits appear less

Table 10.1. Transactional Features of Traumatic Brain Injury in Children

Genetic
– No genetic linkage
– TBI children may not be random group
  • Hyperactivity
  • Antisocial behavioral problems
  • Reading problems, impulsivity, and
    hyperactivity

Environmental
– No known prenatal factors
– Birth process may produce brain damage
– Level of violence in environment
– Parental behaviors place child at risk
  • Child abuse
  • Drinking while driving
  • Not restraining child in car

Neuropsychological Correlates

– Patterns depend on site and type of injury.
– Begin to mimic adult patterns in later childhood.
– Mild injury show few NP deficits.

Intelligence
– Persistent deficits coma (24 hrs +)
– PIQ > VIQ with amnesia
– Low PIQ with low Glascow (7 or less)
– Less specific cognitive deficits
– Lateralized damage not always clear-cut
– Left hemisphere—language deficits
– Right hemisphere—design deficits
– Lateralization of higher level skills not
  always predictable
– Laterilization of sensory—perceptual
  and motor deficits more clear-cut

Perceptual
– Severity of injury
– Timed conditions
– Visual-spatial

Memory
– Common in TBI
– Verbal learning and memory
– Visual-spatial
– Selective reminding
– Memory improves first year
– Verbal learning of new information
  deficits persist with severe injury
– Even mild injury can affect

Attentional and Executive Functions
– Disinhibition
– Impulsivity
– Attentional deficits
– Excessive verbalization
– Socially inappropriate
– Insensitivity

Academic
– Not well researched
– Recognized as handicapping condition
  (IDEA, 1990)
– Problems persist after EEGs and
  neurological exams appear normal
– Language difficulties
– Writing to dictation and copying
– Verbal associations
– Left hemisphere damage—deficits across
  all areas (injury before 5 years of age)

Psychosocial
– Changes in personality
– Increased psychiatric
  disorders in severe
  injury (not mild)

Family
– Disruptive to relationships
– Home environment impacts

specific and not as clearly lateralized. For example, there is only a mild tendency for injury to the left hemisphere to produce language-related deficits and for injury to the right hemisphere to produce deficits in memory for design (McFie, 1961, 1975). Reitan

(1984) states that there does not appear to be a strong relationship between the lateralization of damage and higher level dysfunction in children, although inferences can be drawn based on sensory-perceptual and motor deficits. Further, Chadwick et al. (1981) did not find lateralizing signs on the Wechsler scales, but more diffuse impairment was apparent, particularly with more severe brain injury. However, adolescents begin to show adultlike patterns of lateralizing signs.

Perceptual functions. Perceptual problems appear related to severity of injury, particularly under timed conditions (Bowden, Knights, & Winogron, 1985), and visual and visual-spatial impairment have been identified in children following injury (Levin & Eisenberg, 1979).

Memory functions. Memory deficits appear to be fairly common in children following TBI (Levin & Eisenberg, 1979). Verbal learning and verbal memory (Delis et al., 1994; Levin & Eisenberg, 1979; Levin, Eisenberg, Wigg, & Kobayashi, 1982), visual-spatial (Levin & Eisenberg, 1979; Levin et al., 1982), and selective reminding (Buschke & Fuld, 1974) deficits have been reported in various studies investigating memory functions in children following TBI. Although memory deficits may improve within one year postinjury, difficulties in verbal learning of new information persist in a number of children, particularly those with severe injuries (Levin & Eisenberg, 1979; Levin et al., 1982). However, Levin and Eisenberg (1979) did find that even children with mild injuries (brief coma or no loss of consciousness) evidenced neuropsychological deficits. Verbal learning measures are often powerful for identifying problems associated with TBI.

Attentional and executive control functions. Berg (1986) indicates that closed-head injuries in children can produce changes in personality, academic deterioration, memory deficits, visual-spatial deficits, and processing speed deficits. Brown et al. (1981) found that severe-injury children were more likely to show signs of disinhibition, impulsivity, socially inappropriate behaviors, excessive verbalization, and insensitivity compared to mild-injury and control children. Attentional difficulties, as measured by continuous performance tasks, have also been documented (Chadwick et al., 1981) in children sustaining brain damage.

Academic and School Adjustment

The academic consequences of TBI have not been adequately researched, and this seems particularly problematic given that TBI has recently been recognized as a separate handicapping condition that may require special education support (Individuals with Disabilities Act, 1990). Until 1990, children with TBI did not qualify for special-education services under existing categories (Virginia Department of Education, 1992). However, academic problems may persist in some children long after EEGs and neurological evaluations appear normal (Fuld & Fisher, 1977).

Language-related deficits that accompany some injuries often result in academic difficulties (Ewing-Cobbs, Levin, Eisenberg, & Fletcher (1987) found that children sustaining injury resulting in a loss of consciousness for a minimum of one day or displaying CT abnormalities demonstrated language-related deficits. Deficits were found on tasks measuring writing to dictation, copying, and verbal associations, all of which may adversely affect school performance. Ewing-Cobbs, Fletcher, Levin, and Landry (1985) found that even mild language problems are detrimental to academic performance. Chadwick et al. (1981) also found a slight tendency for children sustaining left-hemisphere damage to show academic deficits across all areas, particularly for those children sustaining injury prior to 5 years of age.

Another major concern related to academic adjustment is that new learning is often affected by TBI. Residual attention, concentration, personality, and behavioral problems also may interact with overall school and academic functioning.

Social-Psychological Adjustment

New psychiatric disorders postinjury appear significantly more often in children with severe head injury (in 50% of cases), whereas children with mild head injury do not differ from a control group (Brown et al., 1981). Most studies investigating head injury in children stress the importance of considering premorbid status in order to assess the full impact of injury on the child (Goldstein & Levin, 1990).

Family and Home Factors

TBI can be disruptive of family interactions (Rourke et al., 1983), and the home environment can have an impact on the recovery process following TBI (Martin, 1990; Rourke et al., 1983). Rourke et al. (1983) describe detailed intervention plans to address these problems.

Implications for Assessment

Due to the various neuropsychological, cognitive, academic, and psychosocial disorders accompanying TBI, a broad-based evaluation is imperative. An approach such as the following is typically recommended (Ewing-Cobbs & Levin, 1990; Rourke, 1994; Silver et al., 1992), including the following: (1) selected, relevant subtests of the Halstead Neuropsychological Test Battery for Children; (2) a measure of intelligence (Wechsler scales); (3) tests of achievement (Woodcock-Johnson Tests); (4) tests of auditory perception, verbal fluency, rapid naming, receptive vocabulary (i.e., Peabody Picture Vocabulary Test, Token Test); (5) tests of visual perception (e.g., Beery Visual-Motor Integration, Rey's Figure); (6) tests of memory and learning (i.e., selective reminding, continuous recognition memory); (7) tests of reasoning and abstraction; and (8) tests of attention (i.e., continuous performance test). Ewing-Cobbs and Fletcher (1990) and Silver et al. (1992) also recommend selected tests of behavioral and psychological adjustment, including the Vineland Adaptive Behavior Scales, the Child Behavior Checklist, and the Personality Inventory for Children. See other measures listed earlier in Table 5.11.

Periodic and ongoing evaluations are particularly important for children following TBI in order to assess the extent of recovery. Berg (1986) suggests that the most rapid recovery occurs during the first year postinjury. Klonoff, Low, and Clark (1977) found that children show abnormal functioning on a majority of neuropsychological measures (65% of all measures) within one year, but that they continue to improve two to five years postinjury. Klonoff et al. (1977) found that 57% eventually showed no measurable

neuropsychological deficits, but improvement continued over a five-year period for these children. Postinjury Full Scale IQ and coma duration were the most powerful predictors for those children with permanent deficits. Approximately 43% of the groups demonstrated significant residual deficits, and one-quarter of this group required special education or failed one or more grades.

Implications for Intervention

Cognitive and personality characteristics of the child, as well as family resources, marital stability, and socioeconomic status, have an impact on outcome variables measuring the child's recovery. With this in mind, developmental history and circumstances in the child's environment must be carefully considered, according to Goldstein and Levin (1990). Further, teacher reports and a review of history help to determine the presence of preexisting disorders like hyperactivity, attentional problems, social interaction, and academic difficulties (Craft et al., 1972). Rutter (1981) cautions that postinjury deficits may in fact reflect premorbid problems rather than being a direct result of the brain trauma. Rutter (1981) also suggest that premorbid characteristics such as impulsivity and hyperactivity may lead to higher injury rates in children who are more likely to take more risks than other children.

The Virginia Department of Education developed Guidelines for Educational Services for Students with Traumatic Brain Injury (1992), emphasizing home—school partnerships. Meeting the needs of families and children is an essential feature of this program. The guidelines cover conducting assessments, making placement decisions, planning and implementing individual educational plans (IEPs) or 504 plans, and improving the behavioral and academic problems with effective strategies and classroom modifications.

In summary, studies indicate the need to integrate data from various sources in order to measure the full impact of head injury on children, and support the need for an integrated paradigm for developing educational and psychosocial treatment programs for brain-injured children.

Prenatal exposure to teratogenic agents, including alcohol and cocaine have been known to produce various neuropsychological, neurocognitive, and neurobehavioral disorders in children. Complications associated with fetal alcohol syndrome and cocaine exposure are reviewed in the following sections.

FETAL ALCOHOL SYNDROME

Fetal alcohol syndrome (FAS) describes children who evidence a growth deficiency, facial anomalies, and CNS dysfunction (Streissguth, 1949). It is caused by prenatal exposure to alcohol. FAS was initially described by Jones and Smith (1973) over two decades ago. Children with FAS frequently show delayed development, overactivity, motor clumsiness, attention deficits, learning problems, cognitive retardation, and seizure disorders. The prevalence of FAS is estimated to be 1 to 3 per 1000 live births (National Institute on Alcohol Abuse and Alcoholism, 1990).

Differences in incidence rates of FAS depend on community, ethnic, and cultural mores, and on geographical area. For example, although the estimated incidence is 1 to 3 per 1000 live births, in Seattle the incidence is 1 per 700 live births (Hanson, Streissguth, & Smith, 1978); and on Native American reservations the incidence ranges from 1 to 97 in 750 live births (May, Hymbaugh, Aase, & Samet, 1983). May (1991) suggests that drinking in Native peoples of North America varies greatly in communities and in relation to specific cultural norms. He suggests that these normative patterns hold the answer to ameliorating maternal alcohol abuse during pregnancy and should be utilized in any intervention program.

Etiology of Fetal Alcohol Syndrome

The type and severity of FAS appears to depend on when gestation the mother drank, how much alcohol was consumed, how frequently it was used, and the age of the mother (Overholser, 1990; Russell et al., 1991). Streissguth, Sampson, and Barr (1989) studied 500 children, of whom 92 had been exposed to alcohol in utero. Moderate exposure to alcohol could

be distinguished on the first day of life and continued throughout development. Children exposed to alcohol prior to birth showed difficulties including cognitive delays, memory and attentional problems, motor difficulties, organizational and problem-solving problems, and social and adaptational behavioral problems.

The threshold for alcohol use during pregnancy appears to be between 7 and 28 drinks per week in early and mid-pregnancy. This level of alcohol intake appears to be highly related to neurobehavioral sequalae (Jacobson & Jacobson, 1994).

Although the mechanism behind FAS is not fully understood, nutritional and metabolic effects of alcoholism along with the teratogenic effects of the alcohol itself are believed to play a role (Williams, Howard, & McLaughlin, 1994). Animal models have begun to be used in order to understand the etiology of FAS. In a study of rats prenatally exposed to alcohol in the third trimester of pregnancy, Melcer, Gonzalez, Barrow, and Riley (1994) found that those who received a high dose of alcohol had resulting overactivity. Haynes, Hess, and Campbell (1992) found that pregnant rats that were fed large daily amounts of alcohol gained less weight during pregnancy, and their pups weighed less and showed less weight gain after birth.

Studies of the brains of children diagnosed with FAS show decreases in total brain size, particularly in the cerebrum and the cerebellum (Mattson, Riley, Jernigan, Garcia, et al., 1994). Moreover, smaller volume of the basal ganglia was also found, with smaller area or nonexistent corpus callosum (Mattson, Riley, Jernigan, Ehlers, et al., 1992; Mattson, Riley, Jernigan, Garcia, et al., 1994). EEGs did not show focal abnormalities for the child's age group (Mattson et al., 1992).

Implications for Assessment and Diagnosis

The diagnosis of FAS is generally accomplished by the medical community. Facial features usually assist in the diagnosis and are more prominent on the left side of the face. The discriminating facial features of FAS include a shorter than expected eye opening, flattening of the mid-face, a short nose, indistinct ridges between nose and mouth, and a tiny upper lip. Associated features include small folded skin at the inner corner of the eye, low nasal bridge, ear anomalies, and an abnormally small jaw (Streissguth, 1994). In addition, the child's growth is generally delayed. The facial features generally become less evident after puberty, and diagnosis at that point becomes problematic (Streissguth, Randels, & Smith, 1991). A small head continues to be a distinguishing feature, with only 28% of samples showing normal head size (Streissguth et al., 1991).

FAS is diagnosed when the facial characteristics are present, a growth deficiency is present, and CNS malfunctioning occurs in conjunction with a maternal history of alcohol abuse. If the child shows some of the facial characteristics of FAS and/or CNS signs along with maternal drinking, the diagnosis of fetal alcohol effect (FAE) is given (Streissguth et al., 1991).

Neuropsychological Aspects of FAS and FAE

The evidence from longitudinal studies of children with FAS indicates that this disorder persists throughout the life span (Streissguth, 1994; Streissguth, Sampson, Olson, et al., 1994). Difficulties are present with cognitive retardation, attention, and adaptive behaviors. Information-processing skills also appear to be significantly affected and sensitive to the effects of maternal binge drinking (Olson, Sampson, et al., 1992).

Newborns of alcoholic mothers have been found to be delayed in their response to the environment and to be born with low birth weights (Day, 1992; Greene et al., 1991). These difficulties continue into adulthood. Early diagnosis of FAS appears to be crucial for later outcome as well as prevention programs for alcoholic women (Niccols, 1994). However, these women responded well to supportive counseling for alcohol control.

There is a high incidence of cognitive retardation and ADHD in children with FAS. A long-term outcome study of children with FAS has found stability in neuropsychological and emotional status. Steinhausen, Wilms, and Spohr (1994) followed 158 children who had been diagnosed with FAS from preschool through adolescence. Intelligence testing found that the majority of children were cognitively retarded as well as having processing problems, attention deficits, sleep disorders, stereotyped and perseverative behaviors, and emotional disturbance. These findings are similar to those reported by Streissguth, Randels, and Smith (1991). These researchers found IQs to remain stable over time.

Attentional problems. Attentional problems are frequently found in children with FAS. In the absence of the full syndrome, findings of attentional problems are equivocal (Boyd et al., 1991). A study that compared Native American children with FAS, those with FAE, and normally developing samples found consistent delays in attention, language, and cognition in the FAS group but not in the FAE or the normally developing groups (Conry, 1990). A further study of attentional deficits compared children with FAS/FAE, ADHD, and typically developing samples on several measures of attention. The FAS/FAE children were found to be similar to the ADHD group in activity level and attentional functioning (Nanson & Hoscock, 1990). Unfortunately, the results of this study are difficult to interpret, as the FAS sample was confounded with FAE children, who most likely show less problematic neuropsychological profiles.

Adaptive behavioral problems. Adaptive behavior skills appear to be most problematic for FAS children. Streissguth, Clarren, and Jones (1985) found that daily living skills, though below expectations for chronological age, were frequently an area of strength for these children, with socialization skills being the most deficient. This finding held true for those children who were *and* those who were not cognitively retarded. Areas that were particularly difficult for children were acting without considering the consequences, problems with initiative, inappropriateness of behaviors due to an inability to read social cues, and inability to establish social relationships (Streissguth, Aase, et al., 1991).

Academic achievement. Academic achievement also poses difficulty for children with FAS. In a major study of adolescents with FAS, Streissguth, Randels, and Smith (1991) found that 6% were in regular education with no support, 28% were in self-contained special education classrooms, 15% were not in school or were at work, and 9% were in sheltered workshops. Academic attainment was at the fourth-grade level in reading, third-grade level in spelling, and second-grade level in arithmetic. Arithmetic skills were most impaired for this group of children and appear to be exquisitely sensitive to the amount of alcohol drunk at one point in time (Streissguth et al., 1994). This finding also held true for word attack skills. Importantly, Streissguth et al. (1994) found that arithmetic and work attack skills were significantly delayed when other confounding variables such as SES, exposure to tobacco and other drugs, and postnatal trauma were covaried.

Language skills. Language skills in FAS children have not been found to be generally deficient. It appears that language development is more closely related to the quality of caretaking independent of SES and/or alcohol exposure (Greene et al., 1990).

Language difficulties seen in children exposed prenatally to alcohol appear to change depending on age considerations. In a study of 10 FAS Native American children and 17 Native American controls, Carney and Chermak (1991) found that the younger FAS children showed global language deficits, whereas the older ones showed syntactic deficits. Although this study was too small in sample size to make generalizable statements, it does sensitize us to the need to compare children within different ethnic groups as well as to recognize the age effects on qualitative language performance. This finding has been replicated, again in a very small sample, by Becker, Warr-Leeper, and Leeper (1990).

Psychosocial Considerations

Many children with FAS come from chaotic home environments where alcohol and other drugs are used. In one longitudinal study, Streissguth, Aase, et al. (1991) found that only 9% of the sample remained with both biological parents, and 3% were still with the biological mother. In fact, 69% of the biological mothers were dead 5 to 12 years after the original evaluation. Streissguth, Aase, et al. (1991) report that approximately 33% of FAS children were given up for adoption or abandoned in the hospital.

Severe behavioral problems are also frequently found in the FAS population. These difficulties make traditional vocational training problematic. Psychopathology appears to create the greatest difficulty in adolescence and later adulthood (Dorris, 1989). Age effects on the expression of psychopathology have been found, with younger children showing difficulty in response inhibition, hyperactivity, and learning, while older children show difficulty with self-regulation, problems understanding social cues, planning and organization, and persistence (Steinhausen et al., 1994; Streissguth, 1994). Many of these deficits appear to be related to a form of disinhibition and executive control problems, particularly where higher level functions are required (e.g., in social relations). It is also difficult to ascertain the degree to which psychopathology is a function of abnormal neuropsychological and cognitive development, and where it reflects the troubled family environment. At any rate, the interaction of these factors should be considered when designing intervention programs.

Implications for Interventions

Studies evaluating interventions with children with FAS are just beginning to establish treatment paradigms. For preschool children, early identification is crucial. Many children are cognitively retarded, show language delays, have problems with attention and memory, and have delayed social skills (Phelps, 1995). Interventions such as early referral by physicians to the school or educational multidisciplinary team is improving (Morse et al., 1992), and medical education in this regard is sorely needed. Early childhood special-education services are invaluable for these children and their families. It is particularly important to involve families in any intervention program (Shriver & Piersel, 1994). Federal regulations provide for Individual Family Service Plans (IFSPs) as part of special education for young children (see P.L. 94-357).

For elementary-aged children, continued special-education services are needed for academic and social support. Medication for distractibility and over-activity may be considered for ADHD symptoms. Social skills training can be helpful to assist with development. Skills training needs to focus on foundational skills of learning social cues and gestures and should be conducted in a school setting or in another setting where natural, ecologically valid social situations serve as the training ground. Minimizing sensory overload, recognizing sleep and eating disorders, and establishing a specialized curriculum have been found to be helpful (Weinner & Morse, 1994).

Emphasis should be placed on appropriate vocational training for adolescents. In addition, structured behavioral and vocational training is crucial for these students because social judgment, consequential thinking, and risk-taking behaviors are problematic for FAS adolescents (Phelps, 1995).

There is no research currently published that evaluates intervention programs with families. Streissguth et al. (1991) report that few children remain with their biological parents. Interventions would differ depending on whether the child remains in a chaotic home or is placed in a more stable environment.

Some success has been found in utilizing cognitive-behavioral techniques for preventing alcohol use in women who are drinking during pregnancy. Peterson and Lowe (1992) have had success with this technique in improving self-esteem and self-efficacy. Additional research is sorely needed in both intervention efficacy and family interventions. Hankin (1994) found that although beverage warning labels are somewhat effective, community-based interventions appear more successful. At any rate, prevention seems to be a more effective way of reducing the very serious deleterious effects to unborn infants, and should be a priority.

Conclusions

FAS is a leading and preventable cause of cognitive retardation in children. Research has pinpointed dif-ficulties for children with FAS, specifically in terms of attention, self-regulation, problem solving, and social awareness. These difficulties continue into adulthood and create significant adjustment problems. Intervention programs have been developed for academic skills, but progress in adaptive behavior skills and basic living skills have been sorely lacking. Research investigating appropriate vocational training is needed, and the need for earlier training in this area is probably necessary. Moreover, using a transactional approach to the neuropsychology of FAS necessitates that interventions be developed for both the child *and* the family. Community-based interventions that recognize the particular values and culture of the community are also needed. Efforts to alert the medical profession to the need for early educational interventions also would be advised.

COCAINE-EXPOSED INFANTS

The incidence of infants born exposed to cocaine has risen in the past decade (U.S. General Accounting Office, 1990). It has been estimated that more than 100,000 babies are born annually with exposure to cocaine and/or other drugs (Chasnoff, Landress, & Barrett, 1990). Research investigating the effects of cocaine exposure to the developing fetus has produced mixed results. Early studies indicated that there were statistically significant abnormalities across many measures of behavior, temperament, and cognition in early development (Singer, Farkas, & Kliegman, 1991). These abnormalities were well publicized, and many believed that the school systems would be flooded with "crack-cocaine children" with severe developmental and behavioral disabilities (Blakeslee, 1990; Chira, 1990). These children were characterized as listless, without affect, difficult to soothe, unmotivated, unable to establish attachments to care-givers, and hyperactive or aggressive.

To place these studies in social context, it is important to recognize that these reports are likely to have been affected by the milieu existing at the time of publication. Coles (1993) declares that the early research was a "scramble for funds and influence, a rush to judgment, and a credulity in the assessment of both clinical and research results which was unprofessional at best" (p. 290). This echoes a sentiment first espoused by Mayes, Granger, Bornstein, and Zuckerman (1992). Hutchings (1993) along with several other commentators (Day & Richardson, 1993; Frank & Zuckerman, 1993), suggests that early research did not evaluate mediating factors such as amount of drug use, nutrition, polydrug use, and lack of appropriate control groups. Moreover, Day and Richardson (1993) suggest that the earliest cases publicized were likely "the most severe, the most complicated, the most obvious, and seldom accurately represent the real natural history of a disease" (p. 293). They also caution about overinterpretation of statistical correlation as "causative" in nature. Many authors in the special issue of *Neurotoxicology and Teratology* (1993) suggest that crack cocaine is but one piece of the puzzle to understanding these children, and that poverty, nutrition, violence, demoralization, and the interaction of these factors may be necessary for a full understanding of the developmental outcome of these children.

Effects of Cocaine

Cocaine is a powerful stimulant that can be ingested by snorting, "freebasing," or smoking. Crack is a form of cocaine that is increasingly popular because of its lower cost. Cocaine or crack produces an intense feeling of euphoria, with increased energy and self-esteem and decreased anxiety. The rebound effects, which include increases in anxiety, exhaustion, and depression, are so emotionally painful that the addicted person will continually smoke cocaine or crack to avoid them. Chronic use is associated with paranoid and affective disorder, weight loss, and poor judgment and insight (Gawin, 1988). Thus, cocaine's effect on the CNS is evident in adults and is related to the chemical properties of the drug.

Cocaine is readily water- and lipid-soluble and passes easily across the placenta (Woods, Plessinger, & Clark, 1987). Moreover, the fetus is exposed for a longer period of time than adults because of a deficiency in the mother's ability to chemically deactivate the drug action (Singer, Garber, & Kliegman,

1991). The cocaine also causes uterine vessel vasoconstriction, which results in reduced blood and oxygen flow to the fetus (Woods et al., 1987).

Variables that are just beginning to be studied include the individual differences in ability to metabolize cocaine, the difference in frequency of use of cocaine, and variations in placental perfusion. Koren (1993) suggests that these variables may account for the variation in expression of severity of symptoms in children prenatally exposed to cocaine. Use of cocaine at high levels and at frequent intervals appears to have more adverse effects on the fetus than does low use (Chasnoff, 1993). Some pregnant women using cocaine appear to have a lower activity level of a primary enzyme (choline esterase) that metabolizes cocaine. For these women's babies, there is an increased risk of high exposure. Additionally, the human placenta also has been found to be variable in its ability to metabolize cocaine (Hoffman et al., 1992). Some fetuses have been found have higher exposures to cocaine compared to others when mothers from both groups consumed equivalent doses (Pellegrini, Koren, & Motherisk, 1990). Moreover, some fetal placental vessels appear to restrict blood and oxygen flow more than others when cocaine is ingested by the mother (Simone, Derewlany, Knie, & Koren, 1992). This variable may have significant effects on the level of exposure to cocaine, regardless of the amount of cocaine taken.

To understand the effect of cocaine on the developing nervous system, it is important to evaluate a number of related variables before describing existing research on behavioral and cognitive outcome for these children. The following sections will discuss environmental variables, pre- and postnatal complications, animal models of the result of cocaine exposure on a fetus, previous studies on the result of cocaine exposure on the fetus, and current knowledge of the behavioral and cognitive status of these children.

Environmental Variables

Socioeconomic status has been frequently cited as an important variable in the evaluation of newborns for cocaine exposure. Many studies used nonrandom subject selection from large urban hospitals that primarily have indigent and minority women as patients. Results from these studies indicated that minority women and poor women were more likely to have drug-exposed children (Singer et al., 1991). In contrast, a recent study found that poor, urban, minority women were no more likely to use illegal drugs than were white middle-class women, with approximately 15% of both groups using such drugs during pregnancy (Chasnoff, Landress, & Barrett, 1990). The drug of choice for these women, however, did differ. Minority women used cocaine more frequently, whereas white women in private care used marijuana.

The use of cocaine in pregnant minority women has been found to interact with such variables as polydrug use, less prenatal care, lower weight at time of delivery, and less weight gain during pregnancy (Frank et al., 1988). Moreover, these women are more likely to be single and have more sexually transmitted diseases (Singer et al., 1991). These women are also found to show to provide a poorer caregiving environment for the infant, possibly due to poor maternal mental status (Cregler & Mark, 1986).

Elliott and Coker (1991) found nonnurturing home environments to be related to prenatal use of crack cocaine. Moreover, the use of crack cocaine has been found to be deterimental to the mother's functioning, a problem that increases in severity over time (Gonzalez & Campbell, 1994). Lester and Tronick (1994) suggest that understanding of the dynamics of cocaine use during pregnancy requires a systems model that interrelates polydrug use with environmental and/or lifestyle issues. These authors caution against shifting to an emphasis on environmental effects and now ignoring drug effects on these children.

Animal Models

Animal models are helpful in understanding the mechanisms underlying the effects of various neurotoxic agents. Application of the results of animal studies to human behavior has been found to be helpful with these agents. A summary of studies looking the effects of various toxins on the nervous systems of animals and humans found that "If a particular agent produced, for example, cognitive or motor deficits in humans, corresponding deficits were also evident in laboratory animals. This was true even when the specific endpoints used to assess these functions were often operationally quite different across species" (Stanton & Spear, 1990, p. 265).

A study of offspring from Sprague-Dawley CD rats given multiple daily doses of cocaine found that exposure to cocaine produced poorer performance on more complicated cognitive tasks when the rats were fully mature (Vorhees et al., 1995). Problem-solving and socialization behaviors have been found to be particularly susceptible to cocaine exposure in utero (Goodwin et al., 1992; Heyser, Spear, & Spear, 1992; Smith, Mattran, Kurkjian, & Kurtz, 1989). Alterations in neural function have also been found, lending support to the hypothesis that cocaine, used frequently and in large doses, acts as a neurobehavioral teratogen (Stanton & Spear, 1990). Controlled studies utilizing animal models have been conducted only in the past six to eight years, and data are continuing to emerge. These findings can inform clinicians as to the possible action of cocaine on the developing nervous system.

Pre- and Postnatal Medical Effects

Neuspiel and Hamel (1991) have hypothesized five mechanisms for the effect of cocaine on the CNS of a developing fetus. Decreased regulation of the receptors for neurotransmitters are believed to result in defective synaptic development, thus altering various structures and cerebral activity. Prenatal vascular disruption has been linked to malformations in various organs and the brain. Fetal and maternal malnutrition can result in growth retardation or microcephaly. All of these effects can significantly alter the child's development. Mayes (1994) suggests that cocaine use in the early portion of pregnancy places the fetus at high risk for experiencing changes in brain growth, synaptic formation, and cell migration. In addition, in postnatal development, exposure to cocaine through breast mile also may interfere with normal brain development (Chasnoff, Lewis, & Squires, 1987).

Increased risk of spontaneous abortions, abrupted placentas, and meconium-stained amniotic fluid has been found to be associated with maternal cocaine use (Frank et al., 1988). Increased rates of prematurity have been found (MacGregor, Keith, Bachicha, & Chasnoff, 1989) and may be related to the early neurodevelopmental effects found in these children (Oro & Dixon, 1987). Singer, Garber, and Kliegman (1991) suggest that premature birth may be a indication that the mother with a history of drug abuse has a heavier use of drugs and/or significant socioeconomic disadvantage.

Intrauterine growth retardation has been found to be present in cocaine-exposed compared to non-cocaine-exposed infants (Chasnoff & Griffith, 1990). Both small head size and slower brain growth have been found in these children (Coles, Platzman, Smith, James, & Falek, 1991; Eisen et al., 1991; Hamel, Hochberg, Green, & Campbell, 1991). When very low birth weight babies were studied on follow-up who had been diagnosed with chronic lung disease, 25% of these babies were found to be cocaine-exposed; double the rate of cocaine exposure generally seen (Singer, Farkas, & Kliegman, 1991). Neurological abnormalities found in these neonates prenatally exposed to cocaine include cerebral infarcts and EEG and BAER abnormalities (Chasnoff et al., 1989; Dixon & Bejar, 1989).

Cognitive and Language Development

The early development of the child exposed to cocaine in utero has been studied more extensively than later development. Most studies have found that at early ages these children showed few global deficits. However, these children did display subtle language delays and problem-solving skills (Hawley, Halle, Drasin, & Thomas, 1995). In a combined study, 93 cocaine-exposed children were studied from birth to age 3 (Griffith, Azuma, & Chasnoff, 1994). This sample was compared to a sample of infants exposed to alcohol or marijuana but not to cocaine, and to 45 drug-free infants. Maternal age, SES, marital status, and use of cigarettes were comparable between

groups. Cocaine-exposed infants were found to have a lower birth weight than the control group; however, this difference was no longer present at age 3 months. Head circumference remained smaller for the cocaine group through 36 months of age. While global scores on the Bayley Scales of Infant Development and the Stanford Binet Intelligence Scale–Fourth Edition did not differ at age 3, a direct relationship was found between prenatal drug exposure and IQ in all drug-exposed groups. Language skills were found to be particularly vulnerable to in utero drug exposure.

In a study of 21 preschool children of mothers participating in a drug treatment program, impairment in a receptive rather than expressive language was found (Malakoff, Mayes, & Schottenfeld, 1994). This difficulty can translate into later problems in new learning as the child has difficulty understanding directions, absorbing new information, or categorizing information into networks. The relationship between early language delays and in utero cocaine exposure has been reported in several studies (Angelilli et al., 1994; van Baar, 1990; van Baar & de Graaff, 1994; Malakoff et al., 1994).

Unfortunately, studies looking at long-term effects have not been conducted, as these children are not old enough to be evaluated. It is very possible that the subtle language deficits currently found may become more evident at later ages, particularly in understanding abstract language and making inferences in written material. Moreover, there are subtle indications of problem-solving difficulties that may translate into later difficulties in executive functioning. These are areas that need to be studied carefully as the opportunity arises, and of which clinicians need to be aware.

Social/Emotional/Behavioral Development

Studies of the neonatal behavior of cocaine-exposed infants have found that these children may show no to mild withdrawal behaviors (Coles et al., 1991; Dixon & Bejar, 1989; Finnegan, Kaltenbach, Weiner, & Haney, 1990). Sensory and behavioral deficits consistently have been found (Chasnoff et al., 1989; Coles et al., 1991; Neuspiel et al., 1991). In particular, these children have been found to have difficulty screening out upsetting stimuli and decreased habituation to environmental stimuli. These difficulties may be related to cocaine-exposed neonates' reported irritability and poor sootheability (Singer, Farkas, & Kliegman, 1991).

Children at 6 months of age who were exposed to cocaine in utero have been found to show temperamental differences, primarily in their difficulties with cooperation, manageability, and responsiveness to routine (Edmondson & Smith, 1994). These children were also less responsive and showed less interest in communication and participation in activity, while their cognitive development did not differ from that of nonexposed 6-month-olds.

Two-year-old children exposed to prenatal drugs were found to be more immature and to show less sustained attention, more deviant behaviors, and fewer positive social interactions than nonexposed children. Although these children were exposed to several drugs in utero, many believe that children exposed to cocaine are frequently born to polydrug mothers (Chasnoff, 1993). It also appears that children with a history of prenatal cocaine exposure may be less passive when not stimulated by an adult (Rotholz, Snyder, & Peters, 1995). A three-year longitudinal study of cocaine-exposed children found that environmental and behavioral factors explained most of the variance of their performance from that of nonexposed children (Chasnoff, 1993).

The finding of behavioral and emotional difficulties in cocaine-exposed children was present in a study of 3 to 5-year-old children. These children were found to show significantly higher T-scores (58.5 versus 46.9) on the Internalizing Scale of the Achenbach Child Behavior Checklist (Achenbach, 1991) than the nonexposed children (Hawley et al., 1995). Externalizing scores, though approaching significance, did not discriminate between the groups.

Attachment to caregivers has also been studied. Insecure and disorganized attachment to the caregiver has been repeatedly found by investigators (Ainsworth, Blehar, Waters, & Wall, 1978; Rodning, Beckwith, & Howard, 1989, 1991). Such problems with attachment to significant persons in the child's life may be an early signal of later difficulties in socioemotional development. These findings are consistent with the concern about these children's difficulty with social cognition.

Tying in with the emerging evidence of behavioral and social difficulties are the findings that the rearing environment plays a primary role in the development of these difficulties. Disturbance in the caregiver—infant dyad has been found and negatively influences the child's ability to regulate his or her behavior on the basis of feedback from the affective environment (Beeghly & Tronick, 1994). Maternal depression and poor psychololgical adjustment have been found to impair mother—child interactions significantly and thus impact on the child's developmental pattern (Chethick, Burns, Burns, & Clark, 1990). In addition, infants and children who suffer physical and emotional neglect by the crack-addicted mother experience more sadness and a more chaotic environment than do nonexposed children (Hawley et al., 1995). In homes where domestic violence, child neglect and abuse, and poor health care are present, children have been found to have significant behavioral and emotional difficulties (Bateman & Heagarty, 1989).

Beckwith et al. (1990) studied home environments of drug-exposed children. Positive early experiences were found to offset later difficulties in caregiving. Prenatally cocaine-exposed children with adequate care in the first year of life were within age expectations at age. Comparisons of these children with drug-exposed children without such care found that they continued to show age-appropriate behaviors at age 2.

Summary

Contrary to the concerns of the 1980s and early 1990s, these children are not showing the long-term global cognitive deficits that were predicted. It is too early to say that these children will have no deficits. Current evidence suggests that cocaine exposure during pregnancy may predispose the child to later difficulties in attention, social development, and emotional regulation and development. Some children appear to evidence subtle language deficits in the preschool years. Abilities that are unable to be measured in the first three years of life may emerge poorly at later ages. The subtle deficits in organization, regulation of behavior, and problem solving may later translate into difficulty with abstract thinking skills. Moreover, one of the best predictors of later social and emotional adjustment is attachment to the caregiver (Stroufe, Fox, & Pancake, 1983). As we have seen from the foregoing review, cocaine-exposed children not only have difficulty with attachment, but their caretakers are frequently unavailable to them because of the addiction.

A transactional approach to understanding these children is paramount. It appears from the emerging research that the environment the child is in may be just as important as whether he or she was exposed to cocaine in utero. Children from impoverished, chaotic, abusive homes will do poorly no matter what the pregnancy history. To understand the functioning of these children, the clinician must take these variables into consideration in interpreting the data. Moreover, these children should be monitored for progress, as early subtle deficits may translate into later difficulties with more complex learning. Although further study is needed on the long-term effects of cocaine exposure, control of these various moderator variables (maternal addiction, poverty, nutrition, etc.) is necessary in order to isolate the effects of cocaine on the fetus.

CHILDHOOD CANCER

Childhood cancers, though relatively rare, are found in children at all ages. the two most common forms of childhood cancer are childhood leukemia and brain tumors. Although the etiologies for these disorders differ, treatment frequently involves chemotherapy and cranial irradiation. The chemotherapy regimen has not been found to have the same effects on later outcome that irradiation produces. It is these "late effects" that most concern the child neuropsychologist. Each of these types of childhood cancers will be discussed in the following sections.

Brain Tumors

Brain tumors are estimated to constitute 20% of malignancies of childhood and are most frequently diagnosed in children between the ages of 3 and 9 years (Carpentieri & Mulhern, 1993). Kun (1992) suggests that between 1200 and 1500 new cases are identified each year, but there have been relatively few studies investigating the psychosocial effects of CNS tumors (Mulhern, Hancock, Fairclough, & Kun, 1992). Treatment protocols often include whole-brain radiation, chemotherapy, and/or surgical interventions, and 50% to 60% of children are cancer-free after 5 years (Carpentieri & Mulhern, 1993).

Associated Features

Etiology. Risk factors that have been associated with the development of brain tumors include: (1) genetic syndromes, including neurofibromatosis and tuberous sclerosis; (2) presence of epilepsy and stroke in families of children with brain tumors; and (3) immunosuppression prior to organ transplant (Cohen & Duffner, 1994). Some environmental toxins (e.g., aromatic hydrocarbons) have been implicated (Zeller, Ivankovic, & Hxx, 1982), as have maternal use of barbituates (Savitz et al., 1988) and prenatal exposure to X-ray (National Radiological Protection Board, 1981).

Types of tumors. The most frequently diagnosed type of tumor is the astrocytoma (Cohen & Duffner, 1994). In an epidemiological study of malignant brain tumors in children under the age of 15, Duffner et al. (1986) found that astrocytomas accounted for 57% of the tumors, while 23% were medulloblastomas and 8% were ependymomas.

Although brain tumors can occur at any age, the 5- to 9-year-old interval shows the largest occurrence of brain tumors, followed closely by ages 0 to 4 years and then by 10 to 14 years of age (Duffner et al., 1986). In children under age 2, the most common types of tumors are medulloblastomas (in the medulla portion of the brain stem), low-grade astrocytomas, and ependymomas (arising from the lining of the ventricles and spinal cord or ependyma). At ages 5 to 9, the most commonly diagnosed tumors are low-grade astrocytomas, medulloblastomas, high-grade astrocytomas, and cerebellar astrocytomas (Cohen & Duffner, 1984). Children with astrocytomas in the cerebellum have been reported to have the highest survival rates, while those with brain stem gliomas have the poorest survival rate (Duffner et al., 1986). Astrocytomas are graded from 1 to 4 depending on the degree of malignancy (Cohen & Duffner, 1994). The lower the grade, the less the malignancy.

Implications for Assessment

Accurate and timely diagnosis of brain tumors is especially important (Price, Goetz, & Lovell, 1992). Clinical manifestations may include changes in personality and cognition, and neuropsychological changes, depending on the type, size, and location of the tumor and on the presence of cerebral edema (e.g., hydrocephalus and/or increased intracranial pressure) (Price et al., 1992). Tumors may be preceded by nausea, headaches, visual deficits (e.g., blurred or double vision, visual field blindness), lateralized sensory or motor impairments, vomiting, or seizures. Presence of these symptoms warrants immediate referral to a child neurologist and may necessitate CT scans or other neuroradiological scans (e.g., MRI). Low-grade tumors often have a slow rather than an acute onset, with neural tissues becoming compressed or displaced at a slow rate (Carpentieri & Mulhern, 1993). Consequently, neurological signs may not always appear early (Price et al., 1992).

Brain tumors have been shown to produce behavioral, personality, academic, intellectual, and neuropsychological deficits in children (Mulhern, Kovnar, Kun, Crisco, & Williams, 1988).

Implications for Intervention

Late effects of treatment. The age at which treatment commences appears to have a significant effect on resulting intelligence test scores (Lockman, 1993). In a study by Radcliffe et al. (1992), children younger than 7 years at diagnosis showed a mean loss of 27

points, while older children showed no such decrease. The decline in IQ points occurred within the first two years. Moreover, children younger than 7 years at diagnosis were receiving special education, whereas the older group required only academic modifications within their regular education programs. In another study by Moore, Copeland, Reid, and Levy (1992), children who had cranial radiotherapy as well as chemotherapy showed more compromised neuropsychological functioning than those with chemotherapy with no radiation or those who received no form of CNS therapy.

Additional studies of children who received cranial radiation have found declines in intelligence, with the steepest decreases found on measures of verbal fluency, visual attention, and the WISC subtests of Picture Arrangement and Block Design (Garcia-Perez et al., 1994). Additional difficulties were found in memory skills. These declines were found to vary with the level of irradiation dose, separate from the effects of the tumor. It was hypothesized by Garcia-Perez et al. (1994) that attentional and memory difficulties were directly related to structures that were irradiated because they were in the path toward the tumor, and include connections with the limbic system, basal ganglia, thalamus, and orbitofrontal regions of the frontal lobe. These results have been replicated by other studies reporting memory, attention, and intelligence deficits (Moore, Ater, & Copeland, 1992; Morrow, O'Conner, Whitman, & Accardo, 1989; Riva, Milani, Pantaleoni, Ballerini, & Giorgi, 1991).

Dennis et al. (1991a) examined the types of memory deficits in children and adolescents with brain tumors. Working memory was not found to be related to age of tumor onset; that is, the later the onset of the tumor, the lower the memory score. Dennis et al. (1991b) found that memory for time sequence appears to be related to structures in the limbic system, hypothalamus, hippocampus, pulvinar nucleus of the thalamus, pituitary, and frontal lobes. Working memory that was less affected appeared to be related to the anterior and medial thalamic nuclei. When there was damage to the putamen and/or globus pallidus, all memory skills were disrupted. This finding led Dennis et al. (1991b) to theorize that the putamen and globus pallidus may involve a "final common pathway" for memory functions (p. 839).

A study by Packer, Meadows, Rourke, Goldwein, and D'Angio (1987) found that long-term survivors of medulloblastomas of the posterior fossa generally had IQs in the average range, with several specific intellectual and academic problems. Academic problems were most pronounced in mathematics, with generally normal reading abilities. Similar to Dennis et al. (1991a, 1991b), Packer et al. (1987) found significant memory deficits in 73% of their sample. Fine motor speed and dexterity were also found to be delayed, as were visual-motor skills. These researchers found that, in general, their sample of children with brain tumors were functioning adequately in the psychosocial domain. In addition, factors such as pre- and postoperative mental status, need for a shunt, extent of the tumor, and postoperative infections were just as important predictors of later neuropsychological outcome as amount of radiation utilized in the treatment.

Summary. Thus, late effects of treatment for brain tumors generally have an impact on academic and neuropsychological functioning. Mediating factors such as amount of radiation, pre- and postoperative status, complications (e.g., shunts, infections), and the extent of the tumor, as well as the age of onset, all affect the child's outcome. Additional study is needed on the quality of life children with brain tumors enjoy and on the level of their psychosocial functioning.

Childhood Leukemia

Children with acute lymphocytic leukemia (ALL) experience significant learning difficulties similar to those of children with brain tumors. ALL accounts for 80% of leukemia in children and is the most common type of cancer in childhood (Poplack, 1985). ALL generally presents with initial symptoms of bleeding, fever, irritability, fatigue, and bone pain. Ninety-five percent of children with ALL survive, and 55% of those continue in remission 5 years after treatment (Diamond & Matthay, 1988). The peak age of onset is between the ages of 3 and 5, and ALL is more common in whites than in African Americans and in boys more than in girls (Poplack, 1985).

Genetics, environmental factors, and viruses have been implicated in the etiology of ALL. There is a 1 in 5 chance that an identical twin of an ALL child also will have the disease. Moreover, Diamond and Matthay (1988) report that many heritable syndromes as well as immunodeficiency disorders appear related to an increased risk of developing leukemia. Exposure to X-rays either pre- or postnatally is also associated with a higher risk for leukemia. Finally, several viral infections seem to co-occur with childhood leukemia (e.g., Epstein-Barr, human T lymphonea-leukemia virus).

Important Variables

Factors that have been found to be important prognostic indicators are initial white blood cell count, sex, age at diagnosis, CNS therapy, degree of lymph node enlargement, hemoglobin level, and platelet count at diagnosis (Robison et al., 1980). Robison et al. (1980) found that the initial white blood cell count (WBC) and age at diagnosis were strong predictors for length of remission and survival. Thus, patients with high WBC and who are younger than 2 or older than 10 have the poorest prognosis.

Implications for Interventions

Treatment differs depending on the risk factors, with patients with more risk factors generally treated more aggressively. In contrast, those children who are felt to be at lower risk are treated by less toxic and less intensive means (Robison et al., 1980). Chemotherapy, either alone or in conjunction with additional chemotherapy agents and/or radiotherapy, is the general treatment for ALL. If leukemia cells reoccur anywhere in the body of a child receiving chemotherapy, the outcome is generally poor (Diamond & Matthay, 1988). In addition, children who have had chemotherapy for ALL are at a higher risk for the development of brain tumors (Meadows et al., 1981).

Late effects. Neuropsychological impairment has been found in children treated with low doses of cranial radiation (1800 rads). Declines in intelligence have been found in children who have undergone cranial radiation, with the most profound effects in the younger and brighter patients.

Attentional deficits that affect the encoding of new materials have been found to be the most significantly affected (Brouwers & Poplack, 1990). An earlier study by Brouwers, Riccardi, Poplack, and Fedio (1987) found slower reaction times for children with ALL after treatment with cranial radiation. These researchers suggested that the decline in IQ is *not* due to cognitive factors but, rather, to a slowing of cognitive processing where children are not given "bonus points" for quick and accurate completion of test items. The results of some studies that have found lower performance scores than verbal scores (Meadows et al., 1981; Schuler et al., 1981) may be due to this cognitive slowing. Moreover, Brouwers et al. (1987) suggest that lower scores on the Arithmetic subtest (a timed test on the Verbal scale) of the Wechsler tests may be due to this cognitive slowing.

Several reviews of the neuropsychological literature on late effects have produced mixed results. Reviews by Fletcher and Copeland (1988), Brouwers et al. (1987), Waters, Said, and Stevens (1988), and Packer et al. (1987) found neuropsychological deficits to be related to the treatment of ALL. In contrast, reviews by Williams and Davis (1986) and Madan-Swain and Brown (1991) did not find such a direct effect.

Butler and Copeland (1993) suggest that significant methodological problems plague these studies and may account for the disparity of findings. When global measures are considered, it is likely that more subtle effects of radiation may be missed. Butler and Copeland (1993) make the telling point that there are more long-term survivors of ALL with subtle neuropsychological deficits that will have an increasingly negative effect on their adaptive behaviors, academic performance, and vocational abilities.

Educational Interventions

A study by Peckham (1991) evaluated the school performance of ALL children whose pre- and posttreatment IQ scores were available. Mathematics skills were found to be most affected, with difficulties in concentration and sustained attention. Consistent with the problems in mathematics, Peckham (1991) found that the posttreatment children had problems remembering, sequencing, and following directions.

At the center Virginia Peckham coordinates at Temple University, treatment has been multidimensional. Inservice training is provided for teachers and parents to inform them of the associated learning difficulties that children with ALL can experience. In addition, educational interventions center on teaching the child strategies for "how to learn." Cognitive-behavioral techniques that stress verbal self-instruction and problem solving have been successful with ALL children. The child is taught to monitor his or her attention, to rehearse new information, to use mnemonic devices, to recall material, to use visualization for recall, and to use multisensory approaches (i.e., seeing, touching, hearing, doing) when learning new material. High school students are taught study techniques and test-taking strategies. These strategies have been adapted from those used by long-term survivors who have been academically successful.

Finally, Peckham (1991) recommends that any child who has had cranial radiation should be considered at risk for academic problems. These problems may show up years after treatment has ended. It is particularly important that school personnel and parents be vigilant about the child's progress, and efforts should be made to assess, periodically and systematically, the effectiveness of the educational interventions that are utilized.

Another program for long-term cancer survivors has been developed by Robert Butler previously at Memorial Sloan-Kettering Cancer Center and now at the Oregon Health Sciences. This program combines cognitive-behavioral therapy with the attention-training program developed by Sohlberg and Mateer (1989). This program is in the developmental stage and is being piloted at several hospitals across the country. Dr. Butler's program involves training specific processes such as attention and concentration while also providing the child with strategies that can assist in the learning process. These strategies may include self-monitoring, rehearsal of new material, overlearning critical material, and organizational strategies such as making lists and keeping an assignment notebook. Several of these techniques are described in more detail in Chapter 11. Further study is progressing on this program, and interested readers may contact Dr. Butler.

Psychosocial issues. Just as the disease and treatment have physical side effects, there are also psychological difficulties that may arise with long-term cancer survivors. The study of these issues generally takes one of two approaches: evaluation for possible psychiatric disturbance and assessment of quality-of-life issues. Chang (1991) reviewed studies of childhood cancer survivors using these broad areas. Although survivors were not found to have significant psychiatric disturbances, these children did have school absences not due to physical reasons and had high rates of school phobia (Lansky et al., 1985). Issues such as fear of death, fear that remission will end, and hope for a cure were the primary areas of concern, not only for the child but also for the parent. Chang (1991) reports that this uncertainty can create havoc for the parent when trying to develop consistent and realistic expectations for the child. Consequently, parents can become overprotective as well as too indulgent with their child, thus promoting the social immaturity that is often seen in these children. Social isolation is also frequently experienced by survivors and adversely affects the normal acquisition of peer interaction skills (Spirto et al., 1990). However, these researchers also found that these social skills improved in older children, particularly in families who encouraged the child to interact with peers and who were not overly protective of the child.

Quality-of-life issues such as educational, vocational, and social attainment are strongly linked to the child's as well as the family's adjustment to this disease. Chang et al. (1987) found that almost three-quarters of the survivors experienced school problems, with 41% being diagnosed as learning disabled and 21% as having severe motivational problems. Following high school graduation, many cancer survivors experience some form of employment discrimination (Counts, Rodov, & Wilson, 1976).

Although it has not been addressed in research to date, cancer survivors may access special-education services under the category "Other Health Impaired." Schools can use this avenue to develop individualized educational plans for children with support services for psychosocial problems that may arise. This particular practice allows for a mechanism to access educational and psychological resources available through the school system, and may ultimately increase overall school and vocational attainment for survivors. Educational practices need further research to test this hypothesis.

Family issues. The ability of parents to cope with the child's disease appears strongly related to the child's level of coping (Pless & Pinkerton, 1975). Some of the difficulties found in these families include increased marital discord, financial difficulty brought on by medical costs, anxiety, sibling adjustment problems, and discordant family life (Bruhn, 1977). Despite all of these stressors, however, Koocher and O'Malley (1981) found that nearly 70% of these parents reported stable and close marriages. These rates may not reflect present divorce rates, which have risen in the general population over this time period.

CNS INFECTIOUS DISEASES: MENINGITIS AND ENCEPHALITIS

Infections of the brain at an early age may result in a variety of outcomes ranging from mental retardation to normal development (Taylor, Schatschneider, & Reich, 1992). Central nervous system infections can be the result of bacterial, viral, and/or fungal invasions of the brain and spinal cord through the sinuses, ears, nose, and mouth. *Meningitis* refers to an inflammation of the meninges or protective layers of the brain and spinal cord, whereas *encephalitis* is a generalized inflammation of the brain. In addition to the medical conditions, social and environmental factors have been found to be predictive of later sequelae from early infections (Kopp & Krakow, 1983). Thus, the infections interface with environmental factors in the resulting deficits, if any, for these children. The social factors cannot, of course, fully account for the deficits, as children with early insults to the brain have constraints placed on their development, and such constraints are tempered by how the environment handles them (Sameroff & Chandler, 1975). Thus, a transactional model for understanding these infectious processes is important. Both meningitis and encephalitis will be discussed briefly.

Meningitis

The meninges, as mentioned in Chapter 2, protect the brain from infections, cushion it from injury, and serve as a barrier to foreign objects. However, they are not impervious to damage or disease, and meningitis results when the meninges become inflamed, particularly in the arachnoid and pia mater layers. Bacterial meningitis, the most common form, affects approximately 40,000 people a year in the United States (Green & George, 1979). The most frequent age at which children are affected with meningitis is between 1 and 5 (Taylor et al., 1992).

The more common sources of bacterial infection are *Escherichia (E.) coli,* which is most common among infants; *Hemophilus (H) influenza type B, Streptococcus pneumoniae,* and *Neisseria meningitidis,* which are most common among children (Hynd & Willis, 1988). The Hemophilus (Hib) meningitis has been found to be related to significant developmental disability (Jadavji, Biggar, Gold, & Prober, 1986; Klein, Feigin, & McCracken, 1986) and to have an incidence of approximately 30 to 70 per 100,000 children (Snyder, 1994). Some ethnic groups have a higher incidence of this disease, with the Navajo and the Alaskan Yupik Eskimos showing the highest incidence (Coulehan et al., 1976; Fraser, 1982).

Usually these infections are spread by the blood as a result of poorly formed blood vessels or neurosurgical procedures. In children, the infection can be related to sinusitis, ear infections, and other types of abscesses. In neonates the infection may be acquired from the mother in the birth canal.

The clinical presentation of meningitis varies with age. In very young children there may be fever, lack

of appetite, nausea, irritability, jaundice, respiratory problems, and a bulging fontanel (Snyder, 1994). In older children there may be fever, headache, generalized seizure activity, nausea, vomiting, a stiff neck, and depressed consciousness. There may also be cranial nerve deficits in that visual field defects and/or facial palsy may be present along with ataxia, paralysis, and seizure activity. Other neurological indicators are present through CT scans, including hydrocephalus, edema, or cortical atrophy with abnormal EEG results (Taylor et al., 1992).

The diagnosis is confirmed by a sample of cerebrospinal fluid (CSF) being taken through a lumbar puncture and bacterium assayed in the sample. In meningitis the CSF is generally cloudy, and pressure is elevated. Treatment generally consists of high doses of antibiotics, frequently ampicillin, for 10 days. Chloramphenicol is frequently also prescribed in the event that the bacteria are resistent to ampicillin (Klein et al., 1986). Fluids are carefully monitored, and CT, MRI, and EEG studies are ordered as needed (Schaad et al., 1990).

The sequelae from meningitis depend on the age of onset, how long before the disorder is diagnosed, the infectious agent and severity of infection, and the treatment used (Weil, 1985). Neonates are at highest risk for mortality from meningitis. Children who experienced coma and subdural infections have been found to evidence the most severe neurological and neuropsychological sequelae (Lindberg, Rosenhall, Nylen, & Ringner, 1977). Moreover, those children who evidenced seizures prior to onset of meningitis, had a longer duration of illness and higher fevers, and were younger at onset had the poorest cognitive result following treatment (Emmett, Jeffrey, Chandler, & Dugdale, 1980; Klein et al., 1986). In a study looking at long-term effects of meningitis, Sell (1983) found that 50% of the children showed significant cognitive and physical difficulty, with language difficulty, hearing problems, cognitive delays, motor delays, and visual impairments being the most frequent complications.

Children who have recovered from the disease process need a comprehensive neuropsychological battery to monitor their progress. Such an assessment should be accomplished serially in order to detect any difficulties. Hearing and vision should be screened repeatedly, and parent and school personnel need to be well versed in attending to possible difficulties in these areas. Moreover, given the importance of parental support and social development, these areas need to be attended to not only in any evaluation but also in any proposed treatment paradigm.

Encephalitis

Encephalitis refers to a generalized inflammatory state of the brain. This disorder is frequently associated with an inflammation of the meninges as well. The incidence of encephalitis is reported to be approximately 1400 to 4300 cases in the United States annually (Ho & Hirsch, 1985). Viruses are frequently the culprit in this disease, which can occur perinatally or postnatally. Encephalitis can be caused by viral diseases such as Herpes simplex or through insect bites. For the majority of cases, however, no cause can be pinpointed (Adler & Toor, 1984).

There are two forms of the disease: acute and chronic. Acute forms are evidenced within days or weeks of infection, whereas chronic forms can take months to become symptomatic. Fever, headache, vomiting, loss of energy, lassitude, irritability, and depressive-like symptoms are frequently seen, with increasing confusion and disorientation seen as the disease progresses. At times speech processes are affected, paralysis or muscle weakness is seen, and gait problems occur (Hynd & Willis, 1988).

Diagnosis is through examination of the CSF for viral agents, with CT scans and EEG analysis also being found useful. Treatment is generally through antiviral agents if a viral cause has been discovered or through the monitoring of the disease process, antibiotics, and fluids no virus has been identified. Sequelae are generally related to the type of infection and the duration of the infectious process. Generally mental retardation, irritability and lability, seizure disorder, hypertonia, and cranial nerve involvement can be seen with the more severe disease process, while in mild to moderate cases there are few, if any, sequelae (Ho & Hirsch, 1985).

SUMMARY AND CONCLUSIONS

Children with various acquired neurological disorders and diseases have become a focus of study, and researchers have investigated the links between psychological, behavioral, and neuropsychological functioning in traumatic injury, infectious diseases, and prenatal exposure to teratogenic agents, including alcohol and cocaine. Children who experience congenital brain dysfunction tend to have problems with neuropsychological development. These difficulties are frequently subtle and appear related to difficulty in learning new material. Attentional and organizational skills are also sensitive to these disorders and may emerge at older ages, when these skills normally develop. These deficits have a negative impact on the adolescent and eventually the adult, and interfere with adjustment and overall adaptation.

In children and adolescents exposed to toxins, childhood cancer, traumatic brain injury, and other CNS infectious diseases, it is recommended that frequent neuropsychological evaluations be conducted to monitor progress and to evaluate possible regression. The use of ability and achievement tests needs to be suspended because the performance of children with neurological problems can *not* be predicted as it can be for typically developing children.

Parents and teachers have been found to play crucial roles in the adjustment and recovery of children with various neurological disorders and diseases. Too often support for the home and school environments is not present although research indicates the need for this type of service in the treatment plan. If the educational needs of the child are not sufficiently impaired to qualify for special education services, modifications of the regular education program are mandated under Section 504 of the Americans with Disabilities Act of 1973. Virginia Peckham, as previously discussed, has provided intervention suggestions that can be implemented in mainstream classrooms. Children with TBI may qualify for services under P.L. 94-142 or Section 504; while children with other neurological diseases/disorders may be considered as "Other Health Impaired" under the same legislation. In any case, regular education teachers need inservice training to assist them in recognizing the needs of neurological-impaired children and in developing effective intervention strategies for the classroom. Parents certainly need support not only for the stress the disorder places on the family but also for planning for the child's long-term development.

A transactional approach to neuropsychological assessment can provide the needed support for the parent, school, and child by assisting not only during the diagnostic phase but also during the diagnostic phase but also during the planning and implementation phase. Serial neuropsychological assessments can be helpful in this process, can assist in this planning, and can be sensitive to the not-always-anticipated changes in the child's development.

CHAPTER 11

NEUROPSYCHOLOGICAL INTERVENTION AND TREATMENT APPROACHES FOR CHILDHOOD AND ADOLESCENT DISORDERS

Information about the child's neuropsychological, cognitive, academic, and psychosocial status forms the basis for designing integrated intervention and treatment plans for children and adolescents with brain-related disorders. Efforts in developing models of neuropsychological intervention have been expanding in recent years. Two models are described in this chapter: the Multistage Neuropsychological Assessment-Intervention Model and the developmental neuropsychological remediation/habilitation framework designed by Rourke (1994). Systematic rehabilitation procedures developed by Reitan and Wolfson (1992) are also briefly reviewed. This chapter presents the underlying features of each model.

Specific techniques for designing intervention programs addressing cognitive, academic, psychosocial, and attentional problems associated with various childhood and adolescent disorders will be explored. Common medications useful for neuropsychiatric disorders of childhood and issues related to medication monitoring, consultation with school staff, and integrated medication protocols will be presented. Issues related to professional and family collaboration will be addressed, including guidelines for developing home—school—physician partnerships for treating childhood and adolescent neuropsychiatric, neurodevelopmental, and brain-related disorders.

MULTISTAGE NEUROPSYCHOLOGICAL MODEL: LINKING ASSESSMENT TO INTERVENTION

While the need for neuropsychological and neuroradiological evaluations may be obvious for conditions where traumatic brain injury or CNS disease is suspected, there also may be reasons to use these techniques for neurodevelopmental disorders, such as learning disabilities and attentional disorders. It is sometimes difficult to determine when to proceed with a comprehensive neuropsychological evaluation, particularly for school-related problems, and how to integrate neuropsychological evaluations into ongoing intervention plans. Teeter (1992) first described a multistage neuropsychological model as a guideline for linking neuropsychological assessment and intervention, and it serves as a foundation for the expanded model to be described (see Table 11.1). The multistage neuropsychological model begins with structured behavioral-observational assessment techniques, and proceeds to more extensive cognitive and psychosocial, neuropsychological and/or neuroradiological evaluations if problems are not effectively remediated at any given stage. This model recommends that systematic interventions be developed and implemented at each stage based on evaluation results.

Table 11.1. Models for Neuropsychological Remediation and Rehabilitation: Linking Assessment to Interventions

MODELS	STAGES	DESCRIPTION
MNM[a]		
	Stage 1: Problem identification	Behavioral assessment
	Stage 2: Behavioral-based intervention	Self-management Contingency-management Learning strategies Peer tutoring
	Stage 3: Cognitive child study	Comprehensive cognitive, academic, psycho-social assessment
	Stage 4: Cognitive-based intervention	Pattern analysis Phonological awareness Activating schemata Organizational strategies
	Stage 5: Neuropsychological assessment	Comprehensive neurocognitive assessment
	Stage 6: Integrated neuropsychological intervention	Compensatory skills Psychopharmacology
	Stage 7: Neurological and neuro-radiological assessment	Neurological, CT, MRI
	Stage 8: Medical-neurological rehabilitation	Rehabilitation and medical management
DNNR (Rourke, 1994)[b]	Step 1: Neuropsychological assets, deficits; academic and psychosiclal assessment	Neuropsychological profile Ecologically based evaluation
	Step 2: Demands of environment	Behavioral, academic, and psychosocial challenges within contextual framework
	Step 3: Short and long-term	Formulate short- and long-range predictions Which deficits will decrease? Specific treatment straegies
	Step 4: "Ideal" remedial plans	"Ideal" plans Monitoring and modification
	Step 5: Availability of resources	Therapeutic goals Prognosis Reduce redundant services
	Step 6: Realistic remedial plan	Compare differences between steps 4 and 5
	Step 7: Ongoing assessment and intervention	
REHABIT (Reitan & Wolfson, 1992)[c]	Tract A: Verbal-language	Materials to increase expressive-receptive skills
	Tract B: Abstraction and reasoning	Materials to increase analysis, organization
	Tract C: General reasoning	Materials for general reasoning
	Tract D: Visual-spatial	Visual-spatial manipulation Sequential skills
	Tract E: Visual-spatial and manipulation	

[a] Multistage Neuropsychological Model (developed by Teeter & Semrud-Clikeman).
[b] Developmental Neuropsychological Remediation/Rehabilitation Model (Rourke, 1994).
[c] Reitan Evaluation of Hemispheric Abilities and Brain Improvement Training (Reitan & Wolfson, 1992).

The following multistage neuropsychological assessment-intervention model (MNM) should be considered when treating children and adolescents with neurodevelopmental and/or neuropsychiatric disorders. This paradigm assumes a linkage between assessment and intervention, where competent evaluation of a problem or disorder leads to effective intervention strategies or plans. It is possible that at early stages of this model effective interventions may eliminate the necessity for further, more in-depth evaluation of the child. However, ongoing treatment evaluation is needed to verify the efficacy of the problem identification—intervention link at all stages. For some childhood problems (e.g., traumatic brain injury, CNS diseases, seizure activity), the clinician is advised to immediately proceed to more advanced stages of the MNM model (i.e., neuropsychological evaluation and neurodiagnostic examination).

The MNM paradigm comprises eight assessment-intervention stages. Stages 1 through 4 can reasonably be conducted by school-based professionals, including school psychologists and educational diagnosticians. Stages 5 and 6 are likely conducted by trained clinical child neuropsychologists in private practice, university, or medical clinics; Stage 7 is reserved for physicians in hospitals or medical centers. Stage 8 most likely requires at least short-term hospitalization in a medical or rehabilitation center.

At each stage of the MNM, accurate diagnosis or problem identification forms the basis for developing specific intervention strategies and for conducting ongoing monitoring and modification of intervention plans. One of the most common errors in implementing intervention programs occurs when treatment strategies are continued long after they are effective. This may occur when evaluations are scheduled years apart without systematic documentation of how the child is actually progressing (e.g., triennial evaluations conducted by schools when children are placed in special-education classrooms). Therefore, ongoing assessment and modification of the intervention plan is essential.

Stage 1: Problem Identification

During Stage 1, children with mild neurodevelopmental disorders (i.e., mild academic delays or deficits) may undergo an initial evaluation using well-established behavioral and curriculum-based assessment (CBA) approaches. There are excellent resources describing these procedures, including work by Shapiro (1989) and Shinn (1989).

Shapiro (1989) provides a flowchart indicating the steps involved in CBA, including (1) a teacher interview; (2) classroom observation and examination of the child's classwork; (3) CBA procedures (e.g., problem identification, problem analysis, problem verification, and remediation); (4) analysis of classroom resources; and (5) remedial decisions. Data gathered from these steps would then be used to develop Stage 2 intervention plans.

Stage 2: Behavioral-Based Intervention Plan

In Stage 2, educational professionals develop and implement an intervention plan based on data derived from the initial behavioral-observational assessment. CBA and ecobehavioral procedures can be helpful for determining a child's instructional, frustrational, and mastery levels for academic materials (Shapiro, 1989). Once specific strategies are selected (e.g., self-management or contingency management techniques), a task analysis of the skill to be taught is conducted. Specific learning strategies may also be the focus of instruction (e.g., summarizing and memory strategies), and other curricular procedures may be implemented (e.g., peer tutoring). Intervention monitoring, use of CBA and behavioral measures, and modification of the instructional plan would be ongoing during this phase.

Curriculum-based procedures contribute a number of important factors to the assessment-intervention process, including a means for (1) identifying current levels of academic skills; (2) monitoring intervention strategies or plans; (3) assessing the instructional context, particularly related to ecobehavioral factors (e.g., rate of presentation, reinforcements, contingencies, prompting, cueing, and feedback mechanisms) that affect learning; (4) assessing mild to moderate reading/learning problems; (5) evaluating skills, particularly at the elementary level; (6) reducing time-consuming and expensive evaluation; and (7) conducting data-based consultation for remediating academic difficulties in children (Shapiro, 1989). These contributions are important and may alleviate the need more in-depth evaluations. In some cases, Stage 1 evaluation and Stage 2 intervention may not be sufficient, and learning problems may persist that require further clinical evaluation and intensive remdiation.

Stage 3: Cognitive Child Study

Some conditions (e.g., reading disabilities resulting from phonological core deficits) may not respond to interventions developed from behavioral assessments and thus may require more in-depth evaluations. In these instances a comprehensive psychoeducational evaluation is warranted. Measures of intellectual, academic, and psychosocial functioning usually make up this phase of assessment. Evaluation at this stage would seek to identify underlying cognitive, perceptual, memory, and reasoning deficits associated with particular academic deficiencies. Word fluency, phonological awareness, prior knowledge (e.g., vocabulary knowledge), and listening comprehension skills are also of interest in this phase. The child's metacognitive strategies and approaches to learning tasks may be helpful for understanding the nature and extent of their learning difficulties.

Intervention plans would incorporate information gleaned during this stage, and may include multiple targets (i.e., academic, cognitive, and psychosocial) for intervention.

Stage 4: Cognitive-Based Intervention Plan

Interventions developed at this stage would address patterns of the child's specific cognitive strengths and weaknesses as the basis for designing effective academic programming. Depending on the patterns of strengths/weaknesses, efforts at this level may include training in phonological awareness for explicit decoding skills, strategic instruction in comprehension (e.g., use of context for gleaning meaning from text), and methods for developing and activating schemata

for learning new information. Study skills and organizational strategies may also be targeted. Specific techniques for various academic deficits (e.g., reading) are discussed in subsequent sections of the chapter.

Attention would also be paid to the child's psychosocial functioning, and attempts to increase the child's self-esteem, social interaction, and psychological well-being may be a focus. Although Stage 4 interventions would systematically address psychosocial factors, these could also be the focus of intervention in Stage 2. In cases where interventions are not initially effective, however, there is an increased probability of the child developing secondary psychological problems, as a cycle of academic failure, social rejection, and low self-esteem often ensues with repeated or prolonged academic deficiencies. Intervention plans would be systematically monitored and modified based on the child's progress.

There are instances in which traditional psychoeducational evaluations and interventions are not sufficient, and some children require more in-depth neuropsychological evaluations.

Stage 5: Neuropsychological Evaluation

Children with severe speech-language, learning, and/or motor difficulties may require neuropsychological evaluations in an effort to assess effectively the nature of their delays or deficits. In these instances clinical child neuropsychological assessment is warranted. The need for neuropsychological assessment is particularly crucial for children who do not respond to the interventions described in earlier stages in the MNM model, or for children who have neurological symptoms associated with their learning and/or psychosocial problems.

Children with traumatic brain injury or CNS diseases also typically require more in-depth neuropsychological evaluations, and would benefit from baseline information about how the brain is functioning and about changes in this baseline with age and effective interventions. Neuropsychological testing also may be necessary for children sustaining birth complications (e.g., prematurity, hypoxia) or exposure to teratogenic agents.

Stage 6: Integrated Neuropsychological Intervention Plan

Interventions developed from neuropsychological data typically address compensatory skills and long-term management. Psychopharmacology may also be needed by some children at this level. See discussions in later sections of the chapter for more details about neuropsychological interventions.

Stage 7: Neurological and/or Neuroradiological Evaluation

Finally, some children may need intensive medical and/or neuroradiological evaluations and interventions. Although only a small portion of children require this stage of evaluation, this stage is crucial for some childhood disorders. Oftentimes children with life-threatening conditions (e.g., tumors, injury, and/or intractable seizures) need ongoing Stage 7 evaluations and medical treatment (e.g., neurosurgery, chemotherapy, and/or CNS irradiation). However, evaluations and interventions described at other levels may also be incorporated into treatment plans for children with these conditions.

Stage 8: Medical-Neurological Rehabilitation

Medical-neurological rehabilitation efforts may be required for a small number of children with severe brain injuries or CNS diseases. These services may require placement in a rehabilitation center for short-term or long-term medical management. In these cases, a medical team including physicians (e.g., pediatric neurologists, neurosurgeons, radiologists, and pediatricians), neuropsychologists, psychologists, speech-language and physical therapists, and social workers design interventions to help remediate or rehabilitate the child's problems. Programs are generally comprehensive in nature and include the child and his or her parent.

In summary, the MNM decribes a process for linking multilpe stages of evaluation into intervention plans. Rourke (1994) describes a remediation model specifically for children with learning disabilities. This model is briefly reviewed below.

DEVELOPMENTAL NEUROPSYCHOLOGICAL REMEDIATION/REHABILITATION MODEL FOR CHILDREN AND ADOLESCENTS

Although Rourke's (1994) Developmental Neuropsychological Remediation/Rehabilitation Model (DNRR) was designed specifically for children with learning disabilities, the basic steps of the model serve as a useful framework for identifying critical elements of a remedial/rehabilitation plan for other brain-related childhood disorders. Rourke et al. (1983) and Rourke, Fisk, and Strang (1986) first introduced this model within a comprehensive assessment paradigm. The DNRR comprises seven major steps, which are described briefly.

Step 1: Interactions of neuropsychological assets/deficits, learning disabilities, academic learning, and psychosocial adaptive function. In the first step, the clinician determines the child's academic capacity and potential for social learning based on his or her neuropsychological profile. During this step, factors that influence learning capacity are assessed. Rourke (1994) recommends using valid neuropsychological assessment techniques within an ecological paradigm. In this paradigm, assessment is broad-based, with the intent of measuring principal areas of brain functioning (content validity or "coverage") and answering the clinical questions at hand. A variety of functions are assessed in order to answer relevant questions about the child's abilities within developmental stages.

Step 2: Demands of the environment. At this step, neuropsychological functioning is related to the behavioral, academic, and psychosocial challenges that face the child. Without understanding the functional status of the child within his or her specific context (classroom, social, cultural, etc.), intervention plans may be rendered meaningless or counterproductive (Rourke, 1994).

Step 3: Short- and long-term behavioral predictions. Short-term and long-term predictions are formulated considering (1) which deficits are expected to decrease regardless of intervention plans and (2) which specific treatment strategies will improve the identified deficits (Rourke, 1994). Neuropsychological assets and deficits are considered as these interact with the developmental challenges, and are influenced by the resources available to the child (family, psychosocial, community, etc.). Rourke (1994) indicates that clinical judgement is important at this step.

Step 4: "Ideal" short- and long-term remedial plans. "Ideal" plans are generated on the basis of evaluation information and the clinical judgment gleaned when proceeding through steps 1 to 3. Particular emphasis is placed on determining or predicting the relationship between short- and long-term intervention strategies, with ongoing monitoring and modification of the plan on an as-needed basis.

Step 5: Availability of remedial resources. Rourke (1994) advocates developing explicit intervention strategies, including identifying specific details about the therapeutic goals, length of intervention, and what to expect over time (prognosis). Specificity at this stage, both in identifying recommendations and in measuring treatment efficacy, is necessary to reduce redundant and expensive services when taking or applying assessment data from the neuropsychologist to the schools.

Step 6: Realistic remedial plan. Realistic plans are constituted by comparing differences that might emerge between steps 4 and 5. Rourke (1994) cautions that without solid data, requests for specific services will most likely be denied because of funding demands/problems.

Step 7: Ongoing relationship between neuropsychological assessment and intervention. In this final step, the neuropsychologist must think of assessment as an ongoing process with the intent of modifying, clarifying or changing intervention plans (Rourke, 1994). This is particularly crucial given that the present state of knowledge about the efficacy of specific remediations is rather limited.

THE REITAN EVALUATION OF HEMISPHERIC ABILITIES AND BRAIN IMPROVEMENT TRAINING (REHABIT)

Reitan (1980) designed REHABIT as an intervention program for rehabilitating brain-related deficits. REHABIT encompasses three stages, including assessment, training with Halstead-Reitan test items, and rehabilitation with special REHABIT materials (Teeter, 1989). Comprehensive evaluation of brain functioning using the Halstead-Reitan neuropsychological test battery is an integral phase of this program. After carefully identifying the child's neuropsychological status, a program is designed to remediate specific brain dysfunction. Techniques for addressing abstract, concept formation, and reasoning deficits are essential components of this program.

REHABIT comprises five tracts for training specific abilities, including verbal-language deficits, abstract reasoning and logical deficits, visual-spatial problems, and right—left hemisphere deficits (Reitan & Wolfson, 1992). Individualized remedial programs can be designed based on the child's neuropsychological profile. REHABIT materials have different levels of difficulty, and training usually begins at a level where the child is successful and then proceeds to more difficult levels. Ongoing evaluation is recommended in an effort to monitor the child's progress throughout the training program.

NEUROPSYCHOLOGICAL FRAMEWORK FOR REMEDIATION

Neuropsychological approaches to remediation often can be classified into three major categories, including approaches that focus on improving the child's neurocognitive deficits, accessing the child's neurocognitive strengths or assets, and a combination approach addressing both neurocognitive assets and deficits (Teeter, 1989). Principles underlying each of these theoretical orientations will be briefly reviewed.

Attacking Neurocognitive Deficits

Attempts to strengthen the child's weaknesses have historically included techniques such as psycholinguistic training, sensory integration, perceptual-motor training, or modality training. These techniques have generally produced little improvement in the child's academic performance, although modest success has been documented with a few specific problems/disorders. For example, in his meta-analysis of psycholinguistic training procedures, Kavale (1990) reported moderate gains for reading-disabled children when given specific instruction in verbal-comprehension and auditory-perceptual skills. In some instances, then, remediation of the weakness may be warranted.

Teaching to Neurocognitive Strengths

This orientation suggests that intervention programs should be designed to access the child's unique neurocognitive strengths and to avoid their deficits/ weaknesses. In some cases where motivation is a significant issue, this approach makes sense (Rourke et al., 1983). Gaddes and Edgell (1994) describe specific situations in which it is imperative to teach to the child's intact brain systems. For example, in children with bilateral cerebral dysfunction, cognitive retardation, and language deficits, techniques that access relatively intact right-hemisphere systems were quite successful in increasing the child's reading abilities.

Combined Treatment Programs

Rourke (1994) recommends intervention approaches that address the child's unique neuropsychological assets and deficits, and are primarily compensatory in nature. Rourke (1994) argues that developmental

stages may also influence which orientation we might initiate. For example, early remedial strategies for children with disorders affecting the white matter may benefit from methods designed to attack the child's deficits. In these cases, intact cortical regions are stimulated and grey matter connections can be facilitated. However, in older children with persistent disorders (e.g., nonverbal learning disabilities), compensatory strategies may be more beneficial.

Regardless of the theoretical orientation of the clinician, there continues to be a need for carefully designed research programs to demonstrate the efficacy of specific approaches. The following section describes techniques that have been found useful in remediating specific deficits in cognitive-intellectual, academic, and psychosocial interventions. Depending on the child's particular pattern of neurocognitive strengths and weaknesses, the clinician may select specific strategies.

SPECIFIC STRATEGIES FOR COGNITIVE-ACADEMIC, PSYCHOSOCIAL, AND ATTENTIONAL DISORDERS

Cognitive and Academic Training

There are number of intervention strategies with documented efficacy for reducing academic deficits in children and adolescents. Techniques for addressing reading, written language, and arithmetic disorders are reviewed, including strategies for teaching study and organizational skills. Social skills training is also discussed briefly.

These techniques are offered as possible strategies based on the child's particular neuropsychological, cognitive, and psychosocial profile, and should not be automatically adopted for every child. Various techniques should be carefully selected following an in-depth evaluation and a clear understanding of the child's neuropsychological assets and deficits, and his or her developmental, cognitive, academic, and social-emotional needs. An in-depth interview with the child's teacher and a record review is critical for determining remedial techniques that have been attempted in the past and have proved effective or ineffective.

Reading Disorders

Phonemic awareness. To date, "the phonological coding deficit is clearly established as the strongest predictor and correlate of reading disabilities" (Wise & Olson, 1991, p. 638). Remedial techniques that have proved most effective incorporate strategies for teaching children phonemic awareness skills and typically include segmenting, blending, and analyzing sounds (Tunmer & Nesdale, 1985; Williams, 1980). Prevention efforts have also shown effective, where preschool children have been successful in developing phonemic awareness skills (Byrne & Fielding-Barnsley, 1993; Lundberg, Frost, & Petersen, 1988). Phonological recoding skills are stressed, where the child is taught to translate letters and letter patterns into phonemes (Iverson & Tunmer, 1993). Knowledge of the grapheme-phoneme correspondences are usually integrated within reading instruction, and are not taught in isolation. Phonograms, common sound elements in word families (e.g., *ight* in *light* and *fight*), may also be stressed in beginning stages to increase vowel generalizations (Iverson & Tunmer, 1993). While children are instructed to categorize words on the basis of their phonemic similarity (Bradley & Bryant, 1983), phonemic awareness is most effective when contextualized using words taken from regular reading lessons (Cunningham, 1989).

Training programs in phonological awareness and phonological recoding often incorporate metacognitve strategies. Children are made aware of the visual and phonological similarities in words, and are taught strategies of how and when to use this knowledge (Iverson & Tunmer, 1993). Cunningham (1990) incorporated similar metacognitive techniques and found this instruction extremely beneficial. Other metacognitive strategy methods have also proved effective (Duffy et al., 1987; Gaskins et al., 1988).

Comprehension. Wise and Olson (1991) reviewed techniques for improving reading including strategies to increase reading comprehension. For example, Palincsar, Brown, and Martin (1987) used a "reciprocal teaching" method whereby teachers used predicting, questioning, and clarifying strategies to improve comprehension skills in slow readers. These skills were maintained two months after instruction and were generalized to other content areas (see Wise & Olson, 1991, for a review).

Bos and Van Reusen (1991) describe several techniques that have been effective for increasing comprehension and vocabulary knowledge, including "interactive learning strategies." This model emphasizes cooperation between the student and the teacher, where the student helps to identify their prior knowledge about a topic and then proceeds to link that prior knowledge with new information. Students are then taught how to scan reading material, to develop "clue lists," "relationship maps" or charts, and to predict relationships across concepts (Bos & Van Reusen, 1991). The teachers role begins as an instructor working together with the student through these stages, then moves to facilitator where students begin to work with each other. These techniques have shown effective in bilingual LD classes for social studies and reading (Bos & Van Reusen, 1991), and for middle-school children for science (Bos & Anders, 1990).

Computer and speech feedback. Olson, Foltz, and Wise (1986) developed a reading program for the microcomputer utilizing a speech synthesizer (i.e. DECtalk). Wise et al. (1989) found that below-average readers (lowest 10% of readers from selected classrooms) improved in phonological coding and word recognition skills using a computer reading program. When children were unable to read a word, segmented feedback was available whereby the computer highlighted and simultaneously "spoke" the word with the child. Comprehension questions were also incorporated into the program, and corrective feedback was provided. These results are promising and efforts are underway to improve these computer-based technologies (Olson et al., 1994; Wise & Olson, 1991).

Lewandowski and his colleagues at the Syracuse Neuropsychology Laboratory have found that reading-disabled students also recall more words when stimuli are presented in two modalities–computer screen and computer voice synthesizer–simultaneously. Montali and Lewandowski (1996) showed a memory advantage for reading-disabled students who experience short-term memory weaknesses, when words were presented bimodally. The performance of the reading-disabled group approached that of normal readers. Further, this performance advantage was also shown for reading conditions. When text was highlighted on the computer screen and the computer also read (spoke) the words at the same time, spontaneous word recall and reading comprehension were improved. Students with reading disabilities expressed a preference for this computer-based reading format.

Steele, Lewandowski, and Rusling (1996) replicated these findings with a mixed (LD, ADHD, and emotionally disturbed) group of children with reading problems. Bimodal facilitation was found in almost every student when data were analyzed using single-subject methodology. In summary, Lewandowski and colleagues suggest that bimodal computer reading methods can be helpful for a variety of poor readers in grades 3 through 12. Future research needs to address the issue of long-term benefits for such methods and to identify which children specifically benefit the most from these procedures. At present, there are a number of commercial computer programs available that combine highlighted and/or bigger text with speak-aloud capacities for spelling, writing, and literacy activities for Macintosh or IBM computers. These commercial programs may prove useful when incorporated into remedial programs for poor readers, and certainly warrant further research.

Whole language programs. Advocates of whole language programs stress the importance of teaching reading as a language activity, linking reading to writing, and incorporating children's literature as a source for reading activities. Wise and Olson (1991) describe whole language techniques as a "strength" approach and further suggest that word recognition and metacognitive techniques can be incorporated into this framework.

Written Language Disorders

Many techniques to improve written language skills use cognitive and metacognitive strategies (Bos & Van Reusen, 1991). Strategy instruction usually involves teaching students how to plan, organize, write, edit, and revise their writing samples (Englert, 1990). Several structured curricular programs are available, including Cognitive Strategy Instruction Writing (Englert, 1990) and Self-Instructional Strategy Training, which teaches story grammar techniques (e.g., who is the main character, when does the story take place, how does the story end), and self-regulation with self-monitoring (Graham & Harris, 1987, 1989). These programs have been shown to increase writing performance in learning-disabled students, although self-regulation training did not appear to have additive effects on performance (Bos & Van Reusen, 1991).

Mathematic Disorders

Mathematic problem-solving skills were not viewed as a priority until the past decade (Bos & Van Reusen, 1991). Reasoning, metacognitive processing, and reading delays have been associated with deficits in solving word problems (Bos & Van Reusen, 1991). Remedial techniques designed to address mathematical problem-solving disorders often reflect cognitive and metacognitive approaches, where students are taught to understand the nature of the problem, plan a solution, carry out the solution, and assess the accuracy of the solution. Similar problem-solving strategy instruction has been shown to be effective in a number of studies (Montague & Bos, 1986; Smith & Alley, 1981).

Fleischner (1994) cautions that few studies with math learning disabilities have adequately addressed the neuropsychological characteristics of the subjects; or, when these data are available, the cognitive strategies employed by the subjects are not described. In this regard, Fleischner (1994) suggests using the Test of Early Mathematics Ability (TEMA-2) or the Diagnostic Test of Arithmetic Strategies to gain information about which strategies are being employed.

On the other hand, Rourke (1989) provides an extensive description of the neuropsychological characteristics of children with specific deficits in the math area, with relative strengths in reading and spelling; and, describes a comprehensive intervention program for this problem.

NLD syndrome. Rourke (1989) and his colleagues (Rourke et al., 1983; Rourke, Del Dotto, Rourke, & Casey, 1990; Rourke & Fuerst, 1991) have described numerous remedial techniques for addressing the academic and psychosocial problems experienced by children with nonverbal learning disabilities (NLD). NLD children have the most difficulty in the academic areas of mathematics reasoning, calculation, and problem solving, with basic social-emotional problems (Rourke, 1989). These problems appear related to a pattern of right-hemisphere weaknesses (e.g., tactile and visual perception, concept formation, novelty, and complex psychomotor skills), with relative strengths in left-hemisphere activities (e.g., phonological skills, verbal abilities, reading, spelling, verbatim memory) (Rourke, 1994).

Rourke (1989) suggests a remedial approach that acknowledges these assets and deficits and encompasses techniques for improving academic skills as well as social relationships. Strang and Rourke (1985) describe a series of teaching strategies to enhance mathematics calculation and reasoning, which involve verbal elaboration of the steps, written cue cards with the rules for solving the problem, and concrete aids (e.g., graph paper and color-coded columns). Students are encouraged to use calculators to check for errors, and teachers use error pattern analysis to modify the remedial plan (Teeter, 1989). Lessons utilize relevant and practical problem solving situations (e.g., shopping).

Further, Rourke (1989) describes techniques for increasing problem-solving skills, generalization of strategies and concepts, appropriate nonverbal skills, accurate self-evaluation, and life skills—preparing for adult life. Because of the very serious psychosocial limitations inherent in the NLD syndrome, Rourke (1989) stresses the need for social problem-solving skills, social awareness, structured peer interactions,

and parent involvement in the treatment plan. Techniques are also developed to increase the child's exploratory behaviors and interactions with the environment. Rourke's (1989) methods emphasize the need for a step-by-step problem-solving approach, in which feedback is provided in a supportive manner. Children are encouraged to "lead with their strong suit" and are also taught more appropriate ways to utilize their relative strengths (i.e., verbal-language skills).

Rourke (1994) has used single-subject investigations to validate his remedial techniques and has found support for treatment plans that are based on a model of identifying the interactions of neuropsychological assets/deficits on academic and psychosocial functioning. Rourke (1994) acknowledges the need for more systematic empirical study of remedial strategies based on neuropsychological findings, particularly to investigate whether interventions should be deficit-driven or compensatory in nature. Developmental considerations appear important in this decision, as Rourke (1994) suggests that when deficits result from early white matter disease or dysfunction, remediation might focus on attacking the deficit. If the diagnosis is made later or if the syndrome persists, compensatory strategies are most likely to be the best approach.

Study and Organizational Skills

Systematic strategy instruction for high school students has been the focus of a program–the Strategies Intervention Model–developed by the University of Kansas Institute for Research on Learning Disabilities (Ellis & Lenz, 1991). This programs was developed to teach students learning strategies to acquire and store knowledge, and to demonstrate this knowledge (Ellis & Friend, 1991). For strategies to be effective, they must be useful, efficient, and memorable. Ellis and Friend (1991) describe several effective strategies, including setting priorities; reflecting on how a task can be attacked and accomplished; and analyzing the task, setting goals, monitoring, and checking to see if goals were accomplished.

Archer and Gleason (1989) also developed Skills

for Success (Grades 3—6), a structured curriculum to teach students study and organization skills. This program features lessons on reading, organizing and summarizing information, test-taking, anticipating test content, how to study, and responding to various test formats (DuPaul & Stoner, 1994). DuPaul and Stoner (1994) also describe a program for organizing school materials, making an assignment calendar, and organizing and completing a paper for children with ADHD. Although these study and organizational skills have not been thoroughly researched, initial evidence suggests that they are promising procedures that can be employed for learning-disabled youth (Ellis & Friend, 1991), and warrant further investigation for children with ADHD (DuPaul & Stoner, 1994).

Social Skills Training

Interest in the remediation of social skills deficits has increased over the years, due to the growing awareness that social skill development is linked to learning disabilities (Semrud-Clikeman & Hynd, 1991b); school dropout, delinquency, and emotional disturbance (Barclay, 1966); and attention deficit disorders (Carlson, Lahey, Frame, Walker, & Hynd, 1987). Specifically, it has been shown that peer rejection as a result of aggression is predictive of criminal behavior later in adulthood (Parker & Asher, 1987). Recently, proposed definitions suggest including social problems as characteristics of learning disabilities (Bryan & Lee, 1990; Gaddes & Edgell, 1994; Lerner, 1993). Advocates of this proposal assert that to focus solely on academic gains in reading and math, while ignoring social interaction skills, will limit the usefulness of our remediation efforts for children with learning disabilities (Bryan, 1991; Rourke, 1994).

Social skills problems appear related to a number of factors including self-efficacy, self-esteem, locus of control, social cognition, comprehension of nonverbal cues, moral development, comprehension of social rules, problem-solving skills, communication disorders, and classroom behaviors (Bryan, 1991). Semrud-Clikeman and Hynd (1991b) further describe several neuropsychological syndromes resulting from involvement of either the right or the left hemisphere. Right-hemisphere dysfunction was postulated in learning-disabled children with a variety of deficits, including math, visual-spatial, and social perception, and left-sided motor weaknesses, with verbal reasoning, social gesturing, and social linguistic problems (Denckla, 1978, 1983). Voeller (1986) also described a group of children with abnormal right-hemisphere signs based on CT scans, EEGs, and neuropsychological measures. These children were unable to interpret others' emotions and had trouble displaying appropriate emotions. Further, there was an increased rate of attentional and hypermotoric behaviors as well in children with right-hemisphere involvement.

There are a number of social skills training programs, including the ACCEPTS program for elementary children (Walker, McConnell, Todis, Walker, & Golden, 1988); and the ACCESS program for adolescents (Walker, Holmes, Todis, & Horton, 1988), to name a few. These programs are highly structured, and have proven efficacy for children with mild to moderate handicaps.

Interventions designed to address social skills deficits in children with various learning and social interaction problems have met with mixed if not disappointing results (Vaughn, McIntosh, & Hogan, 1990). When positive behavioral changes have been noted in children with social skills problems, peers and teachers do not readily acknowledge or perceive these gains (Northcutt, 1987). Another concern that is often raised by researchers is that children "trained" in social skills often display appropriate social skills in controlled, therapeutic settings, but fail to interact appropriately in natural settings.

A couple of therapy caveats illustrate this point. One of the authors conducted a 15-week social skills training program with four monthly booster sessions for children with ADHD. At the end of the 15-week sessions, one 12-year-old girl threw her "graduation" gift on the floor. When confronted by her inappropriate behaviors, she commented, "Well, you told me I should be honest. Did you want me to lie when I didn't like my present?" Despite weeks of modeling, role playing, corrective feedback, videotapings, and behavioral reinforcement on expressing feelings appropriately, when disappointed in a "real-life" situation, she was unable to apply the skills she had demonstrated on numerous occasions during group. When processing the incident, she could generate alternative behaviors, but in the heat of her emotions she was unable to exercise control over her disappointment.

On another occasion, a 13-year-old ADHD male pushed one of his peers and kicked his books across the parking lot on his way out of the hospital. This situation followed an evening when alternatives to anger was the focus of the group session. This adolescent wasn't even an aggressive child, but when he was teased about something that was particularly painful for him, he reacted inappropriately. Not to be overlooked was the other 12-year-old who was baiting his peer. He too was part of the group and obviously was acting inappropriately. Even though both boys were progressing nicely in therapy, in a more natural, less structured situation both were unable to generalize skills that had been the focus of numerous sessions.

In a critical review of 20 studies conducted between 1982 and 1989, Vaughn et al. (1990) did indicate that programs for LD students were most effective when the following conditions were true:

1. LD students received part-time versus full-time LD services.
2. LD were in either elementary or high school; middle school students showed fewer gains.
3. Regular class students were included in the intervention program.
4. Programs were individualized to the student's needs.
5. Children are selected for social skills training on the basis of deficits rather than LD placement alone.
6. Training programs were long term (average 9 weeks, 23.3 hours) and included follow-up sessions.
7. Instruction is conducted in small groups or one-to-one.
8. Programs included coaching, modeling, corrective feedback, rehearsal, and strategy instruction.

La Greca (1993) indicates the need for training programs that address the broader social milieu of the child. Rather than focusing solely on the social skills deficits of the "problem child," programs should also include high-status or nonproblem peers. La Greca (1993) recommends the following: (1) changing peer acceptance through multisystemic intervention models; (2) employing prevention models at the school level; (3) utilizing peer-pairing or cooperative activities with children of mixed social status; (4) changing the ways teachers select groups in the classroom to avoid cliques and child-picked teams; (5) ongoing teacher monitoring of social skills interventions in the classroom; and (6) involving parents in intervention efforts. La Greca (1993) also suggests that one or two close friends might buffer a child who does not enjoy peer acceptance with the larger group. Helping the child develop supportive friendships might be worthwhile for reducing anxiety, stress, depression, and low self-esteem.

In summary, social skills training can be effective when it involves broader goals than increasing skill deficits in the targeted child. By expanding treatment goals to include peers, teachers, and parents, social skills intervention can be helpful for many children with learning problems.

CLASSROOM AND BEHAVIOR MANAGEMENT

Behavior management has long been used as an effective remediation strategy for a variety of learning and behavioral problems in the classroom. The literature base demonstrating the positive effects of behavior management are too extensive to review here. The reader is referred to DuPaul and Stoner (1994) and Witt, Elliott, and Gresham (1988) for a detailed review of research on token economies, contingency contracting, cost response, and time out from positive reinforcement. This section reviews selected strategies that have proved helpful for classroom management and instructional techniques, including self-management, attention training, home-based contingencies, and peer tutoring.

Self-Management/Self-Control Techniques

Self-management techniques have grown in popularity in an effort to help children develop control over their own behavior. Self-control techniques generally include self-assessment (observing one's own behavior), self-evaluation (comparing one's behavior to a "standard"), self-recording, and self-reinforcement (Lloyd & Landrum, 1990). Although these techniques have been used for a variety of behaviors, attending to task has been a major thrust in the literature.

Lloyd and Landrum (1990) surveyed 37 studies using self-recording techniques for children with learning, cognitive, and behavioral disorders from 4 years of age to adolescence. Self-recording was found to be effective for the following variables: increasing attention to task, decreasing disruption, work productivity, work accuracy, task completion, and, sustained schoolwork. Depending on the child's individual needs, self-recording can focus on academic accuracy, productivity, or attention to task; and all areas seem to improve regardless of which is targeted (Lloyd & Landrum, 1990).

Typically self-recording is most effective when cueing occurs (Heins, Lloyd, & Hallahan, 1986), and may take many forms (e.g., tape-recorded beeps at 1-, 2-, or 3-minute intervals, or kitchen timers that ring every 5 minutes). Fading of taped cues is often built into self-recording procedures, and maintenance appears quite good after the treatment has been discontinued (Lloyd & Landrum, 1990). See Shapiro and Cole (1994) for a more in-depth treatment of self-management techniques for the classroom.

Attention Training

Investigations in the field of attention disorders are adopting a componential approach, which recognizes different components of attention. The emphasis has shifted from motoric hyperactivity to determining which aspects of attention discriminate children with attention deficit disoders from normal children (Pennington, 1991).

Attention may well contain multiple aspects, which are arranged in hierarchical order and which may interact with motor, cognitive, and social development (Sohlberg & Mateer, 1989). Thus, disruption of any component may compromise the efficiency of the total attention system. Moreover, disruption of a component will have a negative impact on aspects lower in the hierarchical chain of attention (e.g., ability to shift set may be disturbed and consequently affect responses to temporally presented information or vigilance). It is likely that a breakdown in processing of temporal information would have an impact on classroom learning which requires processing of sequential instructional language.

Differential components of attention may show deficits in various subtypes of attention deficit disorder. Although attention deficit disorder implicates attention as a problem in these children, it is not currently known which aspect or aspects of attention are disordered. Thus, it is likely that no one cognitive task will provide a diagnosis of attention deficit disorder. The tasks that are sensitive to children with attentional disorders are just beginning to be explored.

A system that combines training on the aspects of attention involving selective and sustained attention has been developed by Sohlberg and Mateer (1989). This system teaches the individual to identify targets as quickly and with as few errors as possible. The subject is asked to mark targets embedded in nontargets. For example, a page may consist of several rows of numbers, and the subject is asked to select all the 4's as quickly as possible. As the subject scans the page, he or she utilizes selective attention. The tasks require the subject to use sustained as well as selective attention. The same tasks can also be used to improve divided attention. In this paradigm, the subject is asked to select two targets at the same time.

On the auditory attention training, the subject listens to a cassett tape and is asked to count how many targets he or she hears during the tape. For example, the subject is asked to count how many b's he or she hears from a list of nontarget letters. Or, the subject may be asked to count how many words begin with the letter b from a list of words. This task requires selective as well as sustained attention.

These tasks have been used mostly with head-injured adults, but we have adapted them for use with children displaying significant attentional difficulties (Semrud-Clikeman et al., submitted). The tasks were provided in 24 sessions, with two adults assisting twice a week over a 12-week period. Each child worked in a group of five to six children, and charts were kept of the child's progress. The charts were reviewed at each session, and problem-solving techniques were discussed to help the child consider the most efficient alternative as well as to learn to self-monitor his or her progress. At the end of the 12-week sessions, teachers were asked to report on the child's ability to complete assignments. In 20 of the 22 cases, improvement was seen in the number of completed assignments. Of the 22 children enrolled in the study, approximately 50% were on medication for ADHD. At the end of the study, there was no difference between the medicated and the nonmedicated children in their performance on measures of selective and sustained attention. Moreover, there was a significant improvement in the auditory attention of children who participated in the groups. Such improvement on the auditory attention task was not found for children without attentional problems or for ADHD control children. Therefore, it would appear that children with attention and work completion problems can benefit from direct teaching in problem-solving skills as well as practice in selective attention.

Although this project is a pilot study, it lends credence to the hypothesis that attentional skills can be addressed when specific training is provided. Certainly further investigation into appropriate interventions for children with attentional problems is warranted. Second, the extent to which improvement in attentional skills persists over time is also of interest. Third, although medication helped these children to remain seated, it was not related to measures of sustained and selective attention. This finding is consistent with Barkley's (1990) finding that medication does not improve academic performance. Though preliminary, this research appears promising, and attention training (with problem-solving techniques) may prove useful as an intervention strategy for children with attentional deficits.

Home-Based Contingencies

Home-based contingencies are frequently used as a supplement to school-based token systems (DuPaul & Stoner, 1994). Generally, these procedures employ daily or weekly rating forms that are filled out by the teacher. Several classroom or academic behaviors can be targeted, including attention to task, work completion, homework completion, compliance, and social interactions. The teacher rates the child by class periods or subject areas, using a point scale (e.g., 5 = excellent, 1 = terrible), and provides written comments. The child is responsible for taking the rating form to the parent, and the parent then discusses the child's performance with the child and provides reinforcement based on the points earned at school.

DuPaul and Stoner (1994) indicate that delay of reinforcement can be a problem for children with ADHD, particularly with younger children. However, home-based contingencies have proved effective for increasing school performance, particularly when used with classroom behavior management techniques.

Peer Tutoring

Peer tutoring techniques have been developed for reading, spelling, and math activities, and participants have demonstrated significant gains (Greenwood, Maheady, & Carta, 1991). DuPaul and Stoner (1994) indicate that peer tutoring is an attractive technique because it is time- and cost-efficient. In peer tutoring the class is divided into dyads, and tutor—tutee pairs work together during learning activities (Shapiro, 1989). The Class Wide Peer Tutoring (CWPT) program provides systematic and detailed training guidelines for implementing this intervention technique (Greenwood, Delquardi, & Carta, 1988).

Shapiro (1989) indicates that these procedures have produced positive academic and behavioral gains for children with a variety of disorders, including slow learners, learning-disabled children, and behaviorally disordered children. DuPaul and Henningson (1993) also reported positive gains for a young ADHD child when a classwide peer tutoring program was initiated. The second-grade ADHD child showed less hyperactivity and improved on-task behavior and academic performance in math.

These techniques offer a number of viable strategies for improving the academic, behavioral, and social functioning of children and adolescents with various disorders. Individual educational planning is necessary to decide which of these techniques are most appropriate. These interventions are usually used in combination, and careful monitoring is essential to determine their effectiveness. See DuPaul and Stoner (1994) and Shapiro (1989) for detailed information on intervention monitoring.

Some disorders with biomedical or neuropsychological causes may require biological treatments, usually in the form of psychopharmacology (Pelham, 1993a). The following section reviews selected psychopharmacological interventions for various childhood and adolescent disorders.

PSYCHOPHARMACOLOGICAL INTERVENTIONS

A number of neuropsychiatric disorders of childhood and adolescence are treated with medications. Most of these disorders, however, require combined treatments, and "appropriate psychosocial and psychoeducational interventions should form a component of treatment for most children with these disorders—even those where pharmacotherapy is helpful" (Pelham, 1993a, p. 161). A select list of common medications will be reviewed briefly, including those designed to control for major depressive disorders, psychotic disorders, ADHD, Tourette syndrome, and seizure disorders.

Specific Classes of Medication

Medications are typically classified as stimulants, antipsychotics, tricylic antidepressants, or monoamine oxidase inhibitors (MOIs); antioxiolytics, and anticonvulsants, depending on their behavioral effects on the CNS (Green, 1991). Table 11.2 presents a summary of common medications currently in use to treat children and adolescents, and includes an outline of their potential benefits and side effects.

Psychopharmacological agents may affect more than one neurotransmitter, and specific neurotransmitters may be implicated in more than one neuro-

Table 11.2. Common Uses, Benefits, and Side Effects of Medications for Neuropsychiatric Disorders of Childhood

DRUGS	COMMON USE	MANIFESTATIONS	SIDE EFFECTS
Stimulants			
Methylphenidate (Ritalin)	ADHD	75% children responders Decreased motor activity, impulsivity, and disruptive behaviors Increased attention Improved socialization Improved ratings (teacher, physician, parent) Increased work completion and accuracy Improved test scores (mazes, PIQ, and visual memory)	Insomnia, appetite loss, nausea, vomiting, abdominal pains, thirst, headaches Tachycardia, change in blood pressure Irritability, moodiness Rebound effects Growth suppression (can be monitored) Lower seizure threshold Exacerbate preexisting tics
Dextroamphetamine (D-amphetamine)	ADHD	Similar to methylphenidate Subdued emotional response Increased reflectivity and ability to monitor self Increased interest level Improved school performance Improved parent ratings (conduct, impulsivity, immaturity, antisocial, and hyperactivity)	Similar to methylphenidate Hallucinations, seizures, and drug-induced psychosis (rare occurrences)

(Cont.)

Table 11.2. *(Continued)*

DRUGS	COMMON USE	MANIFESTATIONS	SIDE EFFECTS
Stimulants (Cont.) Magnesium pemoline (Cylert)	ADHD	Similar to methylphenidate Improved teacher ratings (defiance, inattention, and hyperactivity) Improved parent ratings (conduct, impulsivity, and antisocial behaviors) Improved test scores (mazes, PIQ, visual memory)	Similar to methylphenidate
Antipsychotics Haloperidol (Haldol)	Psychosis Tourette Autism PDD ADD with CD	Reduces aggression, hostility, negativity, and hyperactivity Reduces psychotic symptoms Reduces Tourette symptoms Reduces fixations, withdrawal stereotypes, anger, and fidgetiness in autism Increases social responsivity and reality testing in PDD	Behavioral toxicity with pre-existing disorders Dystonia, loss of tone in tongue and trunk) Parkinsonian symptoms (tremors, mask face, and drooling) Dyskinesis (mouth, tongue, and jaw) Dose reduction decreases motor side effects Intellectual dulling and disorganized thoughts
Chlorpromazine (Thorazine)	Psychosis Severe aggression, explosiveness, and hyperexcitability in MR children	Reduces hyperactivity Reduces tantrums, aggression, self-injury Not effective for young autistic	Similar to haloperidol Dermatological problems Cardiovascular problems Lowers seizure threshold Endocrinological problems Ophthalmological problems Hematological problems
Thioridazine (Mellaril)	Psychosis Severe behavior disorders (extreme)	Reduces hyperactivity Improves schizophrenic symptoms Similar to Thorazine	Similar to haldol Sedation, cognitive dulling, and impaired arousal
Thiothixene (Navane)	Psychosis	Similar to Mellaril	Less sedating than Mellaril
Loxapine Succinate (Loxitane)	Psychosis	Similar to haldol	Similar to haldol
Fluphenazine Hydrochloride (Prolixin, Permitil)	Psychosis		
Pimozide (Orap)	Psychosis Tourette (resistant type)	Clinical improvement	High doses–death and seizures
Clozapine (Clozaril)	Severe psychosis (resistant type)	Clinical improvement	Life-threatening Hypertension, tachycardia, and EEG change Seizures

Table 11.2. *(Continued)*

DRUGS	COMMON USE	MANIFESTATIONS	SIDE EFFECTS
Tricyclic Antidepressants			
Imipramine hydrochloride (Tofranil)	Depression Enuresis ADHD School phobia	Improves depression (not severe) Inhibits bladder muscles Reduces hyperactivity Reduces separation anxiety Improves sleep disorders)	Potentially life-threatening cardiovascular problems CNS symptoms (EEG changes, confusion, lowers seizure threshold, incoordination, drowsiness, delusions, and psychosis) Blurred vision, dry mouth, and constipation
Nortriptyline hydrochloride (Pamelor)	Depression	Low rate of clinical improvement in children and adolescents	Withdrawal symptoms
Desipramine hydrochloride (Norpramine)	ADHD ADHD with Tics	Improved ratings (parents and teachers Conners) Clinical improvement	Dry mouth, decreased appetite, tiredness, dizziness, insomnia EEG changes at high doses
Clomipramine hydrochloride (Anafranil)	Obsessive-compulsive disorders Severe ADHD Enuresis School phobia	Reduces obsessions Reduces school phobia/anxiety Reduces aggression, impulsivity, and depressive/affective symptoms	Withdrawal symptoms Seizures Somnolence, tremors, dizziness, headaches, sweating, sleep disorder, gastrointestinal problems, cardiovascular effects, anorexia, and fatigue
Monoamine Osidase Inhibitors			
Fluoxetine hydrochloride (Prozac)	Depression Obsessive-compulsive	Effective for adults Clinical improvement for OCD	Nausea, weight loss, anxiety, nervousness, sweating, sleep disorders
Bupropion hydrochloride (Wellbutrin)	Depression ADHD	Adolescents 18+ improve Improved global ratings Not Conners	Seizures, agitation, dry mouth, insomnia, nausea, constipation, tremors
Anxiolytics			
Chlordiazepoxide (Librium)	Anxiety with hyperactivity and irritability School phobia	Clinical improvement Reduced hyperactivity, fears, enuresis, truancy, bizarreness Decreases emotional overload	Drowsiness, fatigue, muscle weakness, ataxia, anxiety, and depression with high doses
Diazepam (Valium)	Mixed psychiatric DX Anxiety and sleep	Improved global ratings Better results for adolescents	Relatively low toxicity
Alprazolam (Xanax)	Anxiety Panic attacks Separation anxiety	Clinical improvements Responders (premorbid, personality were shy, inhibited, nervous)	Mild drowsiness
Anticonvulsants			
Phenobarbital	Seizure disorders	Reduces seizures	Lethal at high doses Cognitive impairment, rigidity, and depression
Diphenylhydantoin sodium (Phenytoin)	Seizure disorders	Reduces tonic-clonic seizures	Cognitive impairment Drug toxicity

(Cont.)

Table 11.2. *(Continued)*

DRUGS	COMMON USE	MANIFESTATIONS	SIDE EFFECTS
Anticonvulsants (Cont.) Carbamazepine	Seizure disorders Manic-depression	Reduces generalized and tonic-clonic seizures Psychotropic effects	Fewer adverse side effects than other drugs Less cognitive dulling, motoric and affective
Sodium valporate	Seizure disorders	Reduces seizures Petit mal + tonic-clonic	Low cognitive symptoms Relatively nontoxic in adults Rare but potentially fatal hepatoxicity in children

Note: Data taken from Green (1991), Neppe & Tucker (1992), and Dubovsky (1992).

psychiatric disorder (Green, 1991). These CNS affects will be discussed in the following sections.

Stimulants

Stimulant medications are the most common treatment for hyperactivity and attention problems in children and adolescents (DuPaul & Barkley, 1990), and more recently with adults (Weiss & Hechtman, 1993). Although a majority of children with ADHD are considered to be positive responders to psychostimulants, approximately 25% to 30% do not respond favorably (DuPaul & Barkley, 1990). Schaughency and Hynd (1989) suggest that "perhaps there are correlated, parallel, or even orthogonal neurotransmitter systems implicated in ADD" that account for these differences in response rates (p. 436). Further, Hunt, Mandl, Lau, and Hughes (1991) propose that "multiple neurotransmitter systems may be involved in integrated cognitive/behavioral functioning," and "the relative balance of these transmitters and these neurofunctional systems determines the modulation of behavior" (p. 272). Thus, individual response rates may be a function of the ADHD child's primary dysfunction in cognitive/perceptual systems, arousal systems, or inhibitory systems. This perspective still needs further verification in controlled studies.

Disturbances in dopamine (DA) and norepinephrine (NE) levels have been carefully studied in ADHD children, including how stimulants affect these catecholamines for the ultimate control of attention and movement (Zametkin & Rapoport, 1987). DA systems are involved in a variety of cognitive and perceptual functions, including attentional gaiting, sustaining focus, short-term memory, and allocation of memory, while NE systems are involved in cortical arousal, filtering of incoming stimuli, excessive arousal, restlessness, and hyperactivity (Hunt & Mandl, 1991; Hunt, Lau, & Ryu, 1991).

Serotonin has also been implicated in ADHD, particularly as it relates to cortical inhibition, direction of motor activity, control of impulses and aggression, and complex judgment (Hunt, Mandl, et al., 1991; Hunt, Lau, & Ryu, 1991). Increased levels of serotonin produce obsessional thoughts, while decreased levels result in increased impulsivity, aggression, and fragmentation (Hunt, Mandl, et al., 1991). Comings (1990) suggest that serotonin may be less important for understanding ADHD but may be more useful for children with conduct disorders and aggression.

Although biochemical research is difficult to conduct because of developmental changes in neurotransmitters systems, the use of peripheral measures, and the complexity of neurotransmitter action (Zametkin & Rapoport, 1986), several hypotheses have been generated to explain how medications affect various neurotransmitters. For example, medications affect DA, NE, and serotonin in different ways:

1. d-amphetamine may inhibit NE while enhancing DA activity (Shekim, Javid, Davis, & Bylund, 1983).

2. Mmethylphenidate appears to facilitate the release of DA and NE at the presynapse, and may reduce the uptake of DA at the postsynapse (Hunt, Mandl, et al., 1991).
3. Clonidine may inhibit release of NE at the presynapse (Hunt, Brunstetter, & Silver, 1987).
4. Tricylcic antidepressants (e.g., desipramine and imipramine) block the uptake of NE and serotonin (Kolb & Whishaw, 1990).

These various actions facilitate neural transmission by either increasing the amount of neurotransmitters or prolonging the time the transmitters are active at the synapse (Kolb & Whishaw, 1990).

Other medications have been used for children considered nonresponders to stimulant medications, including imipramine (Copeland & Copps (1995), and MAO inhibitors (Zametkin, Rapoport, Murphy, Linnoila, & Ismond, 1985). Desipramine selectively blocks the uptake of NE, and imipramine may block the uptake of serotonin. While antidepressants may increase NE availability at the synapse (Hunt, Mandl, et al., 1991), these are not the front-line medications of choice for most children with ADHD.

The potential benefits of stimulant medications, particularly methylphenidate, are well documented. They include enhanced performance on impulse control, motor coordination, and vigilance (Gadow, 1985); increased academic productivity and accuracy (Balthazor, Wagner, & Pelham, 1991); decreased off-task behaviors (Barkley & Cunningham, 1979b); decreased aggression (Hinshaw, Henker, Whalen, Erhardt, & Dunnington, 1989); improved peer relations (Hinshaw, 1991); fewer negative commands for teachers (Barkley, 1990); and improved interactions with parents (Barkley & Cunningham, 1979b; Pelham, 1993b). Despite these positive results, individual responsivity remains highly variable (DuPaul, Barkley, & McMurray, 1991); and children should be carefully monitored for negative side effects (DuPaul & Barkley, 1990). Also, a number of environmental factors may affect a child's responsivity to medication. For example, Barkley and Cunningham (1980) found that the better the mother—child relationship, the greater the positive response rate in the child. Pelham (1993a) further reports that improvements in peer relations following medication are most evident in situations where other psychosocial and behavioral interventions are in place.

Pelham (1993a) indicates that short-term psychopharmacotherapy is more effective for treating ADHD than are other educational or behavioral treatments. However when behavioral management programs are added to medication regimens, dosage levels may be decreased (Carlson, Pelham, Milich, & Dixon, 1992). Pelham (1993a) recommends establishing baseline data for compliance and work productivity, then varying medication to determine effective doses. Methods for medication monitoring in school and home environments will be discussed in subsequent sections.

Antipsychotics

Two major classes of antipsychotic medications (i.e., neuroleptics or major tranquilizers), phenthiazines (e.g., chlorpromazine), and butyrophenones (e.g., haloperidol), are used to treat a variety of neuropsychiatric disorders in children and adolescents, including schizophrenia (Kolb & Whishaw, 1990); pervasive developmental delays (Joshi, Capozzoli, & Coyle, 1988); chronic motor tics and Tourette (Comings, 1990); severe aggression and conduct disorders (Green, 1991); cognitive retardation with psychotic symptoms (Gadow & Poling, 1988); and excessive or severe hyperactivity, low frustration tolerance, and poor attention (Weizman, Weitz, Szekely, Tyana, & Belmaker, 1984). Although both classes of antipsychotics affect NE and DA systems, benefits appear related to their ability to block DA receptors, thereby reducing psychotic symptoms (Kolb & Whishaw, 1990). However, Kolb and Whishaw (1990) caution that neurotransmitters have intricate interactions with each other that may not be immediately obvious.

Weizman et al. (1984) indicate that neuroleptics, in combination with stimulants, might be effective for a small number of ADHD children who do not respond to either medication alone. Apparently, when these drugs are used in combination, the stimulants increase the release of DA while the neuroleptics block DA thereby suggesting synergetic effects between the two agents (Green, 1991). Zametkin and Rapoport (1987) indicate that antipsychotics are not as effective as stimulants, but these medications do seem to decrease motoric activity and inattention.

Because of the serious side effects associated with neuroleptics, these medications require careful monitoring. Green (1991) suggests that cognitive dulling, sedation, and irreversible tardive dyskinesia (abnormal involuntary movements) are of particular concern when treating children and adolescents. Children and adolescents are prone to exhibit acute dystonic reactions (e.g., neck spasms, mouth and tongue contractions, eyes rolling upward) within the first five hours of ingestion, and are more at risk when taking high-potency, low-dose antipsychotics versus low-potency, high-dose regimens.

Tricyclic Antidepressants/ Monoamine Oxidase Inhibitors (MAOI's)

Tricyclic antidepressants (e.g., imipramine, desipramine, nortriptyline, and clomipramine) act on DA and selectively block the reuptake of NE and serotonin (Kolb & Whishaw, 1990). Tricyclics are effective for treating a variety of childhood and adolescent disorders, including (1) imipramine for depression, enuresis, school phobia, and sleep disorders; (2) desipramine for ADHD and ADHD with tics; (3) nortriptyline for major depressive disorder; and (4) clomipramine for obsessive-compulsive disorders (Green, 1991). Plasma levels should be monitored to identify toxic effects, including affective (mood, concentration, lethargy, social withdrawal), motor (i.e., tremor, ataxia, seizures), psychotic (thought disorders, hallucinations, delusions), and organic (disorientation, memory loss, agitation, confusion) symptoms, or to identify subtherapeutic levels of medication (Green, 1991).

MAOI's have recently been investigated for treating childhood disorders, including Prozac for depression and obsessive-compulsive disorders and Wellbutrin for depression and ADHD (Greene, 1991). Because of their potential for hepatotoxicity, the need of food restrictions, and questionable effectiveness, MAOIs were not commonly administered to children,

although this trend has recently been reversed (Dubovsky, 1992). MAOI-Type A deactivates NE and serotonin; while MAOI-Type B deactivates DA and phenylethylamine (Zametkin & Rapoport, 1987). Prozac does not appear to act on NE or DA uptake, although it does affect the serotonin reuptake pump (Green, 1991). Wellbutrin is not related to other antidepressants, and Green (1991) suggests that MAOIs should be tried before starting a trial on Wellbutrin. Like other antidepressants, MAOIs also require careful plasma-level monitoring.

Antioxiolytics

Antioxiolytics, specifically benzodiazepines (BZDs), are typically administered for the control of severe anxiety, sleep disorders (e.g., insomnia, sleep terrors, and/or sleep walking), and overinhibition disorders (Green, 1991). Relatively little research has been conducted on these medications with children and adolescents, although the American Psychiatric Association Task Force on Benzodiazepines reported that these drugs have low toxicity and abuse potential (Salzman, 1990).

Benzodiazepines appear to affect GABA receptors, which in turn enhance chloride channels to produce hyperpolarization of neurons (Dubovsky, 1992). This neurochemical (BZD-GABA) process has inhibitory affects in arousal and affective brain centers, and thus reduce anxiety. Potential side effects (e.g., sedation, muscle relaxation, and elevated seizure threshold) appear related to the effects BZD receptors have on cortical, pyramidal, and spinal neurons throughout the brain (Dubovsky, 1992). Withdrawal symptoms (e.g., dysphoria, anxiety, heightened sensitivity to light and sound, headaches, sweating, tremors, insomnia, nightmares, delirium, and paranoia) have been reported with BZDs and are similar to the effects of withdrawal from other CNS depressants.

Anticonvulsants

Anticonvulsant medication is the major form of therapeutic intervention for children and adolescents with nonfebrile seizure disorders (Cook & Leventhal,

1992). Phenobarbitol and phenytoin both have adverse affects on academic work, due to their sedative affects. Phenobarbitol has been known to decrease memory in some children and has been known to contribute to disturbed behaviors in other children (Green, 1991). However, when the children are given other anticonvulsants, these behavioral and cognitive side effects improve. Carbamazepine also has adverse side effects, but these seem to be less severe than those of the other two agents. All three medications are commonly used, either in combination or as single agents, and require careful blood level monitoring (Cook & Leventhal, 1992).

Anticonvulsants act as enzyme-inducing agents in the liver, which in turn appears to reduce the "bioavailability of almost all psychotropic agents" (Neppe & Tucker, 1992, p. 417). Anticonvulsants appear to modulate DA, serotonin, and GABA receptor sites.

Monitoring Medication Efficacy

A key question prior to selecting pharmacological intervention is whether medication is warranted. This decision typically requires a comprehensive assessment of the problem and a careful review of the child's medical, educational, and psychosocial history. It is important to determine the exact nature and severity of the disorder prior to medicating and, in some cases, to determine if other psychosocial or behavioral interventions have been attempted. Information concerning previous nonmedical interventions is particularly important for such disorders of children as ADHD, depression, anxiety, and conduct disorders.

When nonmedical interventions are not successful in ameliorating the child's problems, then a controlled trial of medication may be considered. Physicians usually obtain baseline data prior to medication trials, which may include electrocardiogram (ECG); electroencephalogram (EEG); urinalysis; liver, thyroid, and renal function tests; blood pressure; and serum blood levels when administering antipsychotics, antiepileptics, and antidepressants (Green, 1991). Other baseline behavioral data (rating scales, questionnaires, etc.) are also collected in order to measure the effects of medication.

Once psychopharmacotherapy is initiated, objective measures of medication effects are needed to determine individual response rates and to assess the side effects of various medications (Barkley, 1990; DuPaul & Stoner, 1994; Pelham, 1993a). A number of rating scales are available for measuring classroom behaviors and side effects for ADHD (see Barkley, 1990; DuPaul & Stoner, 1994; Pelham, 1993a), but fewer scales are available for other childhood disorders.

Pelham (1993a) suggests that when monitoring medication it is advisable to measure ecologically valid behaviors in order to assess the effects of medication on a child's performance in the classroom and in social situations. Pelham (1993a) employs daily report cards that target behaviors such as work completion, compliance, and accuracy in order to determine the effects of stimulant medications. Although Pelham (1993a) specifically addresses medication monitoring of psychostimulants for ADHD children, ecologically valid measurements would also seem appropriate for other childhood disorders, including depression, anxiety, and conduct-related problems. To assess whether a particular medication is helping a child, the behaviors of concern (e.g., sadness, panic attacks, or anger outbursts) may need to be defined more explicitly and monitored on a regular basis. Thus, for medication monitoring to be ecologically valid, it should occur in the child's natural setting, home and school, and not solely in the clinic or the doctor's office.

Combined Pharmacological and Behavioral Interventions

Psychopharmacotherapy is rarely advised in isolation. Earlier reviews have shown that most childhood and adolescent disorders are complex and affect multiple facets of the child's cognitive, academic, and psychosocial adjustment. Medications also have their limitations and may not uniformly improve all areas of the child's functioning; thus, most physicians combine pharmacological interventions with psychosocial interventions. Psychosocial interventions may include behavioral treatments (e.g., contingency management, home—school notes), individual or group therapy for the child or adolescent, parent training, and family therapy.

Combined therapeutic interventions have been more thoroughly researched with ADHD than with other childhood disorders. For example, medication combined with parent training and behavior management was more effective than either medication or behavior management alone for "normalizing" children with ADHD (Pelham et al., 1988). Low doses of medication (methylphenidate) were considerably enhanced with combined behavioral interventions. Pelham (1993a) suggests that "an important result of combined treatments may be that maximal improvement in behavior may be reached without resorting to high dosages of stimulant medication," which may lower adverse medication effects (p. 220). Further, combined behavioral—medication interventions for children with ADHD appear to complement the shortcomings of either treatment alone (Carlson, Pelham, Milich, & Dixon, 1992), and add incremental effects that do not occur with either intervention alone (Pelham, 1993a).

The extent to which similar effects will be shown for combined pharmacological/psychosocial/behavioral interventions with other childhood disorders needs further investigation. Research investigating combined interventions is needed to determine the short-term and long-term effects of psychopharmacotherapy and individual responsivity to various aspects of the other behavioral, academic, and psychosocial interventions.

Given the need for assessing medication affects in the child's natural setting, there is an increasing need for schools, physicians, and parents to work together to produce the most benefits from pharmacological approaches. The following section discusses these partnerships.

HOME–SCHOOL–PHYSICIAN PARTNERSHIPS

Home—school—physician partnerships are necessary for several reasons. First, children often receive psychosocial, behavioral, and medical interventions from a number of different professionals, and coordination of these services is required. It is not uncommon for a child with a neuropsychiatric disorder to have a psychiatrist or physician prescribe medication, a clinical psychologist conduct therapy, and a school psychologist and/or counselor address school-related academic and psychosocial problems. These various professionals often target the same behaviors and have similar therapy goals, but they may use different techniques. It is important that therapeutic efforts in one setting not be counterproductive to the efforts in another. These situations occur when professionals have diametrically opposed theoretical orientations or utilize drastically different approaches for the same behavioral, psychological, and/or academic problem. Parents may pursue the course recommended by one professional, only to hear a completely opposite opinion from another. This not only creates stress and confusion for the parent, it may set a course of action that is completely counterproductive for the child.

Second, because of the concern over high costs of comprehensive assessments and interventions, duplication of services should be avoided whenever possible. Professionals in different settings may utilize similar evaluation procedures (e.g., rating scales, intellectual measures). It is not uncommon for a child to be assessed using the same instruments, for parents to fill out the same rating scales, and for teachers to respond to the same questionnaires for different professionals (e.g., psychiatrist, clinical psychologist, and school psychologist) within a relatively short period of time. Interventions also may be similar across therapeutic settings. Coordination of services and communication between professionals and parents helps to reduce needless redundancy.

Third, a number of children receive medication on a daily basis. Medication monitoring is an important element of pharmacotherapy and is most helpful when conducted in the child's natural environment—the home or school, where the behaviors of concern can be systematically observed. Physicians need careful and systematic information about how the child is responding to medication, and whether there are side effects at various dosage levels. Properly trained school professionals (e.g., school psychologists) can be extremely helpful in this process. School psychologists may observe the child, collect behavioral data (e.g., work completion rates), and assess psychosocial adjustment at various dosage levels. These data can be communicated directly to the physician (with parental permission) or to the parent for proper medication monitoring. Information concerning individual responsivity needs to be communicated on a regular basis in order to ascertain the child's progress.

Fourth, when children with various brain-related diseases or disorders (e.g., brain tumors, traumatic brain injury) reenter the school system, the professional staff needs to be knowledgeable about the child's medical, psychosocial, academic and behavioral needs. In order to be knowledgeable about the ramifications of brain-related disorders, educational professionals need to be in regular contact with attending physicians (e.g., neurologists, neurosurgeons) and other medical specialists (e.g., speech and physical therapists). Information in these situations needs to be bidirectional –from the physician to the teacher or school psychologist and vice versa. Physicians need information from the school about how the child is progressing and if relapses or other secondary problems are emerging. Educational professionals need to understand the nature and course of recovery of the child's injury or disease.

Fifth, parents and family members may need help in coping with the demands and stresses of dealing with the child's neuropsychiatric disorders, diseases, or trauma. While each professional may play a different role in this process, each may also possess important information that may be useful to the other. Again, communication between the physician and the school is essential.

It is important to remember that when developing home—school—physician partnerships, confidentiality is required. Parental permission is required to obtain and share information, and sensitive or personal information should be discussed only on a need-to-know basis. That is, teachers and other school personnel may be informed when information directly affects the intervention or treatment plan; otherwise, personal information should be kept confidential. A case illustration may help clarify this point. A child had been severely beaten by his mother's boyfriend and sustained serious brain trauma. When the child reenters school, should the source of the child's injury be shared with school personnel (e.g., child's teacher, school psychologist)? If there is continued concern about the safety of the child or concern about the psychological trauma suffered by the child, then sharing this information with the educational professionals is appropriate. If psychoeducational services are needed, then the school psychologist and other educational professionals also may need to know. If the child has already stabilized (i.e., medically, neuropsychologically, and emotionally), then the cause of the injury may not be all that pertinent. Most often the school administrator would be informed under both conditions.

Most of the reasons discussed here suggest the need for communication and coordination of services across agencies. Many parents feel that they have been placed in the role of coordinator of services for their child–a role that parents do not always want to assume. Thus, it is imperative that school and medical professionals discuss these issues and identify an individual who will be responsible for coordinating assessment and intervention plans across the various settings. Regular communication among all parties is needed, and a plan or systematic schedule may be helpful, particularly during the assessment and early intervention stages. Contact may be less frequent once the child stabilizes and shows steady progress in meeting the therapeutic or intervention goals. Regular follow-up at 6-, 12-, 18-, and 24-month intervals may be sufficient in later stages when the child has shown adequate recovery or is progressing on target.

SUMMARY AND CONCLUSIONS

This chapter presented a model for comprehensive, multimethod assessment and intervention for children. Five basic assumptions underlie this model. First, the model assumes that many childhood disorders have a biogenetic basis, such that neuropsychological as well as cognitive, behavioral, and psychosocial factors must be considered for assessment and treatment. Second, a single theoretical paradigm (e.g., behavioral, cognitive, or neuropsychological) is rarely defensible when applied in isolation. One-dimensional explanations for complex, multidimensional conditions are not scientifically founded (Doehring, 1968). Third, many developmental disorders of childhood present symptoms early in life and respond favorably to early intervention. Neurocognitive paradigms offer strong theories and methods for addressing childhood disorders within a developmental framework. Fourth, various paradigms make important contributions for different reasons and, when combined, in-crease the probability of obtaining the best treatment for children with serious disorders. Finally, advancement of a science of childhood disorders will not occur in the form of dramatic discoveries from or within a single paradigm, but will occur through patient working and reworking of complex sets of experimental variables, with clinical validation (Doehring, 1968).

The last chapter presents a number of case studies to illustrate asessment and intervention practices for children with traumatic brain injury and various neuropsychiatric and neurodevelopmental disorders.

CHAPTER 12

CLINICAL CASE STUDIES

Four cases are reviewed in this chapter. Each case represents a childhood disorder that might be referred for a neuropsychological evaluation. The cases were selected to show the variety of assessment protocols that might be used by neuropsychologists, to illustrate issues of comorbidity of disorders, to highlight the importance of serial evaluations, and to present possible treatment options.

INTRACTABLE SEIZURE DISORDER

This case illustrates intractable seizure disorder and the impact of this disorder on a child's learning and overall development. Initially, contact with the school was intermittent, but following indications of ongoing seizure activity, such contact was encouraged and continued for over a year. Initially this child was referred for "attentional" problems, which were actually seizures in disguise. It is particularly important that the attentional difficulties in children with a history of seizure activity be assessed in relationship to the seizures as well as to developmental history. This case also illustrates the importance of serial evaluations that incorporate similar or identical assessment measures to evaluate progress.

Sasha

Sasha was originally referred for neuropsychological evaluation at age 5 1/2. The referral question was to determine the extent of developmental delay and attention problems. Sasha had been diagnosed earlier with partial complex seizures and was initially prescribed Depakote and Zarontin. His early childhood teacher described him as a "slow learner" with attentional difficulties. The Conner's Behavioral Scale

had been completed by his teacher, and his average score did not indicate ADHD. He had received occupational, speech and language therapy. His developmental history was generally normal with his milestones attained within normal limits. Language development had begun normally, but he stopped talking from 18 months to 2 1/2 years of age. At that time he began speaking again in single words, but did not put simple sentences together until the age of 3 1/2 years. During this same time, Sasha began having severe temper tantrums and attentional difficulties. He also experienced difficulty falling asleep, and his motor skills began to be below age expectations, with descriptions of clumsiness and frequent falling. A chromosomal study was negative. Sasha's family history was positive for epilepsy on the maternal side. His mother's epilepsy is successfully treated with Depakote.

Sasha's original evaluation indicated scores in the mildly mentally handicapped range on the K-ABC. Of the seven subtests administered, Sasha was able to perform on Hand Movements (scaled score = 3), Gestalt Closure (scaled score = 3), and Matrix Analogies (scaled score = 7). He was also administered the Stanford Binet Intelligence Scale–Fourth Edition. On this measure he achieved a test composite score of 59. The individual domain scores were as follows:

Verbal Reasoning	68
Abstract/Visual Reasoning	63
Quantitative Reasoning	60
Short-Term Memory	58

Additional language assessment indicated significant difficulties in receptive and expressive language skills. He achieved scores in the mildly mentally handicapped range on several language scales. They were:

Receptive and Expressive Emergent
Language Scale

Comprehension	30 months
Expression	30 months

Peabody Picture Vocabulary Test-Revised

Standard Score	53
Age Equivalent	2—11

Woodcock-Johnson Picture Vocabulary Test

Standard Score	49
Age Equivalent	2—7

Visual motor skills could not be assessed, as Sasha was unable to copy any design successfully. This finding indicated that his skills fell below the 2 year 11 month level–the lowest age measured on this test.

The Vineland Adaptive Behavior Scales were used to assess adaptive behavior skills. Sasha achieved scores in the mildly delayed area, with relative strengths present in socialization.

	Standard Scores
Communication	60
Daily Living Skills	66
Socialization	70

Therefore, at the time of this initial evaluation, Sasha showed relative strengths in nonverbal problem solving for visual-spatial tasks that involved completing pegboards and form boards. Relative strengths also were found in his ability to match colors, shapes, and forms. Weaknesses were most apparent in Sasha's language skills, with his ability to use words falling at the 30-month level and his comprehension skills at the 30- to 35-month level. His gross motor skills (i.e., ability to button clothing, copy designs, cut with a scissors) were relatively well developed, but his fine motor skills were significantly delayed. Although attentional deployment difficulties were also noted, his attentional skills were found to be commensurate with his developmental level. Oppositional behavior was noted, and recommendations were made for the use of behavioral management. No breakthrough of seizures occurred at the time of the evaluation.

Second Evaluation

Sasha was reevaluated six months later. He had continued on Depakote and Zarontin for seizure control, with no noted seizure breakthroughs. An EEG performed at the time of the first evaluation resulted in findings of rhythmic 3.5- to 4-second spikes in the left and right midtemporal regions, with an additional 3.5-second spike and wave activity in the occipital region. Sasha had continued to attend a special education program, and his parents had reported progress. Blood levels for antiepileptic medication had indicated that the Depakote was elevated, and the dose was subsequently lowered. During this evaluation, one 10-second or shorter episode of staring and eye-blinking was noted.

The K-ABC was readministered, and Sasha showed relative strengths in copying hand movements and remembering word order. The raw scores from the first assessment are presented along with those from the second assessment:

	Raw Scores	Scaled Scores	
	First	*Second*	*Second*
Subtest	*Evaluation*	*Evaluation*	*Evaluation*
Hand			
Movement	1	2	4
Gestalt			
Closure	2	1	1
Number			
Recall	0	1	1
Triangles	0	1	5
Word Order	0	1	4

Achievement testing on the K-ABC yielded the following scores:

	Raw Scores	Scaled Scores	
	First	*Second*	*Second*
Subtest	*Evaluation*	*Evaluation*	*Evaluation*
Faces and			
Places	1	1	63
Arithmetic	2	2	58

The PPVT-R was repeated and resulted in a standard score of 50. Of more concern, Sasha's raw score increased only from 22 to 23 in the 6-month interval. The Picture Vocabulary subtest from the Woodcock Johnson Cognitive Battery showed a moderate increase from a raw score of 14 to 19, resulting in a standard score of 67.

Fine motor speed was assessed with the Purdue Pegboard Test. Sasha placed five pegs with each hand, significantly below average for his age. Moreover, his dominant hand, the left, placed significantly fewer pegs than would be expected. Sasha was unable to place pegs using both hands simultaneously.

Conclusions at this time were that little progress had been made in cognitive and academic skills. Concerns were that underlying seizure activity and/or interference from antiepileptic medication was preventing progress. Sasha's behavior continued to be poorly regulated.

Third Evaluation

Sasha was reevaluated six months after the second evaluation. At this time Sasha's behavior had begun to escalate at home, with destructive behavior and aggression toward family members. Behavioral observations indicated several breakthrough seizures that had a significant impact on his performance. Behaviors included eyelid fluttering or slow blinking, lip smacking, face rubbing, blank staring, and general lack of awareness. These behaviors were felt to have a significant impact on Sasha's ability to perform on any of the tests. The Stanford Binet Intelligence Scale–Fourth Edition was administered to compare with scores obtained approximately one year earlier. A comparison of standard scores and raw scores is:

| | Scaled Scores | |
| | First | Third |
Composite	Evaluation	Evaluation
Verbal Reasoning	68	65
Abstract/Visual Reasoning	63	49
Short-term Memory	58	59
Total Composite	59	50

| | Raw Scores | |
| | First | Third |
Composite	Evaluation	Evaluation
Vocabulary	10	13
Comprehension	7	10
Absurdities	2	1
Pattern Analysis	6	6
Copying	4	1
Quantitative	1	0
Bead Memory	4	6
Memory for Sentences	4	7

There had been minimal progress in a year, with some skills showing an increase of 3 raw score points, while others showed either the same score or lower. The largest decrease was found on copying ability. During this subtest Sasha had numerous incidents of seizure breakthrough. Recommendations were for a reassessment by Sasha's neurologist of his medication regimen, as well as behavioral assistance for the parents by the school district. His parents reported that the school district had not followed up on IEP recommendation for behavioral assistance. The neuropsychologist agreed to consult with the special education director to assist with the implementation of such a program. Moreover, recommendation was for one-half day of kindergarten with an aide and one-half day of an early childhood program, as well as speech and language therapy. Further recommendation was made for a return in six months to assess Sasha's improvement.

Fourth Evaluation

Sasha was reassessed approximately 18 months following his first visit. At that time parents reported no further seizure activity. His medication had been changed following the last visit to Depakote sprinkles and 75 milligrams of Dilantin twice daily. Just prior to this visit, Sasha's 2-year-old sister had been diagnosed with partial-complex seizures. Behavioral difficulties had continued at home; the behavioral specialist was sporadic in visiting, and Sasha's parents were frustrated. They also were concerned about his teacher and felt she "just wants Sasha out of her class." He had continued to receive speech and language therapy and occupational therapy. As with the previous evaluation, several incidences of seizure breakthrough were noted that had a negative impact on his performance. Some improvement was found on the K-ABC achievement tests, with Sasha now being able to count using one-to-one correspondence up to 3. His visual motor skills also showed improvement. Previously on this test Sasha had been unable to copy any of the figures; in this session he was able to copy four figures successfully. His raw score on the PPVT-R test declined from 22 to 18.

An MRI was performed and a porencephalic cyst was found in Sasha's right frontal lobe. This cyst was determined not to be responsible for the seizure activity and was to be monitored for growth over the coming months. Moreover, an EEG indicated almost constant seizure activity, some of which showed clinical signs in eye-blinking and lip-smacking. This continual activity had a significant impact not only on Sasha's cognitive and academic development, but also on his emotional and behavioral controls. Recommendations were for a referral to an epilepsy specialist as well as contact with the school to assist with educational programming. The epilepsy specialist recommended a ketogenic diet for the seizure disorder. This diet consists of a significant reduction in fat in the diet, and has been found to be successful in suppression of intractable seizures in some children. It was felt that the diet should be attempted prior to consideration of surgery.

Sasha's teacher indicated that numerous breakthrough seizures occurred at school. The teacher was also concerned about Sasha's poor academic progress. Discussion of the course of his epilepsy, the intractable nature of the seizures, and the impact of these problems on learning assisted the teacher and language therapist in programming for Sasha. The teacher also agreed to assist in obtaining behavioral assistance for Sasha's parents. It was also agreed to contact the neuropsychologist for any unusual or different behaviors. Sasha is due back to the clinic in 6 months following the ketogenic diet routine.

SEVERE DEVELOPMENTAL DYSLEXIA

The following case describes an assessment of a 10-year-old boy who had received excellent special-education services for several years, but who had continued to be unable to read beyond a primer level. The case demonstrates the need to evaluate reading difficulties comprehensively, as well as to obtain a family history.

Allen is a fourth-grade boy who was referred to the clinic for ongoing reading difficulties despite having had three years of special-education services. He had been diagnosed with ADHD and had responded favorably to Ritalin. In kindergarten, Allen was first identified as experiencing difficulty with readiness skills. He was very active and had great difficulty staying in a group and participating in activities. He started taking Ritalin in first grade and was kept in first grade an additional year because of significant delays in academics. Allen was evaluated in second grade and placed in a learning-disability program. Behaviorally and socially he was reported not to experience any difficulties, and was well accepted by his peers. He was also reported to be hard working and motivated.

Allen was the product of a normal full-term birth, labor, and delivery. Developmental milestones were generally attained within normal limits for age. At an early age Allen was noted to display an extreme level of overactivity and inattention. He was diagnosed with ADHD in first grade. His Ritalin dosage has gradually increased from 5 milligrams (mg) twice a day to a current dose of 20 mg in the morning, 20 mg at noon, and 15 mg at 3:00 P.M. His paternal history is remarkable for reading difficulties. His father, his stepsister, a paternal uncle, and a grandfather have all experienced significant reading difficulties, which continued throughout school and into adulthood. Although Allen's father's intelligence is above average, he is unable to read and is currently employed as a grocery stocker. Allen's neurological examination and MRI were normal. He has not had any head injuries, seizures, or serious illnesses.

Evaluation of Allen indicated an average ability

with strengths in vocabulary and comprehension as well as perceptual organization. Relative weaknesses were found in visual memory and motor speed. The following results were obtained on a WIS-III:

Verbal IQ 83   *Performance IQ 89*   *Full Scale IQ 84*

Information	5	Picture Completion	10
Similarities	6	Coding	4
Arithmetic	5	Picture Arrangement	10
Vocabulary	9	Block Design	8
Comprehension	10	Object Assembly	9
Digit Span	4	Symbol Search	6

Achievement testing indicated severe deficits in all areas of reading, with math skills also depressed, particularly in applied problems. The Woodcock-Johnson Achievement Battery–Revised was administered and the following scores obtained:

Subtest	Standard Score
Letter-Word ID	46
Reading Comprehension	64
Word Attach	51
Applied Problems	75
Arithmetic Calculation	83

Allen is a choppy and dysfluent reader. He appeared unsure of vowel and consonant sounds and consequently relied on a "best-guess" strategy for reading (e.g., using a word's visual characteristics as an aid to decoding). The Lindamood Auditory Concepts test was also administered to further evaluate Allen's word attack skills. Allen performed at the mid-first-grade level on this test, with significant difficulties with sound—symbol relationships even at the individual phoneme levels. Blending and the ability to combine sounds were delayed. Allen experienced difficulty at the primary level of distinguishing similar but different sounds at the beginning and ending of words.

Memory skills were found to be deficient on the Children's Version of the California Verbal Learning Test. The following results were obtained:

	Standard Score
Trial 1 Recall	85
Trial 5 Recall	85
Total Recalled A	71
List B Recall	85
Short Delay Free Recall	100
Short Delay Cued Recall	100
Long Delay Free Recall	85
Long Delay Cued Recall	85
Recognition	78
False Positives	92
Perseverative Errors	92

Allen's learning of List A fell significantly below average over the five trials. Although the learning curve rose steadily over the five trials, suggesting that Allen benefited from repetition of the words, the number of items recalled after each trial fell below expectations compared to same-aged peers. Allen's recall of List B also fell below average. Both short-term free recall and cued recall fell within average levels for his age. Allen holds onto information that he has learned. His memory skills are problematic in that Allen has difficulty encoding new information.

Language assessment indicated that Allen has difficulty in both receptive and expressive language skills. The Clinical Evaluation of Language Fundamentals–3 was administered, and the following results were obtained:

	Scaled Score
Receptive Language	
Concepts and Directions	4
Word Classes	9
Semantic Relationships	3
Expressive Language	
Formulated Sentences	5
Recalling Sentences	4
Sentence Assembly	3

This assessment indicated pervasive language problems in Allen's ability to understand and use language. In expressive language, Allen's ability to follow directions using visual cues that increase in complexity was quite poor, and likely a reflection of his previously identified difficulty with adequately encoding verbally based information. Allen's performance on a task that tapped his understanding of comparative, temporal, quantitative, and spatial concepts in language also fell significantly below average. In contrast, Allen's ability to see relationships between words was age-appropriate.

In receptive language, Allen demonstrated significant weakness on a series of structured tasks that required him to create sentences about pictures using stimulus words. He had difficulty integrating words into a relevant sentence while maintaining appropriate grammatical structure. Consistent with his difficulties with encoding verbally mediated information, Allen evidenced a significant weakness in his ability to repeat progressively longer and syntactically complex sentences.

The Test of Variables of Attention (TOVA) was used to measure attentional functioning. Testing was done off Ritalin, on 15 mg of Ritalin, and on 20 mg of Ritalin. Measures of vigilance (omissions), impulsivity and inhibition of responding (commission), speed of information processing (reaction times), and variability of reaction time (variability) were obtained with the following results:

Measure	20 mg	15 mg	Off Ritalin
Omissions	98	98	66
Commissions	90	90	98
Response Time	67	54	34
Variability	63	26	< 25

Results indicated that on his current 20 mg dose, Allen demonstrated age-appropriate gross attention to task and impulse control. In contrast, reaction time and sustained attention fell significantly below expected limits for age. On a 15 mg dose of Ritalin, Allen's gross attention and impulse control were identical to that observed on the higher dose. However, his reaction time and sustained attention were much poorer on the lower dose of Ritalin. With the exception of his impulse control, Allen's performance on the TOVA off medication fell significantly below average on all attentional parameters. Overall results indicated that Allen exhibits a beneficial response to his current Ritalin dose of 20 mg. Even with the higher

dose, however, his response time and ability to sustain and deploy attention consistently fell significantly below average.

Allen's visual-motor integration skills were assessed using the Developmental Test of Visual-Motor Integration. Consistent with teacher reports regarding illegible writing and poor copying skills, Allen's reproductions on this task fell moderately below age expectations (standard scores = 76).

Personality and behavioral assessment indicated no areas of concern. Teacher reports indicated concerns only in the area of academic progress. Both profiles indicated that Allen is perceived as well adjusted, without any behavioral problems.

Summary and Recommendations

Allen is a 10-year-old boy with speech and language problems as well as difficulty with the acquisition of reading skills. He also has a history of ADHD and is currently being treated with Ritalin. This evaluation was requested by his mother to determine current reading skills and to offer treatment recommendations.

Assessment of Allen's academic achievement confirms school and parental reports that he is experiencing persistent and severe difficulties in acquisition of beginning reading skills. Evaluation revealed that his reading skills fell significantly below average, and well below what was to be expected on the basis of his intellectual profile. Allen's reading skills fall approximately at a mid-first-grade level and are limited to inconsistent identification of high-frequency sight words. He shows little in the way of word attack skills and is deficient in other phonological coding skills that have been found to be highly related to the normal acquisition of reading. Relative to an assessment completed more than two years ago, Allen shows little progress. Overall, results from the present testing indicate the presence of a verbally based learning disability. Testing of language functions revealed striking weaknesses in both receptive and expressive language skills. Although parental reports indicated that Allen has made a stable pattern of gains since speech therapy was initiated this year, his language problems are of such severity that they are continuing to have an impact on his ability to use and understand language effectively.

Testing of memory and learning indicated that Allen experienced difficulties in encoding and memorizing verbal information, such as stories and lists of words. Allen's ability to remember verbal information is constrained by problems with encoding and inputting. He does not have difficulty in retrieving and outputting information from memory; that is, once information is encoded into memory, he can retain it for relatively long periods of time. His encoding problems also affect his ability to process verbal material such as instructions adequately. It is important to emphasize that despite his encoding difficulties, Allen has the potential to learn and memorize new information, but he will do so at a rate that is significantly slower than his same-aged peers, and he will require more than the usual amount of repetition. Allen does not appear to have significant difficulty memorizing material that is visual in nature, such as designs and pictures.

Recommendations include an intensive learning disabilities program to work on his phonological coding difficulties while simultaneously strengthening his sight-word vocabulary. Given Allen's good visual-perceptual and visual memory abilities, it is recommended that teaching strategies focus on a sight-word approach with the high-frequency words he encounters. For Allen to become a fully functional reader, it is crucial that he become adept at decoding unknown words. Teaching Allen how to decode words will not be an easy task, given that he lacks a number of the essential phonological-processing skills necessary for effective decoding. To help Allen develop the phonological processing skills that are critical to becoming an effective reader, the Lindamood Auditory Discrimination In Depth Program is recommended. This program, multisensory in nature, recognizes that some children have great difficulty in recognizing and perceiving the association between sequences of sounds in spoken words and sequences of letters in written words. It provides experience at a level prior to that of most beginning phonic programs by teaching sound—symbol correspondences through activities that allow students to hear, see, and feel sound

units of language. The program starts with oral motor activities (e.g., noting the position of the mouth and tongue when a certain sound is produced), and gradually builds up to working with words. For the program to be effective for Allen, it should be intensively incorporated into his reading program. For many children with phonological-processing difficulties, this program has been helpful in diminishing their decoding difficulties. The Lindamood Program, including the associated manual and step-by-step program instructions, can be obtained through Riverside Press.

It is further recommended that Allen be provided with a computer for rehearsing reading skills. Moreover, a language experience approach should be incorporated into Allen's classroom program. This method, which will encourage Allen to use his own words, includes writing his own book by dictating a story to a teacher or aide who provides him with a written transcript. Allen would then read the story back and accumulate flashcards of unknown words that he encounters. Taped books should also be available for Allen. The benefits of taped books are twofold. They will assist with the acquisition of information that would ordinarily be available only through written text. Taped books also provide a way to enhance Allen's reading skills by allowing him to listen to a tape as he follows along in a book. Language therapy is also required to assist with his skill development. Intervention that focuses on his organization of language output, pragmatics, and repair strategies (e.g., using an alternative word or phrase to accommodate his word-finding difficulty), will be especially helpful to him at this point.

These recommendations have been put into place. Allen will return to the clinic in approximately 6 months to assess his progress.

TRAUMATIC BRAIN INJURY

Stan's car was hit head-on by a drunken driver. He was 17 years old at the time of the accident, and he had been a straight A student in his junior year of high school. He was comatose at the accident site but was moving and breathing spontaneously. Intracranial pressure was initially a problem but improved during his hospitalization. An intracerebral hematoma in the left basal ganglia and internal capsule was diagnosed. Stan had right-sided hemiparesis with a mild right facial droop. Oral motor skills were observed to be below average and speech production was difficult. hearing and vision were normal. Stan was hospitalized for five weeks after the accident. He underwent neuropsychological assessment during his stay at the hospital. Findings at that time were difficulties with attention, memory and verbal learning problems, and difficulty with verbal concept formation, with abstract reasoning and visual-spatial skills intact.

Stan was reevaluated three months later by a private neuropsychologist using the WRAML and the Peabody Individual Achievement Test–Reading Subtests. Scores showed average skills in all areas of memory, with relative strengths in visual memory. Achievement testing showed average performance in reading with slight difficulties in writing. Attentional difficulties continued to be present.

Stan was referred for reevaluation eleven months after his discharge from the hospital. He was succeeding in a limited educational program and was slated to graduate from high school that spring. Continued weakness was present in his right arm and leg, and writing was extremely painstaking and difficult for him. He wished for additional information to aid in his selection of a college as well as assistance in obtaining help for his college program. Stan presented as a well-groomed young man with a ready wit and smile. He was cooperative throughout the assessment and was well motivated. Stan's attention was good, and he was not easily distracted by extraneous noises.

Stan achieved a Full Scale IQ of 106 on the WAIS-R, which placed him in the average range of ability for his age. His verbal IQ of 99 was also in the average range, with more well developed skills found on the performance subtests, resulting in an IQ of 116. The following subtest scores were obtained:

Information	9	Picture Completion	15
Digit Span	9	Picture Arrangement	11
Vocabulary	13	Block Design	14
Arithmetic	14	Object Assembly	11
Comprehension	7	Digit Symbol	11
Similarities	11		

Language assessment found Stan's receptive language to be in the above-average range on the PPVT-R (standard score = 115). His ability to name objects also was well within the average range on the Boston Naming Test (raw score = 55). Performance on the Boston Aphasia Screening Test was well within normal levels and showed good ability to compose paragraphs and stories. Verbal fluency scores as measured by the Controlled Word Association test were in the low average range and below what would be expected given his previous history. Stan experienced difficulty naming words beginning with the letters F, A, and S. This finding was consistent with a below-average performance on the Rey Auditory Verbal Learning Test. Stan was able to remember 11 of 15 words over five trials. His performance did not improve with a second trial. When asked to recall these words after a twenty-minute delay, Stan was able to recall 10 correctly, a performance in the average range.

Motor testing indicated significant right-sided weakness. On the Grooved Pegboard, Stan with his right hand performed over two standard deviations below expectations for his age. He had been right-handed prior to the accident. His performance with his left hand was within normal limits. Performance on the VMI with his left hand was well within the normal range (standard score = 115).

Executive function assessment indicated above-average performance on the Wisconsin Card Sorting Test. This finding was consistent with the results of testing during his hospitalization.

Impressions were of a young man with at least average ability who has shown improvement in all areas. Continued difficulty was present in word retrieval and motor skills. These motor difficulties were hampering Stan's progress in school, and it was recommended that a peer note-taker be secured for him and that alternative methods be provided for him to demonstrate his knowledge. Writing could be accomplished on a specially designed computer for ease of writing. It was further recommended that Stan attend a college with support present for students with disabilities. It was also suggested that he take no more than two reading courses per quarter. Follow-up of Stan's progress indicates tht he has made the transition to college, that he has a peer note-taker, and that his professors have adapted their requirements to fit his needs. He continues to be well motivated and has decided to major in special education.

SEVERE EXPRESSIVE APHASIA AND MOTOR APRAXIA WITH PERVASIVE DEVELOPMENTAL DELAY

This last case illustrates the complexity of diagnosing children with severe expressive aphasia with motor apraxia and pervasive developmental delays at an early age. Furthermore, this case demonstrates the need for collaboration between neuropsychologists and public school staff so that neuropsychological findings can be integrated into the classroom.

Initial contact with the child came at the family's request to verify previous evaluations and diagnoses conducted at another neuropsychology clinic and an educational evaluations were conducted to determine the child's neuropsychological, academic, cognitive and social-emotional functioning, and to develop an appropriate intervention program. Serial evaluation results were presented at the school's multidisciplinary team meetings.

Teddy

First and Second Evaluations

Information gathered from the first (age 5 1/2 years) and second (age 7 1/2 years) evaluations was based on observational methods, because Teddy was unable to respond adequately to verbal or nonverbal test items. A number of methods were attempted during the first and second evaluations, including items from the Stanford-Binet, the McCarthy Scales, the Wechsler Scales, the Reitan-Indiana Battery, the French Pictorial Test of Intelligence, and the Leiter International Scales. Severe motor apraxia affected his ability to complete nonverbal measures, and his severe expressive language deficits interfered with verbal measures. On several subtests of the Leiter

Scales, however, Teddy showed near average abilities at the age of 5 1/2 years.

Teddy was enrolled in a preschool program for children with significant developmental delays. He was transferred to a regular elementary school in first grade and received special education services. Speech-language, occupational, and physical therapy were the major interventions in the special-education program at the public school. Although he was taught sign language, which he readily picked up, articulation of vowels and consonant—vowel combinations was the major focus of speech therapy over a four-year period. At the time of the last evaluation, the therapy goal was to attain expressive language to the 5-year-level. After four years of speech therapy, Teddy had not reached his milestone.

Teddy was mainstreamed for part of the day for socialization, but received services for learning disabilities 55% to 60% of the day, 12% to 15% of which were for speech. Although he learned to read, Teddy appeared hyperlexic as his rate and speed of reading outpaced his reading comprehension skills. Despite two years of extensive physical therapy and a full-time aide who helped Teddy trace, cut paper, and draw lines and letters, he was unable to print his name, cut with scissors, or draw simple figures. While he did not approach age-appropriate levels for fine motor skills, Teddy did learn to use a computer and was able to type (one—two finger technique) on the keyboard. Gross motor skills were also delayed but were not as significantly affected.

Attempts to increase his socialization skills showed some progress in that Teddy became more responsive to others. Although he was encouraged to use a combination of speech and sign language for communication, Teddy remained isolated despite attempts to increase socialization with normal and handicapped peers. Recommendations at the end of the second evaluation urged the school to make a transition into computer technology so that Teddy could make better progress with communication and academic skills.

Third Evaluation

The third evaluation was conducted when Teddy was 9-3 years of age, and in the third grade. This was the first evaluation where Teddy was able to complete subtests on standardized assessment measures. During individual testing sessions, Teddy was able to work for periods up to about 45 minutes long. Teddy's attention span was best when activities required reading or when pictures were used to elicit a response.

Teddy was able to indicate when he did not know an answer, and occasionally it appeared that he simply said he didn't know when the answer required a complex verbal response. His expressive language was difficult to understand, and Teddy became frustrated when the examiner could not understand what he was saying. He always repeated his answer, but as the session progressed this was obviously frustrating for him. When speaking, Teddy tried hard to enunciate individul letter sounds, especially the *T* and *C* sounds. On numerous occasions, he used the proper speech inflection and rhythm, but it was difficult to determine if his verbal responses were correct.

Because of severe limitations in responding, formal evaluations may underestimate Teddy's actual level of academic and cognitive development. Portions of the Tests of Cognitive Ability from the Woodcock-Johnson Psychoeducational Test Battery (WJR) were administered in an attempt to determine Teddy's cognitive potential. The following scores were taken from age-based norms and must be analyzed with caution because of Teddy's severe expressive language delays secondary to motor apraxia.

Standard Score		*Grade Level*	*Percentile*
Memory for Names	109	8.2	73
Memory for Names			
(delayed 4 days)	105	8.0	63
Memory for Words	89		
Picture Vocabulary	86		
Visual Closure	79		

Teddy's most outstanding strengths were revealed on tests of associational learning and long-term retrieval. Specifically, Teddy was able to learn associations between unfamiliar auditory and visual stimuli, and scores on the subtest reached the average to high average range of ability. He was able to remember these auditory—visual associations after a four-day delay, and his scores fell within the average range

compared to same-age peers. Further, his associational learning was much better when pictures were used instead of more abstract visual stimuli, like rebus figures.

On another measure of short-term memory, Teddy scored within the average range of ability as he was able to recall a series of unrelated words in the proper order. Teddy also showed at least average potential on a task measuring comprehension-knowledge or crystallized intelligence (standard score = 86). When asked to name familiar and unfamiliar pictured objects Teddy identified "waterfall," "grasshopper," "magnet," and "theater." While Teddy scored within the average range on this subtest, several of his verbal responses were unintelligible. Thus, his academic potential may be higher than can be measured at this time.

Teddy had more difficulty on tasks that required visual processing when objects were distorted or superimposed on other patterns. He also had trouble on a test where he had to remember a series of objects when similar or "distractor" picures were included (standard score = 73). While this test is a measure of visual processing, teddy often did not study the pictures for the full five-second interval before the distractors were presented, so his lack of interest in or attention to this task reduced his score.

Subtest scores on the Stanford Binet Intelligence Scale–Fourth Edition revealed similar patterns as did the WJR Cognitive subtests. Teddy scored above age level on terms where short-term memory for objects was required, and had difficulty on items requiring complex verbal or motor responses.

Educational Implications

Academically, Teddy appears to show improvement in the areas of reading recognition and comprehension. On standardized measures, Teddy identified words such as *special, straight, powder,* and *couple.* While he was able to read sentences, he made errors when responding to questions. For example, he clapped five times instead of two and identified his "eyebrow" instead of his elbow. At other times it was impossible to understand his verbal responses; as a result, Teddy's reading comprehension may be slightly higher than reported. He also showed slightly higher comprehension scores on the Woodcock Reading Mastery Test than on the K-ABC test. According to his teacher, Teddy is reading and understanding vocabulary slightly above grade level and is reading from a fourth-grade book at school.

K-ABC	Standard Score	Grade Level
Reading Decoding Test	93	2.8
Reading Comprehension	79	1.9

Woodcock Reading Mastery Test		
Word Identification Skills		2.6
Passage Comprehension		2.3

Teddy's math skills are less well developed than his reading abilities. While math skills are emerging, this area is a weakness for Teddy (below the 1.0 grade level). Teddy was able to identify numbers and to determine if there were "just as many" puppets and people in different pictures. However, he could not complete simple addition or subtraction, and he was unable to identify the "third" position in a line. Visual-perceptual deficits appear to be having an impact on his ability to develop math skills.

Spelling skills were not formerly measured because severe apraxia interferes with teddy's printing skills. However, Teddy can spell some words with his Touch Talker that he is unable to write. For example he was able to type the words *to* and *be*. At this point he spontaneously remarked, "To be or not to be. Shakespeare." He obviously associated this phrase with something he had learned at home, and he was able to further associate it in the testing session. Severe motor apraxia severely limits Teddy's written expressive skills, and he remains virtually a nonwriter because of his motor limitations.

Classroom Observations

Because standardized assessment tools may be underestimating Teddy's academic progress, a school-based observation was conducted. Teddy seemed aware of the routine and reacted appropriately to directions for small group activities. In large open classroom settings, Teddy was less adaptable, showing more distractibility and off-task behaviors. He was unable to complete worksheets without the help of a teacher's aide, who helped Teddy print the answers on his paper. When working in pairs, Teddy attempted to answer the questions his partner read aloud to him and was more successful when questions were not too complex. Teddy was able to answer 21% (3 out of 14) of the questions read to him and guessed at others. He was unable to print any answers on his worksheet, although his aide traced all the answers with him.

In less structured story time, Teddy sat on the floor with the rest of his class and showed appropriate behaviors. Generally Teddy's behaviors were not distinguishable from those of his peers during story time. He did, however, move close to his teacher and sit up on his knees to see the pictures of the book better. When his classmates signaled for him to sit down, he complied. On several occasions Teddy rested his elbows on his teacher's lap, and he seemed comfortable and close during story time. He smiled spontaneously, and he seemed very attentive throughout this session, which was 25 minutes long.

In speech therapy Teddy was careful when articulating and appeared highly motivated and spontaneous in his interaction with the speech therapist. His articulation of individual sounds was clear, distinct, and at a more normal pace. He played the message on the Touch Talker, and he seemed genuinely spontaneous and interested in interacting. Teddy was able to introduce the neuropsychologist to his teacher when prompted. He practiced muscle control in front of the mirror, and he used the proper hand and finger cues to remind himself where his tongue belonged when reproducing individual sounds. His speech production of individual sounds was about 80% intelligible, while his production of *c-v-c* combinations and words were about 25% to 30% intelligible. He produced the *K* sound at the beginning and end of words, he read out of a "book" he created about Mickey Mouse, and he played a Mickey Mouse game.

Teddy showed some signs of anxiety during the speech therapy session that were not present at any other time during the entire day. Teddy repeatedly stomped his feet, clapped his hands, and laughed out loud. He would stop for a short time when his teacher told him to, but he would continue to act out when frustrated. Despite these problems, Teddy was more intelligible, happy, interactive, and spontaneous during speech therapy then at any other time during the day.

Teddy showed appropriate lunchtime behaviors. He turned in his lunch ticket by himself, carried his tray with some assistance from his aide, ate quietly, and cleaned up by himself. He used his utensils correctly and opened his milk carton on his own. He sat next to his homeroom "buddy" and smiled but did not communicate further with him.

During recess another child gave Teddy a "high five" and he responded appropriately. Other than this 5- or 10-second interchange, Teddy did not interact with anyone else. When left by himself, he walked up and down an asphalt square. His aide told him to play on the equipment, and he methodically walked over to each piece and climbed up a ladder and over two arches. Before climbing over the ladder, Teddy walked around a square area for seven minutes waiting for two children to leave. Once they left, he climbed the ladder once and then left. Although he went through the motions of play, Teddy did not appear enthusiastic or involved.

In the afternoon sessions, Teddy worked on a worksheet counting the number of units of 10 and units of 1. He was able to count the units by himself, but his aide had to trace the numbers on the worksheet with him. When he played a game of Addition Bingo, the aide helped him count problems like $7 + 3$, $1 + 1$, $3 + 0$, $4 + 5$, $3 + 4$, $2 + 3$, and $5 + 1$. Teddy was not independent on any of these problems, but he was able to count out loud when the aide pointed to the edge of each number. No other concrete objects were used during this lesson.

In language arts, Teddy did one computer reading lesson in which he had to read a short passage and answer questions. He was able to turn the computer on, type his first and last name, and select the correct sequence to start the lesson. His accuracy rate was about 75% for the comprehension questions for a story about dinosaurs.

In a small-group reading lesson with his LD teacher and one other student, Teddy read and answered questions in a fourth-grade book. His intelligibility continues to be a problem, but his teacher appears to understand his responses. His inflections and rhythm follow the sentence structure, which suggests that he is processing written material. He was able to answer questions showing that he understood the difference between fiction and nonfiction, and he was able to answer questions such as "Which animal is extinct?" "Why was the place terrible?" "Where did the bugs go?" His teacher also reported that his recognition vocabulary is at the level of the fourth-grade reading book, and that his comprehension skills are improving.

DEVELOPMENTAL PROGRESS

There have been remarkable gains in several areas since Teddy's initial evaluation. First, the most apparent developmental progress is in the area of behavior and classroom adjustment. Teddy seems to be very much aware of classroom expectations, although he is not always able to respond to everything requested of him, especially for writing on worksheets. He is able to walk to his different classes without getting lost, make transitions with relative ease, and sit in his seat and attend to lessons for longer periods of time.

Second, Teddy appears to initiate interactions with teachers and several peers at a rate higher than previously observed. Although Teddy is still isolated because of his communication difficulties, he spontaneously interacts and seeks to communicate more often. Third, Teddy seems more tuned into and aware of his surroundings. He responds more appropriately to the directions of his teachers and he redirects quickly when reminded. Fourth, Teddy spends less time daydreaming and staring off. Although he still has a tendency to watch others, he is more attentive to his lessons and to his teachers. Fifth, Teddy has made remarkable academic gains, especially in reading and in reading comprehension. Math continues to be a weakness.

Sixth, Teddy's expressive skills are improving. His sound repertoire is larger than before and his intelligibility is much better. Teddy is also using speech to communicate. Seventh, Teddy has learned to use the Touch Talker to communicate. This involves sequential associative learning whereby icons and words or sentences are combined to communicate. Finally, Teddy shows more independence for everyday activities, such as going to the bathroom and eating lunch.

Gains are apparent in speech production and Teddy is communicating with a higher frequency than previously noted. His articulation has improved, although he still has a tendency to speak quickly, which reduces his intelligibility. Teddy also appears more mature, and his classroom behaviors are more age-appropriate. Although he still is not fully integrated into his surroundings because of his developmental problems, Teddy responds more appropriately to classroom rules, is more attentive, and is more independent for everyday self-help skills at school.

Although Teddy remains isolated from his peers, he is more spontaneous than ever and he initiates interactions more frequently. He spontaneously interacts with his teachers more often, and he smiles and laughs appropriately. Although he remains delayed in overall social interaction skills, his progress over the last year has been substantial.

SPECIFIC RECOMMENDATIONS

To meet Teddy's needs, it was suggested that the school consider the following shifts in program emphasis:

1. The school staff was encouraged to focus on functional communication skills with an integrated speech-language program rather than primarily a therapy-articulation focus.
2. Augmented speech technology should be incorporated throughout Teddy's academic lessons. At this time, the Touch Talker is used as a secondary rather than primary method for inputting and outputting communication. This should be reversed.
3. The educational environment and expectations should be modified to include computer technology for written and reading lessons. Computer technologies are only intermittently used at present. Again, this should be shifted, with the majority of assignments produced on the computer.

Efforts to encourage Teddy in social interactions with peers were recommended. Social skills training may be initiated to teach appropriate communication and joining-in skills. Teddy should be reinforced for social interactions and should be assigned a "buddy" for portions of the day during recess or lunchtime. Other cooperative learning experiences also should be incorporated into daily lessons. Socialization should be closely monitored and reassessed periodically to determine whether goals and recommendations are realistic.

GLOSSARY

Afferent: Sends impulses toward the cell body; are found throughout the body and transmit sensory information to specific sensory areas.

Amygdala: Located in the temporal lobe and involved in the limbic system. Thought to be involved in reactions of anger and rage.

Angular gyrus: Association fibers that connect the parietal and occipital lobes.

Arachnoid: Spiderlike web that is a delicate network of tissue under the dura mater.

Arcuate fasciculus: Association fibers connecting the frontal and temporal lobe.

Association fibers: Connect cortical regions within each hemisphere.

Astrocytes: A type of neuroglia. Serves to form the blood—brain barrier, support the cellular structure of the brain, and direct the migration of neurons during early development.

Astrocytoma: A type of brain tumor, most frequently found in the cerebellum and brain stem.

Auditory evoked potential: Measures of brain activity from the brain stem to the cortex; one way to assess the integrity of auditory pathways in infants and young children.

Axon: A long projection from the cell body; efferent in nature.

Axon hillock: A slender process close to the cell body where action potentials arise.

Basal ganglia: Includes the caudate nucleus, putamen, and globus pallidus and is intimately involved with motor functions.

Biogenetics: The influence of biology and genetics on the environment of the child.

Brain stem: Comprises the fourth ventricle, medulla oblongata, pons, midbrain, and diencephalon.

Brainstem auditory evoked response (BAER): Early phase of an auditory evoked response; frequently used to map the development of neonates.

Calcarine sulcus: Extends from the occipital pole below to the splenium of the corpus callosum; an anatomical feature of the visual cortex.

Cell body: The life center of the neuron; contains the RNA and DNA of the neuron; serves as the energy-producing region for the cell.

Central nervous system (CNS): Made up of the brain and spinal cord.

Central sulcus: Separates the frontal from the parietal lobe as well as separating the motor cortex from the sensory cortex.

Cerebellum: Connects to the midbrain, pons, and medulla; receives sensory information about where the limbs are in space and signals where muscles should be positioned.

Cerebral lateralization: The degree to which each hemisphere is specialized for processing specific tasks.

Cerebrospinal fluid (CSF): A clear, colorless fluid that fills the ventricles and subarachnoid space. Contains concentrations of sodium, chloride, and magnesium.

Choroid plexus: Located in the fourth ventricle; produces CSF.

Commissure: A connection between brain regions. Three main commissures are present in the cerebral cortex: anterior, posterior, and corpus callosum.

Craniotomies: Surgery of the brain in which the skull is removed in certain regions.

Computed tomography (CT): A narrow X-ray beam that provides for the visualization of the brain anatomy.

Dendrites: Part of the neuron that branches off the cell body and receives impulses from other neurons; dendrites are afferent.

Dendritic arborization: Increasing connections between dendrites; is believed to be affected by environmental exposure.

Dermatomes: Specific body segments that are innervated by sensory and motor spinal nerves.

Developmental dyslexia: A childhood condition wherein reading skills are significantly below ability level; thought to involve deficits in phonological coding.

Diencephalon: Includes the thalamus and hypothalamus, pituitary gland, internal capsule, third ventricle, and the optic nerve.

Dura mater: Tough outer layer surrounding the brain and

spinal cord. A subdural space separates the dura mater from the arachnoid.

Dysplasias: Cells out of place in the cortical layer of the brain.

Dystaxia: Movement disorder in which there is poor co-ordination in smooth coordinated movements.

Ectoderm: A layer of tissue formed during early embryonic development; the outermost layer of the neural tube.

Efferent: Conducts impulses away from the cell body of a neuron; originate in the motor cortex and end in the muscles of the body.

Electroencephalography (EEG): A recording of the electrical activity in the brain through electrodes attached to the scalp; frequently used to diagnose epilepsy.

Endoderm: A layer of tissue formed during early embryonic development; the innermost layer of the neural tube.

Endogeneous components: Later aspects of an ERP thought to be related to cognitive processing.

Event-related potential (ERP): Provides an assessment of later components of brain wave activity; these wave components are thought to be related to higher cognitive functions.

Evoked potential: Brain electrical activity recorded using electrodes connected to a microcomputer and amplifier; thought to be a direct response to external sensory stimulation and relatively free from the influence of higher cortical processes.

Executive functions: Planning, flexibility, inhibition, and self-monitoring; thought to be functions of the prefrontal cortex.

Exogeneous components: Automatic response to stimuli as measured by evoked potentials.

Fissures: Deepest indentations in the cerebral cortex.

Frontal lobe: The most anterior cortical structure; comprises the primary motor cortex, premotor cortex, Broca's area, medical cortex, and prefrontal cortex. Have major motor functions as well as mediating reasoning and planning skills.

Functional MRI (fMRI): A relatively new technique that allows for the mapping of cerebral blood flow or volume.

Gray matter: Comprises neuroglia and blood vessels; includes the corpus striatum, the cortex that covers both hemispheres and the cerebellum.

Gyri: Ridges in the cerebral cortex.

Hippocampus: Portion of the temporal lobe and involved in the limbic system; involved in short-term memory storage.

Hypothalamus: Controls the autonomic nervous system and also has many connections to the limbic system.

Inferior colliculi: Contained in the midbrain; involved in the integration of auditory and kinesthetic impulses.

Internal capsule: Contains fibers connecting the cortex to lower brain regions; connects the frontal cortical regions to the thalamus and the pons.

Interneurons: Small neurons in the spinal cord that connect motor neurons with sensory neurons.

Lateral fissure: Separates the frontal lobe from the temporal lobe.

Limbic system: A complex deep structure in the forebrain consisting of the hippocampus, hypothalamus, septum, and cingulate; serves as an intermediary to cognitive and emotional functions.

Longitudinal fasciculus: Association fibers connecting the temporal and occipital lobes with the frontal lobe.

Magnetic resonance imaging (MRI): A large magnet with a magnetic field that allows the visualization of individual brain structures.

Medulla oblongata: Continuation of the spinal cord. Sensory and motor tracts cross in the medulla; contains the reticular activating system; responsible for respiration, heartbeat, and temperature regulation.

Meninges: Protective layer of tissue surrounding the brain and spinal cord.

Meningitis: Bacterial infection of the meninges with long-term consequences to the developing brain if not caught early and treated.

Microcephaly: Small brain; related to mental retardation.

Microglia: A type of glial cell found mainly in the gray matter; Serve to provide structural support; aid in regeneration of injured nerve fibers; transport gas, water, and metabolites; and remove wastes from cells.

Midbrain: Serves as a major relay function for sensory-motor fibers; includes the tegmentum, substantia nigra, superior colliculi, and inferior colliculi.

Mismatch negativity: Believed to reflect the basic mechanism of automatic attention, switching to stimulus changes without conscious attention.

Myelin: Comprises Schwann cells and surrounds the axon. Allows for impulses to be transmitted rapidly.

Neocortex: Makes up 80% of the brain and is the highest functional division of the forebrain.

Nerve growth factor: A specific protein that stimulates the outward growth of axons.

Neuralation: The process of forming the neural tube; occurs during the second to fourth week of gestation.

Neural tube: Formed in the first two weeks of gestation and develops into the nervous system.

Neuroglia: One of the two major cell types: provides structural support and insulates synapses.

Neuron: The basic cellular structure of the nervous system; transmits nerve impulses through a complex network of interconnecting brain cells; composed of a cell body, dendrites, axon, and axon terminals.

Neuropsychology: The study of brain function and behavior.

Neurotransmitter: A chemical contained in the synaptic knobs that allows for impulses to be carried across synapses.

Node of Ranvier: Gaps in the myelin that allow impulses to skip more quickly along an axon.

Occipital lobe: Plays a central role in visual processing.

Occipital-frontal fasciculus: Association fibers that connect the frontal, temporal, and occipital lobes.

Oligodendroglia: Cells that form and maintain the myelin sheath.

P3b: Late positive wave with a latency of 300 to 800 msec.

Parietal lobe: Plays a central role in the perception of tactile sensory information, including the recognition of pain, pressure, touch, proprioception, and kinesthetic sense.

Peripheral nervous system (PNS): Consists of the spinal, cranial, and peripheral nerves that connect the CNS to the rest of the body.

Pia mater: Surrounds the arteries and veins and serves as a barrier to harmful substances; innermost layer of the meninges; contains small blood vessels.

Pituitary gland: Secretes hormones that regulate bodily functions.

Planum temporale: A structure in the temporal lobes. The left planum temporale is believed to be involved in phonological coding.

Pons: Between the medulla and midbrain, and above the cerebellum; the pons, in conjunction with the cerebellum, receives information concerning movements from the motor cortex and helps modulate movements.

Positron-emission tomography (PET): The use of a radioactive tracer to provide an image of cerebral glucose metabolism.

Processing megativity: The ability to detect targets using ERPs; occurs at approximately 200 msec and is related to selective attention.

Reticular activating system (RAS): Part of the medulla; controls blood pressure, blood volume in organs, heart rate, sleep and wakefulness.

Single photon emission tomography (SPECT): Provides a direct measure of regional cerebral blood flow.

Spinal cord: Comprises gray and white matter; serves two major functions–connecting the brain and body via large sensory-motor tracts and integrating motor activity at subcortical levels.

Sulci: The valleys between the ridges in the cerebral cortex and cerebellum.

Superior colliculi: Contained in the midbrain; involved in vision.

Synapses: Connections between neurons.

Syndehams chorea: Childhood disease resulting from poststreptoccal rheumatic fever characterized by irregular and purposeless movements.

Temporal lobe: Involved in auditory processing, short-term memory, and phonological coding.

Thalamus: Serves as a relay station for many sensory regions, including vision, hearing, sensory, and motor input; contains pathways that go to the several areas of the cerebral cortex.

Teleodendria: The terminal branch of the axon; region where neurotransmitters are released into the synapse.

Ventricles: Large cavities in the brain filled with cerebrospinal fluid.

Visual evoked potentials (VER): Technique to evaluate the integrity of the visual system; can be used to evaluate the integrity of the visual system in the preterm infant.

White matter: Comprises the axons covered by a myelin sheath; is covered by the gray matter in the cerebral cortex.

REFERENCES

Abramowitz, A. J., & O'Leary, S. G. (1990). Effectiveness of delayed punishment in an applied setting. *Behavior Therapy, 21*, 231—239.

Abramowitz, A. J., & O'Leary, S. G. (1991). Behavioral interventions for the classroom: Implications for students with ADHD. *School Psychology Review, 20*, 220—234.

Abreau, F., Templer, D. I., Schuyler, B. A., & Hutchison, H. T. (1990). Neuropsychological assessment of soccer players. *Neuropsychology, 4,* 175—181.

Achenbach, T. (1990). Conceptualization of developmental psychopathology. In M. Lewis & S. Miller (Eds.), *Handbook of developmental psychopathology* (pp. 3—13). New York: Plenum Press.

Achenbach, T. (1991). *Manual for the Child Behavior Checklist and Revised Child Behavior Profile.* Burlington, VT: T. M. Achenbach.

Achenbach, T., & Edelbrock, S. (1987). *Manual for the Youth Self-Report and Profile.* Burlington: University of Vermont, Department of Psychiatry.

Achenbach, T., & McConaughy, S. (1989). *Child Interview Checklist-Self Report Form: Child Interview Checklist Observation Form.* Burlington: University of Vermont, Department of Psychiatry.

Adams, G. B., Waas, G. A., March, J. S., & Smith, M. C. (1995). Obsessive-compulsive disorder in children and adolescents: The role of the school psychologist in identification, assessment, and treatment. *School Psychology Quarterly, 9,* 274—294.

Adler, S. P., & Toor, S. (1984). Central nervous system infections. In J. M. Pellock & E. C. Meyer (Eds.), *Neurologic emergencies in infancy and childhood* (pp. 237—256). New York: Harper & Row.

Aicardi, J. (1990). Epilepsy in brain-injured children with cerebral palsy. *Developmental Medicine in Clinical Neurology, 32,* 191—202.

Ainsworth, M. D. S., Blehar, M. C., Waters, E., & Wall, S. (1978). *Patterns of attachment: A psychological study of the Strange Situation.* Hillsdale, NJ: Lawrence Erlbaum Associates.

Alajouanine, T. H., & L'Hermittee, F. (1965). Acquired aphasia in children. *Brain, 88,* 653—662.

Aldenkamp, A. P., Gutter, T., & Beun, A. M. (1992). The effect of seizure activity and paroxysmal electroencephalographic discharges on cognition. *Acta Neurologia, 86 (Supp. 140),* 111—121.

Alessi, N. E., & Magen, J. (1988). Comorbidity of other psychiatric disturbances in depressed psychiatrically hospitalized children. *American Journal of Psychiatry, 145,* 1582—1584.

Allen, L. F., Palomares, R. S., DeForest, P., Sprinkle, B., & Reynolds, C. R. (1991). The effects of intrauterine cocaine exposure: Transient or teratogenic? *Archives of Clinical Neuropsychology, 6,* 133—146.

Allsop, M., & Verduyn, C. (1990). Adolescents with obsessive compulsive disorder: A case note review of consecutive patients referred to a provincial regional adolescent psychiatry unit. *Journal of Adolescence, 13,* 157—169.

Aman, M. C. (1982). Stimulant drug effects in developmental disorders and hyperactivity: Toward a resolution of disparate findings. *Journal of Autism and Developmental Disorders, 12,* 385—398.

American Psychiatric Association. (1994). *Diagnostic and statistical manual of mental disorders* (4th ed.). Washington, DC: Author.

Anderson, G. M., & Hoshino, Y. (1987). Neurochemical studeis of autism. In D. J. Cohen & A. Donnellan (Eds.), *Handbook of autism and prevasive developmental disorders* (pp. 166—191). New York: Wiley.

Anderson, J. C., Williams, S., McGee, R., & Silva, P. A. (1987). DSM-III disorders in preadolescent children. Prevalence in a large sample from the general population. *Archives of General Psychiatry, 44,* 69—76.

Anderson, L., Ernst, M., & Davis, S. V. (1992). Cognitive abilities of patients with Lesch-Nyhan Syndrome. *Journal of Autism and Developmental Disorders, 22,* 189—203.

Angelilli, M. L., Fischer, H., Delaney-Black, V., et al. (1994). History of in utero cocaine exposure in language-delayed children. *Clinical Pediatrics, 33,* 514—516.

Annett, M. (1985). *Left, right, hand and brain: The right shift theory.* Hillsdale NJ: Lawrence Erlbaum Associates.

Aram, D. M., & Ekelman, B. L. (1988). Scholastic aptitude and achievement among children with unilateral brain lesions. *Neuropsychologia, 26,* 903—916.

Aram, D. M., & Nation, J. E. (1980). Preschool language disorders and subsequent academic difficulties. *Journal of Communication Disorders, 13,* 159—170.

Archer, A., & Gleason, M. (1989). *Skills for school success (grades 3—6).* North Billerica, MA: Curriculum.

Arnold, J. E., Levine, A. G., & Patterson, G. R. (1975). Changes in sibling behavior following family intervention. *Journal of Consulting and Clinical Psychology, 43,* 683—688.

Ashwal, S., Perkin, R. M., Thompson, J. R., Schneider, S., & Tomasi, L. G. (1994). Bacterial meningitis in children: Current concepts of neurological management. *Current Problems in Pediatrics, 24,* 267—284.

Ashwal, S., & Schneider, S. (1994). Neurologic complications of vasculitis disorders of childhood. In K. Swaiman (Ed.), *Pediatric neurology.* St. Louis, MO: Mosby.

Asperger, H. (1944). Die autistischen Psychopathen im Kindesalter. *Archiv fur Psychiatrie und Nervenkrankheiten, 117,* 76—136.

Attwood, A., Firth, U., & Hermelin, B. (1988). The understanding and use of interpesonel gesture by autistic and Down's syndrome children. *Journal of Autism and Developmental Disorders, 18,* 241—258.

Austin, J. K. (1988). Childhood epilepsy: Child adaptation and family resources. *Child and Adolescent Psychiatric Mental Health in Nursing, 1,* 18—24.

Austin, J. K., Risinger, M. W., & Beckett, L. A. (1992). Correlates of behavior problems in children with epilepsy. *Epilepsia, 33,* 1115—1122.

Badian, N. (1988). The prediction of good and poor reading before kindergarten entry: A nine-year follow-up. *Journal of Learning Disabilities, 21,* 98—103.

Baer, L., & Jenike, M. A. (1990). Introduction. In M. A. Jenike, L. Baer, & W. E. Minichiello (Eds.), *Obsessive compulsive disorders: Theory and management* (2nd ed., pp. 3—9). St Louis, MO: Moxby—Year Book.

Bale, P. (1981). Behaviour problems and their relationship to reading difficulty. *Journal of Research in Reading, 4,* 123—135.

Bakker, D. J. (1972). *Temporal order in disturbed reading.* Rotterdam: University Press.

Ball, E. W., & Blackman, B. A. (1991). Does phoneme awareness training in kindergarten make a difference in early word recognition and developmental spelling? *Reading Research Quarterly, 26,* 49—66.

Baltaxe, C. A. M., & Simmons, J. (1983). Communication deficits in the adolescent and adult autistic. *Seminars in Speech and Language, 4,* 27—42.

Balthazor, M. J., Wagner, R. K., & Pelham, W. E. (1991). The specificity of the effects of stimulant medications on classroom-learning related measures of cognitive processing for attention deficit disorder children. *Journal of Abnormal Child Psychology, 19,* 35—52.

Banettini, P. A., Wong, E. C., Jesmanowicz, A., Hinks, R. S., & Hyde, J. S. (1994). Spin-echo and gradient-echo EPI of human brain activation. In F. Schmitt, M. Stehling, & R. Turner (Eds.), *Echo-planar imaging* (pp. 130—140). New York: Springer-Verlag.

Barclay, J. R. (1966). Sociometric choices and teacher ratings as predictors of school dropout. *Journal of Social Psychology, 4,* 40—45.

Barkley, R. A. (1977). The effects of methylphenidate on various measures of activity level and attention in hyperkinetic children. *Journal of Abnormal Child Psychology, 5,* 351—369.

Barkley, R. A. (1989). Attention deficit-hyperactivity disorder. In E. J. Mash & R. A. Barkley (Eds.), *Treatment of childhood disorders* (pp. 39—72). New York: Plenum Press.

Barkley, R. A. (1990). *Attention deficit-hyperactivity disorder: A handbook for diagnosis and treatment.* New York: Guilford Press.

Barkley, R. A. (1994). Assessment of attention in children. In R. Lyon (Ed.), *Frames of references for assessment of learning disabilities* (pp. 117—142). New York: Guilford Press.

Barkley, R.A. (1996). Critical issues in research on attention. In C. R. Lyon & N. A. Krasnegor (Eds.), *Attention, memory, and executive function* (pp. 45—56). Baltimore, MD: Paul Brooks.

Barkley, R. A., & Cunningham, C. E. (1979a). The effects of methylphenidate on the mother—child interactions of hyperactive children. *Archives of General Psychiatry, 36,* 201—208.

Barkley, R. A., & Cunningham, C. E. (1979b). Stimulant drugs and activity level in hyperactive children. *American Journal of Orthopsychiatry, 49,* 491—499.

Barkley, R. A., & Cunningham, C. E. (1980). The parent—child interactions of hyperactive children and their modification by stimulant drugs. In R. Knights & D. Bakker (Eds.), *Treatment of hyperactive and learning disabled children* (pp. 219—236). Baltimore, MD: University Park Press.

Barkley, R. A., DuPaul, G. J., & McMurray, M. B. (1991). Attention deficit disorder with and without hyperactivity: Clinical response to three doses of methylphenidate. *Pediatrics, 87,* 519—531.

Barkley, R. A., Fischer, M., Edelbrock, C. S., & Smallish, L. (1990). The adolescent outcome of hyperactive children diagnosed by research criteria: I. An eight-year prospective follow-up study. *Journal of the American Academy of Child and Adolescent Psychiatry, 29,* 546—557.

Barkley, R. A., Grodzinsky, G., & DuPaul, G. J. (1992). Frontal lobe functions in attention deficit disorder with and without hyperactivity: A review and research report. *Journal of Abnormal Child Psychology, 20,* 163—188.

Barkley, R. A., Karlsson, J., Strzelecki, E., & Murphy, J. (1984). Effects of age and Ritalin dosage on the mother—child interactions of hyperactive children. *Journal of Consulting and Clinical Psychology, 52,* 750—758.

Barnet, A. B., Vincentini, M., & Campos, S. M. (1974). *EEG sensory evoked responses (ERs) in early malnutition.* Paper presented at Society for Neuroscience, St. Louis, Missouri.

Barr, M. L., & Kierman, J. A. (1983). *The human nervous system: An anatomical viewpoint.* Philadelphia: Harper & Row.

Batchelor, E. S., & Dean, R. S. (1993). Empirical derivation and classification of subgroups of children with learning disorders at separate age levels. *Archives of Clinical Neuropsychology, 8,* 1—15.

Bateman, D. A., & Heagarty, M. C. (1989). Passive free base cocaine ("crack") inhalation by infants and toddlers. *American Journal of Diseases in Childhood, 143,* 25—27.

Baxter, L. R., Thompson, J. M., Schwartz, J. M., Guze, B. H., et al. (1987). Trazodone treatment response in obsessive-compulsive disorder. *Psychopathology, 20,* 114—122.

Bear, D. M. (1983). Hemispheric specialization and the neurology of emotion. *Archives of Neurology, 40,* 195—202.

Beardslee, W. R., Keller, M. B., & Kierman, G. D. (1985). Children of parents with affective disorder. *International Journal of Family Psychiatry, 6,* 283—299.

Becker, M., Warr-Leeper, G. A., & Leeper, H. A. (1990). Fetal alcohol syndrome: A description of oral motor, articulatory, short-term memory, grammatical, and semantic abilities. *Journal of Communication Disorders, 23,* 97—123.

Becker, M. G., Isaac, W., & Hynd, G. W. (1987). Neuropsychological development of non-verbal behaviors attributed to "frontal lobe" functioning. *Developmental Neuropsychology, 3,* 275—298.

Beckwith, L., Rodning, C., Norris, D., et al. (1990). Spontaneous play in two-year-olds born to substance-abusing mothers. *Infant Mental Health Journal, 15,* 189—201.

Beeghly, M., & Tronick, E. Z. (1994). Effects of prenatal exposure to cocaine in early infancy: Toxic effects on the process of mutual regulation. *Infant Mental Health Journal, 15,* 158—175.

Befera, M. S., & Barkley, R. A. (1985). Hyperactive and normal girls and boys: Mother—child interactions, parent psychiatric status, and child psychopathology. *Journal of Child Psychology and Psychiatry, 26,* 439—452.

Beidel, D. C. (1988). Psychophysiological assessment of anxious emotional states in children. *Journal of Abnormal Psychology, 97,* 80—82.

Belman, A. L., Lantos, G., Horoupian, D., Novick, B. E., Ultmann, M. H., Dickson, D. W., & Rubinstein, A. (1986). AIDS: Calcification of the basal ganglia in infants and children. *Neurology, 36,* 1192—1199.

Belman, A. L., Ultmann, M. H., Horoupian, D., Lantos, G., Diamond, G., Dickson, D., & Rubinstein, A. (1986). CNS involvement in infants and children with AIDS. *Annals of Neurology, 20,* 405—406.

Bengali, V. (1992). *Head injury in children and adolescents.* Brandon, VT: Clinical Psychology Publishing Company.

Benjamin, C. M., Colley, A., Donnai, D., Kingston, H., Harris, R., & Kerzin-Storrar, L. (1993). Neurofibromatosis type 1: Knowledge, experience, and reproductive decisions of affected patients and families. *Journal of Medical Genetics, 30,* 567—574.

Bennett, T. L., & Krein, L. K. (1989). The neuropsychology of epilepsy: Psychological and social impact. In C. R. Reynolds & E. Fletcher-Janzen (Eds.), *Handbook of clinical child neuropsychology* (pp. 443—474). New York: Plenum Press.

Bennett-Levy, J., & Stores, G. (1984). The nature of cognitive dysfunction in school children with epilepsy. *Acta Neurological Scandinavica, Supplement 99,* 79—82.

Benson, D. F. (1991). The role of frontal dysfunction in attention deficit hyperactive disorder. *Journal of Child Neurology, 6,* Suppl., S9—S12.

Benton, A. L., Hamsher, K. deS., Varney, N. R., & Spreen, O. (1983a). *Contributions to neuropsychological assessment: A Clinical manual.* New York: Oxford University Press.

Benton, A. L., Hamsher, K. deS., Varney, N. R., & Spreen,

O. (1983b). *Facial recognition.* New York: Oxford University Press.

Benton, A. L., Hamsher, K. deS., Varney, N. R., & Spreen, O. (1983c). *Judgment of line orientation.* New York: Oxford University Press.

Berg, R. A. (1986). Neuropsychological effects of closed-head injury in children. In J. E. Obrzut & G. W. Hynd (Eds.), *Child neuropsychology: Volume 2. Clinical Practice* (pp. 113—135). Orlando, FL: Academic Press.

Berk, L. E. (1989). *Child development.* Boston: Allyn and Bacon.

Berman, A., & Siegal, A. (1976). Adaptive and learning skills in juvenile delinquents: A neuropsychological analysis. *Journal of Learning Disabilities, 9,* 51—58.

Berninger, V. W. (1990). Multiple orthographic codes: Key to alternative instructional methodologies for developing the orthographic-phonological connections underlying word identification. *School Psychology Review, 19,* 518—533.

Berninger, V. W., & Abbott, R. D. (1994). Redefining learning disabilities: Moving beyond aptitude—achievement discrepancies to failure to repsond to validated treatment protocols. In G. R. Lyon (Ed.), *Frames of reference for the assessment of learning disabilities: New views on measurement issues* (pp. 163—184). Baltimore, MD: Paul H. Brooks.

Berninger, V. W., & Fuller, F. (1992). Gender differences in orthographic, verbal, and compositional fluency: Implications for assessing writing disabilities in primary grade children. *Journal of School Psychology, 30,* 363—382.

Bernstein, G. A., & Garfinkel, B. D. (1986). School phobia: The overlap of affective and anxiety disorders. *Journal of the American Academy of Child and Adolescent Psychiatry, 2,* 235—241.

Berry, C. A., Shaywitz, S. E., & Shaywitz, B. A. (1985). Girls with attention deficit disorder: A Silent minority? A report on behavioral & cognitive characteristics. *Pediatrics, 76,* 801—809.

Besag, F. M. C. (1995). Epilepsy, learning, and behavior in childhood. *Epilepsia, 36 (Suppl. 1),* S58—S63.

Best, C. T., Hoffman, H., & Glanville, B. B. (1982). Development of right ear asymmetries for speech and music. *Perception and Psychophysics, 31,* 75—85.

Best, C. T., & Queens, H. F. (1989). Baby, it's in your smile: Right hemiface bias in infant emotional expressions. *Developmental Psychology, 25,* 264—276.

Bharucha, N. E., Bharucha, E. P., & Bhabha, S. K. (1995). Bacterial infections. In W. G. Bradley, R. B. Daroff, G.

M. Fenichel, & C. D. Marsden (Eds.), *Neurology in clinical practice* (pp. 1181—1258). Boston: Butterworth-Heinemam.

Biederman, J. (1990). The diagnosis and treatment of adolescent anxiety disorders. *Journal of Clinical Psychiatry, 51,* 20—26.

Biederman, J., Baldessarini, R. J., Wright, V., Knee, D., & Harmatz, J. E. (1989). A double-blind placebo controlled study of desipramine in the treatment of ADD: I. Efficacy. *Journal of the American Academy of Child and Adolescent Psychiatry, 28,* 777—784.

Biederman, J., Faraone, S. V., Benjamin, J., Krifcher, B., Moore, C., et al. (1992). Further evidence for family-genetic risk factors in attention deficit hyperactivity disorder. *Archives of General Psychiatry, 49,* 728—738.

Biederman, J., Faraone, S. V., Keenan, K., Knee, D., & Tsuang, M. T. (1990). Family-genetic and psychosocial risk factors in DSM III attention deficit disorder. *Journal of the American Academy of Child and Adolescent Psychiatry, 29,* 526—533.

Biederman, J., Munir, K., Keenan, K., & Tsuang, M. T. (1991). Evidence of familial association between attention deficit and major affective disorders. *Archives of General Psychiatry, 48,* 633-642.

Biederman, J., Munir, K., & Knee, D. (1987). Conduct and oppositional disorder in clinically referred children with attention deficit disorder: A controlled family study. *Journal of the American Academy of Child and Adolescent Psychiatry, 26,* 724—727.

Bierman, K. L., Miller, C. M., & Stabb, S. (1987). Improving the social behavior and peer acceptance of rejected boys: Effects of social skill training with instructions and prohibitions. *Journal of Consulting and Clinical Psychology, 55,* 194—200.

Bigler, E. R. (1989a). On the neuropsychology of suicide. *Journal of Learning Disabilities, 22*(3), 180—185.

Bigler, E. R. (1989b). Radiological techniques in neuropsychological assessment. In C. R. Reynolds & E. Fletcher-Janzen (Eds.), *Handbook of clinical child neuropsychology* (pp. 247—264). New York: Plenum Press.

Bigler, E. R. (1990). *Traumatic brain injury: Mechanisms of damage, assessment, intervention and outcome.* Austin, TX: Pro-Ed.

Bigler, E. R. (1991). Neuropsychological assessment, neuro- imaging, and clinical neuropsychology: A synthesis. *Archives of Clinical Neuropsychology, 6,* 113—132.

Bigler, E. D., Yeo, R. A., & Turkheimer, E. (1989).

Neuropsychological function and brain imaging. New York: Plenum Press.

Binder, J. R., Rao, S. M., Hammeke, T. A., Frost, J. A., Bandettini, B. S., & Hyde, J. S. (1994). Effects of stimulus rate on signal response during functional magnetic resonance imaging of auditory cortex. *Cognitive Brain Research, 2,* 31—38.

Bishop, D. V. M. (1993). Annotation: Autism, executive functions and theory of mind: A neuropsychological perspective. *Journal of Child Psychology and Psychiatry, 34,* 279—293.

Bishop, D. V. M., Brown, B. D., & Robson, J. (1990). The relationship between phoneme discrimination, speech production, and language comprehension in cerebral-palsied individuals. *Journal of Speech and Hearing Research, 33,* 210—219.

Black, K., & Hynd, G. W. (1995). Epilespy in the school aged child: Cognitive-behavioral characteristics and effects on academic performance. *School Psychology Quarterly, 10,* 345—358.

Blackstock, E. (1978). Cerebral asymmetry and the development of early infantile autism. *Journal of Autism and Developmental Disorders, 8,* 339—353.

Blakeslee, S. (1990, September 17). Crack's toll among babies. *New York Times,* pp. 1, 12.

Blondis, T. A., Roizen, N. J., Snow, J. H., & Accardo, P. J. (1993). Developmental disabilities: A continuum. *Clinical Pediatrics, 32,* 492—498.

Blumberg, S., & Izard, C. (1985). Affective and cognitive characteristics of depression in 10 and 11 year old children. *Journal of Personality and Social Psychology, 49,* 194—202.

Blume, W. H. (1982). *Atlas of pediatric encephalography.* New York: Raven Press.

Boliek, C. A., Obrzut, J. E., & Shaw, D. (1988). The effects of hemispatial and asymmetrical focused attention on dichotic listening with normal and learning-disabled children. *Neuropsychologia, 26,* 417—423.

Boll, T. J. (1974). Behavioral correlates of cerebral damage in children aged 9—14. In R. M. Reitan & L. Davison (Eds.), *Clinical neuropsychology: Current status and application* (pp. 91—120). Washington, DC: V. H. Winston & Sons.

Boll, T. J. (1981). The Halstead-Reitan neuropsychological battery. In S. Filskov & T. Boll (Eds.), *Handbook of clinical neuropsychology* (pp. 577—607). New York: Wiley Interscience.

Boll, T. J., & Barth, J. T. (1981). Neuropsychology of brain damage in childmen. In S. Filskov & T. Boll (Eds.),

Handbook of clinical neuropsychology (pp. 418—452). New York: Wiley Interscience.

Bolter, J. F. (1986). Epilepsy in children: Neuropsychological effects. In J. E. Obrzut & G. W. Hynd (Eds.), *Child neuropsychology: Clinical practice* (pp. 59—81). New York: Academic Press.

Bordarier, C., & Aicardi, J. (1990). Dandy-Walker syndrome and agenesis of the cerebellar vermis: Diagnostic problems and genetic counseling. A review. *Developmental Medicine Child Neurology, 32,* 285—294.

Bos, C. S., & Anders, P. L. (1990). Interactive teaching and learning: Instructional practices for teaching content and strategic knowledge. In T. E. Scruggs & B. Y. L. Wong (Eds.), *Intervention research in learning disabilities* (pp. 166—185). New York: Springer-Verlag.

Bos, C. S., & Van Reusen, A. K. (1991). Academic interventions with learning-disabled students: A cognitive/metacognitive approach. In J. E. Obrzut & G. W. Hynd (Eds.), *Neuropsychological foundations of learning disabilities* (pp. 659—684). San Diego, CA: Academic Press.

Boucher, J., & Warrington, E. K. (1976). Memory deficits in early infantile autism: Some similarities to the amnesic syndrome. *British Journal of Psychology, 67,* 73—87.

Boucugnani, L., & Jones, R. W. (1989). Behaviors analogous to frontal lobe dysfunction in children with attention deficit hyperactive disorder. *Archives of Clinical Neuropsychology, 4,* 161—174.

Bourgeois, B. F. D., Prensky, A. L., Palkes, H. S., Talent, B. K., & Busch, S. G. (1983). Intelligence in epilepsy: A prospective study in children. *Annals of Neurology, 14,* 438—444.

Bowden, H. N., Knights, R., & Winogron, H. W. (1985). Speeded performance following head injury in children. *Journal of Clinical and Experimental Neuropsychology, 7,* 39—54.

Boyd, T. A., Ernhart, C. B., Greene, T. H., Sokol, R. J., et al. (1991). Prenatal alcohol exposure and sustained attention in preschool years. *Neurotoxicology and Teratology, 13,* 49—55.

Boyd, T. A., Tramontana, M. G., & Hopper, S. R. (1986). Cross-validation of a psychometric system for screening neuropsychological abnormality in older children. *Archives of Clinical Neuropsychology, 1,* 387—391.

Bradley, L., & Bryant, P. E. (1983). Categorizing sounds and learning to read–A causal connection. *Nature, 301,* 419—421.

Brady, E. U., & Kendall, P. C. (1992). Comorbidity of anxiety and depression in children and adolescents. *Psychological Bulletin, 111,* 244—255.

Breakey, A., Wilson, J., & Wilson, B. (1974). Sensory and perceptual function in the cerebral palsied: III. Some visual perceptual relationships. *Journal of Nervous Mental Disorders, 158,* 70—77.

Breiner, J. L., & Forehand, R. (1981). An assessment of the effects of parent training on clinic-referred children's school behavior. *Behavioral Assessment, 3,* 31—42.

Brent, D. A., Crumrine, P. K., Varma, R. R., Allan, M. A., & Allman, C. (1987). Phenobaribitol treatment and major depressive disorder in children with epilepsy. *Pediatrics, 80,* 909—917.

Breslau, N. (1985). Psychiatric disorder in children with physical diabilities. *Journal of the American Academy of Child and Adolescent Psychiatry, 24,* 87—94.

Brodal, P. (1992). *The central nervous system: Structure and function.* New York: Oxford Press.

Brouwers, P., & Poplack, D. (1990). Memory and learning sequelae in long-term survivors of acute lymphoblastic leukemia: Association with attention deficits. *American Journal of Pediatric Hematology/Oncology, 12,* 174—181.

Brouwers, P., Riccardi, R., Poplack, D., & Fedio, P. (1987). Attentional deficits in long-term survivors of childhood acute lymphoblastic leukemia. *Journal of Clinical Neuropsychology, 6,* 325—336.

Brown, G., Chadwick, O., Schaffer, D., Rutter, M., & Traub, M. (1981). A prospective study of children with head injuries: III. Psychiatric sequalae. *Psychological Medicine, 11,* 63—78.

Bruhn, J. (1977). Effects of chronic illness on the family. *Journal of Family Practice, 4,* 1057—1060.

Bryan, T. (1991). Social problems and learning disabilities. In B. Y. L. Wong (Ed.), *Learning about learning disabilities* (pp. 195—229). San Diego, CA: Academic Press.

Bryan, T., & Lee, J. (1990). Social skills training with learning disabled children and adolescents: The state of the art. In T. E. Scruggs & B. Y. L. Wong (Eds.), *Intervention research in learning disabilities* (pp. 263—278). New York: Springer-Verlag.

Bryson, S. E., Clark, B. S., & Smith, I. M. (1988). First report of a Canadian epidemiological study of autistic syndromes. *Journal of Child Psychology and Psychiatry, 29,* 433—445.

Bundey, S., & Evans, K. (1969). Tuberous sclerosis: A genetic study of chronic proximal spinal muscular atrophy. *Brain, 98,* 455—472.

Burd, L., Kerbeshian, J., Cook, J., Bornhoeft, D. M., & Fisher, W. (1988). Tourette syndrome in North Dakota. *Neuroscience and Neurobehavioral Review, 12,* 223—228.

Burd, L., Kerbeshian, J., Wikenheiser, M., & Fisher, W. (1986). A prevalence study of Gilles de la Tourette syndrome in North Dakota School-age children. *Journal of American Academy of Child Psychiatry, 25,* 552—553.

Buschke, H., & Fuld, P. (1974). Evaluating storage, retention, and retrieval in disordered memory and learning. *Neurology, 24,* 1019—1025.

Butkowsky, J. S., & Willows, D. M. (1980). Cognitive-motivational characteristics of children varying in reading ability: Evidence for learned helplessness in poor readers. *Journal of Educational Psychology, 72,* 408—422.

Butler, L., Miezitis, S., Friedman, R., & Cole, E. (1980). The effects of two school-based intervention programs on depressive symptoms in preadolescents. *American Educational Research Journal, 17,* 111—119.

Butler, R. W., & Copeland, D. R. (1993). Neuropsychological effects of central nervous system prophylactic treatment in childhood leukemia: Methodological considerations. *Journal of Pediatric Psychology, 18,* 319—338.

Byers, R. K. (1941). Evolution of hemiplegia in infancy. *American Journal of Disabled Children, 61,* 915.

Byrne, B., & Fielding-Barnsley, R. (1993). Evaluation of a program to teach phonemic awareness to young children: A one-year follow-up. *Journal of Educational Psychology, 85,* 104—111.

Cabieses, F., Jeri, R., & Landa, R. (1957). Fatal brainstem shift following hemispherectomy. *Journal of Neurosurgery, 14,* 74—91.

Cadoret, J. R. (1978). Psychopathology in adopted-away offspring of biologic parents with antisocial behavior. *Archives of General Psychiatry, 35,* 176—184.

Cadoret, R. J., Cain, C. A., & Crowe, R. R. (1983). Evidence for gene—environment interaction in the development of adolescent antisocial behavior. *Behavior Genetics, 13,* 301—310.

Cadoret, R. J., Troughton, E., & O'Gorman, T. W. (1987). Genetic and environmental factors in alcohol abuse and antisocial personality. *Journal of Studies on Alcohol, 48,* 1—8.

Caesar, P. (1993). Old and new facts about perinatal brain development. *Journal of Child Psychology and Psychiatry, 34,* 101—109.

Caine, E. D. (1986). The neuropsychology of depression: The pseudodementia syndrom. In I. Grant & K. Adams (Eds.), *Neuropsychological assessment of neuropsychiatric disorders* (pp. 221-243). New York: Oxford University Press.

Cairns, R. B., Cairns, B. D., Neckerman, H. J., Gest, S. D., & Gariepy, J. L. (1988). Social networks and aggressive behavior: Peer support or peer rejection? *Developmental Psychology, 24,* 815—823.

Callaway, E., Holliday, R., & Naylor, H. (1983). Hyperactive children's event-related potentials fail to support underarousal and maturational-lag theories. *Archives of General Psychiatry, 40,* 1243—1248.

Camp, B. W., & Bash, M. A. S. (1985). *Think aloud: Increasing social and cognitive skills–A problem-solving program for children classroom program.* Champaigne, IL: Research Press.

Campbell, M., Adams, P., Small, A. M., McVeigh-Tesch, L., & Curren, E. L. (1988). Naltrexone in infantile autism. *Psychopharmacology Bulletin, 24,* 135—139.

Campbell, M., Fish, B., Korein, J., Shapiro, T., Collins, P., & Co, H. C. (1972). Lithium and chlorpromazine controlled crossover study of hyperactive, severely disturbed young children. *Journal of Autism and Childhood Schizophrenia, 2,* 234—263.

Cantwell, D. P. (1975). Genetics of hyperactivity. *Journal of Child Psychology and Psychiatry and Allied Disciplines, 16,* 261—264.

Cantwell, D. P. (1988). DSM-III studies. In M. Rutter, A. H. Tuma, & I. S. Lann (Eds.), *Assessment and diagnosis in child psychopathology* (pp. 3—36). New York: Guilford Press.

Cantwell, D. P., & Baker, L. (1988). Issues in the classification of child and adolescent psychopathology. *Journal of the American Academy of Child and Adolescent Psychiatry, 27,* 521—533.

Cantwell, D. P., & Baker, L. (1991). Association between attention deficit hyperactivity disorder and learning disorders. *Journal of Learning Disabilities, 24,* 88—95.

Caplan, L. R., Schmahmann, J. D., Kase, C. S., et al. (1990). Caudate infarcts. *Archives of Neurology, 47,* 133—143.

Carlson, C. C., Lahey, B. B., Frame, C. L., Walker, J., & Hynd, G. W. (1987). Sociometric status of clinic-referred children with attention deficit disorders with and without hyperactivity. *Journal of Abnormal Psychology, 15,* 537—547.

Carlson, C. C., Lahey, B. B., & Neeper, R. (1986). Direct assessment of the cognitive correlates of attention deficit disorders with and without hyperactivity.

Journal of Behavioral Assessment and Psychopathology, 8, 69—86.

Carlson, C. L., Pelham, W. E., Milich, R., & Dixon, M. (1992). Single and combined effects of methylphenidate and behavior therapy on the classroom behavior, academic performance, and self-evaluations of children with attention deficit hyperactivity disorder. *Journal of Abnormal Child Psychology, 20,* 213—232.

Carlson, N. R. (1994). *Physiology of behavior.* Boston: Allyn and Bacon.

Carlsson, G., Uvebrant, P. Hugdahl, K., Arvidsson, J., et al. (1994). Verbal and non-verbal function of children with right- versus left-hemiplegic cerebral palsy of pre- and perinatal origin. *Developmental Medicine and Child Neurology, 36,* 503—512.

Carmichael, K. (1970). The onset and early development of behavior. In P. Mussen (Ed.), *Carmichael's manual of child psychology* (Vol. 1, pp. 447—563). New York: Wiley.

Carney, L. J., & Cermak, G. D. (1991). Performance of American Indian children with fetal alcohol syndrome on the test of language development. *Journal of Communication Disorders, 24,* 123—124.

Carpenter, M. B., & Sutin, J. (1983). *Human neuroanatomy* (8th ed.). Baltimore, MD: Williams & Wilkins.

Carpentieri, S. C., Mulhern, R. K., Douglas, S., Hanna, S., & Fairclough, D. L. (1993). Behavioral resiliency among children surviving brain tumors: A longitudinal study. *Journal of Consulting and Clinical Psychology, 22,* 236—246.

Carpentieri, S. C., & Mulhern, R. K. (1993). Patterns of memory dysfunction among children surviving temporal lobe tumors. *Archives of Clinical Neuropsychology, 8,* 345—357.

Carr, E. G. (1985). Behavioral approaches to language and communication. In E. Shopler & G. Mesibov (Eds.), *Communication problems in autism* (pp. 37—57). New York: Plemun Press.

Carr, J. (1994). Annotation: Long term outcome for people with Down's syndrome. *Journal of Child Psychology and Psychiatry, 35,* 425—439.

Case-Smith, J., & Nastro, M. A. (1993). The effect of occupational therapy intervention on mothers of children with cerebral palsy. *American Journal of Occupational Therapy, 47,* 811—817.

Castellanos, F. X., Giedd, J. N., Eckburg, D., et al. (1994). Quantitative morphology of the caudate nucleus in attention deficit hyperactivity disorder. *American Journal of Psychiatry, 151,* 1791—1796.

Castellucci, V. F. (1985). The chemical senses: Taste and smell. In E. R. Kandel & J. H. Schwartz (Eds.), *Principles of neural science* (2nd ed., pp. 409—429). New York: Elsevier.

Cattell, R. B., & Horn, J. L. (1978). A check on the fluid and crystallized intelligence with description of new subtest designs. *Journal of Educational Measurement, 15,* 139—164.

Chadwick, O., & Rutter, M. (1983). Neuropsychological assessment. In M. Rutter (Ed.), *Developmental neuropsychiatry* (pp. 181—212). New York: Guilford Press.

Chadwick, O., Rutter, M., Brown, G., Shaffer, D., & Traub, M. (1981). A prospective study of children with head injuries: II. Cognitive sequelae. *Psychological Medicine, 11,* 49—61.

Chalhub, E. G. (1976). Neurocutaneous syndromes in children. *Pediatric Clinics of North America, 23,* 499—516.

Chang, P. (1991). Psychosocial needs of long-term childhood cancer survivors: A review of the literature. *Pediatrician, 18,* 20—24.

Chang, P. A., Nesbit, M. E., Youngren, N., et al. (1987). Personality characteristics and psychosocial adjustment of long-term survivors of childhood cancer. *Journal of Psychosocial Oncology, 5,* 43—58.

Chase, C. H., & Tallal, P. (1991). Cognitive models of developmental reading disorders. In J. Obrzut & G. W. Hynd (Eds.), *Neuropsychological foundations of learning disabilities* (pp. 199—240). San Diego, CA: Academic Press.

Chasnoff, I. J. (1993). Missing pieces of the puzzle. *Neurotoxicology and Teratology, 15,* 287—288.

Chasnoff, I. J., & Griffith, D. (1990). Cocaine-exposed infants: Two year follow-up. *Pediatric Research, 25,* 249A.

Chasnoff, I. J., Griffith, D., MacGregor, S., Dirkes, K., & Burns, K. (1989). Temporal patterns of cocaine use in pregnancy. *JAMA, 261,* 1741—1744.

Chasnoff, I. J., Landress, H., & Barrett, M. (1990). The prevalence of illicit drug or alcohol use during pregnancy and discrepancies in mandatory reporting in Pinellas County, Florida. *New England Journal of Medicine, 322,* 1202—1206.

Chasnoff, I. J., Lewis, D. E., & Squires, L. (1987). Cocaine intoxication in a breast-fed infant. *Pediatrics, 80,* 836—838.

Chavez, G. F., Mulinare, J., & Cordero, J. F. (1989). Maternal cocaine use during early pregnancy as a risk factor for congenital orogenital anomalies. *Journal of the American Medical Association, 262,* 795—798.

Chelune, G. J., & Edwards, P. (1981). Early brain lesions: Ontogenetic-environmental consideratiosn. *Journal of Consulting and Clinical Psychology, 49,* 777—790.

Chelune, G. J., Fergusson, W., Koon, R., & Dickey, T. (1986). Frontal lobe disinhibition in attention deficit disorder. *Child Psychiatry and Human Development, 16,* 221—234.

Chethick, L., Burns, K., Burns, W., & Clark, R. (1990). The assessment of early relationship dysfunction in cocaine-abusing mothers and their infants. *Infant Behavior and Development, 13,* 312.

Chi, J. G., Dowling, E. C., & Gilles, F. H. (1977). Left—right asymmetries of the temporal speech areas of the human fetus. *Archives of Neurology, 34,* 346—348.

Chiappa, K. H. (1985). *Evoked potentials in clinical medicine.* New York: Raven Press.

Chira, S. (1990, May 25). Crack babies turn five, and schools brace. *New York Times,* pp. A1, A11.

Chiron, C., Dulac, O., Bulteau, C., Nuttin, C., Depas, G., Raynaud, C., & Syrota, A. (1993). Study of region cerebral blood flow in West Syndrome. *Epilepsia, 34,* 707—715.

Chiron, C., Leboyer, M., Leon, F., Jambaque, I., Nuttin, C., & Syrota, A. (1995). SPECT of the brain in childhood autism: Evidence for a lack of hemispheric asymmetry. *Developmental Medicine and Child Neurology, 37,* 849—860.

Christensen, E., & Melchior, J. (1967). Cerebral palsy–a clinical and neuropathological study. *Clinical Developmental Medicine, 25,* 1—10.

Christiansen, K. O. (1974). Seriousness of criminality and concordance among Danish twins. In R. Hood (Ed.), *Crime, criminology and public policy* (pp. 63—67). London: Heinemann.

Chutorian, A. M., Michener, R. C., Defendini, R., et al. (1979). Neonatal polycystic encephalomalacia: Four new cases and review of the literature. *Journal of Neurology, Neurosurgery, and Psychiatry, 42,* 154—160.

Cicchetti, D., & Beeghly, M. (1990). *Down syndrome: A developmental perspective.* Cambridge: England. Cambridge University Press.

Cioni, G., Bartalene, L., Biagioni, E., Boldrini, A., et al. (1992). Neuroimaging and functional outcome of neonatal leukomalacia. Special issue: Normal and abnormal visual development in infants and children. *Behavioral Brain Research, 49,* 7—19.

Clarizio, H. F. (1991). Obsessive-compulsive disorder: The secretive syndrome. *Psychology in the Schools, 28,* 106—115.

Clark, D. A., & Bolton, D. (1985). Obsessive-compulsive adolescents and their parents. *Journal of Child Psychology and Psychiatry and Allied Disciplines, 26,* 267—276.

Clay, M. M. (1993). *Reading recovery : A guidebook for teachers in training.* Portsmouth, NH: Longman.

Cloninger, C. R., Christiansen, K.O., Reich, T., & Gottesman, I. I. (1978). Implications of sex differences in the prevalences of antisocial personality, alcoholism, and criminality for familiar transmission. *Archives of General psychiatry, 35,* 941—951.

Cloninger, C. R., Reich, T., & Guze, S. B. (1975). The multifactorial model of disease transmission: II. Sex differences in the familial transmission of sociopathy (antisocial personality). *British Journal of Psychiatry, 127,* 11—22.

Cohen, D. J., Shaywitz, B. A., Caparulo, B., et al. (1978). Chronic, multiple tics of Giles de la Tourette's disease: CSF acid monoamine metabolities after probenecid administration. *Archives of General Psychiatry, 35,* 245—250.

Cohen, I. L., Campbell, M., Posner, D., Small, A. M., Treibel, D., & Anderson, L. T. (1980). Behavioral effects of haloperidol in young autistic children: An objective analysis using a within-subjects reversal design. *Journal of the American Academy of Child and Adolescent Psychiatry, 19,* 665—677.

Cohen, M. D. (1986). Pediatric magnetic resonance imaging. Philadelphia: W. B. Saunders.

Cohen, M. E., & Duffner, P. K. (1994). Tumors of the brain and spinal cord including leukemic involvement. In K. Swaiman (Ed.), *Pediatric neurology.* St. Louis, MO: Mosby.

Cohen, R. M., Weingarten, H., Smallberg, S. A., & Murphy, D. L. (1982). Effort and cognition in depression. *Archives of General Psychiatry, 39,* 593—597.

Coie, J. D., & Krehbiel, G. (1984). Effects of academic tutoring on the social status of low-achieving, socially rejected children. *Child Development, 55,* 1465—1478.

Colby, C. L. (1991). The neuroanatomy and neurophysiology of attention deficit disorder. *Journal of Child Neurology, 6,* Supplement, S90—S111.

Coles, C. D. (1993). Saying "goodbye" to the "crack baby." *Neurotoxicology and Teratology, 15,* 290—292.

Coles, C. D., Platzman, K., Smith, I., James, M., & Falek, A. (1991). Effects of cocaine, alcohol, and other drugs used in pregnancy on neonatal growth and neurobehavioral status. *Neurotoxicology and Teratology, 13,* 1—11.

Comalli, P., Wapner, S., & Werner, H. (1962). Interference effects of Stroop Color—Word test in childhood, adulthood, and aging. *Journal of Genetic Psychology, 100,* 47—53.

Comings, D. E. (1990). *Tourette syndrome and human behavior.* Durante, CA; Hope Press.

Comings, D. E., Comings, B. G., Cloninger, C. R., & Devor, R. (1984). Detection of major gene for Gilles de la Tourette syndrome. *American Journal of Human Genetics, 36,* 586—600.

Conel, J. (1939—1959). *The postnatal development of the human cerebral cortex* (Vols. 1—6). Cambridge, MA: Harvard University Press.

Conners, C. K. (1969). A teacher's rating scale for use in drug studies with children. *American Journal of Psychiatry, 126,* 884—888.

Conners, C. K. (1982). Parent and teacher rating forms of assessment of hyperkinesis in children. In P. A. Keller & L. G. Ritte (Eds.), *Innovations in clinical practice: A source book* (Vol. 1, pp. 257—264). Sarasota, FL: Professional Research Exchange.

Conners, C. K., & Wells, K. C., (1986). *Hyperactive children: A neuropsychological approach.* Beverly Hills, CA: Sage.

Conners, C. K., & Werry, J. S. (1979). Pharmacotherapy. In H. C. Quay & J. S. Werry (Eds.), *Psychopathological disorders of children* (2nd ed., pp. 336—386). New York: Wiley.

Conry, J. (1990). Neuropsychological deficits in fetal alcohol syndrome and fetal alcohol effects. *Alcoholism: Clinical and Experimental Research, 14,* 650—655.

Conte, R., Kinsbourne, M., Swanson, J., Zirk, H., & Samuels, M. (1986). Presentation rate effects on paired associate learning by attention deficit disordered children. *Child Development, 57,* 681—687.

Cook, E. H., & Leventhal, B. L. (1992). Neuropsychiatric disorders of childhhod and adolescense. In S. C. Yudofsky & R. E. Hales (Eds.), *The American Psychiatric Press textbook of neuropsychiatry* (2nd ed., pp. 639—662). Washington, DC: American Psychiatric Press.

Cook, E. H., Rowlett, R., Jaselskis, C., Leventhal, B. L. (1992). Fluoxetine treatment of patients with autism and mental retardation. *Journal of American Academy of Child and Adolescent Psychiatry, 31,* 739—745.

Coons, H. W., Klorman, R., & Borgstedt, A. D. (1987). Effects of methylphenidate on adolescents with a childhood history of attention deficit disorder: II. Information processing. *Journal of the American Academy of Child and Adolescent Psychiatry, 26,* 368—374.

Cooper, J. R., Bloom, F. E., & Roth, R. H. (1986). *The biochemical basis of neuropharmacology* (5th ed.). New York: Oxford University Press.

Copeland, E. D., & Copps, S. C. (1995). *Medications for attention disorders (ADHD/ADD) and related medical problems: A comprehensive handbook*. Plantation, FL: Specialty Press.

Costello, E. J. (1989). Developments in child psychiatric epidemiology. *Journal of the American Academy of Child and Adolescent Psychiatry, 28,* 836—871.

Coulehan, J., Michaels, R., Williams, K. L. D., North, Q., Welty, T., & Rogers, K. (1976). Bacterial meningitis in Navajo Indians. *Public Health Reports, 91,* 464—468.

Counts, S., Radov, M. H., & Wilson, M. T. (1976). *Attitude of employers and cancer patients towards patients' work ability: Two surveys and an action plan*. (Rehabilitation Program, National Cancer Institute contract No. N01-CN-55070). Pittsburgh, PA: Center for Health Systems, the Fairfax.

Courchesne, E. (1987). A neurophysiological view of autism. In E. Schopler & G. Mesibov (Eds.), *Neurobiological issues in autism* (pp. 285—324). New York: Plenum Press.

Courchesne, E. (1989). Neuroanatomical systems involved in infantile autism: The implications of cerebellar abnormalities. In G. Dawson (Ed.), *Autism: Nature, diagnosis, and treatment* (pp. 120—143). New York: Guilford Press.

Courchesne, E., Lincoln, A. J., Kilman, B. A., & Galambos, R. (1985). Event-related brain potential correlates of the processing of novel visual and auditory information in autism. *Journal of Autism and Developmental Disorders, 15,* 55—75.

Cousens, P., Waters, B., Said, J., & Stevens, M. (1988). Cognitive effects of cranial irradiation in leukemia: A survey and meta-analysis. *Journal of Child Psychology and Psychiatry, 29,* 839—852.

Coutts, R. L., Lichstein, L., Bermudez, J. M., Daigle, M., Mann, R., Charbonnel, T. S., Michaud, R., & Williams, C. R. (1987). Treatment assessment of learning disabled children: Is there a role for frequently repeated neuropsychological testing? *Archives of Clinical Neuropsychology, 2,* 237—244.

Craft, A. W., Shaw, D. A., & Cartlidge, N. E. (1972). Head injuries in children. *British Medical Journal, 4,* 200—203.

Craft, S., White, D. A., Park, T. S., & Figiel, G. (1994). Visual attention in children with perinatal brain injury: Asymmetric effects of bilateral lesions. *Journal of Cognitive Neuroscience, 6,* 165—173.

Cravioto, J., & Arrieta, R. (1983). Malnutrition in childhood. In M. D. Rutter (Ed.), *Developmental neuropsychiatry* (pp. 32—51). New York: Guilford Press.

Cregler, L.L., & Mark, H. (1986). Medical complications of cocaine abuse. *New England Journal of Medicine, 315,* 1495—1500.

Cross-Calvert, S., & McMahon, R. J. (1987). Relation of social fantasy play to social competence in preschoolers. *Developmental Psychology, 20,* 797—806.

Crothers, B., & Paine, R. S. (1959). *The natural history of cerebral palsy*. Cambridge, MA: Harvard University Press.

Crowe, R. (1974). An adoption study of antisocial personality. *Archives of General Psychiatry, 31,* 786—791.

Cull, C. A. (1988). Cognitive function and behavior in children. In M. R. Trimble & E. H. Reynolds (Eds.), *Epilepsy: Behavior and cognitive function* (pp. 97—111). New York: Wiley.

Cull, C. A., & Trimble, M. R. (1989). Effects of anticonvulsant medications on cognitive functioning in children. In B. P. Hermann & M. Seidenberg (Eds.), *Childhood epilepsies: Neuropsychological, psychosocial and intervention aspects* (pp. 83—104). New York: Wiley.

Cunningham, A. (1989). Phonemic awareness: The development of early reading competency. *Reading Research Quarterly, 24,* 471—472.

Cunningham, A. E. (1990). Explicit versus implicit instruction in phonemic awareness. *Journal of Experimental Child Psychology, 50,* 429—444.

Curatolo, P., Arpino, C., Stazi, M. A., & Medda, E. (1995). Risk factors for the co-occurrence of partial epilepsy, cerebral palsy, and mental retardation. *Developmental Medicine and Child Neurology, 37,* 776—782.

Dahl, E. K., Cohen, D. J., & Provence, S. (1986). Clinical and multivariate approaches to the nosology of pervasive developmental disorders. *Journal of American Academy of Child Psychiatry, 25,* 170—180.

Dallas, E., Stevenson, J., & McGurk, H. (1993a). Cerebral-palsied children's interactions with siblings: I. Influence of severity of disability, age, and birth order. *Journal of Child Psychology and Psychiatry and Allied Disciplines, 34,* 621—647.

Dallas, E., Stevenson, J., & McGurk, H. (1993b). Cerebral-palsied children's interactions with siblings: II. Interactional structure. *Journal of Child Psychology and Psychiatry and Allied Disciplines, 34,* 649—671.

Dalldorf, J. S., & Schopler, E. (1981). Diagnosis and management of autism. *Comprehensive Therapy, 7,* 67—73.

Dam, M. (1990). Children with epilepsy: The effect of seizures, syndromes, and etiological factors on cognitive functioning. *Epilepsia, 31 (Suppl. 4),* S26—S29.

Daniel, D. G., Zigin, J. R., & Weinberger, D. R. (1992).

Brain imaging in neuropsychiatry. In Yudofsky, S. C., & Hales, R. E. (Eds.), *The American Psychiatric Press textbook of neuropsychiatry* (2nd ed., pp. 165—186). Washington, DC: American Psychiatric Press.

Daugherty, T. K., & Quay, H. C. (1991). Response perseveration and delayed responding in childhood behavior disorders. *Journal of Child Psychology and Psychiatry, 32,* 453—461.

Davidson, B. L., Tarle, S. A., Van Antwerp, M., Gibbs, D. A., Watts, R. W., Kelly, W. N., & Palella, T. D. (1991). Identification of 17 independent mutations responsible for human hypoxanthineguanine phosphoribosyl-transferase (HGPRT) deficiency. *American Journal of Human Genetics, 48,* 951—958.

Davidson, R. J. (1984). Affect, cognition, and hemispheric specialization. In C. E. Izard, J. Kagan. & R. Zajonc (Eds.), *Emotion, cognition, and behavior.* New York: Cambridge University Press.

Davidson, R. J., & Fox, N. A. (1982). Asymmetrical brain activity discriminates between positive and negative affective stimuli in human infants. *Science, 218,* 1235—1237.

Davidson, R. J., & Fox, N. A. (1989). Frontal brain asymmetry predicts infants' response to maternal separation. *Journal of Abnormal Psychology, 98,* 127—131.

Dawson, G. (1983). Lateralized brain dysfunction in autism: Evidence from the Halstead-Reitan Neuropsychological Battery. *Journal of Autism and Developmental Disorders, 13,* 269—286.

Dawson, G., & Adams, A. (1984). Imitative and social responsiveness in autistic children. *Journal of Abnormal Child Psychology, 12,* 209—225.

Dawson, G., & Castelloe, P. (1995). Autism. In C. E. Walker & M. C. Roberts (Eds.), *Handbook of clinical child psychology.* New York: Plenum Press.

Dawson, G., Finley, C., Phillips, S., & Galpert, L. (1986). Hemispheric specialization and the language abilities of autistic children. *Child Development, 57,* 1440—1453.

Dawson, G., Finley, C., Phillips, S., Galpert, L., & Levy, A. (1990). Reduced P3 amplitude of the event-related brain potential: Its relationship to language ability in autism. *Journal of Autism and Developmental Disorders, 18,* 493—504.

Dawson, G., & Galpert, L. (1986). Enhancing language and communication in autistic children. In G. Dawson (Ed.), *Autism: Nature, diagnosis, and treatment* (pp. 282—309). New York: Guilford Press.

Dawson, G., Grofer Klinger, L., Pangiotides, H., Hill, D., Spieker, S., & Frey, K. (1992). Infants of mothers with depressive symptoms: Electrophysiological and behav-

ioral findings related to attachment status. *Development and Psychopathology, 4,* 67—80.

Dawson, G., & Levy, A. (1989). Arousal, attention, and the socioemotional impairment of individuals with autism. In G. Dawson (Ed.), *Autism: Nature, diagnosis, and treatment* (pp. 49—74). New York: Guilford Press.

Dawson, G., Warrenburg, S., & Fuller, P. (1982). Cerebral lateralization in individuals diagnosed as autistic in early childhood. *Brain and Language, 15,* 353—368.

Dawson, J. (1954). Pulmonary tuberous sclerous. *Quarterly Journal of Medicine, 23,* 113—146.

Day, N. L. (1992). The effects of prenatal exposure to alcohol. *Alcohol Health and Research World, 16,* 238—244.

Day, N. L., & Richardson, G. A. (1993). Cocaine use and crack babies: Science, the media, and miscommunication. *Neurotoxicology and Teratology, 15,* 293—294.

Dean, R. S. (1983). Neuropsychological correlates of total seizures with major motor epileptic children. *Clinical Neuropsychology, 5,* 1—3.

Deaton, A. V. (1990). Behavioral change strategies for children and adolescents with traumatic brain injury. In E. D. Biglin (Ed.), *Traumatic brain injury: Mechanisms of damage, assessment, intervention, and outcome* (pp. 231—250). Austin, TX: Pro-Ed.

Decker, S. N., & Vanderberg, S. G. (1985). Colorado twin study of reading disability. In D. B. Gray & J. F. Kavanaugh (Eds.), *Biobehavioral measures of dyslexia* (pp. 123-135). Parkton, MD: York Press.

DeFries, J. C. (1985). Colorado reading project. In D. B. Gray & J. F. Kavanaugh (Eds.), *Biobehavioral measures of dyslexia* (pp. 107—122). Parkton, MD: York Press.

DeFries J. C., & Fulker, D. W. (1985). Multiple regression analysis of twin data. *Behavior Genetics, 15,* 467.

DeFries, J. C., & Fulker, D. W. (1988). Multiple regression analysis of twin data: Etiology of deviant scores versus individual differences. *Acta Geneticae Medicae et Gemellologiae: Twin Research, 37,* 205—216.

DeFries, J. C., & Gillis, J. J. (1991). Etiology of reading deficits in learning disabilities. In J. Obrzut & G. W. Hynd (Eds.), *Neuropsychological foundations of learning disabilities* (pp. 29—47). San Diego, CA: Academic Press.

Degen, R., Degen, H. E., & Roth, C. (1990). Some genetic aspects of idiopathic and symptomatic absence seizures: Waking and sleep EEGs in siblings. *Epilepsia, 31,* 784—790.

Delgado-Escueta, A. V., Bascal, F. E., & Treiman, D. M. (1982). Complex partial seizures in closed-circuit television and EEG: A study of 691 attacks in 79 patients. *Annals of Neurology, 11,* 292—296.

Delis, D. C., Kramer, J. H., Kaplan, E., & Ober, B. A. (1994). *CVLT-C Children's California verbal learning test: Manual.* San Antonio, TX: The Psychological Corporation.

Dencina, P., Kestenbaum, E. J., Farber, S., Kron, L., et al. (1983). Clinical and psychological assessment of children of bipolar probands. *American Journal of Psychiatry, 140,* 548—558.

Denckla, M. B. (1978). Minimal brain dysfunction. In J. S. Chall & A. F. Mirsky (Eds.), *Education and the brain* (pp. 223—268). Chicago: University of Chicago Press.

Denckla, M. B. (1983). The neuropsychology of social-emotional learning disabilities. *Archives of Neurology, 40,* 461—462.

Denckla, M. B. (1994). Measurement of executive function. In R. Lyon (Ed.), *Frames of reference for assessment of learning disabilities* (pp. 117—142). New York: Guilford Press.

Denckla, M. B. (1996). A theory and model of executive functioin: A neuropsychological perspective. In G. R. Lyon & N. A. Krasnegor (Eds.), *Attention, memory, and executive function* (pp. 263—278). Baltimore, MD: Paul Brooks Publishing.

Denckla, M. B., LeMay, M., & Chapman, C. A. (1985). Few CT scan abnormalities found even in neurologically impaired learning disabled children. *Journal of Learning Disabilities, 18,* 132—135.

Dennis, M. (1991). Frontal lobe function in childhood and adolescence: A heuristic for assessing attention regulation, executive control, and the intentional states important for social discourse. *Developmental Neuropsychology, 7,* 327—358.

Dennis, M., Spiegler, B. J., Hoffman, H. J., Hendrick, E. B., Humphreys, R. P., & Becker, L. E. (1991). Brain tumors in children and adolescents–I. Effects on working, associative, and serial-order memory of IQ, age at tumor onset, and age of tumor. *Neuropsychologia, 29,* 813—827.

Dennis, M., Spiegler, B. J., Hoffman, H. J., Hendrick, E. B., Humphreys, R. P., & Becker, L. E., & Chuang, S. (1991). Brain tumors in children–II. The neuroanatomy of deficits in working, associative, and serial-order memory. *Neuropsychologia, 29,* 829—847.

Department of Health and Human Services. (1989). *Intragency Head Injury Task Force report.* Washington, DC: U.S. Government Printing Office.

Deruelle, C., & de Schonen, S. (1991). Hemispheric asymmetry in visual pattern processing in infants. *Brain and Cognition, 16,* 151—179.

de Schonen, S., Gil de Diaz, M., & Mathivet, E. (1986). Hemispheric asymmetry in face processing in infancy. In H. D. Ellis, M. A. Jeeves, F. Newcome, & A. Young (Eds.), *Aspects of face processing.* Dordrecht: Nijhoff.

Deykin, E. Y., & MacMahon, B. (1980). Pregnancy, delivery, and neonatal complications among autistic children. *American Journal of Diseases in Children, 134,* 860—864.

Diamond, C. A., & Matthay, K. K. (1988). Childhood acute lymphoblastic leukemia. *Pediatric Annals, 17,* 156—170.

Diamond, G. W., Kaufman, J., Belman, A. L., Cohen, L., Cohen, H. J., & Rubinstein, A. (1987). Characterization of cognitive functioning in a subgroup of children with congenital HIV infection. *Archives of Clinical Neuropyschology, 2,* 245—256.

Dill, F. J., Hayden, M. R., & McGillivray, B. (1992). *Genetics.* Baltimore, MD: Williams & Wilkins.

Dill, F. J., & McGillivray, B. (1992). Chromosomal anomolies. In F. J. Dill, M. R. Hayden, B. McGillivray (Eds.), *Genetics.* Baltimore, MD: Williams and Wilkins.

Dishion, T. J. & Loeber, R. (1985). Adolescent marijuana and alcohol use: The role of parents and peers revisited. *American Journal of Drug and Alcohol Abuse, 11,* 1—15.

Dixon, S., & Bejar, R. (1989). Echoencephalographica findings in neonates associated with maternal cocaine and methamphetamine use: Incidence and correlates. *Journal of Pediatrics, 117,* 770—778.

Dodge, K. A. (1993). Social-cognitive mechanisms in the development of conduct disorder and depression. In L. W. Porter & M. R. Rosenzweig (Eds.), *Annual review of psychology* (pp. 559—584). Palo Alto, CA: Annual Reviews, Inc.

Dodge, K. A., Price, J. M., Bachorowski, J., & Newman, J. P. (1990). Hostile attributional biases in severely aggressive adolescents. *Journal of Abnormal Psychology, 99,* 385—392.

Dodrill, C. B. (1981). Neuropsychology of epilepsy. In S. B. Filskov & T. J. Boll (Eds.), *Handbook of clinical neuropsychology* (pp. 366—395). New York: Wiley.

Dodrill, C. B., & Wilkus, R. J. (1978). Neuropsychological correlates of anticonvulsants and epileptiform discharges in adult epileptics. *Electroencephalography and Clinical Neurophysiology, 34,* 259—267.

Dodson, W. E. (1993). Epilepsy and IQ. In W. E. Dodson & J. M. Pellock (Eds.), *Pediatric epilepsy: Diagnosis and therapy* (pp. 373—385). New York: Demos Publications.

Doehring, D. G. (1968). *Patterns of impairment in spe-*

cific reading disability: A neuropsychological investigation. Bloomington: Indiana University Press.

Donnellan, A. M., Mirenda, P. L., Mesaros, R. A., & Fassbender, L. L. (1984). Analyzing the communicative functions of aberrant behavior. *Journal of the Association of Persons with Severe Handicaps, 9,* 201—212.

Dooling, E. C., Chi, J. G., & Gilles, F. H. (1983). Telencephalic development: Changing gyral patterns. In F. H. Gilles, A. Leviton, & E. C. Dooling (Eds.), *The developing human brain: Growth and epidemiologic neuropathology* (pp. 94—104). Boston: John Wright.

Dooley, J. M., Camfield, P. R., Camfield, C. S., et al. (1990). Once-daily ethosuximide in the treatment of absence epilepsy. *Pediatric Neurology, 6,* 38—45.

Dorris, M. (1989). *The broken cord.* New York: Harper & Row.

Douglas, V. I. (1983). Attentional and cognitive problems. In M. Rutter (Ed.), *Developmental neuropsychiatry* (pp. 280—329). New York: Guilford Press.

Douglas, V. I., Barr, R. G., O'Neill, M. E., & Britton, B. G. (1988). Dosage effects and individual responsivity to methylphenidate in attention deficit disorder. *Journal of Child Psychology and Psychiatry, 29,* 453—475.

Douglas, V. I., & Peters, K. G. (1979). Toward a clearer definition of the attentional deficit of hyperactive children. In G. Hale & M. Lewis (Eds.), *Attention and the development of cognitive style* (pp. 173—247). New York: Pergamon Press.

Dreifuss, F. E. (1994). Partial seizures (focal and multifocal). In K. Swaiman (Ed.), *Pediatric Neurology* (pp. 509—530). St. Louis, MO: Mosby.

Drotar, D., & Bush, M. (1985). Mental health issues and services. In N. Hobbs and J. M. Perrin (Eds.), *Issues in the care of children with chronic illness* (pp. 514—550). San Francisco: Jossey-Bass.

Duane, D. (1991). Biological foundations of learning disabilities. In J. Obrzut & G. W. Hynd (Eds.), *Neuropsychological foundations of learning disabilities* (pp. 7—27). San Diego, CA: Academic Press.

Duara, R., Kuschch, A., Gross-Glenn, K., Barker, W., Jallad, B. et al. (1991). Neuroanatomic differences between dyslexic and normal readers on Magnetic Resonance Imaging scans. *Archives of Neurology, 48,* 410—416.

Dubovsky, S. L. (1992). Psychopharmacological treatment in neuropsychiatry. In S. C. Yudofsky & R. E. Hales (Eds.), *The American Psychiatric Press textbook of neuropsychiatry* (2nd ed., pp. 663—702). Washington, DC: American Psychiatric Press.

Duffner, P. K., Cohen, M. E., Horowitz, M., et al. (1986). Postoperative chemotherapy and delayed irradiation in children less than 36 months of age with malignant brain tumors. *Annals of Neurology, 20,* 424—430.

Duffy, F. H., Denckla, M. B., McAnulty, G. B., & Holmes, J. A. (1988). Neurophysiological studies in dyslexia. In F. Plum (Ed.), *Language, communication, and the brain* (pp. 105—122). New York: Raven Press.

Duffy, G., Roehler, L., Sivan, E., Rackliff, G., Book, C., Meloth, M., Vavrus, L., Wesselman, R., Putnam, J., & Bassiri, D. (1987). Effects of explaining the reasoning associated with using reading strategies. *Reading Research Quarterly, 22,* 345—368.

Dumas, J. E. (1989). Treating antisocial behavior in children: Child and family approaches. *Clinical Psychology Review, 9,* 197—232.

Dumas, J. E., & Wahler, R. G. (1985). Indiscriminate mothering as a contextual factor in aggressive-oppositional child behavior: "Damned if you do, damned if you don't." *Journal of Abnormal Child Psychology, 13,* 1—17.

DuPaul, G., & Barkley, R. A. (1990). Medication therapy. In R. A. Barkley (Ed.), *Attention deficit-hyperactivity disorder: A handbook for diagnosis and treatment* (pp. 573—612). New York: Guilford Press.

DuPaul, G., Barkley, R. A., & McMurphy, M. B. (1991). Therapeutic effects of medication on ADHD: Implications for school psychologists. *School Psychology Review, 20,* 203—219.

DuPaul, G., & Henningson, P. N. (1993). Peer tutoring effects on the classroom performance of children with attention-deficit hyperactivity disorder. *School Psychology Review, 22,* 134—143.

DuPaul, G., & Stoner, G. (1994). *ADHD in the schools: Assessment and Intervention strategies.* New York: Guilford Press.

DuPaul, G. J., Stoner, G., Tilly, W. D., & Putnam, D. (1991). Interventions for attention problems. In G. Stoner, M. Shinn, & H. Walker (Eds.), *Interventions for achievement and behavior problems* (pp. 685—714). Washington, DC: National Association for School Psychologists.

Dykens, E. M., Hodapp, R. M., Ort, S., et al. (1989). The trajectory of cognitive development in males with fragile X syndrome. *Journal of American Academy of Child and Adolescent Psychiatry, 28,* 422—426.

Dykman, R. A., Ackerman, P. T., Clements, S. D., & Peters, J. E. (1971). Specific learning disabilities: An attentional deficit syndrome. *Progress in Learning Disabilities, 2,* 56—73.

Dykman, R. A., Ackerman, P. T., & McCray, D. S. (1980). Effects of methylphenidate on selective and sustained attention in hyperactive, reading disabled, and presumably attention disordered boys. *Journal of Nervous and Mental Disease, 168,* 745—752.

Edelbrock, C., Costello, A. J., Dulcas, M. K., Kalas, R., & Conover, N. C. (1986). Parent—child agreement on child psychiatric symptoms assessed via structured interview. *Journal of Child Psychology and Psychiatry, 27,* 181—190.

Edmondson, R., & Smith, T. M. (1994). Temperament and behavior of infants prenatally exposed to drugs: Clinical implications for the mother—infant dyad. *Infant Mental Health Journal, 15,* 368—379.

Ehlers, S., & Gillberg, C. (1993). The epidemiology of Asperger syndrome: A total population study. *Journal of Child Psychology and Psychiatry, 34,* 1327—1350.

Eiben, C. G., Anderson, T. P., Lockman, L., Matthews, D. J., Dryja, R., Martin, J., Burrill, C., Gottesman, N., O'Brien, P., & White, L. (1984). Functional outcome of closed head injury in children and young adults. *Archives of Physical Medicine Rehabilitation, 65,* 168—170.

Eimas, P. D. (1975). Distinctive feature codes in the short-term memory of children. *Journal of Experimental Child Psychology, 19,* 241—251.

Eimas, P. D. (1985). Constraints on a model of infant speech perception. In J. Mehler & R. Fox (Eds.), *Neonate cognition: Beyond the blooming buzzing confusion* (pp. 185—197). Hillsdale, NJ: Lawrence Erlbaum Associates.

Eimas, P. D., & Tartter, V. C. (1979). The development of speech perception. In H. W. Reese & L. P. Lipsitt (Eds.), *Advances in child development and behavior* (Vol. 13, pp. 155—193). New York: Academic Press.

Eisen, L., Field, T., Bandstra, E., et al. (1991). Perinatal cocaine effects on neonatal stress behavior and performance on the Brazelton Scale. *Pediatrics, 88,* 477—480.

Eliason, M. J. (1986). Neurofibromatosis: Implications for learning and behavior. *Journal of Developmental and Behavioral Pediatrics, 7,* 175—179.

Ellenberg, J. H., Hirtz, D. G., & Nelson, K. B. (1984). Age at onset of seizures in young children. *Annals of Neurology, 15,* 27—134.

Ellenberg, J. H., & Nelson, K. B. (1984). Cluster of perinatal events identifying infants at high risk for death or disability. *Journal of Pediatrics, 113,* 546—552.

Elliott, C. D. (1990). *Differential ability scales.* San Antonio, TX: Psychological Corporation.

Elliott, K. T., & Coker, D. R. (1991). Crack babies: Here they come, ready or not. *Journal of Instructional Psychology, 18,* 60—64.

Ellis, E. S., & Friend, P. (1991). Adolescents with learning disabilities. In B. Y. L. Wong (Ed.), *Learning about learning disabilities* (pp. 506—563). San Diego, CA: Academic Press.

Ellis, E. S., & Lenz, B. K. (1991). *The development of learning strategy interventions.* Lawrence, KS: Edge Enterprise.

Emery, A. E. H. (1984). Introduction–the principles of genetic counseling. In A. E. H. Emery & L. Pullen (Eds.), *Psychological aspects of genetic counseling.* New York: Academic Press.

Emmett, M., Jeffrey, H., Chandler, D., & Dugdale, A. (1980). Sequelae of *Hemophilus influenzae* meningitis. *Australian Paediatric Journal, 16,* 90—93.

Englert, C. S. (1990). Unraveling the mysteries of writing through strategy instruction. In T. E. Scruggs & B. Y. L. Wong (Eds.), *Intervention research in learning disabilities* (pp. 186—223). New York: Springer-Verlag.

Enoch, J. M., Itzhaki, A., Lakshminarayanan, V., Comerford, J. P., Lieberman, M., & Lowe, T. (1988a). Gilles de la Tourette syndrome: Visual effects. *Neuro-ophthalmology, 5,* 251—257.

Enoch, J. M., Itzhaki, A., Lakshminarayanan, V., Comerford, J. P., Lieberman, M., & Lowe, T. (1988b). Gilles de la Tourette syndrome: A genetic marker? *Neuro-ophthalmology, 8,* 259—265.

Entus, A. K. (1977). Hemispheric asymmetry in processing of dichotically presented speech and nonspeech stimuli by infants. In S. J. Segalowitz & F. A. Gruber (Eds.), *Language development and neurological theory* (pp. 63—73). New York: Academic Press.

Epstein, H. T. (1978). Growth spurts during brain development: Implications for educational policy and practice. In J. S. Chall & A. F. Mirsky (Eds.), *Education and the brain* (pp. 343—370). Chicago: The University of Chicago Press.

Epstein, H. T. (1979). Correlated brain and intelligence development in humans. In M. E. Hahn, C. Jensen, & B. C. Dudek (Eds.), *Development and evolution of brain size: Behavioral implications* (pp. 111—131). New York: Academic Press.

Epstein, M. A., Shaywitz, S. E., Shaywitz, B. A., & Woolston, J. L. (1992). The boundaries of attention deficit disorder. In S. E. Shaywitz & B. A. Shaywitz (Eds.), *Attention deficit disorder comes of age: Toward the twenty-first century* (pp. 197—220). Austin, TX: Pro-Ed.

Epstein, M. H., Kaufman, J. M., & Cullinan, D. (1986). Patterns of maladjustment among the behavior disorders. II. Boys aged 6—11, boys aged 12-18, girls aged 6—11, and girls aged 12—18. *Behavioral Disorders, 10,* 125—135.

Erickson, J. D., & Bjerkedal, T. (1981). Down's syndrome associated with father's age in Norway. *Journal of Medical Genetics, 18,* 22—28.

Ewing-Cobbs, L., & Fletcher, J. M. (1990). Neuropsychological assessment of traumatic brain injury in children. In E. D. Bigler (Ed.), *Traumatic brain injury: Mechanisms of damage, assessment, intervention and outcome* (pp. 107— 128). Austin, TX: Pro-Ed.

Ewing-Cobbs, L., Fletcher, J. M., & Levin, H. S. (1986). Neurobehavioral sequelae following head injury in children: Educational implications. *Journal of Head Trauma Rehabilitation, 1,* 57—65.

Ewing-Cobbs, L., Fletcher, J. M., Levin, H. S., & Landry, S. H. (1985). Language disorders after pediatric head injury. In J. K. Darby (Ed.), *Speech and language evaluation in neurology: Childhood disorders* (pp. 97—112). Orlando, FL: Grune & Stratton.

Ewing-Cobbs, L., Levin, H. S., Eisenberg, H. M., & Fletcher, J. M. (1987). Language functions following head injury in young children and adolescents. *Journal of Clinical and Experimental Neuropsychology, 9,* 575—592.

Exner, J. E. (1993). *The Rorschach: A comprehensive system* (3rd ed., Vol. 1). New York: Wiley.

Eyman, R. K., Grossman, H. J., Chaney, R. H., et al. (1990). The life expectancy of profoundly handicapped people with mental retardation. *New England Journal of Medicine, 323,* 584—587.

Falconer, M. A., & Rushworth, R. G. (1960). Treatment of encephalotrigeminal angiomatosis (Sturge-Weber disease) by hemispherectomy. *Archives of Disease in Children, 35,* 433—447.

Falconer, J., Wada, J. A., Martin, W., et al. (1990). PET, CT, and MR imaging of neuronal migration abnormalities in epileptic patients. *Canadian Journal of Neurological Science, 17,* 35—39.

Falconer, M. A., & Wilson, P. J. E. (1969). Complications related to delayed haemorrhage after hemispherectomy. *Journal of Neurosurgery, 30,* 413—426.

Faraone, S. V., Biederman, J., Keenan, K., & Tsuang, M. T. (1991). Separation of DSM-III attention deficit disorder and conduct disorder: Evidence from a family-genetic study of American child psychiatric patients. *Psychological Medicine, 21,* 109—121.

Farwell, J. R., Dodrill, C. B., & Batzel, L. W. (1985). Neuropsychological abilities of children with epilepsy. *Epilepsia, 26,* 395—400.

Fedio, P., & Mirsky, A. F. (1969). Selective intellectual deficits in children with temporal lobe or centrencephalic epilepsy. *Neuropsychologia, 7,* 287—300.

Fehrenbach, A. M. B., & Peterson, L. (1989). Parental problem solving skills, stress, and dietary compliance in phenylketonuria. *Journal of Consulting and Clinical Psychology, 57,* 237—241.

Feldman, H. M., Janosky, J. E., Scher, M. S., & Wareham, N. L. (1994). Language abilities following prematurity, perventribular brain injury, and cerebral palsy. *Journal of Communication Disorders, 27,* 71—90.

Felton, R. H. (1993). Effects of instruction on the decoding skills of children with phonological-processing problems. *Journal of Learning Disabilities, 26,* 583—589.

Felton, R. H., & Brown, I. S. (1991). Neuropsychological prediction of reading disabilities. In J. E. Obrzut & G. W. Hynd (Eds.), *Neuropsychological foundations of learning disabilities: A handbook of issues, methods, and practice* (pp. 387—410). San Diego, CA: Harcourt Brace Jovanich.

Felton, R. H., & Pepper, P. P. (1995). Early identification of phonological deficits in kindergarten and early elementary children at risk for reading disability. *School Psychology Review, 24,* 405—414.

Fenton, G. W. (1972). Epilepsy and automatism. *British Journal of Hospital Medicine, 7,* 57—64.

Fergusson, D. M., Fergusson, J. E., Horwood, L. J., et al. (1988). A longitudinal study of dentine lead levels, intelligence, school performance, and behavior: Part 3. Dentine lead levels and attention/activity. *Journal of Child Psychology and Psychiatry, 29,* 811—824.

Ferrari, M. (1989). Epilepsy and its effects on the family. In B. P. Hermann & M. Seidenberg (Eds.), *Childhood epilepsies: Neuropsychological, psychosocial and intervention aspects* (pp. 159—172). New York: Wiley.

Filipek, P. A., & Blickman, J. G. (1992). Neurodiagnostic laboratory procedures: Neuroimaging techniques. In R. B. David (Ed.), *Pediatric neurology for the clinician.* Norwalk, CT: Appleton-Lang.

Filipek, P. A., Kennedy, D. N., & Caviness, V. (1992). Neuroimaging in child neuropsychology. In I. Rapin & S. Segalowitz (Eds.), *Child neuropsychology* (pp. 301—329). Amsterdam: Elsevier Science Publishers.

Filipek, P. A., Kennedy, D. N., & Caviness, V., et al. (1989).

MRI-based brain morphometry: Developmental and application to nromal subjects. *Annals of Neurology, 25,* 61—67.

Filipek, P. A., Semrud-Clikeman, M., Steingard, R. J., Renshaw, P. F., Kennedy, D. N., & Biederman, J. (in press). Volumetric MRI analysis comparing attention-deficit hyperactivity disorder and normal controls. *Neurology.*

Finch, A. J., Jr., Lipovsky, J. A., & Casat, C. D. (1989). Anxiety and depression in children and adolescents: Negative affectivity or separate constructs? In P. C. Kendall & D. Watson (Eds.), *Anxiety and depression: Distinctive and overlapping features* (pp. 171—202). San Diego, CA: Academic Press.

Finn, J. D. (1988). School performance of adolescents in juvenile court. *Urban Education, 23,* 150—161.

Finnegan, L. P., Kaltenbach, K., Weiner, S., & Haney, B. (1990). Neonatal cocaine exposure: Assessment of risk scale. *Pediatric Research, 25,* 10A.

Firth, C. D. (1985). Beneath the surface of developmental dyslexia. In K. E. Patterson, J. C. Marshall, & M. Colheart (Eds.), *Surface dyslexia* (pp. xxx). London: Erlbaum.

Firth, C. D., Stevens, M., Johnstone, E. C., et al. (1983). Effects of ECT and depression on various aspects of memory. *Journal of British Psychiatry, 142,* 610—617.

Firth, U. (1993). Autism. *Scientific American, 268,* 108—114.

Fischer, M., Barkley, R. A., Edelbrock, C. S., & Smallish, L. (1990). The adolescent outcome of hyperactive children diagnosed by research criteria: II. Academic, attentional, and neuropsychological status. *Journal of Consulting and Clinical Psychology, 58,* 580—588.

Flament, M. F., Koby, E., Rapoport, J. L., Berg, C. J., Zahn, T., Cox, C., Denckla, M. B., & Lenane, M. (1990). Childhood obsessive-compulsive disorder: A prospective follow-up study. *Journal of Child Psychology and Psychiatry, 31,* 363—380.

Flament, M. F., Whitaker, A., Rapoport, J. L., Davies, M., Berg, C. Z., Kalikow, K., Sceery, W., & Shaffer, D. (1988). Obsessive compulsive disorder in adolescence: An epidemiological study. *Journal of the American Academy of Child and Adolescent Psychiatry, 27,* 764—771.

Fleischner, J. E. (1994). Diagnosis and assessment of mathematics learning disabilities. In G. R. Lyon (Ed.), *Frames of reference for the assessment of learning disabilities: New views on measurement issues* (pp. 441—458). Baltimore, MD: Paul H. Brooks.

Fleiss, J., & Zubin, J. (1969). On the methods and theory of clustering. *Mulitvariate Behavioral Research, 4,* 235—250.

Fletcher, J. M., & Copeland, D. R. (1988). Neurobehavioral effects of central nervous system prophylactic treatment of cancer in children. *Journal of Clinical and Experimental Neuropsychology, 10,* 495—538.

Fletcher, J. M., Levin, H. S., & Landry, S. H. (1984). Behavioral consequences of of cerebral insult in infancy. In C. R. Almli & S. Finger (Eds.), *Early brain damage: Vol. 1. Research orientations and clinical observations* (pp. 189—214). Orlando, FL: Academic Press.

Fletcher, J. M., & Satz, P. (1985). Cluster analysis and the search for learning disability subtypes. In B. P. Rourke (Ed.), *Neuropsychology of learning disabilities: Essentials of subtype analysis* (pp. 40—64). New York: Guilford Press.

Fletcher, J. M., Shaywitz, B. A., & Shaywitz, S. E. (1994). Attention as a process and a disorder. In G. R. Lyon (Ed.), *Frames of reference for the assessment of learning disabilities: New views on measurement issues* (pp. 69—102). Baltimore, MD: Paul H. Brooks.

Fletcher, J., & Taylor, H. (1984). Neuropsychological approaches to children: Toward a developmental neuropsychology. *Journal of Clinical Neuropsychology, 6,* 39—56.

Fletcher, J., Taylor, H., Morris, R., & Satz, P. (1982). Finger recognition skills and reading achievement: A developmental neuropsychological analysis. *Developmental Psychology, 18,* 124—132.

Flor-Henry, P. (1986). Observations, reflections, and speculations on the cerebral determinants of mood and on the bilaterally asymmetrical distributions of the major neurotransmitter systems. *Acta Neurologica Scandinavica, 74,* 75—89.

Fodor, J. (1983). *The modularity of the mind.* Cambridge, MA: MIT Press.

Folstein, S. E., & Rutter, M. (1987). Autism: Familial aggregation and genetic implications. In E. Schopler & G. Mesibov (Eds.), *Neurobiological issues in autism* (pp. 83—105). New York: Plenum Press.

Foorman, B. R. (1995). Research on "the great debate": Code-oriented versus whole language approaches to reading instruction. *School Psychology Review, 24,* 376—392.

Forehand, R., & Long, N. (1986, November). *A long-term follow-up of parent training participants.* Paper presented at the meeting of the Association for Advancement of Behavior Therapy, Chicago.

Forsythe, I., Butler, R., Berg, I., & McGuire, R. (1991). Cognitive impairment in new cases of epilepsy randomly assigned to carbamazepine, phenytoin and sodium valporate. *Developmental Medicine and Child Neurology, 33,* 524—534.

Fox, N. A., & Davidson, R. J. (1986). Taste-elicited changes in facial signs of emotion and the symmetry of brain electrical activity in human newborns. *Neuropsychologia, 24,* 417—422.

Frame, C., Matson, J. L., Sonis, W. A., Fialkov, M. J., & Kazdin, A. E. (1982). Behavioral treatment of depression in a prepubertal child. *Journal of Behavior Therapy and Experimental Psychiatry, 13,* 239—243.

Francis, G., Last, C. G., & Strauss, C. C. (1992). Avoidant disorder and social phobia in childhood and adolescence. *Journal of the American Academy of Child and Adolescent Psychiatry, 31,* 1086—1089.

Frank, D. A., & Zuckerman, B. S. (1993). Children exposed to cocaine prenatally: Pieces of the puzzle. *Neurotoxicology and Teratology, 15,* 298—300.

Frank, D. A., Zuckerman, B. S., Amaro, H., et al. (1988). Cocaine use during pregnancy: Prevalence and correlates. *Pediatrics, 82,* 888—895.

Fraser, D. (1982). *Haemophilus influenzae* in the community and the home. In S. H. Sell & P. F. Wright (Eds.), *Haemophilus influenzae: Epidemiology, immunology, and prevention of disease* (pp. 11—24). New York: Elsevier Biomedical.

Frick, P. J. & Lahey, B. B. (1991). Nature and characteristics of attention deficit hyperactivity disorder. *School Psychology Review, 20,* 163—173.

Frick, P. J., Lahey, B. B., Christ, M. G., & Loeber, R. (1991). History of childhood behavior problems in biological parents of boys with attention-deficit hyperactivity disorder and conduct disorder. *Journal of Clinical Child Psychology, 20,* 445—451.

Frick, P. J., Lahey, B. B., Christ, M. A. G., Loeber, R., & Green, S. (1991). History of childhood behavior problems in biological relatives of boys with attention-deficit hyperactivity disorder and conduct disorder. *Journal of Clinical Child Psychology, 20,* 445—451.

Frick, P. J., Lahey, B. B., Christ, M. G., McBurnett, K., Loeber, R., Stouthamer-Loeber, M., & Green, S. M. (1990). *Concurrent adjustment and history of childhood behavior problems in biological relatives of boys with attention-deficit hyperactivity disorder and conduct disorder.* Paper presented at the Twenty-fourth Annual AABT convention, San Francisco.

Frick, P. J., Lahey, B. B., Loeber, R., Stouthamer-Loeber,
M., Christ, M. A. G., & Hanson, K. (1992). Familial risk factors to oppositional defiant disorder and conduct disorder: Parental psychopathology and maternal parenting. *Journal of Consulting and Clinical Psychology, 60,* 49—55.

Fried, I., Tanguay, P., Boder, E., Doubleday, C., & Greensite, M. (1981). Developmental dyslexia: Electrophysiological evidence of clnical subgroups. *Brain and Language, 12,* 14—22.

Fried, P. A., Watkinson, B., & Willan, A. (1984). Marijuana use during pregnancy and decreased length of gestation. *American Journal of Obstetrics and Gynecology, 150,* 23—27.

Friedman, J. M., & McGillivray, B. (1992). Genetic paradigms in human disease. In J. M. Friedman, F. J. Dill, M. R. Hayden, & B. McGillivray (Eds.), *Genetics.* Baltimore, MD: Williams & Wilkins.

Friedman, E., & Pampiglione, G. (1971). Prognostic implications of EEG findings of hypsarrhythmia in first year of life. *British Medical Journal, 4,* 323—325.

Friedman, A. S., Utada, A. T., Glickman, N. W., & Morrissey, M. R. (1987). Psychopathology as an antecedent to, and as a "consequence" of, substance abuse, in adolescence. *Journal of Drug Education, 17,* 233—244.

Frith, U. (1985). Beneath the surface of developmental dyslexia. In K. E. Patterson, J. C. Marshall, & M. Coltheart (Eds.), *Surface dyslexia.* London: Erlbaum.

Fuld, P. A., & Fisher, P. (1977). Recovery of intellectual ability after closed head injury. *Developmental Medicine and Child Neurology, 19,* 495—502.

Funderbuck, I. J., Carpenter, J., Tanguay, P., Freeman, B. J., & Westlake, J. R. (1983). Parental reproductive problems and gestational hormonal exposure in autistic and schizophrenic children. *Journal of Autism and Developmental Disorders, 13,* 325—332.

Gaddes, W. H. (1980). *Learning disabilities and brain function: A neuropsychological approach.* New York: Springer-Verlag.

Gaddes, W. H., & Crockett, D. J. (1973). *The Spreen-Benton aphasia tests, normative data as a measure of normal language development* (Research Monograph No. 25). Victoria, BC: University of Victoria, Department of Psychology.

Gaddes, W. H., & Edgell, D. (1994). *Learning disabilities and brain function: A neuropsychological approach* (3rd ed.). New York: Springer-Verlag.

Gadow, K. D. (1985). Relative efficacy of pharmacological, behavioral, and combination treatments for enhancing academic performance. *Clinical Psychology Review, 5,* 513—533.

Gadow, K. D., & Poling, A. G. (1988). *Pharmacotherapy and mental retardation.* Boston: College Hill Press.

Gaffney, G., Kuperman, S., Tsai, L., & Hassanein, K. (1987). Midsagittal magnetic resonance imaging in autism. *British Journal of Psychiatry, 151,* 831—833.

Galaburda, A. M. (1989). Ordinary and extraordinary brain development: Anatomical variation in developmental dyslexia. *Annals of Dyslexia, 39,* 67—80.

Galaburda, A. M. (1993). The planum temporale. *Archives of Neurology, 50,* 457.

Galaburda, A. M., Corsiglia, J., Rosen, G. D., & Sherman, G. F. (1987). Planum temporale asymmetry, reappraisal since Geschwind and Levitsky. *Neuropsychologia, 25,* 853—868.

Galaburda, A. M., & Kemper, T. L. (1979). Cyto-architectonic abnormalities in developmental dyslexia: A case study. *Annals of Neurology, 6,* 94—100.

Galaburda, A. M., Sherman, G. F., Aboitiz, F., & Geschwind, N. (1985). Developmental dyslexia: Four consecutive patients with cortical anomalies. *Annals of Neurology, 18,* 222—233.

Gamble, C. M., Mishra, S. P., & Obrzut, J. E. (1988). Construct validity of neuropsychological instrumentation with a learning disabled population. *Archives of Clinical Neuropsychology, 3,* 359—368.

Garcia-Perez, A., Sierransesumaga, L., Narbona-Garcia, L., Calvo-Manuel, F., & Aguirre-Ventalló, M. (1994). Neuropsychological evaluation of children with intracranial tumors: Impact of treatment modalities. *Medical and Pediatric Oncology, 23,* 116—123.

Gardiner, M. F., & Walter, D. O. (1977). Evidence of hemispheric specialization from infant EEG. In S. Harnad, R. Doty, L. Goldstein, J. Jays, & G. Krauthamer (Eds.), *Lateralization in the nervous system* (pp. 481—500). Orlando, FL: Academic Press.

Gardner, E. (1975). *Fundamentals of neurology,* sixth edition. Philadelphia: W. B. Saunders.

Garg, R. K., Kar, A. M., Agrawal, A., Agrawal, I., & Agrawal, V. (1994). Wilson's disease: Unusual clinical and radiological features. *Journal of Association of Physicians of India, 42,* 253—254.

Garreau, B., Barthelemy, C., Demerech, J., Sauvag, D., Num, J. P., Lelord, G., & Calloway, E. (1980). Disturbances in dopamine metabolism in autistic children: Results of clinical tests and urinary dosages of homovanillic acid (HVA). *Acta Psychiatrica Belgica, 80,* 249—265.

Garty, B. Z., Laor, A., & Danon, Y. L. (1994). Neurofibromatosis type 1 in Israel: Survey of young adults. *Journal of Medical Genetics, 31,* 853—857.

Gaskins, I., Downer, M., Anderson, R., Cunningham, P., Gaskins, R., Schommer, M., & the teachers of the Benchmark School. (1988). A metacognitive approach to phonics: Using what we know to decode what you don't. *RASE: Remedial & Special Education, 9,* 36—66.

Gawin, F. (1988). Chronic neuropharmacology of cocaine: Progress in pharmacotherapy. *Journal of Clinical Psychiatry, 49,* 11—16.

Geary, D. C., Jennings, S. M., Schultz, D. D., & Alper, T. G. (1984). The diagnostic accuracy of the Luria-Nebraska Neuropsychological Battery–Children's Revision for 9 to 12 year old learning disabled children. *School Psychology Review, 13,* 375—380.

Geller, B., Cooper, T. B., & McCombs, H. G. (1989). Double-blind, placebo-controlled study of nortriptyline in depressed children using a "fixed plasma level" design. *Psychopharmocology Bulletin, 25,* 101—108.

Gerberich, S. G., Priest, J. D., Boen, J. R., et al. (1983). Concussion incidences and severity of in secondary school varsity football players. *American Journal of Public Health, 73,* 1370—1375.

German, D. F. (1989). *Test of word finding.* National College of Education, Allen, TX: DLM Teaching Resources.

Gershon, E. S. (1990). Genetics. In F. K. Goodwin & K. R. Jamison (Eds.), *Manic-depressive illness* (pp. 373—401). New York: Oxford University Press.

Geschwind, N. & Galaburda, A. M. (1985). Cerebral lateralization: Biological mechanisms, associations and pathology: I. A hypothesis and a program for research. *Archives of Neurology, 42,* 521—552.

Geschwind, N., & Levitsky, W. (1968). Human brain: Left—right asymmetries in temporal speech regions. *Science, 161,* 186—187.

Ghez, C. (1991). Voluntary movement. In E. R. Kandael, J. Schwartz, & T. Jessel (Eds.), *Principles of neural science* (3rd ed., pp. 609—625). New York: Elsevier.

Gilbert, G. M. (1957). A survey of "referral problems" in metropolitan child guidance centers. *Journal of Clinical Psychology, 13,* 37—42.

Gilger, J. W., Pennington, B. F., & DeFries, J. D. (1992). A twin study of the etiology comorbidity: Attention-deficit hypreactivity disorder and dyslexia. *Journal of American Academy of Child and Adolescent Psychiatry, 31,* 343—348.

Gillberg, C., & Gillberg, I. C. (1983). Infantile autism: A total population study of reduced optimality in the pre-, peri-, and neonatal period. *Journal of Autism and Developmental Disorders, 13,* 153—166.

Gillberg, C., & Gillberg, I. C. (1989). Asperger syndrome–some epidemiological considerations: A research note. *Journal of Child Psychology and Psychiatry, 30,* 631—638.

Gilles, F. H. (1983). Telencephalon medium and the olfactocerebral outpouching. In F. H. Filles, A. Leviton, & E. C. Dooling (Eds.), *The developing human brain: Growth and epidemiologic neuropathology* (pp. 59—86). Boston: John Wright.

Gilmore, D. H., Aitken, D. A. (1989). Specific diagnostic techniques. In M. J. Whittle & J. M. Connor (Eds.), *Prenatal diagnosis in obstretic practice.* Boston: Blackwell Scientific Publications.

Gittelman, R., Mannuzza, S., Shenker, R., & Bonagura, N. (1985). Hyperactive boys almost grown up. *Archives of General Psychiatry, 42,* 937—947.

Goetz, E. T., Hall, R. J., & Fetsco, T. G. (1990). Implications of cognitive psychology for assessment of academic skill. In C. R. Reynolds & R. W. Kamphaus (Eds.), *Handbook of psychological assessment of children: Intelligence and achievement* (pp. 477—503). New York: Guilford Press.

Goff, J., Anderson, H., & Cooper, P. (1980). Distractibility and memory deficits in long-term survivors of acute lymphoblastic leukemia. *Developmental and Behavioral Pediatrics, 1,* 158—163.

Goldberg, E., & Costa, L. D. (1981). Hemisphere differences in the acquisition and use of descriptive systems. *Brain and Language, 14,* 144—173.

Golden, C. J. (1978). *Diagnosis and rehabilitation in clinical neuropsychology.* Springfield, IL: Charles C Thomas.

Golden, C. J. (1981). The Luria-Nebraska Children's Battery: Theory and formulation. In G. W. Hynd & J. E. Obrzut (Eds.), *Neuropsychological assessment and the school-age child: Issues and procedures* (pp. 277—302). Orlando, FL: Grune & Stratton.

Golden, C. J. (1987). *Luria-Nebraska Neurolpsychological Battery: Children's Revision: Manual.* Los Angeles: Western Psychological Services.

Golden, C. J. (1989). The Nebraska Neuropsychological Children's Battery. In C. R. Reynolds & E. Fletcher-Janzen (Eds.), *Handbook of clinical child neuropsychology* (pp. 193—204). New York: Plenum Press.

Golden, C. J., & Wilkening, G. (1986). Neuropsychological basis of exceptionality. In R. Brown & C. Reynolds (Eds.), *Psychological perspectives on childhood exceptionality.* New York: Wiley Interscience.

Goldgarber, D., Lerman, M. I., McBride, O. W., Saffiotti, U., & Gajdusek, D. C. (1987). Characterization and chromosomal location of a DNA encoding brain amyloid of Alzehemer's disease. *Science, 235,* 877—880.

Goldman, R. M., Fristoe, M., & Woodcock, R. (1970). *The Goldman-Fristoe-Woodcock Test of Auditory Discrimination.* Circel Pines, MN: American Guidance Service.

Goldstein, F. C., & Levin, H. S. (1990). Epidemiology of traumatic brain injury: Incidence, clinical characteristics, and risk factors. In E. D. Bigler (Ed.), *Traumatic brain injury: Mechanisms of damage, assessment, intervention and outcome* (pp. 51—68). Austin, TX: Pro-Ed.

Gonzalez, N. M., & Campbell, M. (1994). Cocaine babies: Does prenatal exposure to cocaine affect development? *Journal of the American Academy of Child and Adolescent Psychiatry, 33,* 16—19.

Goodman, R., & Stevenson, J. (1989). A twin study of hyperactivity: II. The aetiological role of genes, family relationships and perinatal adversity. *Journal of Child Psychology and Psychiatry, 30,* 691—709.

Goodwin, F. K., & Jamison, K. R. (1990). *Manic-depressive illness.* New York: Oxford University Press.

Goodwin, G. A., Heyser, C. J., Moody, C. A., et al. (1992). A fostering study of the effects of prenatal cocaine exposure: II. Offspring behavioral measures. *Neurotoxicology and Teratology, 14,* 423—432.

Goodyear, P., & Hynd, G. W. (1992). Attention deficit disorder with (ADD/H) and without (ADD/WO) hyperactivity: Behavioral and neuropsychological differentiation. *Journal of Clinical Child Psychology, 21,* 273—305.

Gordon, M. (1987). *The Gordon Diagnostic System.* DeWitt, NY: Gordon System.

Gorenstein, E. E., & Newman, J. P. (1980). Disinhibitory psychopathology: A new perspective and a model for research. *Psychological Review, 87,* 301—315.

Gourley, R. (1990). Educational policies. *Epilepsia, 31 (Suppl. 4),* S59—S60.

Graham, J. M., Bashir, A. S., Stark, R. E., Silbert, A., & Walzer, S. (1988). Oral and written language abilities of XXY boys: Implications for anticipatory guidance. *Pediatrics, 81,* 795—806.

Graham, P. (1979). Epidemiological studies. In H. C. Quay & J. S. Werry (Eds.), *Psychopathological disorder of childhood* (2nd ed., pp. 185—209). New York: Wiley.

Graham, S., & Harris, K. R. (1987). Improving composition skills of inefficient learners with self-instructional strategy training. *Top. Language Disorders, 7,* 66—77.

Graham, S., & Harris, K. R. (1989). A components analysis of cognitive strategy instruction: Effects on learning disabled student's compositions and self-efficacy. *Journal of Educational Psychology, 81,* 353—361.

Grafman, J., Vance, S., Weingartner, H., Salazar, A., & Amin, A. (1986). The effects of lateralized frontal lesions on mood regulation. *Brain, 109,* 1127—1148.

Gray, J. W., & Dean, R. S. (1989). Approaches to the cognitive rehabilitation of children with neuropsychological impairment. In D. R. Reynolds & E. Fletcher-Janzen (Eds.), *Handbook of clinical child neuropsychology* (pp. 397—408). New York: Plenum Press.

Graziano, A., DeGiovanni, I. S., & Garcia, K. (1979). Behavioral treatment of children's fears: A review. *Psychological Bulletin, 86,* 804—830.

Green, S. H., & George, R. H. (1979). Bacterial meningitis. In F. C. Rose (Ed.), *Pediatric neurology* (pp. 569—581). Oxford: Blackwell Scientific.

Green, W. H. (1991). *Child and adolescent clinical psychopharmacology.* Baltimore, MD: Williams & Wilkins.

Greene, T. H., Ernhart, C. B., Ager, J., Sokol, R. J., et al. (1991). Prenatal alcohol exposure and cognitive development in the preschool years. *Neurotoxicology and Teratology, 13,* 57—68.

Greene, T. H., Ernhart, C. B., Martier, S., Sokol, R. et al. (1990). Prenatal alcohol exposure and language development. *Alcoholism: Clinical and Experimental Research, 14,* 937—945.

Greenwood, C. R., Delquardi, J., & Carta, J. J. (1991). *Classwide peer tutoring.* Seattle: Educational Achievement Systems.

Greenwood, C. R., Maheady, L., & Carta, J. J. (1991). Peer tutoring programs in the regular education classroom. In G. Stoner, M. R. Shinn, & H. M. Walker (Eds.), *Interventions for achievement and behavior problems* (pp. 179—200). Silver Spring, MD: National Association of School Psychologists.

Gresham, F., & Elliott, S. (1990). *Social skills rating system.* Circle Pines, MN: American Guidance Service.

Gresham, F. M., & Gansle, K. A. (1992). Misguided assumptions of DSM-III-R: Impilcations for school psychologists. *School Psychology Quarterly, 7,* 79—95.

Gresham, F. M., & Nagle, R. J. (1980). Social skill training with children: Responsiveness to modeling and coaching as a function of peer orientation. *Journal of*

Consulting and Clinical Psychology, 84, 718—729.

Grether, J. K., Cummins, S. K., & Nelson, K. B. (1992). The California Cerebral Palsy Project. *Paediatric Perinatal Epidemiology, 6,* 339—351.

Griffith, D., Azuma, S. D., & Chasnoff, I. J. (1994).Three-year outcome of children exposed prenatally to drugs. *Journal of the American Academy of Child and Adolescent Psychiatry, 33,* 20—27.

Grumbach, M. M., & Conte, F. A. (1985). Disorders of sexual differentiation. In J. D. Wilson & D. W. Foster (Eds.), *Williams textbook of endocrinology* (7th ed., pp. 312—401. Philadelphia: W. B. Saunders.

Gualteri, T., Evans, R. W., & Patterson, D. R. (1987). The medical treatment of autistic people: Problems and side effects. In E. Schopler & G. Mesibov (Eds.), *Neurobiological issues in autism.* New York: Plenum Press.

Gustavson, J. L., Golden, C. J., Wilkening, G. N., Hermann, B. P., Plaisted, J. R., & MacInnes, W. D. (1981, August). *The Luria-Nebraska Neuropsychological Battery–Children's Revision: Validation with brain damaged and normal children.* Paper presented at the meeting of the American Psychological Association, Los Angeles, California.

Haak, R. A. (1989). Establishing neuropsychology in a school setting. In C. R. Reynolds & E. Janzen (Eds.), *Handbook of clinical child neuropsychology* (pp. 489—502). New York: Plenum Press.

Hadeed, A. J., & Siegel, S. R. (1989). Maternal cocaine use during pregnancy: Effect on the newborn infant. *Pediatrics, 84,* 205—210.

Hagberg, B., Hagberg, G., & Olow, I. (1975). The changing panorama of cerebral palsy in Sweden 1954—1970: II. Analysis of the various syndromes. *Acta Paediatrica Scandinavia, 73,* 433—438.

Hagberg, B., Hagberg, G., & Zetterstrom, R. (1989). Decreasing perinatal mortality–increase in cerebral palsy morbidity? *Acta Paediatrica Scandinavia, 78,* 664—670.

Hagerman, R. J., Murphy, M. A., & Wittenberger, M. D. (1988). A controlled trial of stimulant medication in children with the fragile X syndrome. *American Journal of Medical Genetics, 30,* 377—392.

Hahn, W. K. (1987). Cerebral lateralization of function. From infancy through childhood. *Psychological Bulletin, 101,* 376—392.

Halgren, E. (1990). Insights from evoked potentials into the neuropsychological mechanisms of reading. In A. B. Scheibel & A. F. Wechsler (Eds.), *Neurobiology of higher cognitive function* (pp. 103—150). New York: Guilford Press.

Hamilton, M. (1967). Development of a rating scale for primary depressive illness. *British Journal of Social and Clinical Psychology, 6,* 278—296.

Hammen, C. (1990). Cognitive approaches to depression in children: Current findings and new directions. In B. B. Lahey & A. E. Kazdin (Eds.), *Advances in clinical child psychology* (Vol. 13, pp. 173—202). New York: Plenum Press.

Hammer, M. (1977). *Lateral responses to speech and noise stimuli.* Unpublished Ph.D. dissertation, New York University. *Dissertation Abstracts International, 38*(2), 1439-B.

Hanf, E., & Kling, J. (1973). *Facilitating parent-child interactions: A two-stage training model.* Portland: University of Oregon Medical School.

Hankin, J. R. (1994). FAS prevention strategies: Passive and active measures. *Alcohol Health and Research World, 18,* 62—66.

Hanley, W. B., Linsoa, L., Davidson, W., & Moes, C. A. (1970). Malnutrition with early treatment of phenylketonuria. *Pediatric Research, 4,* 18—27.

Hanson, J. W., Streissguth, A. P., & Smith, D. W. (1978). The effects of moderate alcohol consumption during pregnancy on fetal growth and morphogenesis. *Journal of Pediatrics, 92,* 457—460.

Harden, A., Glaser, G. H., & Pampiglione, G. (1968). Electroencephalographic and plasma changes after cardiac surgery in children. *British Medical Journal, 4,* 210—213.

Hare, R. D., & Jutal, J. (1988). Psychopathy and cerebral symmetry in semantic processing. *Personality and Individual Differences, 9,* 329—337.

Harris, R. (1983). Clinical neurophysiology in paediatric neurology. In E. M. Brett (Ed.), *Paediatric neurology* (pp. 582—600). Edinburgh, Scotland: Churchill Livingstone.

Hart, E. A., Lahey, B. B., Loeber, R., & Hanson, K. (1994). Criterion validity of informants in the diagnosis of disruptive behavior disorders in children: A preliminary study. *Journal of Consulting and Clinical Psychology, 62,* 410—414.

Harter, M. R., & Anllo-Vento, L. (1988). Separate brain potential characteristics in children with reading disability and attention deficit disorder: Color and letter relevance effects. *Brain and Cognition, 7,* 115—140.

Hartlage, L. C., & Hartlage, P. L. (1989). Neuropsychological aspects of epilepsy: Introduction and overview. In C. R. Reynolds & E. Fletcher-Janzen (Eds.), *Handbook of clinical child neuropsychology* (pp. 409—418). New York: Plenum Press.

Hartlage, L. C., & Telzrow, C. F. (1984). Neuropsychological aspects of childhood epilepsy. In R. Tarter & G. Goldstein (Eds.), *Advances in clinical neuropsychology* (pp. 159—179). New York: Plenum Press.

Hashimoto, T., Tayama, M., Miyazaki, M., Fujii, E., Harada, M., Miyoshi, H., Tanouchi, M., & Kuroda, Y. (1995). Developmental brain changes investigated with proton magnetic resonance spectroscopy. *Developmental Medicine and Child Neurology, 37,* 398—405.

Haslam, R. H., Dalby, J. T., Johns, R. D., & Rademaker, A. W. (1981). Cerebral asymmetry in developmental dyslexia. *Archives of Neurology (Chicago), 38,* 679—682.

Hauser, S. L., DeLong, G. R., & Rosman, N. P. (1975). Pneumographic findings in the infantile autism syndrome: A correlation with temporal lobe disease. *Brain, 98,* 677—688.

Hawley, T. L., Halle, T. G., Drasin, R. E., & Thomas, N. G. (1995). Children of addicted mothers: Effects of the "crack epidemic" on the caregiving environment and the development of preschoolers. *American Journal of Orthopsychiatry, 65,* 364—379.

Hayden, A., & Harding, N. (1976). Early intervention for high risk infants and young children: Programs for Down's syndrome children. In T. D. Tjossem (Ed.), *Intervention strategies for high risk infants and young children* (pp. 573—607). Baltimore: University Park Press.

Hayne, H., Hess, M., & Campbell, B. A. (1992). The effect of prenatal alcohol exposure on attention in the rat. *Neurotoxicology and Teratology, 14,* 393—398.

Haynes, J. P., & Bensch, M. (1981). The P > V sign of the WISC-R and recidivism in delinquents. *Journal of Consulting and Clinical Psychology, 49,* 480—481.

Healy, J. M., Halperin, J. M., Newcorn, J., Wolf., L. E., Pascualvaca, D. M., O'Brien, J., Morganstein, A., & Young, J. G. (1987). *The factor structure of ADD items in DSM-III and DSM III-R.* Paper presented at the annual meeting of the American Academy of Child and Adolescent Psychiatry, Los Angeles.

Heaton, R. K. (1981). *A manual for the Wisconsin card sorting test.* Odessa, FL: Psychological Assessment Resources.

Heaton, R. K., Badde, L. E., & Johnson, K. L. (1978). Neuropsychological test results associated with psychiatric disorders in adults. *Psychological Bulletin, 85,* 141—162.

Heaton, R. K., Chelune, G. J., Talley, J. L., Kay, G. G., &

Curtiss, G. (1993). *Wisconsin card sorting test manual.* Odessa, FL: Psychological Assessment Resources.

Heaton, R. K., Grant, I., Anthony, W. Z., & Lehman, R. A. W. (1981). A comparison of clinical and automated interpretation of the Halstead-Reitan Battery. *Journal of Clinical Neuropsychology, 3,* 121—141.

Heffner, R. R. (1995). Pathology of nervous system tumors. In W. G. Bradley, R. B. Daroff, G. M. Fenichel, & C. D. Marsden (Eds.), *Neurology in clinical practice* (pp. 1089—1090). Boston: Butterworth-Heinemann.

Heilman, K. M., & Van Den Abell, T. (1980). Right hemisphere dominance for attention: The mechanisms underlying hemispheric asymmetries of inattention. *Neurology, 30,* 327—330.

Heilman, K. M., Voeller, K. K. S., Nadeau, S. E. (1991). A possible pathophysiological substrate of attention deficit hyperactivity disorder. *Journal of Child Neurology, 6 (Suppl.),* S74—S79.

Heimer, L. (1983). *The human brain and spinal cord.* New York: Springer-Verlag.

Heins, E. D., Lloyd, J. W., & Hallahan, D. P. (1986). Cued and noncued self-recording to task. *Behavior Modification, 10,* 235—254.

Heller, K. W., Alberto, P. A., Forney, P. E., & Schwartzman, M. N. (1996). *Understanding physical, sensory, and health impairments: Characteristics and educational implications.* Pacific Grove, CA: Brooks/Cole.

Heller, W. (1990). The neuropsychology of emotion: Developmental patterns and implications for psychopathology. In N. Stein, B. Leventhal, & T. Trabasso (Eds.), *Psychological and biological approaches to emotion* (pp. 167—214). Hillsdale, NJ: Lawrence Erlbaum Associates.

Hepper, P. G., Shadidullah, S., & White, R. (1991). Handedness in the human fetus. *Neuropsychologia, 29,* 1107—1112.

Herbert, M. (1987). *Conduct disorders of childhood and adolescence: A social learning perspective.* Chichester, UK: Wiley.

Herkert, E. E., Wald, A., & Romero, O. (1972). Tuberous sclerosis and schizophrenia. *Diseases of the Nervous System, 33,* 439—445.

Hermann, B. P., Whitman, S., & Dell, J. (1988). Correlates of behaviour problems and social competence in children with epilepsy, aged 6—11. In B. P. Hermann & M. Seidenberg (Eds.), *Childhood epilepsies: Neuropsychological, psychosocial and intervention aspects* (pp. 143—158). New York: Wiley.

Heyser, C. J., Spear, N. E., & Spear, L. P. (1992). Effects of prenatal exposure to cocaine on conditional discrimination learning in adult rats. *Behavioral Neuroscience, 106,* 837—845.

Hier, D. B., LeMay, M., Rosenberger, P. B., & Perlo, V. P. (1978). Developmental dyslexia: Evidence for a subgroup with a reversal of cerebral asymmetry. *Archives of Neurology, 35,* 90—92.

Hinshaw, S. P. (1991). Stimulant medication and the treatment of aggression in children with attention deficits. *Journal of Clinical Child Psychology, 20,* 301—312.

Hinshaw, S. P., Henker, B., Whalen, C. K., Erhardt, D., & Dunnington, R. E. (1989). Aggressive, prosocial, and nonsocial behavior in hyperactive boys: Dose effects of methylphenidate in naturalistic settings. *Journal of Consulting and Clinical Psychology, 57,* 636—643.

Hinton, G. E. (1993). How neural networks learn from experience. In *Mind and brain: Readings from the Scientific American.* New York: W. H. Freeman.

Ho, D. D., & Hirsch, M. S. (1985). Acute viral encephalitis. *Medical Clinics of North America, 69,* 415—429.

Hoare, P. (1984). The development of psychiatric disorder among school children with epilepsy. *Developmental Medicine and Child Neurology, 26,* 3—13.

Hoare, P., & Kerley, S. (1991). Psychosocial adjustment of children with chronic epilepsy and their families. *Developmental Medicine and Child Neurology, 33,* 201—215.

Hoare, P., & Russell, M. (1995). The quality of life of children with chronic epilepsy and their families: Preliminary findings with a new assessment measure. *Developmental Medicine and Child Neurology, 37,* 689—696.

Hoffman, R. S., Henry, G. C., Howland, M. A., et al. (1992). Association between life threatening cocaine toxicity and pharmacholinesterase activity. *Annuals of Emergency Medicine, 21,* 247—253.

Hoffman, W., & Prior, M. (1982). Neuropsychological dimensions of autism in children: A test of the hemispheric hypothesis. *Journal of Clinical Psychology, 4,* 27—41.

Hofman, K., Harris, E. L., Bryan, R. N., & Denckla, M. B. (1994). Neurofibromatosis type 1: The cognitive phenotype. *Journal of Pediatrics, 124,* S1—S8.

Holcomb, P. J., Ackerman, P. T., & Dykman, R. A. (1985). Cognitive event-related brain potentials in children with attention and reading deficits. *Psychophysiology, 22,* 656-667.

Hollingsworth, C., Tanguay, P., Grossman, L., & Pabst, P. (1980). Long-term outcome of obsessive-compulsive disorder in childhood. Journal of the *American Academy of Child Psychiatry, 19,* 134—144.

Holm, V. A., & Varley, C. K. (1989). Pharmacological treatment of autistic children. In G. Dawson (Ed.), *Autism: Nature, diagnosis, and treatment* (pp. 386—404). New York: Guilford Press.

Hooper, S. R., & Boyd, T. A. (1986). Neurodevelopmental disorders. In J. E. Obrzut & G. W. Hynd (Eds.), *Child neuropsychology (Volume 2): Clinical practice* (pp. 15—58). Orlando, FL: Academic Press.

Horn, C. S., Ater, S. B., & Hurst, D. L. (1986). Carbamazepine-exacerbated epilepsy in children and adolescents. *Pediatric Neurology, 2,* 340—347.

Horn, W. F., & Ialongo, N. (1988). Multimodal treatment of attention deficit hyperactivity disorder in children. In H. E. Fitzgerald, B. M. Lester, & M. W. Yogman (Eds.), *Theory and research in behavioral pediatrics* (Vol. 4, pp. 175—220). New York: Plenum Press.

Horton, A. M., Jr. (1979). Behavioral neuropsychology: Rationale and research. *Clinical Neuropsychology, 1,* 20—23.

Horton, A. M., Jr., & Puente, A. E. (1986). Behavioral neuropsychology in children. In J. E. Obrzut & G. W. Hynd (Eds.), *Child neuropsychology: Vol. 2. Clinical practice* (pp. 299—316). Orlando, FL: Academic Press.

Howard, E. M., & Henderson, S. E. (1989). Perceptual problems in cerebral-palsied children: A real-world example. *Human Movement Science, 8,* 141—160.

Howard, J. (1989). Long-term effects of infants exposed prenatally to drugs. In K. V. Sproat (Ed.), *Special currents: Cocaine babies* (pp. 1—2). Columbus, OH: Ross Laboratories.

Howieson, D. B., & Lezak, M. D. (1992). The neuropsychological evaluation. In S. C. Yudofsky & R. E. Hales (Eds.), *The American Psychiatric Press textbook of neuropsychiatry* (2nd ed., pp. 127-150). Washington, DC: American Psychiatric Press.

Hsu, L. Y. F. (1986). Prenatal diagnosis of chromosomal abnormalities. In A. Milunsky (Ed.), *Genetic disorders and the fetus* (2nd ed.). New York: Plenum Press.

Hudspeth, W. J., & Pribram, K. H. (1990). Stages of brain and cognitive maturation. *Journal of Educational Psychology, 82,* 881—884.

Hugdahl, K., & Carlsson, G. (1994). Dichotic listening and focused attention in children with hemiplegic cerebral palsy. *Journal of Clinical and Experimental Neuropsychology, 16,* 84—92.

Humphreys, P., Kaufman, W. E., & Galaburda, A. M. (1990). Developmental dyslexia in women: Neuropathological findings in three patients. *Annals of Neurology, 28,* 727—738.

Hunt, A. (1983). Tuberous sclerosis: A survey of 97 cases: III. Family aspects. *Developmental Medicine and Child Neurology, 25,* 353—357.

Hunt, R. D., Brunstetter, R., & Silver, L. (1987). Attention deficit disorder: Diagnosis, etiology and neurochemistry. In J. Noshpitz (Ed.), *Basic handbook of child psychiatry* (pp. 337—354, 483—494). New York: Basic Books.

Hunt, R. D., Lau, S., & Ryu, J. (1991). Alternative therapies for ADHD. In L. Greenhill (Ed.), *Ritalin theory and practice* (pp. 75—95). Marryann Leibert Press.

Hunt, R. D., Mandl, L., Lau, S., & Hughes, M. (1991). Neuro- biological theories of ADHD and Ritalin. In L. Greenhill (Ed.), *Ritalin theory and practice* (pp. 267—287). Marryann Leibert Press.

Hutchings, B., & Medwick, S. A. (1975). Registered criminality in the adoptive and biological parents of registered male criminal adoptees. *Proceedings of the Annual Meeting of the American Psychological Association, 62,* 105—106.

Hutchings, D. E. (1993). Response to Commentaries. *Neurotoxicology and Teratology, 15,* 311—312.

Huttenlocher, P. R. (1979). Synaptic density in human frontal cortex: Developmental changes and effects of aging. *Brain Research, 163,* 195—205.

Huttenlocher, P. R., & Hapke, R. J. (1990). A follow-up study of intractable seizures in childhood. *Annals of Neurology, 28,* 699—705.

Hynd, G. W., (1988). *Neuropsychological assessment in clinical child psychology.* Beverly Hills, CA: Sage Publications.

Hynd, G. W. (1992a). Misguided or simply misinformed? Comment on Gresham and Gansle's vitriolic diatribe regarding DSM. *School Psychology Quarterly, 7,* 100—103.

Hynd, G. W. (1992b). *Neuropsychological assessment in clinical child psychology.* Newbury Park, CA: Sage Publications.

Hynd, G. W., & Cohen, M. (1983). *Dylexia: Neuropscyhological theory, research, and clinical differentiation.* Orlando, FL: Grune & Stratton.

Hynd, G. W., Hall, J., Novey, E. S., et al. (1995). Dyslexia and corpus callosum morphology. *Archives of Neurology, 52,* 32—38.

Hynd, G. W., Hern, K. L., Novey, E. S., Eliopulos, D., Marshall, R., Gonzalez, J. J., & Voeller, K. K. (1993). Attention deficit hyperactivity disorder and asymmetry of the caudate nucleus. *Journal of Child Neurology, 8,* 339—347.

Hynd, G. W., Hern, K. L., Voeller, K. K., & Marshall, R. M. (1991). Neurobiological basis of attention-deficit hyperactivity disorder (ADHD). *School Psychology Review, 20,* 174—186.

Hynd, G. W., Lorys, A., Semrud-Clikeman, M., Nieves, N., Huettner, M., & Lahey, B. (1991). Attention deficit disorder without hyperactivity: A distinct behavioral and neurocognitive syndrome. *Journal of Child Neurology, 69,* S35—S41.

Hynd, G. W., Marshall, R. M., & Semrud-Clikeman, M. (1991). Developmental dyslexia, neurolinguistic theory deviations in brain morphology. *Reading and Writing: An Interdisciplinary Journal, 3,* 345—362.

Hynd, G. W., Nieves, N., Connor, R. T., Stone, P., Town, P., Becker, M. G., Lahey, B. B., & Lorys-Vernon, A. (1988). Attention deficit disorder with and without hyperactivity: Reaction time and speed of cognitive processing. *Journal of Learning Disabilities, 20,* 19—36.

Hynd, G. W., & Obrzut, J. E. (Eds.). (1981). *Neuropsychological assessment and the school-age child: Issues and procedures.* New York: Grune & Stratton.

Hynd, G. W., & Obrzut, J. E. (Eds.). (1986). *Child neuropsychology: Vol. 2. Clinical practice.* Orlando, FL: Academic Press.

Hynd, G. W., Quackenbush, R., & Obrzut, J. E. (1980). Training school psychologists in neuropsychological assessment: Current practices and trends. *Journal of School Psychology, 18,* 148—153.

Hynd, G. W., & Semrud-Clikeman, M. (1989). Dyslexia and brain morphology. *Psychological Bulletin, 106,* 447—482.

Hynd, G. W., & Semrud-Clikeman, M. (1992). Neuropsychological batteries in assessment of intelligence. In A. S. Kaufman (Ed.), *Adolescent and adult intelligence testing* (pp. 638—695). New York: Guilford Press.

Hynd, G. W., Semrud-Clikeman, M., Lorys, A. R., Novey, E. S., & Eliopulos, D. (1990). Brain morphology in developmental dyslexia and attention deficit disorder/hyperactivity. *Archives of Neurology, 47,* 919—926.

Hynd, G. W., Semrud-Clikeman, M., Lorys, A. R., Novey, E. S., Eliopulos, D., & Lyytinen, H. (1991). Corpus callosum morphology in attention deficit-hyperactivity disorder: Morphometric analysis of MRI. *Journal of Learning Disabilities, 24,* 141—146.

Hynd, G. W., Semrud-Clikeman, M., Lorys, A. R., Novey, E. S., Eliopulos, D., & Lyytinen, H. (1992). Corpus callosum morphology in attention-deficit hyperactivity disorder (ADHD): Morphometric analysis of MRI. In S. E. Shaywitz & B. A. Shaywitz (Eds.), *Attention*

deficit disorder comes of age: Toward the twenty first century (pp. 245—260). Austin, TX: Pro-Ed.

Hynd, G. W., Semrud-Clikeman, M., & Lyytinen, H. (1991). Brain imaging in learning disabilities. In J. E. Obrzut & G. W. Hynd (Eds.), *Neuropsychological foundations of learning disabilities: A handbook of issues, methods, and practice* (pp. 475—518). San Diego, CA: Academic Press.

Hynd, G. W., Voeller, K. K. S., Hern, K. & Marshall, R. (1991). Neurological basis of attention deficit hyperactivity disorder (ADHD). *School Psychology Review, 20,* 174—186.

Hynd, G. W., & Willis, W. G. (1988). *Pediatric neuropsychology.* Orlando, FL: Grune & Stratton.

Individuals with Disabilities Education Act. *Public Law 101-476,* Section 602(a)(19), (October, 1990). Washington, DC: U.S. Government Printing Office.

Ingram, D. (1975). Motor asymmetries in young children. *Neuropsychologia, 13,* 95—102.

Ingram, T. T. S. (1955). A study of cerebral palsy in the childhood population of Edinburgh. *Archives of Disabled Children, 117,* 395.

Ingram, T. T. S. (1964). *Paediatric aspects of cerebral palsy.* Edinburgh: Churchill-Livingston.

Ingram, T. T. S., Mason, A. W., & Blackburn, I. (1970). A retrospective study of 82 children with reading disability. *Developmental Medicine and Child Neurology, 12,* 271—281.

Isaacson, R. L. (1975). The myth of recovery from early brain damage. In N. R. Ellis (Ed.), *Aberrant development in infancy* (pp. 1—26). Hillsdale, NJ: Lawrence Erlbaum Associates.

Isaacson, R. L. (1976). Recovery "?" from early brain damage. In T. D. Tjossem (Ed.), *Intervention strategies for high risk infants and young children.* Baltimore, MD: University Park Press.

Isaacson, R. L., & Spear, L. P. (1984). Interpretation of early brain damage. In S. Finger & C. R. Almli (Eds.), *Early brain damage: Vol. 2. Neurobiology and behavior* (pp. 73—98). Orlando, FL: Academic Press.

Iversen, S., & Tunmer, W. E., (1993). Phonological processing skills and the reading recovery program. *Journal of Educational Psychology, 85,* 112—126.

Izard, C. E., Kagan, J., & Zajonc, R. B. (1984). Introduction. In C. E. Izard, J. Kagan, & R. B. Zajonc (Eds.), *Emotions, cognitions, and behavior* (pp. 1—14). New York: Cambridge University Press.

Jabbari, B., Maitland, C. G., Morris, L. M., Morales, J., & Gunderson, C. H. (1985). The value of visual evoked potential as a screening test in neurofibromatosis. *Archives of Neurology, 42,* 1072—1074.

Jack, C. R. (1994). MRI-based hippocampal volume measurements in epilespy. *Epilepsia, 35 (supp.),* S21—29.

Jack, C. R., Thompson, R. M., Butts, F. K., Sharbrough, F. W., Kelly, P. J., Hanson, D. P., Rieder, S. J., Ehman, R. L., Handiandreou, N. J., & Cascino, G. D. (1994). Sensory-motor cortex: Correlation of presurgical mapping with functional MR imaging and invasive cortical mapping. *Radiology, 190,* 85—92.

Jacobson, J. L., & Jacobson, S. W. (1994). Prenatal alcohol exposure and neurobehavioral development: Where is the threshold? *Alcohol Health and Research World, 18,* 30—36.

Jacobson, M. (1991). *Developmental neurobiology* (3rd ed.). New York: Plenum Press.

Jadavji, T., Biggar, W., Gold, R., & Prober, C. (1986). Sequelae of acute bacterial meningitis in children treated for seven days. *Pediatrics, 78,* 21—25.

Jankovic, J., Caskey, T. C., Stout, J. T., et al. (1988). Lesch-Nyhan syndrome: A study of motor behavior and cerebrospinal fluid neurotransmitters. *Annals of Neurology, 23,* 466—469.

Jarey, M. L., & Stewart, M. A. (1985). Psychiatric disorder in the parents of adopted children with aggressive conduct disorder. *Neuropsychobiology, 13,* 7—11.

Jasper, H. H. (1958). The ten twenty system of the international federation. *Electroencephalography and Clinical Neurophysiology, 10,* 371—375.

Jernigan, T. L., Hesselink, J. R., Sowell, E., & Tallal, P. A. (1991). Cerebral structure on magentic resonance imaging in language- and learning-impaired children. *Archives of Neurology, 48,* 539—545.

Jessel, T. M. (1991). Reactions of neurons to injury. In E. R. Kandel, J. H. Schwartz, & T. M. Jessel (Eds.), *Principles of neural science* (3rd ed., pp. 258—269). New York: Elsevier.

Johnston, C., & Pelham, W. E. (1986). Teacher ratings predict peer ratings and aggression at three-year follow-up in boys with attention deficit hyperactivity disorder. *Journal of Consulting and Clinical Psychology, 54,* 571—572.

Jones, K. L., & Smith, D. W. (1973). Recognition of the Fetal Alcohol Syndrome in early infancy. *Lancet, 2,* 999—1001.

Joshi, P. T., Cappozzoli, J. A., & Coyle, J. T. (1988). Low-dose neuroleptic therapy for children with child-onset pervasive developmental disorder. *American Journal of Psychiatry, 145,* 335—338.

Juul-Jensen, P., & Foldspang, A. (1983). Natural history of epileptic seizures. *Epilepsia, 24,* 297—303.

Kagan, J., Arcus, D., Snidman, N., & Feng-Wang-Yu (1994). Reactivity in infants. *Developmental Psychology, 30,* 342—345.

Kahn, J. S., Kehle, T. J., Jenson, W. R., & Clark, E. (1990). Comparison of cognitive-behavioral, relaxation, and self modeling interventions for depression among middle-school students. *School Psychology Review, 19,* 196—211.

Kalsbeek, W. D., McLaurin, R. L., Harris, B. S., & Miller, J. D. (1980). The national head and spinal cord injury survey: Major findings. *Journal of Neurosurgery and Psychiatry, 40,* 291—298.

Kamphaus, R., Kaufman, A. S., & Harrison, P. L. (1990). Clinical assessment practice with the kaufman Assessment Battery for Children (K-ABC). In C. R. Reynolds & R. W. Kamphaus (Eds.), *Handbook of psychological and educational assessment of children: Intelligence and achievement* (pp. 259—276). New York: Guilford Press.

Kandel, E. R. (1985). Cellular mechanisms of learning and the biological basis of individuality. In E. R. Kandel & J. H. Schwartz (Eds.), *Principles of neural science* (2nd ed., pp. 816—833). New York: American Elsevier.

Kandel, E. R. (1993a). Brain and behavior. In E. R. Kandel, J. H. Schwartz, & T. M. Jessell (Eds.), *Principles of neural behavior* (4th ed., pp. 1—12). New York: Elsevier.

Kandel, E. R. (1993b). Nerve cell and behavior. In E. R. Kandel, J. H. Schwartz, & T. M. Jessell (Eds.), *Principles of neural behavior* (4rh ed., pp. 18—33). New York: Elsevier

Kandel, E. R., & Jessell, T. M. (1991). Anatomical substrates for somatic sensation. In E. R. Kandel, J. H., Schwartz & T. M.Jessel (Eds.), *Principles of neural science* (3rd ed., pp. 367—384). New York: Elsevier.

Kandel, E. R., & Schwartz, J. H. (1985). *Principles of neural science* (2nd ed.). New York: Elsevier.

Kandel, E. R., Schwartz, J. H., & Jessell. T. M. (1993). *Principles of neural behavior.* New York: Elsevier

Kaplan, E. (1988). A process approach to neuropsychological assessment. In T. Boll & B. K. Bryant (Eds.), *Clinical neuropsychology and brain function* (pp. 125—167). Washington, DC: American Psychological Association.

Kaplan, E., Goodglass, H., & Weintraub, S. (1978). *Boston naming test.* Boston: E. Kaplan & H. Goodglass.

Karras, D., Newlin, D. B., Franzen, M. D., Golden, C. J., Wilkensing, G. N., Rothermel, R. D., & Tramontana,

M. J. (1987). Development of factor scales for the Luria-Nebraska Neuropsychological Battery-Children's Revision. *Journal of Clinical Child Psychology, 16,* 19—28.

Kashani, J. H., Rosenberg, T. K., & Reid, J. C. (1989). Developmental perspectives in child and adolescent depressive symptoms in a community sample. *American Journal of Psychiatry, 146,* 871—875.

Kaslow, N., Rehm, L., & Siegel, A. (1984). Social-cognitive and cognitive correlates of depression in children. *Journal of Abnormal Child Psychology, 12,* 605—620.

Kaufman, A. S., & Kaufman, N. C. (1983). *Interpretative manual for the Kaufman Assessment Battery for Children.* Circle Pines, MN: American Guidance Service.

Kaufman, A. S., & Kaufman, N. C. (1991). *Kaufman Brief Survey of Early Academic and Language Skills.* Circle Pines, MN: American Guidance Services.

Kavale, K. (1990). Effectiveness of special education. In T. B. Gutkins & C. R. Reynolds (Eds.), *The handbook of school psychology* (2nd ed., pp. 868—898). New York, NY: Wiley.

Kazdin, A. E. (1987). *Conduct disorders in childhood and adolescence.* Beverly Hills, CA: Sage Publications.

Kazdin, A. E. (1991). Effectiveness of psychotherapy with children and adolescents. *Journal of Consulting and Clinical Psychology, 59,* 785—798.

Kellam, S. G., & Rebok, G. W. (1992). Building developmental and etiological theory through epidemiologically based intervention trials. In J. McCord & R. E. Tremblay (Eds.), *Preventing antisocial behavior: Interventions from birth through adolescence* (pp. 162—195). New York: Guilford Press.

Kelly, J. P. (1993). Neural basis of perception and movement. In E. R. Kandel, J. H. Schwartz, & T. M. Jessell (Eds.), *Principles of neural behavior* (4th ed., pp. 283—295). New York: Elsevier.

Kelly, J. P., & Dodd, J. (1991). Principles of the functional and anatomical organization of the nervous system. In E. R. Kandel, J. H. Schwartz, & T. M. Jessel (Eds.), *Principles of neural science* (3rd ed., pp. 272—283). New York: Elsevier.

Kendall, P. C., & Braswell, L. (1985). *Cognitive-behavioral therapy for impulsive children.* New York: Guilford Press.

Kennedy, W. A. (1965). School phobia: Rapid treatment of fifty cases. *Journal of Abnormal Psychology, 70,* 285—289.

Keogh, B. K., & Sears, S. (1991). Learning disabilities from a developmental perspective: Early identification and prediction. In B. Y. L. Wong (Ed.), *Learning about learning disabilities* (pp. 486—505). San Diego, CA: Academic Press.

King, G. A., Schultz, I. Z., Steel, K., Gilpin, M. et al. (1993). Self-evaluation and self-concept of adolescents with physical disabilities. *American Journal of Occupational Therapy, 47,* 132—140.

King, N. J., Ollendick, T. H., & Gullone, E. (1991). Negative affectivity in children and adolescents: Relations between anxiety and depression. *Clinical Psychology Review, 11,* 441—459.

Kinney, D. K., Woods, B. T., & Yurgelun-Todd, D. (1986). Neurologic abnormalities in schizophrenic patients and their families. *Archives of General Psychiatry, 43,* 665—668.

Kinsbourne, M. (1989). Mechanisms and development of hemisphere specialization in children. In C. R. Reynolds & E. Fletcher Janzen (Eds.), *Handbook of clinical child neuropsychology* (pp. 69—86). New York: Plenum Press.

Kirk, U., & Kelly, M. (1986). Children's differential performance on selected dorsolateral prefrontal and posterior cortical function: A developmental perspective. *Journal of Clinical Experimental Neuropsychology, 7,* 604.

Klauber, M. R., Barrett-Connor, E., Hofstetter, C. R., & Micik, S. H. (1986). A population-based study of non-fatal childhood injuries. *Preventive Medicine, 15,* 139—149.

Klein, J., Feigin, R., & McCracken G. J. (1986). Report of the task force on diagnosis and management of meningitis. *Pediatrics, 78,* 959—982.

Klein, S. P., & Rosenfield, W. D. (1980). The hemispheric specialization for linguistic and non-linguistic tactile stimuli in third grade children. *Cortex, 16,* 205—212.

Klicpera, C. (1983). Poor planning as a characteristic of problem-solving behavior in dyslexic children. *Acta Paedopsychiatrica, 49,* 73—82.

Klonoff, H., Low, M. D., & Clark, C. (1977). Head injuries in children: A five year follow-up. *Journal of Neurology, Neurosurgery, and Psychiatry, 40,* 1211—1219.

Klonoff, H., & Paris, R. (1974). Immediate, short-term, and residual effects of acute head injuries in children: Neuropsychological and neurological correlates. In R. M. Reitan & L. A. Davison (Eds.), *Clinical neuropsychology: Current status and applications* (pp. 179—210). New York: Wiley.

Klorman, R. (1991). Cognitive event-related potentials in attention deficit disorder. *Journal of Learning Disabilities, 24,*

Klorman, R., Brumaghim, J. R., Borgstedt, A. D., & Salzman, L. F. (1994). How event-related potentials help to understand the effects of stimulants of attention deficit hyperactivity disorder. In J. R. Jennings, P. Ackles, & M. G. H. Coles (Eds.), *Advances in psychophysiology* (Vol. 4). New York: JAI Press.

Klorman, R., Brumaghim, J. T., Salzman, L. F., Strauss, J., Borgstedt, A. D., McBride, M., & Loeb, S. (1988). Clinical and cognitive effects of methylphenidate on attention deficit hyperactivity disorder with and without aggressive/noncompliant features. *Journal of Abnormal Psychology, 97,* 413—422.

Klove, H. (1989). The hypoarousal hypothesis: What is the evidence? In T. Sagvolden & T. Archer (Eds.), *Attention deficit disorder: Clinical and basic research* (pp. 131—136). Hillsdale, NJ: Lawrence Erlbaum Associates.

Kloza, E. M. (1990). Low MSAFP and new biochemical markers for Down syndrome: Implications for genetic counselors. In B. A. Fine, E. Gettig, K. Greendale, B. Leopold, & N. W. Paul (Eds.), *Strategies in genetic counseling: Reproductive genetics and new technologies.* White Plains, NY: March of Dimes Defects Foundation.

Knee, K., Mittenburg, W., Burns, W. J., DeSantes, M., & Keenan, M. (1990). Memory indices of LD readers using the CVLT-C. *The Clinical Neuropsychologist, 4,* 278.

Knights, R., & Norwood, J. (1980). *A neuropsychological test battery for children: Exmainer's manual.* Ottawa, KS: Knights Psychological Consultants.

Knott, V., Waters, B., Lapierre, Y., & Gray, R. (1985). Neurophysiological correlates of sibling pairs discordant for bipolar affective disorder. *American Journal of Psychiatry, 142,* 248—250.

Koegel, R. L., Firestone, P. B., Kremme, K. W., & Dunlop, G. (1974). Increasing spontaneous play by supressing self-stimulation in autistic children. *Journal of Applied Behavioral Analysis, 7,* 521—525.

Koegel, R. L., & Johnson, J. (1989). Motivating language use in autistic children. In G. Dawson (Ed.), *Autism: Nature, diagnosis, and treatment* (pp. 310—325). New York: Guilford Press.

Kohn, J. G. (1990). Issues in the management of children with spastic cerebral palsy. *Pediatrician, 17,* 230—236.

Kokkonen, J., Saukkonen, A. L., Timonen, E., Serlo, W. et al. (1991). Social outcome of handicapped children as adults. *Developmental Medicine and Child Neurology, 33,* 1095—1100.

Kolb, B., & Fantie, B. (1989). Development of the child's brain and behavior. In C. R. Reynolds & E. F. Janzen (Eds.), *Handbook of clinical child neuropsychology* (pp. 17—40). New York: Plenum Press.

Kolb, B., & Taylor, L. (1990). Neocortical substrates of emotional behavior. In N. Stein, B. Leventhal, & T. Trabasso (Eds.), *Psychological and biological approaches to emotion* (pp. 115—144). Hillsdale, NJ: Lawrence Erlbaum Associates.

Kolb, B., & Whishaw, I. Q. (1985). *Fundamentals of human neuropsychology* (2nd ed.). San Francisco: W. H. Freeman & Co.

Kolb, B., & Whishaw, I. Q. (1990). *Fundamentals of human neuropsychology* (3rd ed.). San Francisco: W. H. Freeman & Co.

Kolvin, I., Berney, P., & Bhate, S. R. (1984). Classification and diagnosis of depression in school phobia. *British Journal of Psychiatry, 145,* 347—357.

Koocher, G. P., & O'Malley, J. E. (1981). *The Damocles syndrome: Psychological consequences of surviving childhood cancer.* New York: McGraw-Hill.

Koots, J. P., Marinelli, B., & Cohen, D. J. (1982). Modulation of response to environmental stimulation in autistic children. *Journal of Autism and Developmental Disorders, 12,* 185—193.

Kopp, C., & Kralow, J. (1983). The developmentalist and the study of biological residual in children after recovery from bacterial meningitis. *Archives of Pediatrics, 79,* 63—71.

Koren, G. (1993). Cocaine and the human fetus: The concept of teratophilia. *Neurotoxicology and Teratology, 15,* 301—304.

Korkman, M., & Peltomaa, A. K. (1993). Preventive treatment of dyslexia by a preschool training program for children with language impairments. *Journal of Clinical Child Psychology, 22,* 277—287.

Kovacs, M. (1979). *Children's Depression Inventory.* Pittsburgh, PA: University of Pittsburgh School of Medicine.

Kovacs, M. (1985). The natural history and course of depressive disorders in childhood. *Psychiatry Annals, 15,* 387—389.

Kovacs, M. (1989). Affective disorders in children and adolescents. *American Psychologist, 44,* 209—215.

Kovaks, M., & Beck, A. T. (1977). An empirical-clinical approach toward a definition of childhood depression. In J. G. Schulterbrandt & A. Raskin (Eds.), *Diagnosis, treatment, and conceptual models* (pp. 1—25). New York: Raven Press.

Kovacs, M., Feinberg, T. L., Crouse-Novak, M.,

Paulauskas, S. L., Pollock, M., & Finkelstein, R. (1984). Depressive disorders in childhood: II. A longitudinal study of the risk for a subsequent major depression. *Archives of General Psychiatry, 41,* 229—237.

Krageloh-Mann, I., Hagberg, B., Petersen, D., et al., (1992). Bilateral spastic cerebral palsy–pathogenetic aspects from MRI. *Neuropediatrics, 23, 46—48.*

Kramer, A. D., & Feiguine, R. J. (1981). Clinical effects of amitriptyline in adolescent depression: A pilot study. *Journal of the American Academy of Child and Adolescent Psychiatry, 20,* 636—644.

Kratochwill, T. R., & Bergan, J. R. (1990). *Behavioral consultation in applied settings: An individual guide.* New York: Plenum Press.

Kratochwill, T. R., & Plunge, M. (1992). DSM-III-R, treatment validity, and functional analysis: Further considerations for school psychologists. *School Psychology Review, 7,* 227—232.

Kraus, J. F. (1987). Epidemiology of head injury. In P. R. Cooper (Ed.), *Head injury* (2nd ed., pp. 1—19). Baltimore, MD: Williams & Wilkins.

Kraus, J. F., Black, M. A., Hessol, N., Ley, P., Rokaw, W., Sullivan, C., Bowers, S., Knowlton, S., & Marshall, L. (1984).The incidence of acute brain injury and serious impairment in a defined population. *American Journal of Epidemiology, 119,* 186—201.

Kun, L. E. (1992). Brain tumors in children. In A. Perez & W. Brady (Eds.), *Principles and practices of pediatric oncology* (pp. 1417—1441). Philadelphia: Lippincott.

Kupfermann, I. (1991). Learning and memory. In E. R. Kandel, J. H., & T. M. Jessel (Eds.), *Principles of neural science* (3rd ed., pp. 997—1008). New York: Elsevier.

Lachar, D. (1990). *Personality inventory for children (PIC): Revised format manual.* Los Angeles: Western Psychological Association.

Lachar, D., Kline, R. B., & Boersma, D. C. (1986). The Personality Inventory for Children: Approaches to actuarial interpretation in clinic and school settings. In H. M. Knoff (Ed.), *The assessment of child and adolescent personality* (pp. 273—308). New York: Guilford Press.

Ladd, G. S., Hart, C. H., & Price, J. M. (1990). Preschoolers' behavioral orientations and patterns of peer control: Predictive of peer status? In S. R. Asher & J. D. Coie (Eds.), *Peer rejection in childhood* (pp. 35—52). Cambridge: Cambridge University Press.

La Greca, A. M. (1993). Social skills training with children: Where do we go from here? Presidential Address. *Journal of Clinical Child Psychology, 22,* 288—298.

Lahey, B. B., Pelham, W. E., Schaughency, E. A., Atkins, M. S., Murphy, A., Hynd, G. W., Russo, M., Hartdagen, S., & Lorys Vernon, A. (1988). Dimensions and types of attention deficit disorder. *Journal of the American Academy of Child and Adolescent Psychiatry, 27,* 330—335.

Lahey, B. B., Piacentini, J. C., McBurnett, K., Stone, P., Hartdagen, S., & Hynd, G. (1987). Psychopathology in the parents of children with conduct disorder and hyperactivity. *Journal of the American Academy of Child and Adolescent Psychiatry, 27,* 163—170.

Lahey, B. B., Schaughency, E. A., Frame, C. L., & Strauss, C. C. (1985). Teacher ratings of attention problems in children experimentally classified as exhibiting attention deficit disorders with and without hyperactivity. *Journal of the American Academy of Child and Adolescent Psychiatry, 24,* 613—616.

Lahey, B. B., Schaughency, E. A., Hynd, G. W., Carlson, C. L., & Nieves, N. (1987). Attention deficit disorder with and without hyperactivity: Comparison of behavioral characteristics of clinic-referred children. *Journal of American Academy of Child and Adolescent Psychiatry, 26,* 718—723.

Lambert, N. M., & Sandoval, J. (1980). The prevalence of learning disabilities in a sample of children considered to be hyperactive. *Journal of Abnormal Child Psychology, 8,* 33—50.

Lansky, S. B., List, M. A., Ritter-Sterr, C., et al. (1985). Late effects: Psychosocial. *Clinical Oncology, 4,* 239—262.

Larsen, J. P., Hoien, T., Lundberg, I., & Odegaard, H. (1990). MRI evaluation of the size and symmetry of the planum temporale in adolescents with developmental dyslexia. *Brain and Language, 39,* 289—301.

Larsen, J. P., Hoien, T., Odegaard, H. (1992). Magnetic resonance imaging of the corpus callosum in developmental dyslexia. *Cognitive Neuropsychology, 9,* 123—134.

Last, C. G., Hersen, M., Kazdin, A. E., Finkelstein, R., & Strauss, C. C. (1987). Comparison of DSM-III separation anxiety and overanxious disorders: Demographic characteristics and patterns of comorbidity. *Journal of the American Academy of Child Psychiatry, 26,* 527—531.

Laufer, M. W., & Denhoff, E. (1957). Hyperkinetic behavior syndrome in children. *Journal of Pediatrics, 50,* 463—474.

Laurent, J., Hadler, J. R., & Stark, K. D. (1995). A multiple stage screening procedure for the identification of childhood anxiety disorders. *School Psychology Quarterly, 9,* 239—255.

Leark, R. A., Snyder, T., Grove, T., & Golden, C. J. (1983, August). *Comparison of the K-ABC to standardized neuropsychological batteries: Preliminary results.* Paper presented at the American Psychological Association, Anaheim, California.

Lechtenberg, T. (1984). *Epilepsy and the family.* Cambridge, MA: Harvard University Press.

Le Couteur, A., Rutter, M., Lord, C., Rios, P. Robertson, S., Holdgrafer, M., & McLennan, J. (1989). Autism Diagnostic Interview: A standardized investigator-based instrument. *Journal of Autism and Developmental Disorders, 19,* 363—388.

LeFrancois, G. R. (1995). *An introduction to child development* (8th ed.). Belmont, CA: Wadsworth.

LeMay, M. (1976). Morphological cerebral asymmetries of modern man, fossil man, and nonhuman primates. *Annals of New York Academy of Sciences, 280,* 349—366.

Leonard, C. M., Voeller, K. K., Lombardino, L. J., Morris, M. K., Hynd, G. W., Alexander, A. W., Andersen, H. G., Honeyman, J. C., Mao, J., Agee, F., & Staab, E. V. (1993). Anomalous cerebral structure in dyslexia revealed with magnetic resonance imaging. *Archives of Neurology, 50,* 461—469.

Leonard, H. L., & Swedo, S. E. (1979). Obsessive compulsive disorder. In J. Noshpitz (Ed.), *Basic handbook of child psychiatry.* New York: Wiley.

Lerner, J. (1993). *Learning disabilities: Theories, diagnosis, & teaching strategies* (6th ed.). Boston: Houghton Mifflin.

Lester, B. M., & Dreher, M. (1989). Effects of marijuana use during pregnancy on newborn cry. *Child Development, 60,* 765—771.

Lester, B. M., & Tronick, E. Z. (1994). The effects of prenatal cocaine exposure and child outcome. *Infant Mental Health Journal, 15,* 107—120.

Levin, H. S., Culhane, K. A., Hartman, J., Evankovich, K., Mattson, A. J., Haward, H., Ringholz, G., Ewing-Cobbs, L., & Fletcher, J. M. (1991). Developmental changes in performance on tests of frontal lobe functioning. *Developmental Neuropsychology, 7,* 377—395.

Levin, H. S., & Eisenberg, H. M. (1979). Neuropsychological impairment after closed head injury in children and adolescents. *Journal of Pediatric Psychology, 4,* 389—402.

Levin, H. S., Eisenberg, H. M., Wigg, N. R., & Kobayashi, K. (1982). Memory and intellectual ability after head injury in children and adolescents. *Neurosurgery, 11,* 668—673.

Levine, M. D. (1993). *Developmental variation and learning disorders.* Cambridge, MA: Educators Publishing Service.

Leviton, A., & Paneth, W. (1990). White matter damage in preterm newborns–An epidemiologic perspective. *Early Human Development, 24,* 1—22.

Lewis, R. D., Hutchens, T. A., & Garland, B. L. (1993). Cross-validation of the discriminative effectiveness of the Luria Nebraska neuropsychological battery for learning disabled adolescents. *Archives of Clinical Neuropsychology, 8,* 437—447.

Lezak, M. D. (1983). *Neuropsychological assessment.* New York: Oxford University Press.

Lezak, M. D. (1994). *Neuropsychological assessment* (4th ed.). New York: Oxford University Press.

Liberman, I. Y., & Liberman, A. M. (1990). Whole language vs. code emphasis: Underlying assumptions and their implications for reading instruction. *Annals of Dyslexia, 40,* 51—76.

Liberman, I. Y., & Shankweiler, D. (1985). Phonology and the problems of learning to read and write. *Remedial and Special Education, 6,* 8—17.

Liberman, I. Y., Shankweiler, D., Blachman, B., Camp, L., & Werfelman, M. (1980). Steps toward literacy. Report prepared for Working Group on Learning Failure and Unused Learning Potential, President's Commission on Mental Health, November 1, 1977. In P. Levinson & C. H. Sloan (Eds.), *Auditory processing and language: Clinical and research perspectives* (pp. 189—215). New York: Grune & Stratton.

Liberman, I. Y., Shankweiler, D., Fisher, F. W., & Carter, B. (1974). Explicit syllable and phoneme segmentation in the young child. *Journal of Experimental Child Psychology, 18,* 201—212.

Lindberg, J., Rosenhall, U., Nylen, O., & Ringner, A. (1977). Long-term outcome of *Hemophilus influenzae meningitis* related to antibiotic treatment. *Pediatrics, 60,* 1—6.

Lindsay, J., Ounstead, C., & Richards, P. (1979). Long-term outcome in children with temporal lobe seizures: III. Psychiatric aspects in childhood and adult life. *Developmental Medicine and Child Neurology, 21,* 630—636.

Linnoila, M., Virkkunen, M., Scheinin, M., Nuutila, A., Rimon, R., & Goodwin, F. K. (1983). Low cerebrospinal fluid 5-hydroxyindolacetic acid concentration differentiates impulsive form nonimpulsive violent behavior. *Life Sciences, 33,* 2609—2614.

Linz, T. D., Hooper, S. R., Hynd, G. W., Isaac, W., & Gibson, L. J. (1990). Frontal lobe functioning in conduct disorder juveniles: Preliminary findings. *Archives of Clinical Neuropsychology, 5,* 411—416.

Listernick, R., & Charrow, J. (1990). Neurofibromatosis type 1 in childhood. *Journal of Pediatrics, 116,* 845—853.

Litman, T. (1974). The family as a basic unit in health and medical care: A social-behavioral overview. *Social and Scientific Medicine, 8,* 495—519.

Little, R. E., Anderson, K. W., Ervin, C. H., Worthington Roberts, B., & Clarren, S. K. (1989). Maternal alcohol use during breast-feeding and infant mental and motor development at one year. *New England Journal of Medicine, 321,* 425—430.

Liu, D. T. (1991). Introduction and historical perspectives. In D. T. Liu (Ed.), *A practical guide to chorion villus sampling.* New York: Oxford University Press.

Livingstone, M., Rosen, G. D., Drislane, F. W., & Galaburda, A. M. (1991). Physiological and anatomical evidence for a magnocellular defect in developmental dyslexia. *Proceedings of the National Academy of Science, 88,* 7943—7947.

Lloyd, J. E., & Landrum, T. J. (1990). Self-recording of attending to task: Treatment components and generalization of effects. In T. E. Scruggs & B. Y. L. Wong (Eds.), *Intervention research in learning disabilities* (pp. 235—262). New York: Springer-Verlag.

Lochman, J. E., Lampron, L. B., Gemmer, T. C., & Harris, S. R. (1987). Anger coping intervention with aggressive children: A guide to implementation in school settings. In P. A. Keller & S. R. Heyman (Eds.), *Innovations in clinical practice: A source book* (pp. 339—356).

Lockman, L. A. (1993, November). *Pediatric brain tumors: The role of the Pediatric Brain Tumor Task Force.* Paper presented at the Cancer Center Symposium on Cancer and the Nervous System, Minneapolis, MN.

Lockman, L.A. (1994a). Absence seizures. In K. Swaiman (Ed.), *Pediatric Neurology* (pp. 531—536). St. Louis, MO: Mosby.

Lockman, L. A. (1994b). Nonabsence generalized seizures. In K. F. Swaiman (Ed.), *Pediatric neurology* (2nd ed., pp. 261—270). St. Louis, MO: Mosby.

Loeber, R. (1990). Development and risk factors of juvenile antisocial behavior and delinquency. *Clinical Psychology Review, 10,* 1—42.

Loeber, R., & Dishion, T. J. (1983). Early predictors of male delinquency: A review. *Psychological Bulletin, 94,* 68—99.

Loge, D. V., Staton, R. D., & Beatty, W. W. (1990a). Performance of children with ADHD on tests sensitive to frontal lobe dysfunction. *Journal of the American Academy of Child and Adolescent Psychitry, 29,* 540—545.

Loge, D. V., Staton, R. D., & Beatty, W. W. (1990b). Performance of children with ADHD on tests sensitive to frontal lobe functions. *Journal of Learning Disabilities, 20,* 19—36.

Loiseau, P., Pestre, M., Dartigues, J. F., et al. (1983). Long-term prognosis in two forms of childhood epilepsy: Typical absence seizures and epilepsy with Rolandic (centrotemporal) EEG foci. *Annals of Neurology, 13,* 642—648.

Loiselle, D. L., Stamm, J. S., Maitinsky, S., & Whipple, S. C. (1980). Evoked potential and behavioral signs of attentive dysfunctions in hyperactive boys. *Psychophysiology, 17,* 193—201.

Lombroso, C. (1985). Neonatal EEG. In J. B. Cracco, R. P. Brenner, & B. F. Westmoreland (Eds.), *State of the science of EEG–1985* (pp. 2—18). Atlanta: American Electroencephalographic Society.

Lord, C., Rutter, M., Goode, S., et al. (1989). Autism Diagnostic Schedule: A standardized observvation of communicative and social behavior. *Journal of Autism & Developemtnal Disorders, 19,* 185—212.

Lord, C., & Schopler, E. (1985). Differences in sex ratios in autism as a function of measured intelligence. *Journal of Autism and Developmental Disorders, 15,* 185—193.

Lorys, A. R., Hynd, G. W., & Lahey, B. B. (1990). Do neurocognitive measures differentiate attention deficit disorder (ADD) with and without hyperactivity? *Archives of Clinical Neuropsychology, 5,* 119—135.

Lou, H. C. (1991). Cerebral glucose metabolism in hyperactivity (letter to the editor). *New England Journal of Medicine, 324,* 1216.

Lou, H. C., Henriksen, L., & Bruhn, P. (1984). Focal cerebral hypoperfusion in children with dysphasia and/or attention deficit disorder. *Archives of Neurology, 41,* 825—829.

Lou, H. C., Henriksen, L., Bruhn, P., Borner, H., & Nielson, J. B. (1989). Striatal dysfunction in attention deficit and hyperkinetic disorder. *Archives of Neurology, 46,* 48—52.

Lovaas, O. I. (1987). Behavioral treatment and normal educational and intellectual functioning of young autistic children. *Journal of Consulting and Clinical Psychology, 55,* 3—9.

Lovell, M. R., & Starratt, C. (1992). Cognitive rehabilitation and behavior therapy of neuropsychiatric disorders. In S. C. Yudofsky & R. E. Hales (Eds.), *The American Psychiatric Press textbook of neuropsychiatry* (2nd ed., pp. 639—662). Washington, DC: American Psychiatric Press.

Lubs, H. A., Rabin, M., Carlan-Saucier, K., Gross-Glenn, K., Duara, R., Levin, B., & Lubs, M. L. (1991). Genetic bases of developmental dyslexia: Molecular studies. In J. E. Obrzut & G. W. Hynd (Eds.), *Neuropsychological foundations of learning disabilities: A handbook of issues, methods, and practice* (pp. 49—78). San Diego, CA: Harcourt Brace Jovanovich.

Lundberg, I., Frost, J., & Petersen, O. P. (1988). Effects of an extensive program for stimulating phonological awareness in preschool children. *Reading Research Quarterly, 23,* 267—284.

Luria, A. R. (1973). *The working brain.* New York. Basic Books.

Luria, A. R. (1980). *Higher cortical functions in man* (2nd. ed.). New York: Basic Books.

Luria, A. R., & Majovski, L. V. (1977). Basic approaches used in American and Soviet clinical neuropsychology. *American Psychologist, 32,* 959—968.

Luxenberg, J. S., Swedo, S. E., Flament M. F., et al. (1988). Neuroanatomical abnormalities in obsessive-compulsive disorders detected with quantitative X-ray computed tomography. *American Journal of Psychiatry, 145,* 1089—1093.

Lyon, G., & Gadisseux, J. F. (1991). Structural abnormalities of the brain in developmental disorders. In M. Rutter & P. Caesar (Eds.), *Biological risk factors for psychological disorders* (pp. 1—19). Cambridge: University Press.

MacArthur, C., & Graham, S. (1987). Learning disabled students' composing with three methods: Handwriting, dictation, and word processing. *Journal of Special Education, 21,* 22—42.

MacAuslan, A. (1975). Physical signs in association with depressive illness in childhood. *Child-Care-Health Development, 1,* 225—232.

MacGregor, S., Keith, L., Bachicha, J., & Chasnoff, I. J. (1989). Cocaine use during pregnancy: Correlation between prenatal care and perinatal outcome. *Obstetrics and Gynecology, 74,* 882—885.

Madan-Swain, A., & Brown, R. T. (1991). Cognitive and psychosocial sequelae for children with acute lymphocytic leukemia and their families. *Clinical Psychology Review, 11,* 267—294.

Magill-Evans, J. E., & Restall, G. (1991). Self-esteem of persons with cerebral palsy: From adolescence to adulthood. *American Journal of Occupational Therapy, 45,* 819—825.

Majnemer, A., Rosenblatt, B., & Riley, P. (1994). Predicting outcome in high-risk newborns with a neonatal neurobehavioral assessment. *American Journal of Occupational Therapy, 48,* 723—732.

Majovski, L. V. (1989). Higher cortical functions in children: A developmetnal perspective. In C. R. Reynolds & E. Fletcher Janzen (Eds.), *Handbook of clinical child neuropsychology* (pp. 41—67). New York: Plenum Press.

Malakoff, M. E., Mayes, L. C., & Schottenfeld, R. S. (1994). Language abilities of preschool-age children living with cocaine-using mothers. *American Journal of Addictions, 3,* 346—354.

Malaspina, D., Quitkin, H. M., & Kaufman, C. A. (1992). Epidemiology and genetics of neuropsychiatric disorders. In S. Yudofsky & R. E. Hales (Eds.), *The American Psychiatric Press textbook of neuropsychiatry* (2nd ed., pp. 187—226). Washington, DC: American Psychiatric Press.

Mandoki, M. W., & Sumner, G. S. (1991). Klinefelter Syndrome: The need for early identification and treatment. *Clinical Pediatrics, 3,* 161—164.

Mann, V. (1986). Why some children encounter reading problems. In J. Torgesen & B. Wong (Eds.), *Psychological and educational perspectives on learning disabilities* (pp. 133—159). New York: Academic Press.

Mann, V. (1991). Language problems: A key to early reading problems. In B. Y. L. Wong (Ed.), *Learning about learning disabilities* (pp. 130—163). San Diego, CA: Academic Press.

Mann, V., & Liberman, I. Y. (1984). Phonological awareness and verbal short-term memory: Can they presage early reading success? *Journal of Learning Disabilities, 17,* 592—598.

Marsh, R. W. (1985). Phrenoblysis: Real or chimera? *Child Development, 56,* 1059—1061.

Marteau, T., Drake, H., & Bobrow, M. (1994). Counseling following diagnosis of a fetal abnormality: The differing approaches of obstetricians, clinical geneticists, and genetic nurses. *Journal of Medical Genetics, 31,* 864—867.

Martin, D. A. (1990). Family issues in traumatic brain injury. In E. D. Bigler (Ed.), *Traumatic brain injury: Mechanisms of damage, assessment, intervention and outcome* (pp. 381—395). Austin, TX: Pro-Ed.

Martin, R. (1988). *Assessment of child personality and behavior.* New York: Guilford Press.

Martin, R. C. (1993). Short-term memory and sentence processing: Evidence form neuropsychology. *Memory and Cognition, 21,* 176—183.

Mash, E. J., & Johnston, C. (1982). A comparison of the mother—child interactions of younger and older hyperactive and normal children. *Child Development, 53,* 1371—1381.

Mash, E. J., & Terdal, L. G. (1988). *Behavioral assessment of childhood disorders.* New York: Guilford Press.

Matthews, K. A., Manuck, S. B., & Saab, P. G. (1986). Cardiovascular responses of adolescents during a naturally occurring stressor and their behavioral and psychophysiological predictors. *Psychophysiology, 23,* 198—209.

Matthews, W. S., Barabas, G., & Ferrai, M. (1982). Emotional concomitants of childhood epilepsy. *Epilepsia, 23,* 671—681.

Matthews, W. S., Barabas, G., & Ferrai, M. (1983). Achievement and school behavior in children with epilepsy. *Psychology in the Schools, 26,* 10—13.

Matthews, W. S., Solan, A., & Barabas, G. (1995). Cognitive functioning in Lesch-Nyhan syndrome. *Developmental Medicine and Child Neurology, 37,* 715—722.

Mattingly, I. G. (1972). *Language by ear and eye: The relationship between speech and reading.* Cambridge, MA: MIT Press.

Mattson, S. N., Riley, E. P., Delis, D. C., Stern, C., & Jones, K. L. (submitted). *Verbal learning and memory in children with fetal alcohol syndrome.* Submitted for publication.

Mattson, S. N., Riley, E. P., Jernigan, T. L., Ehlers, C. L., et al. (1992). Fetal alcohol syndrome: A case report of neuropsychological, MRI, and EEG assessment of two children. *Alcoholism: Clinical and Experimental Research, 16,* 1001—1003.

Mattson, S. N., Riley, E. P., Jernigan, T. L., Garcia, A., et al. (1994). A decrease in the size of the basal ganglia following prenatal alcohol exposure: A preliminary report. *Neurotoxicology and Teratology, 16,* 283—289.

Mattson, S. N., Jernigan, T. L., & Riley, E. P. (1994). MRI and prenatal alcohol exposure: Images provide insight into FAS. *Alcohol Health and Research World, 18,* 49—52.

Mautner, V. F., Tatagiba, M., Outhoff, R., Samii, M., & Pulst, S. M. (1993). Neurofibromatosis 2 in the pediatric age group. *Neurosurgery, 33,* 92—96.

May, P. A. (1991). Fetal alcohol effects among North American Indians: Evidence and implications for society. *Alcohol Health and Research World, 15,* 239—248.

May, P. A., Hymbaugh, K. J., Aase, J. M., & Samet, J. M. (1983). Epidemiology of fetal alcohol syndrome among American Indians of the Southwest. *Social Biology, 30,* 374—387.

Mayes, L. C. (1994). Neurobiology of prenatal cocaine exposure effect on developing monoamine systems. *Infant Mental Health Journal, 15,* 121—133.

Mayes, L. C., Granger, R. H., Bornstein, M. H., & Zuckerman, B. (1992). The problem of prenatal cocaine exposure: A rush to judgment. *JAMA, 267,* 406—408.

McBurnette, K., Lahey, B. B., Frick, P. J., Risch, C., et al. (1991). Anxiety, inhibition, and conduct disorder in children. *Journal of American Academy of Child and Adolescent Psychiatry, 30,* 192—196.

McCord, J. (1991). The cycle of crime and socialization practices. *Journal of Criminal Law and Criminality, 82,* 211—228.

McCubbin, H. I., & Patterson, J. M. (1983). The family stress process: The double ABCX model of adjustment and adaptation. *Marriage and Family Review, 6,* 7—37.

McFie, J. (1961). Intellectual impairment in children with localized post-infantile cerebral lesions. *Journal of Neurology, Neurosurgery, and Psychiatry, 24,* 361—365.

McFie, J. (1975). *Assessment of organic impairment.* London: Academic Press.

McGee, R., Silva, P. A., & Williams, S. M. (1984). Perinatal, neurological, environmental and developmental characteristics of seven-year-old children with stable behavior problems. *Journal of Child Psychology and Psychiatry and Allied Disciplines, 25,* 573—586.

McGinnis, E., & Forness, S. (1988). Psychiatric diagnosis: A further test of the special education eligibility hypothesis. *Severe Behavior Disorders Monograph, 11,* 3—10.

McIntosh, D. E., & Gridley, B. E. (1992). Differential Ability Scales: Profiles of learning disabled subtypes. *Psychology in the Schools, 30,* 11—24.

McIntosh, D. E., & Gridley, B. E. (1993). Differential ability scales: Profiles of learning disabled subtypes. *Psychology in the schools, 30,* 11—24.

McKay, S. E., Stelling, M. W., Baumann, R. J., Carr, W. A., Walsch, J. W., & Gilmore, R. L. (1985). Assessment of frontal lobe dysfunction using the Luria-Nebraska Neuropsychological Battery–Children's Revision: A case study. *Journal of Clinical Neuropsychology, 7,* 23—27.

McKissock, W. (1953). Infantile hemiplegia. *Proceedings of the Royal Society of Medicine, 46,* 431—434.

McMahon, R. J., & Forehand, R. (1984). Parent training for the noncompliant child: Treatment outcome, generalization and adjunctive therapy procedures. In R. F. Dangel & R. A. Polster (Eds.), *Parent training: Foun-*

dations of research and practice (pp. 298—328). New York: Guilford Press.

Meadows, A. T., Gordon, J., Massari, D. J., Littman, P., Ferguson, J., & Moss, K. (1981). Declines in IQ scores and cognitive dysfunctions in children with acute lymphocytic leukemia treated with cranial irradiation. Lancet, 2, 1015—1016.

Mednick, S. A., & Hutchings, B. (1978). Genetic and psychophysiological factors in asocial behaviour. In R. D. Hare & D. Schalling (Eds.), Psychopathic behavious: Approaches to research (pp. 239—253). Chichester, England: John Wiley & Sons.

Meichenbaum, D. H., Bream, L. A., & Cohen, J. C. (1985). A cognitive-behavioral perspective of child psychopathology: Implications for assessment and training. In R. J. McMahon & R. DeV. Peters (Eds.), Childhood disorders: Behavioral developmental approaches (pp. 36—52). New York: Brunner/Mazel.

Melcer, T., Gonzalez, D., Barron, S., & Riley, E. P. (1994). Hyperactivity in preweaning rats following postnatal alcohol exposure. Alcohol, 11, 41—45.

Mendelson, W., Johnson, N., & Stewart, M. A. (1971). Hyperactive children as teenagers: A follow-up study. Journal of Nervous and Mental Disease, 153, 273—279.

Mendlewicz, E. J., Brown, G., Minichiello, M., Millican, F., & Rapoport, J. (1984). EEG and neuroendocrine parameters in pubertal and adolescent depressed children: A case report study. Journal of Affective Disorders, 6, 265—272.

Menkes, J. H. (1985a). Metabolic diseases of the nervous system. In J. H. Menkes (Ed.), Textbook of child neurology (pp. 28—138). Philadelphia: Lea & Febiger.

Menkes J. H. (1985b). Textbook of child neurology. Philadelphia: Lea & Febiger.

Menkes, J. H. (1990). Metabolic diseases of the central nervous system. In J. H. Menkes (Ed.), Textbook of child neurology (pp. 28—138). Philadelphia: Lea & Febiger.

Mesibov, G. B., Schopler, E., Shaffer, B., et al. (1989). Use of the Childhood Autism Rating Scale with autistic adolescents and adults. Journal of the American Academy of Child and Adolescent Psychiatry, 28, 538—541.

Metrakos, J. D., & Metrakos, K. (1970). Genetic factors in epilepsy. In E. Niedermeyer (Ed.), Epilepsy: Modern problems in pharmacopsychiatry (pp. 312—335). Basel: Karger.

Michaels, K., Lopus, M., & Matalon, R. (1988). Phenylalanine metabolites as indicators of dietary compliance in children phenylketonuria. Biochemical Medicine and Metabolic Biology, 39, 18—23.

Milberg, W. B., & Blumstein, S. E. (1981). Lexical decisions and aphasia: Evidence for semantic processing. Brain and Language, 28, 154—168.

Milberg, W. B., Hebben, N., & Kaplan, E. (1986). The Boston Process Approach to neuropsychological assessment. In I. Grant & K. M. Adams (Eds.), Neuropsychological assessment and neuropsychiatric disorders (pp. 65—86). New York: Oxford University Press.

Milich, R., & Landau, S. (1989). The role of social status variables in differentiating subgroups of hyperactive children. In L. M. Bloomingdale & J. Swanson (Eds.), Attention deficit disorder: Current concepts and emerging trends in attentional and behavioral disoders of childhood (Vol. 5, pp. 1—16). Elmsford, NY: Pergamon Press.

Milich, R., Loney, J., & Landau, S. (1982). The independent dimensions of hyperactivity and aggression: A validation with playroom observation data. Journal of Abnormal Psychology, 91, 183—198.

Miller, G., & Cala, L. A. (1989). Ataxic cerebral palsy—Clinico-radiological correlations. Neuropediatrics, 20, 84—89.

Miller, M., & Hall, J. G. (1978). Possible maternal effect on severity of neurofibromatosis. Lancet, 2, 1071—1073.

Minde, K., Lewin, D., Weiss, G., Lavigueur, H., Douglas, V., & Sykes, E. (1971). The hyperactive child in elementary school: A five-year, controlled, follow-up. Exceptional Children, 38, 215—221.

Minkoff, H., Deepak, N., Menez, R., & Firkig, S. (1987). Pregnancies resulting in infants with acquired immunodeficiency syndrome of AIDS-related complex: Follow-up of mothers, children, and subsequently born siblings. Obstetrics and Gynecology, 69, 288—291.

Minshew, N. J., & Goldstein, G. (1993). Is autism an amnesic disorder? Evidence from the California Verbal Learning Test. Neuropsychology, 7, 209—216.

Mirsky, A. F. (1987). Behavioral and psychophysiological markers of disordered attention. Environmental Health Perspectives, 74, 191—199.

Mitchell, W. G., Chavez, J. M., Lee, H., & Guzman, B. L. (1991). Academic underachievement. Journal of Child Neurology, 6, 65—72.

Moffitt, T. E. (1988). Neuropsychology and self-reported early delinquency in an unselected birth cohort: A preliminary report from New Zealand. In T. Moffitt, S. Mednick, & S. A. Stack (Eds.), Biological contributions to crime causation (pp. 93—120). New York: Martinus Nijhoff Press.

Moffitt, T. E. (1993). The neuropsychology of conduct

disorder. *Development and Psychopathology, 5,* 135—151.

Moffitt, T. E., & Henry, B. (1989). Neuropsychological assessment of executive functions in self-reported delinquents. *Development and Psychopathology, 1,* 105—118.

Molfese, D. L., Freeman, R. B., & Palermo, D. S. (1975). The ontogeny of brain lateralization for speech and nonspeech stimuli. *Brain and Language, 2,* 356—368.

Molfese, D. L., & Molfese, V. J. (1979). Hemisphere and stimulus differences as reflected in the cortical responses of newborn infants to speech stimuli. *Developmental Psychology, 15,* 505—511.

Molfese, D. L., & Molfese, V. J. (1986). Psychophysiological indices of early cognitive processes and their relationship to language. In J. E. Obrzut & G. W. Hynd (Eds.), *Child neuropsychology: Theory and research* (pp. 95—115). New York: Academic Press.

Molfese, D. L., & Molfese, V. J. (1994). Short-term and long-term developmental outcomes. In G. Dawson & K. W. Fischer (Eds.), *Human behavior and the developing brain* (pp. 493—517). New York: Guilford Press.

Molter, J. (1993). *The effects of phonemic awareness training on delayed readers.* Unpublished doctoral dissertation, University of Wisconsin—Milwaukee.

Monod, N., & Garma, L. (1971). Auditory responsivity of the human premature. *Biology of the Neonate, 17,* 292.

Montague, M., & Bos, C. (1986). The effect of cognitive strategy training on verbal math problem solving performance of learning disabled adolescents. *Journal of Learning Disabilities, 19,* 26—33.

Montali, J., & Lewandowski, L. (1996). Bimodal reading: Benefits of a talking computer for average and less skilled readers. *Journal of Learning Disabilities, 29,* 271—279.

Montgomery, J. W. (1992). Easily overlooked language disabilities during childhood and adolescence: A cognitive lingusitic perspective. *Pediatric Clinics of North America, 39,* 513—524.

Montgomery, J. W., Windsor, J., & Stark, R. E. (1991). Specific speech and language disorders. In J. E. Obrzut & G. W. Hynd (Eds.), *Neuropsychological foundations of learning disabilities: A handbook of issues, methods, and practice* (pp. 573—601). San Diego, CA: Harcourt Brace Jovanovich.

Moore, B. D., Ater, J. L., & Copeland, D. R. (1992). Improved neuropsychological functioning in children with brain tumors diagnosed during infancy and treated without cranial irradiation. *Journal of Child Neurology, 7,* 281—290.

Moore, B. D., Copeland, D. R., Reid, H., & Levy, B. (1992). Neurophysiological basis of cognitive deficits in long-term survivors of childhood cancer. *Archives of Neurology, 49,* 809—817.

Moore, K. L. (1983). *Before we are born* (2nd ed.). Philadelphia: W. B. Saunders.

Morgan, A. E., & Hynd, G. W. (submitted). *Anatomical variations of the planum temporale: Implications for dyslexia and inguistic ability. Brain Imaging and Behavior.*

Morris, G. L., Mueller, W. M., Yetkin, F. Z., Haughton, V. M., Hammeke, T. A., Swanson, S., Rao, S. M., Jesmanowicz, A., Estowski, L. D., Bandettini, P. A., Wong, E. C., & Hyde, J. S. (1994). Functional magnetic resonance images in partial epilepsy. *Epilepsia, 35,* 1194—1198.

Morris, J., & Bigler, E. (1985, January). *An investigation of the Kaufman Assessment Battery for Children (K-ABC) with neurologically impaired children.* Paper presented at the meeting of the International Neuropsychological Society, San Diego, CA.

Morris, R., Blashfield, R., & Satz, P. (1986). Developmental classification of reading-disabled children. *Journal of Clinical and Experimental Neuropsychology, 8,* 371—392.

Morrison, S. R., & Siegel, L. S. (1991). Learning disabilities: A critical review of definitional and assessment issues. In J. E. Obrzut & G. W. Hynd (Eds.), *Neuropsychological foundations of learning disabilities: A handbook of issues, methods, and practice* (pp. 79—98). San Diego, CA: Harcourt Brace Jovanovich.

Morrow, J., O'Connor, D., Whitman, B., & Accardo, P. (1989). CNS irradiation and memory deficit. *Developmental Medicine and Child Neurology, 31,* 690—691.

Morse, B. A., Idelson, R. K., Sachs, W. H., Weiner, L. et al. (1992). Pediatrician's perspectives on fetal alcohol syndrome. *Journal of Substance Abuse, 4,* 187—195.

Moskowitz, A., & Sokol, S. (1980). Spatial and temporal interaction of pattern evoked cortical potentials in human infants. *Vision Research, 20,* 699—707.

Mulder, H. C. & Suurmeijer, T. P. (1977). Families with a child with epilepsy: A sociological contribution. *Journal of Biosocial Science, 9,* 13—24.

Mulhern, R. K., Hancock, J., Fairclough, D., & Kun, L. E. (1992). Neuropsychological status of children treated for brain tumors: A critical review and integration. *Medical and Pediatric Oncology, 20,* 181—192.

Mulhern, R. K., Kovnar, E. H., Kun, L. E., Crisco, J. J., & Williams, J. M. (1988). Psychologic and neurologic function following treatment for childhood temporal lobe astrocytoma. *Journal of Child Neurology, 7,* 1660—1666.

Muller, D., & Zeller, J. (1988). Some aspects of pediatric and specialist outpatient management of preschool and school children. *Arztliche Jugenkinde, 79,* 264—269.

Mundy, P., & Sigman, M. (1989). The theoretical implications of joint-attention deficits and autism. *Development and Psychopathology, 1,* 173—183.

Munir, K., Biederman, J., & Knee, D. (1987). Psychiatric comorbidity in patients with attention deficit disorder: A controlled study. *Journal of the American Academy of Child and Adolescent Psychiatry, 26,* 844—848.

Myers, deR., Sweet, J. J., Deysach, R., & Meyers, F. C. (1989). Utility of Luria-Nebraska neuropsychological battery–children's revision in the evaluation of reading disabled children. *Archives of Clinical Neuropyschology, 4,* 201—215.

Naatanen, R. (1990). The role of attention in auditory information processing as revealed by event-related potentials and other brain measures of cognitive function. *Behavior and Brain Sciences, 13,* 112—130.

Nadich, T. P. (1992). Imaging of the developing brain (special issue). *AJNR, 13,* 419—828.

Nanson, J. L., & Hiscock, M. (1990). Attention deficits in children exposed to alcohol prenatally. *Alcoholism: Clinical and Experimental Research, 14,* 656—661.

Nasrallah, H. (1992). The neuropsychiatry of schizophrenia. In S. C. Yudofsky & R. E. Hales (Eds.), *The American psychiatric press textbook of neuropsychiatry* (2nd ed., pp. 621—638). Washington, DC: American Psychiatric Press.

National Institute of Neurological and Communicative Disorders and Stroke. (NINCDS) (1979). *Technical document of the panel on developmental neurological disorders to the national advisory neurological and communicative disorders and stroke council.* Bethesda, MD: U.S. Department of Health and Human Services.

National Institute on Alcohol Abuse and Alcoholism. (1990). *Seventh special report to the U.S. Congress on Alcohol and Health₂* DHHS Pub. No. (ADM) 90-1656. Washington, DC: U.S. Government Printing Office.

National Radiological Protection Board (1981). *Radiological Protection Bulletin, 39,* 3—10.

Nelson, K. B. (1991). Prenatal origin of hemiparetic cerebral palsy: How often and why? *Pediatrics, 88,* 1059—1062.

Nelson, K. B., & Leviton, A. (1991). How much of neonatal encephalopathy is due to birth asphyxia? *American Journal of Disabled Children, 145,* 1325—1331.

Nelson, K. B., Swaiman, K. F., & Russman, B. S. (1994). Cerebral palsy. In K. F. Swaiman (Ed.), *Pediatric neurology* (pp. 471—488). St. Louis, MO: Mosby.

Neppe, V. M. (1985). Epilepsy and psychiatry: Essential links. *Psychiatric Insight, 2,* 18—22.

Neppe, V. M., & Tucker, G. J. (1992). Neuropsychiatric aspects of seizure disorders. In S. C. Yudofsky & R. E. Hales (Eds.), *The American Psychiatric Press textbook of neuropsychiatry* (2nd ed., pp. 397—425). Washington, DC: American Psychiatric Press.

Netley, C. (1987). Predicting intellectual functioing in 47, XXY boys from characteristics of siblings. *Clinical Genetics, 32,* 24—27.

Neurotoxicology and Teratology. (1993). Special issue on cocaine, *15.*

Neuspiel, D. R., & Hamel, S. C. (1991). Cocaine and infant behavior. *Journal of Developmental Behavioral Pediatrics, 12,* 55—64.

Neuspiel, D. R., Hamel, S. C., Hochberg, E., Green, J., & Campbell, D. (1991). Maternal cocaine use and infant behavior. *Neurotoxicology and Teratology, 13,* 229—233.

Newby, R. F., & Lyon, R. (1991). Neuropsychological subtypes of learning disabilities. In J. E. Obrzut & G. W. Hynd (Eds.), *Neuropsychological foundations of learning disabilities: A handbook of issues, methods, and practice* (pp. 355-386). San Diego, CA: Harcourt Brace Jovanovich.

Newby, R. F., & Matthews, C. G. (1986). Relationship between the "cognitive triad" from the personality inventory for children and an extended Halstead-Reitan neuropsychological battery. *Archives of Clinical Neuropsychology, 1,* 157—164.

Newman, J. P., Patterson, C. M., & Kosson, D. S. (1987). Response perseveration in psychopaths. *Journal of Abnormal Psychology, 96,* 145—148.

Niccols, G. A. (1994). Fetal alcohol syndrome: Implications for psychologists. *Clinical Psychology Review, 14,* 91—111.

Nielsen, J. (1991). *Klinefelter's syndrome: An orientation* (2nd ed.). Denmark: Novo Nordisk A/S.

Nieves, N. (1991). Childhood psychopathology and learning disabilities. In J. E. Obrzut, & G. W. Hynd (Eds.), *Neuropsychological foundations of learning disabilities: A handbook of issues, methods, and practice* (pp. 113—145). San Diego, CA: Harcourt Brace Jovanovich.

Nodine, B. F., Barenbaum, E., & Newcomer, P. (1985). Story composition by learning disabled, reading disabled, and normal children. *Learning Disability Quarterly, 8,* 167—179.

Nolan, D. R., Hammeke, T. A., & Barkley, R. A. (1983). A comparison of the patterns of the neuropsychological performance in two groups of learning disabled children. *Journal of Clinical and Child Psychology, 12,* 13—21.

North, K., Joy, P., Yuille, D., Cocks, N., & Hutchins, P. (1995). Cognitive function and academic performance in children with neurofibromatosis type 1. *Developmental Medicine and Child Neurology, 37,* 427—436.

Northcutt, T. E. (1987). The impact of a social skills training program on the teacher—student relationship. *Dissertation Abstracts International, 46,* 1231A.

Nussbaum, N. L., & Bigler, E. D. (1986). Halstead-Reitan test batteries for children. In C. R. Reynolds & E. Fletcher-Janzen (Eds.), *Handbook of clinical child neuropsychology* (pp. 181—192). New York: Plenum Press.

Nussbaum, N. L., Bigler, E. D., & Koch, W. (1986). Neuropsycholgocially derived subgroups of learning disabled children: Personality behavioral dimensions. *Journal of Research and Development in Education, 19,* 57—67.

Nussbaum, N. L., Bigler, E. D., & Koch, W. R., Ingram, J. W., Rosa, L., & Massman, P. (1988). Personality/behavioral characteristics in children: Differential effects of putative anterior versus posterior cerebral asymmetry. *Archives of Clinical Neuropsychology, 3,* 127—135.

Nyhan, W. L. (1976). Behavior in the Lesch-Nyhan syndrome. *Journal of Autism and Childhood Schizophrenia, 6,* 235—252

Obrzut, J. E. (1988). Deficient lateralization in learning-disabled children: Developmental lag or abnormal cerebral organization? In D. L. Molfese & S. J. Segalowitz (Eds.), *Brain lateralization in children: Developmental implications* (pp. 567—589). New York: Guildford Press.

Obrzut, J. E. (1991). Hemispheric activation and arousal asymmetry in learning-disabled children. In J. E. Obrzut & G. W. Hynd (Eds.), *Neuropsychological foundations of learning disabilities: A handbook of issues, methods, and practice* (pp. 179—198). San Diego, CA: Harcourt Brace Jovanovich.

Obrzut, J. E., Conrad, P. E., & Boliek, C. A. (1989). Verbal and nonverbal auditory processing among left- and right-handed good readers and reading disabled children. *Neuropsychologia, 27,* 1357—1371.

Obrzut, J. E., Conrad, P. E., Bryden, M. P., & Boliek, C. A. (1988). Cued dichotic listening with right-handed, left-handed, bilingual and learning-disabled children. *Neuropsychologia, 26,* 119—131.

Obrzut, J. E., & Hynd, G. W. (1986). *Child neuropsychology: Vol. 2. Clinical practice.* Orlando, FL: Academic Press.

Obrzut, J. E., & Hynd, G. W. (1990). Cognitive dysfunction and psychoeducational assessment in traumatic brain injury. In E. D. Bigler (Eds.), *Traumatic brain injury: Mechanisms of damage, assessment, intervention and outcome* (pp. 165—180). Austin, TX: Pro-Ed.

Obrzut, J. E., & Hynd, G. W. (1991). *Neuropsychological foundations of learning disabilities: A handbook of issues, methods, and practice.* San Diego, CA: Harcourt Brace Jovanovich.

Ochs, J., Mulhern, R., Fairclough, D., Parvey, L., et al. (1991). Comparison of neuropsychologic functional and clinical indicators of neurotoxicity in long-term survivors of childhood leukemia given cranial radiation or parenteral methotextrane: A prospective study. *Journal of Clinical Oncology, 9,* 145—151.

O'Donnell, J. P. (1991). Neuropsychological assessment of learning disabled adolescents and young adults. In J. E. Obrzut & G. W. Hynd (Eds.), *Neuropsychological foundations of learning disabilities: A handbook of issues, methods, and practice* (pp. 331—354). San Diego, CA: Academic Press.

Office of Special Education Programs. (1988). *Eleventh Annual Report to Congress on the Implementation of Public Law 94-142: The Education for All Handicapped Children Act.* Washington, DC: U.S. Department of Education.

Ogawa, T., Sugujama, A., Isheiwa, S., Sujuki, M., Ishiara, T., & Sato, K. (1982). Ontogenic development of EEG-asymmetry in early infantile autism. *Brain and Development, 4,* 439—449.

Ojemann, G. A., Cawthon, D. F., & Lettich, E. (1990). Localization and physiological correlates of language and verbal memory in human lateral temporoparietal cortex. In A. B. Scheibel & A. F. Wechsler (Eds.), *Neurobiology of higher cognitive function* (pp. 185—202). New York: Guilford Press.

O'Leary, D. S., & Boll, T. J. (1984). Neuropsychological correlates of early generalized brain dysfunction in children. C. R. Almli & S. Finger (Eds.), *Early brain damage: Vol. 1. Research orientations and clinical observations.* Orlando, FL: Academic Press.

O'Leary, D. S., Seidenberg, M., Berent, S., & Boll, T. J. (1981). The effects of age of onset of partial and generalized seizures on neuropsychological performance in children. *Journal of Nervous and Mental Disease, 141,* 624—629.

Olson, H. C., Sampson, P. D., Barr, H., Streissguth, A. P., et al. (1992). Prenatal exposure to alcohol and school problems in late childhood: A longitudinal prospective study. *Development and Psychopathology, 4,* 341—359.

Olson, R. (1994). Language deficits in "specific" reading disability. In M. Gernsbacher (Ed.), *Handbook of psycholinguistics.* New York: Academic Press.

Olson, R., Foltz, G., & Wise, B. (1986). Reading instruction and remediation with the aid of computer speech. *Behavior Research Methods, Instruments, & Computers, 18,* 93—99.

Olson, R., Fosberg, H., Wise, B., & Rack, J. (1994). Measurement of word recognition, orthographic, and phonological skills. In G. R. Lyon (Ed.), *Frames of reference for the assessment of learning disabilities: New views on measurement issues* (pp. 243—278). Baltimore, MD: Paul H. Brooks.

Olson, R., Kriegl, R., Davidson, B., & Foltz, G. (1985). Individual and developmental differences in reading disability. In T. Waller (Ed.), *Reading research: Advances in theory and practice* (Vol. 4, pp. 1—64). London: Academic Press.

Olson, R. K., Conners, F., DeFries, J., & Fulker, D. (1990). Genetic etiology of individual differences in reading disability. In L. Feagaus, E. Short, & L. Meltzer (Eds.), *Subtypes of learning disabilities* (pp. 113—135). Hillsdale, NJ: Erlbaum.

Olson, R., Wise, B., Conners, F., & Rack, J. (1990). Organization, heritability, and remediation of component word recognition and language skills in disabled readers. In T. H. Carr & B. A. Levy (Eds.), *Reading and its development: Component skills approaches* (pp. 261—322). New York: Academic Press.

Olson, R., Wise, B., Conners, F., Rack, J., & Fulker, D. (1989). Specific deficits in component reading and language skills. Genetic and environmental influences. *Journal of Learning Disabilities, 22,* 339—348.

Oro, A. S., & Dixon, S. D. (1987). Perinatal cocaine and methamphetamine exposure: Maternal and neonatal correlates. *Journal of Pediatrics, 111,* 571—578.

Osterreith, P. A. (1944). La test de copie d'une figure complexe. *Archives de psychologie, 30,* 206—356.

Ottman, R., Annegers, J. F., Hauser, W. A., et al. (1989). Seizure risk in offspring of parents with generalized versus partial epilepsy. *Epilepsia, 30,* 157—165.

Overholser, J. C. (1990). Fetal alcohol syndrome: A review of the disorder. *Journal of Contemporary Psychotherapy, 20,* 163—176.

Ovsiew, F. (1992). Bedside neuropsychiatry: Eliciting the clinical phenomena of neuropsychiatric illness. In S. C. Yudofsky & R. E. Hales (Eds.), *The American psychiatric press textbook of neuropsychiatry* (2nd ed., pp. 89-126). Washington, DC: American Psychiatric Press.

Ozonoff, S., Pennington, S. F., & Rogers, S. J. (1990). Are there emotion perception deficits in young autistic children? *Journal Of Child Psychology and Psychiatry and Allied Disciplines, 31,* 343-361.

Ozonoff, S., Pennington, S. F., & Rogers, S. J. (1991). Executive function deficits in autistic individuals: Relationship to theory of mind. *Journal of Child Psychology and Psychiatry and Allied Disciplines, 32,* 1081—1105.

Packer, R. K., Meadows, A. T., Rourke, L. B., Goldwein, J. L., & D'Angio, G. (1987). Long-term sequelae of cancer treatment on the central nervous system in childhood. *Medical and Pediatric Oncology, 15,* 241—253.

Palincsar, A., Brown, A., & Martin, S. (1987). Peer interaction in reading comprehension instruciton. *Educational Psychologist, 22,* 231—253.

Pampiglione, G. (1964). Prodomal phase of measles: Some neurophysiological studies. *British Medical Journal, 2,* 1296—1300.

Pampiglione, G., & Pugh, E. (1975). Infantile spasms and subsequent appearance of tuberous sclerous syndrome. *Lancet, 2,* 1046.

Pandya, D., & Yeterian, E. H. (1990). Architecture and connections of cerebral cortex: Implications for brain evolution and function. In A. B. Scheibel & A. F. Wechsler (Eds.), *Neurobiology of higher cognitive function* (pp. 53—84). New York: Guilford Press.

Panksepp, J. (1982). Toward a general psychological theory of emotions. *Behavioral Brain Science, 5,* 407—422.

Papalia, D., & Olds, S. W. (1992). *Human development* (5th ed.). New York: McGraw-Hill.

Parker, J. G., & Asher, S. R. (1987). Peer relations and later personal adjustment: Are low-accepted children at risk? *Psychological Bulletin, 102,* 357—389.

Parkins, R., Roberts, R. J., Reinarz, S. J., & Varney, N. R. (1987, January). *CT asymmetries in adult developmental dyslexics.* Paper presented at the annual meeting of the International Neuropsychological Society, Washington, DC.

Passler, M., Isaac, W., & Hynd, G. W. (1985). Neuropsychological development of behavior attributed to frontal lobe functioning in children. *Developmental Neuropsychology, 1,* 349—370.

Patterson, G. R. (1982). *Coercive family process.* Eugene, OR: Castalia Publications.

Patterson, G. R. (1983). Stress: A change agent for family process. In N. Garmezy & M. Rutter (Eds.), *Stress, coping, and development in children* (pp. 235—264). New York: McGraw Hill.

Patterson, G. R. (1986). Performance models for antisocial boys. *American Psychologist, 41,* 432—444.

Patterson, G. R., & Chamberlain, P. (1988). Treatment process: A problem at three levels. In L. C. Wynne (Ed.), *The state of the art in family therapy research: Controversies and recommendations* (pp. 189—223). New York: Family Process Press.

Patterson, G. R., DeBaryshe, B. D., & Ramsey, E. (1990). A developmental perspective on antisocial behavior. *American Psychologist, 44*, 329—335.

Patterson, G. R., & Fleischman, M. J. (1979). Maintenance of treatment effects: Some considerations concerning family systems; and follow-up data. *Behavior Therapy, 10*, 168—185.

Patterson, G. R., Reid, J. B., Jones, R. R., & Conger, R. W. (1975). *A social learning approach to family intervention* (Vol. 1). Eugene, OR: Castalia Publications.

Pauls, D. L., & Leckman, J. F. (1986). The inheritance of Gilles de la Tourette syndrome and associated behaviors: Evidence for autosomal dominant transmission. *New England Journal of Medicine, 315*, 993—997.

Pazzaglia, P., & Frank-Pazzaglia, L. (1976). Record in grade school of pupils with epilepsy: An epidemiological study. *Epilepsia, 17*, 361—366.

Peckham, V. C. (1991). Educational deficits in survivors of childhood cancer. *Pediatrician, 18*, 25—31.

Pelham, W. E. (1993a). Pharmacotherapy for children with attention deficit—hyperactivity disorder. *School Psychology Review, 22*, 199—227.

Pelham, W. E. (1993b). Recent developments in pharmacological treatment for children and adolescent mental health disorders. *School Psychology Review, 22*, 158—161.

Pelham, W. E., Carlson, C., Sams, S. E., Vallano, G., Dixon, M. J., & Hoza, B. (1993). Separate and combined effects of methylphenidate and behavior modification on boys with attention deficit—hyperactivity disorder in the classroom. *Journal of Consulting and Clinical Psychology, 61*, 506—615.

Pelham, W. E., Schnedler, R. W., Bender, M. E., Miller, J., Nilsson, D., Budow, M., Ronnei, M., Paluchowski, C., & Marks, D. (1988). The combination of behavior therapy and methylphenidate in a treatment of hyperactivity: A therapy outcome study. In L. Bloomingdale (Ed.), *Attention deficit disorders* (pp. 29—48). London: Pergamon Press.

Pellegrini, E., Koren, G., & Motherisk, I. (1990). A new model for counseling in reproductive toxicology. In G. Koren (Ed.), *Maternal—fetal toxicology: A clinician's guide* (pp. 355—372). New York: Marcel Dekker.

Penfield, W., & Jasper, H. (1954). *Epilepsy and the functional anatomy of the human brain.* New York: Macmillan.

Pennington B. F. (1991). *Diagnosing learning disorders.* New York: Guilford Press.

Pennington, B., Bender, B., Puck, M., Salbenblatt, J., & Robinson, A. (1982). Learning disabilities in children with sex chromosome anomalies. *Child Development, 53*, 1182—1192.

Pennington, B. F., & Bennetto, L. (1993). Main effects or transactions in the neuropsychology of conduct disorder? Commentary on "The neuropsychology of conduct disorder." *Development and Psychopathology, 5*, 153—164.

Perlstein, M., & Hood, P. (1955). Infantile spastic hemiplegia. *American Journal of Medicine, 34*, 391—396.

Perrin, E. C., Ayoub, C. C., & Willett, J. B. (1993). In the eyes of the beholder: Family and maternal influences on perceptions of adjustment of children with chronic illness. *Journal of Developmental and Behavioral Pediatrics, 14*, 94—105.

Peterson, P. L., & Lowe, J. B. (1992). Preventing fetal alcohol exposure: A cognitive behavioral approach. *International Journal of the Addictions, 27*, 613—626.

Petti, T. A., Bornstein, M., Dalamater, A., & Conners, C. K. (1980). Evaluation and multimodality treatment of a depressed prepubertal girl. *Journal of the American Academy of Child Psychiatry, 19*, 690—702.

Pettit, G. S., Bates, J. E., & Dodge, K. (1993). Family interaction patterns and children's conduct problems at home and school: A longitudinal perspective. *School Psychology Review, 22*, 403—420.

Pharoah, P. O. D., Cooke, T., Cooke, R. W. I., et al. (1990). Birthweight specific trends in cerebral palsy. *Archives of Disabled Children, 65*, 602—609.

Phelps, L. (in press). *A practitioner's handbook of health-related disorders in children.* New York: Guilford Press.

Phelps, L. (1995). Psychoeducational outcomes of Fetal Alcohol Syndrome. *School Psychology Review, 24*, 200—212.

Phillips, S. A., & Shanahan, R. J. (1989). Etiology and mortality of status epilepticus in children: A recent update. *Archives of Neurology, 46*, 74—76.

Pimm, P. (1992). Cerebral palsy: "A non-progressive disorder?" *Educational and Child Psychology, 9*, 27—33.

Pincus, J., & Tucker, G. (1978). Violence in children and adults. *Journal of the American Academy of Child Psychiatry, 17*, 277—288.

Pirrozzolo, F. J. (1981). Language and brain: Neuropsychological aspects of developmental reading disability. *School Psychology Review, 10,* 350—355.

Plaisted, J. R., Gustavson, J. C., Wilkening, G. N., & Golden, C. J. (1983). The Luria-Nebraska Neuropsychological Battery–Children's Revision: Theory and current research findings. *Journal of Clinical Child Psychology, 12,* 31—21.

Pless, I. B., & Pinkerton, P. (1975). *Chronic childhood disorder: Promoting patterns of adjustment.* London: Kimpton.

Plomin, R., Chipuer, H. M., & Loehlin, J. C. (1990). Behavioral genetics and personality. In L. A. Pervin (Ed.), *Handbook of personality theory and research* (pp. 225—243). New York: Guilford Press.

Polyakov, G. I. (1961). Some results of research into the devolopment of the neuronal structure of the cortical ends of the analyzers in man. *Journal of Comparative Neurology, 117,* 197—212.

Poplack, D. G. (1985). Acute lymphoblastic leukemia in childhood. *Pediatric Clinics of North America, 32,* 69—697.

Poplin, M. S., Gary, R., Larsen, S., Nanikowski, A., & Mehring, T. (1980). A comparison of written language expression abilities in learning disabled and non—learning disabled students at three grade levels. *Learning Disabilities Quarterly, 3,* 46—53.

Porges, S. W., Walter, G. F., Korb, R. J., & Sprague, R. L. (1975). The influence of methylphenidate on heart rate and behavioral measures of attention in hyperactive children. *Child Development, 46,* 727—733.

Porrino, L. J., Rapoport, J. L., Behar, D., Sceery, W., Ismond, D. R., & Bunney, W. E. (1983). A naturalistic assessment of the motor activity of hyperactive boys. *Archives of General Psychiatry, 40,* 681—687.

Posner, M. I. (1988). Structures and function of selective attention. In T. Boll & B. K. Bryant (Eds.), *Clinical neuropsychology and brain function: Research, measurement, and practice,* (pp. 169—202). Washington, DC: American Psychological Association.

Posner, M. I., & Boies, S. J. (1971). Components of attention. *Psychological Review, 78,* 391—409.

Posner, M. I., & Peterson, S. E. (1990). The attention system of the human brain. *Annual Review of Neuroscience, 13,* 25—42.

Posner, M. I., & Raichle, M. E. (1994). *Images of mind.* New York: Scientific American Library.

Poznanski, E., Grossman, J. A., Buchsbaum, Y., Banegas, M., Freeman, L., & Gibbons, R. (1984). Preliminary studies of the reliability and validity of the Children's Depression Rating Scale. *Journal of the American Academy of Child Psychiatry, 23,* 191—197.

Preakey, A., Wilson, J., & Wilson, B. (1974). Sensory and perceptual function in the cerebral palsied: III. Some visual perceptual relationships. *Journal of Nervous Mental Disease, 158,* 70—78.

Preskorn, S. H., Weller, E. B., & Hughes, C. W. (1987). Depression in prepubertal children: Dexamethasone nonsuppression predicts differential response to imipramine vs. placebo. *Psychopharmocology Bulletin, 23,* 128—133.

Preskorn, S. H., Weller, E. B., & Weller, R. A. (1982). Depression in children: Relationship between plasma imipramine levels and response. *Journal of Clinical Psychiatry, 43,* 450—453.

Pribram, K. H. (1992). *Brain and perception: Holonomy and structure in figural processes.* Hillsdale, NJ: Lawrence Erlbaum Associates.

Price, T. P., Goetz, K. L., & Lovell, M. R. (1992). Neuropsychiatric aspects of brain tumors. In S. C. Yudofsky & R. E. Hales (Eds.), *The American Psychiatric Press textbook of neuropsychiatry* (2nd ed., pp. 473—498). Washington, DC: American Psychiatric Press.

Prior, M. R., & Bradshaw, J. L. (1979). Hemispheric functioning in autistic children. *Cortex, 15,* 73—81.

Prizant, B. M., & Wetherby, A. M. (1987). Enhancing language and communication in autism. In G. Dawson (Ed.), *Autism: Nature, diagnosis, and treatment* (pp. 282—309). New York: Guilford Press.

Puig-Antich, J. (1982). Psychobiological correlates of major depressive disorder in children and adolescents. In L. Grinspoon (Ed.), *Psychiatry, 1982: Annual review* (pp. 288—296). Washington, DC: American Psychiatric Press.

Puig-Antich, J., & Chambers, W. J. (1978). *The Schedule for Affective Disorders and Schizophrenia for School-Age Children (Kiddie-Sads).* New York: New York Psychiatric Institute.

Puig-Antich, J., & Gittelman, R. (1982). Depression in childhood and adolescence. In E. S. Paykel (Ed.), *Handbook of affective disorders* (pp. 379-392). New York: Guilford Press.

Puig-Antich, J., Perel, J. M., Lupatkin, W., Chambers, W. J., Tabrizi, M. A., King, J., Johnson, R., & Stiller, R. (1987). Imipramine in prepubertal major depression. *Archives of General Psychiatry, 44,* 81—89.

Pullis, M. (1991). Practical considerations of excluding

conduct disordered students: An empirical analysis. *Behavior Disorders, 17,* 9—22.

Purpura, D. P. (1975). Dendritic differentiation in human cerebral cortex: Normal and aberrant developmental patterns. In G. W. Kreuzberg (Ed.), *Advances in neurology* (Vol. 12, pp. 115—141). New York: Raven Press.

Quay, H. C. (1986a). Conduct disorder. In H. C. Quay & J. S. Werry (Eds.), *Psychopathological disorders of childhood* (3rd ed., pp. 35—72). New York: Wiley.

Quay, H. C. (1986b). A critical analysis of DSM-III as a taxonomy of psychopathology in childhood and adolescence. In T. Millon & G. L. Klerman (Eds.), *Contemporary directions in psychopathology: Toward the DSM-IV* (pp. 151—165). New York: Guilford Press.

Rachman, S. J., & Hodgson. (1991). Consequences of panic. *Journal of Cognitive Psychotherapy, 5,* 187—197.

Rack, J. P., Snowling, M. J., & Olson, R. K. (1992). The nonword reading deficit in developmental dyslexia: A review. *Reading Research Quarterly, 27,* 28—53.

Radcliff, J., Packer, R. J., Atkins, T. E., Bunin, G. R., Schut, J., Goldwein, J. W., & Sulton, L. N. (1992). Three- and four-year cognitive outcome in children with noncortical brain tumors treated with whole-brain radiotherapy. *Annals of Neurology, 32,* 551—554.

Raine, A., O'Brien, M., Smiley, N., Scerbo, A., & Chan, C. (1990). Reduced lateralization in verbal dichotic listening in adolescent psychopaths. *Journal of Abnormal Psychology, 99,* 272, 277.

Rakic, P., & Riley, K. P. (1983). Overproduction and elimination of retinal axons in the fetal rhesus monkey. *Science, 219,* 1441—1444.

Rapoport, J. L. (1986). Childhood obsessive compulsive disorder. *Journal of Child and Psychology and Psychiatry and Allied Disciplines, 27,* 289—295.

Rapoport, J. L., Elkins, R., Langer, D. H., Sceery, W., Buchsbaum, M. S., Gillin, J. C., Murphy, D. L., Zahn, T. P., Lake, R., Ludlow, C., & Mendelson, W. (1981). Childhood obsessive-compulsive disorder. *American Journal of Psychiatry, 138,* 1545—1554.

Rasmussen, T., & Milner, B. (1977). The role of early left-brain injury in determining lateralization of cerebral speech functions. In S. J. Diamond & D. A. Blizard (Eds.), Evolution and lateralization of the brain. Orlando, FL: Academic Press.

Ratcliffe, S. G., Butler, G. E., & Jones, M. (1990). Edinburgh study of growth and development of children with sex chromosome abnormalities. In J. A. Evans, J. L. Hamerton, & A. Robinson (Eds.), *Birth defects: Original article series: Vol. 26. Children and*

young adults with chromosome aneuploidy (pp. 1—44). New York: Wiley-Liss.

Raymond, G., Bauman, M., & Kemper, T. (1989). The hippocampus in autism: Golgi analysis. *Annals of Neurology, 26,* 483—484.

Rayport, S. G. (1992). Cellular and molecular biology of the neuron. In S. C. Yudofsky & R. E. Hales (Eds.), *The American psychiatric press textbook of neuropsychiatry* (2nd ed., pp. 3—28). Washington, DC: American Psychiatric Press.

Realmuto, G. M., Garfinkel, B. D., Tuchman, M., et al. (1986). Psychiatric diagnosis and behavioral characteristics of phenylketonuric children. *Journal of Nervous and Mental Disorders, 174,* 536—540.

Reid, W. H., & Morrison, H. L. (1983). Risk factors in children of depressed parents. In H. L. Morrison (Ed.), *Children of depressed parents: Risk, identification, and intervention* (pp. 33—46). New York: Grune & Straton.

Reinis, S., & Goldman, J. M. (1980). *The development of the brain: Biological and functional perspectives.* Springfield, IL: Charles C Thomas.

Reiss, A. L., & Freund, L. (1990). Fragile X syndrome. *Biological Psychiatry, 27,* 223—240.

Reitan, R. M. (1962). Psychological deficit. *Annual Review of Psychology, 13,* 415—444.

Reitan, R. M. (1969). *Manual for administration of neuropsychological test batteries for adults and children.* Indianapolis, IN: Author.

Reitan, R. M. (1971). Sensorimotor functions in brain-damaged and normal children of early school age. *Perceptual and Motor Skills, 33,* 671—675.

Reitan, R. M. (1980). *REHABIT–Reitan evaluation of hemispheric abilities and brain improvement training.* Tucson: Reitan Neuropsychology Laboratory and University of Arizona.

Reitan, R. M. (1984). *Aphasia and sensory-perceptual deficits in children.* Tucson, AZ: Neuropsychological Press.

Reitan, R. M. (1986a). *Theoretical and methodological bases of the Halstead-Reitan Neuropsychological Test Battery.* Tucson, AZ: Neuropsychological Press.

Reitan, R. M. (1986b). Theoretical and methodolgical bases of the Halstead-Reitan Neurological Test Battery. In I. Grant & K. M. Adams (Eds.), *Neuropsychological assessment of neuropsychiatric disorders* (pp. 3—30). New York: Oxford University Press.

Reitan, R. M. (1987). *Neuropsychological evaluation of children.* Tucson, AZ: Neuropsychological Press.

Reitan, R. M., & Boll, T. (1973). Neuropsychological correlates of miminal brain dysfunction. *Annals of the New York Academy of Sciences, 203,* 65—88.

Reitan, R. M., & Davison, L. A. (1974). *Clinical neuropsychology: Current status and clinical applications.* New York: V. H. Winston & Sons.

Reitan, R. M., & Herring, S. (1985). A short screening device for identification of cerebral dysfunction in children. *Journal of Clinical Psychology, 41,* 643—650.

Reitan, R. M., & Wolfson, D. (1985a). *The Halstead-Reitan Neuropsychological Battery: Theory and clinical interpretation.* Tucson, AZ: Neuropsychological Press.

Reitan, R. M., & Wolfson, D. (1985b). *Neuroanatomy and neuropathology: A clinical guide for neuropsychologists.* Tucson, AZ: Neuropsychology Press.

Reitan, R. M., & Wolfson, D. (1992). *Neuropsychological evaluation of older children.* Tucson, AZ: Neuropsychology Press.

Reschly, D. J., & Gresham, F. M. (1989). Current neuropsychological diagnosis of learning problems: A leap of faith. In C. R. Reynolds & E. Fletcher-Janzen (Eds.). *Handbook of clinical child neuropsychology* (pp. 503—520). New York: Plenum Press.

Reynolds, C. R. (1989). Measurement and statistical problems in neuropsychological assessment of children. In C. R. Reynolds & E. Fletcher-Janzen (Eds.), *Handbook of clinical child neuropsychology* (pp. 147—177). New York: Plenum Press.

Reynolds, C. R. (1990). Conceptual and technical problems in learning disability diagnosis. In C. R. Reynolds & R. W. Kamphaus (Eds.). *Handbook of psychological and educational assessment of children: Intelligence and Achievement* (pp. 571—592). New York: Guilford Press.

Reynolds, C. R., & Kamphaus, R. W. (Eds.). (1990). *Handbook of psychological and educational assessment of children: Intelligence and Achievement.* New York: Guilford Press.

Reynolds, C. R., & Kamphaus, R. (1992). *The Behavioral Assessment Scale for Children.* Circle Pines, MN: AGS.

Reynolds, C. R., & Richmond, B. O. (1978). What I Think and Feel: A revised measure of children's manifest anxiety. *Journal of Abnormal Child Psychology, 6,* 271—280.

Reynolds, W. M. (1989). *Reynolds Child Depression Scale.* Odessa, FL: Psychological Assessment Resources.

Reynolds, W. M. (1990a). Depression in children and adolescents: Nature, diagnosis, assessment, and treatment. *School Psychology Review, 19,* 158—173.

Reynolds, W. M. (1990b). Introduction to the nature and study of internalizing disorders in children and adolescents. *School Psychology Review, 19,* 137—141.

Riccardi, V. M. (1992). *Neurofibromatosis, natural history, and pathogenesis.* Baltimore, MD: John Hopkins University Press.

Riccio, C. A., Hynd, G. W., Cohen, M. J., & Gonzalez, J. J. (1993). Neurobiological basis of attention deficit hyperactivity disorder. *Exceptional Children, 60,* 118—124.

Rimland, B. (1964). *Infantile autism.* New York: Appleton-Century-Crofts.

Rincker, J. L. (1990). Academic and intellectual characteristics of adolescent juvenile offenders. *Journal of Correctional Education, 41,* 124—131.

Ritvo, E. R., Freeman, B. J., Mason-Brothers, A., Mo, A., & Ritvo, A. M. (1985). Concordance for the syndrome of autism in 40 pairs of afflicted twins. *American Journal of Psychiatry, 142,* 74—77.

Ritvo, E. R., Mason-Brothers, A., Freeman, B. J., et al. (1990). The UCLA—University of Utah epidemiological survey of autism: The etiologic role of rare diseases. *American Journal of Psychiatry, 147,* 1614—1621.

Riva, D., Milani, N., Pantaleoni, C., Ballerini, E., & Giorgi, C. (1991). Combined treatment modality for medulloblastoma in childhood: Effects on neuropsychological functioning. *Neuropediatrics, 22,* 36—42.

Roa, S. M., Bandettini, P. A., Wond, E. C., Yetkin, F. Z., Hammeke, T. A., Mueller, W. M., Goldman, R. S., Morris, G. L., Antono, P. G., Estkowski, L. D., Haughton, V. M., & Hynde, J. S. (1992). Gradient echo EPI demonstrates bilateral superior temporal gyrus activation during passive word presentation. *Book of Abstracts, 11 Annual Meeting, Society for Magnetic Resonance in Medicine.* Berlin, Germany.

Robin, A. L., & Foster, S. (1989). *Negotiating parent-adolescent conflict.* New York: Guilford Press.

Robins, L. N. (1966). *Deviant children grown up.* Baltimore: Williams & Wilkins.

Robinson, A., Bender, B., & Linden, M. (1990). Summary of clinical findings in children and young adults with chromosome anomalies. In J. A. Evans, J. L. Hamerton, & A. Robinson (Eds.), *Birth defects: Original article series: Vol. 26. Children and young adults with sex chromosome aneuploidy* (pp. 225—228). New York: Wiley-Liss.

Robinson, R. (1973). The frequency of other handicaps in children with cerebral palsy. *Developmental Medicine in Child Neurology, 15,* 305—312.

Robinson, L. L., Nesbit, M. E., Sather, H. N., et al. (1980).

Assessment of the interrelationships of prognostic factors in childhood acute lymphoblastic leukemia. *American Journal of Hematology and Oncology, 2,* 5—13.

Rochford, J., Weinapple, M., & Goldstein, L. (1981). The quantitative hemispheric EEG in adolescent psychiatric patients with depressive or paranoid symptomatology. *Biological Psychiatry, 16,* 47—54.

Rodning, C., Bechwith, L., & Howard, J. (1989). Characteristics of attachment organization and play organization in prenatally drug-exposed toddlers. *Developmental Psychopathology, 1,* 277—289.

Rodning, C., Bechwith, L., & Howard, J. (1991). Quality of attachment and home environments in children prenatally exposed to PCP and cocaine. *Development and Psychopathology, 3,* 351—366.

Rosen, G. D., Galaburda, A. M., & Sherman, G. F. (1990). The ontogeny of anatomic asymmetry: Constraints derived from basic mechanisms. In A. B. Scheibel & A. F. Wechsler (Eds.), *Neurobiology of higher cognitive function* (pp. 215—238). New York: Guilford Press.

Rosenbaum, J. F. (1988). Course and treatment of manic depressive illness. *Journal of Clinical Psychiatry, 49,* Supplement.

Rosman, N. P. (1994). Acute brain injury. In K. F. Swaiman (Ed.), Pediatric neurology, (pp. 951—976). St. Louis, MO: Mosby.

Ross, A. O. (1981). *Child behavior therapy. Principles, Procedures and empirical basis* (pp. 251—289). New York: Wiley.

Ross, E. M., Peckham, C. S., West, P. B., et al. (1980). Epilepsy in childhood: Findings from the National Child Development Study. *British Medical Journal, 1,* 207—210.

Rotholz, D. A., Snyder, P., & Peters, G. (1995). A behavioral comparison of preschool children at high adn low risk from prenatal cocaine exposure. *Education and Treatment of Children, 18,* 1—18.

Rourke, B. P. (1981). Neuropsychological assessment of children with learning disabilities. In S. B. Filskov & T. J. Boll (Eds.), *Handbook of clinical child neuropsychology.* New York: Wiley Interscience.

Rourke, B. (Ed.). (1985). *Neuropsychology of learning disabilities: Essentials of subtype analysis.* New York: Guilford Press.

Rourke, B. (1989). *Nonverbal learning disabilities: The syndrome and the model.* New York: Guilford Press.

Rourke, B. (Ed.). (1991). *Neuropsychological validation of learning disabilities subtypes.* New York: Guilford Press.

Rourke, B. (1994). Neuropsychological assessment of children with learning disabilities: Measurement issues. In C. R. Lyon (Ed.), *Frames of reference for the assessment of learning disabilities: New views on measurement issues* (pp. 475—514). Baltimore, MD: Paul H. Brooks.

Rourke, B., Bakker, D., Fisk, J., & Strang, J. (1983). *Child neuropsychology: An introduction to theory, research, and clinical practice.* New York: Guilford Press.

Rourke, B., Del Dotto, J. E., Rourke, S. B., & Casey, J. E. (1990). Nonverbal learning disabilities: The syndrome and a case study. *Journal of School Psychology, 28,* 361—385.

Rourke, B., & Finlayson, M. A. J. (1978). Neuropsychological significance of variations in patterns of academic performance: Verbal and visual-spatial abilities. *Journal of Abnormal Child Psychology, 6,* 121—133.

Rourke, B., Fisk, J. L., & Strang, J. D. (1986). *Neuropsychological assessment of children: A treatment-oriented approach.* New York: Guilford Press.

Rourke, B., & Fuerst, D. R. (1991). *Learning disabilities and psychosocial functioning: A neuropsychological perspective.* New York: Guilford Press.

Rourke, B., & Strang, J. D. (1978). Neuropsychological significance of variations in patterns of academic performance: Motor, psychomotor, and tactile-perceptual abilities. *Journal of Pediatric Psychology, 3,* 62—66.

Rourke, B., & Strang, J. D. (1983). Subtypes of reading and arithmetic disabilities: A neuropsychological analysis. In M. Rutter (Ed.), *Developmental neuropsychiatry* (pp. 473—488). New York: Guilford Press.

Rourke, B., Young, G. C., & Leenaars, A. A. (1989). A childhood learning disability that predisposes those afflicted to adolescent and adult depression and suicide risk. *Journal of Learning Disabilities, 22,* 169—175.

Roussounis, S. H., Hubley, P. A., & Dear, P. R. (1993). Five-year-follow-up of very low birthweight infants: Neurological and psychological outcome. *Child Care, Health and Development, 19,* 45—49.

Rowan, N., & Monaghan, H. (1989). Reading achievement in pupils with cerebral palsy (hemiplegia). Special Issue: Dyslexia: Current research issues. *Irish Journal of Psychology, 10,* 615—621.

Rowland, L. P. (1991). Blood-brain behavior, cerebrospinal fluid, brain edema, and hydrocephalus. In E. R. Kandel, J. H. Schwartz, & T. M. Jessel (Eds.), *Principles of neural science* (3rd ed., pp. 1050—1073). New York: Elsevier.

Rowland, L. P., Fink, M. E., & Rubin, L. (1994). Cerebrospinal fluid: Blood-brain barrier, brain edema, and hydrocephalus. In E. R. Kandel, J. H. Schwartz, & T. M. Jessell (Eds.), *Principles of neural behavior* (pp. 1050—1060). New York: Elsevier

Rubin, H., & Liberman, I. (1983). Exploring the oral and written language errors made by language disabled children. *Annals of Dyslexia, 33,* 111—120.

Rumsey, J. M., Dorwart, R., Vermess, M., Denkla, M. B., Kruesi, M. J. P., & Rapoport, J. L. (1986). Magnetic resonance imaging of brain anatomy in severe developmental dyslexia. *Archives of Neurology, 43,* 1045—1046.

Russell, M., Czarnecki, D. M., Cowan, R., McPherson, E., et al. (1991). Measures of maternal alcohol use as predictors of development in early childhood. *Alcoholism: Clinical and Experimental Research, 15,* 991—1000.

Rutter, M. (1978a). Diagnosis and definition. In M. Rutter & E. Schopler (Eds.), *Autism: A reappraisal of concepts and treatments.* New York: Plenum Press.

Rutter, M. (1978b). Language disorder and infantile autism. In M. Rutter & E. Schopler (Eds.), *Autism: A reappraisal of concepts and treatments* (pp. 85—104). New York: Plenum Press.

Rutter, M. (1981). Psychological sequelae of brain damage in children. *American Journal of Clinical Neuropsychology, 138,* 1533—1544.

Rutter, M. (1983a). Behavioral studies: Questions and findings on the concept of a distinctive syndrome. In M. Rutter (Ed.), *Developmental neuropsychiatry* (pp. 259—279). New York: Guilford Press.

Rutter, M. (1983b). Issues and prospects in developmental neuropsychiatry. In M. Rutter (Ed.), *Developmental neuropsychiatry* (pp. 557—598). New York: Guilford Press.

Rutter, M. (1985). Infantile autism. In D. Schaffer, A. A. Ehrhardt, & L. L. Greenhill (Eds.), *The clinical guide to child psychiatry* (pp. 48—78). New York: Free Press.

Rutter, M., Chadwick, O., & Shaffer, D. (1983). Head injury. In M. Rutter (Ed.), *Developmental neuropsychiatry* (pp. 83—111). New York: Guilford Press.

Rutter, M., & Lockyear, L. (1967). A five to fifteen year follow-up study of infantile psychosis. I. Description of sample. *British Journal of Psychiatry, 113,* 1169—1182.

Rutter, M., MacDonald, H., LeCouteur, A., Harington, R., Bolton, P., & Bailey, A. (1990). genetic factors in child psychiatric disorders: II. Empirical findings. *Journal of Child Psychology and Psychiatry, 31,* 39—83.

Rutter, M., & Yule, W. (1975). The concept of specific reading retardation. *Journal of Child Psychology and Psychiatry, 16,* 181—197.

Sachs, H. T., & Barrett, R. P. (1995). Seizure disorders: A review for school psychologists. *School Psychology Review, 24,* 131—145.

Sachs, P. R., & Redd, C. A. (1993). The Americans with Disabilities Act and individuals with neurological impairments. Special Issue: The implications of the Americans with Disabilities Act of 1990 for psychologists. *Rehabilitation Psychology, 38,* 87—101.

Sackheim, H. A., Decina, P., & Malitz, S. (1982). Functional brain asymmetry and affective disorders. *Adolescent Psychiatry, 10,* 320—335.

Safilios-Rothchild, C. (1970). *The sociology and social psychology of disability and rehabilitation.* New York: Random House.

Sagvolden, T., & Archer, T. (1989). *Attention deficit disorder: Clinical and basic research.* Hillsdale, NJ: Lawrence Erlbaum Associates.

Salzman, C. (1990). Benzodiazepine dependency: Summary of the APA task force on benzodiapines. *Psychopharmacology Bulletin, 26,* 61—62.

Sameroff, A. (1975). Transactional models in early social relations. *Human Development, 18,* 65—79.

Sameroff, A., & Emde, R. N. (1998). *Relationship disturbances in early childhood: A developmental approach.* New York: Basic Books.

Sameroff, A. J., & Chandler, M. J. (1975). Reproductive risk and the continuum of caretaking casualty. In F. D. Horowitz (Ed.), *Review of child development research* (Vol. 4, pp. 187—244). Chicago: University of Chicago Press.

Samuels, J. W., & Samuels, N. (1986). *The well pregnancy book.* New York: Summit.

Sandberg, D., & Barrick, C. (1995). Endocrine disorders in childhood: A selective survey of intellectual and educational sequelae. *School Psychology Review, 24,* 146—170.

Sargeant, J. A., & Scholten, C. A. (1985a). On data limitations in hyperactivity. *Journal of Child Psychology and Psychiatry, 26,* 111—124.

Sargeant, J. A., & Scholten, C. A. (1985b). On resource strategy limitations in hyperactivity: Cognitive impulsivity reconsidered. *Journal of Child Psychology and Psychiatry, 26,* 97—109.

Sarnat, H. (1995). Developmental disorders of the nervous system. In W. G. Bradley, R. B. Daroff, G. M. Fenichel, & C. D. Marsden (Eds.), *Neurology in clinical practice* (pp. 1459—1482). Boston: Butterworth-Heinemann.

Sato, S., Dreifuss, F. E., Penry, J. K. et al. (1983). Long-term follow-up of absence seizures. *Neurology, 33,* 1590—1600.

Sato, S., White, B. G., Penry, J. K., et al. (1982). Valporic acid versus ethosuximide in the treatment of absence seizures. *Neurology, 32,* 157—165.

Satterfield, J. H., Schell, A. M., & Backs, R. W. (1988). Topographic study of auditory event related potentials in normal boys and in boys with attention deficit disorder with hyperactivity. *Psychophysiology, 25,* 591—606.

Sattler, J. (1988). *Assessment of children (3rd ed.).* San Diego, CA: Jerome M. Sattler.

Satz, P. (1991). The Dejerine hypothesis: Implications for an etiological reformation of developmental dyslexia. In J. E. Obrzut & G. W. Hynd (Eds.). *Neuropsychological foundations of learning disabilities: A handbook of issues, methods, and practices* (pp. 99—112). San Diego, CA: Academic Press.

Satz, P, & Morris, R. (1981). Learning disabilities subtypes: A review. In F. Pirozzolo & M. Wittrock (Eds.), *Neuropsychological and cognitive processes in reading.* New York: Academic Press.

Satz, P., & Sparrow, S. S. (1970). Specific developmental dyslexia: A theoretical formulation. In D. Bakker & P. Satz (Eds.), *Specific reading disability: Advances in theory and method.* Rotterdam: Rotterdam University Press.

Savitz, D. A., Wachtel, H., Barnes, F. A., et al. (1988). Case-control study of childhood cancer and exposure to 60 hz magnetic fields. *American Journal of Epidemiology, 128,* 21—26.

Saxby, L., & Bryden, M. P. (1984). Left-ear superiority in children for processing auditory material. *Developmental Psychology, 20,* 72—80.

Saxby, L., & Bryden, M. P. (1985). Left-visual field advantage in children for processing visual emotional stimuli. *Developmental Psychology, 21,* 253—261.

Scarborough, H. (1990). Very early language deficits in children. *Child Development, 61,* 1728—1743.

Scarr, S., & McCartney, K. (1983). How people make their own environments: A theory of genotype—environment correlations. *Child Development, 54,* 424—435.

Schaad, U., Suter, S., Gianella-Borradori, A., Pfenninger, J., Auckenthaler, R., Bernath, O., Cheseaux, J. J., & Wedgewood, J. (1990). A compairson of ceftriaxone and cefuroxime for treatment of bacterial meningitis in children. *New England Journal of Medicine, 322,* 141—147.

Schachar, R. J., Tannock, R., & Logan, G. (1993). Inhibitory control, impulsiveness, and ADHD. *Clinical Psychology Review, 13,* 721—789.

Schaughency, E. A., & Hynd, G. W. (1989). Attentional control systems and the attentional deficit disorders (ADD). *Learning and Individual Differences, 4,* 423—449.

Schaughency, E. A., Lahey, B. B., Hynd, G. W., Stone, P. A., Piacentini, J. C., & Frick, P. J. (1989). Neuropsychological test performance and the attention deficit disorders: Clinical utility of the Luria-Nebraska Neuropsychological Battery Revision. *Journal of Clinical and Consulting Psychology 57,* 112—116.

Schaughency, E. A., & Rothlind, J. (1991). Assessment and classification of attention-deficit hyperactivity disorders. *School Psychology Review, 20,* 187—202.

Scheibel, A. B. (1990). Dendritic correlates of higher cognitive function. In A. B. Scheibel & A. F. Wechsler (Eds.), *Neurobiology of higher cognitive function* (pp. 239—270). New York: Guilford Press.

Schmitt, B. D. (1975). The minimal brain dysfunction myth. *American Journal of Diseases of Children, 129,* 1313—1318.

Schopler, E., Mesibov, G., Shigley, H., & Bashford, A. (1984). Helping autistic childrn through their parents: The TEACCH model. In E. Schopler & G. Misibov (Eds.), *The effects of autism on the family* (pp. 65—81). New York: Plenum Press.

Schuler, D., Polcz, A., Revesz, T., Koos, R., Bakos, M., & Gal, N. (1981). Psychological late effects of leukemia in children and their prevention. *Medical and Pediatric Oncology, 9,* 191—194.

Schwaab, D. F. (1991). Relation between maturation of neurotransmitter systems in the human brain and psychosocial disorders. In M. Rutter & P. Caesar (Eds.), *Biological risk factors for psychosocial disorders* (pp. 50—66). New York: Cambridge University Press.

Seidenberg, M. (1988). Neuropsychological functioning of children with epilepsy. In B. P. Hermann & M. Seidenberg (Eds.), *Childhood epilepsies: Neuropsychological, psychosocial and intervention aspects* (pp. 71—81). New York: Wiley.

Seidenberg, M., Beck, N., Geisser, M., Giordani, B., et al. (1986). Academic achievement of children with epilepsy. *Epilepsia, 27,* 753—759.

Seidman, D. S., Paz, I., Laor, A., et al. (1991) Apgar scores and cognitive performance at 17 years of age. *Obstetrics and Gynecology, 77,* 875—878.

Seigel, L. S. (1989). IQ is irrelevant to the definition of learning disabilities. *Journal of Learning Disabilities, 22,* 469—479.

Sell, S. H. (1983). Long term sequelae of bacterial meningitis in children. *Pediatric Infectious Disease, 2,* 90—93.

Selz, M., & Reitan, R. (1979a). Neuropsychological test performance of normal, learning-disabled, and brain-damaged older children. *Journal of Nervous and Mental Disorders, 167,* 298—302.

Selz, M., & Reitan, R. (1979b). Rules for neuropsychological diagnosis: Classification of brain function in older children. *Journal of Consulting and Clinical Psychology, 47,* 258—264.

Semrud-Clikeman, M., Biederman, J., Sprich-Buckminster, S., Lehman, B., Faraone, S., & Norman, D. (1992). Comorbidity between ADHD and learning disability: A review and report in a clinically referred sample. *Journal of the American Academy of Child and Adolescent Psychiatry, 31,* 439—448.

Semrud-Clikeman, M., Filipek, P. A., Biederman, J., et al. (1994). Attention deficit hyperactivity disorder: Magnetic resonance imaging morphometric analysis of the corpus callousm, *Journal of the American Academy of Child and Adolescent Psychiatry, 33,* 875—881.

Semrud-Clikeman, M., Harrington, K., Parle, N., Clinton, A., & Connor, R. (submitted). Innovative interventions with children with attentional difficulties in the school setting. *School Psychology Quarterly.*

Semrud-Clikeman, M., & Hynd, G. W. (1991a). Review of issues and measures in childhood depression. *School Psychology International, 12,* 275—298.

Semrud-Clikeman. M., & Hynd, G. W. (1991b). Specific nonverbal and social skills deficits in children with learning disabilities. In J. E. Obrzut & G. W. Hynd (Eds.), *Neuropsychological foundations of learning disabilities: A handbook of issues, methods, and practice* (pp. 603—630). San Diego, CA: Academic Press.

Semrud-Clikeman, M., & Hynd, G. W. (1993). Assessment of learning and cognitive dysfunction in young children. In J. L. Culbertson and D. J. Willis (Eds.), *Testing young children* (pp. 11—28). Austin, TX: Pro-Ed.

Semrud-Clikeman, M., Hynd, G. W., Lorys, A. R., & Lahey, B. B. (1993). Differential diagnosis of children with ADHD and ADHD/with co-occurring conduct disorder. *School Psychology International, 14,* 361—370.

Semrud-Clikeman. M., Hynd, G. W., Novey, E. S., & Eliopulos, D. (1991). Dyslexia and brain morphology: Relationships between neuroanatomical variation and neurolinguistic tasks. *Learning and Individual Differences, 3,* 225—242.

Semrud-Clikeman, M., & Teeter, P. A. (1995). Personality, intelligence, and neuropsychology in the diagnosis and treatment of clinical disorders.In D. H. Zaklofske & M. Zeidner (Eds.), *International handbook of personality and intelligence* (pp. 651—672). New York: Plenum Press.

Shah, A., & Frith, U. (1993). Why do autistic individuals show superior performance on Block Design task? *Journal of Child Psychology and Psychiatry, 34,* 1351—1364.

Shankweiler, D., & Liberman, I. Y. (1989). *Phonology and reading disability.* University of Michigan Press, Ann Arbor.

Shankweiler, D., Liberman, I. Y., Mark, L. S., Fowler, C. A., & Fischer, F. W. (1979). The speech codeand learning to read. *Journal of Experimental Psychology: Human Perceptual Performance, 5,* 531—545.

Shapiro, B. (1992). Normal and abnormal development. In M. L. Batshaw & Y. M. Perret (Eds.), *Children with disabilities: A medical primer.* Baltimore, MD: Paul H. Brooks.

Shapiro, D. K. & Dotan, N. (1985, October). *Neuropsychological findings and the Kaufman Assessment Battery for Children.* Paper presented at the National Academy of Neuropsychologists. Philadelphia.

Shapiro, E. S. (1989). *Academic skills problems: Direct assessment and intervention.* New York,: Guilford Press.

Shapiro, E. S., & Cole, C. L. (1994). *Self-management interventions for classroom behavior change.* New York: Guilford Press.

Shapiro, S. K., Quay, H. C., Hogan, A. E., & Schwartz, K. P. (1988). Response perseveration and delayed responding in undersocialized conduct disorder. *Journal of Abnormal Psychology, 97,* 371—373.

Shatz, C. J. (1993). The developing brain. In *Mind and brain: Readings from the Scientific American* (pp. 15—26). New York: W. H. Freeman.

Shaw, E. D., & Beals, R. K. (1992). The hip joint in Down's syndrome: A study of its structure and associated disease. *Clinical Orthopaedics and Related Research, 278,* 100—107.

Shaw, J. A. (1988). Childhood depression. *Medical Clinics of North America, 72,* 831—845.

Shaywitz, S. E., Escobar, M. D., Shaywitz, B. A., Fletcher, J. M., & Makuch, R. (1992). Evidence that dyslexia may represent the lower tail of a normal distribution of reading ability. *The New England Journal of Medicine, 326,* 145—150.

Shaywitz, S. E., Shaywitz, B. A., Fletcher, J. M., &

Escobar, M. D. (1990). Prevalence of reading disability in boys and girls: Results of the Conneticut Longitudinal Study. *Journal of the American Medical Association, 264,* 998—1002.

Shear, P. K., Tallal, P., & Delis, D. C. (1992). Verbal learning and memory in language-impaired children. *Neuropsychologia, 30,* 451—458.

Shekim, W. O., Javid, J., Davis, J. M., & Bylund, D. B. (1983). Urinary MHPG and HVA excretion in boys with attention deficit disorder and hypreactivity treated with D-amphetamine. *Biological Psychiatry, 18,* 707—714.

Shepard, G. M. (1994). *Neurobiology* (3rd ed.). New York: Oxford University Press.

Shepherd, L. (1988). Discussion. In J. E Kavanaugh & T. J. Truss (Eds.), *Learning disabilities: Proceedings of the national conference* (pp. 164—167). Parkton, MD: York Press.

Sheshow, D., & Adams, W. (1990). *Wide Range Assessment of Memory and Learning.* Wilmington, DE: Jastak Associates.

Sheslow, D., & Adams, W. (1990). Wide Range Assessment of Memory and Learning. Wilmington, DE: Jastak Associates.

Shinn, M. R. (1989). *Curriculum-based measurement: Assessing special children.* New York: Guilford Press.

Short, R. J., & Shapiro, S. K. (1993). Conduct disorders: A framework for understanding and intervention in schools and communities. *School Psychology Review, 22,* 362—375.

Shriver, M. D., & Piersel, W. (1994). The long-term effects of intrauterine drug exposure: Review of recent research and implications for early childhood special education. *Topics in Early Childhood Special Education, 14,* 161—183.

Shucard, D. W., Cummins, K. R., & McGee, M. G. (1984). Event-related brain potentials differentiate normal and disabled readers. *Brain and Language, 21,* 318—324.

Shurtleff, H. A., Fay, G. E., Abbott, R. D., & Berninger, V. W. (1988). Cognitive and neuropsychological correlates of academic achievement: A levels of analysis assessment model. *Journal of Psychoeducational Assessment, 6,* 298—308.

Sidman, R. L., & Rakic, P. (1973). Neuronal migration, with special reference to the developing human brain: A review. *Brain Research, 62,* 1—35.

Sillanpaa, M. (1992). Epilepsy in children: Prevalence, disability and handicap. *Epilepsia, 33,* 444—449.

Silver, L. B. (1988). The scope of the problem in children and adolescents. In J. G. Looney (Ed.), *Chronic mental illness in children and adolescents* (pp. 39—51). Washington, DC: American Psychiatric Press.

Silver, J. M., Hales, R. E., & Yudofsky, S. C. (1992). Neuropsychiatric aspects of traumatic brain injury. In S. C. Yudofsky & R. E. Hales (Eds.), *The American Psychiatric Press textbook of neuropsychiatry* (2nd ed., pp. 363—395). Washington, DC: American Psychiatric Press.

Silverstein, F. S., & Johnston, M. V. (1990). Neurological assessment of children: The damaged child. In R. D. Eden, F. H. Boehm, & M. Haire (Eds.), *Assessment and care of the fetus: Physiological, clinical, and methodlogical principles.* Norwalk, CT: Appleton & Lange.

Simeonsson, R. J., Olley, J. G., & Rosenthal, S. L. (1987). Early intervention for children with autism. In M. J. Guralnick & F. C. Bennet (Eds.), *The effectiveness of early intervention for at-risk and handicapped children* (pp. 275—296). New York: Academic Press.

Simone, C., Derewlany, L., Knie, B., & Koren, G. (1992). Can the human placenta biotransform cocaine? *Clinical Investigations in Medicine, 15,* A19.

Singer, H. S., Brown, J., Quaskey, S., Mellits, E. D., Denckla, M. B., & Rosenberg, L. A. (1991). The treatment of attention deficit hyperactivity disorder in Tourette Syndrome: A double-blind placebo-controlled study with clonidine and desipramine. *Annals of Neurology, 30,* 485.

Singer, L. T., Farkas, K., & Kliegman, R. (1991). Childhood medical and behavioral consequences of maternal cocaine use. *Journal of Pediatric Psychology 17,* 389—406.

Singer, L. T., Garber, R., & Kliegman, R. (1991). Neurobehavioral sequelae of fetal cocaine exposure. *The Journal of Pediatrics, 119,* 667—672.

Singhi, P. D., Bansal, U., Singhi, S., & Pershad, D. (1992). Determinants of IQ profile in children with idiopathic generalized epilepsy. *Epilepsia, 33,* 1106—1114.

Smalley, I. L., Asarnow, R. F., & Spence, M. A. (1988). Autism and genetics: A decade of research. *Archives of General Psychiatry, 45,* 953—961.

Smith, A., Walker, M. L., & Myers, G. (1988). Hemispherectomy and diaschisis: Rapid improvement in cerebral functions after right hemispherectomy in a six year old child. *Archives of Clinical Neuropsychology, 3,* 1—8.

Smith, D. W., & Wilson, A. A. (1973). *The child with Down's syndrome (Mongolism).* Philadelphia: Saunders.

Smith, E., & Alley, G. (1981). *The effect of teaching sixth graders with learning disabilities a strategy for solving verbal math problems.* (Research Report No. 39). Lawrence University of Kansas, Institute for Research in Learning Disabilities.

Smith, M. N. (1989). Reading without speech: A study of children with cerebral palsy. Special Issues: Dyslexia: Current research issues. *Irish Journal of Psychology, 10,* 601—614.

Smith, R. F., Mattran, K. M., Kurkjian, M. F., & Kurtz, S. L. (1989). Alterations in offspring behavior induced by chronic prenatal cocaine dosing. *Neurotoxicology and Teratology, 11,* 35—38.

Smith, S. D., Penington, B. F., Kimberling, W. J., & Lubs, H. A. (1983). A genetic analysis of specific reading disability. In J. A. Cooper & C. L. Ludlow (Eds.), *Genetic aspects of speech and language disorders.* New York: Academic Press.

Smith, T. B., Innocenti, M. S., Boyce, G. C., & Smith, C. S. (1993). Depressive symptomatology and interaction behaviors of mothers having a child with disabilities. *Psychological Reports, 73,* 1184—1186.

Snead, O. C. III. (1985). Gamma-hydroxybutyrate model of generalized absence seizures: Further characterization and comparison with other absence models. *Epilepsia, 29,* 361—365.

Snow, J. H., & Hynd, G. W. (1985a). Factor structure of the Luria Nebraska Neuropsychological Battery–Children's Revision. *Journal of School Psychology, 23,* 271—276.

Snow, J. H., & Hynd, G. W. (1985b). A multivariate investigation of the Luria Nebraska Neuropsychological Battery–Children's Revision with learning disabled children. *Journal of Psychoeducational Assessment, 3,* 101—109.

Snow, J. H., Hynd, G. W., & Hartlage, L. H. (1984). Differences between mildly and more severely learning disabled children on the Luria-Nebraska Neuropsychological Battery–Children's Revision. *Journal of Psychoeducational Assessment, 2,* 23—28.

Snyder, R. D. (1994). Bacterial meningitis of infants and children. In K. Swaiman (Ed.), *Principles of neurology* (pp. 611—642). St. Louis, MO: Mosby.

Sohlberg, M. M., & Mateer, C. A. (1989). *Introduction to cognitive rehabilitation.* New York: Guilford Press.

Soubrie, P. (1986). Reconciling the role of central serotonin in human and animal behavior. *Behavioral Medical Science, 9,* 319—364.

Spirto, A., Stark, L. J., Cobella, C., Drigan, R., et al. (1990). Social adjustment of children successfully treated for cancer. *Journal of Pediatric Psychology, 15,* 359—371.

Spivack, G., Platt, J. J., & Shure, M. B. (1976). *The problem solving approach to adjustment.* San Francisco: Jossey-Bass.

Spreen, O. (1989). The relationship between learning disability, emotional disorders, and neuropsychology: Some results and observations. *Journal of Clinical and Experimental Neuropsychology, 11,* 117—140.

Spreen, O., & Benton, A. L. (1969). *Neurosensory center comprehensive examination for aphasia (NCCEA).* Victoria, B.C.: University of Victoria.

Spreen, O., & Benton, A. L. (1977). *Neurosensory center comprehensive examination for aphasia (NCCEA)- revised.* Victoria, B.C.: University of Victoria.

Spreen, O., & Gaddes, W. H. (1969). Developmental norms for 15 neuropsychological tests age 6 to 15. *Cortex, 5,* 170—191.

Spreen, O., & Strauss, E. (1991). *A compendium of neuropsychological tests.* New York: Oxford University Press.

Spreen, O., Tupper, D., Risser, A., Tuokko, H., & Edgell, D. (1984). *Human developmental neuropsychology.* New York: Oxford University Press.

Stahl, S. A., & Kuhn, M. R. (1995). Does whole language or instruction matched to learning styles help children learn to read. *School Psychology Review, 24,* 393—404.

Stanley, F. J. (1994). The aetiology of cerebral palsy. *Early Human Development, 36,* 81—88.

Stanovich, K. E. (1986). Matthew effects in reading: Some consequences of individual differences in the acquisition of literacy. *Reading Disability Quarterly, 21,* 360—406.

Stanovich, K. E. (1988). Explaining the differences between the dyslexic and garden-variety poor reader: The phonological-core variable-difference model. *Journal of Learning Disabilities, 21,* 590—612.

Stanovich, K. E. (1989). Has the learning disabilities field lost its intelligence? *Journal of Learning Disabilities, 22,* 487—492.

Stanovich, K. E. (1992). Speculations on the causes and consequences of individual differences in early reading acquisition. In P. Gough, L. Ehri, & R. Trieman (Eds.), *Reading acquisition* (pp. 307—342). Hillsdale, NJ: Lawrence Erlbaum Associates.

Stanovich, K. E. (1993). The construct validity of discrepancy definitions of reading disability. In C. R. Lyon, D. B. Gray, J. F. Kavanagh, & N. A. Krasnegor (Eds.), *Better understanding learning disabilities: New views from research and their implications for education and public policies* (pp. 273—308). Baltimore, MD: Paul H. Brooks.

Stanovich, K. E., Cunningham, A., & Cramer, B. (1984). Assessing phonological awareness in kindergarten children: Issues of task comparability. *Journal of Experimental Child Psychology, 38,* 175—190.

Stanovich, K. E., Cunningham, A., & Freeman, D. J. (1984). Intelligence, cognitive skills, and early reading progress. *Reading Research Quarterly, 19,* 278—303.

Stanovich, K. E., Nathan, R., & Vala-Rossa, M. (1986). Developmental changes in the cognitive correlates of reading ability and the developmental lag hypothesis. *Reading Research Quarterly, 21,* 267—283.

Stanovich, K. E., & West, R. F. (1989). Exposure to print and orthographic processing. *Reading Research Quarterly, 24,* 402—433.

Stanton, M. E., & Spear, L. P. (1990). Workshop on the qualitative and quantitative comparability of human and animal developmental toxicity, Work Group I Report: Comparability of measures of developmental neurotoxicity in humans and laboratory animals. *Neurotoxicology and Teratology, 12,* 261—267.

Stark, K. D., Reynolds, W. M., & Kaslow, N. J. (1987). A comparison of the relative efficacy of self-control therapy and a behavioral problem-solving therapy for depression in chidlren. *Journal of Abnormal Child Psychology, 15,* 91—113.

Stark, R. E. (1988). Implications for clinical management: A perspective. In R. E. Stark & P. Tallal (Eds.), *Language, speech, and reading disorders in children: Neuropsychological studies* (pp. 169—180). Boston: College-Hill.

Stark, R. E., & Tallal, P. (1988). *Language, speech, and reading disorders in children: Neuropsychological studies.* Boston, MA: College-Hill Publication.

Staton, R. D., Wilson, H., & Brumback, R. A. (1981). Cognitive improvement associated with tricyclic antidepressant treatment of childhood major depressive illness. *Perceptual and MotorSkills, 53,* 219—234.

Stechler, G., & Halton, A. (1982). Prenatal influences on human development. In B. B. Wolman (Ed.), *Handbook of developmental psychology* (pp. 175—189). Engelwood Cliffs, NJ: Prentice-Hall.

Stedman, J., Van Heyningen, R., & Lindsey, J. (1982). Educational underachievement and epilepsy: A study of children from normal schools admitted to a special hospital for epilepsy. *Early Childhood Development Care, 9,* 65—82.

Steingard, R., Biederman, J., Doyle, A., & Sprich-Buckminster, I. (1992). Psychiatric comorbidity in attention deficit disorder: Impact on the interpretation of child behavior checklist results. *Journal of American Academy of Child and Adolescent Psychiatry, 31,* 449—454.

Steingard, R., Biederman, J., Spencer, T., Wilens, T., & Gonzalez, A. (1993). Comparison of clonidine response in the treatment of ADHD. *Journal of the American Academy of Child and Adolescent Psychiatry, 32,* 350—353.

Steinhausen, H. C., Willms, J., & Spohr, H. L. (1993). Long-term psychopathological and cognitive outcome of children with fetal alcohol syndrome. *Journal of the American Academy of Child and Adolescent Psychiatry, 32,* 990—994.

Steinhausen, H. C., Willms, J., & Spohr, H. L. (1994). Correlates of psychopathology and intelligence in children with fetal alcohol syndrome. *Journal of Child Psychology and Psychiatry and Allied Disciplines, 35,* 323—331.

Steinmetz, H., & Galaburda, A. M. (1991). Planum temporale asymmetry: In-vivo morphometry affords a new perspective for neuro-behavioral research. *Reading and Writing: An Interdisciplinary Journal, 3,* 331—343.

Steinmetz, H., Rademacher, J., Huang, Y., Hefter, H., Zilles, K., Thron, A., & Freund, H. (1989). Cerebral asymmetry: MR planimetry of the human planum temporale. *Journal of Computer Assisted Tomography, 13,* 996—1005.

Sternberg, R. (1985). *Beyond IQ: A triarchic theory of human intelligence.* Cambridge, England: Cambridge University Press.

Stewart, M. A., deBlois, C. S., & Cummings, C. (1980). Psychiatric disorder in the parents of hyperactive boys and those with conduct disorder. *Journal of Child Psychology and Psychiatry, 21,* 283—292.

Strain, P. S., Jamieson, B. J., & Hoyson, M. H. (1985). Learning experiences. . . . An alternative program for preschoolers and parents: A comprehensive service system for the mainstreaming of autistic-like preschoolers. In C. J. Meisel (Ed.), *Mainstreamed handicapped children: Outcomes, controversies, and new directions* (pp. 251—269). Hillsdale, NJ: Lawrence Erlbaum Associates.

Strang, J. D., & Rourke, B. (1983). Concept-formation/nonverbal reasoning abilities of children who exhibit specific academic problems in arithmetic. *Journal of Clinical Child Psychology, 12,* 33—39.

Strang, J. D., & Rourke, B. (1985). Adaptive behavior of children with specific arithmetic disabilities and associated neuropsychological abilities and deficits. In B. P. Rourke (Ed.), *Neuropsychology of learning disabilities: Essentials of subtype analysis* (pp. 302—328). New York: Guilford Press.

Strauss, C. C. (1990). Anxiety disorders of childhood and adolescence. *School Psychology Review, 19,* 142—157.

Strauss, C. C., Frame, C. L., & Forehand, R. L. (1987). Psychosocial impairment associated with anxiety in children. *Journal of Clinical Child Psychology, 1,* 235—239.

Strauss, C. C., Last, C. G., Hersen, M., & Kazdin, A. (1988). Association between anxiety and depression in children and adolescents with anxiety disorders. *Journal of Abnormal Child Psychology, 15,* 57—68.

Streissguth, A. P. (1994). A long-term perspective of FAS. *Alcohol Health and Research World, 18,* 74—81.

Streissguth, A. P., Aase, J. M., Clarren, S. K., Randels, S. P., LaDue, R. A., & Smith, D. F. (1991). Fetal alcohol syndrome in adolescents and adults. *Journal of the American Medical Association, 265,* 1961—1967.

Streissguth, A. P., Barr, H. M., Olson, H. C., Sampson, P. D., Bookstein, F. L., & Burgess, D.ÊM. (1994). Drinking during pregnancy decreases word attack and arithmetic scores on standardized tests: Adolescent data from a population-based prospective study. *Alcoholism: Clinical and Experimental Research, 18,* 248—254.

Streissguth, A. P., Clarren, S. K., & Jones, K. L. (1985). Natural history of the fetal alcohol syndrome: A ten-year follow-up of eleven patients. *Lancet, 2,* 85—91.

Streissguth, A. P., Randels, S. P., & Smith, D. F. (1991). A test—retest study of intelligence in patients with fetal alcohol syndrome: Implications for care. *Journal of the American Academy of Child and Adolescent Psychiatry, 30,* 584—587.

Streissguth, A. P., Sampson, P. D., & Barr, H. M. (1989). Neurobehavioral dose—response effects of prenatal alcohol exposure in humans from infancy to adulthood. Conference of the Behavioral Teratology Society, the National Institute on Drug Abuse, and the New York Academy of Sciences: prenatal abuse of licit and illicit drugs. *Annals of the New York Academy of Sciences, 562,* 145—158.

Streissguth, A. P., Sampson, P. D., Olson, H. C., Bookstein, F. L., Barr, H. M., Scott, M., Feldman, J., & Mirsky, A. F. (1994). Maternal drinking during pregnancy: Attention and short-term memory in 14-year-old offspring–A longitudinal prospective study. *Alcoholism: Clinical and Experimental Research, 18,* 202—218.

Strom, D. A., Gray, J. W., Dean, R. S., & Fischer, W. E. (1987). The incremental validity of the Halstead-Reitan Neuropsychological Battery in predicting achievement for learning-disabled children. *Journal of Psychoeducational Assessment, 2,* 157—165.

Stroufe, L. A., Fox, N. E., & Pancake, V. R. (1983). Attachment and dependency in developmental perspective. *Child Development, 54,* 1615—1627.

Surgeon General's Advisory on Alcohol and Pregnancy (1981). FDA *Drug Bulletin, 11,* 9—10.

Sutherland, R. J., Kolb, B., Schoel, W. M., Whishaw, I. Q., & Davies, D. (1982). Neuropsychological assessment of children and adults with Tourette's syndrome: A comparison with learning disabilities and schizophrenia. *Advances in Neurology, 35,* 311—322.

Swaiman, K. F. (1994a). Cerebellar dysfunction and ataxia in childhood. In K. F. Swaiman (Ed.), *Pediatric neurology* (2nd ed., pp. 261—270). St. Louis, MO: Mosby.

Swaiman, K. F. (1994b). *Pediatric neurology* (2nd ed., pp. 261—270). St. Louis, MO: Mosby.

Swanson, H. L. (1989). Central processing strategy differences in gifted, average, learning disabled, and mentally retarded children. *Journal of Experimental Child Psychology, 47,* 370—397.

Sykes, D. H., Douglas, V. I., & Morgenstern, G. (1973). Sustained attention in hyperactive children. *Journal of Child Psychology and Psychiatry, 14,* 213—220.

Sykes, D. H., Douglas, V. I., Weiss, G., & Minde, K. K. (1971). Attention in hyperactive children and the effect of methylphenidate. *Journal of Child Psychology and Psychiatry, 12,* 129—139.

Szatmari, P. (1991). Asperger's syndrome: Diagnosis, treatment, and outcome. *Psychiatric Clinics of North America, 14,* 81—93.

Szymonowicz, W., Preston, H., & Yu, V. Y. (1986). The surviving monozygotic twin. *Archives of Disabled Children, 61,* 454—458.

Tallal, P. (1988). Developmental language disorders. In J. F. Kavanagh & T. J. Truss (Eds.), *Learning disabilities: Proceedings of the National Conference* (pp. 181—272). Parkton, MD: York Press.

Tallal, P., & Percy, M. (1973). Developmental aphasia: Impaired rate of nonverbal processing as function of sensory modality. *Neuropsychologia, 11,* 389—398.

Tallal, P., Miller, S., Bedi, G., Byma, G., Wang, X., et al. (1996). Language comprehension in language-learning impaired children improved with acoustically modified speech. *Science, 271,* 81-84.

Tanguay, P. E. (1976). Clinical and electrophysiological

research. In E. R. Ritvo (Ed.), *Autism: Diagnosis, current research, and management* (pp. 75—84). New York: Spectrum.

Tanner, C. M., & Goldman, S. M. (1994). Epidemiology. *Current Opinion in Neurology, 7,* 340—345.

Tanoue, Y., Oda, S., Asano, F., & Kawashima, K. (1988). Epidemiology of infantile autism in southern Ibaraki, Japan: Differences in prevalence rates in birth cohorts. *Journal of Autism and Developmental Disorders, 18,* 155—166.

Taylor, H. G. (1984). Minimal brain dysfunction in perspective. In R. tarter & G. Goldstein (Eds.), *Advances in clinical neuropsychology* (Vol. 2, pp. 207—229). New York: Plenum Press.

Taylor, H. G., Schatschneider, C., & Reich, D. (1992). *Sequelae of Haemophilus influenzae meningitis: Implications for the study of brain disease and development.* In M. G. Tramontana and S. Hooper (Eds.), *Advances in child neuropsychology: Vol. I* (pp. 109—137). New York: Springer-Verlag.

Teeter, P. A. (1985). A neurodevelopmental investigation of academic achievement: A report of years 1 and 2 of a longitudinal study. *Journal of Consulting and Clinical Psychology, 53,* 709—717.

Teeter, P. A. (1986). Standard neuropsychological batteries for children. In J. E. Obrzut & G. W. (Eds.), *Child neuropsychology, Volume 2: Clinical practice* (pp. 187—228). Orlando, FL: Academic Press.

Teeter, P. A. (1989). Neuropsychological approaches to the remediation of educational deficits. In C. R. Reynolds & E. Fletcher-Janzen (Eds.), *Handbook of clinical child neuropsychology* (pp. 357—376). New York: Plenum Press.

Teeter, P. A. (1991). Attention-deficit hyperactivity disorder: A psychoeducational paradigm. *School Psychology Review, 20,* 266—280.

Teeter, P. A. (1992, March). *Medical and behavioral paradigms: A false dichotomy.* Symposia conducted at the meeting of the National Association of School Psychologists, Washington, DC.

Teeter, P. A. (in preparation). *Developmental interventions for attention deficit hyperactivity disorder.* New York: Guilford Press.

Teeter, P. A., & Semrud-Clikeman, M. (1995). Integrating neurobiological, psychosocial, and behavioral paradigms: A transactional model for the study of ADHD. *Archives of Clinical Neuropsychology, 10,* 433—461.

Teeter, P. A., & Smith, P. L. (1993). WISC-III and WJR: Predictive and discriminant validity for students with severe emotional disturbance. *Journal of Pyschoeducational Assessment,* WISC-III Monograph, 113—124.

Teeter, P. A., Uphoff, C. A., Obrzut, J. E., & Malsch, K. (1986). Diagnostic utility of the critical level formula and clinical summary scales of the Luria-Nebraska Neuropsychological Battery–Children's Revision with learning disabled children. *Developmental Neuropsychology, 2,* 125—135.

Templer, D. I. (1972). The obsessive-compulsive neurosis: Review of research findings. *Comprehensive Psychiatry, 13,* 375—383.

Thatcher, R. W. (1991). Maturation of the human frontal lobes: Physiological evidence for staging. *Developmental psychology, 7,* 397—419.

Thatcher, R. W. (1994). Cyclic cortical reorganization: Origins of human cognitive development. In G. Dawson & K. W. Fischer (Eds.), *Human behavior and the developing brain* (pp. 232—268). New York: Guilford Press.

Thomas, C. L. (1985). *Taber's cyclopedic medical dictionary.* Philadelphia: W. B. Saunders.

Thomas, C., Englert, C., & Gregg, S. (1987). An analysis of erros and strategies in the expositiory writing of learning disabled students. *Remedial and Special Education, 8,* 21—30.

Thompson, R. F. (1975). *Introduction to physiological psychology.* New York: Harper & Row.

Tisher, M. (1983). School refusal: A depressive equivalent? In D. P. Cantwell & G. A. Carlson (Eds.), *Affective disorders in children and adolescents.* New York: Spectrum Publications.

Torgesen, J. K. (1977). The role of nonspecific factors in the task performance of learning-disabled children: A theoretical assessment. *Journal of Learning Disabilities, 10,* 27—34.

Torgesen, J. K. (1986). Genetic factors in moderately severe and mild affective disorders. *Archives of General Psychiatry, 43,* 222—226.

Torgesen, J. K. (1988). Studies of children with learning disabilities who perform poorly on memory span tasks. *Journal of Learning Disabilities, 21,* 605—612.

Torgesen, J. K. (1991a). Cross-age consistency in phonological processing. In S. Bradley & D. Shankweiler (Eds.), *Phonological processes in literacy* (pp. 187—193). Hillsdale, NJ: Lawrence Erlbaum.

Torgesen, J. K. (1991b). Learning disabilities: Historical and conceptual issues. In B. Y. L. Wong (Ed.), *Learning about learning disabilities* (pp. 3—37). San Diego, CA: Academic Press.

Torgesen, J. K. (1993). Variations on theory in learning disabilities. In G. Reid Lyon, D. Gray, J. Kavanagh, & N. Krasnegor (Eds.), *Better understanding learning disabilities: New views from research and their implications for education and public policies.* Baltimore, MD: Paul H. Brooks.

Torgesen, J. K., & Bryant, B. R. (1993). *Test of phonological awareness.* Austin, TX: Pro-Ed.

Torgesen, J. K., Dahlem, W. E., & Greenstein, J. (1987). Using verbatim text recordings to enhance reading comprehension in learning disabled adolescents. *Learning Disabilities Focus, 30,* 30—38.

Tramontana, M., & Hooper, S. (1987). Discriminating the presence and pattern of neuropsychological impairment in child psychiatric disorders. *International Journal of Clinical Neuropsychology, 9,* 111—119.

Tramontana, M., & Hooper, S. (1989). Neuropsychology of child psychopathology. In C. R. Reynolds & E. Fletcher-Janzen (Eds.), *Handbook of clinical child neuropsychology* (pp. 87—106). New York: Plenum Press.

Tramontana, M., Hooper, S., & Nardillo, E. M. (1988). Behavioral manifestations of neuropsychological impairment in children with psychiatric disorders. *Archives of Clinical Neuropsychology, 3,* 369—374.

Tramontana, M., & Sherrets, S. D. (1985). Brain impairment in child psychiatric disorders: Correspondences between neuro-psychological and CT scans. *Journal of American Academy of Child Psychiatry, 24,* 590—596.

Tramontana, M., Sherrets, S. D., & Golden, C. J. (1980). Brain dysfunction in children with psychiatric disorders: Application of Selz-Reitan rules for neuropsychological diagnosis. *Clinical Neuropsychology, 2,* 118—123.

Tranel, D. (1992). Functional neuroanatomy: Neuropsychological correlates of cortical and subcortical damage. In S. C. Yudofsky & R. E. Hales (Eds.), *The American Psychiatric Press textbook of neuropsychiatry* (2nd ed., pp. 57—88). Washington, DC: American Psychiatric Press.

Trauner, D. (1994). Increased intracranial pressure. In K. F. Swaiman (Ed.), *Pediatric neurology: Principles and practice* (pp. 197—204). St. Louis, MO: Mosby.

Treiman, R., & Hirsch-Pasek, K. (1985). Are there qualitative differences in reading behavior between dyslexics and normal readers? *Memory and Cognition, 13,* 357—364.

Tremblay, R. E., Masse, B., Perron, D., Leblanc, M.,

Schwartzman, A. E., & Ledingham, J. E. (1992). Early disruptive behavior, poor school achievement, delinquent, and delinquent personality: Longitudinal analyses. *Journal of Consulting and Clinical Psychology, 60,* 1—10.

Trommer, B. L., Hoeppner, J. B., Lorber, R., & Armstrong, K. J. (1988). The go-no-go paradigm in attention deficit disorder. *Annals of Neurology, 24,* 610—624.

Tsyvaer, A. (1992). Head and neck injuries in soccer: Impact of minor trauma. *Sports Medicine, 14,* 200—213.

Tysvaer, A. T., Storli, O. V., & Bachen, N. I. (1989). Soccer injuries to the brain: A neurologic and electroencephalographic study of former players. *Acta Neurology Scandanavia, 80,* 151—156.

Tuma, J. M., & Pratt, J. M. (1982). Clinical child psychology practice and training: A national survey. *Journal of Clinical Child Psychology, 11,* 27—34.

Tunmer, W. E., & Nesdale, A. R. (1985). Phonemic segmentation skill and beginning reading. *Journal of Educational Psychology, 77,* 417—427.

Tunmer, W. E., & Rohl, M. (1991). Phonological awareness and reading acquisition. In D. Sawyer & B. Fox (Eds.), *Phonological awareness in reading: The evolution of current perspectives* (pp. 1—30). New York: Springer-Verlag.

Ultmann, M. H., Belman, A. L., Ruff, H. A., Novick, B. E., Cone-Wesson, B., Cohen, H. J., & Rubinstein, A. (1985). Developmental abnormalities in infants and children with acquired immune deficiency syndrome (AIDS) and AIDS-related complex. *Developmental Medicine and Child Neurology, 27,* 563—571.

Ultmann, M. H., Diamond, G. W., Belman, A. L., Novick, B. E., Rubinstein, A. & Cohen, H. J. (1987). Developmental abnormalities in infants and children with acquired immune deficiency syndrome (AIDS): A follow-up study. *International Journal of Neuroscience, 32,* 661—667.

Urion, D. K. (1988). Nondextrality and autoimmune disorders among relatives of language-disabled boys. *Annals of Neurology, 24,* 267—269.

U.S. Department of Health and Human Services. (1989). *Traumatic brain injury.* Washington, DC: U.S. Government Printing Office.

U.S. General Accounting Office Report (1990). *Drug exposed infants: A generation at risk.* Washington, DC: U.S. Government Printing Office.

Uvebrandt, P. (1988). Hemiplegic cerebral palsy aetiology and outcome. *Acta Paediatrica Scandanavia, 345* (Suppl.), 1—100.

Vaughn, S., McIntosh, R., & Hogan, A. (1990). Why social skills training doesn't work: An alternative model. In T. E. Scruggs & B. Y. L. Wong (Eds.), *Intervention research in learning disabilities* (pp. 263—278). New York: Springer-Verlag.

van Baar, A. (1990). Development of infants of drug-dependent mothers. *Journal of Child Psychology and Psychiatry, 31*, 911—920.

van Baar, A., & de Graaff, B. M. T. (1994). Cognitive development at preschool-age of infants of drug-dependent mothers. *Developmental Medicine and Child Neurology, 36*, 1063—1075.

Van Bourgondien, M. E., & Mesibov, G. (1989). Diagnosis and treatment of adolescents and adults with autism. In G. Dawson (Ed.), *Autism: Nature, diagnosis and treatment* (pp. 367—385). New York: Guilford Press.

van Praag, H. M. (1982). Neurotransmitters and CNS disease. *Lancet, 2*, 1259—1264.

Vellutino, F. R., & Scanlon, D. M. (1987). Phonological coding, phonological awareness, and reading ability: Evidence from a longitudinal and experimental study. *Merrill Palmer Quarterly, 33*, 321—363.

Vining, E. P. G., Mellits, D., Dorsen, M. M., et al. (1987). Psychologic and behavioral effects of antiepileptic drugs in children: A double-blind comparison between phenobarbitol and valporic acid. *Pediatrics, 80*, 165—174

Virginia Department of Education (1992). *Guidelines for educational services for children with traumatic brain injury*. Richmond, VA: Author.

Voeller, K. K. S. (1986). Right hemisphere deficit syndrome in children. *American Journal of Psychiatry, 143*, 1004—1011.

Voeller, K. K. S. (1991). Toward a neurobiologic nosology of attention deficit hyperactivity disorder. *Journal of Child Neurology, 6(Suppl.)*, S2—S8.

Voeller, K. K. S. (1995). Clinical neurologic aspects of the right hemisphere deficit syndrome. *Journal of Child Neurology, 10*, 516—522.

Volger, G. P., Defries, J. C., & Decker, S. N. (1984). Family history as an indicator of risk for reading disability. *Journal of Learning Disabilities, 10*, 616.

Volpe, J. J. (1987). *Neurology of the newborn* (2nd ed.). Philadelphia: W. B. Saunders.

Volpe, J. J. (1992). Value of MR in definition of the neuropathology of cerebral palsy in vivo. *American Journal of Neuroradiology, 13*, 79—84.

Volpe, J. J. (1995). *Neurology of the newborn* (3rd ed.). Philadelphia: W. B. Saunders.

Vonofakos, D., Marcu, H., & Hacker, H. (1979). Oligodendrogliomas: CT patterns with emphasis on features indicating malignancy. *Journal of Computer-Assisted Tomography, 3*, 783—788.

Vorhees, C. V., Reed, T. M., Acutt-Smith, K. D., et al. (1995). Long-term learning deficits and changes in unlearned behaviors following in utero exposure to multiple daily doses of cocaine during different exposure periods and maternal plasma cocaine concentrations. *Neurotoxicity and Teratology, 17*, 253—264.

Waber, D. P., & Holmes, J. M. (1986). Assessing children's copy productions of the Rey-Osterreith Complex Figure. *Journal of Clinical and Experimental Neuropsychology, 8*, 563—580.

Wada, J. A., Clark, R., & Hamm, A. (1975). Cerebral hemispheric asymmetry in humans. *Archives of Neurology, 32*, 239—246.

Wadsworth, J. S., & Harper, D. S. (1993). The social needs of adolescents with cerebral palsy. *Developmental Medicine and Child Neurology, 35*, 1019—1022.

Wagner, R. K., & Torgeson, J. K. (1987). The nature of phonological processing and its causal role in the acquisition of reading skills. *Psychological Bulletin, 101*, 192-212.

Wald, S. L. (1995). Disorders of the cerebrospinal fluid circulation and brain edema. In W. G. Bradley, R. B. Daroff, G. M. Fenichel, & C. D. Marsden (Eds.), *Neurology in clinical practice* (pp. 1431—1458). Boston: Butterworth-Heinemam.

Walker, H. M., McConnell, S. R., Todis, B., Walker, J., & Golden, H. (1988). *The Walker social skills curriculum: The ACCEPTS program*. Austin, TX: Pro-Ed.

Walker, H. M., Holmes, D., Todis, B., & Horton, G. (1988). *The Walker Social Skills Curriculum. The ACCESS Program: Adolescent curriculum for communication and effective social skills*. Austin, TX: PRO-ED.

Wallander, J. L., Varni, J. W., Babani, L., Banis, T., & Wilcox, K. (1989). Family resources as resistance factors for psychological maladjustment in chronically ill children. *Journal of Pediatric Psychology, 14*, 157—173.

Walsh, K. (1994). *Neuropsychology*. Edinburgh, Scotland: Churchill Livingston.

Walzer, S. (1985). X chromosome abnormalities and cognitive development: Implications for understanding normal human development. *Journal of Child Psychology and Psychiatry, 26*, 177—184.

Waterman, G .S., & Ryan, N. D. (1993). Pharmocological treatment of depression and anxiety. *School Psychology Review, 22*, 228—242.

Watts, R. W., Spellacy, E., Gibbs, D. A. et al. (1982). Clinical, post-mortem, biochemical and therapeutic observations on the Lesch-Nyhan syndrome with particular reference to the neurological manifestations. *Quarterly Journal of Medicine, 51,* 43—78.

Webster-Stratton, C. (1984). Randomized trial of two parent training programs for families with conduct disordered children. *Journal of Consulting and Clinical Psychology, 52,* 666—678.

Webster-Stratton, C. (1985). Mother perceptions and mother-child interactions: Comparison of a clinic-referred and a non-clinic group. *Journal of Clinical Child Psychology, 14,* 334—339.

Webster-Stratton, C. (1989). Systematic comparison of consumer satisfaction of three cost-effective parent training programs for conduct problem children. *Behavior Therapy, 20,* 103—115.

Webster-Stratton, C. (1990). Long-term follow-up of families with young conduct problem children: From preschool to grade school. *Journal of Clinical Child Psychology, 19,* 144—149.

Webster-Stratton, C. (1993). Strategies for helping early school-aged children with oppositional defiant and conduct disorders: The importance of home—school partnerships. *School Psychology Review, 22,* 437—457.

Webster-Stratton, C., Hollinsworth, T., & Kolpacoff, M. (1989). The long-term effectiveness and clinical significance of three cost-effective training programs for families with conduct problem children. *Journal of Consulting and Clinical Psychology, 57,* 550—553.

Wechsler, D. (1991). *WISC-III manual.* San Antonio, TX: Psychological Corporation.

Weil, M. L. (1985). Infections of the nervous system. In J. H. Menkes (Ed.), *Textbook of child neurology* (3rd ed., pp. 316— 431). Philadelphia: Lea & Febiger.

Weinberger, D. R. (1987). Implications of normal brain development for the pathogenesis of schizophrenia. *Archives of General Psychiatry, 44,* 660—669.

Weingartner, H., Gold, P., Ballenger, J. D., et al. (1981). Effects of vasopressin on human memory functions. *Science, 211,* 601—603.

Weinner, L., & Morse, B. A. (1994). Intervention and the child with FAS. *Alcohol Health and Research World, 18,* 67—72.

Weintraub, S., & Mesulam, M. M. (1983). Developmental learning disabilities and the right hemisphere: Emotional, interpersonal and cognitive components. *Archives of Neurology, 40,* 463-468.

Weiss, G., & Hechtman, L. (1993). *Hyperactive children grown up* (2nd ed.). New York: Guilford Press.

Weiss, G., & Hechtman, L. (1986). *Hyperactive children grown up.* New York: Guilford Press.

Weiss, G., Kruger, E., Danielson, U., & Elman, M. (1975). Effect of long-term treatment of hyperactive children with methylphenidate. *Canadian Medical Association Journal, 112,* 159—165.

Weiss, I. P., Barnet, A. B., & Reutter, S. A. (1984). Visual evoked potentials to flash in high-risk premature infants. In R. H. Nodar and C. Barber (Eds.), *Evoked Potentials II* (pp. 526—535). London: Butterworth Publishers.

Weissmann, M. M. (1987). Assessing psychiatric disorders in children. *Archives of general psychiatry, 44,* 747—753.

Weizman, A., Weitz, R., Szekely, G. A., Tyana, S., & Belmaker, R. H. (1984). Combination of neuroleptic and stimulant treatment in attention deficit disorder with hyperactivity. *Journal of American Academy of Child Psychiatry, 23,* 295—298.

Wells, K. C., & Forehand, R. (1985). Conduct and oppositional disorder. In P. H. Bornstein & A. E. Kazdin (Eds.), *Handbook of clinical behavior therapy with children* (pp. 36—65). Homewood, IL: Dorsey.

Welsh, M. C., Pennington, B. F., & Grossier, D. B. (1991). A normative developmental study of executive function: A window on prefrontal function in children. *Developmental Neuropsychology, 7,* 131—139.

Wender, P. (1974). Some speculations concerning a possible biochemical basis of minimal brain dysfunction. *Life Sciences, 14,* 1605—1621.

Werner, E. E., & Smith, R. S. (1982). *Vulnerable but invincible: A study of resilent children.* New York: McGraw-Hill.

Werry, J. S., Reeves, J. S., & Gail, S. (1987). Attention deficit, conduct, oppositional, and anxiety disorders in children. *Journal of the American Academy of Child and Adolescent Psychiatry, 26,* 133—143.

West, D. J. (1982). *Delinquency: Its roots, careers and prospects.* London: Heinemann.

Wheeler, L., & Reitan, R. M. (1962). The presence of laterality of brain damage predicted from responses to short aphasia screening test. *Perceptual and Motor Skills, 15,* 783—799.

Whitaker, H. A., & Noll, J. D. (1972). Some linguistic parameters of the Token Test. *Neuropsychologia, 10,* 395—404.

White, D. A., Craft, S., Hale, S., & Park, T. S. (1994).

Working memory and articulation rate in children with spastic ciplegic cerebral palsy. *Neuropsychology, 8,* 180—186.

White, J., Moffitt, T. E., Caspi, A., Bartusch, D. J. & Needles, D. J. (1994). Measuring impulsivity and examining its relationship to delinquency. *Journal of Abnormal Psychology, 103,* 192—205

White, J., Moffitt, T., Earls, F., & Robins, L. (1990). Preschool predictors of persistent conduct disorder and delinquency. *Criminology, 28,* 443—454.

Wiklund, L. M., Uvebrandt, P., & Floodmark, O. (1991). Computed tomography as an adjunct in etiological analysis of hemiplegia cerebral palsy: I. Children born preterm. *Neuropediatrics, 22,* 50—56.

Wilkinson, J. L. (1986). *Neuroanatomy for medical students.* Bristol BSI: John Wright & Son Ltd.

Williams, B. F., Howard, V. F., & McLaughlin, T. F. (1994). Fetal alcohol syndrome: Developmental characteristics and directions for futrue research. *Educational Treatment of Children, 17,* 86—97.

Williams, D. (1989). *A process-specific training program in the treatment of attention deficits in children.* Unpublished doctoral dissertation, University of Washington.

Williams, J. M., & Davis, K. S. (1986). Central nervous system prophylactic treatment for childhood leukemia: Neuropsychological outcome studies. *Cancer Treatment Reviews, 13,* 113—127.

Williams, J. P. (1980). Teaching decoding with an emphasis on phoneme analysis and phoneme blending. *Journal of Educational Psychology, 72,* 1—15.

Williams, J. R. (1993). *Neuroanatomy foundations.* Odessa, FL: Psychological Asessment Resources.

Williamson, M. L., Koch, R., Azen, C., & Chang, C. (1981). Correlates of intelligence test results in treated phenylketonuric children. *Pediatrics, 68,* 161—167.

Wilson, E. R., Mirra, S., & Schwartz, J. F. (1982). Congenital diencephalic and brain stem damage: Neuropathologic study of three cases. *Acta Neuropathologica, 57,* 70—74.

Winogron, H. W., Knights, R. M., & Bowden, H. N. (1984). Neuropsychological deficits following head injury in children. *Journal of Clinical Neuropsychology, 6,* 269—286.

Wise, B. W., & Olson, R. K. (1991). Remediating reading disabilities. In J. E. Obrzut & G. W. Hynd (Eds.), *Neuropsychological foundations of learning disabilities: A handbook of issues, methods, and practice* (pp. 631—658). San Diego, CA: Academic Press.

Wise, B. W., Olson, R. K., Anstett, M., Andrews, L., Terjak, M., Schneider, V., Kostuch, J., & Kriho, L. (1989). Implementing a long-term remedial reading study in the public schools: Hardware, software, and real world issues. *Behavior Research Methods, & Instrumentation, 21,* 173—180.

Witelson, S. (1977). Anatomic asymmetry in the temporal lobes: Its documentation, phylogenesis and relationship to functional asymmetry. *Annals of the New York Academy of Sciences, 299,* 328—354.

Witelson, S. (1983). Bumps on the brain: Right—left asymmetry as a key to functional asymmetry. In S. J. Segalowitz (Ed.), *Language functions and brain organization* (pp. 117—143). New York: Academic Press.

Witelson, S. (1987a). Brain asymmetry: Functional aspects. In G. Adelman (Ed.), *Encyclopedia of neuroscience* (pp. 152—156). Cambridge: Birkhauser Boston.

Witelson, S. (1987b). Neurobiological aspects of language in children. *Child Development, 58,* 653—688.

Witelson, S. (1989). Hand and sex differences in the isthmus and genu of the human corpus callosum. *Brain, 112,* 799—835.

Witelson, S. (1990). Structural correlates of cognitive function in the human brain. In A. B. Scheibel & A. F. Wechsler (Eds.), *Neurobiology of higher cognitive function* (pp. 167—184). New York: Guilford Press.

Witelson, S. F., & Kigar, D. L. (1988). Anatomical development of the corpus callosum in humans: A review with reference to sex and cognition. In D. F. Molfese & S. J. Segalowitz (Eds.), *Brain lateralization in children: Developmental implications* (pp. 35—57). New York: Guilford Press.

Witelson, S., & Pralle, W. (1973). Left hemisphere specialization for language in the newborn: Neuroanatomical evidence of asymmetry. *Brain, 96,* 641—646.

Witol, A., & Webbe, F. (1994). Neuropsychological deficits associated with soccer play. *Archives of Clinical Neuropsychology, 9,* 204—205.

Witt, J. C., Elliot, S., & Gresham, F. (1988). *Handbook of behavior therapy in education.* New York: Plenum Press.

Witt, J. C., Heffer, R. W., & Pfiffer, J. (1990). Structured rating scales: A review of self-report and informant rating processes, procedures, and issues. In C. R. Reynolds & R. W. Kamphaus (Eds.), *Handbook of psychological and educational assessment of children* (pp. 364—394). New York: Guilford Press.

Wolf, M. M., Braukmann, C. J., & Ramp, K. A. (1987). Serious delinquent behavior as part of a significantly handicapping condition: Cures and supportive environments. *Journal of Applied Behavior Analysis, 20,* 347—359.

Wolf, M. M., & Goodglass, H. (1986). Dyslexia, dysnomia, and lexical retrieval: A longitudinal investigation. *Brain and Language, 28,* 154—168.

Wolf-Schien, E. G. (1992). On the association between Fragile X chromosome, mental handicap, and autistic disorder. *Developmental Disabilities Bulletin, 20,* 13—30.

Woods, B. T., & Tueber, H. C. (1973). Changing patterns of childhood aphasia. *Annals of Neurology, 3,* 273—280.

Wong, B. Y. L. (1991). *Learning about learning disabilities.* San Diego, CA: Academic Press.

Wong, B. Y. L., & Jones, W. (1982). Increasing metacomprehension in learning disabled and normally-achieving students through self-questioning training. *Learning Disability Quarterly, 5,* 228—240.

Woodcock, R. W. (1990). Theoretical foundations of the WJ-R measures of cognitive ability. *Journal of Psychoeducational Assessment, 8,* 231—258.

Woodcock, R. W., & Johnson, M. B. (1977). *Woodcock-Johnson Psycho-Educational Battery.* Allen, TX: DLM.

Woodcock, R. W., & Johnson, M. B. (1989). *Woodcock-Johnson Tests of Cognitive Ability: Examiner's manual.* Allen, TX: DLM.

Woods, B. T., & Teuber, H.-L. (1978). Mirror movements after childhood hemiparesis. *Neurology, 28,* 1152—1158.

Woods, J. R., Plessinger, M. A., & Clark, K. E. (1987). Effects of cocaine on uterine blood flow and fetal oxygenation. *JAMA, 257,* 957—961.

Woolsey, C. N. (1958). Organization of somatic and motor areas of the cerebral cortex. In H. F. Harlow & C. N. Woolsey (Eds.), *Biological and biochemical bases of behavior* (pp. 63—81). Madison: University of Wisconsin.

Yakovlev, P. E., & Lecours, A. R. (1967). The myelogenetic cycles of regional maturation of the brain. In A, Minowski (Ed.), *Regional development of the brain in early life* (pp. 3—70). Philadelphia: Davis.

Yokochi, K., Aiba, K., Kodama, M., & Fujimoto, J. M. (1991). Magnetic resonance imaging in athetotic cerebral palsied children. *Acta Paediatrica Scandinavia, 80,* 818—823.

Yokochi, K., Hosoe, A., Shimabukuro, S., & Kodama, K. (1990). Gross motor patterns in children with cerebral palsy and spastic diplegia. *Pediatric Neurology, 6,* 245—250.

Young, G., Segalowitz, J., Misek, P., Alp, I. E., & Boulet, R. (1983). Is early reaching left-handed? Review of manual specialization research. In G. Young, S. J. Segalowitz, C. Corter, & S. E. Trehaub (Eds.), *Manual specialization and the developing brain* (pp. 13—32). New York: Academic Press.

Young, R. S. K., Ropper, A. H., Hawkes, D., et al. (1983). Pentobarbital in refractory status epilepticus. *Pediatric Pharmocology, 3,* 63—67.

Ysseldyke, J. E., Algozzine, B., Shinn, M., & McGue, M. (1982). Similarities and differences between underachievers and students labeled learning disabled. *Journal of Special Education, 16,* 73—85.

Yudofsky, S. C., & Hales, R. E. (1992). *The American Psychiatric Press textbook of neuropsychiatry* (2nd ed.). Washington, DC: American Psychiatric Press.

Zaidel, E., Clark, M., & Suyenobu, B. (1990). Hemispheric independence: A paradigm case for cognitive neuroscience. In A. B. Scheibel & A. F. Wechsler (Eds.), *Neurobiology of higher cognitive function* (pp. 297—356). New York: Guilford Press.

Zambelli, A. J., Stamm, J. S., Maitinsky, S., & Loiselle, D. L. (1977). Auditory evoked potentials and selective attention in formerly hyperactive adolescent boys. *American Journal of Psychiatry, 134,* 742—747.

Zametkin, A. J., & Cohen, R. M. (1991). Cerebral glucose metabolism in hyperactivity (letter to the editor). *New England Journal of Medicine, 324,* 1216—1217.

Zametkin, A. J., Nordahl, T. E., Gross, M., King, A. C., Semple, W. E., Rumsey, J., Hamburger, S., & Cohen, R. M. (1990). Cerebral glucose metabolism in adults with hyperactivity of childhood onset. *New England Journal of Medicine, 323,* 1361—1366.

Zametkin, A. J., & Rapoport, J. L. (1986). The pathophysiology of attention deficit disorder with hyperactivity. In B. B. Lahey & A. E. Kazdin (Eds.), *Advances in clinical child psychology* (Vol. 9, pp. 177—216). New York: Plenum Press.

Zametkin, A., & Rapoport, J. L. (1987). Noradrenergic hypothesis of attention deficit disorder with hyperactivity: A critical review. In H. Y. Meltzer (Ed.), *Psychopharmacology: The third generation of progress* (pp. 837—842). New York: Raven Press.

Zametkin, A., Rapoport, J. L., Murphy, D. L., Linnoila, M., & Ismond, D. (1985). Treatment of hyperactive children with monamine oxidase inhibitors: I. Clinical efficacy. *Archives of General Psychitry, 42,* 962—966.

Zeller, W. J., Ivankovic, S., Habs, M., et al. (1982). Experimental chemical production of brain tumors. *Annals of the New York Academy of Science, 381,* 250—256.

Zigler, E., & Hodapp, R. M. (1991). Behavioral functioning in individuals with mental retardation. *Annual Review of Psychology, 42,* 166—174.

Zuckerman, B., Frank, D., Hingson, R., Amaro, H., Levenson, S. M., Kayne, H., Parker, S., Vince, R., Aboagye, K., Fried, L., Cabral, H., Timberi, R., & Bauchner, H. (1989). Effects of maternal marijuana and cocaine use on fetal growth. *The New England Journal of Medicine, 320,* 233—240.

NAME INDEX

SUBJECT INDEX